Modern Theories of Money

The Nature and Role of Money in Capitalist Economies

Edited by

Louis-Philippe Rochon

Kalamazoo College and Center for Policy Studies, USA

and Sergio Rossi

University of Fribourg and Università della Svizzera italiana, Switzerland

Edward Elgar
Cheltenham, UK • Northampton, MA, USA

Published by
Edward Elgar Publishing Limited
Glensanda House
Montpellier Parade
Cheltenham
Glos GL50 1UA
UK

Edward Elgar Publishing, Inc.
136 West Street
Suite 202
Northampton
Massachusetts 01060
USA

A catalogue record for this book
is available from the British Library

Library of Congress Cataloguing in Publication Data
Modern theories of money : the nature and role of money in capitalist economies /
edited by Sergio Rossi and Louis-Philippe Rochon.
    p. cm.
    Includes index.
    1. Money. 2. Capitalism. 3 Keynesian economics. I. Rossi, Sergio. II.
Rochon, Louis-Philippe.

HG220.A2 M54 2003
332.4'01—dc21

2002037920

ISBN 1 84064 789 2 (cased)

Printed and bound in Great Britain by MPG Books Ltd, Bodmin, Cornwall

Contents

PART 3 THE THEORY OF MONEY EMISSIONS

PART 4 FURTHER CONTRIBUTIONS TO MONETARY ANALYSIS

Figures

Tables

Contributors

Jean-Luc Bailly is Associate Professor of Economics at the University of Burgundy in Dijon, France, and a Member of the Research Laboratory of Monetary Economics at the Centre for Banking Studies in Lugano, Switzerland. Among his publications are: 'Le modèle IS–LM en économie fermée', in M. Montoussé (ed.), *Macroéconomie* (Bréal, 1999); 'La pensée de Keynes', in M. Montoussé (ed.), *Histoire de la pensée économique* (Bréal, 2000); 'La politique monétaire', in M. Montoussé (ed.), *Économie monétaire et financière* (Bréal, 2000).

Santonu Basu is Senior Lecturer in Economics at the Business School, South Bank University, London, UK. Among his publications are: 'Why institutional credit agencies are reluctant to lend to the rural poor: a theoretical analysis of the Indian rural credit market' (*World Development*, 1997), 'Incomplete information and asymmetric information' (*Zagreb International Review of Economics and Business*, 2001), 'Financial globalisation: some conceptual problems' (*Eastern Economic Journal*, 2002, with P. Arestis), *Financial Liberalization and Intervention: A New Analysis of Credit Rationing* (Edward Elgar, 2002).

Riccardo Bellofiore is Professor of Economics at the University of Bergamo, Italy, where he teaches monetary economics, macroeconomics, and history of economic thought. He edited *Marxian Economics: A Reappraisal* (Macmillan, 1998) and *Global Money, Capital Restructuring and the Changing Patterns of Labour* (Edward Elgar, 1999). Together with Piero Ferri he has recently published two collections of papers on the economic legacy of Hyman Minsky: *Financial Keynesianism and Market Instability* and *Financial Fragility and Investment in the Capitalist Economy* (Edward Elgar, 2000). Among his publications there is also a book on the Italian Marxist scholar Claudio Napoleoni (Unicopli, 1991).

Heinrich Bortis is Professor of Economics at the University of Fribourg, Switzerland, where he teaches economic theory, economic history, and history of economic thought. Among his recent publications are: *Institutions, Behaviour and Economic Theory: A Contribution to Classical–Keynesian Political Economy* (Cambridge University Press, 1997), 'A note on Keynesian long-period theory' (*History of Economic Ideas*, 1998), 'Political economy, economics and social science', in S.B. Dahiya (ed.), *The Current State of Economic Science* (Spellbound, 1999), 'Some considerations on structure and change' (*Structural Change and Economic Dynamics*, 2000), 'Notes on institutions, political economy and economics', in P.L. Porta, R. Scazzieri and A. Skinner (eds), *Knowledge, Social Institutions and the Division of Labour* (Edward Elgar, 2001), 'Piero Sraffa and the revival of classical political economy' (*Journal of Economic Studies*, 2002).

Biagio Bossone is Advisor to the Executive Director (Italy) at the International Monetary Fund, Washington DC, US, and Associate Director at the Banca d'Italia, Rome, Italy. Among his publications are: 'Can saving be scarce?' (*International Review of Economics and Business*, 1998), 'Circuit theory of banking and finance' (*Journal of Banking and Finance*, 2001), 'A proposal to deregulate banking: comment on Thomas' (*Cato Journal*, 2001), 'Do banks have a future? A study on banking and finance as we move into the third millennium' (*Journal of Banking and Finance*, 2001).

Xavier Bradley is Associate Professor of Economics at the University of Burgundy in Dijon, France, and a Member of the Research Laboratory of Monetary Economics at the Centre for Banking Studies in Lugano, Switzerland. Among his publications are: 'La "finance" et le circuit de la monnaie' (*Revue française d'économie*, 1993); 'Le multiplicateur d'investissement et l'épargne des revenus' (*Recherches économiques de Louvain*, 1994); 'From Keynes's to the modern analysis of inflation', in A. Cencini and M. Baranzini (eds), *Inflation and Unemployment: Contributions to a New Macroeconomic Approach* (Routledge, 1996).

Alvaro Cencini is Professor of Economics at the Università della Svizzera italiana and at the Centre for Banking Studies in Lugano, Switzerland, where he is also Co-founder and Director of the Research Laboratory of Monetary Economics. Among his publications are: *Money, Income and Time: A Quantum-Theoretical Approach* (Pinter Publishers, 1988); *Monetary Theory, National and International* (Routledge, 1995/1997); *Inflation and Unemployment: Contributions to a New Macroeconomic Approach*

(Routledge, 1996, as co-editor); *Monetary Macroeconomics: A New Approach* (Routledge, 2001).

Curzio De Gottardi is a Postdoctoral Research Student at the University of New York (Stern School of Business) and a Member of the Research Laboratory of Monetary Economics at the Centre for Banking Studies in Lugano, Switzerland. He is the author of *Offre et demande: équilibre ou identité?* (Fribourg University Press, 2000).

Giuseppe Fontana is Lecturer in Economics at the University of Leeds, UK. His research interests are in the areas of macroeconomics, monetary economics, history of economic thought and methodology. He is the author of *Money, Uncertainty and Time in the Post Keynesian Tradition* (Routledge, forthcoming) and has recently published a number of articles in the *American Journal of Economics and Sociology*, *Cambridge Journal of Economics, Journal of Post Keynesian Economics* and *Review of Social Economy*.

Claude Gnos is Associate Professor of Economics at the University of Burgundy in Dijon, France, and Director of the *Centre d'Études Monétaires et Financières*. He is the author of *Production, répartition et monnaie* (Dijon University Press, 1992), *L'euro* (Editions Management et Société, 1998) and *Les grands auteurs en économie* (Editions Management et Société, 2000). He has contributed to *Inflation and Unemployment: Contributions to a New Macroeconomic Approach* (Routledge, 1996) and to *Historical Perspectives on Macroeconomics: Sixty Years After the General Theory* (Routledge, 1998).

Marc Lavoie is Professor of Economics at the University of Ottawa, Canada. He has published two books on the economics of ice hockey and two graduate textbooks on post Keynesian economics, the latest being *Foundations of Post-Keynesian Economic Analysis* (Edward Elgar, 1992). He has co-edited a book on the works of Milton Friedman and he was an associate editor of the *Encyclopedia of Political Economy* (Routledge, 1999). He has published over 100 articles in refereed journals and books. He is in search of coherent features between the various heterodox schools, particularly in the fields of pricing, money, employment and growth.

Virginie Monvoisin is a full-time research instructor at the *Institut Universitaire des Maîtres* in Lyon, France. She is currently completing her Ph.D. dissertation on the macroeconomic nature of money in contemporary economic theories, and is a member of the *Centre d'Études Monétaires et Financières* at the University of Burgundy in Dijon, France. Her research interests are mainly directed towards the endogeneity of money. In addition to her doctoral dissertation she has presented a number of papers in this area at international academic conferences in Europe and in the United States, giving the prevalence to post Keynesian economics, the definition of money and the money creation process.

Alfonso Palacio-Vera is Lecturer in Economics at the Universidad Complutense de Madrid, Spain. His research interests are in the areas of economic dynamics, post Keynesian economics, monetary economics and macroeconomics. He has recently published articles on monetary theory and policy in the *Journal of Post Keynesian Economics* and *Metroeconomica*.

Thomas I. Palley is Director of the Globalisation Reform Project at the Open Society Institute, Washington, US. He is the author of *Post Keynesian Economics: Debt, Distribution and the Macro Economy* (Macmillan, 1996) and *Plenty of Nothing: The Downsizing of the American Dream and the Case for Structural Keynesianism* (Princeton University Press, 2000). His recent articles include: 'The economics of social security: an old Keynesian perspective' (*Journal of Post Keynesian Economics*, 1998), 'The case for equilibrium low inflation: some financial market considerations with special attention to the problems of Japan' (*Eastern Economic Journal*, 2000), and 'Destabilizing speculation and the case for an international currency transactions tax' (*Challenge*, 2001).

Alain Parguez is Professor of Economics at the University of Besançon, France, and is associated with the Economics Department at the University of Ottawa, Canada. He has written extensively on monetary theory, crisis theory and economic policy. He was the editor of the 'Monnaie et Production' series of *Économies et Sociétés*, and has written numerous articles and books. He is currently writing a book on the general theory of the monetary circuit.

Corinne Pastoret is Lecturer in Economics at the University of Burgundy in Dijon, France. She is currently completing her Ph.D. dissertation on the role of banks in Keynesian economics and has presented a number of papers at international academic conferences in Europe and elsewhere on 'Post Keynesian monetary controversies from the perspective of Keynes's *Treatise on Money*', 'Controversies over the dual role of banks, creators of money and credit institutions' and 'Modifications and crisis of monetary and financial systems in South-East Asia'.

Pierre Piégay is Assistant Professor of Economics at the University of Burgundy in Dijon, France, and a Member of the Research Laboratory of Monetary Economics at the Centre for Banking Studies in Lugano, Switzerland. He is the author of 'The new and post Keynesian analyses of bank behavior: consensus and disagreement' (*Journal of Post Keynesian Economics*, 1999–2000) and 'Offre de monnaie endogène et comportement bancaire: une interprétation des controverses post-keynésiennes' (*Économie appliquée*, 2001).

Riccardo Realfonzo is Professor of Economics at the University of Sannio, Italy, where he teaches history of economic analysis, monetary economics, and international economics. Among his publications are *Money and Banking: Theory and Debate (1900–1940)* (Edward Elgar, 1998) and several papers in international journals and books about the theory of the monetary circuit, Marxian economics, the macroeconomic debate of the first half of the twentieth century and Italian economic thought. He also edited, together with Augusto Graziani, the first editions of works by the Italian inter-war scholars M. Fanno (Esi, 1992) and G. Del Vecchio (Utet, 1997).

Louis-Philippe Rochon is the Stephen B. Monroe Assistant Professor of Economics and Banking at Kalamazoo College, Michigan, US, where he is also the Director of the Center for Policy Studies. He is the author of *Credit, Money and Production: An Alternative Post-Keynesian Approach* (Edward Elgar, 1999), and co-editor of *Credit, Interest Rates and the Open Economy: Essays on Horizontalism* (Edward Elgar, 2001, with M. Vernengo), *Macroeconomics without Supply and Demand: A Horizontalist Synthesis* (Edward Elgar, forthcoming, with M. Vernengo) and *Les théories keynésiennes de la monnaie* (Economica, forthcoming, with P. Piégay). He has also published a number of articles on credit and money, and on macroeconomics, in the *Review of Political Economy*, *Journal of Economic Issues*, *Metroeconomica*, and the *European Journal of the History of Economic Thought*.

Sergio Rossi is Assistant Professor of Economics at the University of Fribourg and at the Università della Svizzera italiana, Lugano, Switzerland, and also a Member of the Research Laboratory of Monetary Economics at the Centre for Banking Studies in Lugano, Switzerland. He has a D.Phil. degree of the University of Fribourg, Switzerland, and a Ph.D. degree of the University of London (University College). His publications include: *La moneta europea: utopia o realtà?* (Meta-Edizioni, 1996); *Modalités d'institution et de fonctionnement d'une banque centrale supranationale: le cas de la Banque Centrale Européenne* (Peter Lang, 1997); *Money and Inflation* (Edward Elgar, 2001). He has also published articles on monetary and public sector economics in *Studi economici, Public Choice* and *Kyklos*.

Malcolm Sawyer is Professor of Economics at the University of Leeds, UK. He is the author of ten books on macroeconomics, political economy and industrial economics. He has edited 15 books including *The UK Economy* (Oxford University Press, 2001) and *Economics of the Third Way* (Edward Elgar, 2001, with P. Arestis). He has published nearly 100 articles on a wide range of topics including industrial policy, macroeconomics, inflation and income distribution. Some recent articles include 'Explaining the euro's initial decline' (*Eastern Economic Journal*, 2001, with P. Arestis, I. Biefang-Frisancho Mariscal and A. Brown), 'The economic analysis underlying the "third way"' (*New Political Economy*, 2001, with P. Arestis), 'Kalecki on imperfect competition, inflation and money' (*Cambridge Journal of Economics*, 2001).

Bernard Schmitt is Emeritus Professor of Economics at the University of Burgundy in Dijon, France, and at the University of Fribourg, Switzerland. He is also Co-founder and Director of the Research Laboratory of Monetary Economics at the Centre for Banking Studies in Lugano, Switzerland. Among his publications are: *Monnaie, salaires et profits* (Presses Universitaires de France, 1966); *Macroeconomic Theory: A Fundamental Revision* (Castella, 1972); *Théorie unitaire de la monnaie, nationale et internationale* (Castella, 1975); *Inflation, chômage et malformations du capital* (Economica and Castella, 1984).

Mario Seccareccia is Professor of Economics at the University of Ottawa, Canada, and Lecturer at the Labour College of Canada. He has published numerous articles and contributed to books in the areas of macroeconomics and monetary theory, labour economics, history of economic thought and economic history. Among his recent publications are: *Vers le plein emploi* (University of Montreal Press, 1998; co-edited with P. Paquette), *North American Monetary Integration: Should Canada Join the Dollarization Bandwagon?* (Canadian Centre for Policy Alternatives, forthcoming), and a volume on the question of the European Economic and Monetary Union and

North American monetary integration (Routledge, forthcoming; co-edited with L.-P. Rochon).

Matias Vernengo was born in Argentina and raised in Brazil. He obtained his B.Sc. and M.Sc. degrees at the Universidade Federal do Rio de Janeiro, Brazil, and his Ph.D. at the New School for Social Research in New York, US. He is Assistant Professor of Economics at Kalamazoo College, Michigan, US, and has taught at the Universidade Federal do Rio de Janeiro, the Graduate Faculty of Political and Social Sciences of the New School for Social Research, and has also been Visiting Professor at the University of Burgundy in Dijon, France, and at the Facultad Latino Americana de Ciencias Sociales in Ecuador. He has also been an external consultant of the International Labour Organisation. His research focuses on the effects of external liberalisation on growth, income distribution, social policies and the environment in developing countries. He has co-edited a book on *Credit, Interest Rates and the Open Economy: Essays on Horizontalism* (Edward Elgar, 2001, with L.-P. Rochon), and has published in *Cuestiones Económicas*, the *Brazilian Journal of Political Economy*, the *European Journal of the History of Economic Thought*, *Latin American Perspectives*, and the *Review of Political Economy*.

L. Randall Wray is Professor of Economics at the University of Missouri–Kansas City, US. He has published widely in journals and is the author of *Money and Credit in Capitalist Economies: The Endogenous Money Approach* (Edward Elgar, 1990) and *Understanding Modern Money: The Key to Full Employment and Price Stability* (Edward Elgar, 1998). His recent articles include: 'The 1966 financial crisis: financial instability or political economy?' (*Review of Political Economy*, 1999), 'Public service employment: full employment without inflation' (*Economic and Labour Relations Review*, 2000), and 'Did the rising tide eliminate our "surplus" population?' (*Journal of Economic Issues*, 2001).

Alberto Zazzaro is Professor of Economics at the University of Ancona, Italy. Among his recent publications are: 'Innovation, human capital destruction and firms' investment in training' (*Manchester School*, 2000, with M.R. Carillo), 'Bank's inefficiency and economic growth: a micro–macro approach' (*Scottish Journal of Political Economy*, 2001, with R. Lucchetti and L. Papi), 'Group reputation and persistent (or permanent) discrimination in credit markets' (*Journal of Multinational Financial Management*, 2001, with D. Scalera), and 'The discouraged entrepreneur: a model of self-employment with financial constraints' (*International Journal of Applied Economics and Econometrics*, 2001).

Acknowledgements

The editors would like to thank Edward Elgar and his collaborators in Camberley and Cheltenham for their enthusiastic and professional support during the development of this book. They are also grateful to Nunzio F. Canova (Università della Svizzera italiana, Switzerland) and Gérald Gavillet (University of Lausanne, Switzerland) for their bibliographic assistance.

L.-P.R.
S.R.

Introduction

Louis-Philippe Rochon and Sergio Rossi

Since Keynes, Kalecki and Sraffa, the progress of macroeconomics and of monetary theory in particular has not been overwhelmingly positive. While some aspects of new Keynesian economics offer glimmer of hope, with their emphasis on banks and the credit channel, macroeconomics has generally returned to pre-Keynesian economics.

Most macroeconomic models today are market-clearing equilibrium models or models that mimic exchange/barter economies where the price mechanism guarantees convergence to a steady position of equilibrium. Scarcity plays a central role, and prices and quantities are determined within existing markets. Economics is defined as the 'efficient allocation of scarce resources'. In all cases, money is neutral in the long run. In the short run money is allowed to play a role, but this is usually attributed to the existence of some imperfections, such as sticky wages and prices, asymmetric information, unanticipated shocks, or credit rationing. In the short run, therefore, the economy can deviate from its long-run position, which is usually associated with a non-accelerating inflation rate of unemployment (NAIRU). The real and monetary sides of the economy are assumed largely independent from one another. Further, rules of conduct for (homogeneous) households and entrepreneurs (atomistic agents) are dictated by principles outlined by marginalism mostly within perfectly competitive markets. Economic agents are maximisers of their respective objectives (utility and profit). Aggregation of these agents constitutes the macroeconomic worldview of neoclassical theory. Macroeconomics is thus rooted in microeconomic foundations. The causality runs from microeconomic to macroeconomic phenomena, while never acknowledging the possibility of reverse causality.

These models, however, stand in stark contrast with models of production that take into consideration institutions, time, history, income distribution, class relations and hierarchy, and technological change. Realism is at the root of these latter models, which attempt to explain the real world from observations and stylised facts. Such models are inherently dynamic, and do not gravitate toward any specific position of equilibrium. Many would claim that such models are anti-equilibrium or without equilibrium. Kaldor (1985, p. 12) in particular sees 'the economy as a continually evolving system whose path cannot be predicted any more than the evolution of an ecological system in biology'.

In this second group of models, unemployment is the normal state of the economy and is not caused by imperfections, but rather by the lack of aggregate demand (with or without the existence of uncertainty), which affect production and investment decisions, bank lending decisions, productivity, and hence employment. An activist government sector is therefore a requirement for full employment and economic growth. Further, money matters, in both short-run and long-run analysis. It is neither because money creation may be inflationary, nor because increases in the money supply are anticipated or not. Rather, money matters because production cannot take place without it. In pure exchange models, the wheels of production turn; money is simply the grease that allows for smoother motion. By contrast, for post Keynesian and circuit writers the wheels of production cannot turn without money.

In these models money matters for another important reason. The purpose of production is to sell goods against the expectation of future revenues. In an entrepreneurial economy, production is undertaken to make monetary profits. Money is thus both the starting and ending points of the analysis. This raises the question of the role of the rate of interest. While the interest rate is a purely exogenous variable in the sense that it is controlled by the central bank, its role is not always properly assessed. In this sense, it has a dual role, both important for the production process. Firstly, interest enters into the costs of production. While the rate of interest may not have a direct influence on investment, as postulated by the downward-sloping investment demand curve, it is an important determinant of the costs of production. Secondly, the rate of interest may also have an indirect effect on output via its distributional effects. As interest rates rise and effective demand is affected, this may have a negative effect on sales and production, and possibly on employment levels.

Production economies are thus monetary and credit-based economies, and imply a specific sequence of irreversible events. The real and monetary sides of the economy are not independent, hence the explanation for the endogenous nature of money. The possibility of full employment without inflation is accepted, as long as it is understood within a class-based model.

Heterogeneous households and firms are not maximisers, but rather satisfiers, and meet economic needs (a hierarchy of needs; see Robinson, 1956) rather than wants in a lexicographic fashion. Because of uncertainty, they follow rules of bounded rationality (Lavoie, 1992).

With the publication of the works of Keynes, Kalecki and Sraffa, macroeconomics was off to a good start. Macroeconomics was independent of microeconomic behaviour and emphasised the role of aggregate demand in determining output and growth. Together, their works offered a critical analysis of neoclassical theory while also offering a clear alternative to mainstream thought, based on institutions, time, uncertainty, social classes and imperfect markets. Unfortunately, none of these three economists worked together to present a coherent whole. Hence the Keynesian – or Kaleckian – revolution was aborted. Attention seemed to have focused on Keynes's *General Theory*, ignoring the more heterodox-grounded work of Kalecki. As for Sraffa, his publications were too few to have had much impact on the profession at large. Had the work of Kalecki or Sraffa been at the centre of the debate, the revolution may have taken on a very different nature.

Focusing on the *General Theory* led to some problems, which begin with the book itself. While Keynes presented it as a 'struggle to escape', it still owed too much to neoclassical theory. Keynes still accepted the labour supply curve, the exogeneity of money, and perfectly competitive markets, to name a few. In this sense, the *General Theory* may best be described as an unfinished work. This is consistent with Keynes's own assessment. For example, in the German edition of the *General Theory*, Keynes described it as a 'transition', thereby implying that much still had to be done (see Rochon, 1999a). Hence Keynes's first mistake was to retain too much of the neoclassical edifice.

Irrespective of the reasons for which Keynes borrowed elements of neoclassical theory (see Robinson, 1970; Dow and Dow, 1989), the fact remains that while his story of aggregate demand and the multiplier got across, it paved the way for what came afterwards, namely, Hicks (1937) and his IS–LM interpretation of Keynes's *General Theory*. While Keynes was arguing against neoclassical theory (at least in principle), Hicks was trying to reconcile it with Keynes's theory of effective demand, thereby paving the way for the elaboration of the so-called neoclassical synthesis. Although Hicks (1980–81) would later recant his approach, the damage was done, thereby aborting the Keynesian revolution. Since then, macroeconomics has continued to develop along pre-Keynesian lines, and the IS–LM model remains a central component of Keynesian macroeconomics. Needless to say, the blame cannot be laid entirely at Hicks's feet. After all, Keynes did treat the money supply as exogenous in the *General Theory*, and never repudiated Hicks's model although he was given the opportunity to do so when Hicks solicited Keynes's comments on his 1937 paper. One may wonder how different macroeconomics may have turned out had Keynes forcefully denounced the Hicks model, both before and after it was published. This was Keynes's second mistake.

The IS–LM model had a tremendous impact on the profession and on policy makers. It proposed a synthesis of Keynes and neoclassical ideas, but unfortunately had little to do with Keynes's objective of replacing neoclassical theory, made explicitly clear in the preface to the *General Theory*. After all, Hicks's model was conceived before Keynes's most famous book. Hicks had modelled first the Walrasian framework, and only after the publication of the *General Theory* he sought to see whether it was compatible with Keynes. As Hicks (1980–81, pp. 141–2) tells us, 'the idea of the IS–LM diagram came to me as a result of the work I had been doing on three-way exchange, conceived in a Walrasian manner. . . . So it was natural for me to think that a similar device could be used for the Keynes theory'.

The IS–LM model became synonymous with Keynesian economics. After all, it did emphasise aggregate demand and argued that fiscal policy could have a multiplier effect on output. But Keynesians argued in terms of a liquidity trap and of sticky nominal wages. This did not sit well with Keynes's model. To be sure, Keynes admitted the possibility of a liquidity trap but made clear that he could think of no period when a liquidity trap actually occurred. Keynes also let nominal wages float in Chapter 19 of the *General Theory* and showed that we could still have unemployment. Somehow, these elements did not find their way into Hicks's and the Keynesians' interpretation (and later on in Modigliani's model).

Monetarists responded to Hicks, not to Keynes. Monetarists also emphasised aggregate demand, but placed the emphasis on money supply. In this sense, they were very much Keynesian, accepting the IS–LM model and the exogenous nature of money. Rational expectationists searched for microfoundations of macroeconomics and developed models devoid of any institutional structure. Rational agents choose to optimise. In this respect new Keynesians fare better, emphasising the importance of effective demand and the role of credit and banks, but still fall back on a theoretical model that is essentially neoclassical while at the same time accepting the need for microfoundations. Credit rationing still implies the scarcity of bank loans, and banks are still financial intermediaries channelling savings to investment according to the loanable funds view (deposits make loans).

Two overall themes run among all these models. Firstly, aggregate demand is essentially assigned a passive or short-run role, if present at all. Indeed, the IS–LM model is only a short-run model. Aggregate demand only explains temporary deviations from long-run levels of output, as well as demand-pulled inflation. The supply side of the model dictates the equilibrium or natural levels of employment and output, that is, the NAIRU. Growth is explained by changes on the supply side of the model. Either way, demand is a passive player adjusting itself to the supply conditions of the model. Secondly, these models essentially consider the money supply as set by the central bank. Money is exogenous. If there is an excess demand for money, then the existing supply must be rationed, as in new Keynesian models. The rate of interest is endogenous and determined within the money market, that is, it is dictated by supply of and demand for money.

This is hardly comforting for those economists who regard aggregate demand as pivotal, both in the short and long run, and who consider that money is endogenous at all times. The theory of effective demand needs to be reconstructed along lines more consistent with Keynes's and Kalecki's models, and the endogeneity of money needs to be carefully explained. In fact, for many economists these two elements are one and the same. A proper theory of effective demand, based on a monetary theory of production, must rely on a theory of endogenous money. In this setting, money cannot be exogenous. Hence the IS–LM model that artificially separates the real sector from the monetary sector cannot be accepted, even if one makes the LM curve dependent on the IS curve, as in Davidson (1972/1978).

A number of economists remained therefore faithful to the works of Keynes and Kalecki. Advocating the need to incorporate institutional elements and some realism into the theory of money and effective demand, they largely rejected the IS–LM framework, and continued to develop Keynesian and Kaleckian models on firmer, more heterodox grounds. As Deleplace and Nell (1996, p. 5) write, '[t]he "Monetary Theory of Production" . . . has finally to be developed without compromises'.

The purpose of this volume is twofold. Firstly, it is to continue to offer insights into this heterodox tradition by developing views consistent with the principles of effective demand and endogenous money. To do this, we must rebuild Keynes, using Kalecki and Sraffa, and therefore 'complete the unfinished Keynesian revolution' (Arestis, 1992, p. 88). Secondly, as the focus of the book is on money and monetary theory, it also aims at continuing the tradition of reconciliation. Since the early publication of the 'Monnaie et Production' series in *Économie et Sociétés*, it became evident, in fact, that there were two distinct groups of economists who shared a similar interpretation of Keynes's and Kalecki's theory of a monetary economy of production: post Keynesians and circuitists. Proponents of both groups pledged allegiance to Keynes (and some also to Kalecki and Sraffa), while also rejecting the neoclassical synthesis as being a 'bastard' version of Keynes's *General Theory*.

Because of their emphasis on production and time, post Keynesians and proponents of the monetary circuit approach place money at the very centre of their analyses of investment and output. For them, it is inconceivable, for the most part, to separate real analysis from monetary factors (see Rogers, 1989). In this sense, there is a complete rejection of barter systems or models based on pure exchange. In the real world, production, investment and money are integrally linked through the banking system. This is the very sense of Keynes's and Kalecki's notion of a monetary theory of production. Money is endogenised through the needs of the economic system to reproduce itself and grow.

Now, while post Keynesian and circuit theories have many elements in common, they also have important differences. This is complicated by the fact that it is difficult to clearly identify who is post Keynesian, or what post Keynesians stand for. The same argument applies to advocates of the monetary circuit approach.

Among post Keynesians, in fact, we can identify four strands of monetary thought. Firstly, we have the American post Keynesians, for whom uncertainty and time play an important role. The writings of Davidson, along with the *Journal of Post Keynesian Economics*, are central to this group. The existence of money is linked directly to the pervasiveness of uncertainty. Capitalist economies are not necessarily prone to crises, but uncertainty prevents economies from gravitating toward full employment (see for instance Davidson, 1972/1978; Cardim de Carvalho, 1995; Dalziel, 1995). Secondly, we can identify the Minskian post Keynesians, or the structuralists, for whom fluctuations in output and employment can be attributed to financial reasons. For these authors, capitalist economies are prone to periodic crises, although modern institutions would prevent 'it' from happening again (Minsky, 1982; Pollin, 1991; Palley, 1996). Financial innovations, both the liability and asset types, play an important part in explaining the endogeneity of money and the resulting weaker role of the central bank in controlling the money supply. Thirdly, we can identify the Cambridge post Keynesians. While they are generally assumed to focus primarily on growth theory and business cycles, some had clear notions of endogenous money (Robinson, 1956; Kahn, 1958/1972).[1] Kaldor (1980, 1982) may be added to this group as well.[2] Finally, we find horizontalists, who focus on the nature of money and the role of interest rates in monetary economies of production (Moore, 1988; Lavoie, 1992; Seccareccia, 1996; Rochon, 1999a). These authors emphasise that banks lend money only to creditworthy customers and, far from being passive, are active players in the endogenous money-creation process.

As the reader will notice, there are a number of key themes common to all these groups, namely, the demand-determined importance of output, the role of banks, endogenous money and uncertainty. In particular, the creation of money results from a demand for loans that are granted by banks. Moreover, key elements from each group can be placed together to form a coherent approach, as we discuss below.

Among circuit writers we can identify different schools, too. In fact, there are three independent schools. Firstly, we find the proponents of the French circuit school who follow the early writings of Parguez (1975, 1982, 1984, 1986, 1987). This group is mainly concerned with policy-oriented issues focusing on the level of economic activity, unemployment and stabilisation policies, with an interest in situating the monetary circuit approach in the history of economic thought (see Vallageas, 1985). More recently, Parguez (1996, 2001, 2002) and Parguez and Seccareccia (2000) have returned to theoretical issues such as the nature and origin of money, integrating in their analysis many aspects of the neo-chartalist view (see Wray, 1998, 2000; Bell, 2000, 2001). Secondly, in Italy the followers of Graziani (1990, 1996, 1997) emphasise the sequential nature of monetary flows in the circular process of production–consumption involving the set of firms and the set of households with the intervention of the banking system taken as a whole. A number of authors in this tradition work toward incorporating elements of Marx and Schumpeter within the theory of the monetary circuit (Bellofiore, 1985, 1989, 1992, 1998; Messori, 1985, 1997; Realfonzo, 1998; Bellofiore et al., 2000).[3] Finally, following the work of Schmitt (1959, 1966, 1972, 1973, 1975, 1984) we find the Dijon–Fribourg school, explaining the asset–liability nature of modern money by its being a double-entry in banks' balance sheets, and investigating the nature of national as well as international macroeconomic problems like inflation, unemployment and external debt servicing (Cencini, 1988, 1995, 1996, 2001; Gnos and Schmitt, 1990; Cencini and Schmitt, 1991; Gnos, 1992a, 1998; Schmitt, 1996a, 1996b; Rossi, 1998, 2001a).

Like the post Keynesian approach, the so-called monetary circuit approach encompasses different lines of thought that cannot be considered as a unified strand of monetary thinking. In particular, Parguez's and Schmitt's views on money and monetary macroeconomics strongly differ and are in sharp contrast to one another. The differences are so deep that Schmitt has come to refuse the label 'circuitist' to define the paradigm he has been working on since 1956 (see Gnos and Rasera, 1985). These two views therefore are kept separate also in this volume, where the second part is on the theory of the monetary circuit *à la* Graziani–Parguez, while the third part is on what we call the theory of money emissions (the Schmitt school).

Now, while there are similarities and differences among the proponents of the post Keynesian monetary approach as well as among those of the theory of the monetary circuit, there are also similarities and differences between these two camps. At times, these differences may appear to be irreconcilable. But this should not discourage post Keynesians and circuitists to seek to work together to build a consistent theory of monetary production economies. We believe, in fact, that many differences may be more the result of emphasis than substance. We believe therefore that there are sufficient similarities to warrant a continued effort at reconciliation. This effort is worthwhile and some economists have been for a few years now trying to bridge the gap (Lavoie, 1992; Rochon, 1999a; Fontana, 2000; Parguez and Seccareccia, 2000). After all, in his *mea culpa*, Moore (2001, p. 13) now acknowledges that the debate between horizontalists and structuralists was the 'quintessential "storm in a teacup"'. As he correctly argues, this debate unnecessarily prevented post Keynesians from presenting the merits of their innovative approach to mainstream audiences. In fact, descendants of Keynes, Kalecki and Sraffa must not repeat the fatal mistake that their progenitors did, that is, not to cooperate. There is clearly a need to present a coherent alternative to mainstream models, and now more than ever. It is becoming more evident to some orthodox economists, especially those interested in policy matters, that the rate of interest is exogenous and that the 'money stock' (their expression) may not be as easily controlled by the central bank. We thus find the beginning of an interesting argument. The challenge is now to let them see the rest of the analysis, and especially the policy implications of the post Keynesian and circuit approaches to money, credit and banking. A dialogue between these two strands of thinking may therefore be seminal for the further construction of a realistic and policy-oriented theory of the working of modern capitalist systems.

A DIALOGUE

The success of Deleplace and Nell's (1996) *Money in Motion* has brought to the fore the importance of a dialogue between the various heterodox schools of thought on the nature and role of money, and the relevance of monetary policy in influencing output and employment. Post Keynesians, on the one hand, and proponents of the monetary circuit approach, on the other hand, agree on a variety of issues. All share Keynes's and Kalecki's emphasis on money, credit and production. All try to explain the integration of money into the real economy, although their explanations may differ. They all reject to a large degree Hicks's interpretation of Keynes's *General Theory* as a system of simultaneous equations in favour of a system set in historical time. But the attempt at building a larger body of consistent thought requires at the very best some degree of generality. It is perhaps inconceivable to have full agreement and consensus on a theory that delves too much into intricate details. Consensus therefore requires generality; otherwise debate may distract us from the overall objective, or even lead to abandoning it altogether, as was the case with the Trieste summer school. It is thus important to remember that the purpose of monetary heterodoxy is to reconcile post Keynesians and circuitists, integrating their analyses into a coherent theoretical structure.

At this juncture, however, an important point must be made. In their Introduction, Deleplace and Nell (1996) made us aware of the general arguments of the two groups. That was then. It is now time to go further and try to convince each group that much still needs to be done, especially in light of the weaknesses of each approach, to form a body of consistent thought. Such a statement needs to be explained.

Many post Keynesians, even some horizontalists, still make use of some orthodox arguments, either some Marshallian elements or some rules of marginalism. This needs to be addressed and, hopefully, abandoned (see Winnett, 1992). In part, it was Keynes's reluctance or inability to fully rid himself of the vestigial traces of neoclassical theory that contributed to the ensuing Hicksian interpretation. So, while post Keynesians have a theory of endogenous money, a number of them have been distracted by arguments regarding the evolution of the banking system (Chick, 1986), and whether money is endogenous only when the economy is growing (Davidson and Weintraub, 1973; Chick, 1995). Chick (1986) argues that money became endogenous only late in the development of banks, although there is no real evidence that this was the case. Other observers have hinted that money has always been endogenous, irrespective of the historical period (see Lavoie, 1992). What post Keynesians therefore need to do is develop their theory of endogenous money on firmer and more heterodox grounds by focusing on the nature of money. On the other hand, circuit writers have too far emphasised the nature of money and have neglected the useful discussion over the role and importance of institutions and financial markets. Their discussion over the nature of money has often bordered on the esoteric and has resulted in marginalising many post Keynesians.

We have now reached a stage in the evolution of heterodox monetary thinking where the weaknesses of post Keynesians (on the nature of money, for instance) can be answered by the writings of the proponents of the monetary circuit approach. Similarly, the weaknesses of circuit theory, more specifically institutional arguments and stylised facts, can be replaced by elements discussed in post Keynesian literature. We have therefore a great opportunity of creating a coherent whole. This book is intended to be a step forward in this direction. It represents a confrontation between the various approaches, but one that is direct, open and serene. Its purpose is to solidify the elements all these approaches have in common, and possibly clear the air on some remaining differences. The result hoped for is to agree on a heterodox approach to the creation, circulation and destruction of money that may inform a policy-oriented study of the pathologies affecting modern capitalist economies.

Let us introduce more closely the reader to the different heterodox views on money and monetary theory presented in this volume, before summarising the contributions that make up its different parts.

THE POST KEYNESIAN MONETARY APPROACH

The early criticism of the orthodox theories of money occurred with Keynes's post-*General Theory* articles on the finance motive (see Rochon, 1997). Keynes's arguments though were ambiguous. While he argued that banks were at the centre of the lending process supplying firms with the necessary finance, the point of these articles was not to develop a theory of endogenous money. Rather, it was to argue that firms need no *ex ante* stock of saving in order to carry out investment decisions. Keynes (1937/1973, p. 216) saw this as an 'improvement' in his analysis, and it very much was: he linked the production process to bank lending, and discussed the importance of the overdraft system and credit lines.[4]

Keynes certainly comes close to a theory of endogenous money, and his arguments can be made consistent with such an approach (Graziani, 1987; Bradley, 1993; Rochon, 1997). Overall, though, there are still a few arguments missing. In essence, the central bank is missing from Keynes's analysis: the emphasis is squarely on the role of banks. Yet, the conspicuous absence of a central bank is problematic. What is its role? After all, Keynes argued in the *General Theory* that money was exogenous and controlled by the central bank. Is this the case? Could Keynes not be arguing in terms of a money multiplier with reserves supplied by the central bank and multiplied through the bank lending process? The analysis is not complete.

The next phase of the post Keynesian analysis arouse with the Radcliffe Report, and in particular with the contributions of Kahn (1958/1972) and Kaldor (1958/1964). Yet, their contributions also were not about developing a theory of endogenous money. Rather, they were arguing in terms of a variable velocity of money and the ineffectiveness of monetary policy in controlling inflation. The quantity theory of money was thus an unreliable theory, and the causality between money and inflation could not be sustained. Kaldor in particular still argued in terms of causality from money to income, but noted that this causality was unreliable (see Moore, 1991). In this respect, one can also include Minsky's (1957a, 1957b) early papers. But then again, the same criticism applies to Minsky as it does to the early Kaldor. Minsky was attempting to show the importance of liability management and the unreliability of monetary policy. Minsky's origins are rooted in the loanable funds view (Lavoie, 1997) and therefore do not sit well within the framework of endogenous money. These early articles cannot be considered as being consistent with post Keynesian thought.

Overall, therefore, the early post Keynesian contributions did not lead to developing a theory of endogenous money, although one exception that stands out is Robinson (1956). In *The Accumulation of Capital*, Robinson is clear on the endogenous nature of money, the role of bank loans to finance production, and the role played by the reflux mechanism in extinguishing money and debt. In fact, Robinson (1956) ought to be considered the founder of the post-Keynes school of endogenous money (see Rochon, 2001b). It would be naïve to deny, however, that today the endogenous money view is encumbered by a number of differences that stand in the way to build a unified, and consistent, theory of money and monetary economies.

Differences

As noted above, there are four distinct schools within post Keynesian monetary economics. This certainly complicates any attempt at presenting a coherent whole. Nonetheless, certain common characteristics can be discerned. These four schools, in fact, can be reduced to two groups. These are structuralists and horizontalists (Pollin, 1991). In general, we may claim that American post Keynesians and Minskian post Keynesians can be labelled structuralists, while Cambridge post Keynesians (including Robinson, 1956) and horizontalists can properly be labelled horizontalists.

This dichotomy is a familiar one, having been discussed at length in the literature of the 1990s (see Moore, 1991, 1995; Palley, 1991, 1994, 1996; Pollin, 1991, 1996; Rochon, 1999a). The debate between these two circles goes beyond establishing whether the money supply curve is horizontal or upward sloping. Traditionally, the debate centres on the availability of reserves and the liquidity of banks, and the riskiness of expanding banks' balance sheets. Structuralists generally argue that banks are not as passive as horizontalists claim, and have more control over bank lending than argued by Moore (1988). In this connection, Lavoie (1996) has shown that banks do not necessarily become more illiquid or riskier as loans are made. Further, Rochon (2001a) has shown that much of the criticism of horizontalism rests on a misinterpretation and misreading of the horizontalist literature.

In particular, structuralists argue three points. Firstly, they argue that money is only partially endogenous, or rather that the total money supply is both endogenous and exogenous (Davidson, 1972/1978; Minsky, 1991). Secondly, they argue that bank credit is only required when the economy is growing. Money is endogenous only when output is increasing (Wells, 1983; Davidson, 1986; Bibow, 1995; Chick, 1995). Thirdly, as banks grant credit to firms, they become increasingly illiquid, thereby raising interest rates to compensate for the riskiness of their illiquidity. Horizontalists, on the other hand, reject all three assumptions. Firstly, they claim that money is fully endogenous. In other words, the whole money supply is always and everywhere an endogenous phenomenon: no component of the money supply is exogenous. How can it be? Even if the central bank increased reserves, there must be borrowers willing to enter into debt. This is the significance of Moore's (1988) expression that money is 'credit-led and demand-determined'. In this sense, there can never be an excess supply of money. Secondly, bank credit is always required, even when the economy is not expanding. This is because bank borrowers must repay their bank loans with the proceeds of their sales on the market for produced goods, and, in order to begin production anew, must borrow again.[5] Thirdly, as Lavoie (1996) argues, banks do not necessarily become riskier as loans expand. After all, if banks keep lending only to creditworthy borrowers, they should remain risk-free. Of course, as Rochon (1999a, Ch. 8) argues, banks may face a macro-uncertainty shock that would affect all agents in the economy.

Similarities

Despite the differences, a strong argument can nonetheless be made that a common approach exists among all post Keynesians. Elements from each group can therefore be put together to form a coherent alternative to neoclassical theory. The first two key elements are the role of effective demand and endogenous money, which form the cornerstone of the post Keynesian approach. Indeed, if production is carried out through bank loans, and if wages are paid before production begins, then the theory of effective demand and endogenous money are flip sides of the same coin. Thus, all post Keynesians recognise the endogenous component to money, although they disagree on the degree of money endogeneity. Money is always the result of a bank loan, and loans create deposits that create reserves in the process. Banks only look for reserves later. Financial innovations, as argued by structuralists (see Pollin, 1996), give us an account of how banks can find reserves (although see Rochon, 1999a, for a horizontalist interpretation of financial innovations).

With these two key elements, it becomes easier to incorporate other elements of the post Keynesian analysis into a consistent whole. For instance, income distributional elements must be allowed to play a role in affecting aggregate demand. If economic growth is demand-determined, then elements affecting effective demand must be incorporated into the story. In this sense, higher investment, public spending and higher wages will have a positive impact on aggregate demand. The rate of interest, set by the central bank, may also have a role to play. Interest rates may not play a direct role on aggregate demand through investment, but may have an indirect impact through income distribution. Financial markets must also be brought to the fore. What is their precise role? Do they have an effect on aggregate demand, and if so, how? To be sure, post Keynesians, except Minsky and some structuralists, have not properly incorporated financial markets into their analysis of money and aggregate demand. Finally, uncertainty must also play an important role. Fear of the future may delay investment and consumption, and may thus have a negative effect on aggregate demand. Uncertainty may also raise financial markets' instability. More importantly, uncertainty may affect directly not only the demand for bank loans, but also the supply of bank loans. This does not mean that money is supply-determined. Banks can only lend to those who demand a loan. However, uncertainty may make banks more pessimistic about borrowers' ability to pay back their loans. Thus in periods of uncertainty banks become more pessimistic, and this is usually associated with a downturn in aggregate demand and output. In general, all economics agents – be it the government, the central bank, commercial banks, firms or households – operate under fundamental uncertainty. The world is non-ergodic (Davidson, 1972/1978). This will affect the agents' decisions to save, lend, consume, invest, and so on.

THE THEORY OF THE MONETARY CIRCUIT

The circular flow analysis of production and consumption by macroeconomic sets of agents (namely, firms and workers, with or without the intervention of banks) is as old as economics. Its origin can be traced back to the work of Quesnay, the Louis XV personal surgeon who gave rise to the physiocratic school in eighteenth-century France (see Deleplace, 1999). Since then, a number of European-based economists such as Böhm-Bawerk, Leontief, Marx, Schumpeter and Wicksell, to name only the most celebrated, used this approach in their analyses of the economic process within the framework of a money-using economy (see Vallageas, 1985; Bellofiore, 1992; Realfonzo, 1998).[6] More recently, the monetary circuit approach has been advocated by Le Bourva (1962), who referred to the work of Schmitt (1960) to point out the flow nature of money and to analyse the circular flow of income. Le Bourva (1992, p. 455) observed that a direct link exists between the formation and the use of income on the one hand, and the creation and destruction of money on the other. His work was inspired by the well-known controversy between the banking and the currency schools spawning the eighteenth-century history of economic thought. This controversy was revived in the nineteenth century in the debate between metallists and chartalists, which regained momentum in the first half of the twentieth century. In particular, Le Bourva brought to the fore the efflux–reflux mechanism that lies behind the creation, circulation and destruction of bank money, and that logically precludes any possibility for the money multiplier to be other than unity, a point on which circuitists largely agree. As its name indicates, the theory of the monetary circuit is therefore, first of all, a theory explaining the circular flow of money from its creation by the banking system to its destruction by the same system (Realfonzo, 1999). This flow occurs in logical time and circuit writers separate it into a number of sequential phases ranging from the opening to the closing of the circuit of money. Hence the need arises for them to consider the time span of this circuit, and in particular the problems elicited by its being temporarily open. As Realfonzo (1998, p. 16) puts it, '[u]ntil the moment in which firms are in a position to repay the banks, a stock of money remains in existence, leaving open a double debit/credit relation between firms and banks on the one hand, and between banks and workers on the other'.

Circuit theorists consider that the formation of a money stock poses a problem for the firms – considered here as a whole – because it obliges them to renegotiate their loan commitments with banks. This may lead to less favourable borrowing conditions for those firms that are not able to extinguish their bank debts. As a result, these firms must support greater costs for producing a given output in the following period(s). At a macroeconomic level, in fact, failure to repay bank debt may lead firms to cut back their wage bill, hence employment, with the ensuing possibility of generating a crisis in the whole system (see Parguez, 1975; 1987; Poulon, 1982). This framework has a number of similarities with the post Keynesian monetary approach, although some differences may also be noted.

Similarities

The theory of the monetary circuit and the post Keynesian monetary approach share many characteristics. Firstly, they both emphasise the importance of bank credit for the production process to be set in motion and expand. Although for the former theory the creation of money is congenital to production while for the latter approach it only is necessary when the economy is growing, both agree that banks are essential for production and consumption, so much so that bank money is endogenous because it is credit-led and demand-determined. In particular, within post Keynesian monetary economics horizontalism is very close to the theory of the monetary circuit: the tenets of both are the same as regards the creation, circulation and destruction of money within a modern capitalist economy of production (see Moore, 1988; Graziani, 1990; Lavoie, 1999; Rochon, 1999a, 1999b). Secondly, post Keynesians as well as circuit writers favour partial and sequential analysis of macroeconomic phenomena, rejecting the neoclassical search for general and simultaneous equilibria. Although monetary post Keynesians focus on time and uncertainty while circuit theorists address the macroeconomic role of different classes of agents, both are interested in part–whole relationships affecting aggregate demand and income distribution within a monetary economy of production. As a result, they both reject methodological individualism and try instead to construct a macroeconomic theory that can explain the observed microeconomic forms of behaviour in terms of reverse causality. Thirdly, both groups consider that the rate of interest is an exogenous variable, which central banks can control much better than the total money supply (an endogenous magnitude indeed) for policy matters. In particular, in case of an economic downturn the central bank can act on the bank (or federal funds) rate to enhance recovery and boost employment, rather than to manipulate the money supply, which is largely out of its control.

Differences

The similarities between the post Keynesian monetary approach and the theory of the monetary circuit do not fully extend to the 'first principles' of monetary economics. In particular, between the two camps there is still disagreement on the function that the thing called money performs in modern times. Post Keynesian authors focus on money as a stock of (liquid) wealth, which, as Keynes noted, allows agents to bridge the gap between the present and the future in a non-ergodic world characterised by fundamental uncertainty and liquidity preference. By contrast, circuit writers emphasise that money is the means of final payment within an economic system of production and exchange, in which there may also exists a group of individuals who have no access to it because of their social (low) profile. This raises the need to forge ahead the distinction between these two money functions while seeking to construct a general theory of monetary production economies explaining money as a means of payment as well as money as a stock of wealth (see Graziani, 1996). Today, both approaches still disagree to a large extent on the principal function of money, although some authors are trying to bridge the gap, integrating also an appraisal of banks' liquidity preference within a macro-theoretical framework (Rochon, 1999a, 1999b; Fontana, 2000). What remains to be settled, in fact, is the nature of money. All the rest is ancillary to that. If money is a store of wealth, it clearly is a stock magnitude. If money is a means of payment whose creation, circulation and destruction occurs in a circular flow, then money is a flow. Still it must be explained whether the stock is the efficient cause of the flow, or vice versa. The general answer that money is both a flow and a stock, depending on the focus of the analysis, cannot be deemed satisfactory unless one can objectively explain the dual nature of money referring to conceptual logic. This is the ground on which the Schmitt school has founded its quantum-theoretical approach to monetary macroeconomics, developing an original monetary theory to analyse, positively as well as normatively, the working of modern capitalist systems of production and consumption. This theory is reminiscent of Keynes's (1930/1971, p. 134) statement that '[h]uman effort and human consumption are the ultimate matters from which alone economic transactions are capable of deriving any significance; and all other forms of expenditure only acquire importance from their having some relationship, sooner or later, to the effort of producers or to the expenditure of consumers'.

THE THEORY OF MONEY EMISSIONS

The theory of money emissions has been developed independently of the monetary circuit approach followed over the last thirty years in Italy, France and Canada by circuit writers. In fact, these two frameworks have many differences and very few similarities, although their focus is the same, namely, the working of our monetary economies of production. Led by Schmitt, the Dijon–Fribourg school argues that the circuit of money is instantaneous, because money is a flow in the form of a numerical double-entry recorded in a bank's bookkeeping system of accounts. The integration of money into the real economy occurs through production: it is the payment of wages that allows for the association of money – a numerical form – and output – its real content.[7] Schmitt puts forward a new interpretation of Keynes's concept of the wage-unit, to show that money and output are the twin faces of the same reality: produced goods exist as wage-units from the moment wages are paid out by firms to workers – through banks, which record them as bank deposits – to the moment these deposits are spent on the market for produced goods (Schmitt, 1975; Cencini, 1988; Rossi, 2001b). The value of money results therefore from the integration of banking and production systems into a unique macroeconomic structure, which is real as well as monetary. In this new framework, money income is the instantaneous result of a production monetised by banks, although it refers to a finite period of time, as the Robertson 'day' (see Schmitt, 1982). Production, hence its result, that is, output, is measured by the number of wage-units paid out to workers (factor costs), so that, following Keynes, labour is the sole factor of production in the theory of money emissions. Further, the payment of wages is an emission in as much as money and the corresponding output are one and the same object, namely, money income defining an exchange-value that exists in the form of a bank deposit. This deposit results from a loan that banks grant to firms to finance production, and is destroyed as soon as an equivalent output is sold on the market for produced goods. In the meantime, it may circulate in financial transactions that depositors are not necessarily aware of and that are the result of banks' financial intermediation (see Gnos, 1998).

Elaborating on these principles, the Schmitt school puts forward a new theory of effective demand, where the determination of the wage bill as well as the formation of value occurs in a circular flow process. More precisely, according to the theory of money emissions, 'effective demand is defined as a two-way flux, firms "giving" and "receiving" the same product' (Schmitt, 1986, p. 117). Hence income formation (that is, total supply) and income expenditure (total demand) are two identical magnitudes in this framework, for otherwise they could not exist (see Schmitt, 1988). This does not mean, however, that full employment can always be attained, or that this approach applies exclusively to a Say's Law economy in the traditional interpretation of this law, as claimed by Lavoie (1987, p. 87). The Schmitt school, in fact, explains that structural anomalies of capital accumulation may lead to inflation and unemployment, because today the banks' bookkeeping structure does not yet differentiate between redistributed and invested profits (see Cencini, 1996; Baranzini and Cencini, 2001; Rossi, 2001a). A further set of issues concern the international economy, namely, the problems raised by the introduction of the European single currency (see Schmitt, 1973, 1975; Cencini and Schmitt, 1992; Gnos, 1992b; Rossi, 1996, 1997) and by external debt servicing (see Cencini and Schmitt, 1991; Cencini, 1995).

Similarities

Despite its originality the theory of money emissions has a number of affinities with the background of the post Keynesian tradition and the monetary circuit approach. All these schools address the main problems of modern economies of production. In fact, the focus on unemployment associated with a lack of total demand (deflation) is a central theme in post Keynesian, circuitist as well as Schmittian analyses. Another issue on which the Schmitt school and the other heterodox approaches to monetary theory focus is capital accumulation and functional income distribution. All these schools also agree on the view that considers macroeconomics not being based on microeconomic foundations. Macroeconomic phenomena and relationships cannot be reduced to, and analysed by, economic aggregates. There exist therefore several themes that all these heterodox approaches have in common, although the similarities between Schmitt's and the other schools mainly concern the issues addressed while the differences are substantial, for they lie in the very conceptual framework within which these issues are analysed.

Differences

The theory of money emissions is based on a conception of production and income that is radically different from the post Keynesians' and circuitists' conception, which resembles the neoclassical one. Schmitt and his followers do not consider income as a flow of expenditure through time, but as a stock, that is, the result of a constantly renewed process of creation involving money and production of goods and services. The traditional idea of income formation as a continuous or discontinuous function of time is rejected and replaced by what the Dijon–Fribourg school calls a 'quantum theory of production': in the payment of wages, output is emitted as a quantum that is simultaneously real and monetary. It is real in so far as it is the result of a physical process of transformation (matter and energy) that creates value-in-use, and it is monetary in so far as it is emitted within the payment of money wages – which are the measure of output in economic terms. Income is formed when wage earners are credited with a sum of bank deposits, and is destroyed when these deposits are spent on the goods market. In this framework, as Deleplace (1999, p. 475) points out, neither production nor income distribution creates a link between periods, so that the multiplier is necessarily equal to one. Further, Keynes's identity between income and output is established on the grounds of conceptual logic. It becomes therefore logically impossible to explain either inflation or unemployment by referring to a disequilibrium between total demand and total supply, or between saving and investment. As was already noted by Keynes (1936/1973, p. 81) in the *General Theory*, '[t]he prevalence of the idea that saving and investment, taken in their straightforward sense, can differ from one another, is to be explained, I think, by an optical illusion due to regarding an individual depositor's relation to his bank as being a one-sided transaction, instead of seeing it as the two-sided transaction which it actually is'. The Schmitt school offers an alternative explanation of inflation and unemployment with respect to post Keynesian and circuitist analyses, on the basis of an original reading of Keynes's work (the *Treatise on Money* as well as the *General Theory*). For example, the main cause of inflation is attributed to today's structure of domestic and cross-border payment systems, whose working does not yet conform to the double-entry definition of modern money and to its conceptual distinction from income and capital. Inflation, defined by the Schmitt school as a loss of purchasing power suffered by each unit of money, does not depend therefore on microeconomic behaviour. It is a macroeconomic disturbance that has a 'monetary-structural' cause (see Rossi, 2001a, Ch. 6). According to Schmitt and his followers in Dijon, Fribourg and Lugano, macroeconomics has nothing to do with the agents' behaviour and there is no point in considering uncertainty or liquidity preference for the explanation of crisis. A truly macroeconomic theory has to focus on the structure underneath the economic system, to discover the logical laws governing its working so as to propose a positive as well as a normative analysis of modern capitalist economies.

THE CONTRIBUTIONS

As we have pointed out, while all contributions in this book qualify as heterodox, not all would be considered as post Keynesian, even defined broadly. It is for this reason that we avoid using the label 'post Keynesian' in the title of the volume. Although many authors contained herein would proudly wear it, others would not so readily adhere to this paradigm. For instance, Lavoie has requested his chapter be placed in neither the post Keynesian part nor the part on the circuit school. In this respect, Sawyer (1999, 2002) has often made the plea that post Kaleckian is a better label than post Keynesian, although his contribution appears in the part developing the post Keynesian monetary approach. As for the circuit school, perhaps this label is also misleading given the differences between the work of Parguez and that of Schmitt.

In spite of these differences, some of which are more apparent than real, there are nonetheless some fundamental similarities to all the approaches presented in this book. What unites the authors herein is their rejection of orthodoxy (that is, the notion that money is a veil, either in the short or in the long run) as well as their attention to the role played by effective demand and endogenous money within a class-based macro-theoretical framework. In an attempt at representativeness, we have invited contributions from leading economists in Europe, Canada and the United States, to give a flavour of the research work currently done all around the world on heterodox monetary theory. We have also given space to some younger economists, to ensure continuity between the so-called old guard and the emerging generation of heterodox economists. We have nevertheless included a number of prominent authors, and we believe that all contributions presented in what follows will prove enlightening and thought provoking, so as to open new avenues for monetary research in the third millennium. We are thus grateful to all contributors for their scholarly efforts in providing arguments that will hopefully raise a renewed interest in the nature and role of money in capitalist economies, one of the most controversial, and therefore fascinating, area of economics.

The book is divided into four parts.

Part one is devoted to the post Keynesian monetary approach. It contains six chapters dealing with specific aspects of this approach, or with similarities between various groups within the post Keynesian camp, namely, the so-called structuralists and horizontalists. The first chapter is contributed by Malcolm Sawyer, who argues that an important distinction should be made between money as a means of payment and money as a store of wealth, and that very different analyses of money follow from regarding it as one or the other, especially in terms of the measurement of money. In particular, those who place importance on the need to measure the demand for money must justify what exactly they are measuring. Sawyer argues that the distinction between a means of payment and a store of wealth is crucial because the same financial asset can generally not fulfil both functions.

Chapter two, written by Virginie Monvoisin and Corinne Pastoret, explores Keynes's liquidity preference theory. The authors note that while a number of endogenous money theorists have taken a renewed interest in liquidity preference theory and in particular in the liquidity preference of banks, post Keynesians initially turned to other Keynesian concepts, such as the finance motive, to construct a theory of endogenous money. As Monvoisin and Pastoret argue, liquidity preference can explain a number of points of that theory including the behaviour of households and of banks (with respect to money and credit respectively). The authors ask whether this is the theory of liquidity preference as set out in Keynes's *General Theory* or something different. Are households' liquidity preference and banks' liquidity preference consistent with the concept of endogenous money? Monvoisin and Pastoret claim that the distinction between liquidity and money allows post Keynesians to elaborate a more general theory of money and finance and so to reconcile a theory of liquidity preference with a theory of money. It is the difference between money and liquidity, or the lack of any such conceptual difference, that underlies the debates among post Keynesians. The disagreements about the determination of the interest rate, about the supply of money, and about the role of the central bank stem explicitly or implicitly from disagreements about the distinction between liquidity and money.

In the third chapter, Giuseppe Fontana and Alfonso Palacio-Vera explore the inconsistencies within the theoretical framework of monetarism. In particular, the authors address the controversial issues related to the new consensus in monetary theory and policy. After giving a brief summary of the main tenets of monetarism, Fontana and Palacio-Vera examine and discuss the instruments of monetary policy within that approach. A thorough critical discussion enables them to show that the post Keynesian theory of endogenous money may offer a valid alternative to monetarism.

In Chapter four, Thomas I. Palley investigates the need for developing a new system of financial regulation predicated upon the use of asset-based reserve requirements (ABRR), which, according to the author, would restore effective monetary control in a system with endogenous money and financial innovations. While such a system represents a shift in regulatory focus away from the traditional concern with the liabilities side of financial intermediaries' balance sheets, it nonetheless has both significant macroeconomic and microeconomic advantages. At the macroeconomic level, ABRR can provide policy makers with multiple additional independent policy instruments. Palley argues that this is particularly useful in light of recent concerns about the dangers of asset price inflation and the need to target asset prices. ABRR can also help restore the traction of monetary policy at a time when banks are becoming a smaller part of the financial landscape. At the microeconomic level, ABRR can be used to discourage excessive risk taking by financial intermediaries. Finally, they can also raise considerable seigniorage revenues. To be fully effective, a system of ABRR should be applied against all financial intermediaries on the basis of the assets they hold rather than the business in which they are nominally.

In his contribution as Chapter five, L. Randall Wray continues the development of the so-called chartalist view of money according to which money exists because of state taxes. In this chapter, Wray discusses domestic issues related to chartalism, but also extends the analysis to the open economy and explores the supposed hegemony of the US dollar. His analysis begins with a comparison of what the author calls the seigniorage view with the sovereignty view (that is, chartalism). Wray argues that the first view is irrelevant in today's world (if it existed at all), and that the sovereignty view is more applicable to modern monetary systems.

In Chapter six, Santonu Basu examines the new Keynesian approach to money and credit based on the presence of adverse selection and incentive effects owing to the existence of asymmetric information. While agreeing with many aspects of the credit-rationing model put forth by Stiglitz and Weiss, Basu argues that this model is not adequate to explain why many small businesses do not have access to credit during periods of restrictive monetary policy. Basu claims that there is a need to revisit the theory of credit rationing and to develop a better model to explain its effects on the national economy as a whole.

While the first part of this volume explores post Keynesian themes, the second part is more specific to ideas within the theory of the monetary circuit. Once confined to France and Italy, many of these ideas have slowly been found also in the writings of some North-American and Canadian post Keynesians. This part contains six chapters, each elaborating and developing a number of themes within the monetary circuit tradition.

As argued above, there is much that unites the post Keynesian and the monetary circuit approaches. Chapter seven, by Louis-Philippe Rochon, argues just this point. The author compares both the post Keynesian and the circuit approaches to credit and endogenous money and argues that, while different, these approaches are nonetheless compatible. Rochon notes that post Keynesians have traditionally emphasised the relationship between banks and the central bank, while circuit writers have placed more emphasis on the relationship between banks and firms. This has led the former to defend the functions of money, whereas the latter have focused on the nature of money. In the end, Rochon claims that to have a truly general theory of endogenous money, both approaches need to adopt elements of each other's approach.

In Chapter eight, Biagio Bossone investigates the implications that derive from thinking the economy as a circuit when the underlying theoretical framework is elaborated to incorporate the microeconomic and financial dimensions of the economy. As he notes, the theory of the monetary circuit has largely ignored the function that banks and non-bank intermediaries play as core links of individual decisions and agent interactions, and has left unexplored relevant areas of banking and finance, such as the impact of banks and non-bank intermediaries on economic efficiency and stability, the role of non-bank intermediation in coordinating individual choices in the markets for funds and capital goods, and the differential welfare cost of alternative banking regulatory regimes. More generally, the theory has disregarded the role of non-bank finance in the overall circuit process and, in particular, in determining the economy's equilibrium. Bossone sets out to show how the adapted framework works, making explicit the choice structure and the interrelationships of agents operating in a multi-sector, sequential economy with risk and uncertainty. He thus discusses the implications of the adapted circuit framework, including: the possibility for the economy to achieve multiple equilibria, the existence of various sources and transmission mechanisms of financial instability across the circuit, the identification of the different role of banks and non-bank intermediaries, and the effect of alternative regulatory regimes for banks and payment systems on the efficiency of the money supply process. He then uses the adapted circuit framework to speculate on the future of banking in a rapidly changing financial environment.

Mario Seccareccia is the author of Chapter nine, where he explores two aspects of the flux–reflux principle that is at the core of the theory of the monetary circuit. The author begins by investigating the ways by which investment is financed, and the role of banks. The financing of investment by bank credit has largely been ignored by circuit writers (with the exception of Parguez). Seccareccia also explores the related phenomenon of internal financing of investment and pricing. Next, he addresses the issue of price formation within the monetary circuit tradition. He then offers some preliminary empirical evidence, based on Canadian and North-American observations, that provides a useful insight into the nature of the mechanism of money and credit creation.

In Chapter ten, Riccardo Bellofiore and Riccardo Realfonzo explore Marx's monetary theory in light of the monetary circuit approach, to show that the Marxian description of the capitalist process as a monetary sequence is compatible with a theory of banks as providers of finance to production. To this end, the authors investigate the working of a monetary production economy using a class-based model in which capitalists, on the one side, and workers, on the other side, interact via the banking system within a triangular scheme. In this framework, banks advance money-capital and firms use it to buy labour power from workers. Money available in advance becomes therefore a condition essential to the production of commodities; it is first of all finance to production issued by banks. This purchasing power does not exist before bank loans are granted. For the banking sector as a whole, loans make deposits, and the authors note that Marx was well aware of this 'reverse causality' in the third volume of his *Capital*. In this work, published posthumously, Marx (who initially defines banking in terms of pure intermediation) realised that a metal base is not necessary, and that it is possible to maintain that banks create money *ex nihilo*. In this framework bank deposits have a twofold nature. On the one hand, they are loans made to banks by savers, which in turn banks loan out and are thus not to be found in the banks' safes. On the other hand, they are mere book entries in the banks' balance sheets. This re-reading of Marx's work leads Bellofiore and Realfonzo to conclude that Marx understood that banking cannot be defined in terms of pure intermediation, but also entails money creation, and that in a capitalist system the money-creation process is crucial for the working of a monetary production economy.

In Chapter eleven, Alberto Zazzaro argues that in order to lend greater empirical content and full internal consistency to the theory of the monetary circuit requires: (1) that the chartalist theory of money be revised and a new institutional theory of the origin of money be developed; (2) to introduce microeconomic elements into the analytical framework of the monetary circuit. He addresses these issues in turn, beginning with an analysis of the nature and origin of money linked to the controversy between chartalists and metallists in the history of monetary thought. Zazzaro argues that both chartalists and metallists have recognised that money has the nature of a social institution identifying a credit right on existing resources. Both chartalists and metallists understood money as the record of a purchasing power whose support tends to change in time with customs and technology, there being no logical link between the form or support that money takes and its intrinsic essence. With respect to the origin of money, the author argues that the divergence between metallists and chartalists is far more pronounced than their controversy over the nature of money. Whatever the function of money one considers essential, metallism and chartalism encounter the same logical difficulty of having to precede money with the existence of an adequately developed system of exchange and market mentality. According to Zazzaro, only in this case would the introduction of money be able to ensure considerable saving of resources in exchange (metallists) or to represent an effective tool of seigniorage (chartalists). Turning to the rejection of methodological individualism as the hallmark of heterodox monetary thinking, Zazzaro argues that a weak individualist perspective is not at odds with it and may even be necessary to forge ahead modern circuit theory. He claims that to extend the empirical significance of the theory of the monetary circuit and especially to lend greater realism and consistency to the crucial phase of circuit closure, it is indispensable to supplement the aggregate analysis of the macro-social circuit with a microeconomic analysis of micro-social circuits. His argument is that by explicitly introducing the individual component into the analysis, one may provide a consistent, realistic solution to the main difficulty of circuit theory, namely, that of the formation of aggregate monetary profits and the payment of bank interest.

Chapter twelve, contributed by Pierre Piégay, examines the post Keynesian controversies on banks' liquidity preference and its consequences on the creation of endogenous money. The author aims to propose an alternative interpretation to these controversies between structuralists and horizontalists. He argues that these two schools focus on two distinct levels of analysis that are not clearly distinguished within post Keynesian monetary theory. He then sets out to make these distinctions clear in light of the monetary circuit approach. The first difference that Piégay brings forward is the distinction between a microeconomic and a macroeconomic line of thought, a point that is also noted by Zazzaro. There is, however, a second distinction between horizontalists and structuralists pointed out by Piégay, a distinction that concerns the twofold function of the banking system. Horizontalists focus on the role of banks as creators of money while structuralists focus on their role as financial intermediaries. Piégay concludes that the controversy between horizontalists and structuralists ultimately reflects the difficulty of post Keynesian monetary analysis in distinguishing between monetary and financial operations carried out by banks. As he argues, this difficulty arises because post Keynesians still regard money as if it were an asset.

The idea that money is an asset is firmly rejected by the theory of money emissions, developed by Schmitt and his school over the last fifty years. This theory is presented in the third part of the volume, whose opening chapter is contributed by Bernard Schmitt and Curzio De Gottardi, who set out to prove that general equilibrium theory is logically inconsistent. The authors show that this theory is founded on a central illogical reasoning, and that, once logic is restored, equilibrium relative prices cannot be determined. To this end, Schmitt and De Gottardi consider the Walrasian model of a pure exchange economy with two agents and two commodities, assuming that this model satisfies the hypotheses required to guarantee the mathematical existence of equilibrium, that is, the mathematical existence of the relative price. The authors show that in this model the demonstration of the existence of equilibrium is illogical, and that the relative price cannot be determined. They also show that this outcome can be generalised to a pure exchange model with n agents and n commodities. Their conclusion is that relative prices do not exist in theory as well as in the real world. Economic analysis must begin anew to determine monetary prices.

In Chapter fourteen, Alvaro Cencini aims to provide the elements for a new criticism of the IS–LM framework, which has become the quintessence of the so-called neoclassical synthesis. Cencini sets out to prove that the IS–LM analysis suffers from a logical inconsistency that deprives it of any heuristic value. He reaches this goal by first analysing the reasons that have made Hicks's interpretation of Keynes's *General Theory* so successful, and then explaining why the post Keynesian criticism of IS–LM has failed to prove objectively beyond dispute. In fact, post Keynesians have not provided an internal criticism to the IS–LM analysis. As Cencini argues, their point of view would be very much reinforced if it were possible to show that Hicks's interpretation suffers from an internal contradiction. Indeed, Cencini shows that the IS–LM approach is logically flawed on several grounds, which are closely related to the shortcomings of the neoclassical theory it stems from. Referring to Keynes's post-*General Theory* articles, Cencini explains that for any given level of income, that is, of production, the amount globally saved can never be different from what has been globally invested. Even if one were to accept the existence of *ex ante* S and I in the form of planned saving and planned investment, this would not imply that their actual or realised values will result from their reciprocal adjustment. Cencini provides a new interpretation in which Keynes's fundamental identity of S and I is made to coexist with their *ex ante* variation, if only within the boundaries of the income actually formed. Interpreted along the Cencini lines, Keynes's analysis reveals its deep-seated opposition to the neoclassical approach and to any attempt to integrate it into a neoclassical synthesis like the IS–LM scheme.

Claude Gnos is the author of Chapter fifteen, where he sets out to show that the theory of the monetary circuit has been misunderstood by a number of post Keynesian writers. Gnos argues that the emphasis placed by circuit theorists on firms as bank borrowers and on households as deposit takers is not some arbitrary device or a priori assumption, but it derives from the deep structures and relationships underpinning modern capitalist economies. In this respect, Gnos compares the way circuit theory depicts the relationships between banks, firms and households with the diversity of observable relationships and practices. His objective is to show that the latter are 'surface phenomena' complying with the deep structure and the causal factors established by the former. His approach considers, first, the financing of firms' and households' expenditure, then the emphasis placed by circuit authors on the flux and reflux of money wages faced with the actual diversity of firms' expenses and the formation of profits. A first issue relates to the flux. In fact, firms pay not only for wages but also for capital goods they use in the production process. A second issue relates to the reflux and the formation of profits. Gnos asks how firms would be able to make profits from the sale of the goods produced if they inject only wages into the economy. His argument is that the start of production entails the superposition of different individual circuits: when buying manufactured goods, firms spend pre-existing incomes. This spending is part of the reflux phase of a circuit previously initiated. Simultaneously, the payment of wages initiates a new circuit. As Gnos shows, profit is the firms' income, derived from sales in the market for produced goods where it is made at the expense of buyers. Firms benefit from a transfer from buyers that is both nominal and real. They take the place of wage earners on the liabilities side of banks' balance sheets and then spend the corresponding income in their place. So, profits, nominal and real, are included in the circuit of money wages.

Chapter sixteen is written by Sergio Rossi, who aims to expand on the essence of money and banking in a monetary production economy. In particular, Rossi attempts to build a bridge between the liquid store of wealth and the means of payment conceptions of money, emphasised respectively by post Keynesians and circuitists. He goes back to the distinction between money proper and money's worth put forth by Smith in *The Wealth of Nations*, to disentangle, at the conceptual level, the two functions that the thing called 'money' carries out within a modern production economy. To reach this goal, Rossi addresses the two functions of modern banking, namely, the emission of money as such and the transfer of money balances between economic agents. The author asks two questions. Firstly, can one and the same 'thing' be a means of payment as well as a temporary abode of purchasing power? In the negative, what does it bring to distinguish analytically the two 'things' that carry out these two functions at different points in time? Rossi's argument leads to the conclusion that in modern banking there is a positive distinction between money and deposits. Monetary macroeconomics must therefore consider this distinction to analyse the working of modern capitalist economies, in order to propose the appropriate solution to macroeconomic problems such as inflation and unemployment.

In Chapter seventeen, contributed by Jean-Luc Bailly, the focus is on the macroeconomic relationship between wages and prices. The author argues that this relationship derives from the very definition of the unit of measurement in a monetary economy of production. This unit is the wage-unit. Bailly's argument is that, having been formed in the production process, the sum total of income cannot be different when spent on the market for produced goods. As he shows, the sum total of prices charged cannot differ from the sum total of wages. The wage bill defines an area with strictly defined borders within which current prices are determined. Hence the system of prices practised cannot vary infinitely. However, prices have an essential function in that they allow the distribution of output between wage income and non-wage income. Whereas wages express the share that workers take in the formation of output, prices charged in the goods market bring out the share of the current output to be paid to capital, that is, profit. Bailly notes, however, that profit is not monetised separately from the remainder of current output, but when wages are paid. So, if profit is a 'telescopic' category of wages, it comes up against an objective limit: the amount of profit cannot be greater than that of wages and therefore the volume of profit goods cannot exceed half of aggregate output. Bailly's conclusion is that the stickiness of wages and prices arises essentially because profit cannot come from anywhere but wages, the amount of which fulfils the principle of effective demand.

Chapter eighteen closes the part on the theory of money emissions. It is written by Xavier Bradley, who investigates the relationship between investment and involuntary unemployment. Investment, that is, the process of capital accumulation, plays a key role for the explanation of unemployment. This is particularly the case for Keynes, who tried to prove that a lack of investment is responsible for the existence of involuntary unemployment. Bradley's contribution to the analysis of unemployment is to identify why at crucial points Keynes did not stand by his own objective, and propose a solution consistent with a macroeconomic analysis of money income. As he notes, Keynes's solution to the unemployment problem emphasised the need to overcome psychological barriers that prevent investment from reaching its optimum level. This approach weakened considerably Keynes's concept of involuntary unemployment by transferring the responsibility of unemployment from the employees to that of the investors or the *rentiers*. Bradley argues that if the concept of involuntary unemployment is to play a significant role in economic analysis, a genuine structural deficiency – whatever the behaviour of economic agents – must be identified in the process of capital accumulation. Keynes was not able to reach this objective because, as attested by his analysis of the investment multiplier, he failed to discriminate between producing and investing. According to Bradley, the remedy to this shortcoming lies in the assignment of a precise orientation in the circuits of money income with a definite direction to every payment in the economy. By giving a more accurate account of the formation and amortisation of the stock of fixed capital, this will enable to understand the origin of the structural malfunction in the economy.

The last part of this volume comprises four chapters that forge ahead monetary heterodoxy. In this respect, Marc Lavoie and Matias Vernengo requested that their contributions be placed in this part because they did not want to figure in any of the other parts. This fact is particularly interesting in itself, and certainly goes a long way in supporting our view that there is a need to integrate the post Keynesian and the monetary circuit approaches into a single, coherent view that Lavoie (1992) has labelled 'post-classical'.

In Chapter nineteen, Heinrich Bortis sets out to combine the classical (Ricardian) theory of value and distribution, which is rooted in production, and Keynes's theory of employment, interest and money conceived of as a part of a monetary theory of production. This implies considering long-period equilibrium situations, where market prices coincide with Sraffian prices of production and profit rates are the same in all sectors. The problem that the author addresses is to adapt the behavioural elements of Keynes's short-period theory to a long-period institutional basis and to combine it with long-period classical system theory. Bortis aims to build a classical–Keynesian system of economic theory of which classical and Keynesian theory would constitute different aspects. He also intends to clarify the analytical links existing between horizontal Sraffa–Leontief interindustry land models and vertically integrated Ricardo–Pasinetti labour models. In fact, Bortis's analysis is of a long-period nature: only permanent or slowly evolving factors (technology and institutions) are considered, abstracting thus from more or less rapidly changing short- and medium-term behavioural elements associated with the market place or with business cycles respectively. Moreover, since his investigation is at the level of pure theory, Bortis does not consider concrete institutional set-ups but only examines how the institutional and technological system works in principle.

In his contribution as Chapter twenty, Alain Parguez takes on the monetary views of Hyman P. Minsky. The point that Parguez elaborates is that Minsky's theory of crisis cannot be considered within the post Keynesian tradition. The author claims that Minsky could never rid himself of his neoclassical upbringing, and this has led to a confused theory of money, credit and crisis. Parguez concludes that the key to understanding Minsky is the perverse role played by savings in Minsky's financial explanation of the working of the macroeconomy.

In Chapter twenty-one, Marc Lavoie combs over the various steps within the theory of endogenous money by incorporating in his analysis commercial banks' balance sheets. The author begins his analysis from a simple model with no central bank, no government and within a closed economy. As the analysis progresses, Lavoie slowly opens up his model to incorporate elements of the real world. His conclusion is that irrespective of the conditions, money is always and everywhere an endogenous phenomenon.

In Chapter twenty-two, Matias Vernengo explores the gold standard period that corresponds to the dominance of the commodity export model of development in the peripheral countries. The international division of labour implied centre countries exporting manufactured goods and importing commodities from the periphery. Export revenues were crucial to service foreign debts and for importing essential goods to accelerate the development process. A fall in the terms of trade implied the impossibility to serve the debt, and a forced default that led to abandonment of the gold standard. Hence, peripheral countries were for most of the time off the gold standard system, and effectively in a gold exchange system. Vernengo analyses the main effects of this hybrid system on the balance of payments' adjustment mechanism of central and peripheral countries. He argues that the conventional wisdom that assumed a smooth and symmetrical adjustment of the balance of payments in the centre and in the periphery is not correct.

NOTES

1. See Rochon (2001b).
2. See Lavoie (1999).
3. See also Cencini and Schmitt (1976, 1977) for a critical appraisal of Marx's theory using a circular flow approach.

4. Rochon (1999a) has argued that Keynes's 1937 articles on the finance motive should not be considered an extension of his *General Theory* but rather a new beginning.
5. Pressman (2000) criticises the reflux mechanism claiming that firms do not repay their loans in the real world. But as Rochon (2000) has shown, this changes nothing to the theory since it still requires the tacit approval of the bank.
6. See Schmitt and Greppi (1996) for an extensive exploration of circular flow analyses by twentieth-century German-speaking writers.
7. Devillebichot (1969, p. 693; our translation) notes that in this framework 'money is distinct from its purchasing power "as blood is distinct from its oxygen"'. This analogy points out that blood (money) is the vehicle of oxygen (money's worth, that is, produced goods and services). Notice here the similarity with the idea of 'the great wheel of [output] circulation' put to the fore by Smith (1776/1970, pp. 385–6).

REFERENCES

Arestis, P. (1992), *The Post-Keynesian Approach to Economics: An Alternative Analysis of Economic Theory and Policy*, Aldershot and Brookfield: Edward Elgar.

Baranzini, M. and A. Cencini (2001), 'Foreword', in S. Rossi, *Money and Inflation: A New Macroeconomic Analysis*, Cheltenham and Northampton: Edward Elgar, viii–xli.

Bell, S. (2000), 'Do taxes and bonds finance government spending?', *Journal of Economic Issues*, **34** (3), 603–20.

Bell, S. (2001), 'The role of the state and the hierarchy of money', *Cambridge Journal of Economics*, **25** (2), 149–63.

Bellofiore, R. (1985), 'Money and development in Schumpeter', *Review of Radical Political Economics*, **17** (1–2), 21–40.

Bellofiore, R. (1989), 'A monetary labor theory of value', *Review of Radical Political Economics*, **21** (1–2), 1–25.

Bellofiore, R. (1992), 'Monetary macroeconomics before the *General Theory*: the circuit theory of money in Wicksell, Schumpeter and Keynes', *Social Concept*, **6** (2), 47–89.

Bellofiore, R. (1998), 'Between Wicksell and Hayek: Mises' theory of money and credit revisited', *American Journal of Economics and Sociology*, **57** (4), 531–78.

Bellofiore, R., G. Forges Davanzati and R. Realfonzo (2000), 'Marx inside the circuit: discipline device, wage bargaining and unemployment in a sequential monetary economy', *Review of Political Economy*, **12** (4), 403–17.

Bibow, J. (1995), 'Some reflections on Keynes's "finance motive" for the demand for money', *Cambridge Journal of Economics*, **19** (5), 647–66.

Bradley, X. (1993), 'La "finance" et le circuit de la monnaie', *Revue française d'économie*, **8** (1), 67–88.

Cardim de Carvalho, F.J. (1995), 'Post Keynesian developments of liquidity preference theory', in P. Wells (ed.), *Post Keynesian Economic Theory*, London: Kluwer Academic Publishers, 17–33.

Cencini, A. (1988), *Money, Income and Time: A Quantum-Theoretical Approach*, London and New York: Pinter Publishers.

Cencini, A. (1995), *Monetary Theory, National and International*, London and New York: Routledge.

Cencini, A. (1996), 'Inflation and deflation: the two faces of the same reality', in A. Cencini and M. Baranzini (eds), *Inflation and Unemployment: Contributions to a New Macroeconomic Approach*, London and New York: Routledge, 17–60.

Cencini, A. (2001), *Monetary Macroeconomics: A New Approach*, London and New York: Routledge.

Cencini, A. and B. Schmitt (1976), *La pensée de Karl Marx: critique et synthèse, Volume 1: La valeur*, Albeuve: Castella.

Cencini, A. and B. Schmitt (1977), *La pensée de Karl Marx: critique et synthèse, Volume 2: La plus-value*, Albeuve: Castella.

Cencini, A. and B. Schmitt (1991), *External Debt Servicing: A Vicious Circle*, London and New York: Pinter Publishers.

Cencini, A. and B. Schmitt (1992), 'Per la creazione di uno spazio monetario europeo garante della sovranità di ogni singolo paese', in R. Chopard (ed.), *Europa '93! E la piazza finanziaria svizzera?*, Bellinzona: Meta-Edizioni, 99–136.

Chick, V. (1986), 'The evolution of the banking system and the theory of saving, investment and interest', *Économies et Sociétés* ('Série Monnaie et Production', 3), **20** (8–9), 111–26.

Chick, V. (1995), 'Is there a case for post Keynesian economics?', *Scottish Journal of Political Economy*, **42** (1), 20–36.

Dalziel, P. (1995), 'The Keynesian multiplier, liquidity preference, and endogenous money', *Journal of Post Keynesian Economics*, **18** (3), 311–31.

Davidson, P. (1972/1978), *Money and the Real World*, New York: John Wiley and Sons.

Davidson, P. (1986), 'Finance, funding, saving, and investment', *Journal of Post Keynesian Economics*, **9** (1), 101–10.

Davidson, P. and S. Weintraub (1973), 'Money as cause and effect', *Economic Journal*, **83** (332), 1117–32.

Deleplace, G. (1999), 'Des hétérodoxies diverses', in *Histoire de la pensée économique: du 'royaume agricole' de Quesnay au 'monde à la Arrow–Debreu'*, Paris: Dunod, 433–79.

Deleplace, G. and E.J. Nell (eds) (1996), *Money in Motion: The Post Keynesian and Circulation Approaches*, London and New York: Macmillan and St. Martin's Press.

Devillebichot, G. (1969), 'Note sur les travaux de Bernard Schmitt', *Revue d'économie politique*, **79** (3), 693–702.

Dow, A.C. and S.C. Dow (1989), 'Endogenous money creation and idle balances', in J. Pheby (ed.), *New Directions in Post-Keynesian Economics*, Aldershot and Brookfield: Edward Elgar, 147–64.

Fontana, G. (2000), 'Post Keynesians and Circuitists on money and uncertainty: an attempt at generality', *Journal of Post Keynesian Economics*, **23** (1), 27–48.

Gnos, C. (1992a), *Production, répartition et monnaie*, Dijon: Éditions Universitaires de Dijon.

Gnos, C. (1992b), 'La transition vers l'union économique et monétaire: les vertus négligées de la monnaie commune', *Revue du Marché commun et de l'Union européenne*, 360, 621–6.

Gnos, C. (1998), 'The Keynesian identity of income and output', in P. Fontaine and A. Jolink (eds), *Historical Perspectives on Macroeconomics: Sixty Years After the General Theory*, London and New York: Routledge, 40–8.

Gnos, C. and J.-B. Rasera (1985), 'Circuit et circulation: une fausse analogie', *Cahiers de la Revue d'économie politique*, special issue, 41–57.

Gnos, C. and B. Schmitt (1990), 'Le circuit, réalité exhaustive', *Économies et Sociétés* ('Série Monnaie et Production', 6), **24** (2), 63–74.

Graziani, A. (1987), 'Keynes' finance motive', *Économies et Sociétés* ('Série Monnaie et Production', 4), **21** (9), 23–42.

Graziani, A. (1990), 'The theory of the monetary circuit', *Économies et Sociétés* ('Série Monnaie et Production', 7), **24** (6), 7–36.

Graziani, A. (1996), 'Money as purchasing power and money as a stock of wealth in Keynesian economic thought', in G. Deleplace and E.J. Nell (eds), *Money in Motion: The Post Keynesian and Circulation Approaches*, London and New York: Macmillan and St. Martin's Press, 139–54.

Graziani, A. (1997), 'The Marxist theory of money', *International Journal of Political Economy*, **27** (2), 26–50.

Hicks, J.R. (1937), 'Mr. Keynes and the "classics": a suggested interpretation', *Econometrica*, **5** (2), 147–59. Reprinted in J.R. Hicks (1982), *Money, Interest and Wages: Collected Essays on Economic Theory*, Oxford: Basil Blackwell, vol. II, 100–15.

Hicks, J.R. (1980–81), 'IS–LM: an explanation', *Journal of Post Keynesian Economics*, **3** (2), 139–54. Reprinted in J.R. Hicks (1982), *Money, Interest and Wages: Collected Essays on Economic Theory*, Oxford: Basil Blackwell, vol. II, 318–31.

Kahn, R.F. (1958), 'Memorandum of evidence submitted to the Radcliffe committee'. Reprinted in R.F. Kahn (1972), *Selected Essays on Employment and Growth*, Cambridge: Cambridge University Press, 124–52.

Kaldor, N. (1958), 'Monetary policy, economic stability and growth', Memorandum submitted to the Committee on the Working of the Monetary System (Radcliffe Committee), June 23. Reprinted in N. Kaldor (1964), *Essays on Economic Policy*, New York: Norton, vol. I, 128–53.

Kaldor, N. (1980), *Origins of New Monetarism*, Cardiff: University College Cardiff Press.

Kaldor, N. (1982), *The Scourge of Monetarism*, Oxford: Oxford University Press.

Kaldor, N. (1985), *Economics Without Equilibrium*, Armonk: M.E. Sharpe.

Keynes, J.M. (1930/1971), *A Treatise on Money* (vol. I *The Pure Theory of Money*), London: Macmillan. Reprinted in *The Collected Writings of John Maynard Keynes*, Vol. V, London and Basingstoke: Macmillan.

Keynes, J.M. (1936/1973), *The General Theory of Employment, Interest and Money*, London: Macmillan. Reprinted in *The Collected Writings of John Maynard Keynes*, Vol. VII, London and Basingstoke: Macmillan.

Keynes, J.M. (1937/1973), 'The "ex ante" theory of the rate of interest', *Economic Journal*, **47** (188), 663–9. Reprinted in *The Collected Writings of John Maynard Keynes*, Vol. XIV, London and Basingstoke: Macmillan, 215–23.

Lavoie, M. (1987), 'Monnaie et production: une synthèse de la théorie du circuit', *Économies et Sociétés* ('Série Monnaie et Production', 4), **21** (9), 65–101.

Lavoie, M. (1992), *Foundations of Post-Keynesian Economic Analysis*, Aldershot and Brookfield: Edward Elgar.

Lavoie, M. (1996), 'Horizontalism, structuralism, liquidity preference and the principle of increasing risk', *Scottish Journal of Political Economy*, **43** (3), 275–

300.

Lavoie, M. (1997), 'Loanable funds, endogenous money and Minsky's financial fragility hypothesis', in A.J. Cohen, H. Hagemann and J. Smithin (eds), *Money, Financial Institutions and Macroeconomics*, Boston: Kluwer Academic Publishers, 67–82.

Lavoie, M. (1999), 'The credit-led supply of deposits and the demand for money: Kaldor's reflux mechanism as previously endorsed by Joan Robinson', *Cambridge Journal of Economics*, **23** (1), 103–13.

Le Bourva, J. (1962), 'Création de la monnaie et multiplicateur du crédit', *Revue économique*, **13** (1), 29–56.

Le Bourva, J. (1992), 'Money creation and credit multipliers', *Review of Political Economy*, **4** (4), 447–66.

Messori, M. (1985), 'Le circuit de la monnaie: acquis et problémes non résolus', in R. Arena and A. Graziani (eds), *Production, circulation et monnaie*, Paris: Presses Universitaires de France, 207–46.

Messori, M. (1997), 'The trials and misadventures of Schumpeter's treatise on money', *History of Political Economy*, **97** (4), 639–67.

Minsky, H.P. (1957a), 'Monetary systems and accelerator models', *American Economic Review*, **47** (6), 859–83.

Minsky, H.P. (1957b), 'Central banking and money market changes', *Quarterly Journal of Economics*, **71** (2), 171–87.

Minsky, H.P. (1982), *Can 'It' Happen Again? Essays on Instability and Finance*, Armonk: M.E. Sharpe.

Minsky, H.P. (1991), 'The endogeneity of money', in E.J. Nell and W. Semmler (eds), *Nicholas Kaldor and Mainstream Economics: Confrontation or Convergence?*, New York: St. Martin's Press, 207–20.

Moore, B.J. (1988), *Horizontalists and Verticalists: The Macroeconomics of Credit Money*, Cambridge: Cambridge University Press.

Moore, B.J. (1991), 'Marx, Keynes, Kalecki and Kaldor on the rate of interest as a monetary phenomenon', in E.J. Nell and W. Semmler (eds), *Nicholas Kaldor and Mainstream Economics: Confrontation or Convergence?*, New York: St. Martin's Press, 225–42.

Moore, B.J. (1995), 'The exogeneity of short-term interest rates: a reply to Wray', *Journal of Economic Issues*, **29** (1), 258–66.

Moore, B.J. (2001), 'Some reflections on endogenous money', in L.-P. Rochon and M. Vernengo (eds), *Credit, Interest Rates and the Open Economy: Essays on Horizontalism*, Cheltenham and Northampton: Edward Elgar, 11–30.

Palley, T.I. (1991), 'The endogenous money supply: consensus and disagreement', *Journal of Post Keynesian Economics*, **13** (3), 397–403.

Palley, T.I. (1994), 'Competing views of the money supply process: theory and evidence', *Metroeconomica*, **45** (1), 67–88.

Palley, T.I. (1996), 'Beyond endogenous money: toward endogenous finance', in G. Deleplace and E.J. Nell (eds), *Money in Motion: The Post Keynesian and Circulation Approaches*, London and New York: Macmillan and St. Martin's Press, 516–31.

Parguez, A. (1975), *Monnaie et macroéconomie: théorie de la monnaie en déséquilibre*, Paris: Economica.

Parguez, A. (1982), 'La monnaie dans le circuit ou le voile déchiré', *Économie appliquée*, **35** (3), 231–65.

Parguez, A. (1984), 'La dynamique de la monnaie', *Économies et Sociétés* ('Série Monnaie et Production', 1), **18** (4), 83–118.

Parguez, A. (1986), 'Au cœur du circuit ou quelques réponses aux énigmes du circuit', *Économies et Sociétés* ('Série Monnaie et Production', 3), **20** (8–9), 23–39.

Parguez, A. (1987), 'La crise dans le circuit, ou l'intégration de la finance et de la production', *Économie appliquée*, **40** (4), 755–70.

Parguez, A. (1996), 'Beyond scarcity: a reappraisal of the theory of the monetary circuit', in G. Deleplace and E.J. Nell (eds), *Money in Motion: The Post Keynesian and Circulation Approaches*, London and New York: Macmillan and St. Martin's Press, 155–99.

Parguez, A. (2001), 'Money without scarcity: from the horizontalist revolution to the theory of the monetary circuit', in L.-P. Rochon and M. Vernengo (eds), *Credit, Interest Rates and the Open Economy: Essays on Horizontalism*, Cheltenham and Northampton: Edward Elgar, 69–103.

Parguez, A. (2002), 'Victoria Chick and the theory of the monetary circuit: an enlightening debate', in P. Arestis, M. Desai and S. Dow (eds), *Money, Macroeconomics and Keynes: Essays in Honour of Victoria Chick*, London and New York: Routledge, vol. I, 45–55.

Parguez, A. and M. Seccareccia (2000), 'The credit theory of money: the monetary circuit approach', in J. Smithin (ed.), *What is Money?*, London and New York: Routledge, 101–23.

Pollin, R. (1991), 'Two theories of money supply endogeneity: some empirical evidence', *Journal of Post Keynesian Economics*, **13** (3), 366–96.

Pollin, R. (1996), 'Money supply endogeneity: what are the questions and why do they matter?', in G. Deleplace and E.J. Nell (eds), *Money in Motion: The Post Keynesian and Circulation Approaches*, London and New York: Macmillan and St. Martin's Press, 490–515.

Poulon, F. (1982), *Macroéconomie approfondie: équilibre, déséquilibre, circuit*, Paris: Cujas.

Pressman, S. (2000), 'A note on money and the circuit approach', *Journal of Economic Issues*, **34** (4), 969–73.

Realfonzo, R. (1998), *Money and Banking: Theory and Debate (1900–1940)*, Cheltenham and Northampton: Edward Elgar.

Realfonzo, R. (1999), 'French circuit school', in P.A. O'Hara (ed.), *Encyclopedia of Political Economy*, London and New York: Routledge, vol. I, 375–8.

Robinson, J. (1956), *The Accumulation of Capital*, London: Macmillan.

Robinson, J. (1970), 'Quantity theories old and new', *Journal of Money, Credit, and Banking*, **2** (4), 504–12.

Rochon, L.-P. (1997), 'Keynes's finance motive: a re-assessment. Credit, liquidity preference and the rate of interest', *Review of Political Economy*, **9** (3), 277–93.

Rochon, L.-P. (1999a), *Credit, Money and Production: An Alternative Post-Keynesian Approach*, Cheltenham and Northampton: Edward Elgar.

Rochon, L.-P. (1999b), 'The creation and circulation of endogenous money: a circuit dynamique approach', *Journal of Economic Issues*, **33** (1), 1–21.

Rochon, L.-P. (2000), 'The creation and circulation of endogenous money: a reply to Pressman', *Journal of Economic Issues*, **34** (4), 973–9.

Rochon, L.-P. (2001a), 'Horizontalism: setting the record straight', in L.-P. Rochon and M. Vernengo (eds), *Credit, Interest Rates and the Open Economy: Essays on Horizontalism*, Cheltenham and Northampton: Edward Elgar, 31–65.

Rochon, L.-P. (2001b), 'Cambridge's contribution to endogenous money: Robinson and Kahn on credit and money', *Review of Political Economy*, **13** (3), 287–307.

Rogers, C. (1989), *Money, Interest and Capital: A Study in the Foundations of Monetary Theory*, Cambridge: Cambridge University Press.

Rossi, S. (1996), *La moneta europea: utopia o realtà?*, Bellinzona and Lausanne: Meta-Edizioni.

Rossi, S. (1997), *Modalités d'institution et de fonctionnement d'une banque centrale supranationale: le cas de la Banque Centrale Européenne*, Bern and Paris: Peter Lang.

Rossi, S. (1998), 'Endogenous money and banking activity: some notes on the workings of modern payment systems', *Studi economici*, **53** (3), 23–56.

Rossi, S. (2001a), *Money and Inflation: A New Macroeconomic Analysis*, Cheltenham and Northampton: Edward Elgar.

Rossi, S. (2001b), 'The meaning of bank deposits', *Quaderni di ricerca*, Centre for Banking Studies/Research Laboratory of Monetary Economics, Lugano, no. 6.

Sawyer, M. (1999), 'Kalecki on money and finance', Leeds University Business School, unpublished.

Sawyer, M. (2002), 'Economic policy with endogenous money', in P. Arestis, M. Desai and S. Dow (eds), *Money, Macroeconomics and Keynes: Essays in Honour of Victoria Chick*, London and New York: Routledge, vol. I, 35–44.

Schmitt, B. (1959), 'L'équilibre de la monnaie', *Revue d'économie politique*, **69** (5), 921–50.

Schmitt, B. (1960), *La formation du pouvoir d'achat*, Paris: Sirey.

Schmitt, B. (1966), *Monnaie, salaires et profits*, Paris: Presses Universitaires de France (also Albeuve: Castella, 1975).

Schmitt, B. (1972), *Macroeconomic Theory, a Fundamental Revision*, Albeuve: Castella.

Schmitt, B. (1973), *New Proposals for World Monetary Reform*, Albeuve: Castella.

Schmitt, B. (1975), *Théorie unitaire de la monnaie, nationale et internationale*, Albeuve: Castella.

Schmitt, B. (1982), 'Time as quantum', in M. Baranzini (ed.), *Advances in Economic Theory*, Oxford and New York: Basil Blackwell and St. Martin's Press, 115–25.

Schmitt, B. (1984), *Inflation, chômage et malformations du capital*, Paris and Albeuve: Economica and Castella.

Schmitt, B. (1986), 'The process of formation of economics in relation to other sciences', in M. Baranzini and R. Scazzieri (eds), *Foundations of Economics: Structures of Inquiry and Economic Theory*, Oxford and New York: Basil Blackwell and St. Martin's Press, 103–32.

Schmitt, B. (1988), 'The identity of aggregate supply and demand in time', in A. Barrère (ed.), *The Foundations of Keynesian Analysis*, London and Basingstoke: Macmillan, 169–93.

Schmitt, B. (1996a), 'A new paradigm for the determination of money prices', in G. Deleplace and E.J. Nell (eds), *Money in Motion: The Post Keynesian and Circulation Approaches*, London and New York: Macmillan and St. Martin's Press, 105–38.

Schmitt, B. (1996b), 'Unemployment: is there a principal cause?', in A. Cencini and M. Baranzini (eds), *Inflation and Unemployment: Contributions to a New Macroeconomic Approach*, London and New York: Routledge, 75–105.

Schmitt, B. and S. Greppi (1996), 'The national economy studied as a whole: aspects of circular flow analysis in the German language', in G. Deleplace and E.J. Nell (eds), *Money in Motion: The Post Keynesian and Circulation Approaches*, London and New York: Macmillan and St. Martin's Press, 341–64.

Seccareccia, M. (1996), 'Post Keynesian fundism and monetary circulation', in G. Deleplace and E.J. Nell (eds), *Money in Motion: The Post Keynesian and Circulation Approaches*, London and New York: Macmillan and St. Martin's Press, 400–16.

Smith, A. (1776/1970), *The Wealth of Nations*, Harmondsworth: Penguin.

Smithin, J. (1999), 'Fundamental issues in monetary economics', in S.B. Dahiya (ed.), *The Current State of Economic Science, Volume 2: Microeconomics, Macroeconomics, Monetary Economics*, Rohtak: Spellbound, 1075–91.

Vallageas, B. (1985), 'Les circuits dans les analyses de Marx, Boehm-Bawerk, Hayek et Keynes', *Économies et Sociétés* ('Série Monnaie et Production', 2), **19** (8), 47–68.

Wells, P. (1983), 'A Post Keynesian view of liquidity preference and the demand for money', *Journal of Post Keynesian Economics*, **5** (4), 523–36.

Winnett, A. (1992), 'Some semantics of endogeneity', in P. Arestis and V. Chick (eds), *Recent Developments in Post-Keynesian Economics*, Aldershot and Brookfield: Edward Elgar, 47–63.

Wray, L.R. (1998), *Understanding Modern Money: The Key to Full Employment and Price Stability*, Cheltenham and Northampton: Edward Elgar.

Wray, L.R. (2000), 'Modern money', in J. Smithin (ed.), *What is Money?*, London and New York: Routledge, 42–66.

PART ONE

THE POST KEYNESIAN MONETARY
APPROACH

1. Money: Means of Payment or Store of Wealth?

Malcolm Sawyer[1]

INTRODUCTION

This chapter argues that a sharp distinction should be drawn between the functions of means of payment and store of wealth, which are generally ascribed to money. It is further argued that, in general, the same financial asset does not serve as both a means of payment and as a store of wealth. Some of the differences for economic analysis that flow from money being regarded as a means of payment and as a store of wealth are also indicated.

Money is generally described as having three functions. The first function is sometimes described as medium of exchange and at other times as means of payment. The term medium of exchange clearly suggests that the role of money is to facilitate exchange, and the existence of money is seen to overcome the problem of the double coincidence of wants. The term means of payment indicates that money is used to settle payments and debts. We will use the term means of payment since the *defining* characteristic of money is that it is the generally accepted means of payment.

> The most important [function of money] is that it acts as a specialised means of payment. Final payment is made whenever a seller of a good, or service, or another asset, receives something of equal value from the purchaser, which leaves the seller with no further claim on the buyer. Money is the asset which specialises in this role, being generally used for the settlement of transactions. As such it must, by definition, be a store of value and, in general, it proves efficient to treat the means of payment as the unit of account (Goodhart, 1975, p. 2).

This means of payment function of money is well expressed by saying that 'money buys goods and goods buy money; but goods do not buy goods' (Clower, 1967/1969, pp. 207–8).

3

The second function is sometimes described as a store of value and sometimes as a store of wealth. A store of value is taken to mean that whatever serves as money must retain most of its value over the period of time for which it is held between its receipt and its disbursement, though it is envisaged that the time between receipt and disbursement is relatively short: 'A moment's reflection will indicate that money is able to perform its medium of exchange function *primarily* because it acts as a store of value' (Shaw, McCrostie and Greenaway, 1997, p. 76; emphasis added).

The notion of store of wealth is rather different from the notion of store of value. The notion of store of wealth is taken to mean that individuals hold money as part of their asset portfolio for the holding of wealth, and intend to hold money as such for some significant period of time. The return on money (in a broad sense) is then compared with the returns on other assets that are also stores of wealth as alternative ways in which an individual can indeed keep his/her wealth.

The third function is that money acts as the unit of account, that is, as the abstract unit in terms of which prices, contracts and debts are expressed. This function differs from the previous two in that the unit of account is an abstract one whereas the two other functions are not abstract in that way even if they do not involve a physical embodiment. However, Tobin and Golub note some of the differences between money as a unit of account and money as a means of payment:

> It was natural, therefore, to seek the explanation of the value of money in the factors determining the quantity of money supplied and demanded. But except in economies with very primitive financial systems, this approach involves a vast mistake of identification, a 'fallacy of misplaced concreteness', to use Alfred North Whitehead's concept. The value of money is the value of a unit of account, for example, the dollar, in terms of which all kinds of private and public contracts are denominated. Money in the sense of means of payment – currency and demand deposits – is far from the only asset that changes in value when the index of consumer prices rises or falls. There is no obvious presumption that the value of the dollar is determined by the supply of and demand for means of payment, to the exclusion of all the other assets also denominated in dollars (Tobin and Golub, 1998, p. 57).

This third function of money is not central to the rest of the chapter, except to say that a distinction is drawn between those financial assets that have a price of unity in terms of the unit of account and those that do not. The argument of this chapter is that in general the two functions of means of payment and store of wealth are not generally satisfied by any single financial asset. The two functions are indeed in a considerable degree of conflict and it is doubtful whether the same financial (or other) asset can satisfy both functions. The key attribute of money is argued to be as a means of payment, which has been central to the circuitist analysis (together with the idea that money is credit money created by the banking, or equivalent, system).[2] Money as a means of payment is generally a poor store of wealth.

It is clear that there are (at least) two rather distinct ways in which economists have analysed money. One approach has emphasised money's unique characteristic as the means of payment, while the other has focused on money as a store of wealth. Graziani has pointed out that:

> The transition from a definition of money as purchasing power to a definition of money as a stock of wealth was considered as a fundamental acquisition in the progress of economic theory. Nowadays, supporters of the previous conception of money are few in the Anglo-Saxon world. Many more are active however in present-day France, most of them being supporters of the so-called French school of the Monetary Circuit (Graziani, 1996, p. 139).

He argues further that:

> It was then clear that money, if defined as mere purchasing power, could only be endowed with an indirect utility, originating from the utility of the goods money could buy on the market. On the other hand, if money had to yield utility on its own, it had to be useful not only when spent upon commodities but also when kept as a store of wealth. Money had consequently to be defined as a stock of liquid wealth (ibid., p. 139).

Graziani points to the analytical consequences that flow from treating money as store of wealth and money as purchasing power. As a store of wealth, money appears as an observable variable, and 'the definition of money can be extended to any kind of resource, provided it is accepted by agents as part of their liquid balances' (ibid., p. 140). Graziani also argues that with a 'rigorous definition of equilibrium', which includes no debts pending, then bank money disappears from equilibrium. If bank loans and deposits are eliminated, interest paid by firms also disappears, and 'any possible conflict between the world of industry and the world of finance is automatically eliminated' (ibid., p. 140). This 'disappearance of the money market gives rise to the further idea that the financial market might perform the role of bringing new liquidity to firms' (ibid., p. 140).

By contrast, when money is defined as a means of payment, no rational agent would keep idle balances in the absence of uncertainty, and a 'puzzling consequence would be that money ... would disappear from the equilibrium position and would no longer be an observable variable' (ibid., p. 141).

However, if 'the existence of a certain amount of debts among agents [is taken] as being consistent with equilibrium ... [then] nothing prevents bank money from being in existence even in full equilibrium' (ibid., p. 141). Money is restricted to cash, notes and bank deposits. At least two interest rates have to be considered, namely short-term rate of interest paid by firms to banks and long-term rate of interest paid by firms to savers. The role of banks is to create the means of payment, and the financial market is no longer 'a source of fresh liquidity to firms as a whole' (ibid., p. 141).

Graziani's argument raises the differences between money as a means of payment and money as a store of wealth to another level. It is then not only a question of whether a single financial asset can serve both functions, but also that '[t]he choice between one or the other of the two conceptions of money produces a number of analytical consequences' (ibid., p. 139).

MEANS OF PAYMENT VS. STORE OF WEALTH

When money is viewed as a means of payment, it is presented as a useful social convention which facilitates trade through the avoidance of the double coincidence of wants problem involved in a barter economy. Further, contracts are expressed in terms of money as a unit of account, and these contracts can be discharged by money as a means of payment. However, and whether or not what is used as money has any intrinsic value, money as a means of payment is held in order to dispose of it – that is, to use the money to buy goods and services, financial and other assets, and so on. This makes for some difficulty of terminology in respect of the demand for money. An individual holds money and may do so willingly but the intention is for the holding of money to be temporary. The money is held in order to dispose of it. Further money will be received to replenish the holding, which in turn will be disposed of. As the traditional presentation of the transactions demand for money makes clear (as the holding of money by an individual rises on receipt of income and gradually declines as expenditure takes place, followed by a replenishment when income is again received), the demand for money is an average concept (over a period).

From the observation that an individual holds money, it cannot be inferred that she has a demand for that amount of money in any meaningful sense of demand. The receipt of money may have been unanticipated, and the holding is temporary until the individual has both time and opportunity to use it. It may be that if a person is observed to be holding money, this must imply that she has a demand for money – for otherwise she would have already passed the money on to someone else. This is rather like the dollar bill on the pavement story. A neoclassical economist would claim that you can never encounter someone simply observing a dollar bill on the pavement: surely someone would pick it up! In a world of uncertainty and transactions costs, it may take some time (albeit this may be a relatively short period of calendar time) before a person passes on money received to someone else. But when money is viewed as a means of payment, then money is generally held to be later discarded. Thus the demand for money is unlike (almost) any other demand – it is a demand to have something in order to dispose of it.

Money is discussed as a store of wealth as far as the individual holding the money is concerned. Money is not a store of wealth at the aggregate level. Money is an asset for the holder but a liability for the financial institution concerned (which may be the central bank). Also, bank deposits enter on one side of the balance sheet of the banks and loans on the other side of the balance sheet, and there is a rough equality between loans and deposits.

In Keynes's analysis (Keynes, 1936/1973) the transactions and precautionary motives are clearly linked with the flow level of income and expenditure, while the speculative motive is linked with the level of wealth (as well as the rate of interest). Money is compared with bonds as a way of holding wealth.

> In this connection we can usefully employ the ancient distinction between the use of money for the transaction of current business and its use as a store of wealth. . . . But, given that the rate of interest is never negative, why should anyone prefer to hold his wealth in a form which yields little or no interest to holding it in a form which yields interest (assuming, of course, at this stage, that the risk of default is the same in respect of a bank balance as of a bond)? (Keynes, 1936/1973, p. 168).

This is more forcefully expressed as follows: 'it is a recognized characteristic of money as a store of wealth that it is barren; whereas practically every other form of storing wealth yields some interest or profit. Why should anyone outside a lunatic asylum wish to use money as a store of wealth?' (Keynes, 1937a/1973, p. 116) – to which he answered in terms of the uncertainty surrounding the returns on bonds as compared with the certain, if barren, yield from money.

The idea of viewing money as a store of wealth, as indicated in the above quote from Graziani (1996), has been much further developed and, in some respects, has become the dominant approach. Tobin (1958), for example, provided a formal model in which money and bonds were viewed as alternative modes of holding wealth, and were compared in terms of both their expected return and the variance of their respective return (where the frequency distribution of returns to the assets was assumed to be known to each individual). Friedman (1969, p. 52) argued that 'the quantity theory is in the first instance a theory of the *demand* for money. It is not a theory of output, or of money income, or of the price level'. According to him, the demand for money is a function of permanent income, wealth, a vector of the rates of return and *u*, which stands 'for any such variables that can be expected to affect tastes and preferences' (ibid., p. 56). Further, 'to the ultimate wealth-owning units in the economy, money is one kind of asset, one way of holding wealth' (ibid., p. 52).

Patinkin (1965, p. 79) wrote that 'our concern is with the *utility of holding money*, not with that of *spending* it. This is the concept implicit in all cash-balance approaches to the quantity theory of money; and it is the one that will be followed explicitly here'. But Patinkin (ibid., p. 80) also argues that 'the security which money balances provide against either of these types of inconvenience [defaulting temporarily on a payment or replenish balances by redemption of bonds] is what is assumed to invest them with utility'.

Money as a store of wealth leads readily to the notion of a stock demand for money, linked with the level of wealth and the relative returns. In contrast with money as a means of payment, money as a store of wealth is held for the returns from money and with the intention of holding the money for a substantial period of time (though individuals may frequently rearrange their wealth portfolio as their perception of relative returns changes).

Keynes (1936/1973) postulated the transactions, the precautionary and the speculative motive for holding money (to which he later added the finance motive; see Keynes, 1937b/1973). The first two of these motives could be seen to relate to money's function as means of payment, whereas the last one relates to its role as a store of wealth. It has often been argued that money 'balances held for one motive may also go to satisfy the need to hold money for the other purpose' (Goodhart, 1975, p. 21). It is also the case that a commodity may have a variety of uses (that is, serve a number of functions): a car may be valued for its speed, its comfort, its status symbol, and so on. As argued above, money is held as a means of payment with the intention of disposing of it relatively quickly. Holding money in this way brings us utility only because we will soon be spending it. Money is held as a store of wealth for the utility that its holding provides. The intention is to hold such money for a significant period of time.

Thus the reasons for holding money as a means of payment are quite different from the reasons for holding money as a store of wealth. But, of course, different people can have quite different reasons for demanding a particular item. Later, we will argue that these different types of reasons for holding money lead to the view that there are different types of money satisfying the role of means of payment and the role of store of wealth.

THE MEASUREMENT OF MONEY

There have been endless debates as to what constitutes money (at a particular time and in a specific society). But whether money is regarded as a means of payment or as a store of wealth leads to quite different measures of money. Money as a store of wealth could be regarded as any financial asset with a fixed nominal value that can be converted into money as a means of payment relatively quickly and at a small cost. The imprecision of the terms 'relatively quickly' and 'small cost' leaves room for some debate over what is money as a store of wealth at any particular time. In this form money as a store of wealth does not involve any nominal price uncertainty (in that its price is always unity), though it does involve uncertainty over its future value (because of inflation) and over its rate of return (since the rates of interest on these financial assets generally vary over time).

Money as a means of payment would, of course, be defined as the financial assets that are readily accepted for payment and are readily transferable between one individual and another. Here, again, there will be some room for debate as to what constitutes money as a means of payment at a point in time.

Keynes (1936/1973, p. 167, fn. 1) indicated, albeit in a footnote, that money can be defined differently for different purposes:

> we can draw the line between 'money' and 'debts' at whatever point is most convenient for handling a particular problem. For example, we can treat as *money* any command over general purchasing power which the owner has not parted with for a period in excess of three months, and as *debt* what cannot be recovered for a longer period than this; or we can substitute for 'three months' one month or three days or three hours or any other period; or we can exclude from *money* whatever is not legal tender on the spot. It is often convenient in practice to include in *money* time-deposits with banks and, occasionally, even such instruments as (*e.g.*) treasury bills. As a rule, I shall . . . assume that money is co-extensive with bank deposits.

The argument here is rather different, namely that money needs to be precisely defined, and different financial assets given different names (and assigned different properties in the analysis). The financial asset that serves as a means of payment (assumed to have a fixed price in terms of the unit of account) will be labelled here money (mp). In current circumstances this concept of money (mp) may be seen as approximately measured by M1. The financial asset that has a fixed nominal price and serves as an effective store of wealth (and receiving a significant rate of interest) is labelled money (sw). This concept of money may overlap with money (mp), and this is further discussed below. In current circumstances money (sw) may be seen as approximately measured by some aggregate, such as M2, M3 or M4, other than that which is contained in M1.

There is always a question in macroeconomics (and indeed in economic analysis more generally) as to how much aggregation to use. In macroeconomic analysis it has been customary to use an aggregate called money and often another financial aggregate called bonds. It is postulated here that four types of financial assets, which are often put under the heading of money, should be distinguished. The first is money (mp), corresponding to the liabilities of banks that are transferable directly from one person to another (with notes and coins being liabilities of the central bank). Banks are those financial institutions some of whose liabilities serve as means of payment. The second corresponds to banks' other liabilities that have a fixed nominal price but which do not serve as a means of payment. These liabilities may be transferable into money as a means of payment by the individual at relatively low cost of time and money. There is no simple name for them, and we could label them bank money (sw).

The third type are deposits with non-bank financial institutions that have a fixed nominal price. These deposits correspond to a broad notion of money such as M4 minus M2. Both the second and third types of financial assets form the liabilities of financial institutions, which would also have a stock of loans on the other side of their balance sheet. This raises the complication that if the demand for either of these types of assets rises and is satisfied, then the holding of loans also has to increase. As some are increasing their holding of deposits, others have to increase their holding of loans.

The fourth type of financial assets is all other financial assets that typically have a variable price. For the purpose of our discussion it is not necessary to further distinguish between these financial assets, and we could follow tradition and label these financial assets as 'bonds'.

The distinction between the various financial assets which have a fixed nominal price is made for a number of reasons. First, it should then become clear that some analyses (such as the circuitist and most of the post Keynesian endogenous money literature) relate only to money as a means of payment, and hence only directly to those financial assets that circulate as a means of payment. But other analyses which focus on money as a store of wealth, such as that of Keynes and Davidson, would seem to apply to all financial assets with fixed nominal price. This would then suggest that often analyses of money are non-comparable because they involve different perceptions of the nature of money.

Second, when banks create loans, they thereby create deposits, but these are deposits of money (mp). The existence of bank money (sw) complicates the reflux process and loans can remain in existence provided that bank deposits, whether money as means of payment or as a store of wealth, also remain in existence.

CAN A FINANCIAL ASSET BE BOTH A MEANS OF PAYMENT AND STORE OF WEALTH?

The question is not really whether money as a means of payment can be used as a store of wealth, for clearly it can: there is nothing to prevent someone using money as a store of wealth. Rather, it is whether money can in some sense act as a 'good' store of wealth, as well as being used as a means of payment. In general, there exists a range of financial assets that have a fixed nominal price in terms of money as a unit of account, and that yield a positive rate of interest. When money as a means of payment yields a zero or very low interest rate, then these financial assets with fixed nominal price will generally be a superior store of wealth as compared with money. Thus, it can be argued that 'the asset menus of the United States and other developed economies include assets that dominate money and exclude it from any place in permanent portfolios beyond the share it merits for reasons of inertia' (Tobin and Golub, 1998, p. 56). Further, Keynes's 'speculative motive is a reason for holding time deposits or other short-term obligations that dominate means of payment: it is not a reason for holding means of payment. Perhaps Keynes was either ignoring these intermediate assets or lumping them all together with means of payment as money' (ibid., p. 57).

Thus it is argued that at the present time money (mp) is a different financial asset than money (sw), and that there is virtually no overlap between the two types of financial assets. We say 'virtually no overlap', for some may use (say) cash as a store of wealth for reasons such as ignorance, inertia and avoidance of the checks by tax authorities and others when bank accounts are used. Two questions now arise. First, is it just a feature of the present arrangements that there is little overlap between money (mp) and money (sw) or is it a more general feature? Second, what significance should be given to the fact that money (mp) and bank money (sw) are both liabilities of the banking system?

To seek an answer to the first question we can draw on the own-rate of interest as defined by Keynes. He wrote that 'the total return expected from the ownership of an asset over a period is equal to its yield *minus* its carrying cost *plus* its liquidity-premium, *i.e.* to $q - c + l$. That is to say, $q - c + l$ is the own-rate of interest of any commodity, where q, c and l are measured in terms of itself as the standard' (Keynes, 1936/1973, p. 226). The return on money (mp) can be written as $q_1 - c_1 + l_1$ and on money (sw) as $q_2 - c_2 + l_2$. For banks money (mp) involves greater costs of transferring deposits from one person to another and the holding of a higher reserve ratio. It could be argued that the liquidity premia on the two types of money differ only a little. Money as a means of payment is held in order to dispose of it and it could then be argued that it is an inevitable feature of money (mp) that it imposes significantly greater costs than money (sw). It may be possible to envisage further technological changes with electronic transfer which would take the costs of transfer close to zero. In that event and if banks could operate with similar reserve ratios against the different types of money, then it could be envisaged that $q_1 - c_1$ and $q_2 - c_2$ become close in value, at which point money (mp) would become a store of wealth. But until that time arrives, it would seem that money (mp) would remain a poor store of wealth and the distinction between money (mp) and money (sw) maintained.

Turning now to the second question, the notion that 'loans make deposits' refers in the first instance to money (mp), and hence it is only money (mp) that comes into existence as a result of the granting of loans. It may, of course, be the case that as money circulates, it reaches someone who wishes to save in the form of bank money (sw) (that is, under present circumstances shifts from a demand deposit to a time deposit).

Banks generally have different reserve ratios for money (mp) and bank money (sw). An individual may be able to switch relatively easily between bank money (sw) and money (mp), and as such the two financial assets would appear to be readily substituted for one another. But any significant shift between money (mp) and bank money (sw) would lead the banks to have to respond. The banks' total deposits remain unchanged but the composition of their deposits changes, along with different reserve requirements. As a result, the effective cost of their deposits changes (since the rate of interest on money (sw) is much greater than the rate of interest on money (mp) though the banks' costs of operating the latter are greater than for the former). Provided that the central bank is willing to supply reserves then the shift in the composition of banks' liabilities can occur and the volume of outstanding loans remains unchanged. However, the banks could respond to the shift in demand by changing the relative interest rates on different types of deposits and on loans.

MONEY AND UNEMPLOYMENT

There are considerable implications for the analysis of unemployment arising from whether money is regarded as a means of payment or a store of wealth. When money is regarded as a means of payment, and money is created through the loan process, then banks' decisions on whether or not to grant loans have consequences on whether or not expenditure can take place. The level and structure of investment expenditures depend on decisions made by banks as to whom they will lend and on what conditions. This was expressed by Kalecki (1990, p. 489) in the following way:

> [T]he possibility of stimulating the business upswing is based on the assumption that the banking system, especially the central bank, will be able to expand credits without such a considerable increase in the rate of interest. If the banking system reacted so inflexibly to every increase in the demand for credit, then no boom would be possible on account of a new invention, nor any automatic upswing in the business cycle. . . . Investments would cease to be the channel through which additional purchasing power, unquestionably the *primus movens* of the business upswing, flows into the economy.

In a similar vein, he argues that:

> if this rate [of interest] were to increase sufficiently fast for the influence of the increase in gross profitability to be fully offset, an upswing would prove impossible. There is thus a close connection between the phenomenon of the business cycle and the response of the banking system to the increase in demand for money in circulation, at a rate of interest which is not prohibitive to the rise in investment' (Kalecki, 1990, p. 473).

In an endogenous money approach, the major impact of money on the levels of employment and output comes when that money is created through the loan process. The level and structure of loans impacts on the level and structure of investment, and thereby over time on the level and structure of the capital stock. In this context the question as to whether money is neutral or non-neutral is impossible to answer for what is the 'base case' against which a comparison could be made. It is difficult to envisage a decentralised market economy which did not involve money and finance. In the absence of a financial sector, then savings has to be undertaken in the form of the acquisition of goods and Say's Law would operate. When there is a financial sector, the operation of the banks and other financial institutions will necessarily determine the level and structure of investment.

When money is considered as a means of payment, unemployment can be seen to occur for many reasons. A major one would, of course, be that investment decisions fall short of full employment savings, and the shortfall of investment can arise from a combination of the incentives to invest (profitability and so on) and the ability of enterprises to finance their investment plans. But unemployment may also arise from a lack of sufficient productive capacity in the economy.

Money considered as a store of wealth is often seen as a (often *the*) major cause of unemployment. 'Unemployment develops . . . because people want the moon; – men cannot be employed when the object of desire (*i.e.* money) is something which cannot be produced and the demand for which cannot be readily choked off' (Keynes, 1936/1973, p. 235). Similarly, Davidson (2000, p. 15) argues that:

> To complete Keynes's general theory it is necessary to explain why, in an entrepreneurial, money-using economy, the propensity to save does not give rise to a market demand for readily reproducible durable products of industry. Why do savers *not* use producible durable goods as vehicles for carrying their saving to the future? To explain why, Keynes [1936/1973, ch. 17] introduced the 'essential properties' of money (and all other liquid assets) that distinguishes buying (and holding) liquid assets from buying (and holding) producible durables.

Also, Fontana (2000, p. 32) makes a similar point:

> The existence of a liquid store of wealth with those characteristics means that the critical link between supply of, and demand for, resources, as expressed by Say's Law, is broken. As Keynes saw it, that liquid store of wealth stands as a barrier to full employment. Unemployment results because 'the owners of wealth demand what cannot be produced (money) and do not demand what can be produced (other forms of wealth)' (Dillard, 1955, p. 16). Agents react to what is seen as an uncertain future by hoarding money.

> Keynes is usually considered as the economist who most explicitly and coherently pursued the idea that money matters only in so far as it is kept as a form of wealth. In fact, in the Keynesian model, the level of aggregate demand is influenced by the choice between real capital goods and cash balances, while sudden increases in liquidity preference may determine demand failures and unemployment (Graziani, 1996, p. 142).

> The trouble arises, therefore, because the act of saving implies, not a substitution for present consumption of some specific additional consumption which requires for its preparation just as much immediate economic activity as would have been

required by present consumption equal in value to the sum saved, but a desire for 'wealth' as such, that is for a potentiality of consuming an unspecified article at an unspecified time (Keynes, 1936/1973, p. 211).

[T]here is always an alternative to the ownership of real capital-assets, namely the ownership of money and debts; so that the prospective yield with which the producers of new investment have to be content cannot fall below the standard set by the current rate of interest. And the current rate of interest depends . . . not on the strength of the desire to hold wealth, but on the strengths of the desires to hold it in liquid and in illiquid forms respectively, coupled with the amount of the supply of wealth in the one form relatively to the supply of it in the other (ibid., pp. 212–13).

However, as a number of the above quotes hint, the difficulties over insufficient aggregate demand (to maintain full employment) arise from the existence of financial (and some other) assets, which do not require resources (including labour) for their production. As Davidson (2000, p. 15) has expressed it, money does not grow on trees. But then neither do bonds, equities, and so on. The decision to save is (usually) closely linked with a decision to acquire a financial asset, but not with a decision to acquire a durable asset, the production of which requires labour.

Liquidity preference may be seen to influence the allocation of wealth (and the increments of wealth, that is, savings) between different financial assets, which would have varying degrees of liquidity (see Davidson, 2000, Figure 1). A shift in liquidity preference would change the relative demands for the different financial assets, and some corresponding changes in the relative returns and prices of the financial assets could be anticipated. But in so far as the volume of deposits with banks and non-banks changes, there are consequent changes on the other side of the balance sheet, namely that the volume of loans outstanding has to change. For example, a shift away from financial assets such as bonds or equity would lower the price of these assets and raise the yield on them. A shift towards money (as a store of wealth) would mean that individuals wish to see the amount of bank deposits rise. But this can only occur with the participation of banks. On the other side of the banks' balance sheet are loans, and a change in the amount of deposits has to go alongside a corresponding change in loans. The banks could respond by cutting the rate of interest on deposits and also on loans. The difficulty arises that the shift in liquidity preference may mean a reluctance to take on loans, and banks cannot lower the loan interest rate low enough for sufficient take-up of loans to match the demand for deposits.

CONCLUSION

It is widely recognised that what is considered money changes over time (and differs across societies) and that the measurement of money (however defined) presents difficulties. In this chapter we have argued that a definition of money in terms of means of payment and the definition of money in terms of a store of wealth would lead to measures of money which are quite different. At present, the means of payment view would lead to a measure like M1, while the store of wealth view would imply a measure such as M3 or M4 (other than M1). This would mean that if the estimation of a demand for money function is regarded as interesting, it should be made clear which definition of money is being used in the derivation of the demand for money and the statistical measure of money to be used chosen accordingly (rather than looking for some notion of 'best fit'). Further, confusion arises from the use of the same term ('money') for different concepts and different measures.

The idea has been advanced here that the financial assets that serve as a means of payment have little overlap with the financial assets which serve as a store of wealth. Money as a store of wealth is one of many financial assets, and the demand for such money depends on the relative attractiveness of money and the other financial assets. Whilst a shift in liquidity preference would alter the relative demands and thereby the relative prices of the financial assets, such a shift would not itself lead to a change in the level of aggregate demand.

NOTES

1. The author is grateful to Giuseppe Fontana for discussions on the subject matter of this chapter.
2. See, for example, Graziani (1990) and Rochon (1999, ch. 1) for overviews of the circuitist approach, and Fontana (2000) for seeking to bring together post Keynesian and circuitist approaches.

REFERENCES

Clower, R.W. (1967), 'A reconsideration of the microfoundations of monetary theory', *Western Economic Journal*, **6** (1), 1–8. Reprinted in R.W. Clower (ed.) (1969), *Monetary Theory: Selected Readings*, Harmondsworth: Penguin, 202–11.
Davidson, P. (2000), 'There are major differences between Kalecki's theory of employment and Keynes's general theory of employment interest and money', *Journal of Post Keynesian Economics*, **23** (1), 3–26.

Dillard, D. (1955), 'The theory of a monetary economy', in K.K. Kurihara (ed.), *Post-Keynesian Economics*, London: Allen & Unwin, 3–30.

Fontana, G. (2000), 'Post Keynesians and Circuitists on money and uncertainty: an attempt at generality', *Journal of Post Keynesian Economics*, **23** (1), 27–48.

Friedman, M. (1969), 'The quantity theory of money: a restatement', in *The Optimum Quantity of Money and Other Essays*, London: Macmillan, 51–68.

Goodhart, C.A.E. (1975), *Money, Information and Uncertainty*, London: Macmillan.

Graziani, A. (1990), 'The theory of the monetary circuit', *Économies et Sociétés* ('Série Monnaie et Production', 7), **24** (6), 7–36.

Graziani, A. (1996), 'Money as purchasing power and money as a stock of wealth in Keynesian economic thought', in G. Deleplace and E.J. Nell (eds), *Money in Motion: The Post Keynesian and Circulation Approaches*, London and New York: Macmillan and St. Martin's Press, 139–54.

Kalecki, M. (1990), *The Collected Works of Michael Kalecki*, Vol. I *Capitalism: Business Cycles and Full Employment*, Oxford: Clarendon Press.

Keynes, J.M. (1936/1973), *The General Theory of Employment, Interest and Money*, London: Macmillan. Reprinted in *The Collected Writings of John Maynard Keynes*, Vol. VII, London and Basingstoke: Macmillan.

Keynes, J.M. (1937a/1973), 'The general theory of employment', *Quarterly Journal of Economics*, **51** (2), 209–23. Reprinted in *The Collected Writings of John Maynard Keynes*, Vol. XIV, London and Basingstoke: Macmillan, 109–23.

Keynes, J.M. (1937b/1973), 'The "ex ante" theory of the rate of interest', *Economic Journal*, **47** (188), 663–9. Reprinted in *The Collected Writings of John Maynard Keynes*, Vol. XIV, London and Basingstoke: Macmillan, 215–23.

Patinkin, D. (1965), *Money, Interest and Prices*, New York: Harper International, 2nd edition.

Rochon, L.-P. (1999), *Credit, Money and Production: An Alternative Post-Keynesian Approach*, Cheltenham and Northampton: Edward Elgar.

Shaw, G.K., M.J. McCrostie and D. Greenaway (1997), *Macroeconomics: Theory and Policy in the UK*, Oxford: Basil Blackwell, 3rd edition.

Tobin, J. (1958), 'Liquidity preference as behaviour towards risk', *Review of Economic Studies*, **25** (67), 65–86.

Tobin, J. and S.S. Golub (1998), *Money, Credit and Capital*, Boston: McGraw-Hill.

2. Endogenous Money, Banks and the Revival of Liquidity Preference

Virginie Monvoisin and Corinne Pastoret

INTRODUCTION

A number of endogenous money theorists are taking a renewed interest in liquidity preference theory and in particular in the liquidity preference of banks. Although post Keynesians initially turned to other Keynesian concepts, such as the finance motive, to construct a theory of endogenous money, liquidity preference can explain a number of points of that theory including the behaviour of households with regard to money and the behaviour of banks with regard to credit.

Is this a renewal of interest in liquidity preference as set out in the *General Theory* or is it something different? Are households' liquidity preference and banks' liquidity preference consistent with the conception of endogenous money?

The next section looks at the liquidity preference theory developed by Keynes in the *General Theory* so as to evaluate subsequent changes in this concept.[1] We will emphasise how liquidity preference was supplanted by concepts justifying the endogenous nature of money and how it can be reincorporated into the theory of endogenous money. The third section examines the liquidity preference of banks, which some authors claim is related to Keynes's concept of liquidity preference. We will question whether this is legitimate and we will try to show that banks' liquidity preference, in fact, encompasses other aspects of Keynes's theory of money. The fourth section compares and contrasts the liquidity preference of households and of banks. The overall picture of behaviour with respect to liquidity will allow us to reconcile the concepts of endogenous money and liquidity preference. The last section concludes with some final remarks.

KEYNES'S LIQUIDITY PREFERENCE THEORY

Before scrutinising banks' liquidity preference, let us first delimit the concept of liquidity preference in the narrow sense defined by Keynes. We will then be able to gauge just how faithful recent developments of liquidity preference theory have remained to the initial concept and to examine how the theory of endogenous money has positioned itself in reaction to Keynes's theory of money demand.

Recent debate about liquidity preference has often been organised around the theory of endogenous money. Although endogenous money theorists initially disregarded liquidity preference theory, a number of them have subsequently attempted to include it in the theory. Such inclusion entails a change in the concept of liquidity preference and focusing on certain aspects of it, and even extending it to banks.

The Traditional Theory of Liquidity Preference

By setting out liquidity preference as defined by Keynes, we can assess how much the concept has changed. Initially the corner stone of liquidity preference was uncertainty. Keynes set out three motives for holding money by way of explanation of how the demand for money was structured. What is unusual about this concept is that Keynes's overall scheme is clearly macroeconomic, whereas microeconomic arguments are used to explain liquidity preference; it is the behaviour of economic agents that underpins this theory of money demand.

The theoretical context that Keynes constructs and describes is profoundly marked by the uncertainty that economic agents feel in what is by definition an uncertain environment. Keynes incorporates historical time into the argument and opts for a dynamic rather than a static mode of analysis. When they come to make decisions, such as whether or not to invest, entrepreneurs are confronted with the question of time and therefore of short- and long-term uncertainty. Any investment decision is itself dependent on two variables that in turn involve uncertainty: the marginal efficiency of capital and the interest rate.

Consumers too feel uncertainty. For one thing, they are in an uncertain environment: the marginal propensity to consume may be affected by unpredictable changes in tax policy, by differences between future and current income, or by the value of capital. Keynes makes allowance for the effects of unpredictable variations and of forecasts on economic computations. In addition, economic agents, whether entrepreneurs or consumers, feel uncertainty. At this point Keynes remarks that agents resort to a means of reducing this feeling of uncertainty in the form of contracts. For entrepreneurs, the contract is a way of considering that the present state of affairs will obtain in the future. It may be that faith in the contract, as a long-term forecast, is rather limited (Keynes, 1936/1973, pp. 148–53). As economic agents invariably operate within an uncertain environment, they will feel less uncertain. Liquidity preference theory can be understood in this uncertain framework, as holding money is one way of guarding against uncertainty. This is so because money is a bridge between the present and the future.[2]

Keynes therefore constructed a theory of money demand based on an understanding of the behaviour of economic agents. The study of why people hold money involves analysing liquidity preference, as liquidity is an essential feature of money.

> Liquidity-preference is a potentiality or functional tendency, which fixes the quantity of money which the public will hold when the rate of interest is given; so that if r is the rate of interest, M the quantity of money and L the function of liquidity-preference, we have $M = L(r)$. This is where, and how, the quantity of money enters into the economic scheme (Keynes, 1936/1973, p. 168).

Liquidity functions are designed to include two elements. Firstly, they include the behaviour of individuals, L_1, accounting for the cash holdings that agents hope to use for their future spending and to guard against the uncertainty of the future. Secondly, they also include L_2, accounting for uncertainty about the interest rate.[3] This behaviour toward money is categorised into three possible reactions, that is, three motives that prompt the individual to hold money:

1. the transactions motive, that is, the need of cash for current transactions of personal and business exchanges;[4]
2. the precautionary motive, that is, the desire for security as to the future cash equivalent of a certain proportion of total resources;[5]
3. the speculative motive, that is, the object of securing profit from knowing better than the market what the future will bring forth (Keynes, 1936/1973, p. 170).[6]

These motives are based on expectations, income, and the rate of interest. They are at one and the same time the result of economic activity and related to economic data. The behaviour of economic agents may be taken as an aggregate and it is likely that Keynes intends liquidity functions to be taken as a whole as he refers to the 'public' rather than to the 'agent', although this alters neither the method nor its outcome. Cash holdings are idle for individuals in microeconomic terms (Léonard and Norel, 1991, p. 155).

Liquidity preference theory therefore remains a theory of allocation of money, as it indicates how agents perceive the demand for money. Money as cash holdings allows the agent to respond to all motives of demand for liquidity and to face up to uncertainty. Of all the forms of stores of value (real assets, financial assets, or cash assets) money is the one that can be used most effectively to make choices in time and space.[7]

Liquidity Preference Neglected by Endogenous Money Theory

Keynes's liquidity preference is a theory of money allocation that helps us to understand how economic agents perceive the demand for money. Post Keynesians, however, emphasised the shortcomings of liquidity preference theory as a theory of money. They drew on Keynes's (1930/1971) *Treatise on Money* and his papers on the finance motive[8] to go beyond the *General Theory*[9] and to serve as a foundation for their theory of money demand, which differs in principle from liquidity preference theory. The exposition of the theory of endogenous money will serve as a framework for analysing liquidity preference in the fourth section.

To understand the importance of this separation and the construction of endogenous money theory, the theoretical conditions should be clarified. These consist in two points: (i) the distinction between savings and money, and (ii) the dominant role of the entrepreneur, of production, and of the way it is financed. To do this, Keynes identifies the two functions of banks by virtue of the distinction between savings and liquidity. These two functions are financial intermediation and money creation.[10]

Keynes describes two ways in which money is created: active and passive creation, which depends on the form of money demand. Money is created actively when firms apply for credit from banks, which create money. The second mode of money creation stems from surplus deposits that banks recycle among each other. Keynes first clarifies his conception of credit. For him, it is important to look at the demand for money as such, not at borrowing,[11] moving away from the theory of loanable funds. This conception has far-reaching implications for banks and we shall return to it in the next section. At this stage, it is noteworthy that Keynes ties together investment, credit, and money demand through firms and banks. He claims in fact that, 'if decisions to invest are (e.g.) increasing, the extra finance involved will constitute an additional demand for money' (Keynes,

1937a/1973, p. 209). He further states that '[s]urely nothing is more certain than that the credit or "finance" required by *ex ante* investment is not mainly supplied by *ex ante* saving' (Keynes, 1937b/1973, p. 217).

Investment by the entrepreneur requires a prior demand for money. A project is financed because banks supply credit to start production. Banks are the starting point of the production process, as post Keynesians were to argue. Money incorporated within the production system is endogenous. Now, as Wells (1981, p. 587) recalls, there is 'a motive [that is, the finance motive] which Davidson's pioneering studies (1965, 1972) made clear apart from and in addition to the transactions, precautionary and speculative motives for demanding money'. This motive supplements the other three liquidity preference motives, although it does not generate any specific amount in terms of cash holdings. Cash holding for the finance motive is compounded with that engendered for the transactions motive. However, the effect of the finance motive on the analysis of cash holdings is of little importance; all that matters are the consequences of its presence, the motives behind it. What needs to be understood is how the demand for money and credit are involved in the production process.

For post Keynesians, the finance motive alone explains the demand for credit, which is the basis of money creation, and the relations between firms and banks. The other motives for holding money described in liquidity preference theory provide no explanation about the creation of money and the production process. Now, post Keynesians set out to explain where money comes from, as it is money that allows production to be implemented. The entrepreneur uses it to finance output and to pay his employees. Commercial banks provide credit, which they create in part or in full. Money is endogenous in that it results from demand within the economic system itself and not from the volition of some external institution.

Goux (1996, pp. 72–3) lists the characteristics of money by identifying a number of common theoretical points: money is integrated by virtue of production, the creation of new debts gives rise to the creation of money, money is a social convention (just like the interest rate), money is a flow, money is endogenous, potentially created and destroyed. The mechanism of supply of credit money is the same for all post Keynesians: money demand determines the amount of credit, loans make deposits, and deposits make resources.

Although post Keynesians have become involved in many controversies about the money supply, there is a common theoretical corpus attempting to define the mechanisms by which money is created.[12] However, other discussions about the demand for money and liquidity preference have arisen.

Liquidity Preference, Uncertainty and Post Keynesian Monetary Theory

Liquidity preference reappears in the framework of endogenous money when post Keynesians come to make allowance for uncertainty. Returning to the Keynesian principle whereby money is a connection between the present and the future, post Keynesians observe that money affects decisions about production, as it is a suitable tool for combating uncertainty. Given the need for forward planning of production in a monetary economy, money is present in the entrepreneur's calculations from the outset and allows him to forecast interest rates and spending. Likewise, the decisions that banks make are affected by uncertainty. Banks adjust the terms for granting credit in line with their expectations. Money exists because it is a bulwark against uncertainty allowing economic agents to fulfil their expectations. Its existence is related to the behaviour and reactions of economic agents. Money is held because of uncertainty and it reduces the impression of uncertainty, as uncertainty creates the need for money and holding money is a way of arming oneself against uncertainty.

The importance of uncertainty affects the post Keynesian view of the functions of money.[13] This approach is adopted more specifically by the structuralists[14] or the liquidity preference school. They set about reinterpreting the use that agents make of money.

> The complex division of labour and ramified interdependence-via-exchange that characterise a capitalist economy are unthinkable without money as a universal medium of exchange. . . . Further, money as universal medium of exchange in spot transactions is not adequate in itself. Production takes time, and the capitalist who would undertake a given production process needs financing to bridge the gap between his initial purchases of means of production and the eventual realisation of sale revenue (Cottrell, 1994, p. 592).

> The fact that almost every society employs some money is in itself a response to uncertainty. Denominating contracts in an intermediate commodity, money, allows a sharing of uncertainty between the buyer and the seller (Dow, 1993, p. 19).

This, in fact, takes us back to a definition of money functions dependent on liquidity preference theory. The store of value function of money explains how uncertainty justifies the precautionary motive for holding money.

Analysis of uncertainty is informative about the significance ascribed to the study of liquidity. While Davidson concentrates on the precautionary motive, other structuralists extend their theory of credit money to explain the speculative motive. As Dow (1996, p. 503) argues: 'Credit is created not only to finance productive investment but also to finance speculation'.

This approach is not neutral for the conception of endogenous money. The analysis of liquidity preference as a demand for money by households does not seem to square with the theory of endogenous money, which is based on the demand for money by firms through bank credit. This issue is addressed in the fourth section.

Through Davidson we have examined how endogenous money theorists interpret uncertainty. We shall see later on that the different interpretations of uncertainty and therefore of liquidity lead to contrasting conclusions:

> There is no shortage of theories of liquidity preference that lay claim to a Keynesian parentage. I consider three here, those of Tobin (1958), Davidson (1988) and Makowski (1989), concentrating on the referents of the theory in each case, what uncertainty and liquidity are taken to be, and on the way uncertainty is represented analytically. Tobin's aptly titled 'Liquidity Preference as Behaviour Towards Risk' remains the received view on Keynesian liquidity preference. Liquidity, for Tobin, is synonymous with cash ... Davidson is concerned to highlight the use of money and money contracts as a means of 'getting by' and facilitating economic activity in a world of uncertainty ... Makowski ... defines uncertainty as 'risk plus the possibility of learning' (Runde, 1994, pp. 137–8).

Before examining this point, we must first look at what makes up banks' liquidity preference so as to assess the consequences of such a view of money.

BANKS' LIQUIDITY PREFERENCE AND ITS SOURCES IN KEYNES'S WRITINGS

The concept of liquidity preference developed in the *General Theory* has been extended to banks. This reflects the intention to include banks in the analytical framework of the *General Theory*, and more specifically to study the microeconomic behaviour of banks and the macroeconomic impact of that behaviour. More generally, close scrutiny of the role played by banks allows us to inquire into the connection between the way banks grant credit and the endogenous nature of money.

We will look at whether banks' liquidity preference is truly a new concept or whether it 'merely' brings together under the same heading factors that were already to be found in Keynes's writings. We will thus bring out the connections between banks' liquidity preference as defined by post Keynesians and other concepts defined by Keynes in the *Treatise on Money* and in the *General Theory*.

Banks' Liquidity Preference

We approach banks' liquidity preference through the study of how banks manage two major risks: the risks of illiquidity and insolvency. We show the connections between managing these two risks and rationing bank credit. We work with the definition of liquidity preference given by Le Héron (1986; 2002), who considers that banks' liquidity preference consists in guarding against the risk of insufficient liquidity and the risk of insolvency of the bank.

Commercial banks' liquidity preference is aimed at reducing the two major microeconomic risks related to their activity, namely:

– A crisis of liquidity specific to banks' conversion activity, that is, to the fact that banks' monetary liabilities are highly liquid compared with their assets. Any massive demand for money to be repaid to another bank may cause the bank to fail for insufficient liquidity as its assets cannot be mobilized swiftly enough.
– A crisis of solvency if the bank as a business concern is not cost-effective enough and its assets are not of sufficient value compared with its liabilities, leading to bankruptcy (Le Héron, 2002, p. 10).

The illiquidity risk

Poor management of the illiquidity risk may lead the bank to run short of liquidity, or even to bankruptcy, if it cannot meet its liquid commitments towards other banks. This will lead to very strict credit rationing that may have devastating effects for economic activity.

The post Keynesian model of bank behaviour The management of the illiquidity risk can be studied by using a post Keynesian model of bank behaviour. For example, Dymski (1988) attempts to explain how banks manage this risk in an uncertain environment by using a model similar to that developed by Tobin in 1982. Within this analytical framework, so as to avoid finding themselves faced with a shortage of liquidity, banks must anticipate the volume of future deposits available to them before they grant loans. Hence banks choose to create a certain volume of credit on the basis of estimates of their future liquidity.

> Bank loan rate and volume decisions in the loan period are based partly on assessments of the availability of banking system liquidity in the adjustment period; in effect, expected liquidity considerations influence current credit-creation activities. Second, as noted, banks may be unable to meet all loan-contract obligations if the banking system is faced with a shortage of liquidity in the adjustment period (Dymski, 1988, p. 517).

Adjustments that banks must make in the future also affect economic activity, particularly when banks' forecasts of their future liquidity have been overly optimistic: 'dual banks are susceptible to sustained disequilibria, and the adjustment behavior of dual banks will be among the causes of upturns and downturns' (ibid., p. 501).

The forecast of future liquidity determines banks' decisions as to whether or not to grant credit and may give rise to credit rationing: 'Not only are the bank's functions interdependent: they may conflict. The more credit banks create to satisfy loan demand, the fewer funds are available for redistribution to meet depositor demands for liquidity' (ibid., p. 516).

Dymski (1988) essentially analyses the way in which the risk of illiquidity is managed by forecasting the level of future deposits available to the bank. Another approach is for banks to manage their risk of illiquidity by managing their assets and liabilities: 'Banks' liquidity preference is expressed by their intention to reduce uncertainty and so by a specific composition of their balance sheets' (Le Héron, 2002, p. 11).

It must be remembered that banks hold highly liquid deposits and must grant loans thereby restricting their liquidity. More specifically, they may decide to finance firms through the financial market instead of doing so directly. This strategy allows them to reduce their exposure to the risk of illiquidity, as securities can more readily be made liquid. However, banks must forecast changes in the market value of such securities, fluctuations that are subject to uncertainty just like future bank liquidity is.

Real time and uncertainty: the problem of evaluating the bank's future liquidity Let us further emphasise that Dymski (1988) introduces real time and uncertainty into the model proposed by Tobin. These additional points, Dymski argues, allow the construction of a post Keynesian model of bank behaviour. The new assumptions mean that it is impossible for banks to determine *ex ante* any point of equilibrium for granting credit and allocating deposits: 'But as agents cannot coordinate their actions in advance, some banks may have difficulties in performing their supply of liquidity function. In other words, they would then be unable to meet the demand for liquidity from depositors' (Dymski, 1988, p. 504).

The uncertainty of the environment in which agents operate explains the existence of a future demand for money by bank depositors that banks must endeavour to anticipate: 'The stochastic hypothesis is sufficient to give a role to money and to banks: this creates a precautionary demand for liquid reserves – an analytic role for money' (ibid., p. 504).

The bank must therefore manage its illiquidity risk over several periods before deciding how much credit to grant. The assumption of radical uncertainty of the environment dear to post Keynesians does not mean that agents do not make decisions. Accordingly Dymski (1988) considers that in an uncertain environment agents (here banks) make forecasts, with the risk of making mistakes, as if they were in an ergodic universe. They put diminishing faith in their forecasts when the economy is moving towards a crisis situation.

As we have just explained, banks' management of the illiquidity risk reflects their need to anticipate demand for deposits by depositors. A further aspect of illiquidity risk management involves the study of relations between banks. In contrast with Tobin's model, this means that deposits are not only financial assets held as protection against uncertainty but are also means of payment. This casts fresh light on relations between banks.

Illiquidity risk and relations between banks A bank's illiquidity has several consequences. Dymski (1988) emphasises two factors. First, the bank may be unable to meet the demand for deposits from depositors for making payments. Dymski speaks of instantaneous conversion of deposits into reserves or into money to explain this phenomenon. In the same way, he highlights what the difficulty is in granting new credits. Le Héron (2002) emphasises the consequence of illiquidity for the bank within the banking system. When the bank is unable to honour its commitments with its counterparts, '[a]ny massive demand for money to be repaid to another bank may cause the bank to fail for insufficient liquidity as its assets cannot be mobilized swiftly enough' (Le Héron, 2002, p. 10). The same point was raised by Dymski (1988, p. 516), as quoted above: 'Not only are the bank's functions interdependent: they may conflict. The more credit banks create to satisfy loan demand, the fewer funds are available for redistribution to meet depositor demands for liquidity'.

At this point we must raise two issues that will be examined more closely later on. In concentrating on bank behaviour, Dymski (1988) overlooks the ability of each bank to influence the future liquidity of all economic agents, including banks themselves. In addition, the illiquidity risk is closely bound up with the limits imposed on money creation by the central bank. Without these institutional constraints, we might wonder whether banks' liquidity preference is still meaningful, short of restricting illiquidity risk management to a strategy for maximising bank profits. This would be another matter though. Moreover, in his 1986 paper Le Héron considers that there is no such thing as banks' liquidity preference in the absence of quantitative constraints imposed by the central bank. However, even in this perspective, the other aspect of banks' liquidity preference, insolvency risk, is paramount, in particular when it comes to explaining credit rationing. We will ask, however, to what extent it can be tied in with the actual concept of banks' liquidity preference.

The insolvency risk

When banks grant loans, they must face up to the risk of illiquidity and also manage the insolvency risk. This essentially entails the bank evaluating the projects that it decides to finance directly. The bank attempts to evaluate the cost-effectiveness of the project, and in particular its associated returns, to determine whether the borrower is able to make the repayments at the due dates. Like all economic agents, the bank operates in an environment characterised by radical uncertainty. Nonetheless, as when assessing future liquidity, it can try to make predictions by assuming that the future is to some extent foreseeable.

This was a subject of controversy debated in several papers published by the *Journal of Post Keynesian Economics*. The issue was to seek out any common ground among the approaches in terms of asymmetric information of the new Keynesians and the assessment of lender's risk by the bank in an uncertain universe. Dymski (1988) views these approaches as consistent in terms of asymmetric information and a post Keynesian conception of the role of banks.

Banks may also become insolvent by acquiring unprofitable shares or government bonds; the bank is then exposed to the risks of the market and of income.[15]

It should be noted that post Keynesians include insolvency risk under the concept of the banks' liquidity preference. If a borrower defaults, the bank may be short of liquidity, after being insolvent; conversely, it may become insolvent or go bankrupt as a result of a liquidity crisis. The interaction of these two risks justifies including insolvency risk within the banks' liquidity preference theory, although a priori it does not relate directly to bank liquidity.

Banks' Liquidity Preference Includes Elements from the *Treatise on Money* and the *General Theory*

At first sight the banks' liquidity preference appears to be an innovative concept, extending to banks the concept of households' liquidity preference as presented by Keynes in the *General Theory*. Without going so far as to deny the relevance of the concept of banks' liquidity preference, we show that it includes elements from the *Treatise on Money* and from the *General Theory*. The lender–borrower relationship and lending and borrowing risks are related to banks' management of insolvency risk. The practical problem of the banker is related to illiquidity risk management. Keynes, however, does not forget to emphasise the macroeconomic effect of banks' microeconomic behaviour.

The lender–borrower relationship in the *General Theory* and its origins in the *Treatise on Money*: insolvency risk management

Before granting a loan, banks assess the borrower's creditworthiness and the cost-effectiveness of the project to be funded. This assessment is related to insolvency risk management, which is an integral part of the concept of banks' liquidity preference.

In his *Treatise on Money*, Keynes observes that banks rely in part on their relationship with the borrower to decide whether or not to grant the loan. Banks choose which potential borrowers will secure credit on the basis of their standing with their banker. A subjective element is introduced into the selection of successful and unsuccessful applicants that increases the unsatisfied fringe of borrowers, 'the amount lent to any individual being governed not solely by the security and the rate of interest offered, but also by reference to the borrower's purposes and his standing with the bank as a valuable or influential client' (Keynes, 1930/1971, p. 327).

The lender–borrower relationship is then clarified, in Chapter 11 of the *General Theory*, by the definition of the two risks that influence the scale of investment, the borrower risk and the lender risk (Keynes, 1936/1973, p. 144). The borrower risk derives from the borrower's doubts about the actual returns he may get from his investment. The lender risk may arise either from the borrower's deliberate attempt to escape his commitment to pay back the loan (dubbed the moral risk) or from statutory provisions that might release him from his commitment, or from unintentional failure because of disappointed expectations as to returns. As Keynes (1930/1971, p. 21) puts it in *A Treatise on Money*, '[h]ow banks manage these two risks is an integral part of the concept of banks' liquidity preference'.[16] In the same work, Keynes deals also with the way the bank manages illiquidity risk through 'the practical problem of the banker'.

The practical problem of the banker: managing the risk of illiquidity

In *A Treatise on Money* Keynes shows that banks have potentially unlimited power to create money. He takes the view that loans make deposits with the result that banks may lend more than their available deposits. However, even if they can create money, banks must manage their liquidity. While, on the one hand, they must grant loans, they must also, on the other hand, take into account the requirements and behaviour of depositors, and settle their debts with other banks. In other words, to use the terminology employed earlier on, banks must manage their illiquidity risk.

As stated above, Keynes distinguishes two ways in which banks make deposits – active and passive creation – with differing impacts on banks' liquidity and financial standing. Banks actively create deposits when they grant loans. They passively create money when they receive liquid resources from depositors or from other banks.

> It follows that the rate at which the bank can, with safety, *actively* create deposits by lending and investing has to be in a proper relation to the rate at which it is *passively* creating them against the receipt of liquid resources from its depositors. For the latter increase the bank's reserves even if only a part of them is ultimately retained by the bank, whereas the former diminish the reserves even if only a part of them is paid away to the customers of other banks (Keynes, 1930/1971, pp. 21–2).

Even if actively and passively created deposits appear similar, the consequences of creating them are different for the bank's liquidity and profitability. This asymmetry can be explained as follows:

1. When a bank passively creates a deposit, it acquires a claim on another bank that increases its reserves even if some of these reserves are subsequently transferred to other banks. The bank takes no risk in creating deposits in this way.
2. Contrariwise, when a bank actively creates deposits, if these deposits are transferred to other banks, they give rise to a debt owed to the receiving bank by the issuing bank. The creation of this type of deposits makes the bank creating the deposit more fragile inasmuch as, even if most of the deposits created were to remain with this bank, it would be weakened by them. Conversely, passive creation can only strengthen the bank's standing or at worst keep it unchanged. The amount of credit that banks can grant without it affecting liquidity is measured in relative terms and not by referring to the amount of deposits they hold.

> But it is equally clear that the rate at which an individual bank creates deposits on its own initiative is subject to certain rules and limitations; – it must keep step with the other banks and cannot raise its own deposits relatively to the total deposits out of proportion to its quota of the banking business of the country (Keynes, 1930/1971, pp. 26–7).

This raises a practical problem that any banker must attempt to resolve:

> Now it is evident that the bank must so conduct its business that these opposite processes can be approximately offset against one another ... The practical problem of the banker consists, therefore, in so managing his affairs that his daily accruing assets in the shape of cash and claims shall be as nearly as possible equal to his daily accruing liabilities in these forms (Keynes, 1930/1971, p. 21).

One point is worth making here even if it is to be dealt with more closely in the next section, namely that Keynes emphasises the connection between the microeconomy and the macroeconomy. Keynes illustrates the impact of money creation by a single bank on the other banks. More generally, he shows that a bank's liquidity is the outcome of the aggregate behaviour of this bank and of the banking system as a whole:

> Every movement forward by an individual bank weakens it [the banking system], but every such movement by one of its neighbour banks strengthens it; so that if all move forward together, no one is weakened on balance. Thus the behaviour of each bank, though it cannot afford to move more than a step in advance of the others, will be governed by the average behaviour of the banks as a whole – to which average, however, it is able to contribute its quota small or large (Keynes, 1930/1971, p. 23).

The practical problem of the banker is therefore a source of inspiration for post Keynesians dealing with illiquidity risk and more generally with banks' liquidity preference. For example, Dymski's (1988) model of bank behaviour formalises and extends Keynes's idea in the *Treatise on Money*. Dymski, in particular, emphasises the incongruence between deposits created and deposits available to the bank in the future. Le Héron (2002) concentrates on how debts and claims between banks affect bank liquidity. The macroeconomic consequences of bank behaviour seem nonetheless to be underestimated in the concept of banks' liquidity preference. A return to the *Treatise on Money* will allow us to show in the next section the need to construct a macroeconomic theory of banking.

BANKS' LIQUIDITY PREFERENCE, HOUSEHOLDS' LIQUIDITY PREFERENCE AND THE ENDOGENOUS MONEY SUPPLY

As we have seen, banks' liquidity preference brings together a number of elements of the monetary and financial theory developed by Keynes in the

Treatise on Money and in the *General Theory*. The use of the term liquidity preference when applied to banks may seem surprising. However, the extension of the concept of liquidity preference has the major advantage of focusing on the role of banks. First, we look at the connections and interactions between the two forms of liquidity preference. What is at stake here is the inclusion of the role of banks in the liquidity preference theory set out by Keynes in the *General Theory*. One of the major criticisms levelled at this work is the absence of banks, even if Keynes argues that he covered the matter in the *Treatise* and does not go over the same ground in the *General Theory*. Thereafter, we emphasise the integration of the two forms of liquidity preference in the theory of endogenous money. This will involve asking questions about the compatibility of these two concepts.

Households' Liquidity Preference and Banks' Liquidity Preference Contrasted

We will examine the connections and interactions between banks' liquidity preference and households' liquidity preference. Dymski's (1988) post Keynesian model of bank behaviour forges a first link between these two forms of liquidity preference. Through households' future demand for deposits, households' liquidity preference affects banks' illiquidity risk and the volume of bank credit. We will draw a distinction between deposits as financial assets and deposits as a means of payment. Wray (1992) highlights a second tie between the two forms of liquidity preference in conceiving of households' holding of deposits as unexercised buying power. We will show that households' liquidity preference affects banks' lending risk through the medium of effective demand.

Portfolio theories from Tobin to Dymski: households' liquidity preference restricts banks' capacity to grant loans

The theory of banks' liquidity preference states that banks must anticipate their future liquidity. In particular, they must anticipate households' liquidity preference or, in other words, households' choices about holding a part of their income in the form of deposits. In view of the way they evaluate future liquidity, they will grant loans or on the contrary restrict credit.

Banks' liquidity preference is closely linked to households' liquidity preference. It follows from this that even households' decisions may in part explain the amount of credit allocated to the economy. Tobin explains that the main limit on granting bank credit lies in the agents' willingness to hold deposits created by banks. Deposits appear, in this perspective, to be highly liquid financial assets that an agent must be prepared to hold.

A number of post Keynesians, notably Dymski (1988), have picked up on Tobin's 1982 model and applied it in an uncertain environment with real time integrated. The conclusions remain similar to those drawn by Tobin: 'Not only are the bank's functions interdependent: they may conflict. The more credit banks create to satisfy loan demand, the fewer funds are available for redistribution to meet depositor demands for liquidity' (Dymski, 1988, p. 516). Nonetheless, these changes affect the nature of deposits. Dymski includes in depositors' demand for deposits both deposits held as financial assets and deposits required for making payments ('conversion of deposits into money' or 'to be converted into reserves') and probably for paying debts between banks. It seems therefore necessary to make a distinction between the monetary and financial aspect of deposits and the motives for creating these deposits. A deposit, before acting as a store of value, is the result of a payment. Could it be, as Tobin suggests, that there are unwanted deposits?

Some economists see a difference between loans granted and deposits: if loans make deposits in accordance with the principle of endogenous money, the forms of demand they express are different, as the motives for contracting loans and the motives for holding deposits do not relate to the same economic agents. They make a distinction between demand for credit, on one side, and the desire to hold money that is materialised by the holding of deposits, on the other side. These deposits, resulting from the spending of loans, vary with the agents' portfolio decisions.

> The (flow) demand for new bank lending, on which the endogeneity case focuses, originates with one set of agents while the (new) deposits that are created by this lending have to be held by a different set. The first set ('deficit unit') is a subset of the latter ('wealthholders'). For the former, what is involved is an income-expenditure decision; for the latter it is a portfolio consideration (Arestis and Howells, 1996, pp. 540–1).

Here, by virtue of its function as a store of value and of its link with uncertainty, money is a factor in households' portfolio decisions (Rochon, 1999, p. 217). Money is conceived of as one of a number of financial assets. Households look to hold their savings and their wealth in less liquid assets than money in line with the principle of liquidity preference.

In the second section we recalled what households' liquidity preference entailed. Post Keynesians have adopted this approach emphasising and enhancing some of these aspects so as to include it in their banking theory. Here, the demand for money or deposits is the decisive factor behind banks' liquidity and therefore behind the amount of credit they can allocate.

Connections between liquidity preference and evaluation of lender's risk

The portfolio allocation models we have just referred to consider that an increase in households' liquidity preference allows banks to create more loans. In effect, depositors will hold the deposits that banks create. The banks will not find themselves short of liquidity.

Wray (1992) also discusses the connection between the liquidity preferences of households and of banks in the broader framework of macroeconomics. He reverses the relationship between the liquidity preference of banks and of households: 'rising liquidity preference will be associated with reductions of planned spending, with a shift of public preferences toward the most liquid bank liabilities, and with rising reserve requirements coupled with a reserve drain at the individual bank level' (Wray, 1992, p. 303). Indeed, increased preference for liquidity by households goes hand in hand with increased risks for lender and borrower. The bank is therefore impelled not to grant any more loans. Such a change in the behaviour of households goes along with a downturn in consumption and a fall in effective demand. The economy takes a turn for the worse and lender and borrower risks increase.

However, Wray studies the relationship between the two liquidity preferences in a macroeconomic context and at a different level of analysis from Tobin and from Dymski, who both take a microeconomic view, which accounts for their apparent differences. Here Wray is more concerned about the question of bank insolvency while Dymski and Tobin concentrate on the issue of bank illiquidity. Wray works with the conception of deposits as a means of paying for consumption. This approach makes it possible to allow for the relations between deposits, production – through the principle of effective demand – and consumption.

Liquidity Preference in the Framework of Endogenous Money

In what has been said, difficulties have appeared when it comes to including households' and banks' liquidity preferences within the framework of endogenous money, as well as in accommodating the two forms of liquidity preference. We will investigate whether such integration can be achieved and how. In doing this we work on the principles of post Keynesian theory whereby the central bank does not control the money supply mechanism. Commercial banks alone have the task of creating money.

Economists dealing with banks' liquidity preference acknowledge the banks' ability to create money. Dymski (1988), for instance, accepts the idea that loans make deposits. However, it is future liquidity alone that governs the decisions to grant bank loans. Banks' expectations as to this future liquidity imply that something is known about it. Now, liquidity in the banking system is not a given but an end-result, the outcome of money creation by all the banks.[17] Dymski (1988) proposes what is essentially a microeconomic theory of bank behaviour, which post Keynesians consider inconsistent with the theory of endogenous money. Nonetheless, it seems difficult to forego a theory of bank behaviour under the endogenous money approach, as money is created by banks.[18] Graziani's (1990) attempt to construct a 'macroeconomic theory of banking' is part of this approach. Banks' liquidity preference may be rendered consistent with the theory of endogenous money when allowance is made for the connection between micro- and macroeconomic theories of banking.

Post Keynesians have emphasised the shortcomings of households' liquidity preference theory as a theory of money. Now, as we saw in the second section, while they abandoned this concept for another definition of the demand for money with the finance motive, they continue to use the idea of liquidity preference. This, however, is a contradiction in appearance only. Money demand for the finance motive and for liquidity preference covers quite separate cases. The former concerns firms' demand for credit from banks and falls within the sphere of production. The latter relates to the demand for liquidity (for cash holdings), for 'public' securities, and is bound up with the financial sphere of the economy. 'The finance motive, however, focused on the demand for money not for a stock of assets but a business demand for a flow of credit' (Rousseas, 1986, p. 200).

Thus, liquidity preference is perfectly consistent and does not interfere with the process of creating endogenous money as long as the distinction is drawn between the demand for money, that is, the finance motive, and the demand for liquidity, that is, liquidity preference.

Finally, it now seems that the connection between the liquidity preference of banks and of households can be reconciled with the theory of endogenous money. The role of uncertainty in post Keynesian analysis rehabilitates the liquidity preference approach as an explanatory factor for holding money. By extension, the liquidity preference of households, expressed through deposits, is of primary significance. Banks must anticipate it to guard against the risk of illiquidity. By making allowance for the difference between liquidity and money, if money is created *ex nihilo*, in macroeconomics loans depend on demand from firms and deposits are the consequence of loans granted by banks. It is perfectly coherent to consider that the money supply responds to an endogenous process through the creation of loans, and that banks, individually, have to face up to difficulties in managing this.

The decision of households with respect to liquidity preference is not between saving and consumption, but rather on how to divide their saving between hoards and other financial assets. ... Liquidity preference arises therefore out of the creation of income. It is thus a decision on how best to allocate saving between hoards and other assets. It is a portfolio decision (Rochon, 1999, p. 292).

Hence liquidity preference analysis can be included within the framework of endogenous money. The most commonly used approach in this respect is to describe the relationship between commercial banks and the central bank.[19] The second approach to endogenous money allows us to remove the ambiguity about liquidity and saving by making a distinction between liquidity and money. This approach favours the connection between money and production by emphasising the role of loans to firms and the payment of wages.[20] Here, money, liquidity, saving, and consumption are included in an overall production process with separate logical stages.

CONCLUSION

Many recent papers by post Keynesians have addressed the theory of liquidity preference. The renewed interest in this concept stems from the intensification and enhancement of a number of points about households' liquidity preference theory such as the specific conception of households' deposits. However, renewed interest also derives from the generalisation of liquidity preference to banks. Although this interest for liquidity preference may seem on the face of it to be in contradiction with the theory of endogenous money, we have noted that under certain circumstances this is not so.

The distinction between liquidity and money allows us to reconcile the two concepts within a more general theory of money and finance, and so to reconcile a theory of liquidity and a theory of money. Now, the definition of the difference between money and liquidity, or the lack of any such definition, underlies the debate among post Keynesians. The disagreements about the determination of the interest rate, about the supply of money, and about the role of the central bank stem explicitly or implicitly from disagreements about the distinction between liquidity and money.

NOTES

1.   In this chapter, unless otherwise specified, liquidity preference is taken to mean households'

liquidity preference.

2. '*For the importance of money essentially flows from its being a link between the present and the future*' (Keynes, 1936/1973, p. 293).

3. L_1 is an increasing function of income as it results from the demand for money for the transactionary and precautionary motives. L_2 is a decreasing function of the interest rate as it results from the demand for money for the speculative motive.

4. This motive is, in fact, two separate motives: the income motive, corresponding to the demand for money as a function of income and the time between it coming in and going out, and the business motive, corresponding to the demand for money by firms as a function of current income (production) and the time between incurring expenses and collecting the proceeds of sales.

5. Liquidity preference for the precautionary motive is different from saving, which is the leftover of income.

6. The speculative motive, which also expresses a fear of the future, consists in a comparison with the interest rate so as to maintain the level of earnings.

7. See the properties of money in Keynes (1936/1973, pp. 229–34).

8. Keynes (1937a/1973, 1937b/1973, 1938/1973, 1939/1973).

9. In some respects, dealt with extensively elsewhere, the neglect of liquidity preference by post Keynesians looks like a criticism. For example, the consequences of liquidity preference for determining the interest rate are clearly criticised and dismissed. The same can be said of the conceptions underlying the *General Theory* and liquidity preference as to the nature of money, the money supply, and the role of the central bank, these conceptions being de facto superseded by post Keynesian ideas.

10. The distinction between liquidity and saving implicitly determines the two functions of banks. The first is readily identifiable as financial intermediation and the control of savings. The second relates to the control of cash deposits. The issue of how these deposits are created and how they relate to output is raised (Keynes, 1930/1971, p. 27).

11. 'For it is concerned with changes in the *demand for bank borrowing*, whereas I am concerned with changes in the *demand of money*' (Keynes, 1937a/1973, p. 207).

12. First, banks respond to the demand for loans and not to a demand for deposits. Since the demand for loans, at a given level of interest rates, collateral requirements, and the like is determined by prices and output, loans (and deposits) are endogenously determined. We also agree that loans and deposits are different things and that, while deposits are held by the mass of the population, loans are demanded by a subset of deposit holders acting from different motives. We also agree that the role of the central bank is to set the lender-of-last-resort rate of interest and that banks then set their loan (deposit) rates by a mark-up (discount) on this rate. Banks meet all loan demands that satisfy their prevailing collateral requirements and the central bank reserves. Deposits are universally acceptable as a medium of exchange. Finally, we recognise the elementary point that when individuals exchange deposits for other assets, this merely redistributes deposits; the aggregate volume of deposits only changes when there is a corresponding change in the aggregate volume of loans (Howells, 1997, p. 429).

13. From this point of view, Wray's writings are somewhat atypical as he concentrates on money as a unit of account rather than as a store of value, and he engages in lengthy developments of money as a form of debt (Wray, 1990).

14. This is probably the most prolific strand in post Keynesian monetary thought with its many representatives including Chick, Davidson and Palley.

15. See Le Héron (2002, p. 11) for details of these risks and how banks cope with them.

16. We may even support Wolfson's view that the importance Keynes ascribes to the lender–borrower relationship is a variation on the asymmetric information approach developed by new Keynesians: 'This insight [of Keynes] seems to be at variance with the asymmetric information approach: wouldn't the borrower's relationship with the bank be one way of distinguishing between good and bad borrowers, which the bank is supposed to be incapable

of doing?' (Wolfson, 1996, p. 449, fn. 7).

17. Considering deposits as a given magnitude is obviously a simplification, which is legitimate in itself, but liable to sever any connection between microeconomic and macroeconomic theories of banking (Graziani, 1990, p. 60).
18. This is strange, since post Keynesians have placed considerable emphasis on the credit creation role of banks, and on the fact that commercial banks hold the key to economic expansion. Yet, they have largely ignored the microeconomic behaviour of banks (Rochon, 1999, p. 215).
19. Endogenous money theory can be interpreted at two levels: that of commercial banks and that of central banks. At each level, supply can be said to be adapted to demand, to the price set (Lavoie, 1985, pp. 171–2). See also Rochon (this volume).
20. See Lavoie (1996).

REFERENCES

Arestis, P. and P. Howells (1996), 'Theoretical reflections on endogenous money: the problem with "convenience lending"', *Cambridge Journal of Economics*, **20** (5), 539–51.

Arestis, P. and P. Howells (1999), 'The supply of credit money and the demand for deposits: a reply', *Cambridge Journal of Economics*, **23** (1), 115–19.

Cottrell, A. (1994), 'Post-Keynesian monetary economics', *Cambridge Journal of Economics*, **18** (6), 587–605.

Dow, S.C. (1993), *Money and the Economic Process*, Aldershot and Brookfield: Edward Elgar.

Dow, S.C. (1996), 'Horizontalism: a critique', *Cambridge Journal of Economics*, **20** (4), 497–508.

Dymski, G.A. (1988), 'A Keynesian theory of bank behavior', *Journal of Post Keynesian Economics*, **10** (3), 499–526.

Dymski, G.A. (1989), 'Keynesian versus credit theories of money and banking: a reply to Wray', *Journal of Post Keynesian Economics*, **12** (1), 157–63.

Dymski, G.A. (1993), 'Keynesian uncertainty and asymmetric information: complementary or contradictory?', *Journal of Post Keynesian Economics*, **16** (1), 49–54.

Dymski, G.A. (1994), 'Fundamental uncertainty, asymmetric information, and financial structure: "new" versus "post" Keynesian microfoundations', in G.A. Dymski and R. Pollin (eds), *New Perspectives in Monetary Macroeconomics: Essays in the Tradition of Hyman Minsky*, Ann Harbor: University of Michigan Press, 77–104.

Fazzari, S. and A.M. Variato (1994), 'Asymmetric information and Keynesian theories of investment', *Journal of Post Keynesian Economics*, **16** (3), 351–69.

Goux, J.-F. (1987), 'La théorie monétaire de la "finance" chez Keynes: une réinterprétation', *Revue d'économie politique*, **97** (5), 592–612.

Goux, J.-F. (1996), 'Une explication monétaire non monétariste: la théorie post-keynésienne', *Revue française d'économie*, **11** (3), 69–94.

Graziani, A. (1990), 'La théorie du circuit et la théorie macro-économique de la banque', *Économies et Sociétés* ('Série Monnaie et Production', 6), **24** (2), 51–62.

Heise, A. (1992), 'Commercial banks in macroeconomic theory', *Journal of Post*

Keynesian Economics, **14** (3), 285–95.

Howells, P.G.A. (1995), 'The demand for endogenous money', *Journal of Post Keynesian Economics*, **18** (1), 89–106.

Howells, P.G.A. (1997), 'The demand for endogenous money: a rejoinder', *Journal of Post Keynesian Economics*, **19** (3), 429–35.

Keynes, J.M. (1930/1971), *A Treatise on Money*, London: Macmillan. Reprinted in *The Collected Writings of John Maynard Keynes*, Vols V and VI, London and Basingstoke: Macmillan.

Keynes, J.M. (1936/1973), *The General Theory of Employment, Interest and Money*, London: Macmillan. Reprinted in *The Collected Writings of John Maynard Keynes*, Vol. VII, London and Basingstoke: Macmillan.

Keynes, J.M. (1937a/1973), 'Alternative theories of the rate of interest', *Economic Journal*, **47** (186), 241–52. Reprinted in *The Collected Writings of John Maynard Keynes*, Vol. XIV, London and Basingstoke: Macmillan, 201–15.

Keynes, J.M. (1937b/1973), 'The "ex ante" theory of the rate of interest', *Economic Journal*, **47** (188), 663–9. Reprinted in *The Collected Writings of John Maynard Keynes*, Vol. XIV, London and Basingstoke: Macmillan, 215–23.

Keynes, J.M. (1938/1973), 'Mr. Keynes and "finance"', *Economic Journal*, **48** (190), 314–22. Reprinted in *The Collected Writings of John Maynard Keynes*, Vol. XIV, London and Basingstoke: Macmillan, 229–33.

Keynes, J.M. (1939/1973), 'The process of capital formation', *Economic Journal*, **49** (195), 569–74. Reprinted in *The Collected Writings of John Maynard Keynes*, Vol. XIV, London and Basingstoke: Macmillan, 278–85.

Lavoie, M. (1985), 'La thèse de la monnaie endogène face à la non-validation des crédits', *Économies et Sociétés* ('Série Monnaie et Production', 2), **19** (8), 169–95.

Lavoie, M. (1996), 'Monetary policy in an economy with endogenous credit money', in G. Deleplace and E.J. Nell (eds), *Money in Motion: The Post Keynesian and Circulation Approaches*, London and New York: Macmillan and St. Martin's Press, 532–45.

Le Héron, E. (1986), 'Généralisation de la préférence pour la liquidité et financement de l'investissement', *Économies et Sociétés* ('Série Monnaie et Production', 3), **20** (8–9), 67–93.

Le Héron, E. (2002), 'La préférence pour la liquidité des banques: une analyse post-keynésienne du comportement bancaire', *Les Cahiers Lillois d'Économie et de Sociologie*, forthcoming.

Léonard, J. and P. Norel (1991), 'Système monétaire et préférence pour la liquidité: Keynes et la macro-économie des comportements', *Économie appliquée*, **44** (2) 153–62.

Rochon, L.-P. (1999), *Credit, Money and Production: An Alternative Post-Keynesian Approach*, Cheltenham and Northampton: Edward Elgar.

Rousseas, S. (1986), 'The finance motive, Keynes, and the post-Keynesians', *Économies et Sociétés* ('Série Monnaie et Production', 3), **20** (8–9), 189–201.

Runde, J. (1994), 'Keynesian uncertainty and liquidity preference', *Cambridge Journal of Economics*, **18** (2), 129–44.

Tobin, J. (1963), 'Commercial banks as creators of "money"', in D. Carson (ed.), *Banking and Monetary Studies*, Homewood: Irwin, 408–19.

Tobin, J. (1982), 'The commercial banking firm: a simple model', *Scandinavian Journal of Economics*, **84** (4), 495–530.

Wells, P. (1981), 'Keynes' demand for finance', *Journal of Post Keynesian Economics*, **3** (4), 586–9.

Wolfson, M.H. (1996), 'A Post Keynesian theory of credit rationing', *Journal of Post Keynesian Economics*, **18** (3), 443–70.

Wray, L.R. (1989), 'A Keynesian theory of banking: a comment on Dymski', *Journal of Post Keynesian Economics*, **12** (1), 152–6.

Wray, L.R. (1990), *Money and Credit in Capitalist Economies: The Endogenous Money Approach*, Aldershot and Brookfield: Edward Elgar.

Wray, L.R. (1992), 'Commercial banks, the central bank, and endogenous money', *Journal of Post Keynesian Economics*, **14** (3), 297–310.

3. Modern Theory and Practice of Central Banking: An Endogenous Money Perspective

Giuseppe Fontana and Alfonso Palacio-Vera[1]

INTRODUCTION

To commemorate the new millennium and its first fifty issues, the editors of the *Journal of Economic Perspectives* commissioned a series of essays, among other reasons, to provide insights into key developments in both the economy and economic thinking in the twentieth century. One of these essays has a very tempting title and a rather controversial announcement. According to De Long (2000, pp. 83–4), '[t]he story of 20th century macroeconomics begins with Irving Fisher . . . [who] fuelled the intellectual fire that became known as monetarism. . . . But what has happened to monetarism at the end of the 20th century?'. De Long claims that the influence of monetarism over current macroeconomics is profound and widespread. In particular, he argues that the emergence of monetary policy as one of the most critical government responsibilities is the result of the triumph of classic monetarism as developed, for instance, by Friedman and Schwartz (1963).

A similar sort of evocation of monetarism is also at the core of a recent paper by Laidler (2002, p. 1) on the transmission mechanism: 'Conventional opinions about monetary policy are nowadays very monetarist, as that term is usually understood, not least among policy makers'.

Some post Keynesians would agree with these assessments. They would offer further evidence that modern monetary policy is monetarist in nature, despite some deception by current policy makers (see Parguez, 1999). Other post Keynesians, however, would disagree with these conclusions altogether. For instance, Dalziel (2002, p. 1) has recently argued that:

the recent announcement of the 'triumph of monetarism' is misplaced, on the grounds that the cornerstone of monetarism, the quantity theory of money, is no longer used by central banks in practice. Instead, modern monetary policy is based on maintaining aggregate demand growth that is compatible with supply-side capacity growth, a framework that can be traced to Chapter 21 of Keynes's (1936) *General Theory*.

Does current monetary policy then mark the triumph of Friedman and monetarism, or is it rather the triumph of Keynes and post Keynesianism? This chapter invites a non-dualistic response to the question and also aspires to make the post Keynesian camp less heterogeneous. The main tenet of the new monetarist consensus is twofold: (a) monetary policy is the major direct determinant of inflation and (b) low and stable inflation is critically important for economic growth (Bernanke et al., 1999). The theoretical framework supporting these propositions is the 'targets-and-instrument approach' (Blinder, 1997) and is based on an often-tacit combination of elements that are derived from the work of Keynes, Friedman and their followers. The main aim of this chapter is thus to show the basic features of that framework and some of the controversial issues related to the new consensus in monetary policy.

Readers are also warned that this chapter is grounded on the idea that the endogenous money hypothesis (EMH hereafter) represents the core of a non-mainstream approach to monetary issues encompassing, among others, horizontalists, structuralists, and circuitists. Notwithstanding important differences between these views, the EMH in our opinion is general enough to represent the post Keynesian camp (for a theoretical and methodological explanation of this use, see Fontana, 2000, and Fontana and Gerrard, 2002a).

The structure of the chapter is as follows. The next section reviews the modern practice of central banking. The third section discusses the 'targets-and-instrument approach'. The fourth section proposes an alternative approach to central banking based on the EMH. Then there is a section relating these two approaches to different views on the nature of money. Finally, the last section concludes.

THE MODERN PRACTICE OF CENTRAL BANKING

The first proposition of the new consensus on monetary policy is that monetary policy is the major direct determinant of inflation (Bernanke et al., 1999, p. 3). According to a prominent monetary economist this means that most central bankers around the world would undoubtedly subscribe to the following equation (Laidler, 2002, p. 3):

$$dP/dt = dM/dt + dv/dt - dy/dt \qquad (3.1.A)$$

The logarithmic growth rate of prices, that is, the inflation rate[2] is equal to the logarithmic rate of growth of some representative monetary aggregate, plus the logarithmic rate of change in the velocity of circulation of money, minus the logarithmic growth rate of real income.[3] According to Laidler (2002), central bankers would also accept that in the long run (a) changes in the money supply do not affect real income and (b) changes in the velocity of circulation of money are outside their control, so that for central banking policy purposes equation (3.1.A) can be written in the following way:

$$dP/dt = dM/dt \qquad (3.1.B)$$

Equation (3.1.B) is thus the basic long-run equation driving what Laidler (2002) considers to be the new consensus approach to monetary policy. For what matters, this equation is perfectly compatible with the standard monetarist propositions that (a) changes in the money supply have a substantial effect on aggregate demand and (b) any change in the money supply monetary authorities succeed in bringing about manifests itself in the long run in higher prices but not in higher real output. But does it really matter that equation (3.1.B) could be made consistent with a monetarist approach to monetary policy? What do central bankers really do in the day-to-day setting of monetary policy? Again, according to Laidler (2002) the same central bankers would surely agree that in the short run they use roughly a set of three equations, namely an expectations-augmented Phillips curve, an IS curve and a Fisher equation:

$$dP/dt - (dP/dt)^e = g(Y - Y^*) \qquad (3.2)$$
$$Y - Y^* = h(r, X) \qquad (3.3)$$
$$r = i - (dP/dt)^e \qquad (3.4)$$

where $(Y - Y^*)$ measures the output gap (for the problematic nature of the value of this variable see Dalziel, 2002), $(dP/dt)^e$ is the expected value of the inflation rate, r and i are the real and nominal rate of interest respectively, and X is a vector of variables that shift the IS curve.

As Laidler promptly recognises, however, there is an unresolved tension over the way the new consensus literature approaches the setting of monetary policy: 'Equation (3.1.A) makes money all important for inflation in the long run while equations (3.2)–(3.4) treat it as irrelevant in the short run' (Laidler, 2002, p. 5). From a monetarist perspective, equation (3.3) is a Trojan horse in the citadel of the quantity theory of money. What a true monetarist would like to see in its place is the following equation, namely a positively sloped LM curve:

$$M/P = m(i, Y) \tag{3.5}$$

where M/P indicates the equilibrium real money balances of our economy.

Of course, there is a good, though often neglected, reason for explaining the use of an IS curve rather than a LM curve. It is related to the so-called instrument problem (IP hereafter), a major component of the 'targets-and-instrument approach' that is currently used by most central bankers (see Blinder, 1997). The long and intense debate around the IP began with Poole's seminal work (Poole, 1970). The crux of the matter was to determine the conditions under which an interest rate (r) policy was preferred to a monetary aggregate (M) policy. The main result of the debate was that, *in theory*, the latter policy tends to represent an optimal choice of monetary policy when the variance of shocks to the commodity market is larger than the variance of shocks to the monetary sector. The controversy between advocates of r targets and advocates of M targets was then finally settled *in practice*. As argued by Blinder (1997, p. 7), 'these [theoretical] conditions then arose in practice, and one central bank after another abandoned M targets in favor of r targets'.

This is all well known and the controversy over the optimal choice of monetary policy instruments is now history. There remains a problem with this argument and the often-quoted successful interaction between theory and practice of central banking. Consistency with the 'targets-and-instrument approach' requires that, were the practical conditions ever be reversed, it would again be appropriate to use monetary aggregates as intermediate targets. This possibility may justify, among other things, keeping the base money-multiplier approach as the essential tool for explaining the money supply process in standard textbooks. But post Keynesians, like Moore (1988) and Wray (1998) as well as leading monetary practitioners like Goodhart (2002), have openly talked about the myth of the money multiplier. As is shown in the next sections these authors maintain that a money supply-based monetary policy strategy is unfeasible, let alone undesirable.

Before moving to the problems of the current use of the 'targets-and-instrument' approach, it is worthwhile to note that there is much more than a numerical substitution in having an IS curve rather than a positively sloped

LM curve in the set of equations (3.2)–(3.4). For the day-to-day setting of monetary policy, central bankers seem to have lost any confidence in the ability of a monetary aggregate strategy to deliver price stability. It is now the central bank key interest rate that is seen as the instrument to hit the desired inflation rate through its effects on aggregate demand (see Bank of England, 1999b). Recent work by Arestis and Sawyer (2002) on current monetary policy in the United Kingdom confirms this view. They argue that 'monetary policy (in the form of the setting of a key interest rate) now has little to do with money. The supply of money is not mentioned, and the demand for money is either viewed as unstable (Treasury) or is treated residually (Bank of England)' (Arestis and Sawyer, 2002, p. 12). Thus, what Laidler (2002) defines as an unresolved tension in the modern setting of monetary policy is simply evidence of the large bridge that has for a long time separated theory from practice of central banking. If from a practical point of view equation (3.1.A) really mattered, then it would necessarily follow that central banks ought to use open market operations (or the bank rate) to determine the quantity of bank reserves and, via the multiplier, the quantity of money, whose long-run impact would be on prices only. But is this a policy choice really open to a central bank? As Wray (1998, p. 98) explains '[t]he central bank never has controlled, nor could it ever control, the quantity of money; neither can it control the quantity of reserves in a discretionary manner' (see also Goodhart, 2002). For the current setting of monetary policy, equation (3.1.A) is then simply a relic of what theorists suggested that central banks should do, and what these same central banks could not do.

A more general or encompassing interpretation of equation (3.1.A) would be that, in the long run and in the absence of persistent changes in the velocity of circulation of money, the money supply would move in line with nominal income. Similarly, the implied direction of causation, if any, in equation (3.1.B) would then be from changes in the price level to changes in the stock of money. As explained in a recent report by the Bank of England (1999a, p. 13), 'sustained increases in prices cannot occur without an accompanying increase in the money stock. That does not mean that money causes inflation. When the short-term nominal interest rate is viewed as the policy instrument, both money and inflation are jointly caused by other variables' (see also Arestis and Sawyer, 2002, p. 7).

MAINSTREAM THEORY OF CENTRAL BANKING: THE INSTRUMENT PROBLEM VIEW

The instrument problem (IP) of monetary policy arises because of the need to specify how central banks implement open market operations. In particular, the IP consists in the choice of a variable that will be set directly by central bankers via purchasing and selling securities. A central bank may buy or sell a certain amount of securities, thereby providing or withdrawing the equivalent amount of bank reserves. Alternatively, a central bank may purchase or sell whatever amount of securities other market participants want to exchange at a specified price. In this case, central banks would let the market determine the quantity of bank reserves to be held at that price. Literature regarding the choice of monetary policy instruments, beginning with Poole (1970), laid down the conditions under which a price variable, for instance an interest rate, was to be preferred to a quantity variable like borrowed (BOR) or non-borrowed bank reserves (NBOR).

In Poole's seminal contribution (Poole, 1970), a stochastic IS–LM framework is formulated where the commodity and monetary sectors are subjected to exogenous random shocks. The monetary policy strategy that minimises a loss function, presented as the quadratic deviation of current from desired level of output, will be the preferable one:

$$L = E[(Y - Y^*)]^2 \qquad (3.6)$$

If σ_v is the standard deviation of disturbances to the money demand function, σ_u the standard deviation of disturbances to the commodity sector, and b_1 the income elasticity of the demand for money, a sufficient condition for a money-targeting regime to be preferable to an interest-rate-targeting regime is $\sigma_v / \sigma_u \prec b_1$ (Poole, 1970, p. 206). Targeting money supply damps the impact on income of disturbances to aggregate demand whereas targeting the interest rate damps the impact of disturbances to money demand. Graphically, the controversy between the two different targeting policies is represented in terms of the range of output changes due to real (Figures 3.1 and 3.2) and monetary (Figures 3.3 and 3.4) random shocks.

In Figure 3.1 the central bank targets the stock of money and holds it constant through, for instance, open market operations. Random shocks to the commodity market (that is, the IS curve) produce changes in r and Y. In particular in Figure 3.1 income changes are in the range Y_1–Y_2.

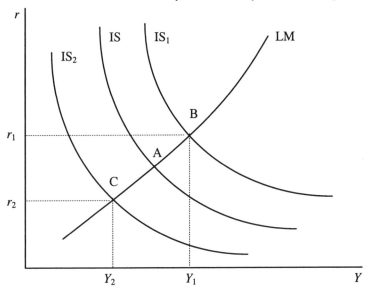

Figure 3.1. Shocks to the commodity sector with a money-targeting policy

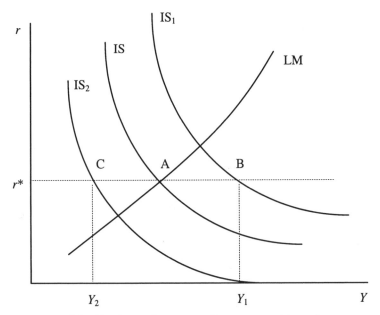

Figure 3.2. Shocks to the commodity sector with an interest-rate-targeting policy

In Figure 3.2 the interest rate r^* is the target of the central bank. Shocks to the IS curve produce again changes in Y but the range of income changes is greater than in the previous case. Thus, if shocks emanate from the commodity market, an interest-rate-targeting policy produces greater fluctuations in income than a money-supply-targeting policy.

In Figures 3.3 and 3.4 random shocks arise form the money market (that is, the LM curve) and are due to changes in the demand for money. In Figure 3.3 the central bank targets the stock of money. Shifts of the LM curve produce changes in r and Y in the range Y_1-Y_2.

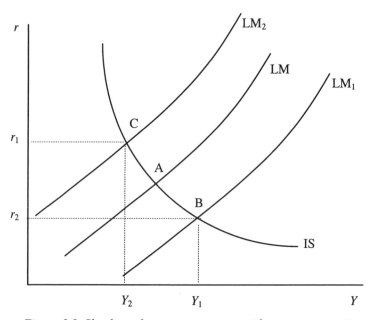

Figure 3.3. Shocks to the monetary sector with a money-targeting policy

In Figure 3.4 the central bank targets the interest rate (for instance r^*). This means that changes in money demand (for instance the L_1 curve) have to be accommodated by changes in money supply (for instance the M_1 curve). In terms of the overall money market, changes in the L curve shift the LM curve but then the accommodative movements of the M curve would take it back to the initial position. The equilibrium level of income is then in both cases Y_0. Thus, if shocks emanate from the money market, a money-supply-targeting policy produces greater fluctuations in income than an interest-rate-targeting policy.

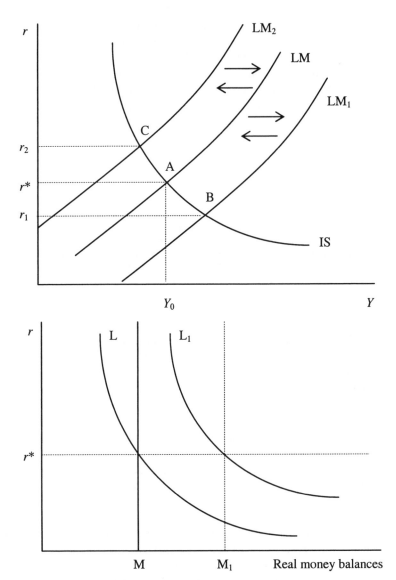

Figure 3.4. Shocks to the monetary sector with an interest-rate-targeting policy

In general, the choice of the monetary policy instrument depends on the values of σ_v and σ_u, the structural parameters of the model determining the slopes of the IS and LM functions, and the covariance of disturbances to the commodity and monetary sectors. Given the values of the three behavioural parameters of the model and the covariance of shocks, a larger variance of disturbances to the commodity sector makes the money stock more likely to be the preferable instrument, and vice versa.[4] As a result, as Friedman (1990, p. 1191) notes, 'in the end, however, the choice is inherently empirical'. Although more complicated models bring in other factors, yet the essential results remain unchallenged.[5] For instance, after reviewing the literature on the IP under different theoretical scenarios, Friedman (1990, pp. 1199–200) concludes that:

> the basic insight of the Poole analysis – relating the choice of instrument of monetary policy to the relative variances of different categories of disturbances affecting the economy, as well as to the values of specifically identifiable parameters of economic behavior – carries over to models incorporating nontrivial aggregate supply behavior, as long as there is some contradiction of perfectly classical assumptions that prevents the economy from automatically equilibrating on its own in the first place (and, at the same time, renders monetary policy non-neutral).

From a post Keynesian perspective, Poole's approach suffers from several problems, not least that it ignores the interdependence between the commodity market (IS curve) and the money market (LM curve). (For an earlier example of this critique see Davidson, 1965, and further developments by Rochon, 1999, pp. 132–9.) The focus of this chapter, however, is only on two issues.

Firstly, Poole's analysis implicitly assumes that central banks have full control of the money supply. Most of the money used by the public, however, either as a means of payment or as a liquid store of value, represents the liabilities of private depository institutions. Although central banks may have some influence over the money-creating activities of these institutions, they cannot fix the stock of money in a country. Therefore, as is shown in the next section, the money supply is not an exogenously set policy variable. When a central bank sets a quantity variable, it may at best fix the level of bank reserves or the monetary base (reserves plus currency). But once the level of bank reserves or the monetary base has been decided, the stock of money will be the result of the portfolio decisions of the bank and non-bank private sector. Thus, even if a central bank can directly set the value of its own liabilities, the money supply is endogenously determined as a residual of the economic process. Allegedly, in an extension of Poole's analysis by

Modigliani et al. (1970), the money supply process incorporates two types of disturbances. First, there are the standard shocks affecting the aggregate demand function and the money demand function. Second, and importantly, the model also includes shocks hitting the relationship between NBOR and the money supply. The difference with Poole's analysis is that targeting interest rates damps the effect of monetary disturbances that could, in principle, consist of variations in either BOR or the money multiplier as well as shocks to the money demand function, whereas targeting NBOR now damps, to a lesser extent, the effects on income of real disturbances.

The second analytical shortcoming of Poole's approach is that the standard deviation of disturbances to the monetary sector, no matter whether they affect the portfolio decisions of the bank or the non-bank private sector, is assumed to be *independent* of the monetary policy regime implemented. But the variance of disturbances to the monetary sector σ_m^2 is likely to be a function of the monetary policy regime pursued by a central bank. In particular, implementation of a money-targeting regime will tend to rise σ_m^2. Therefore, the problem is not choosing between two alternative monetary policy regimes according to an empirical criterion, for instance the variance and covariance of disturbances to the commodity and monetary sectors and several behavioural parameters. Rather, the problem is that σ_m^2 is itself a function of the monetary policy regime actually implemented. As a result, the choice is likely to be self-defeating. Would then the implementation of a money-targeting policy regime rise σ_m^2 as much as to make an interest-rate-targeting regime preferable? The experience with money-targeting regimes suggests a positive answer. The next section is devoted to explain why implementation of a money-targeting regime will tend to increase σ_m^2.

Finally, it was suggested above that, when the monetary policy instrument is an interest rate, the money supply is endogenous. In contrast, when the monetary policy instrument is a monetary aggregate, the interest rate is the endogenous variable. Recently, there has been an interesting theoretical development related to these conclusions. The so-called 'information variable' approach to monetary policy has recognised the inferiority of using some endogenous variable – like the money supply – as an intermediate target when compared to a more general feedback rule linking the value of the monetary policy instrument to the observed value of that variable. Referring to this approach, Friedman (1990, p. 1210) remarks that '[u]nder such a rule, the endogenous variable is not an intermediate target but an "information variable"'. All that matters is whether observed values of, for instance, the money supply provide information that helps to predict future movements of the ultimate objectives of monetary policy. The basic rule being that, since it is optimal to exploit all relevant sources of information, there is no reason to limit the focus of central banks on one single endogenous variable. There may be circumstances under which, say, the money stock may in fact provide useful information for setting the policy instrument. For instance, if individuals tend to accumulate money in advance of actual spending, then the observed value of the money stock at any particular time conveys some information about the future behaviour of aggregate demand. Again, when the ability to spend of households or firms relies on their access to credit, and bank loans actually precede spending, then the observed volume of credit conveys important information about the future state of aggregate demand. Thus, in all these cases the value of variables like money or credit has an important role to play in setting the optimal value of the policy instrument of a central bank. Of course, the case can be only made stronger when this information is available on a timelier basis than observations of variables like income and prices (ibid., p. 1203).

Notwithstanding the analytical shortcomings of money targeting, beginning in the 1970s central banks in an increasing number of countries have adopted monetary aggregate targets. However, Bernanke et al. (1999, p. 304) argue that, in practice, no central bank has ever adopted a rigid rule for determining money growth. Even those countries traditionally associated with money-targeting regimes, for instance Germany and Switzerland, have willingly deviated from their announced monetary targets in order to meet other short-term objectives, such as stabilisation of output or the exchange rate. In addition, the announced monetary targets were adjusted from year to year to reflect economic conditions and competing objectives of the monetary authorities. On the theoretical front, the shortcomings of money targeting apparently tended to go unconsidered in the literature on controlling monetary aggregates. In this literature, the problem was to hit a target for a monetary aggregate, where the target was usually taken as given. As such, the problem encompassed both control of bank reserves (and the monetary base) and forecast of money multipliers. Therefore, little or no attention at all was paid to control problems posed by disturbances to the income velocity of money. In the next section all these problems are addressed.

AN ALTERNATIVE THEORY OF CENTRAL BANKING: THE ENDOGENOUS MONEY APPROACH

This section shows why money-targeting regimes are undesirable, if not unfeasible. For a money-targeting regime to be viable, at least two conditions must be met: (a) central banks have full control of the money supply and (b) there is a stable relationship between the money supply and money income. In turn, if condition (a) is to hold, two additional conditions must be fulfilled, namely, (a_1) central banks control the monetary base (or the level of bank reserves) and (a_2) there is a stable relationship between the monetary base and the money supply, that is, the base money-multiplier is stable. The discussion below intends to show that, in practice, most (if not all) of these conditions do not hold in economies with modern financial systems.

Firstly, central banks may not have full control of bank reserves (condition (a_1)). For instance, Kaldor (1985, p. 10) argues that central banks cannot close the discount window since the maintenance of the *solvency* of the banking system is their most important function. Similarly, Moore (1988) and Goodhart (1994) have highlighted several institutional features of the US and UK monetary policy frameworks respectively, which make attempts at controlling the monetary base ineffective, at least in the short run. For example, Goodhart (1994, p. 1425) argues that:

> If the CB [central bank] tried to run a system of monetary base control, it would fail. Much, perhaps most, of the time it would still be *accommodating* the day-to-day demand of the banking system for reserves at a penal interest rate of its own choice, whenever its Mo [monetary base] target was below the system's demand for reserves. Otherwise when its target was *above* the system's demand, overnight rates would fall to near zero.

Similarly, for the United States, Moore (1988, p. 122) argues that, by keeping unsatisfied the demand of NBOR, the Fed controls the amount of discount-window borrowing. As the demand for BOR rises, the marginal *effective* total cost (discount rate plus frown costs) of obtaining reserves rises above the discount rate. As a result, the federal funds rate rises *pari passu* above the discount rate. Increases in NBOR relative to total reserves (TR = BOR + NBOR) operate in the opposite direction, reducing BOR and, therefore, short-term interest rates. Thus, central banks set the supply price but *not* the total supply of reserves. The reserve supply function may be viewed as *horizontal* in the market period, at an interest rate *exogenously* administered by central banks (Moore, 1988, p. 405).

Secondly, the base-money multiplier is not stable (condition (a_2)). The explanation for the instability and hence for the fundamental uncertainty attached to any forecast of money multipliers relies on the idea that the money supply in modern monetary production economies is credit driven and demand determined.[6] Credit money is created when loans are granted by the banking system to the non-bank private sector, and is extinguished when loans are repaid, so that the level and the rate of expansion of the money supply are ultimately a decision of the private sector of the economy. The rate of monetary expansion is determined by the level of aggregate net deficit spending (Moore, 1988, Ch. 12). If a central bank increases NBOR through open market operations, banks may voluntarily opt not to increase lending, if they do not identify any profitable outlet, and, instead, increase their level of excess reserves (ER). Similarly, non-bank private sector units, that is, firms and households, can easily dispose of any unwanted money balances through loan repayment (the reflux mechanism). In these cases, an increase in NBOR will be offset by a decrease in the money multiplier. Thus, any attempt by central banks to impose a rate of monetary expansion upon the private sector through, for instance, an increase in NBOR will be ineffective. This rate is indeed determined by lending and/or deficit-spending decisions of the private sector.

Similarly, attempts by central banks to restrain the level of bank reserves below either the level of required reserves (RR) (where TR = BOR + NBOR = RR + ER) or total reserves would encourage banks to look for reserves in wholesale markets. For instance, banks may borrow from the discount window or on the inter-bank market. In any case, inter-bank market interest rates will tend to rise and banks will only be able to obtain additional reserves at a higher cost. As a result, banks will now have an impetus for implementing portfolio adjustments through the search for alternative sources of funds with lower reserve requirements. These adjustments are commonly known as liability management practices (Earley and Evans, 1982; Evans, 1984; Goodhart, 1984, Ch. 3; Podolski, 1986; De Cecco, 1987).

As these funds are obtained, banks transform their balance sheets, allowing them to increase their loan/reserve and deposit/reserve ratios (Pollin, 1991; Palley, 1996, 1998; Moore, 1998).[7] As recognised among others by Moore (1998) and Palley (1998), banks, as profit maximisers, continually seek to raise their deposit/reserve ratio by discovering new financial products, thus making money multipliers and money velocity exhibit an upward trend. In addition, as interest rates rise (fall), banks feel more (less) pressure to search for alternative sources of funds with lower reserve requirements such that, other things being the same, the rate of financial innovation will tend to speed up (slow down) (Palacio-Vera, 2001). As a result of this process, money multipliers and the income velocity of monetary aggregates will also exhibit a pro-cyclical pattern. In this way, financial innovation loosens the connection between reserves and lending (Earley and Evans, 1982; Evans, 1984, p. 444). Finally, since central banks cannot know in advance either the rate or the pattern of financial innovation, they will not be able to accurately predict the rate of growth of base money necessary to obtain a given growth rate of the monetary aggregate selected as intermediate target.

Finally, the idea of a stable relationship between the money supply and nominal income (condition (b)) has not enjoyed much empirical support in recent times. As argued by Blinder (1997, p. 7; 1998, pp. 26–9), beginning in the 1970s, the instabilities showing up in money demand functions in the United States, in the United Kingdom, and in many other countries, led academics and policy makers alike to conclude that a money-targeting regime was not a viable option.[8] For instance, in a recent study Estrella and Mishkin (1997) conclude that the empirical relationships involving monetary aggregates, nominal income, and inflation are not sufficiently strong and stable in the United States and Germany to support a straightforward role for monetary aggregates in the conduct of monetary policy. Similar results are presented by Friedman and Kuttner (1992, 1996). A common explanation for the abandonment of money-targeting regimes is the notion that the relationship between the money supply and money income has proven to be unstable (Friedman, 1984, 1988; Goodhart, 1986, 1989; Friedman and Kuttner, 1992, 1996; Bernanke et al., 1999, p. 305). In more formal terms, the unstable nature of the relationship between monetary aggregates and money income shows up in the empirical observation that the various monetary aggregates are not co-integrated with nominal income, that is, velocity is *non-stationary* (Goodhart, 1989, p. 316).

Under such circumstances, any attempt to run a money-targeting regime is bound to lead to severe short-run volatility in interest rates and, perhaps, even in money growth, as the 'monetarist' experiment in the United States revealed (see for instance Friedman, 1984, and 1988, p. 55).[9] In turn, the break-up of this relationship is attributed to a combination of deregulation of financial markets, improvements in transactions technology and, especially, financial innovation (Hester, 1981; Minsky, 1982, Ch. 7; Goodhart, 1984, Ch. 3, 1986, 1989; Podolski, 1986; De Cecco, 1987; Arestis and Howells, 1992; Clarida et al., 1999, p. 1685). It is now commonplace to conclude that changes in financial markets in the last three decades have made the growth rate of the money supply much less controllable and predictable. For instance, Podolski (1986, p. 162) argues that:

> the financial system has become less dependent on the central bank as the lender of last resort, in the sense that it is now easier for financial institutions to equate the demand for funds with the supply by operating in the wholesale markets. By the same token, the capacity of financial institutions to circumvent central bank operations or regulations has increased.

Endogenous money theorists have emphasised the role of liability management practices in enhancing the ability of banks to accommodate loan demand in a scenario where the central bank attempts to restrain banks' reserves (Minsky, 1982; Evans, 1984; Rousseas, 1986; Wray, 1990; Pollin, 1991; Palley, 1996). Liability management practices allow banks to capture non-deposit funds in wholesale markets by paying market interest rates. In turn, as argued in the previous discussion on the money multiplier, the way these non-deposit funds alter the structure of the liability side of the balance sheets of banks is difficult to predict. As Podolski (1986, p. 164) explains:

> theoretically, the demand for an aggregate is likely to shift depending on whether new funds are likely to be attracted to it or whether there would be a net escape of funds in a given set of circumstances. Thus, the impact of liability management and associated innovations is likely to be uncertain and unpredictable. The fall in interest sensitivity [of the demand for money] may be accompanied by an upward or a downward shift in the demand schedule of an aggregate. Given a menu of aggregates, there are likely to be relative shifts in the aggregates, making the relationship between them difficult to predict and interpret.

In short, financial innovation and liability management practices have made *both* the relationship between reserves (or base money) and deposits (or the money supply) *and* between money and nominal GDP an unstable one.

A closely related explanation for the break-up of the money–income relationship is Goodhart's Law. According to it, any observed statistical regularity will tend to collapse once pressure is placed upon it for control purposes (Goodhart, 1984, p. 96). In the context of the discussion on the IP presented above, Goodhart's Law and the ability of banks to avert central bank-imposed reserve constraints by adopting liability management practices means that, were a central bank to ever adopt a money-targeting regime, the variance of random disturbances to the monetary sector σ_m^2 would tend to rise. One reason is that, as the 1979–82 'monetarist' experiment in the United States showed, the implementation of a money-targeting regime substantially increases volatility in short-term interest rates (see Friedman, 1988, p. 55). This volatility raises the degree of uncertainty about the expected future marginal cost of funds to banks, thereby encouraging them to hedge against it. As quoted by Goodfriend (1991, p. 14), according to Cukierman (1991), since loan rates are determined prior to the determination of the cost of funds to banks, 'unanticipated credit or money demand shocks after banks have entered into loan commitments create a negative correlation between competitive deposit rates and bank profits'. As a result, smoothing of short-term interest rates by central banks protects banks against the risk of widespread insolvencies. In the absence of interest rate smoothing – as will be the case when a money-targeting regime is being implemented – resort to liability management practices allows banks to reduce this uncertainty but, as shown above, this is likely to increase instability in the relation between reserves and the money supply on the one hand, and between money and money income on the other hand. As pointed out by Goodhart (1995, p. 259):

> a system which caused short-term volatility in interest rates might develop mechanisms for shifting financing flows between banks and non-bank intermediaries. In consequence, monetary growth rates might be stabilised while inducing greater variability in the relationship between money and nominal incomes.

Another reason why σ_m^2 will tend to rise is that, if the income velocity of money is not sufficiently interest elastic, implementation of a money-targeting regime does not only cause short-run volatility in interest rates but may also lead to higher real interest rates than otherwise. This will occur if, for instance, the central bank attempts to impose on the private sector a rate of monetary growth that is lower than the rate desired by the latter. Several authors have argued that high real interest rates stimulate financial innovation thereby rising σ_m^2. For instance, Hester (1981, p. 183) argues that 'the one clear lesson from recent history is that financial institutions innovate whenever customer relationships are jeopardized by slow monetary growth'. Likewise, Minsky (1982, pp. 171–2) argues that:

> the higher interest rates, in turn, induce institutional changes in the money market which have the effect of increasing lending ability. ... Since the significant institutional innovations during a period of monetary constraint will be those which tend to increase velocity, they can be represented as shifting the velocity-interest rate relationship to the right.

The increased ability of banks to avert central-bank-imposed reserve constraints has led to the view that, under the current institutional framework, central banks can only affect money supply growth *indirectly*, that is, through variations in short-term nominal interest rates (Niggle, 1990, p. 445; Arestis and Howells, 1992, p. 147).[10] For instance, Goodhart (1995, p. 252) suggests that, with a few possible exceptions, no central bank has ever run a true system of monetary base control and that, 'instead, central banks sought to control the level of interest rates in order to affect the rate of monetary expansion indirectly'. Interestingly, Mishkin (1998, pp. 489–90) argues that, in reality, the Fed 'monetarist' experiment in the period 1979–82 was a *smokescreen* that was used by Paul Volcker to divert attention away from interest rates. In this way, the setting of targets for the growth rates of monetary aggregates allowed the Fed to set interest rates high enough as to bring inflation down. Similarly, Goodhart (1989, p. 296, 2002, pp. 16–18) argues that the policies adopted in the early 1980s did allow the authorities freedom to raise interest rates to levels that did subdue inflation. Finally, von Hagen (1999) argues that money-targeting strategies are helpful in solving internal and external coordination problems for central banks. When reviewing the experience of the Bundesbank, he argues that the adoption of a money-targeting regime was a signal that the previous monetary regime had been overcome, and a means to define the role of monetary policy vis-à-vis other players in the macroeconomic policy game, and to structure the internal policy debate.

Thus these results lead to the view that control of the rate of expansion of the money supply ultimately rests on the ability of central banks to affect bank lending to the non-bank private sector. This is a proposition that has long been advocated by endogenous money theorists like Kaldor and Trevithick (1981), Chick (1986), Moore (1988), Niggle (1991), Arestis and Howells (1992), Dow (1993) and Goodhart (1995). Within an endogenous money framework, the key question is how variations in interest rates impinge on the decisions to deficit spend by the non-bank private sector and the willingness to lend by the banking system. In this respect, Arestis and Howells (1992, p. 149) argue that 'it is clear that the U.K. authorities now see interest rate changes as having an impact upon aggregate demand through a number of diverse channels. These include the cost of borrowing, income and wealth effects, and the exchange rate'. Likewise, as quoted in Taylor (1998, p. 14, 1999, p. 326):

> in commenting on a money growth strategy, Alan Greenspan reasoned: 'Because the velocity of such an aggregate [M1] varies substantially in response to small changes in interest rates, target ranges for M1 growth in [the FOMC's] judgement no longer were reliable guides for outcomes in nominal spending and inflation.' He adds that 'in response to an unanticipated movement in spending and hence the quantity of money demanded, a small variation in interest rates would be sufficient to bring money back to path but not to correct the deviation in spending' (Greenspan, 1997, pp. 4–5).

According to Taylor (1999, p. 326), in Greenspan's view the interest elasticity of the income velocity of money is so large that, under a money-targeting regime, the interest rate would respond by too small an amount to an increase in output. In summary, the type of institutional arrangements characteristic of modern economies with developed financial markets make it very unlikely that conditions necessary to run successfully a money-targeting regime will be fulfilled.

DIFFERENT VIEWS ON THE NATURE OF MONEY: A DIGRESSION

Post Keynesian scholars have often argued that money is mainly the standard of value in which contractual obligations for the organisation of economic activities are made (see for instance Dow and Smithin, 1999). This is considered the primary role of money and it is usually related to a particular theory of the nature of money. Money has the nature of a very special commodity. Money is a social convention. This idea has a long tradition in the history of economics but confusion often arises in terms of the implications of adopting this view.

According to the mainstream–individualist school (see for example Menger, 1892), money is a natural outcome of the market. Money was first a special commodity selected for its particular properties (for instance, salt), then replaced by coins made of a precious metal, with an exchange value approximately equal to the value of the metal in the coin. Later on money was minted in order to identify the quantity and quality of the metal. Finally, money became paper money, bank money and in recent times electronic money. In all these stages money is always and forever a commodity that promotes efficient reductions in the cost of transacting. Money is thus selected by market operators for its properties of, for instance, divisibility, durability and portability. This is still today the most popular and well-respected theory of the evolution of money (see Mishkin, 1998, pp. 52–7). Against it Keynes always voiced his own opposition (see for instance Keynes, 1914/1973, p. 406). Similarly, Schumpeter (1954/1994) argued that a theory of commodity money is logically untenable. He argued for a confusion between logical and historical origins of money and, in fact, he discriminated between theoretical metallism (untenable) and practical metallism (acceptable).

> The error involved consists in a confusion between the historical origin of money – which, in very many cases, although perhaps not universally, may indeed be found in the fact that some commodities, being particularly saleable, come to be used as the medium of exchange – and its nature or logic – which is entirely independent of the commodity character of its material (Schumpeter, 1954/1994, p. 289, fn. 5; see also Ingham, 2000, pp. 17–23).

Money is a social relation, hence 'it is not essential to the nature of money that it *consists* of precious metal or be covered by it' (Schumpeter, 1970, p. 213, as quoted in Realfonzo, 1998, p. 38; see also Ingham, 1996).

The alternative view on the nature of money is the so-called chartalist view. According to this view, money is never the exclusive product of the market; rather it is a creature of law. This idea was made popular by Knapp's book *The State Theory of Money* (1924) and was enthusiastically endorsed by Keynes (1914/1973). The state determines the currency of the country by declaring what it would accept for discharging tax liabilities. The theory became so widely accepted that very few economists felt the need to refer to it or to critically discuss it. The notable exception is Schumpeter, who never kept secret the limitations of Knapp's theory of money. Schumpeter acknowledged Knapp's aversion to the idea of commodity money but he complained about the lack of adequate theoretical arguments to support that opposition to the individualist theory of the value of money. As he maintained, Knapp's theory 'was simply a theory of the "nature" of money considered as the legally valid means of payment. Taken in this sense it was as true and as false as it is to say, for example, that the institution of marriage is a creature of law' (Schumpeter, 1954/1994, p. 1090).

In more recent times this theory has been defended and developed by the Kansas City school (see Wray, 1998, Ch. 3; Bell, 2001) to promote the use of counter-cyclical fiscal policy for achieving full employment. All chartalist scholars are unified by the aim of providing a non-market theory of money grounded on the social rather than natural origin of money. As suggested by Davidson (1977/1999, p. 196), 'it is a social custom *supported by social behavior and/or legislation* that gives money its unique importance where as Clower noted "goods trade for money and money trades for goods, but goods do not trade directly for goods"'. The chartalist view of money, and indeed of the economic activity in general, opens up new avenues. In the first place, money is more than the medium of exchange of an economy. It is mainly a unit of account and on the basis of this function it plays the essential roles of store of wealth and of means of final payment. Second, and more importantly for the purpose of this chapter, the most significant transactions in modern economies are not spot transactions but involve a myriad of overlapping and concomitant nominal forward contracts that are usually made in conditions of fundamental uncertainty. This means that by using the discount rate as their main monetary instrument – and with the important proviso that in a world of endogenous money they could not logically do differently – central bankers are only aiming to qualify the terms on which the social convention called money rests. They can only hope that their price signals affect the behaviour of agents in financial and money markets. But as recently argued, 'the signal may or may not be taken seriously. . . . Because the *same monetary policy* may produce different effects as it might produce different expectational responses on behalf of economic agents, monetary policy influence on liquidity cannot be seen as being deterministic' (Dow and Rodríguez-Fuentes, 1998, p. 6).

CONCLUSION

This chapter started asking the question if current monetary policy marks the triumph of Friedman and monetarism, or it is rather the triumph of Keynes and post Keynesianism. After reviewing current interpretations of theory and practice of central banking, it was shown that there is a not fully resolved tension in the modern setting of monetary policy. In the long run, money, at least for some authors, is made all-important for inflation but in the short run it is treated as irrelevant. However, this tension is quickly solved when a distinction is made between what some mainstream theorists suggested that central banks should do, and what these same central banks could not do.

In theory targeting a monetary aggregate damps the impact on income of disturbances to aggregate demand, whereas targeting the interest rate damps the impact of disturbances to money demand. Thus, a monetary aggregate policy tends to be preferred to an interest rate policy when the variance of shocks to the commodity market is larger than the variance of shocks to the monetary sector. This is the so-called instrument problem view (see Poole, 1970), a major component of the mainstream 'targets-and-instrument approach'.

In practice, however, central banks consider the interest rate as their only instrument to hit the desired inflation rate through its effects on aggregate demand (see Bank of England, 1999b). In today's world of financial innovation and liability management practices, central banks know that *both* the relationship between reserves (or base money) and deposits (or the money supply), *and* between money and nominal income (or GDP) is a very unstable one. A monetary aggregate policy is simply not feasible.

This is what post Keynesians have been claiming for a long time (see for instance Moore, 1988). Money is a residual of the economic process. The rate of change in monetary aggregates is in fact a function of the level of net deficit spending in the economy, which is, in turn, a function of the interest rate set by the central bank. In short, monetary aggregates are credit driven and demand determined. Does current monetary policy then mark the triumph of Friedman and monetarism, or is it rather the triumph of Keynes and post Keynesianism? *In theory* there is an often-tacit combination of elements that are derived from the work of Keynes, M. Friedman and their followers. This is the source of some unresolved tensions in modern central banking. But *in practice* central banks do know what they cannot do. A more encompassing interpretation of the modern setting of monetary policy would then be that, in the long run, and in the absence of persistent changes in the velocity of circulation of money – a very unlikely scenario anyway – the money supply will move in line with nominal income. The implied direction of causation, if any, would then be from changes in nominal income to changes in the stock of money.

NOTES

1. The authors are grateful to Malcolm Sawyer for continuous support in the development of this chapter and constructive observations on its final draft.
2. For a critical appraisal of the methodological issues involved in the measurement of inflation, see Rossi (2001, Chs 1–2).
3. As Laidler (2002) explains, this is a very rough description of modern monetary policies. A serious policy model would also include a foreign sector, an interest term structure and take account of complex lag relations between these variables.
4. Poole (1970, pp. 208–9) also demonstrates that there exists a 'combination' policy rule that dominates either the simple interest rate instrument or the simple money stock instrument. In particular, a central bank can set the level of the loss function at a value that is at least as low as under any of the two extreme regimes by supplying money neither perfectly elastically nor perfectly inelastically. However, as Friedman (1990, p. 1192) points out, despite the greater generality of the finite-elasticity response policy, in practice 'it is impossible to say a priori whether this optimal response policy is to supply money with positive or negative interest elasticity. The choice is again empirical'.
5. An exploration of the instrument problem in the spirit of Poole (1970) that takes into account the problems posed by money endogeneity can be found in Moore (1972).
6. In a similar vein, after analysing the monetarist experiment in the United States, Baghestani and Mott (1988, p. 492) argue that 'the Fed should never assume that the money supply process is invariant to changes in its operating procedures' and that there may be another conclusion warranted, that is, 'that attempts by the Fed to rein in the prevailing degree of (short-run at least) endogeneity or demand-determination of the money supply will always be met by actions on the part of the banking system to re-create this degree of endogeneity'.
7. As is well known, the deposit/reserve ratio is one of the two behavioural parameters that enter into the determination of the value of money multipliers, the other one being the currency/deposit ratio.
8. Friedman (1988, p. 57) argues that instabilities in the income–money relationship had actually begun to become more pronounced as early as the mid-1970s, and their appearance had already spawned a large body of empirical literature even before the new monetary experiment in the United States commenced in October 1979.
9. Nelson (1993) provides an exhaustive list of the main practical arguments put forward by central bankers and economists working at central banks to reject the implementation of money-targeting regimes.

10. Interestingly, Goodfriend (1991, p. 8) argues that 'except for the period from 1934 to the end of the 1940s when short-term interest rates were near zero or pegged, the Fed has always employed either a direct or an indirect Federal funds rate policy instrument'.

REFERENCES

Arestis, P. and P. Howells (1992), 'Institutional developments and the effectiveness of monetary policy', *Journal of Economic Issues*, **26** (1), 135–57.

Arestis, P. and M. Sawyer (2002), 'The Bank of England macroeconomic model: its nature and implications', Paper presented at the Post Keynesian Study Group Winter Seminar, University of Leeds.

Baghestani, H. and T. Mott (1988), 'The money supply process under alternative Federal Reserve operating procedures: an empirical examination', *Southern Economic Journal*, **55** (2), 485–93.

Bank of England (1999a), *Economic Models at the Bank of England*, London: Bank of England.

Bank of England (1999b), 'The transmission mechanism of monetary policy', *Bank of England Quarterly Bulletin*, **39** (2), 1–12.

Bell, S. (2001), 'The role of the state and the hierarchy of money', *Cambridge Journal of Economics*, **25** (2), 149–63.

Bernanke, B.S., T. Laubach, F.S. Mishkin and A.S. Posen (1999), *Inflation Targeting: Lessons from the International Experience*, Princeton: Princeton University Press.

Blinder, A.S. (1997), 'What central bankers could learn from academics – and vice versa', *Journal of Economic Perspectives*, **11** (2), 3–19.

Blinder, A.S. (1998), *Central Banking in Theory and Practice*, Cambridge (MA): MIT Press.

Chick, V. (1986), 'The evolution of the banking system and the theory of saving, investment and interest', *Économies et Sociétés* ('Série Monnaie et Production', 3), **20** (8–9), 111–26. Reprinted in M. Musella and C. Panico (eds) (1995), *The Money Supply in the Economic Process: A Post Keynesian Perspective*, Cheltenham and Brookfield: Edward Elgar, 412–27.

Clarida, R., J. Galí and M. Gertler (1999), 'The science of monetary policy: a New Keynesian perspective', *Journal of Economic Literature*, **37** (4), 1661–707.

Cukierman, A. (1991), 'Why does the Fed smooth interest rates?', in M.T. Belongia (ed.), *Monetary Policy on the 75th Anniversary of the Federal Reserve System: Proceedings of the Fourteenth Annual Economic Policy Conference of the Federal Reserve Bank of St. Louis*, Dordrecht: Kluwer Academic, 111–47.

Dalziel, P. (2002), 'The triumph of Keynes: what now for monetary policy research?', Paper presented at the Post Keynesian Study Group Winter Seminar, University of Leeds.

Davidson, P. (1965), 'Keynes's finance motive', *Oxford Economic Papers*, **17** (1), 47–65.

Davidson, P. (1977/1999), 'Can money be neutral even in the long run? Chartalism vs. monetarism', in L. Davidson (ed.), *The Collected Writings of Paul Davidson, Volume 3: Uncertainty, International Money, Employment and Theory*, London and New York: Macmillan and St. Martin's Press, 196–210.

De Cecco, M. (ed.) (1987), *Changing Money: Financial Innovation in Developed Countries*, Oxford: Basil Blackwell.

De Long, J.B. (2000), 'The triumph of monetarism?', *Journal of Economic Perspectives*, **14** (1), 83–94.

Dow, S.C. (1993), *Money and the Economic Process*, Cheltenham and Brookfield: Edward Elgar.

Dow, S.C. and C. Rodríguez-Fuentes (1998), 'The political economy of monetary policy', in P. Arestis and M.C. Sawyer (eds), *The Political Economy of Central Banking*, Cheltenham and Northampton: Edward Elgar, 1–19.

Dow, S.C. and J. Smithin (1999), 'The structure of financial markets and the "first principles" of monetary economics', *Scottish Journal of Political Economy*, **46** (1), 72–90.

Earley, J.S. and G.R. Evans (1982), 'The problem is bank liability management', *Challenge*, **24** (6), 54–6.

Estrella, A. and F.S. Mishkin (1997), 'Is there a role for monetary aggregates in the conduct of monetary policy?', *Journal of Monetary Economics*, **40** (2), 279–304.

Evans, G.R. (1984), 'The evolution of financial institutions and the ineffectiveness of modern monetary policy', *Journal of Economic Issues*, **18** (2), 439–48.

Fontana, G. (2000), 'Post Keynesians and Circuitists on money and uncertainty: an attempt at generality', *Journal of Post Keynesian Economics*, **23** (1), 27–48.

Fontana, G. (2001), 'Rethinking endogenous money: a constructive interpretation of the debate between accommodationists and structuralists', *Economic Discussion Paper Series*, Leeds University Business School, E01/02.

Fontana, G. and B. Gerrard (2002a), 'The encompassing principle as an emerging methodology for post Keynesian economics', in P. Arestis, M. Desai and S. Dow (eds), *Methodology, Microeconomics and Keynes: Essays in Honour of Victoria Chick*, London and New York: Routledge, vol. II, 95–105.

Fontana, G. and B. Gerrard (2002b), 'The monetary context of economic behaviour: a post Keynesian–Circuitist perspective', *Review of Social Economy*, **60** (2), forthcoming.

Friedman, B.M. (1984), 'Lessons from the 1979–82 monetary policy experiment', *American Economic Review*, **74** (2), 382–7.

Friedman, B.M. (1988), 'Lessons on monetary policy from the 1980s', *Journal of Economic Perspectives*, **2** (3), 51–72.

Friedman, B.M. (1990), 'Targets and instruments of monetary policy', in B.M. Friedman and F.H. Hahn (eds), *Handbook of Monetary Economics*, Amsterdam: Elsevier Science B.V., vol. II, 1185–230.

Friedman, B.M. and K.N. Kuttner (1992), 'Money, income and interest rates', *American Economic Review*, **82** (3), 472–92.

Friedman, B.M. and K.N. Kuttner (1996), 'A price target for U.S. monetary policy? Lessons from the experience with money growth targets', *Brookings Papers on Economic Activity*, (1), 77–146.

Friedman, M. and A.J. Schwartz (1963), *A Monetary History of the United States, 1867–1960*, Princeton: Princeton University Press.

Goodfriend, M. (1991), 'Interest rates and the conduct of monetary policy', *Carnegie–Rochester Conference Series on Public Policy*, **34** (1), 7–30.

Goodhart, C.A.E. (1984), *Monetary Theory and Practice: The UK Experience*,

London: Macmillan.

Goodhart, C.A.E. (1986), 'Financial innovation and monetary control', *Oxford Review of Economic Policy*, **2** (4), 79–102.

Goodhart, C.A.E. (1989), 'The conduct of monetary policy', *Economic Journal*, **99** (396), 293–346.

Goodhart, C.A.E. (1994), 'What should central banks do? What should be their macroeconomic objectives and operations?', *Economic Journal*, **104** (435), 1424–36.

Goodhart, C.A.E. (1995), 'Money supply control: base or interest rates', in K. Hoover and S. Sheffrin (eds), *Monetarism and the Methodology of Economics*, Cheltenham and Brookfield: Edward Elgar. Reprinted in C.A.E. Goodhart (1995), *The Central Bank and the Financial System*, London: Macmillan, 249–62.

Goodhart, C.A.E. (2002), 'The endogeneity of money', in P. Arestis, M. Desai and S. Dow (eds), *Money, Macroeconomics and Keynes: Essays in Honour of Victoria Chick*, London and New York: Routledge, vol. I, 14–24.

Greenspan, A. (1997), 'Remarks at the 15th anniversary conference of the Center for Economic Policy Research', Stanford University, 5 September.

Hester, D.D. (1981), 'Innovations and monetary control', *Brookings Papers on Economic Activity*, (1), 141–99.

Ingham, G. (1996), 'Money is a social relation', *Review of Social Economy*, **54** (4), 507–29.

Ingham, G. (2000), 'Babylonian madness: on the historical and sociological origins of money', in J. Smithin (ed.), *What is Money?*, London and New York: Routledge, 16–41.

Kaldor, N. (1985), 'How monetarism failed', *Challenge*, **28** (2), 4–13.

Kaldor, N. and J. Trevithick (1981), 'A Keynesian perspective on money', *Lloyds Bank Review*, (139), 1–19.

Keynes, J.M. (1914/1973), 'Review of "What is money" by A.M. Innes', reprinted in *The Collected Writings of John Maynard Keynes*, Vol. XI, London and Basingstoke: Macmillan, 404–6.

Laidler, D. (2002), 'The transmission mechanism with endogenous money', in P. Arestis, M. Desai and S. Dow (eds), *Money, Macroeconomics and Keynes: Essays in Honour of Victoria Chick*, London and New York: Routledge, vol. I, 25–34.

Menger, K. (1892), 'On the origins of money', *Economic Journal*, **2** (6), 239–55.

Minsky, H.P. (1982), *Can 'It' Happen Again? Essays on Instability and Finance*, Armonk: M.E. Sharpe.

Mishkin, F.S. (1998), *The Economics of Money, Banking, and Financial Markets*, Harlow: Addison Wesley, fifth edition.

Modigliani, F., R. Rasche and J.P. Cooper (1970), 'Central bank policy, the money supply, and the short-term rate of interest', *Journal of Money, Credit and Banking*, **2** (2), 166–218.

Moore, B.J. (1972), 'Optimal monetary policy', *Economic Journal*, **82** (325), 116–39.

Moore, B.J. (1988), *Horizontalists and Verticalists: The Macroeconomics of Credit Money*, Cambridge: Cambridge University Press.

Moore, B.J. (1998), 'Accommodationism versus structuralism: a note', *Journal of Post Keynesian Economics*, **21** (1), 175–8.

Nelson, C.L. (1993), 'Monetary policy officials' views about setting monetary targets', *Journal of Economic Issues*, **27** (4), 1181–93.

Niggle, C.J. (1990), 'The evolution of money, financial institutions, and monetary economics', *Journal of Economic Issues*, **24** (2), 443–50.

Niggle, C.J. (1991), 'The endogenous money supply theory: an institutionalist appraisal', *Journal of Economic Issues*, **25** (1), 137–51.

Palacio-Vera, A. (2001), 'The endogenous money hypothesis: some evidence from Spain (1987–1998)', *Journal of Post Keynesian Economics*, **23** (3), 509–26.

Palley, T.I. (1996), *Post Keynesian Economics: Debt, Distribution and the Macro Economy*, London and New York: Macmillan and St. Martin's Press.

Palley, T.I. (1998), 'Accommodationism, structuralism, and superstructuralism', *Journal of Post Keynesian Economics*, **21** (1), 171–3.

Parguez, A. (1999), 'The expected failure of the European economic and monetary union: a false money against the real economy', *Eastern Economic Journal*, **25** (1), 63–70.

Podolski, T.M. (1986), *Financial Innovation and the Money Supply*, Oxford: Basil Blackwell.

Pollin, R. (1991), 'Two theories of money supply endogeneity: some empirical evidence', *Journal of Post Keynesian Economics*, **13** (3), 366–95.

Poole, W. (1970), 'Optimal choice of monetary policy instruments in a simple stochastic macro model', *Quarterly Journal of Economics*, **84** (2), 197–216.

Realfonzo, R. (1998), *Money and Banking: Theory and Debate (1900–1940)*, Cheltenham and Northampton: Edward Elgar.

Rochon, L.-P. (1999), *Credit, Money and Production: An Alternative Post-Keynesian Approach*, Cheltenham and Northampton: Edward Elgar.

Rossi, S. (2001), *Money and Inflation: A New Macroeconomic Analysis*, Cheltenham and Northampton: Edward Elgar.

Rousseas, S. (1986), *Post Keynesian Monetary Economics*, Armonk: M.E. Sharpe.

Schumpeter, J.A. (1954/1994), *History of Economic Analysis*, London and New York: Routledge.

Schumpeter, J.A. (1970), *Das Wesen des Geldes*, Göttingen: Vandenhoeck and Ruprecht.

Taylor, J.B. (1998), 'Applying academic research on monetary policy rules: an exercise in translational economics', *The Manchester School*, **66** (supplement), 1–16.

Taylor, J.B. (1999), 'A historical analysis of monetary policy rules', in J.B. Taylor (ed.), *Monetary Policy Rules*, Chicago and London: University of Chicago Press, 319–41.

von Hagen, J. (1999), 'Money growth targeting by the Bundesbank', *Journal of Monetary Economics*, **43** (3), 681–701.

Wray, L.R. (1990), *Money and Credit in Capitalist Economies: The Endogenous Money Approach*, Aldershot and Brookfield: Edward Elgar.

Wray, L.R. (1998), *Understanding Modern Money: The Key to Full Employment and Price Stability*, Cheltenham and Northampton: Edward Elgar.

4. Monetary Control in the Presence of Endogenous Money and Financial Innovation: The Case for Asset-Based Reserve Requirements

Thomas I. Palley

INTRODUCTION

A cornerstone of post Keynesian economics is the endogeneity of the money supply. To date, the bulk of discussion among post Keynesian monetary theorists has concerned the technicalities of the process of monetary accommodation (Palley, 1994, 1996a).[1] At the policy level, the one notable implication of post Keynesian monetary theory has been the impossibility of effective monetary policy predicated on controlling the money stock. Beyond this 'negative' policy recommendation, post Keynesians have had little to say.

This chapter seeks to fill this gap and describes a policy framework based on asset-based reserve requirements (ABRR). Such a framework, which involves constructing tethers to the expansion of the assets side of financial intermediary balance sheets, can restore monetary control in an environment of endogenous money and financial innovation.

THE CASE FOR ASSET-BASED RESERVE REQUIREMENTS

The last two decades have witnessed significant financial innovation within the US economy and a feature of this has been a relative decline in the size of the banking sector. One problem posed by innovation and banking disintermediation is that the conduct of monetary policy may have become more difficult owing to reduced bank demand for liabilities of the central bank (Friedman, 1999). A second problem concerns asset price inflation. Such inflation can have large effects on aggregate demand owing to wealth effects, and it can also contribute to the build up of financial fragility to the extent that agents borrow against increased asset values. However, other than by raising the general level of interest rates, central banks have little power to control asset price inflation. This poses a dilemma since cooling over-heated asset markets may require cooling the economy as a whole so that the cure may be as bad as the disease.

This chapter proposes a new regulatory framework of asset-based reserve requirements which can enhance and sharpen domestic monetary control in the new era. Under the proposed framework, financial intermediaries would be obliged to hold reserves against different types of assets, with the reserve requirement being adjustable at the discretion of the monetary authority. These reserves would consist of liabilities of the central bank, but their definition could also be widened to include government bonds.[2] Moreover, the new system would apply to all financial intermediaries and not just banks. This contrasts with the existing system of liability based regulation which has banks being required to hold reserves against deposit liabilities, and which has banks being required to satisfy shareholder capital requirements that vary with the nature of the assets they hold.

Before turning to the details of a system of ABRR, it is important to recognise that the welfare justification for such a system rests upon a meta-view that maintains there is benefit from discretionary policy interventions – a view that is also implicit in existing monetary policy arrangements which emphasise control over short-term interest rates. The foundation for this position is that either the monetary authority has an information advantage relative to market participants, or that decentralised markets result in socially sub-optimal outcomes that can be improved upon by discretionary intervention. Absent this, the monetary authority would be unable to improve on outcomes by adjusting reserve requirements.

The proposed system of ABRR has significant macroeconomic and microeconomic policy advantages. At the macroeconomic level, ABRR can provide monetary authorities with multiple independent additional tools of monetary control that can supplement existing control over the short-term interest rate. In terms of Tinbergen's (1952) targets and instruments approach to macroeconomic stabilisation policy, ABRR can provide additional independent policy instruments that allow policy makers to focus on additional economic targets. This can be especially useful when fiscal policy is constrained by budgetary concerns. It can also be useful for controlling asset price inflation since ABRR offer a new policy instrument that can be independently targeted on the stock market, thereby avoiding having to slow the entire economy.

At the microeconomic level there are also significant advantages. One long-recognised advantage is that ABRR can be used to guide the allocation of credit toward areas deemed socially deserving (Thurow, 1972; Pollin, 1993). This credit allocation function links with recent discussions about stabilising the international financial system. There is now an emerging awareness that much of the problem of financial instability arises from inappropriate asset allocations. Thus, the 1997 East Asian financial crisis is now widely attributed to excessive reliance on short-term lending, combined with overly risky portfolio investment by investors who chased yield with less than full regard to risk. This in turn suggests shifting the focus of financial regulation away from its traditional concern with the liabilities side of financial intermediaries' balance sheets toward an increased concern with the assets side. ABRR do this and can be used to discourage excessive investment and lending in areas deemed to be unduly risky. Thus, by imposing higher reserve requirements on short-term loans, ABRR can raise the cost of short-term loans relative to longer-term loans, thereby discouraging short-term borrowing. Similarly, by making risky foreign country portfolio investments subject to reserve requirements, ABRR can lower returns to such investments, thereby discouraging holdings.[3]

A last microeconomic advantage of ABRR concerns their financial crisis properties. In particular, ABRR have valuable incentive-consistent properties that can help stabilise financial systems. In recent years, monetary authorities have emphasised the need for bank risk-adjusted capital requirements to mitigate the problem of moral hazard in lending. However, such requirements may be highly pro-cyclical and exacerbate the business cycle. This is because banks are forced to look for additional capital in recessions when loan quality deteriorates and default increases: yet this is exactly when bank capital is hardest to raise. This can produce a credit crunch that amplifies the downturn. Contrastingly, a system of ABRR can guard against moral hazard by having reserve requirements be contingent upon loan riskiness, yet ABRR are less destabilising since reserves are automatically freed up when borrowers default.

A final point concerns the issue of who the regulatory system should apply to. Within the US economy, the earlier New Deal system of financial regulation was based on the principle of industry segmentation which divided the financial sector into banking, insurance and securities underwriting. A system of fire walls ensured that firms did not mix these three types of business, and each segment was subjected to different regulatory rules. Banks were especially singled out regarding the need for reserve requirements on certain types of liabilities. This system of regulation has now been significantly undone by the repeal of the Glass–Steagall Act, which was prompted by the fact that financial innovation had steadily whittled away distinctions between financial intermediaries. Not only do nominally different types of intermediary now compete in the same markets, but even where products differ, they can be decomposed through the use of derivatives, and shown to possess many shared attributes. For these reasons, the New Deal distinctions between financial intermediaries became increasingly less relevant. However, this blurring of distinctions suggests that a new system of ABRR should be applied to all financial intermediaries including banks, insurance companies and mutual funds. Under such a comprehensive regulatory umbrella reserve requirements would be set by asset type, and not by who holds the asset.[4] This would ensure that the incidence of reserve requirements was determined by the asset configuration of different financial intermediaries, and would remove the incentive to shift business to avoid requirements – which was a problem that afflicted the earlier New Deal regulatory regime.

MICROECONOMIC FOUNDATIONS: ABRR WITHIN THE GENERIC FINANCIAL FIRM

Given that the proposed system of ABRR is intended to apply to all financial intermediaries, the model that is developed below uses the construct of a generic financial firm. This firm is most easily identified with a bank which takes in deposits (bank liabilities) and makes loans (bank assets). However, it can also be identified with a mutual fund which issues variable price deposits (mutual fund liabilities) and invests the proceeds in equities (mutual fund assets). The asset allocation consequences of ABRR work through their impact on relative rates of return, and these are conceptually the same for both types of firm. The principal difference between banks and other financial intermediaries is that banks receive a pre-determined interest payment, whereas other financial intermediaries hold equity which puts them in the position of residual claimants. This also means they bear correspondingly more risk.

The interest rate effects of different systems of reserve requirements can be shown through the following heuristic model of a perfectly competitive generic financial firm with constant returns technology and non-stochastic withdrawals. The assumption of constant marginal costs is a simplifying assumption that facilitates incorporation of the micro model into the subsequent macro model.[5]

Under the current system of liability-based reserve requirements (LBRR) the representative firm's profit maximisation programme is given by:

$$\text{Max } V = i_L L + i_H H - [a_L + p_L]L - [a_H + p_H]H - [i_D + a_D]D - [i_T + a_T]T - [i_F + a_F]F \quad (4.1.\text{A})$$

subject to:

$$L + H = [1 - k_D]D + [1 - k_T]T + F \qquad (4.1.B)$$

where:

L = investment loans
H = consumer loans
D = short-term deposits
T = long-term deposits
F = money market borrowing $(F > 0)$ or lending $(F < 0)$
i_j = interest rate $(j = L, H, D, T, F)$
a_j = constant marginal cost per dollar of administering loans and
     liabilities $(j = L, H, D, T, F)$
p_j = probability per dollar of default on loans $(j = L, H)$
k_j = reserve requirement ratio $(j = D, T)$, $k_D > k_T$

Equation (4.1.A) is the profit function, while equation (4.1.B) is the balance sheet constraint. Substituting the constraint into (4.1.A) and differentiating with respect to the choice variables (D, T, H, F) yields four first-order conditions. Satisfaction of these conditions then implies the following structure of interest rates expressed in terms of the money market rate:

$$i_L = i_F + a_F + a_L + p_L \qquad (4.2.A)$$
$$i_H = i_F + a_F + a_H + p_H \qquad (4.2.B)$$
$$i_T = [1 - k_T][i_F + a_F] - a_T \qquad (4.2.C)$$
$$i_D = [1 - k_D][i_F + a_F] - a_D \qquad (4.2.D)$$

The money market rate, which is set by the monetary authority, underpins the entire structure of interest rates.[6] The rates on investment and consumer loans are established as mark-ups over the money market rate. These mark-ups take account of the respective costs of administering loans, as well as the respective expected loan default losses.

The rates on short- and long-term deposits are also established by reference to the money market rate. The effect of LBRR is to reduce the interest rate paid on both short- and long-term deposit rates: the larger the reserve requirement ratio, the lower the rate paid. The logic is as follows. Money market funds, short-term deposits and long-term deposits are all alternative sources of funds, and firms will therefore seek to equate the marginal cost of funds across these different sources. Reserve requirements mean that part of each dollar of deposits has to be retained as reserves, so that financial firms have to acquire more than a dollar of deposits to make a dollar of loans. In effect, reserve requirements raise the effective marginal cost of deposits as a source for funding loans, and firms therefore lower the rate paid to depositors.

The effects of a system of LBRR can be contrasted with those of a system of ABRR. In this case, the representative firm's maximisation programme is given by:

$$\text{Max } V = i_L L + i_H H - [a_L + p_L]L - [a_H + p_H]H - [i_D + a_D]D - [i_T + a_T]T - [i_F + a_F]F \quad (4.3.A)$$

subject to:

$$[1 + k_L]L + [1 + k_H]H = D + T + F \quad (4.3.B)$$

The one change concerns the structure of the balance sheet constraint, in which required reserves are now held against assets. Comparing the two constraints reveals how reserve requirements are really a form of balance sheet regulation. Substituting the constraint into (4.3.A) and differentiating with respect to the choice variables (*L*, *H*, *D*, *T*) again yields four first-order conditions. Satisfaction of these conditions then implies the following structure of interest rates expressed in terms of the money market rate:

$$i_L = [i_F + a_F][1 + k_L] + a_L + p_L \quad (4.4.A)$$
$$i_H = [i_F + a_F][1 + k_H] + a_H + p_H \quad (4.4.B)$$
$$i_D = i_F + a_F - a_D \quad (4.4.C)$$
$$i_T = i_F + a_F - a_T \quad (4.4.D)$$

Once again, the money market rate serves to underpin the entire structure of rates. However, reserve requirements now affect the structure of rates in dramatically different fashion. In a LBRR system, reserve requirements affect the relative rates paid on liabilities and have no effect on loan rates. In an ABRR system, they have no effect on the rates paid on liabilities, and instead affect the relative rates charged on loans. A higher required reserve ratio raises loan rates. The reason is that ABRR oblige banks to borrow more than a dollar to make one dollar of loans, and they now charge borrowers for the extra that they must borrow.

Comparison of equations (4.2.A)–(4.2.D) with (4.4.A)–(4.4.D) reveals the different microeconomic allocative effects of LBRR and ABRR. LBRR penalise financial intermediary depositors by reducing the worth of deposits to financial firms, and they then reduce the amount they are willing to pay for deposits.

ABRR require firms to acquire additional funds to make loans, and they pass on the costs of these additional funds to borrowers.

Differential reserve requirements therefore provide a means of influencing the composition of the financial firms' assets and liabilities. In a system of LBRR, reserve requirements reduce the yield on firm liabilities and reduce the total demand for such liabilities. If reserve requirements differ across liabilities, then demand for the liability with the higher reserve requirement will fall relative to that with the lower reserve requirement. In a system of ABRR, reserve requirements raise loan rates and reduce the overall demand for loans from firms. If reserve requirements differ by loan type, then the demand for loans with the higher reserve requirement will fall relative to that with the lower reserve requirement.

The above mechanism reveals how ABRR can be used to influence the microeconomic allocation of credit. This is done by changing the relative price of different types of credit without changing the general level of interest rates. Such a credit allocation effect has some similarity with selective credit controls. However, selective credit controls are a 'quantity'-based regulation, which leads to rationing problems associated with how to allocate the fixed quantity of credit. ABRR allows the market to allocate credit at a price that is implicitly determined by the monetary authority.

If the menu of assets available to the financial intermediary is further disaggregated, the monetary authority can in principle make even finer decisions about pricing of credit and asset returns. Thus, over-heating of real estate markets may have amplified business cycle fluctuations (Case, 2000). Under LBRR, controlling such over-heating requires raising the general level of interest rates, with all its adverse consequences for the entire macroeconomy. In a system with ABRR, the monetary authority can narrowly target the property sector by raising reserve requirements on mortgage loans. Indeed, such interventions could even be arranged so as to distinguish between commercial, residential and industrial property loans, or to distinguish by region. In this fashion, property markets that are over-heated could be cooled without slowing the whole economy.

Finally, the ability of ABRR to influence the allocation of credit indicates its usefulness as a tool for regulating international financial flows. The recent currency crisis in South East Asia has been substantially attributed to excessive international short-term lending. South East Asian economies were allowed to build up large foreign currency denominated debts, and a run on their currencies resulted when creditors realised they were going to have difficulty servicing these debts. Capital market failure associated with excessive extension of short-term credit was at the heart of the problem. A system of ABRR could potentially be used to prevent such outcomes since domestic monetary authorities could impose requirements on short-term loans in general, or just on loans to countries that they deem to be over-borrowed.

TARGETS AND INSTRUMENTS: THE MACROECONOMIC ADVANTAGES OF ABRR

The previous section analysed the microeconomic relative interest rate pricing effects of alternative systems of reserve requirements. This section analyses the implications of alternative systems of reserve requirements for macroeconomic stabilisation. It shows how a system of ABRR can provide a useful additional instrument for purposes of macroeconomic stabilisation, which can be particularly useful when governments are constrained in their use of fiscal policy, or when they have additional financial sector targets such as the exchange rate. ABRR can be a useful instrument because they can be used to control consumption spending while leaving investment spending unaffected.

The above claims can be illustrated in the following Keynesian general equilibrium IS–LM model:

$$y = C(i_H, i_D, i_T, [1-t]y) + I(i_L) + G + NX \tag{4.5}$$
$$NX = NX(e, y) \tag{4.6}$$
$$e = e(i_F/i_{F*}) \tag{4.7}$$
$$L + H = [1 - k_D]D + [1 - k_T]T \tag{4.8}$$
$$k_L L + k_H H = B \tag{4.9}$$
$$L = L(i_L, y) \tag{4.10}$$
$$H = H(i_H, i_D, i_T, [1-t]y) \tag{4.11}$$
$$D = D(i_H, i_D, i_T, [1-t]y) \tag{4.12}$$
$$T = T(i_H, i_D, i_T, [1-t]y) \tag{4.13}$$

All quantities are real quantities. The definition of variables is as follows:

y = output
C = consumption spending
I = investment spending
G = government spending
NX = net exports
e = exchange rate
i_{F*} = foreign money market rate
B = monetary base

Equation (4.5) is the goods market equilibrium condition. Equation (4.6) determines the level of net exports. Equation (4.7) determines the exchange rate which is a function of relative cross-country money market interest rates. Equations (4.8)–(4.13) describe the financial sector. Equation (4.8) is the aggregate banking sector balance sheet constraint, and federal funds borrowings are therefore zero in aggregate. Equation (4.9) is the market equilibrium condition for the market for monetary base, and it is assumed for simplicity that non-bank currency holdings are zero. Equations (4.10)–(4.13) determine household demand for loans, corporate demand for loans, household demand for demand deposits, and household demand for time deposits.

Equation (4.5), the goods market equilibrium condition, has the level of output being determined by the level of demand. The level of demand is in turn determined by consumption, investment, government spending and net exports. The level of consumption spending depends on the consumer loan interest rate, the demand and time deposit rates, the money market interest rate, and after-tax income. The influence of the demand deposit and time deposit rates on consumption spending reflects the conventional transmission mechanism whereby the general level of yields on financial assets affects household saving. This effect is negative if the substitution effect dominates the income effect. The influence of the consumption loan rate reflects the credit channel. Investment spending depends on the investment loan rate which reflects the cost of credit channel.

The determination of interest rates and monetary aggregates depends on the system of reserve requirements and the monetary authorities' target variable. For current purposes the analysis is restricted to the case where the central bank is targeting the money market interest rate. In this case the supply of base is endogenous, and the system of equations given by (4.5)–(4.13) is block recursive, with equations (4.5)–(4.7) constituting one block and equations (4.8)–(4.13) constituting another.

If the financial system is governed by LBRR, interest rates are determined according to equations (4.2.A)–(4.2.D). Substituting in equations (4.5)–(4.7), this yields the following system:

$$y = C + I + G + NX \qquad (4.5.A)$$
$$NX = X(e, y) \qquad (4.6.A)$$
$$e = e(i_F/i_{F*}) \qquad (4.7.A)$$

where:

$$C = C(i_F + a_F + a_H + p_H,\ [1-k_D][i_F + a_F] - a_D,\ [1-k_T][i_F + a_F] - a_T,\ [1-t]y)$$

$$I = I(i_F + a_F + a_L + p_L)$$

The endogenous variables are y, NX and e. The policy instruments are i_F, k_D, k_T, t and G.

From a policy standpoint, the target variables are usually the level of output, y, and the level of net exports, NX. If policy makers have control over both monetary and fiscal policy, then they have sufficient instruments (i_F, G and t) to both lower final demand and change its composition such that the level of investment spending is maintained. This can be done by tight fiscal policy (higher t and lower G) and easy monetary policy (lower i_F). In terms of the IS–LM model, such a policy shifts the IS left and lowers the LM.

However, difficulties arise when fiscal policy is constrained. In this case, conventional wisdom is that policy makers have only one instrument, namely control over the money market interest rate. If policy makers wish to slow the economy to avoid inflationary pressures, then they have to raise the money market rate. This results in higher consumer loan rates, which reduces consumption demand by reducing consumer borrowing and increasing saving. However, it also raises investment loan rates and reduces investment spending, which slows the rate of growth of potential output. Thus, using higher interest rates to slow the economy and prevent inflation carries a heavy cost in terms of reduced investment and capital accumulation. Finally, higher rates cause a deterioration in the trade balance owing to their effect on the exchange rate, and this can have serious negative consequences for the manufacturing sector.

A system of ABRR offers policy makers a way out of these dilemmas. In such a system interest rates are determined by equations (4.4.A)–(4.4.D). Substituting in equations (4.5)–(4.7) yields the following system:

$$y = C + I + G + NX \tag{4.5.B}$$
$$NX = X(e, y) \tag{4.6.B}$$
$$e = e(i_F / i_{F*}) \tag{4.7.B}$$

where:

$$C = C([i_F + a_F][1 + k_H] + a_H + p_H, \ i_F + a_F - a_D, \ i_F + a_F - a_T, \ [1-t]y)$$
$$I = I([i_F + a_F][1 + k_L] + a_L + p_L)$$

Inspection of this system shows that if policy makers want to twist the composition of aggregate demand by reducing consumption, they can do this by raising consumer loan reserve requirements. This immediately translates into higher consumer loan rates and reduced consumption spending, which reduces aggregate demand and output. Since money market rates are unchanged, the investment loan rate is unchanged and investment spending is not directly affected. Moreover, the exchange rate is also unchanged since the money market interest rate is unchanged. This means that the tightening vis-à-vis consumer spending is accomplished without an adverse exchange rate impact on net exports.

It is even possible that the monetary authority could lower the exchange rate and stimulate investment while simultaneously discouraging consumption. This can be done by lowering the money market interest rate while raising the reserve requirement on consumer loans even higher. If done appropriately, the consumer loan rate would rise and the investment loan rate fall. Moreover, the lower money market interest rate would depreciate the exchange rate, which would raise exports, lower imports and improve the current account.

In sum, using asset-based reserve requirements to twist the structure of consumer and investment loan rates, provides a powerful policy tool for lowering consumption without lowering investment. For this reason ABRR are a valuable instrument of stabilisation policy.

ABRR AND THE NEW PROBLEM OF ASSET PRICE INFLATION

Recently, particularly in the United States, concerns have arisen about the macroeconomic consequences of asset price inflation. Thus, Federal Reserve Chairman Alan Greenspan (1999) has noted how asset price inflation can produce a large wealth effect on consumption, and it can also generate financially fragile balance sheets if individuals take on debt to purchase other flexible price assets. For the monetary authority this poses a dilemma since using interest rates to control asset prices puts the general level of economic activity at risk.

ABRR offer a way out of this dilemma by enabling the monetary authority to directly target asset prices. This can be seen from the following asset price augmented IS–LM model. Asset prices, q, enter as a positive argument in the consumption function. The goods market equilibrium, net export and exchange rate equations become:

$$y = C + I + G + NX \qquad (4.5.C)$$
$$NX = X(e, y) \qquad (4.6.C)$$
$$e = e(i_F/i_{F*}) \qquad (4.7.C)$$

where:

$$C = C([i_F+a_F][1+k_H]+a_H+p_H, i_F+a_F-a_D, i_F+a_F-a_T, [1-t]y, q)$$
$$I = I([i_F+a_F][1+k_L]+a_L+p_L)$$

The price of equities is determined by discounted profits per share. Assuming for simplicity a steady perpetual stream of profits, V, this implies:

$$q = V/i_q \qquad (4.14)$$

where i_q is the rate of return on equities. Finally, portfolio equilibrium requires that the risk-adjusted rates of return to holding equities equal the safe return on holding deposits. This implies:

$$i_q[1 + k_q] = i_D + z \qquad (4.15)$$

where:

k_q = ABRR imposed on equity holdings
z = equity premium

Substituting (4.15) into (4.14) shows that an increase in the reserve requirement on equities drives down equity prices. This in turn reduces consumption spending and imports in equations (4.5.C) and (4.6.C), but the general level of interest rates remains unchanged. Consequently, asset prices can be specifically targeted without having negative spill-over effects on investment spending and the exchange rate.

STABILITY ADVANTAGES OF ABRR

Another advantage of ABRR is their superior macroeconomic stability properties. Reserve requirements have traditionally been imposed against bank liabilities, with the scale of requirements depending on the perceived likelihood of net withdrawals. This design reflects an earlier belief that bank runs were caused by panic withdrawals of deposits, and reserve requirements could help mitigate this likelihood. However, to the extent that bank runs are triggered by deterioration in the assets side of banks' balance sheets, the best way of protecting against bank runs may be strengthening the assets side of balance sheets. Moreover, this may be especially desirable given that deposit insurance reduces depositor discipline on banks, thereby contributing to a moral hazard problem that has banks engage in excessively risky lending.

The Basle agreement of 1988 introduced risk-based equity requirements to counter this moral hazard, the aim being to discourage banks from adopting excessively risky asset compositions by obliging them to put up more capital as the riskiness of their lending increased. However, a problem with these requirements is that they are potentially unstable. In a recession, loan default wipes out equity, and this requires banks to raise more equity capital. Yet, this is exactly when it is most difficult for banks to raise more equity. As a result, risk-based capital requirements may act as an 'automatic destabiliser' that amplifies business cycle downturns by contributing to credit crunches.

ABRR do not have this problem, but they can still help combat moral hazard. Thus, ABRR can be structured according to risk, thereby making risky loans relatively more costly and discouraging excessive risky lending. If a risky loan defaults, the reserves on that loan are freed up, giving banks the liquidity they need when most needed. Moreover, it is also easier to expand the banking system's capacity to lend in times of recession under a system of ABRR than under a system of capital requirements. Under ABRR the monetary authority can inject reserves through standard open market operations thereby giving banks the liquidity to back further lending, whereas a system of risk-based capital requirements requires that equity holders stump up more capital. However, as noted above, recessions make equity holders reluctant to supply capital, thereby making counter-cyclical management of the banking system more difficult.[7]

FURTHER ADVANTAGES OF ABRR

Two further advantages of ABRR concern their implications for collection of seigniorage and the conduct of monetary policy. Under existing arrangements, government collects seigniorage on cash held by the public and through reserve requirements levied on bank deposits. Over the last decade, as cash needs have fallen owing to the introduction of new transactions technologies (such as credit cards), and as bank holdings of reserves have fallen away owing to lowering of reserve requirement ratios and reduced demand for bank deposits, seigniorage collection has declined. Introduction of ABRR on the spectrum of financial assets held by financial intermediaries would reverse this, and hugely increase the demand for reserves. In doing so, it would create a seigniorage windfall that would benefit the public purse. Moreover, seigniorage revenues would grow as the economy's holdings of financial assets grew.

With regard to monetary policy, the declining significance of banks threatens to make the future conduct of monetary policy more difficult.[8] Monetary policy works through central banks exchanging government bonds for reserves, and thereby altering the supply of reserves. A key requirement is that there be a demand for reserves, so that the change in supply causes a market imbalance that in turn causes interest rates to adjust. However, the demand for reserves has been shrinking as banks have shrunk relative to the overall financial sector, and as reserve requirements on deposits have been lowered. This means that central banks (including the Fed) have an increasingly tenuous hold on the economy because their policies work via the banking system, and banks are increasingly small relative to the financial system. This trend will likely persist, making the conduct of future monetary policy more difficult. Imposing a system of ABRR on all financial intermediaries would re-establish the Fed's hold over the entire financial sector, and monetary policy would work rapidly and forcefully since any change in the supply of reserves would be felt by all financial intermediaries across the board.

CONCLUSION

This chapter has argued for a new comprehensive system of financial sector regulation centered on asset-based reserve requirements. Such a system can be used to combat financial instability by giving policy makers the instruments needed to discourage excessive risk taking. It also facilitates the task of macroeconomic management by providing policy makers with multiple additional independent instruments which can allow them to hit additional targets, including stock market prices. It can also be used to affect the allocation of credit, including discouraging excessive short-term foreign lending. ABRR also possess highly desirable stability properties in that liquidity is automatically released in times of financial distress. Lastly, ABRR can raise significant seigniorage, and can enhance the traction of monetary policy in a world in which banks are becoming a smaller part of the financial landscape.

With regard to operationalising such a system, ABRR should be uniformly applied across all financial intermediaries. In the past, reserve requirements have been imposed on just banks, and this has placed banks at a competitive disadvantage versus other financial intermediaries and provided an incentive to shift financial intermediation outside the banking sector, thereby diminishing the effectiveness of monetary control. Both of these problems would persist if ABRR were placed on just banks. For these reasons, they should be placed on all financial intermediaries on the basis of the assets they hold.

Within the United States, the financial regulatory framework of the New Deal era has been largely bypassed by financial innovation and legal repeal. There now exists a significant regulatory gap that has diminished policy makers' abilities to control financial markets. A comprehensively applied system of ABRR can fill this void, and contribute to the restoration of stable financial markets and effective monetary control.

If ABRR are placed only on firms operating in the domestic market, this stands to create an incentive to shift business offshore – much as banks' desires to escape reserve requirements on deposits contributed to the growth of the euro-dollar market in the 1960s. The best way to avoid such jurisdictional shopping is to have ABRR adopted by all major countries – as has been the case for bank capital requirements under the Basle agreements. However, absent this, a system of ABRR may still feasible on a go-it-alone basis. First, shifting business to avoid ABRR imposes costs on financial intermediaries, and these costs act to limit the incentive to shift. Second, decisions about business location depend on a range of factors including business environment, the network of other support services and ancillary markets, availability of qualified personnel, and the soundness of the regulatory system governing the conduct of business. All of these factors work to the advantage of the United States, so that application of ABRR need not be decisive regarding business location. Third, it may also be possible to make ABRR stick on foreign financial intermediaries by having the validity of domestic collateralised loan agreements and loan guarantees depend on compliance with ABRR regulations. The same holds for domestic assets, as proper legal title registration at time of purchase could require compliance with ABRR regulations. Such measures would then give foreign financial intermediaries an incentive to comply, and they illustrate how domestic financial market regulation is still feasible despite the international mobility of financial capital.

Finally, as with any system of regulation, an ABRR system will need to be periodically updated in response to financial innovation. All effective regulation implicitly prevents profit-maximising firms from doing what they would like to do, and thereby sets up an incentive to innovate and evade regulation. Over time, firms are inevitably successful in this process, so that good regulation always sows the seeds of its own destruction. In a system of ABRR, financial firms stand to introduce new asset categories and methods of transacting that are outside the ambit of existing regulation, and this means the system will need to be periodically updated. This is not a criticism of ABRR *per se*, but rather a systemic feature of all regulation.

NOTES

1. Palley (1996b) explores the implications of endogenous money for the Cambridge theory of income distribution, while Palley (1997) explores the role of endogenous money in the business cycle.
2. Having government bonds qualify would increase the demand for bonds and lower the interest rate paid by government. Qualifying bonds could be restricted to short-term issues, or could be both short- and long-term issues.
3. This proposal has recently been advanced by D'Arista and Griffith-Jones (2001) and represents a specific application of ABRR.
4. Some asset categories might be zero rated.
5. The assumption of constant marginal costs means that the size of the individual firm is indeterminate. If pinning down the size of the firm is an important object, then rising marginal costs of intermediation are needed. This would cause the short-run market loan supply schedule to be upward sloping, and the loan rate would rise with the extent of lending. However, such a modification would not change the core implication that the pattern of relative interest rates is impacted by the reserve requirement regime. An example of how the size of the individual financial firm can be determined is the following demand deposit cost function for the ith firm, $C_i = a_0 - a_1 D_i + a_2 D_i^2$. Total deposit taking costs are a quadratic function in the level of demand deposits. This implies an equilibrium level of demand deposits at the ith bank of $D_i = a_1/2a_2$. The number of firms, N, in equilibrium is given by $ND_i = D$, where D is the aggregate level of deposits.
6. If the monetary authority is targeting the monetary base, there will be a similar effect on the structure of rates. The one difference is that the 'general level' of rates would shift up and down as the federal funds rate varied with fluctuations in the demand base. However, it is now widely agreed that central banks in fact target short-term interest rates and allow monetary quantities to adjust endogenously (Goodhart, 1989; Blinder, 1998; Friedman, 2000).
7. Capital requirements have allocative properties that are similar to ABRR. Since shareholder capital is the most expensive type of capital, they tend to discourage banks from accumulating assets that carry high capital requirements. There is now discussion of making capital requirements more subject to activist discretionary change, and using them to manage the financial business cycle. Their big drawback relative to ABRR is their pro-cyclical character.
8. This is an issue that has been recently raised by Friedman (1999).

REFERENCES

Blinder, A. (1998), *Central Banking in Theory and Practice*, Cambridge: MIT Press.

Case, K. (2000), 'Real estate and the macroeconomy', *Brookings Papers on Economic Activity*, (2), 119–45.

D'Arista, J. and S. Griffith-Jones (2001), 'The boom of portfolio flows to emerging markets and its regulatory implications', in S. Griffith-Jones, M.F. Montes and A. Nasution (eds), *Short Term Capital Flows and Economic Crises*, Oxford: Oxford University Press, 52–69.

Friedman, B. (1999), 'The future of monetary policy: the central bank as an army with only a signal corps?', *NBER Working Papers*, 7420.

Friedman, B. (2000), 'The role of interest rates in Federal Reserve policymaking', *NBER Working Papers*, 8047.

Goodhart, C.A.E. (1989), 'The conduct of monetary policy', *Economic Journal*, **99** (396), 293–346.

Greenspan, A. (1999), 'New challenges for monetary policy', Symposium sponsored by the Federal Reserve Bank of Kansas City in Jackson Hole, Wyoming, August.

Palley, T.I. (1994), 'Competing views of the money supply: theory and evidence', *Metroeconomica*, **45** (1), 67–88.

Palley, T.I. (1996a), 'Accommodationism versus structuralism: time for an accommodation', *Journal of Post Keynesian Economics*, **18** (4), 585–94.

Palley, T.I. (1996b), 'Inside debt, aggregate demand, and the Cambridge theory of distribution', *Cambridge Journal of Economics*, **20** (4), 465–74.

Palley, T.I. (1997), 'Endogenous money and the business cycle', *Journal of Economics*, **65** (2), 133–49.

Pollin, R. (1993), 'Public credit allocation through the Federal Reserve: why it is needed; how it should be done', in G.A. Dymski, G.A. Epstein and R. Pollin (eds), *Transforming the U.S. Financial System: Equity and Efficiency for the 21st Century*, Armonk: M.E. Sharpe, 321–54.

Thurow, L. (1972), 'Proposals for rechanneling funds to meet social priorities', in Federal Reserve Bank of Boston (ed.), *Policies for a More Competitive Financial System*, Boston: Federal Reserve Bank of Boston, 179–89.

Tinbergen, J. (1952), *On the Theory of Economic Policy*, Amsterdam: North-Holland.

5. Seigniorage or Sovereignty?

L. Randall Wray

INTRODUCTION

In this chapter, we will explore two competing approaches to the analysis of national currency emission. We will call one the seigniorage view, to be contrasted with what we will call the sovereignty view. Before proceeding, let us say that we are not interested in presenting a historical analysis, nor will we pursue the etymology of these terms. We will define each of these terms as we will be using them, and then will identify the views associated with each. We will argue that the sovereignty view is more useful for understanding the operation of most modern national currencies. While much of the discussion will focus on the domestic use of the currency, we will also explore issues surrounding an 'open economy' and foreign currency reserves, and will discuss the supposed 'hegemony' of the United States.

SEIGNIORAGE

Seigniorage is usually defined by reference to a supposed earlier stage in which full-bodied coins were minted by the state (Haslag, 1998). Each coin would contain an amount of precious metal equal in value as a commodity to the coin's exchange value as well as to the nominal value stamped on the coin. The state's mint would accept gold for coining, assessing a fee, called a seigniorage charge. So long as that fee exceeded the mint's costs, the state would receive net revenue from its minting operation, that is, seigniorage revenue. If, for example, a gold miner brought a pound of gold to the mint for coining, the state might charge a fee equivalent to one ounce of gold and provide fifteen one-ounce coins. If minting costs were equal to the value of half an ounce of gold, the state would gain in purchasing power an amount equal to half an ounce of gold. In turn, the gold miner would have gained purchasing power equal to 15 ounces of gold, less mining costs.

This speculative history leads quite naturally to what Goodhart (1998) has called the 'metallist' view, that is, the notion that the value of a currency depends on the value of the commodity from which it is coined. Note, however, that there is a problem that requires resolution, because we must somehow transform the relative commodity value of gold to a nominal value. This means that even if this speculative history were accurate, and even if coins were full-bodied, there is still room for what Goodhart calls the 'cartalist' view – or what Knapp (1905/1924) called the state money approach – because it might be the state that fixes the nominal value of gold – an ounce of gold is equivalent to so many dollars.

The next logical step would be for the state to try to cheat at the mint, by debasing coins. If the state kept for itself five ounces of gold in addition to the one-ounce seigniorage fee, but gave to the gold miner 15 coins containing only 10 ounces of gold, it might be able to fool the miner. It would retain six ounces of gold, which could be minted as six full-bodied coins, or a greater number of debased coins. However, markets would soon recognise the debased coins, whose purchasing power would fall. Debasement would thus only lead to inflation and would not, over the long run, increase seigniorage. To increase long-run seigniorage, the state would have to raise its minting charges, but this might be limited owing to competition from alternative mints, including private mints or foreign mints, or from circulation of unminted gold.

Such a strict interpretation of the concept of seigniorage, however, suffers from two problems. Firstly, there is scant historical evidence in its favour, but we will leave that to the side, as it is not necessary to engage in historical debate. More importantly, even if such a system existed in the distant past, it is not relevant to any economy today. Hence, the definition of the term has been extended to the use of paper money backed by reserves of precious metals and, more importantly, to paper 'fiat' monies that are not backed by precious metal reserves. The last case should be divided into subclasses, the first dealing with a fiat money in a fixed exchange rate system and the second encompassing a fiat money with a floating exchange rate.

The typical extension of the concept begins with the recognition that transactions costs could be reduced by circulating paper rather than gold coins. Some gold would be held as a reserve against the paper notes, but the rest of it could be released to alternative uses. As Black (1989, p. 314) argues, '[t]he use of a paper money instead of full-bodied coin by modern governments generates a very large social saving in the use of the resources that would otherwise have to be expended in mining and smelting large quantities of money'. This then generates seigniorage, the value of which 'can be measured by considering the aggregate demand curve for currency, as a function of the rate of interest' (ibid., p. 314). Assuming a fractional gold reserve held against the currency, seigniorage to the state would equal the purchasing power of its total note issue less the cost of providing the paper currency, which includes the opportunity cost of holding the gold reserves. There still remains the potential problem of inflation resulting from state note issue, which forces us to make a distinction between real and nominal seigniorage, but we will ignore that because it is of secondary interest.

The notion of seigniorage is also frequently extended to the international sphere. According to Black (1989, p. 314):

> Substitution of fiduciary reserve assets such as Special Drawing Rights created by the International Monetary Fund or United States dollars for gold would generate a substantial social gain in the form of seigniorage equal to the excess of the opportunity cost of capital over the costs of providing the fiduciary asset.

The issuer of the 'currency' used as a reserve asset internationally would reap all the seigniorage gain unless interest were paid on holdings, in which case 'the seigniorage is split between the issuer and the holder' (ibid., p. 314). Given current international realities, it is often claimed that the United States gains significant seigniorage because the dollar is used as the primary reserve around the world, a topic to be explored below.

Let us return to the domestic economy and briefly consider a closed economy in which government issues a fiat money that is not backed by a precious metal reserve. This is supposed to generate significant seigniorage income to the government, but it is not clear why anyone accepts this fiat money. In the 'pure' gold standard case, one can understand why the public accepts paper notes that are convertible on a fixed ratio to gold, as they can be exchanged for gold that has intrinsic value. However, if the fiat money is not convertible, it is not clear why it is accepted. There are two possible solutions that have been articulated. The first relies on convention: agent Tom accepts fiat money from the government because he expects that agent Sally will accept that same fiat money in payment. There is an obvious logical, infinite regress problem that should make this unappealing, as it is difficult to see how such a convention became established. Another possibility, apparently accepted by at least some post Keynesians, is that the public simply views government fiat money as a government liability that will be retired later. In this case, government fiat money is not essentially different from any other (including private) liability, and the government's position is no different from that of any other economic agent. When the government emits money to purchase something, it has not finished the transaction, but remains in debt, which it will have to settle at a later date. For example, Rossi (1999, p. 484) argues that no economic agent ('even as powerful as a government might be') can purchase 'by simply letting its own IOUs circulate'. He continues arguing that, '[a]s a matter of fact, it is plain that no agent whatsoever can really pay by acknowledging his/her debt to another agent. . . . The emission of modern money is never a purchase for the issuer' (ibid., p. 484). In a somewhat similar vein, Mehrling (2000, p. 401) argues that 'state money is not a fiat outside money . . . but, rather, an inside credit money'. Hence, Mehrling insists that we should think of government-issued money as nothing but 'a promise to pay'.

A problem immediately arises for Rossi and Mehrling, however. When a private party issues a liability there is a clear 'hierarchy of monies', and their analyses correctly predict that one must retire one's liability by delivering another liability – usually, one issued by an agent higher in the hierarchy. Liabilities of firms are mostly extinguished by delivering liabilities of banks; and banks extinguish their liabilities by delivering liabilities of the central bank. It should be obvious, but it usually does not appear to be so (see, for example Mehrling's (2000) confused discussion), that central bank liabilities do not differ in any significant degree from treasury liabilities. In other words, we can treat both as essentially 'high-powered money' or liabilities of the state (a point to which we will return below). But what is the state liable *for*? Rossi (1999) provides no clue, but Mehrling (2000) provides an attempt at an answer: The state is *liable* to deliver foreign currencies to extinguish its own liabilities. According to Mehrling (2000), when the state issues its 'fiat money', it is implicitly pledging to convert this to foreign currency. But why would the domestic agent accept the domestic currency solely because it will be converted to a foreign currency at a fixed exchange rate? We again encounter the infinite regress problem: we accept domestic currency that is convertible because foreigners will accept the foreign currency in payment; hence, we can use the foreign currencies to purchase imports or foreign assets.

Mehrling (2000) tries to finesse this by offering an argument that is not consistent with his general orientation, and which, more importantly, would seem to apply only to exceptional cases. In his view, government is nothing more than a giant firm that offers goods and services for sale – perhaps a giant Microsoft. The modern state is 'the one entity with which every one of us does ongoing business. We all buy from it a variety of services. . . . Just as we are each individually willing to extend temporary credits to individual business associates to whom we expect to be making payments in the future, so too we are all willing to extend credit to the government' (Mehrling, 2000, pp. 402–3). Hence, one accepts government fiat money because one knows one can buy goods and services from government by delivering the same government fiat money in payment. While this is not theoretically implausible, it does require that the government, like Microsoft, be a producer and not a consumer of the non-governmental sector's output. There may well be governments like that in the real world, but Mehrling's theory is not obviously applicable to the case of most governments around the world, which do provide some goods and services, but which are consistently very large net consumers of private sector output.

We now turn to the final issue, the exchange rate regime. In a fixed exchange rate regime, including a gold standard, the state promises to convert its fiat money to the reserve (foreign currency or gold) at a pre-arranged exchange rate. It must, therefore, hold reserves and its seigniorage is thereby reduced by the costs of maintaining this reserve. Further, it must carefully manage its emission of currency so as not to threaten its reserve holdings. Mehrling (2000), as noted above, advances the argument that one accepts the domestic fiat money because one's government promises to convert it to foreign currencies. Ignoring the infinite regress problem, this argument is plausible only for a fixed exchange rate system. In a floating currency system, the government makes no such promise. Certainly, those who hold the domestic currency probably do expect that they will be able to convert it to foreign currency in exchange markets, at whatever exchange rate happens to exist at the time the conversion is made. Further, they may well hold some expectations that government will intervene to try to stabilise exchange rates should their currency appreciate or depreciate significantly. But it would be quite a stretch to argue that they accept a fiat money from their state *because* they probably will be able to convert it in foreign exchange markets at an exchange rate that will not deviate wildly from today's exchange rate. Why not simply demand the foreign currency in payment today, and eliminate all the uncertainty? This is not to deny that the state might want to hold foreign currency reserves in order to minimise currency instability, that it might indeed give up its reserves to maintain orderly convertibility to foreign currencies, or that it might limit its emission of its fiat money in an attempt to avoid currency devaluation. However, it seems to be an exceedingly weak argument to maintain that a fiat money with no intrinsic value is accepted in payment for state purchases simply because the fiat money is expected to be marketable in foreign exchange markets in the future at an unguaranteed rate.

SOVEREIGNTY

We can develop an alternative view, one that is related to Goodhart's (1998) 'cartalist' or Knapp's (1905/1924) state money approach. In this view, the value of a currency is not linked to the value of the material from which it is produced. Nor is its value determined by reserves of precious metals or foreign currencies into which it might be converted. Note that the alternative view does not necessarily deny all of the logic of the metallist approach – one can envision a system in which the government issues a full-bodied coin or a paper money fully backed by precious metals (or foreign currencies) and at a fixed exchange rate. In such a system, one could imagine that the government could indeed obtain seigniorage by charging a coinage fee. Again, this is not the place to debate the historical accuracy of this speculative history. However, the alternative denies that this is helpful in developing an understanding of a modern nation, such as the United States or Japan, that operates on a 'fiat money' and a flexible exchange rate. We will call the alternative view the sovereignty approach because it links the state's ability to issue a currency denominated in the unit of account it has chosen, and without any explicit guarantee that the currency will be converted to anything (including precious metals or foreign currencies), to a fundamental power that is directly associated with sovereign nations. And, tellingly, this form of sovereign power is almost exclusively held by nation states and their delegates. It is a power that not even a Microsoft can hope to attain.

The easiest way to draw a contrast between the seigniorage approach and the sovereignty approach is to return to our discussion of fiat money as a 'liability' of the state. According to the seigniorage approach, so long as the government can emit a currency with greater purchasing power than required to produce it, seigniorage is obtained. And, as discussed above, we are left with the perplexing question as to why the non-state sector accepts a fiat money when it is not clear exactly what the state is 'liable' for. By contrast, the sovereignty approach, following Knapp (1905/1924), insists that the state is liable only to accept its fiat money in payments made to itself. The state might decide to make itself liable to deliver precious metals or foreign currencies at a fixed exchange rate, if it so chooses. Thus, in that special case, the state's liability goes beyond its agreement to accept its 'liabilities' in payments to the state to include other, self-imposed conditions. However, as discussed above, this special case is not relevant for most countries today (with the obvious exception of countries operating a currency-board type arrangement, as well as some others that operate with a somewhat less constraining exchange rate peg).

The general case today is one in which fiat money is a state 'liability' only in the sense that the state agrees to accept it at state pay offices. For what payments is the state accepting its fiat money in payment? We have already rejected Mehrling's (2000) belief that the state is nothing but a giant Microsoft, supplying goods and services to markets and accepting its liabilities in payment. It is clear that in the real world, most payments to the state consist of payments of taxes, fees, fines and interest. In all modern states, taxes are by far the most significant payments to the state, and easily dwarf sales by the state to the non-state sector.

For our purposes, sovereignty can be defined as the ability to impose tax liabilities, although in the past the ability to impose fees, fines, tithes and interest was more important than imposition of tax liabilities. Clearly, these payments are not voluntary at the individual level, although in democratic nations tax liabilities are at least in theory imposed by consensus. It should be emphasised that this ability to impose liabilities on the population does not presuppose an autocratic or fascistic state (as several critics – including Mehrling – have claimed). Even the most democratic of states impose taxes; indeed, it is somewhat paradoxical that the social democratic states (Scandinavian nations, for example) tend to impose relatively larger tax liabilities than do more oligarchically controlled states (the United States or Japan). All sovereign nations impose involuntary liabilities on their populations in the sense that the individual cannot choose to avoid the liabilities owed, even if the imposition of taxes is democratic. Of course, many kinds of taxes can be avoided by refraining from behaviour that is subject to taxation (by not earning income, one avoids an income tax; by eschewing tobacco, one avoids the cigarette tax, and so on). The simplest tax, the head tax or poll tax, is the most difficult to avoid; a residence tax could be avoided, but only at the cost of a serious diminution of comfort. Unavoidable taxes are probably better from the perspective that they distort behaviour to a lesser extent, and might better motivate the demand for the currency.

Our concept of sovereignty requires one further extension. It is not sufficient that the state is able to impose tax liabilities, for it must be able to designate the manner in which tax liabilities are to be 'worked off' or met. In all modern states, one eliminates one's tax liability by delivering the state's own liability – what we have been calling fiat money – at state pay offices. Why does one accept the state's liability? Because one is indebted to the state as a result of imposition of tax liabilities, and the state agrees to accept its own liabilities in retirement of the tax liabilities it imposes as a result of its sovereignty.

The sovereignty approach has several advantages over the seigniorage approach. Firstly, it avoids any infinite regress problem: all that is required is the ability to impose an unavoidable liability (such as a tax on one's head) and to name what must be delivered in tax payment. Secondly, it resolves the nominal, or unit of account, problem: the state names the unit of account (the dollar), imposes tax liabilities in that unit (a five-dollar head tax), and denominates its own 'fiat money' liabilities in that account (a one-dollar note).

We have not yet explained why the fiat money will have any purchasing power in terms of commodities produced in the non-state sector. If, for example, the state imposed a five-dollar head tax, but then distributed buckets of dollar-denominated fiat money about, free for the taking, then all could meet their tax liabilities without offering anything to the state. In this situation, the value of the fiat dollar would be close to zero, just sufficient to cover the cost and effort involved in locating buckets of 'free' money. More generally, the 'real' value of the dollar will be determined by the 'effort' involved in obtaining it, that is, the labour services or basket of commodities one must provide to obtain a fiat money dollar. For example, let us presume that the state only wants to purchase labour services – it hires police and fire-fighters to provide public safety services, soldiers to provide national defence, and IRS agents to collect the taxes it imposes – and offers to pay a dollar of state notes per hour of labour services hired. Setting to the side obvious labour heterogeneity complications, the fiat money dollar will be worth an hour of labour. If the state announces that it will offer two dollars per hour of labour, it will devalue the purchasing power of the dollar by half; if it lowers wages to half a dollar an hour, it will double the purchasing power of the dollar. Obviously, things are much more complicated in the real world, but further examination is not required to establish our point that 'real' purchasing power is maintained by ensuring it is 'difficult' to obtain the fiat money that is required to retire tax liabilities.

There are two real world complications that require brief analysis. Firstly, most payments in modern economies do not involve use of a fiat money; indeed, even taxes are almost exclusively paid using bank money. Secondly, fiat money is not emitted into the economy solely through treasury purchases of goods and services. In fact, the central bank supplies most of our currency, and it appears to supply almost all of the bank reserves that are from the point of view of the non-bank public perfect substitutes for treasury liabilities. Obviously if we simply consolidate the central bank and the treasury, calling the conglomerate 'the state', and combine treasury and central bank liabilities into a 'high-powered money' or 'fiat money', we eliminate these complications. When one uses a bank liability to pay 'the state', it is really the bank that provides the payment services, delivering the state's fiat money that results in a debit of the bank's reserves. When the state spends, it provides a check that once deposited in a bank leads to a credit to the bank's reserves. If one subsequently withdraws cash, bank reserves are debited. Note that payments using bank money within the private sector merely cause reserves to shift pockets from one bank to another, and thus can be entirely ignored. Ignoring for a second actions initiated by the central bank, only payments to the treasury or cash withdrawals from banks cause a reduction of banking system reserves, while payments by the treasury result in reserve credits to the banking system as a whole.

But the treasury is not the only source of reserve injections or deductions. Central banks principally provide reserves at the discount window or through open market purchases of sovereign debt, foreign currencies, or gold. They also can drain reserves by reversing these actions: unwinding loans at the discount window, or through open market sales of sovereign debt, foreign currencies or gold. In addition, central banks engage in various transactions with their treasury. However, these internal actions have no implications for the non-state sector. For example, a central bank might buy treasury debt and credit the treasury's deposit at the central bank, but this has no impact on banking system reserves until the treasury uses its deposit – for example, by purchasing labour or non-state sector output. Hence, strictly internal actions involving only the central bank and treasury should be ignored, which is the main justification for consolidating their accounts.

Just as the 'external' world does not care about the accounting manoeuvres practised by husband and wife within the household, the internal accounting machinations between the central bank and the treasury are not important for our analysis. Many economists find all this very confusing, because they do not understand the nature of the internal accounting procedures followed by the central bank and the treasury – procedures that they have imposed on themselves and which are not dictated by logical necessity. For example, the treasury spends by drawing on an account it holds at the central bank, relying on the central bank to debit its account and credit a bank's reserves. It would be more transparent, but would change nothing of significance, if the treasury simply spent by crediting a private bank account directly. Similarly, taxpayers send checks to the treasury, which deposits them at the central bank, leading to a credit to the treasury's account and a debit to the private bank's reserves. Again, it might be easier for economists to follow the steps if the payment of taxes simply led to a direct reduction of bank reserves by the treasury. Things are made even more complex because the treasury maintains accounts at private banks, depositing its tax receipts, then moving the deposits to the central bank to offset concurrent spending. Obviously, so long as treasury deposits are held within the banking system, there is no impact on banking system reserves, and, hence, treasury deposits at private banks can be ignored, because the bank simply debits the taxpayer's account and credits the treasury's account.

We do not want to devote a lot of space to all this accounting, as it has already been examined in detail by Wray (1998) and Bell (2000). The only logic that is necessary to grasp is that the state 'spends' by emitting its own liability (mostly taking the form of a credit to banking system reserves). On the state's consolidated balance sheet, its liability increases by the amount of the purchase, and its asset increases by the amount of the purchase. The non-state sector records an offsetting action: its asset is reduced by the transfer of its production to the state, but its balance sheet is credited by the amount of the sale. A tax payment is just the opposite: the state's asset (a tax liability owed by the non-state sector) is reduced, as is the state's liability (banking system reserves); for the non-state sector, the tax liability owed is reduced, and its reserves held as an asset are debited. And all this works only because the state has first exerted its sovereignty by imposing a tax liability on the non-state sector. The state's ability to purchase by emitting its liabilities is only the second step; by ignoring the state's sovereign power to impose tax liabilities in the first place, analysts like Rossi (1999) and Mehrling (2000) wrongly conclude that the state's position is no different from that of any other agent that issues liabilities. The state is different because it uses its sovereign power to impose liabilities.

Treasury procedures followed for its issues of interest-paying debt add another layer of complication that befuddles economists like Mehrling and Rossi. Economists have long believed that the government must either 'print money' or 'borrow' whenever it deficit spends. However, as we have shown, government always spends by crediting reserves to the banking system. Taxes drain these reserves, but a government deficit means that some of the created reserves are not drained by taxes. The non-bank public absorbs some of these net reserves as it draws down deposits (obtaining currency), resulting in a clearing drain from the banking system. Banks, in turn, use reserves for clearing of accounts among one another (which merely shifts reserves from pocket to pocket), and for clearing with the government (which reduces banking system reserves). At any point in time, the banking system will likely desire to hold a net reserve position, as each bank holds a positive reserve position to deal with anticipated clearing drains (with the public, with other banks, and with the state). In systems like that of the United States, in which reserves do not earn interest, profit-seeking behaviour of banks will lead to minimisation of net reserve holdings.

When an individual bank holds more reserves than desired, it will seek to lend the excess in overnight markets (the federal funds market in the United States). As is documented in every money and banking textbook, the United States also imposes required reserve ratios on banks, against certain kinds of deposits. While much is made of this, it adds nothing of substance to our analysis. If desired reserve holdings are above legal reserve requirements (as they now are for many banks in the United States), then it is only the excess above desired holdings (and not the excess above legally required holdings) that will place downward pressure on overnight interest rates. If legal requirements are above what is desired by banks for clearing, then only the excess above legally required reserves will pressure overnight rates. Much has also been made of contemporaneous versus lagged reserve accounting. Contemporaneous reserve accounting simply eliminates any 'slop', that is, any excess reserve leads to immediate impacts on overnight rates. Lagged reserve accounting builds a very small 'buffer' into the system, because banks can try to adjust balance sheets during a brief settlement period in order to bring reserve holdings into line with deposits held at some point in the past.[1] However, the reality is that regardless of the accounting method used, excess reserves above what is legally required or desired will cause overnight rates to fall, while insufficient reserves cause overnight rates to rise.

Post Keynesians have gone to great lengths to demonstrate that reserves are not discretionary from the point of view of the central bank, which supplies reserves 'horizontally' or on demand. If it did not do so, it would not be able to hit its overnight interest rate target. This has been examined sufficiently that no further exposition is warranted. What has been largely ignored, however, is that 'horizontal' central bank operations that add reserves through open market purchases, or that drain reserves through open market sales, account for a rather small proportion of adjustments to bank reserve positions. They are absolutely dominated by treasury impacts on reserve positions. As discussed above, government spending adds reserves, while taxes drain them; hence, deficits result in net credits and surpluses result in net debits. While the central bank can offset such actions if they create excess or insufficient reserves, the central bank's interventions are necessarily limited. Continuous open market sales to drain excess reserves created by deficit spending are most problematic, because the central bank will eventually run out of treasury debt to sell. However, informal procedural rules also limit central bank purchases, although there is no limit implied by double entry bookkeeping (since the central bank buys assets by crediting banks with reserves, there is no theoretical limit to its ability to do this).

In any case, in all modern economies, there is a division of responsibilities such that the central bank is responsible for draining/adding reserves on a day-to-day basis (often referred to as offsetting operating factors), while the treasury is responsible for draining/adding reserves over a longer run. It does this by selling/retiring sovereign debt. Whenever it runs a sustained deficit, it will be adding reserves to the system, which will likely generate excess reserve positions. Sales of new sovereign debt then drain the excess reserves. Banks will almost always prefer interest-earning treasury debt over non-interest earning excess (undesired and/or unrequired) reserves, hence there is no problem selling the treasury debt. Note, also, that if there were a problem, the treasury would simply avoid selling the debt, and, indeed, would not need to sell the debt as the banks preferred in this instance to hold non-interest-earning reserves.

In other words, far from requiring the treasury to 'borrow' by selling new issues, government deficits only require the central bank and treasury to drain excess reserves to avoid downward pressure on overnight interest rates.[2] On the other hand, sustained budget surpluses drain reserves and can eventually cause bank reserve positions to fall short of what is desired and/or required. Over the short run, the central bank provides needed reserves through open market purchases; over the longer run, the treasury rectifies the reserve drain by retiring outstanding debt. In effect the public surrenders its interest-earning sovereign debt in order to pay 'excessive' taxes that result from budget surpluses and that would otherwise drain required and/or desired reserves from the banking system.[3] Treasury debt could be eliminated entirely if the central bank were to simply pay interest on reserves, or if the central bank were to adopt zero as its overnight interest rate target. In either case, the central bank would be able to hit its target regardless of the size of the treasury's deficit; hence, there would be no need for sales of sovereign debt. In such a system, budget surpluses would trigger central bank loans of reserves, at the overnight rate.

This brings us back to the final issue, which is the relation between the exchange rate system and sovereignty. In a flexible exchange rate system operating with a fiat money, the overnight interest rate is exogenous, set by the monetary authorities. The treasury 'borrowing' rate will be closely aligned with this rate as arbitrage will keep rates on short-term debt essentially equal to the overnight rate target, and long-term sovereign debt will have a rate that is largely determined by expectations of future overnight rate targets. No amount of deficit or surplus spending by the treasury will cause overnight rates to move away from the central bank's target, nor will international capital flows impact the overnight rate – although they may affect exchange rates. On the other hand, a nation that uses a fiat currency but that adopts a fixed exchange rate (based on a gold standard, or a peg against other rates, or a currency board) will not, in general, be able to exogenously set its overnight rate. Because the state in such a system will have to maintain reserves (of gold or of other currencies, depending on the type of fixed exchange rate adopted) in order to maintain its peg, it faces the probability that it will have to adjust interest rates to try to retain sufficient reserves. An actual or expected drain of reserves (again, of gold or foreign currency) will likely lead to an increase of the overnight interest rate target to stem the drain. For similar reasons, the treasury of such a nation will be constrained in its ability to deficit spend, fearing that deficits that are too large could result in an economy so robust as to generate a clearing drain with other nations (resulting, for example, from a trade deficit).

Even in the absence of a trade deficit, the government operating with a fixed exchange rate would face a constraint, because its deficit would result in domestic currency emission. On a strict gold standard (with 100 per cent gold reserves) or a strict currency board arrangement, government spending would be rigidly constrained by its accumulation of gold or foreign currency (respectively). But even in a more flexible system (with a pegged exchange rate, but without 100 per cent reserves), government would fear deficits because these would leverage its reserve holdings. Hence, government spending on a fixed exchange rate system is constrained, in addition to the constraints imposed on monetary policy by exogenous interest rates, as discussed above – both fiscal and monetary policy are constrained. In a very real sense, a country that adopts fixed exchange rates surrenders a great deal of its sovereignty.

As we have seen, in a nation that operates with a fiat money on a floating exchange rate, treasury debt is really nothing more than reserves that pay interest, and the purpose of sovereign debt issue is to drain excess reserves to allow the central bank to hit its overnight interest rate target. This really cannot be called a borrowing operation – it makes no sense to argue that a government operating in such a system needs to 'borrow' its own liabilities in order to deficit spend. Hence, it also makes no sense to speak of 'default risk' of home-currency-denominated sovereign debt issued by a nation operating a floating exchange rate. Such a government will always be able to pay interest and retire principal by crediting banking system reserves. In contrast, a government operating in a fixed exchange rate regime may be forced to default on its commitment to convert its liabilities to the reserve asset at a fixed exchange rate – whether that reserve is gold or foreign currencies.

Hence, there is default risk on sovereign debt issued in a fixed exchange rate regime. Similarly, if a state issues liabilities denominated in a foreign currency, its sovereign debt is subject to default risk for the simple reason that it will not be able to pay interest and retire principal by crediting bank reserves.

Any sovereign state that has the ability to impose mostly unavoidable tax liabilities will be able to issue a fiat money. It will be able to exogenously maintain overnight interest rates so long as it adopts a floating exchange rate. It will be able to deficit spend, purchasing goods and services by crediting bank reserves. It will never need to borrow before it can spend, although if it wishes to maintain overnight rates at a positive level, it will need to offer an interest-bearing alternative to non-interest-earning excess reserves. This does not mean that deficit spending is always desirable, nor does it mean that government should ignore impacts of deficits or exogenously set low interest rates on domestic inflation or on exchange rates. While I believe that most economic theories regarding the impact of government spending and monetary policy on inflation, long-term interest rates, and exchange rates are largely wrong-headed, this lies beyond the scope of the present chapter. Here, it is only necessary to establish the minimum possibilities for the operation of sovereign power.

Many nations have chosen not to exercise sovereign power up to these minimum limits, however. They have chosen to fix exchange rates, to issue government debt denominated in a foreign currency, or to operate with a currency board. When a country chooses, say, to operate a currency board based on the US dollar, it allocates to the United States a measure of its sovereignty. Its government will have to borrow dollars or obtain dollars through its tax system (which, ultimately, must come from exports, asset sales, or borrowing) in order to spend. Economists often claim this gives seigniorage revenue to the United States, because the demand for dollars allows the United States to buy the exports of the nation operating the dollar currency board without ever supplying real goods and services in return. The United States is said to get a 'free lunch'. There is some truth in this claim, particularly if we ignore the negative impacts on the US economy (possible loss of jobs and industry, depression of aggregate demand) that result only if the United States does not adopt policy to ensure full employment at home. If we think of US exports as a 'cost' and US imports as a 'benefit' to Americans, then a trade deficit that is produced by nations wanting dollars to hold as reserves does generate a free lunch for the US economy taken as a whole, all else equal. By extension, even those nations that have chosen to float their currencies but that attempt to accumulate dollars as a liquid reserve (perhaps to be used as desired to dirty the float) provide some free lunches to the US economy.

There are two misconceptions about this that must be addressed, however. Firstly, it is necessary to determine who in the United States reaps this 'seigniorage income'. Secondly, it is necessary to determine whether other nations can reap 'seigniorage income' or does the United States alone gain such income through its 'hegemonic' power, as is often claimed. We will examine these issues in the last section.

THE SEIGNIORAGE INCOME OF THE UNITED STATES

Within any sovereign nation that operates with a domestic currency and a floating rate regime, only the state has the power to impose tax liabilities. As we have claimed, this is a critical component of sovereign power – although by no means is it the only power claimed by the sovereign. By imposing taxes, the state can move resources to itself. All modern states rely heavily on a monetary system, first imposing taxes to create a demand for the currency, then issuing the currency to buy desired resources. The use of money by the state is what disguises the nature of sovereign power. When the state seizes financial and real assets (sometimes for failure to pay taxes, sometimes as fines for criminal activity, and sometimes through use of eminent domain), the veil of money obscuring the nature of sovereignty is removed. All other economic agents in the sovereign nation must use income or issue debt or rely on charitable giving (including that of the state) or engage in petty production to obtain resources. No other economic agent can issue liabilities that represent final means of payment for itself. Hence, even though the rest of the world wishes to accumulate dollars, this gives no particular advantage to any non-sovereign economic agent in the United States. When a US non-sovereign consumer purchases an imported Toyota, she either gives up income or sells an asset or issues a liability to finance the purchase. The Japanese exporter holds a dollar claim on a US bank that will probably be converted in the market to a yen claim on a Japanese bank, which in turn will go to the market to convert a dollar reserve to a yen reserve at the Bank of Japan.[4] When all is said and done, the American holds a new auto and someone (the Japanese bank, or a domestic or foreign non-bank entity, or possibly the Bank of Japan) holds dollar reserves at the Fed. However, from the perspective of the American owning the new Toyota it certainly does not feel like she got 'something for nothing' – she used her income, or sold an asset, or committed herself to payments on debt. As economists are fond of saying, there is no free lunch. And if the United States does not operate an enlightened full employment policy at home, the net result of all this could be lost automobile manufacturing jobs in the United States.

By contrast, if the US government chooses to import a Toyota, it truly can 'get something for nothing' – issuing dollar reserves that eventually find their way to the Bank of Japan. But is this seigniorage? Not really, or, in any case, it is no different from a domestic purchase by a sovereign state. Any sovereign state obtains 'something for nothing' by imposing a tax liability and then issuing the currency used by those with tax liabilities to meet the obligation. The only difference in our example is that the US government has obtained output produced outside the United States, by those who are not subject to its sovereign power – in other words, by those not subject to US taxes. However, even within any nation there can be individuals who avoid and evade taxes imposed by the sovereign power, but who are still willing to offer their output to obtain the sovereign's currency. This is so because those who are not able to avoid and evade taxes need the currency, hence, are willing to offer their own output to obtain the currency. The US dollar has value outside the United States because US taxpayers need the currency. By this we do not mean to imply that US currency is only used to pay taxes, or that those who hold US currency or reserve deposits at the Fed do so on the knowledge that US taxpayers want high-powered money to pay taxes. Analytically, however, it is the sovereign power of the US government that allows it to issue currency and reserves that are demanded domestically and abroad. Take away the US treasury's sovereign power to impose dollar taxes, and the world demand for dollars would wither away. Hence, whatever 'seigniorage' there is, it is at bottom derived from sovereign power.

The question is whether the US government is alone in its ability to issue sovereign currency accepted by those who are not subject to the sovereign's taxes. Obviously, it is not. Other sovereign states operating on a floating exchange rate regime and with a domestic currency are able to obtain the same 'seigniorage income' that the US government can obtain. And, just as in the case of the United States, the ability to obtain 'seigniorage income' is at bottom related to sovereignty – only the state has this power. Surely this cannot be controversial. Still, it can be argued that the United States reaps far more 'seigniorage income' than other nations, because dollar reserves (broadly defined to include US treasury debt as well as US currency and reserves held at the Fed) relative to the size of the US economy might be larger than the relative size of foreign holdings of sovereign debt for most other nations. Here, however, we should distinguish between sovereign purchases and non-sovereign purchases. While 'seigniorage income' is sometimes equated to the total quantity of net imports, as we have shown above imports purchased by the non-sovereign population do not provide any 'free lunch'. It is only the portion of a trade deficit that is due to sovereign purchases that can be said to provide a free lunch and seigniorage income to the sovereign power. Properly defined, then, US 'free lunches' are not nearly so large as commonly claimed by reference to the United States as the 'world's largest debtor nation'.

The remaining question is whether these free lunches result from US hegemonic power, or do they result mostly from self-imposed rules adopted by other nations. Let us first recognise that the United States is the lone remaining superpower and that it exercises military and political power in its perceived interest. It could probably force any nation to adopt a currency board based on the dollar. It could probably annex any nation and subject the population to all the sovereign power imposed on US citizens. This could be done, perhaps has been done, to relatively weak Latin American nations, and with very few global repercussions. It would be more difficult to do this to large OECD nations, and it is doubtful that the United States has attempted to do so, or even would attempt to do so.[5] It seems far more probable that most nations (and individuals) around the world that are holding large dollar reserves (again, including US treasury debt and deposits at the Fed) are doing so on the basis of what they see to be in their own self interest.

This is probably due, in part, to the sheer size of the US economy – the world's elephant. However, the desire to hold dollar reserves could never be satisfied if the United States did not run trade deficits (particularly given the low levels of official aid offered by the United States). US trade deficits, in turn, require that the rest of the world, taken as a whole, desires to sell more output to the United States than it is willing to buy from the United States. It takes two to tango. Given the rest of the world's desire to accumulate dollar reserves and its lack of desire to consume US output, the United States is 'forced' to reap seigniorage income.[6] If, say, Japan and Euroland decided to pump up their economies sufficiently to eliminate their trade surpluses, they, too, would be 'forced' to reap some seigniorage income, and US seigniorage income would probably decline as exports to these nations rose. The counter argument is that only the United States can run persistent trade deficits without causing exchange rate depreciation. Perhaps – but this, too, requires 'two to tango'. So long as the rest of the world wants more dollar reserves, the dollar will remain strong even in the presence of a US trade deficit. Under the current 'rules of the game' adopted by most nations of the world, national economic success is measured by the quantity of dollar reserves accumulated, just as mercantilist nations measured success by gold inflows. Perhaps if economists understood the principles of sovereignty, the game would be played differently.

NOTES

1. See Wray (1990) for a detailed discussion.
2. In the United States complicated procedures are followed, often involving specially designated private banks, but this changes nothing of substance. The treasury attempts to minimise any effects on reserves by selling sovereign debt concurrently with its deficit spending. If it correctly gauges the exact size and timing of its receipt of taxes, as well as private sector deposits of its checks into the banking system, it will be able to place sovereign debt at just the right time and in just the right magnitude to ensure that there will be no impact on banking system reserves. In that case, the Fed will not have to intervene. In practice, this is quite difficult to do. However, the Fed can easily determine whether there are too many, or too few, reserves by watching the overnight rate. See Bell (2000).
3. Again, the treasury can pre-emptively retire debt concurrently with its surplus tax collection so that no central bank intervention is required to restore reserves when the government runs surpluses.
4. Alternatively, the Japanese bank could keep dollar reserves, or could convert them to US treasury debt, which is essentially just interest-earning reserves. Note also that these transactions could have implications for exchange rates, which might induce Bank of Japan or Fed interventions into foreign exchange markets – something we can ignore.
5. It is indeed probable that attempts to manage a far-flung empire would actually reduce 'free lunches' because of the costs incurred.
6. Fiscal austerity such as that adopted during the 1990s reduces the seigniorage income.

REFERENCES

Bell, S. (2000), 'Do taxes and bonds finance government spending?', *Journal of Economic Issues*, **34** (3), 603–20.

Black, S. (1989), 'Seigniorage', in J. Eatwell, M. Milgate and P. Newman (eds), *The New Palgrave: Money*, New York and London: Norton, 314.

Goodhart, C.A.E. (1989), *Money, Information and Uncertainty*, Cambridge: MIT Press.

Goodhart, C.A.E. (1998), 'The two concepts of money: implications for the analysis of optimal currency areas', *European Journal of Political Economy*, **14** (3), 407–32.

Haslag, J.H. (1998), 'Seigniorage revenue and monetary policy', Federal Reserve Bank of Dallas *Economic Review*, third quarter, 10–20.

Knapp, G.F. (1905), *Die Staatliche Theorie des Geldes*, München and Leipzig. English edition: *The State Theory of Money*, Clifton: A.M. Kelley, 1924.

Mehrling, P. (2000), 'Modern money: fiat or credit?', *Journal of Post Keynesian Economics*, **22** (3), 397–406.

Rossi, S. (1999), 'Review of Wray's *Understanding Modern Money: The Key to Full Employment and Price Stability*', *Kyklos*, **52** (3), 483–5.

Wray, L.R. (1990), *Money and Credit in Capitalist Economies: The Endogenous*

Money Approach, Aldershot and Brookfield: Edward Elgar.

Wray, L.R. (1998), *Understanding Modern Money: The Key to Full Employment and Price Stability*, Cheltenham and Northampton: Edward Elgar.

6. Asymmetric Information, Credit Rationing and the Stiglitz and Weiss Model

Santonu Basu

INTRODUCTION

The theoretical explanation of credit rationing principally emerged from the failure of the 'availability doctrine', which attempted to provide an alternative explanation of how monetary policy works in the presence of interest inelastic investors. The essential argument was that the suppliers of loanable funds are more sensitive to changes in the interest rate than their borrowers. Thus even if investors are less sensitive to changes in the interest rate, monetary policy still works via the suppliers' sensitivity to changes in the interest rate, and as a result they will reduce the supply of loans when the interest rate increases.[1] This paradoxical statement challenges the very fabric of the rationality of entrepreneurs upon which much of our economic theory rests. Therefore, the availability doctrine had the formidable task of explaining why rational profit-maximising bankers in the presence of excess demand chose to introduce a non-price rationing device rather than raise the interest rate. In other words, when bankers have the opportunity to increase their profit by increasing the interest rate, why do they decide to reduce the supply of loans? This literature could not provide a satisfactory explanation to the above question.[2] It soon became clear that there was a need to develop a theory of credit rationing.[3]

The essential argument of the credit rationing literature is that the capacity to repay the loan does not rise proportionately with the rise in the contractual payment, which emerges as a result of an increase either in the interest rate or in the size of the loan, thereby introducing default risk. Thus an increase in the interest rate or in the size of the loan will not necessarily in all circumstances increase the expected profitability. In fact, it often may reduce the expected profitability, and as a result banks on these occasions introduce a non-price form of rationing. Thus the essence of the argument is that higher interest rates or larger loans increase the default risk, thereby reducing bankers' expected profitability and thus banks introduce a non-price rationing device.[4] This result was derived from the well-known theoretical argument that while the rates of return on an investment project increase as the size of the investment increases, beyond a certain point the return increases at a declining rate, reaches an optimality point, and then falls. In other words, this is based on the second-order condition of differential equations, which is that the rate of return and the size of the investment are not monotonically related. But the contractual payment is an increasing function of the interest rate or size of the loan. This means that the contractual payment must converge to the rate of return of an investment project before reaching the optimality point of the investment project. As the investment ceases at the optimality point, the issue of rationing does not arise. This leads to an interesting question: why do borrowers (that is, investors) not cease to borrow at the convergence point or just before it, since at that point investors' net return will be zero? In particular, when borrowers know that in the event of default, as Jaffee and Modigliani (1969) point out, the lender becomes the owner of the firm, why does a borrower, knowing the outcome of the default, wilfully invite such an outcome? This leaves theoreticians with an uneasy question to resolve. There thus appears to be a need to provide a rationale as to why default risk increases, given the situation described above.

Stiglitz and Weiss's (1981) theoretical explanation of credit rationing is an attempt to remove this weakness that follows from Hodgman (1960) to Jaffee and Modigliani (1969). Stiglitz and Weiss's basic argument is that changes in the interest rate adversely affect the amalgam of good and bad borrowers and, as a result, banks introduce a non-price rationing device. Following the development of their explanation, Blinder and Stiglitz (1983) subsequently attempt to provide an alternative explanation of the working of monetary policy in the light of Stiglitz and Weiss's model. In this chapter we will carefully and critically re-examine the Stiglitz and Weiss model.

THE STIGLITZ AND WEISS MODEL

Stiglitz and Weiss's argument rests on the notion that while borrowers' capacity to pay may be known to the bankers from the borrowers' expected return from their projects, what is not known to bankers is the borrowers' risk. This is because of the presence of asymmetric information, which addresses the uncertainty that often emerges when one agent either deliberately distorts or does not disclose all the relevant information to another agent during their interaction phase.[5] On this occasion, the individual does not reveal his/her attitude towards risk, which is assumed to be a function of the individual's pecuniary situation. Accordingly, Stiglitz and Weiss (1981) argue that an increase in the interest rate may adversely affect the combination of good and bad borrowers owing to the presence of two effects, referred to as the adverse selection and incentive effects. The adverse selection effect states that those who have a preconceived notion that their probability to repay the loan is low are more likely to remain in the pool of loan applicants at a higher interest rate. The incentive effect suggests that as the higher interest rate reduces the expected net return of projects that succeed, borrowers or firms may be induced to switch from so-called low-risk to high-risk projects, where the probability of success is low, and where the return will be high in the event of success. Thus the essence of the argument is that, although capacity to pay may be known from the investment project, what is not recognised is that changes in the interest rate may bring about the above two effects, thereby altering the risk structure of the loan portfolio, and thus introducing the possibility of adversely affecting the borrowers' capacity to pay. In other words, changes in the interest rate may adversely affect the quality of loans, thereby reducing banks' expected profitability. Thus in the presence of excess demand a rational profit-maximising banker, instead of raising the interest rate, introduces a non-price form of rationing.[6]

Blinder and Stiglitz (1983) attempted to build on this model by providing an alternative explanation of how monetary policy works. Thus the essence of this argument is similar to that presented by the 'availability doctrine', which is that the suppliers of loanable funds are sensitive to changes in the interest rate: at higher rates of interest, suppliers of loanable funds may reduce the supply of loans. Thus monetary policy works via a reduction in the supply of loans.

Blinder and Stiglitz (1983) argue that individual banks have more information about their own clients than their competitors. If the interest rate increases and a bank decides to deny loans to some of their clients, these borrowers would be unable to receive loans from other lenders as it provides a signal to other banks that they are bad borrowers; otherwise their own bank would have offered loans to them. Borrowers would therefore have no other choice than to reduce their investment expenditures. This in turn would slow down economic activity.

However, information reveals that this is not necessarily the case; in fact, borrowers who have been denied loans indeed receive loans from other finance companies.[7] In fact, a variety of financial institutions have emerged to finance borrowers who traditionally have been denied loans from banks (see, for example, the Bangladesh Gramin bank). This not only raises doubts about Blinder and Stiglitz's explanation in relation to how the mechanism of monetary policy works, but more importantly raises the question of whether their explanation of credit rationing is adequate. This is the issue to which we turn now.

As the central argument is based on two key assumptions, that is, the adverse selection and incentive effects, we will confine our examination to these two assumptions, and explore whether they are adequate to establish why rationing emerges in the operation of the credit market.

RE-EXAMINING THE STIGLITZ AND WEISS MODEL

The adverse selection effect states that for those who have a preconceived notion that their probability to repay the loan is low, a higher interest rate is not likely to deter them from borrowing. As the interest rate increases, low-risk borrowers will leave the pool of loan applicants, thereby leaving only risky borrowers. Thus the interest rate itself acts as a screening device to identify risky borrowers, who then will be rationed by banks. But the problem with this assumption is that borrowers' riskiness is determined only by the fact that they have a preconceived notion of their low probability to repay the loan. In turn, they are unlikely to be concerned about the level of the interest rate, and are thus likely to remain in the pool of loan applicants when the interest rate is low. The higher interest rate may be able to identify high-risk borrowers, but lower interest rates cannot do the same. This means that high-risk borrowers are quite likely to receive loans when the interest rate is low. We should expect therefore a higher default rate at low interest rates. Furthermore, as far as rationing is concerned, the less-risky borrowers leave the pool of loan applications, leaving only the risky borrowers to be rationed.[8] This raises the question of whether bankers would not raise the interest rate because of the borrowers' interest elastic demand for loans, or because of their fear that it may increase the riskiness of the loans. Freimer and Gordon (1965, p. 416) argue that offering loans at a higher interest rate may not generate much demand, 'while it may encourage borrowers to negotiate loans within this limit at a lower interest rate'.

Stiglitz and Weiss's second assumption states that as the higher interest rate reduces investors' net return for projects that succeed, this may induce borrowers or firms to switch from a low-risk project to a high-risk project where the probability of success is low, and where the return will be high in the event of success. But Stiglitz and Weiss overlook two important factors that a firm may consider when making the decision to switch between projects following changes in the interest rate: (a) there is a cost associated with selection and switching between projects, and (b) the possibility of an adverse impact from the crowding out effect. The issue of the switching cost arises owing to the fact that investment expenditures are largely irreversible, and consist mostly of sunk costs. If a firm wishes to switch from a low-return to a high-return project, which may involve switching from either one industry to another or from a cheaper product to an expensive product, it must take into consideration the net loss that would accrue as a result of the sunk costs from the old project. A firm's capital (that is, plant and equipment), marketing and advertising techniques are to some extent specific to given projects. In principle, a firm should be able to sell its plant and equipment to any other firm that is involved in that specific project within that industry. However, as the value of plant and equipment will be about the same for all firms within this industry, it is unlikely that one firm will gain much, if anything at all, from selling it.

Furthermore, in the event of changes in the interest rate, if a firm considers that its net return from the current project is not sufficient in comparison with the high interest rate, then this view is quite likely to be shared by other firms operating in that industry. Therefore, all firms from that industry would have the same inducement effect, that is, they all would like to switch from low-return to high-return projects. In these circumstances, firms either will have no buyers for their plant and equipment, or will be forced to sell well below the current market value in order to induce other firms to buy. In either case, this suggests that a switch between projects involves a substantial loss to a firm, due to the irreversible costs.[9] It follows that once we consider the incorporation of the switching cost as well as the selection cost, the firm's net expected rate of return may not rise sufficiently to induce it to switch from a low- to a high-return project, even when the new project offers a higher expected rate of return.

On the other hand, if we assume that switching between projects does not necessarily imply switching from one industry to another industry, the sunk costs may be small but we cannot ignore the adverse impact of the crowding out effect. If all firms within the industry decide to switch from low-return projects to high-return projects (that is, from low-return products to high-return products), then this movement will in turn not only reduce the return of the so-called high-return projects, but also increase the risk of the projects, because of the greater competition that emerges as a result of the greater supply of firms. This is equally applicable in the case of switching between industries.

The above argument suggests that switching between projects in the event of changes in the interest rate is possible provided we assume capital is malleable[10] (since malleable capital has properties that eliminate the additional costs involved in switching) and there exists an unlimited demand in the market to absorb all additional firms without adversely affecting the price of the product. It follows that if the switching between projects involves satisfying the above two conditions, then it is unlikely that existing firms that are already committed to projects will be in a position to make any possible additional gain by switching from those with low returns to those with higher returns. Thus the possibility of receiving a lower expected net return remains high in the event of high interest rates, irrespective of the choice of projects, that is, irrespective of whether firms choose to continue with the old project or switch to a new one. This leaves us to deal with firms that are yet to commit to any project. The question is whether a higher interest rate will induce these firms to switch from a low-risk to a high-risk project. But the problem is that as interest rates oscillate (virtually from month to month), the process of production from its initial state to the completion period in general takes a longer period, during which the variation in the interest rate will cause the expected net return of a project to oscillate too. Consequently, it becomes impossible for the investor to calculate the expected net return of his project with any precision. In the absence of knowledge of the future oscillation of the interest rates, he must wait until the completion of the production process. The problem is that the level of the interest rate is one of the many factors that play a role in the decision to invest in any project, and therefore it may be too demanding to suggest that an investor's decision to invest in any project will be influenced by the level of interest rate alone.

Furthermore, the higher expected rate of return and the risk are not the only two criteria on the basis of which entrepreneurs select their projects. Entrepreneurs are also influenced by their knowledge and familiarity with that project. In most cases, entrepreneurs do not have sufficient information in relation to all projects available to them, leading them to select the project they know best, and this is to some extent irrespective of the level of the interest rate. This therefore suggests that there are limitations in the selection of a project even after changes in the interest rate, owing either to unfamiliarity with other available projects or to the additional cost that will be involved in switching between projects.

Thus it is difficult to establish the proposition that an increase in the interest rate will bring about the possibility of a large-scale incentive effect, thereby introducing the possibility of adversely affecting borrowers' capacity to pay. Thus a careful examination of the two assumptions devised by Stiglitz and Weiss to explain why bankers, in the presence of excess demand, do not raise the interest rate, suggests that neither provides a convincing reason for the possible adverse effect of interest rate increases on borrowers' capacity to pay. This perhaps suggests that the Stiglitz and Weiss model is not adequate to explain why bankers' ration credit. There is therefore a limitation in extending this model to explain the working of monetary policy.

CONCLUSION

It is not our view that the process of credit rationing has nothing to contribute to our understanding of the working of monetary policy. In fact, during tight monetary policy, smaller borrowers' access to the loan market is normally reduced, and as a result we observe many small business failures. To show why this occurs we need to develop a new analysis of credit rationing. The Stiglitz and Weiss model is not adequate for this analysis.

The fundamental problem in the Stiglitz and Weiss model is that it attempts to determine the direction of the risk on an a priori basis. In order to do this, Stiglitz and Weiss use the individual's pecuniary position as a proxy for the determination of the direction of risk, and this appears to be demanding too much. Stiglitz and Weiss assume that if in an investment project a borrower's own wealth constitutes a small fraction of the total investment, then this borrower is likely to take a greater risk, since he has less to lose in the event of project failure. The interpretation here is that the attitude towards risk is inversely related to the borrower's pecuniary position. Thus, although an individual's attitude towards risk is not known, if we know his/her pecuniary position, then the direction of the attitude towards risk can be predicted. This is what we call the hidden variable approach to uncertainty analysis. But this is not sufficient; one must have the opportunity to make an additional gain from undertaking additional risk. The problem with this approach is that once we incorporate further information or re-arrange the information set within the frame of hidden variable analysis, our result will change, as shown above. This raises the question whether uncertainty is associated with hidden variables or arises owing to missing information. In reality, of course, we know neither what governs an individual's attitude towards risk nor the impact of external variables, such as the pecuniary position, upon an internal variable such as the attitude towards risk. Further, an individual's attitude towards risk changes over time and space, independently of the state of his/her pecuniary position. Therefore, whatever our subjective opinion may be about the individual's attitude towards risk, it cannot be predicted accurately from the individual's pecuniary position, although we cannot ignore the importance of the latter factor in the consideration of the loan equation. The problem of uncertainty is not associated with some hidden variable, but arises from the incomplete nature of our information.

This may suggest that prior to investigating why borrowers' access to the loan market differs, we are required to investigate how the loan market operates in the presence of uncertainty. In other words, we require a new theory of credit rationing, as the existing theory does not take us far on this issue.[11]

NOTES

1. See Rosa (1951) and Tobin (1953) for elaboration on this line of argument.
2. See Smith (1956), Kareken (1957) and Scott (1957a, 1957b), all of whom searched for a satisfactory answer to the above question, but recognised themselves that their answer remained incomplete.
3. See Hodgman (1960) on this issue.
4. See Hodgman (1960), Chase (1961), Freimer and Gordon (1965) and Jaffee and Modigliani (1969) for elaboration on credit rationing.
5. See Basu (2001) for further elaboration on this issue.
6. See also Keeton (1979), Diamond (1984), Myers and Majluf (1984), Bester (1985, 1995), Williamson (1986), Besanko and Thakor (1987), Riley (1987), Bernanke and Gertler (1989), Gale (1989), Calomiris and Hubbard (1990), Jaffee and Stiglitz (1990), Gertler (1992), Bhattacharya and Thakor (1993), and Gertler and Gilchrist (1994) on this line of research.
7. See Bird and Juttner (1976) and Storey (1982) for further details on this finding.
8. Riley (1987, p. 226) points out that, 'the extent of rationing implied by the Stiglitz and Weiss model is not likely to be very important empirically'.
9. See Pindyck (1991) for more details on this issue.
10. See Garegnani (1978), who argues that at any given instant available physical capital cannot be fluid, so it cannot take an appropriate form to adjust to the new level of interest rates.
11. For further details on these issues see Basu (2002).

REFERENCES

Basu, S. (2001), 'Incomplete information and asymmetric information', *Zagreb International Review of Economics and Business*, **4** (2), 23–48.

Basu, S. (2002), *Financial Liberalization and Intervention: A New Analysis of Credit Rationing*, Cheltenham and Northampton: Edward Elgar.

Bernanke, B.S. and M. Gertler (1989), 'Agency costs, net worth, and business fluctuation', *American Economic Review*, **79** (1), 14–31.

Besanko, D. and A.V. Thakor (1987), 'Collateral and rationing: sorting equilibria in monopolistic and competitive credit markets', *International Economic Review*, **28**

(3), 671–89.

Bester, H. (1985), 'Screening vs. rationing in credit markets with imperfect information', *American Economic Review*, **75** (4), 850–5.

Bester, H. (1995), 'A bargaining model of financial intermediation', *European Economic Review*, **39** (2), 211–28.

Bhattacharya, S. and A.V. Thakor (1993), 'Contemporary banking theory', *Journal of Financial Intermediation*, **3** (1), 2–50.

Bird, R.G. and D.J. Juttner (1976), 'Financing problems of small firms in the manufacturing sector: the Australian case', *Kredit und Kapital*, **9** (3), 384–415.

Blinder, A. and J.E. Stiglitz (1983), 'Money, credit constraints, and economic activity', *American Economic Review*, **73** (2), 297–302.

Calomiris, C.W. and R.G. Hubbard (1990), 'Firm heterogeneity, international finance, and "credit rationing"', *Economic Journal*, **100** (399), 90–104.

Chase, S.B. (1961), 'Credit risk and credit rationing: comment', *Quarterly Journal of Economics*, **75** (2), 319–27.

Diamond, D.W. (1984), 'Financial intermediation and delegated monitoring', *Review of Economic Studies*, **51** (3), 393–414.

Freimer, M. and M.J. Gordon (1965), 'Why bankers ration credit', *Quarterly Journal of Economics*, **79** (3), 397–416.

Gale, W.G. (1989), 'Collateral, rationing and government intervention in credit markets', *NBER Working Paper*, 3083.

Garegnani, P. (1978), 'Notes on consumption, investment and effective demand: I', *Cambridge Journal of Economics*, **2** (4), 335–53.

Garegnani, P. (1979), 'Notes on consumption, investment and effective demand: II', *Cambridge Journal of Economics*, **3** (1), 63–82.

Gertler, M.L. (1992), 'Financial capacity and output fluctuations in an economy with multi-period financial relationships', *Review of Economic Studies*, **59** (3), 455–72.

Gertler, M.L. and S.G. Gilchrist (1994), 'Monetary policy, business cycles, and the behavior of small manufacturing firms', *Quarterly Journal of Economics*, **109** (2), 309–40.

Hodgman, D.R. (1960), 'Credit risk and credit rationing', *Quarterly Journal of Economics*, **74** (2), 258–78.

Jaffee, D.M. and F. Modigliani (1969), 'A theory and test of credit rationing', *American Economic Review*, **59** (5), 850–72.

Jaffee, D.M. and J.E. Stiglitz (1990), 'Credit rationing', in B.M. Friedman and F.H. Hahn (eds), *Handbook of Monetary Economics*, Amsterdam: Elsevier Science B.V., vol. I, 837–88.

Kareken, J.H. (1957), 'Lenders' preferences, credit rationing, and the effectiveness of monetary policy', *Review of Economics and Statistics*, **39** (3), 292–302.

Keeton, W.R. (1979), *Equilibrium Credit Rationing*, New York: Garland.

Myers, S.C. and N.S. Majluf (1984), 'Corporate financing and investment decisions when firms have information that investors do not have', *Journal of Financial Economics*, **13** (2), 187–221.

Pindyck, R.S. (1991), 'Irreversibility, uncertainty, and investment', *Journal of Economic Literature*, **29** (3), 1110–48.

Riley, J. (1987), 'Credit rationing: a further remark', *American Economic Review*, **77** (1), 224–7.

Rosa, R.V. (1951), 'Interest rates and the central bank', in *Money, Trade and*

Economic Growth: Essays in Honor of John Henry Williams, New York: Macmillan, 270–95.

Scott, I.O. (1957a), 'The availability doctrine: theoretical underpinnings', *Review of Economic Studies*, **25** (1), 41–8.

Scott, I.O. (1957b), 'The availability doctrine: development and implications', *Canadian Journal of Economics and Political Science*, **23** (4), 532–9.

Smith, W.L. (1956), 'On the effectiveness of monetary policy', *American Economic Review*, **46** (4), 588–606.

Stiglitz, J.E. and A. Weiss (1981), 'Credit rationing in markets with imperfect information', *American Economic Review*, **71** (3), 393–410.

Storey, D.J. (1982), *Entrepreneurship and the New Firm*, London: Croom Helm.

Tobin, J. (1953), 'Monetary policy and the management of the public debt: the Patman inquiry', *Review of Economics and Statistics*, **35** (2), 118–27.

Williamson, S.D. (1986), 'Costly monitoring, financial intermediation, and equilibrium credit rationing', *Journal of Monetary Economics*, **18** (2), 159–79.

PART TWO

THE THEORY OF THE MONETARY CIRCUIT

7. On Money and Endogenous Money: Post Keynesian and Circulation Approaches

Louis-Philippe Rochon[1]

INTRODUCTION

Post Keynesians and circuitists have been dialoguing for several years now on possible ways of reconciling their respective views on Keynes and related issues. The fruits of this initial dialogue appeared in *Économies et Sociétés* (a French journal edited by Alain Parguez), and culminated in *Money in Motion*, a book edited by Ghislain Deleplace and Edward J. Nell (1996). Despite best efforts, however, it appears that today much of the dialogue fell on deaf ears. In part, this is because of the different vocabulary and concepts used by each school, and also because of various degrees of emphasis on certain issues. For instance, post Keynesians place uncertainty at the very heart of their approach, while circuitists acknowledge the presence of uncertainty but tend to give it just lip service.

This has led to the conclusion that perhaps both schools are irreconcilable. This would be unfortunate since, at the core, there really is much in common between the two schools. Differences tend to be more a matter of emphasis than substance. For instance, on monetary issues, each school sees money as endogenous and the rate of interest as exogenous, determined by the policies of the central bank. These two elements alone should awaken us to the rich possibility of a reconciliation between the two schools, and to the fact that proponents of each school have much to learn from one another. In this sense, it is worth considering their respective contributions, though not all, in the areas of credit, money and interest rates.

In his recently edited book, Smithin (2000) asks the pertinent question, what is money? As he correctly points out, since production economies are monetary economies, then it becomes all the more important to discuss the nature of money. To be true to Keynes, in a 'monetary economy of production', money must be linked to production and cannot be added simply at any time or anywhere in the analysis (Lavoie, 1992). After all, this is the very definition of 'endogenous' money. Modern money is bank money or credit issued for the purpose of production. As Keynes asserted clearly in his post-*General Theory* articles (but see also his *Treatise on Money*), production begins only once firms have received credit from banks (see Rochon, 1997). Money is never neutral: neither in the short run nor in the long run.

Unfortunately, most economists do not give interesting or relevant answers to the question of what money is. Neoclassical economists simply treat money as an afterthought, assigning it roles and functions that have little to do with the economic process of production. In this sense, money can be analysed without any references to real factors.

Post Keynesians, on the other hand, have offered interesting insights into the relationship between money and production. They have correctly argued that money is endogenous. Modern credit money, income and the real economy are linked through the process of production. Despite recognising this, however, post Keynesians answer the question of what money is by focusing too narrowly on the roles and functions of money, that is, they have emphasised the demand for money for transactions, precautionary and speculative purposes, and discussed whether money is foremost a unit of account, a store of value or a medium of exchange.[2] The discussion has centered on the importance of uncertainty in its relation to the demand for money (Davidson, 1972/1978).

While this is certainly a useful debate, the discussion is premature in the sense that discussion over the roles and functions of money must come second. In the first instance, discussion must emphasise the creation of money, and only after discuss what this newly created money does. In other words, before money can be used for transactions, it must first be created.

Whereas post Keynesians emphasise the demand for money, circuit writers have emphasised the creation of money through the demand for bank credit. They have little to say about the roles and functions of money. According to circuitists, money is also endogenous, and the existence of money is tied to bank debt. In this literature, the link between credit, money, debt, income and production is carefully analysed. Like post Keynesians, circuit theorists emphasise the role of banks in the creation of money, but their approach to money is based primarily on the nature of money. They focus on the relationship between banks and firms, as the principal relationship, and only later look at the roles and functions of money, once created.

The purpose of this chapter is to suggest a marriage of post Keynesian and circuit approaches to credit and money, debt and banks. In doing so, however, we will keep the sequential analysis of economics advocated by circuit writers. This should pose no problems to post Keynesians who also emphasise the concept of historical time. This approach will hopefully help us to clarify some of the underlying debates. In the end, the differences are more apparent than real and a synthesis of both approaches can be reached leading to a more heterodox theory of endogenous money.

This chapter will analyse and contrast the contributions of post Keynesians and circuitists. By post Keynesians, we mean those authors more commonly associated with either the horizontalist tradition (in particular Moore, 1988; but also Kaldor, 1982) or the structuralist approach, defined broadly (Davidson, 1972/1978; Wray, 1990; Palley, 1994; Pollin, 1996). By circuitists, we mean Graziani (1984, 1996), Parguez (1996) and their followers. Of course, it is never an easy task to reduce the vast and at times conflicting contributions of the post Keynesians and circuitists, thus making the task of summarising that much more difficult.

Both approaches see money as resulting from specific social interactions. Money endogeneity is seen as a natural outcome. This said, post Keynesians and circuitists approach the issues in different ways. For instance, post Keynesians, both horizontalists and structuralists, see money endogeneity as essentially the result of some institutional feature, such as central bank accommodation, financial innovations or stages in the evolution of banking and central banking. Hence, money *became* endogenous given the specific institutional and economic structure. We will call this *institutional endogeneity*. By contrast, for the proponents of the theory of the monetary circuit the endogenous nature of money does not depend on any institutional feature but rather it depends on an hierarchical relationship inherent in monetary economies of production. In this sense, money is always and everywhere an endogenous phenomenon: money is endogenous irrespective of the stages of development of the banking system or of central banking, or of accommodation or financial innovations. This is precisely what Lavoie argues. 'Money is in some way endogenous *whether* central banks are dynamic or not' (Lavoie, 1984, p. 778; our translation). This is because money flows from debt and exists because economic agents are willing to enter into a debt relationship – the result of an existing hierarchy in the production process. Production cannot begin, and hence income cannot be formed, without the existence of debt issued by a third agent: banks.[3] Money is created by debt. As Bellofiore and Seccareccia (1999, p. 754) argue, '[m]oney is a credit instrument in a triangular transaction in which payments are settled by means of promises to pay from a third agent (a bank)'. Banks have the ability to create money because their liabilities, sanctioned by the state, are recognised as means of payment. This is *natural endogeneity* or, as Rochon (1999a) has called it, *revolutionary endogeneity*.

One possible way of reconciling both approaches is by referring to Lavoie's (1985) two poles of endogeneity. In this article, Lavoie argues that money endogeneity exists at two points in the analysis. For Lavoie, money is endogenous because of the relationship between firms and banks, on the one hand, and between banks and the central bank, on the other. So, we may argue that in debating the merits of endogenous money post Keynesians and circuitists refer to different poles of the analysis, and hence often debating at cross wits. While both poles are equally important, they are, in historical time, necessarily sequential in the analysis. The first pole is of primary emphasis (the creation of money), while the second pole is secondary, although by no means unimportant (the roles and functions of money). Circuitists emphasise the first pole of endogenous money (money *ab ovo*) while post Keynesians concentrate more on the second (money *ex post*).[4]

The implications of this chapter ought to be clear. Post Keynesian and circuit theories, far from being incompatible, are complementary. Proponents of each approach have much to learn from the other. Aspects of both can be merged together to form a single, coherent, heterodox theory of endogenous money, to which other issues, like financial markets and speculation, can be successfully added.

The remainder of this chapter is divided into three parts. The first part analyses the notions of money in post Keynesian and circuit approaches. As these notions are different, so are their respective views on how to define a theory of endogenous money, which is the topic of the second part. The last part brings the analysis together and concludes.

MONEY

The Post Keynesian Approach: The Functions of Money

For many post Keynesians money is a curiosity. Like their neoclassical counterparts, post Keynesians still define money according to its roles and functions: 'Money is what money does' (Hicks, 1967, p. 1). Post Keynesians define money foremost as a store of value and a unit of account, with uncertainty playing a central role. Given uncertainty, the debate was reduced to whether money is used mainly for speculative (see O'Donnell, 1989), precautionary (Chick, 1983) or transactions purposes. These discussions tell us nothing about the creation of money. They only apply to money once it has been created. 'What is money?' and 'where does money come from?' are two questions that are analysed separately: *what* money is (a unit of account, a medium of exchange, or a store of value) is different than *where* money comes from (bank loans). By compartmentalising the two questions, this may have contributed to unnecessary debates on the existence of money and on the meaning of endogenous money.[5]

The point of departure for post Keynesians is the discussion over the importance of uncertainty with respect to the demand for money for households and firms. Both agents seek, in an uncertain world, a way to make crucial decisions on how best to store wealth. Transactions costs reduce the effective yield of such assets and may prevent agents from holding them. Hence, the demand for money as a store of value has to do with the precautionary and the speculative demand for money (Davidson, 1972/1978, p. 189). Firms may see production costs rising in the uncertain future and may want to hold on to money for precautionary reasons. This seems to mean that money is primarily a stock that somehow must be allocated among the various reasons for which agents may demand it. This is precisely Wray's (1996, p. 440) conclusion as well: 'In contrast [to circuitists], most Post Keynesians have emphasized money as a stock'.

One possible reason for this is that post Keynesians appear to be primarily interested in arguing why money is not neutral – even in the long run – as opposed to how it is created. According to Davidson (1996, p. 62), '[t]he existence of the societal institution of legally enforceable forward contracts denominated in nominal (not real!) terms [creates] a monetary environment that is not neutral, even in the long run'. Uncertainty is the key argument.

The emphasis on the demand for money as a store of value (and presumably a supply) is a fundamental difference between post Keynesians and circuitists. Money is demanded because of its functions, and is somehow supplied to accommodate these needs. This leads to see money as some sort of good (or asset) that has a demand and supply function varying with its price. Changes in the rate of interest ought to eliminate any excesses. This is the inevitable acceptance of the existence of a money market. Emphasis is therefore on stock adjustments.

Accepting supply and demand analysis of money carries a number of implications. Winnett (1992, p. 48) notes that 'in posing the problem in terms of demand and supply functions for money, they [post Keynesians] have already made very large concessions to the neo-classical point of view, and they have denied themselves many possibilities for showing how their assumptions might form a coherent alternative'. This conclusion is close to that reached by Deleplace and Nell (1996, p. 8), who state that the theoretical foundations of the argument are methodologically derived from the quantity theory equation. Whether the demand for money is vertical (in the absence of a speculative demand for money) or downward-sloping (depending on the prevalence of the Keynesian speculative demand for money) is largely irrelevant. Secondly, supply and demand analysis is primarily static, and is interested in the overall allocation of a given stock of money or liquid assets, a portion of which is held in money: the money market must clear.

But the process of endogenous money in post Keynesian analysis is a dynamic process set within the context of historical time. Credit and money are flows that respond to the needs of the economy to reproduce itself and grow. If credit and money are flows, how then can we reconcile this with an apparatus that analyses economic magnitudes in terms of stocks? (The same logic applies to the IS–LM model.) This was the argument made by Arestis (1997, p. 56), who claims that there 'is a logical objection to trying to represent an analysis of flows in a diagram designed to show the behaviour of stocks'.

Finally, supply and demand analysis recognises the existence of a money *market*, where demand and supply functions determine a price and a quantity, as well as an equilibrium position. It also recognises the possible existence of excess demands and supplies of money, eliminated through changes in the rate of interest (Howells, 1995), irrespective of whether the supply curve is vertical or upward-sloping.[6]

Separately, each function has its problems, too. By drawing a demand curve, post Keynesians acknowledge that the demand for money, for instance, is inversely related to the rate of interest. Money is an asset among many others that is held for reasons of liquidity. Since it has no return (or less than most other assets),[7] holding money carries opportunity costs. It enters the theory of portfolio allocation, or what Nell (1967, p. 386) calls the 'theory of choice'. If this is the case, then an explanation must be offered for why money is held.

Post Keynesians link money to the existence of uncertainty. Households prefer holding bonds to money because the future is by definition uncertain (unknown and unknowable in a non-ergodic world). Dow (1996) believes that increased information (hence less uncertainty) leads to the increased weight of an argument. This then translates into a fall in the demand for money as an asset.

> Weight is derived from the relative amount of relevant evidence brought to bear on the (generally unquantifiable) estimation of probability. The greater the amount of relevant evidence, the greater the degree of confidence with which expectations

may be held as to the relative returns on alternative assets, and thus the less the demand for money which earns no monetary return. New evidence, therefore, which increases confidence in expectations thus reduces money's liquidity relative to the expected return on alternative assets, and may also reduce the discount on the expected return on alternative assets, both encouraging a fall in the demand for money (Dow, 1996, p. 38).

Money exists *because* of uncertainty (see also Davidson, 1972/1978). According to Dow (1996, p. 36), '[m]oney's role itself is the product of uncertainty'. As Dymski (1996, p. 385) correctly points out, uncertainty is the 'entry point' of Davidson's post Keynesianism. Indeed, for Davidson (1972/1978, p. 144), '[i]t is only in a world of uncertainty and disappointment that money comes into its own'. Money's perfect liquidity and its ability to deal with uncertainty give money intrinsic value (Davidson, 1972/1978; Dymski, 1996). According to Dow (1996, p. 37), '[l]iquidity preference thus follows from money's central economic role as the asset whose value is most certain'. Dymski (1996, p. 381) claims that 'exogenous uncertainty creates a need for a store of value: agents' willingness to undertake time-using activities may entail a desire simply to hold resources in reserve'.

This position is traced back to Keynes (1973b, p. 116), who maintained that households keep money balances because of 'calculations and conventions concerning the future. . . . The possession of actual money lulls our disquietude; and the premium which we require to make us part with money is the measure of the degree of our disquietude'. This is why 'anyone outside a lunatic asylum' would hold on to money.

Rousseas (1992, pp. 12, 15) also makes this claim, arguing that 'money . . . is what binds the present and the future in a world of uncertainty. . . . It is the capitalist response to uncertainty that gives money its peculiarity'. Moreover, according to Rousseas (1992, p. 22), '[i]n a non-barter monetary economy, it is the continued presence of uncertainty in all markets, to a lesser or greater extent, that permits money to serve as a store of wealth or value, that is to be used as a hedge against uncertainty'.[8]

Linking the existence of money to uncertainty, however, has two obvious problems. First, it undermines the role played by banks in the creation of money in the financing of production through the extension of credit. If money is endogenous, then it exists because of bank loans. Then again, post Keynesians tell us that money exists because of uncertainty. Which is it? We cannot have two seemingly mutually inconsistent explanations of the existence of money. Secondly, this view assumes that in a world of perfect certainty (which granted cannot exist) there would be no need for money: the study of economics could be done in terms of barter and real analysis. It leaves therefore the impression that the one distinguishing feature between post Keynesian and neoclassical theory is the pervasiveness of uncertainty.[9]

Moreover, many post Keynesians claim that the finance motive is a component of the demand for money, that is, the fourth motive for holding money (Keynes, 1973b; Davidson, 1965). If it is used primarily to finance the costs of production and investment, then the demand for money function becomes quasi-synonymous with the demand for investment funds: firms demand money to finance on-going investment.[10] A downward-sloping curve becomes the monetised embodiment of the downward-sloping investment demand function. Post Keynesians therefore seem oblivious to the lessons drawn from the capital debates that there cannot be an inverse relationship between the rate of interest and investment.

With respect to the supply of money, two arguments can be made. First, money may be measured at any given point in time as a stock. For instance, at time t there is a given quantity of money in existence. But money itself is a flow the creation of which responds to the needs of the economy. Yet, supply and demand analysis is incapable of representing the second argument. Demanding and then supplying credit or money is necessarily a dynamic process, as argued by Arestis (see above). Thus, in a world of stocks, the acceptance of a supply function implies the notion that money is somehow scarce and that it must be rationed. The supply of money becomes limited by the function itself. At any given rate of interest, only one possible quantity of money supplied exists (unless we adopt the horizontalist position). Anything to the right of the money supply schedule cannot exist unless the curve is somehow shifted, through policy.[11] This contrasts with the broadest notion of endogenous money by which supply adapts itself to demand. Secondly, and related to the first point, a supply function at the macro level makes little sense. If money is truly endogenous, then there cannot be a function relating quantity to price. If the supply is demand-constrained, then it cannot be an increasing function of the rate of interest. If anything, it can be drawn horizontally.

The acceptance of demand and supply functions of money is therefore a static interpretation of a dynamic process. These functions embody the very notion of scarcity at the heart of neoclassical theory. They tell us nothing about the source or origins of money. The discussion over money is done without referring to the role played by commercial banks. Supply and demand analysis reinstates the simultaneous determination of price and quantity. The theory of the determination of the rate of interest becomes simultaneously a theory of the determination of the quantity of money. These theories are no longer separate: what determines money determines the rate of interest and vice versa.[12] But in post Keynesian theory, price and quantity ought to be determined separately, through different forces.[13] There is general consensus that the rate of interest is exogenous and that the supply of credit, in the broadest sense, adapts to demand.

The post Keynesian notion of money is therefore lacking in this important respect, and offers very little that is different from neoclassical theory, except that money is the result of uncertainty. Uncertainty is necessary for the existence of money. Even this point, however, is problematic since it still treats money as a stock/asset and relies on portfolio allocation. If uncertainty can be eliminated, then we are back to neoclassical theory (Davidson, 1972/1978).

The Monetary Circuit Approach

Circuitists see money first and foremost as debt, within the context of a generalised monetary theory of production. They emphasise the *nature* of money (as debt), and only after look at the roles and functions of money. In this sense, *what* money is (debt issued by banks) is the same as *where* money comes from (bank loans). The inevitable conclusion is that money is always and everywhere an endogenous phenomenon. This is not to say, of course, that money has no functions, for clearly it has. Money *is* of course a unit of account, and it *is* indeed a medium of exchange and a store of value. But this analysis should be secondary in a theory of endogenous money. Only once money is created can we look at its functions and roles. Thus circuitists are interested in the nature of money *ab ovo*, and the functions of money *ex post*.

For the proponents of the theory of the monetary circuit (see Graziani, 1984, 1996; Parguez, 2001; Lavoie, 1992; Realfonzo, 1998; Rochon, 1999b; Parguez and Seccareccia, 2000) money, income and production are intimately linked through the discussion over banks and bank behaviour. Capitalist economies are debt economies: production cannot be separated from the discussion over credit, banks and debt. The starting point is Keynes's reference in the *Treatise* that money 'comes into existence along with debts' (Keynes, 1930/1971, p. 3; see Davidson, 1972/1978, p. 147). While money is simultaneously a stock and a flow, it is first a flow that responds to the needs of the economy, circulates and then is partly destroyed. The *stock* of money that is left represents the demand for money at the end of the production period.

The theory of the monetary circuit begins with the distinction between credit and money. From the perspective of double-entry bookkeeping, it is clear that credit is an asset of banks while money is a liability (Parguez and Seccareccia, 2000). Money and credit are seen as different. The demand for credit cannot be a component of the demand for money since money is the result of the demand for – and subsequent supply of – bank credit. Money results from credit.[14] Money is created at the very instant credit is used by firms. As Parguez and Seccareccia (2000, p. 101) claim, '[m]oney appears both causally and historically as a result of prior debt and credit relations'.

Money is not seen primarily as an asset (although it can be one, see below). Its primary function is to allow production to begin and goods to circulate. Money is first a flow. This is achieved by giving firms and the state access to finance in order to hire labour and purchase other means of production – thus creating income. Credit and money therefore are first and foremost flows responding to the needs of the economy. Credit and money are the *sine qua non* of monetary production economies.

Two important points of departure for circuit writers are the following. Firstly, they emphasise first and foremost the nature of money, rather than its roles or functions (Gnos, 1999). Secondly, they do not link the existence of money to uncertainty. Money exists irrespective of whether there is uncertainty. Let us consider these arguments in turn.

The nature of money
The analysis of the theory of the monetary circuit is set within a specific hierarchy of relations, with a given irreversible sequence in the production process between five players in the system: households (workers and rentiers), firms (producing consumption goods and capital goods), banks, the central bank and the state. Firms cannot begin production without first hiring workers, who cannot consume without first receiving an income. Banks cannot lend without an *ex ante* demand for credit. The central bank is the financial agent of the state that sanctions the currency thereby converting bank deposits into money (Wray, 1998). It is this act that gives banks the ability to supply credit, creating deposits and money in the process (see below). The role of the central bank is to set the rate of interest, to act as the financial agent of the state, and to ensure the financial survival of the economic system. Within this role, the central bank also acts as a clearing house for banks, thus ensuring the convertibility of bank deposits from one bank to another at par (more on this in the next section).

In fact, money is a constant reminder of the existence of debt. Each of the hierarchical relationships revolves around debt. Money is the result of intricate debt relationships. In this sense, money exists within a specific social relationship of financial indebtness, bipolar in nature: there must always be a debtor whenever there is a creditor. This analogy holds at every stage of the monetary circuit. Within a period of production, there are parallel circuits of debt, all revolving around the notions of money and income. Firms enter into debt towards banks, the state enters into debt towards the central bank (both of these being by far the most important ones), households towards the firms and the state, and finally banks with respect to the central bank. Hence, this hierarchy of debt sets into motion an intricate pattern of monetary creation, circulation and destruction that ends with the cancellation of the initial debt. In other words, money exists because of debt, circulates because of debt, and is extinguished in the reimbursement of debt. This pattern is divided characteristically between efflux and reflux.

At the beginning of the circuit, for instance, firms request credit to cover expenses such as wages (short-term credit) and investment (long-term credit), based on firms' expectations of the future (short-term expectations for production purposes, and long-term expectations for investment). Banks, on the other hand, agree to extend credit based on their expectations of effective demand and the general creditworthiness of individual firms. Firms are initially in debt towards banks. But the beginning of the monetary circuit also includes the activities of the state that must finance its expenditures by borrowing from the central bank. The central bank is the financial agent of the state. The state needs credit to remunerate its workforce, but also to 'purchase' other factors of 'production' such as the payment of dividends on its existing debt, the purchase of equipment, and to meet social programme expenditures, and so on.

Banks and the central bank are able to do this without pre-existing saving because their liabilities (bank deposits) are recognised as money and sanctioned by the state. This confers onto all banks a special status: that of creators of money. Banks and the central bank create money *ex nihilo*; they create purchasing power. Banks and the central bank are able to do this by indebting themselves towards themselves (Parguez and Seccareccia, 2000). They bet on the ability of firms and the state to repay their initial debt. Hence, when a firm borrows from a bank, or when the state borrows from the central bank, four debts are created. First, the debt of productive firms to the banks; second, the debt of commercial banks to themselves; third, the debt of the state to the central bank; finally, the debt of the central bank to itself. Together, all four debts make up what Graziani (1984) calls the initial debt of the system – debts that allow production and the activities of the state to begin.

Once credit is granted, money is instantaneously created: here lies the existence of the money supply. It is true that the central bank has a role in the creation of the money supply, but this is entirely different than in other (more mainstream) theories. In this framework, the central bank creates money in response to the needs of the state. In fact, the entire money supply is created in response to the needs of the economic system. Banks and the central bank can never exogenously increase the money supply since their decision to grant credit is demand-determined by firms and the state (see below).

Once credit is granted, firms and the state use it to remunerate workers, pay dividends and purchase capital goods. In every instance, incomes are created for workers, rentiers and capital- and consumption-goods firms. The creation of money is synonymous with the creation of debt and income. This is the crucial efflux stage of the monetary circuit.

At this stage, the bank accounts of households, rentiers, and capital- as well as consumption-goods firms are increased. The total value of money created does not change, although its composition does. Initially, the money supply consisted entirely of the bank accounts of firms and the state. Now, this money has shifted to recipients of income. Although the composition of the money supply has changed, its nature remains the same: it still represents the debt of firms and the state to banks and the central bank. Just as credit was created because of 'production flows', money now circulates because of transactions flows.

But now, a second phase of the monetary circuit begins. The creation of income sets into motion the necessary creation of secondary debts but this time involving households. This is the beginning of the reflux stage of the monetary circuit, or what Graziani (1984) calls final finance.

As households – workers and rentiers – consume, money is shifted around from their bank accounts to those of consumption-goods firms. Consumption can be seen as a temporary debt. When households consume, they buy a bundle of goods and thus temporarily enter into a debt position towards firms. This debt is then reimbursed according to the criteria of firms: either instantly, through the payment of the goods in full, or over time, through the extension of (store) credit. Similarly, the creation of income involves the necessary payment of taxes. As households pay their taxes, they are transferring money from their bank accounts to those of the state. Taxes also represent the debt of households towards the state, extinguished when households pay their taxes. Hence, at this stage, households enter various debt positions with firms and the state, which are extinguished through the creation of income for the state and consumption-goods firms. Money flows back to both consumption-goods firms and the state as income.

The final stage of the monetary circuit involves the cancelling of the initial debts and the destruction of money. Firms and the state use the proceeds from consumption and taxes to repay banks and the central bank. Debts are cancelled, and in the process money is destroyed.

At another level, there is another debt relationship that must be analysed. Above, we noticed four hierarchies of debt. The passages above discussed the debt of firms towards banks, of the state towards the central bank, and of households towards firms and the state. Missing was the debt of banks towards the central bank. This last debt corresponds to Lavoie's (1985) second pole. Indeed, as deposits are created in the process of debt, banks must demand reserves, that is, bank deposits at the central bank (an asset for banks and a liability for the central bank). Banks are therefore indebted towards the central bank that must deliver to them a given amount of reserves, which the central bank supplies on demand, fully or partially.[15] Lavoie's 'second pole' arises thus at the end of the analysis.[16] The standard post Keynesian debate between so-called horizontalists and structuralists enters here (Moore, 1988; Wray, 1990).

From the above discussion, we can observe that production involves an intricate system of debts and incomes, resulting from the creation, circulation and destruction of money. Money is created through debt; it is circulated through debt; it is cancelled through debt. Money is therefore primarily a flow.

Three crucial conclusions arise from the theory of the monetary circuit.

First, consumption and taxes cannot finance anything. Rather, they must be seen as part of the reflux phase. Their role is to allow firms and the state to reimburse bank debt. In this sense, once debt is reimbursed, firms and the state must borrow anew, or have their existing agreement extended into a new round of production and expenditures (Rochon, 2000). Hence, Keynes's finance motive or bank credit is needed irrespective of whether the economy or costs of production are rising, as postulated by many post Keynesians (Davidson, 1972/1978; Wells, 1983; Chick, 1995).

Secondly, money exists irrespective of uncertainty. In contrast to post Keynesians, even if we envisage a world of perfect certainty, firms and the state would still need access to bank credit. There is no need for uncertainty to understand the nature and existence of money, although uncertainty plays a key role when firms and banks anticipate the unknown future. The theory of the monetary circuit is therefore perfectly compatible with the pervasive nature of uncertainty. The theory of the monetary circuit is set within a context of historical time and uncertainty (see below).

Thirdly, circuit theorists make no use of supply and demand analysis. Although there is certainly a demand and supply of credit, they are independent, and do not interact together to determine a price and quantity of credit: there is no credit or money market. The price of credit, that is, the rate of interest, is determined exogenously by the central bank (in an environment of uncertainty), while the supply of credit is determined by the demand for credit, given the banks' criteria for lending.[17] Supply *is* demand (Parguez, 1985, p. 273). According to Di Ruzza (1984, p. 1; our translation):

> the use of supply and demand analysis with respect to money gives rise to more inconveniences than to advantages. . . . To consider supply and demand functions for money, irrespective of their characteristics, implies foremost the definition and acceptance of a certain separation between money and the 'real' economy. . . . If we assume that the supply of money is endogenous, and determined by demand, the notion of supply itself loses all its significance. The only quantity of money foreseeable, possible and normal, would be the 'desired' quantity, i.e. that arising from the internal economic needs of the system.

While Di Ruzza's argument is in terms of supply and demand for money, it can certainly be applied to credit, too. This led Lavoie to argue that for 'many circuitists, the notions of supply and demand (of money) as such are non-existent' (Lavoie, 1987, p. 91; our translation).

The nature of money is tied to the source and creation of money. While this point will be discussed below, it is worth mentioning here that there are no references, at this stage, to the functions of money. In fact, at the financing stage of production, there is really no need to discuss any of these. Production and debt are the necessary and sufficient conditions for the existence of money.

Money and uncertainty

The discussion above has emphasised the notion of bank credit and debt. As stated earlier, we should first discuss the nature of money and only then look at what happens to it once it is created. Circuit writers have done this, too. There is no denying that money is a medium of circulation allowing goods to circulate. It is also a unit of account in which all goods and debts are denominated. But what about the function of money as a store of value? If money exists because of debt, how can we reconcile the notion of uncertainty with that of money, rather than credit?[18] Is there a role for uncertainty in a theory of *money*?

We saw above that uncertainty enters into the decisions of firms and banks in demanding and then supplying credit. With respect to uncertainty and money, it concerns the decisions by economic agents to remain liquid, at the very end of the monetary circuit.

Having received an income, households will be left, after consumption, with a stock of saving that they will then allocate between various assets. It is at this point that money becomes a stock and an asset. Households' decisions to allocate saving between, say, bonds and shares on the one hand (financial saving) and money on the other (hoarded saving) may be the result of uncertainty since money is perfectly liquid and is a store of value. This is households' demand for *money*. If households are uncertain about future levels of interest rates, or simply have a desire to remain liquid for precautionary reasons, they will hold on to more money rather than to other assets (the demand for money rises). But this demand for money, like saving, is not causal, and is a residual of the system (Lavoie, 1992).

As households purchase bonds, however, money is channeled back to the state. Similarly, as households purchase financial shares, money is refluxed back to firms. The state and firms use these sums to repay their initial debt with banks and the central bank. There are therefore two sources of reflux: consumption and financial savings. Keynes (1973c, p. 276) defended this very position, '[f]or the purpose of restoring liquidity consumption is just as good as saving'. The conclusion is, as Graziani (1984) explains, that financial markets can never be a source of fresh finance. Rather, they are a component of the reflux phase of the monetary circuit.

The quantity of money hoarded by households (liquidity) corresponds to the amount of money firms were not able to recapture from households through the selling of commodities or financial shares. This remaining stock of money that stays in the banking system represents the final (or permanent) debt of firms towards banks (Lavoie, 1992). As Parguez (1997, p. 7) notes, '[w]hen there is an increase in the demand for money as an asset, firms cannot repay their whole short-term debt to banks'.[19]

Firms may also have a demand for money. If they have profits after repayment of their debt, firms must decide how much to keep as retained earnings and how much to give to shareholders. Once again, the demand for money arises at the end of the monetary circuit. It is a decision, as in the case of households, on how to allocate existing saving. Increased uncertainty about the future may force firms to remain more liquid.

The post Keynesian discussion of money and uncertainty is not necessarily wrong as it is misplaced, and above all overemphasised. The relationship between money and uncertainty, as opposed to the relationship between credit and uncertainty, arises at the end of the monetary circuit. Furthermore, uncertainty does not explain *why* money exists, but rather *why money remains in the system*. Money is therefore both a flow/liability and a stock/asset.

The difference that arises between post Keynesians and circuit theorists concerns primarily the sequence of time. The circuitist approach to uncertainty and money does not stand much in contradiction with the post Keynesian argument, except that the argument is placed within its logical and sequential place. It is in this sense that the discussion of money is secondary.

ENDOGENOUS MONEY

Having discussed the concept of money from the point of view of post Keynesians and circuit theorists, it is now appropriate to turn the discussion over to the notion of endogenous money. As discussed above, post Keynesians separate the dual question of *what* money is from *how* money is created. For circuit theorists these questions are the same, as the previous section should have made clear.

It is often difficult to define endogenous money. Is it sufficient, for instance, to define it as simply the inability of central banks to control the *stock* of money? If this is so, then many schools of thought have a theory of endogenous money, including New Keynesians. For example, it would be possible to claim that endogenous money is present in the writings of Romer and Romer (1990), Bernanke and Blinder (1992), Gertler (1992), and Kashyap and Stein (1994). Yet, these authors all retain a neoclassical foundation to monetary theory: exogenous reserves, deposit–loan causality, and so on. But they claim that financial innovations allow banks to circumvent the authority of the central bank, which has lost control over the money supply.

For instance, Kashyap and Stein (1994, p. 223) have argued that:

> The quantitative importance of the lending channel is likely to be sensitive to a number of institutional characteristics of the financial markets. . . . Thus understanding the lending channel is a prerequisite to understanding how innovations in financial institutions might influence the potency of monetary policy.

Romer and Romer (1990, p. 157) claim that banks are able to 'greatly mitigate any direct impact of tight monetary policy on their lending by issuing CDs subject to low reserve requirements in response to a decline in the quantity of transactions balances caused by a reduction in reserves'.

The above quotes are in fact close to the view of many post Keynesians. Even in the *General Theory*, Keynes has a variable velocity, which some would interpret as being equivalent to endogenous money. Minsky's early views (1957a, 1957b) implied a similar model based on financial innovations.

The large difference rests in the theoretical underpinnings of such approach. The salient question, therefore, is the following: is it possible to have endogenous money within an otherwise neoclassical framework? If we define endogenous money simply as the inability of central banks to control the supply of money, then the answer is yes. If, however, endogenous money is defined differently, then the question cannot be answered in the affirmative.

This section will consider the meaning of endogenous money in light of the discussion of money in the previous section. It will show that post Keynesians rely heavily on institutional features to explain the endogenous nature of money. In this sense, post Keynesians, both structuralists and horizontalists, share a similar view of endogenous money.

The Post Keynesians

The notion of endogenous money is central to post Keynesians. It is true that post Keynesians consider the money-creation process through bank loans. But this view is too often under-emphasised or under-developed. Endogenous money rather takes on the stature of a mere statement, after which post Keynesians are more interested in the functions and roles of money, and its links with uncertainty. This is somewhat regrettable, for it is precisely the endogenous nature of money that could provide a clear opportunity to distinguish post Keynesians from neoclassical economists. The discussion on uncertainty and the roles of money is too closely related to that of neoclassical theory.

Despite their acknowledgement of the endogenised process, post Keynesians do not always make clear what is meant by endogenous money. Rochon (1999a, p. 63) defines endogenous money according to the following five characteristics:

1. Reverse causality between money and income, specifying that the causality runs from expected (or desired) income of firms, to the demand for credit, to money and effective income.
2. Reverse causality between savings and investment, meaning thereby that firms finance investment before savings are generated.
3. Reverse causality between reserves, deposits and loans, where reserves are endogenous and have no causal influence on loans.
4. The rate of interest is set exogenously by the central bank according to its economic objectives (expected inflation, output, and so on) – there is no natural rate of interest.

5. The money supply is credit-led and demand-determined.

Rochon (1999a) indicates that this corresponds to a revolutionary theory of endogenous money. After some deeper reflection, however, I believe that this definition needs to be somewhat amended in light of the discussion above on the nature of money.

To a more or less degree, these characteristics are found in the post Keynesian literature, of the structuralist and horizontalist pedigrees, with some minor changes. For instance, structuralists still see the relationship between reserves and loans as 'bi-causal' (Palley, 1994; Pollin, 1996), a source of some concern (see Rochon, 1999a, Ch. 6).

While these characteristics are present in post Keynesian economics, however, there can be no doubt that they are the result of institutional characteristics, resulting from the development of the banking system. In this sense, money only became endogenous over time. For instance, Chick (1986) argues that in the early stages of banking, money was entirely exogenous. Banks were neoclassical and the causality ran from deposits to reserves, and finally to loans. The supply of credit was thus pre-determined; the principle of scarcity applied. Banks were pure financial intermediaries. It is only when the central bank 'fully accepted responsibility for the stability of the financial system', in the fourth stage of banking development, that banks were able to expand lending beyond their reserve capacity. It is the accommodative role of the central bank, that is, the removal of reserve constraints, that rendered money endogenous.[20] Endogenous money is thus the result of institutional changes, defined as the ability of the economy to expand without a prior expansion of reserves (Wray, 1990, p. 135). Stage five, the introduction of liability management, is simply a less extreme version of money endogeneity where banks actively seek to pursue financial innovations in order to expand the supply of credit. This last stage arose only because the central bank may not fully accommodate the demand for bank reserves. In both stages, however, the result is the same: banks no longer depend on deposits or reserves to lend.

The main conclusion in this analysis is that money is endogenous or exogenous according to the historical period. Moore (1996) agrees on this point. According to him, the debate over exogenous versus endogenous money is misleading since 'both views are correct, but . . . apply to a *different* historical period' (Moore, 1996, p. 89; see also Davidson, 1972/1978; Guttmann, 1990, p. 82; Minsky, 1991, p. 89; Niggle, 1991).

Strangely enough, Moore (1988, 1996) also shares Chick's view in the sense that money is endogenous as the result of a purely accommodative central bank. This explains why Moore (1979, p. 126) ranks 'the supportive responsibilities of central banks above their control duties'. Money is endogenous because central banks are 'impotent in their ability to restrict the rate of growth of the money stock' (Moore, 1985, p. 112).

Yet, if money is said to be purely exogenous in early periods, it is also claimed to be only partially endogenous today. In fact, all post Keynesians agree that the money supply is only partly endogenous. For instance, Davidson (1972/1978) claims that 'the money supply can be expanded exogenously (i.e. by the deliberations of the Central Bank) or endogenously when the banking system responds to an increase in the demand for money' (see also Weintraub, 1978, p. 75; Davidson, 1989, p. 489; Rousseas, 1989, p. 478; Minsky, 1991, p. 208; Niggle, 1991, p. 143).[21] This is the same position defended by Moore (1988, 1996) when he argues that the central bank can always increase the money supply by injecting additional reserves into the system. According to Moore (1996, p. 89), '[t]he monetary authorities are always able to increase the money supply at their initiative by the purchase of securities in the open market. . . . The money supply can always be increased, by some multiple, of the growth of bank reserves, at the initiative of the central bank'. Arestis (1992, p. 180) concurs with this view: 'Monetary authorities are generally able to increase the money supply on their own initiative except in conditions of severe and extreme slump when economic agents would not wish to hold any extra money injected into the system, occasions when the monetary authorities may really wish to increase the money supply'. This is also the case for Pollin (1995, p. 11). Pollin sees an increase in central bank reserves as an increase in the banks' liquidity and their loan supply (see also Palley, 1994). It therefore appears that the money supply is not only demand-determined, but supply-determined, too (see also Cottrell, 1988, p. 295).

This confusion and asymmetry arise because post Keynesians still adhere to an orthodox concept to define endogeneity: high-powered reserves. The notion of endogenous money is equated with that of endogenous reserves: money is endogenous *because* reserves are endogenous, resulting from the accommodative policy of central banks or financial innovations. This is why the horizontalist versus structuralist debate centred on central bank accommodation. Structuralists argued that the lack of central bank accommodation invalidated the horizontalist (full or complete endogeneity) argument, and rendered money partly exogenous. If the central bank refused to fully accommodate, then banks would have to cut back or call back loans (Pollin, 1996) and the money supply would decrease.

Rousseas (1989) links endogenous money to the accommodative nature of the central bank directly. According to him, 'the money supply is endogenous to a marked degree without being perfectly so. *Demand does create, to a greater or lesser extent but never perfectly so, its own supply!* The degree to which the supply of money is positively sloped depends on the discretionary policies of the Federal Reserve' (Rousseas, 1989, p. 478; italics in the original).

The institutional dimension to endogenous money is also present in the structuralist arguments. In the structuralist tradition, money becomes endogenous because of financial innovations. Liability management gives banks the ability of extending credit beyond the central bank's targeted money supply, thereby frustrating central bank policy. Money is created over and above what the central bank targeted; money is endogenised.

Both arguments, rather than being contradictory as the horizontalist versus structuralist debate often made it out to be (and I am guilty of this, too), are in fact quite complementary. Endogenous money is only that part of the money supply that is allowed to be so by the central bank. But the argument is the same as in Moore (1988): money *would be* fully endogenous *provided* that the central bank accommodated. Since structuralists do not see reserves as fully endogenous, as pointed out by Screpanti (1997, p. 567), money is only partly endogenous. But given financial innovations and liability management, it is made more endogenous given banks' ability to circumvent the central bank. Nonetheless, the argument confuses the endogeneity of *reserves* with endogenous *money*. It is for this reason that we refer to this version as *institutional endogeneity*.

The Circuitist Tradition

In the previous section, it was argued that the theory of the monetary circuit is linked to the theory of production and the creation of debt. The creation of money emanates from the need of the economy to reproduce itself, and to grow. As firms and the state borrow money to hire labour and purchase other means of production, incomes are created in the process. The creation of money is analogous to the creation of money income.

The endogenous nature of money is a result of the nature of money as bank debt, resulting from the needs of the system. In this sense, it is *natural* endogeneity since it does not depend on any institutional arrangements. While these arrangements may be of considerable importance in discussing relevant innovations in banking practices, they do not alter the pre-eminent nature of money as bank debt, and do not make money endogenous. In other words, money is endogenous irrespective of the accommodative nature of central banks or of liability management, as noted by Lavoie (1984, p. 238). According to him, '[a]ccommodation or the lack of it, liability management or the lack of it, and financial innovation or the lack of it are second-order phenomena to the crucial causal story that goes from debt to the supply of means of payment' (Lavoie, 1996, p. 533). For circuitists, therefore, institutional developments are not part of the essential argument. They are useful, however, to further justify their primary argument and to give a more realist interpretation to their notion of endogenous money.

Money is debt, as discussed above. It represents a hierarchy of debts. First, it is a debt of firms to banks and a debt of the state to the central bank as they begin production and finance expenditures. It is also a debt of banks to themselves as they agree to lend to firms (Parguez, 2001). Since money is viewed as debt, it must be reimbursed, thus explaining the emphasis on the notion of money creation and destruction, and the cancellation of debt.

The role of the central bank is also not to be minimised, but its operations are part and parcel of the monetary system. Its primary role is not to set the money supply, or impose quantity constraints on the state or banks. Rather, it is to act as a clearing house for banks, and to act as the financial arm of the state.

With respect to the first argument (the second argument was discussed at length in the previous section), the central bank acts as a clearing house for banks to settle interbank debts. In a multi-bank system, it is clear that deposits will move from one bank to another given transactions flows, as the composition of the money supply changes. In other words, deposits will circulate as payments are made and incomes are created. A problem arises because someone must ensure that the liabilities of one bank are exchanged at par with those of another – which may be called an internal or interbank exchange rate. By allowing banks to settle their accounts through it, the central bank ensures the convertibility of bank deposits through its role as a clearing house. It ensures a unique exchange rate: it does not make money endogenous. In this light, its reserves operations are seen largely as a way of ensuring the financial stability of the system, providing reserves on demand to those banks that need them. This position is quite consistent with the post Keynesian literature.

Of course, the five characteristics listed above are crucial to the understanding of a theory of endogenous money. Together, they explain the importance of banks in the production process, in a modern framework. They also help to explain the rejection of the principle of scarcity. According to the theory of the monetary circuit, therefore, money cannot be simultaneously endogenous and exogenous, nor can it be endogenous or exogenous according to different historical periods.

Because of this view, money is naturally endogenous. It cannot be otherwise. This gives heterodox economists a further distinctive approach to money and monetary macroeconomics than neoclassical theory. Although much work still needs to be done to explore these meanings, this approach offers a more interesting beginning.

CONCLUSION

The purpose of this chapter was to show that both post Keynesians and circuit theorists have much to learn from one another. Post Keynesians have not fully incorporated into their theory the notion of money as bank debt, while circuitists lack discussion of banking institutional details, vital for understanding the mechanics of endogeneity. Both approaches therefore need to be further developed. When both approaches have been properly combined, then a coherent heterodox programme may begin.

NOTES

1. The first draft of this chapter was written while the author was Visiting Professor at the University of Burgundy at Dijon, France, in the Fall 2000, and was presented at the Kalamazoo College–University of Notre Dame conference on post Keynesian economics, May 13–14, 2001. The author would like to thank, without implicating them, Per Gunnar Berglund, Amitava Dutt, Claude Gnos, John King, Marc Lavoie, Virginie Monvoisin, Corinne Pastoret, Jean-François Ponsot, John Smithin and Matias Vernengo.

2. This has led some economists to question whether post Keynesians have a theory of money at all. Moreover, because of their emphasis on the functions of money, this had led others to ask how different their theory is from neoclassical theory. For instance, Heinsohn and Steiger (1983, p. 5) have claimed that '[t]he explanation of money by Post Keynesians, if they have one at all, does not differ from classical and neoclassical economists. . . . The Post Keynesian's lack of "radicality" results in the retention of an inadequate theory concerning the origin of money, the rise of monetary economies and, therefore, of the role of money in the real world of capitalist societies'.

3. While savings can be used to finance production, we must remember that existing saving was the result of some initial investment some time in the past. The same applies to financial markets. While Lavoie (1992) recognises that production can be financed by bank credit (debt), savings and financial markets, he also recognises precisely that the use of non-bank credit was created by debt in the past.

4. In personal correspondence with the author, Smithin argues that both poles are simultaneous in the sense that what allows banks to grant credit is precisely the special relationship they enjoy with the central bank. To this we would suggest that banks grant credit not necessarily because of their relationship with the central bank but rather because their deposits are accepted as means of payment.

5. Moore (1988) does not begin his analysis in this way. For him, the existence of money is

linked to the productive needs of the economy to finance working capital. Wray (1990) also analyses the important link between money and debt.

6. The least that can be said about the horizontalist position is that it conveys the appropriate message about the exogeneity of the rate of interest and the notion that there cannot be an excess supply or demand for money.

7. To claim that money has no return is less true today than it was in earlier times when money was essentially notes and coins. Deposits are now interest-bearing money, although they carry less return than other assets.

8. Another post Keynesian who has emphasised this point is Arestis. Claiming that uncertainty is 'one of the central elements' of post Keynesian theory, Arestis (1990, p. 228) argues that money becomes a link between the irreversible past and the unknown future, as Keynes argued in the *General Theory* (1936/1973a, p. 294). According to Arestis (1990, p. 229), '[i]t is precisely the kind of uncertainty inherent in historical time that is both necessary and sufficient conditions for the existence of money'. This is also the interpretation that Dutt and Amadeo (1990, p. 112) have of post Keynesian theory: 'The institution of money can be thought of as a response to uncertainty, as a way of postponing the making of actual decisions, without uncertainty there would be no need to hold money except for normal transactions purposes'.

9. At a speech given at the New School University, Davidson admitted this saying that the only difference between neoclassical and post Keynesian theories is the existence of uncertainty. Getting rid of uncertainty, he claimed, was going back to neoclassical economics.

10. In Moore (1988), bank credit is used to finance working capital only.

11. Post Keynesians claim that the central bank can always increase the money supply exogenously, thereby shifting the curve. Such a solution can hardly be deemed revolutionary and is certainly more akin to neoclassical theory than to post Keynesian economics.

12. By drawing the supply curve as horizontal, horizontalists at least avoid this problem.

13. Horizontalists understood this clearly. Kaldor (1982) and Moore (1988) made the rate of interest exogenous. Demand determined the quantity of money, and this had no feedback effect on the price.

14. The implication here is that Keynes's finance motive is therefore not a fourth motive for holding money but rather a motive to demand bank credit, which then leads to the endogenous creation of money.

15. Banks can reduce their indebtness to the central bank by adopting financial innovations that reduce the demand for reserves by creating new types of deposits that require little or no reserves. Hence, financial innovations are not meant to increase the quantity of loans, as in some versions of post Keynesian theory (see Pollin, 1996), but rather reduce the demand for reserves and the indebtness of banks towards the central bank.

16. In some countries (Canada, Australia, Sweden, and the United Kingdom) required reserves are zero.

17. Banks are not passive. They set minimum creditworthiness standards that borrowers must meet. Provided that they do so, firms are granted credit. These bank-determined criteria change depending on the optimism or pessimism of banks regarding the unknown and unknowable future. See Rochon (1999a, Ch. 8).

18. It should be obvious by now that circuit theorists do not see the demand for credit as a demand for money. They are different notions altogether.

19. It is at this stage – and this stage only – that banks are financial intermediaries. They agree to lend the hoarded savings of households to firms in order for them to refinance their permanent debt (Lavoie, 1992).

20. According to this definition, Chick also includes Tobin among the proponents of the new endogenised approach, as does Wray (1990) for the same reason.

21. As noted in Rochon (1999a), the proper terminology should be to consider the demand for *credit*, not *money*.

REFERENCES

Arestis, P. (1990), 'Post Keynesianism: a new approach to economics', *Review of Social Economy*, **48** (3), 222–46.

Arestis, P. (1992), *The Post Keynesian Approach to Economics: An Alternative Analysis of Economic Theory and Policy*, Aldershot and Brookfield: Edward Elgar.

Arestis, P. (1997), 'PKE theoretical aspects of money and finance', in *Money, Pricing, Distribution and Economic Integration*, London and New York: Macmillan and St. Martin's Press, 55–73.

Bellofiore, R. and M. Seccareccia (1999), 'Monetary circuit', in P.A. O'Hara (ed.), *Encyclopedia of Political Economy*, London and New York: Routledge, vol. II, 753–6.

Bernanke, B.S. and A.S. Blinder (1992), 'The Federal funds rate and the channels of monetary transmission', *American Economic Review*, **82** (4), 901–21.

Chick, V. (1983), *Macroeconomics after Keynes: A Reconsideration of the General Theory*, Cambridge: MIT Press.

Chick, V. (1986), 'The evolution of the banking system and the theory of saving, investment and interest', *Économies et Sociétés* ('Série Monnaie et Production', 3), **20** (8–9), 111–26.

Chick, V. (1995), 'Is there a case for post Keynesian economics?', *Scottish Journal of Political Economy*, **42** (1), 20–36.

Cottrell, A. (1988), 'The endogeneity of money: reply', *Scottish Journal of Political Economy*, **35** (3), 295–7.

Davidson, P. (1965), 'Keynes's finance motive', *Oxford Economic Papers*, **17** (1), 47–65.

Davidson, P. (1972/1978), *Money and the Real World*, New York: John Wiley and Sons.

Davidson, P. (1989), 'On the endogeneity of money once more', *Journal of Post Keynesian Economics*, **11** (3), 488–90.

Davidson, P. (1996), 'What are the essential elements of post Keynesian monetary theory?', in G. Deleplace and E.J. Nell (eds), *Money in Motion: The Post Keynesian and Circulation Approaches*, London and New York: Macmillan and St. Martin's Press, 48–69.

Deleplace, G. and E.J. Nell (eds) (1996), *Money in Motion: The Post Keynesian and Circulation Approaches*, London and New York: Macmillan and St. Martin's Press.

Di Ruzza, R. (1984), 'Quelques commentaires sur la communication du Professeur Davidson', University of Ottawa/ISMEA Conference, October, mimeo.

Dow, S.C. (1996), 'Horizontalism: a critique', *Cambridge Journal of Economics*, **20** (4), 497–508.

Dutt, A. and E. Amadeo (1990), *Keynes's Third Alternative: The Neo-Ricardians and the Post Keynesians*, Aldershot and Brookfield: Edward Elgar.

Dymski, G. (1996), 'Money as a "time machine" in the new financial world', in P. Arestis (ed.), *Keynes, Money and the Open Economy: Essays in Honour of Paul Davidson*, Cheltenham and Lyme: Edward Elgar, vol. I, 85–104.

Gertler, M. (1992), 'Financial capacity and output fluctuations in an economy with multi-period financial relationships', *Review of Economic Studies*, **59** (3), 455–72.

Gnos, C. (1999), 'The endogenous view of money: the nature of money in question',

University of Burgundy at Dijon, mimeo.

Graziani, A. (1984), 'The debate on Keynes's finance motive', *Economic Notes*, **1** (1), 15–33.

Graziani, A. (1996), 'Money as purchasing power and money as a stock of wealth in Keynesian economic thought', in G. Deleplace and E.J. Nell (eds), *Money in Motion: The Post Keynesian and Circulation Approaches*, London and New York: Macmillan and St. Martin's Press, 139–54.

Guttmann, R. (1990), 'The regime of credit-money and its current transition', *Économies et Sociétés* ('Série Monnaie et Production', 7), **24** (6), 81–105.

Heinsohn, G. and O. Steiger (1983), 'Private property, debts and interest or: the origin of money and the rise and fall of monetary economies', *Studi economici*, **36** (21), 3–55.

Hicks, J.R. (1967), *Critical Essays in Monetary Theory*, Oxford: Clarendon Press.

Howells, P.G.A. (1995), 'The demand for endogenous money', *Journal of Post Keynesian Economics*, **18** (1), 89–106.

Kaldor, N. (1958), 'Monetary policy, economic stability and growth', Memorandum submitted to the Committee on the Working of the Monetary System (Radcliffe Committee), June 23. Reprinted in N. Kaldor (1964), *Essays on Economic Policy*, New York: Norton, vol. I, 128–53.

Kaldor, N. (1982), *The Scourge of Monetarism*, Oxford: Oxford University Press.

Kashyap, A.K. and J.C. Stein (1994), 'Monetary policy and bank lending', in N.G. Mankiw (ed.), *Monetary Policy*, Chicago and London: University of Chicago Press, 221–56.

Keynes, J.M. (1930/1971), *A Treatise on Money: The Pure Theory of Money*, in *The Collected Writings of John Maynard Keynes*, Vol. V, London and Basingstoke: Macmillan.

Keynes, J.M. (1936/1973a), *The General Theory of Employment, Interest and Money*, in *The Collected Writings of John Maynard Keynes*, Vol. VII, London and Basingstoke: Macmillan.

Keynes, J.M. (1973b), *The Collected Writings of John Maynard Keynes*, Vol. XIV *The General Theory and After: Part II Defence and Development*, London and Basingstoke: Macmillan.

Keynes, J.M. (1973c), *The Collected Writings of John Maynard Keynes*, Vol. XXIX *The General Theory and After: A Supplement*, London and Basingstoke: Macmillan.

Lavoie, M. (1984), 'Un modèle post-keynésien d'économie monétaire fondé sur la théorie du circuit', *Économies et Sociétés* ('Série Monnaie et Production', 1), **18** (4), 233–58.

Lavoie, M. (1985), 'La thèse de la monnaie endogène face à la non-validation des crédits', *Économies et Sociétés* ('Série Monnaie et Production', 2), **19** (8), 169–95.

Lavoie, M. (1987), 'Monnaie et production: une synthèse de la théorie du circuit', *Économies et Sociétés* ('Série Monnaie et Production', 4), **21** (9), 65–101.

Lavoie, M. (1992), *Foundations of Post-Keynesian Economic Analysis*, Aldershot and Brookfield: Edward Elgar.

Lavoie, M. (1996), 'Monetary policy in an economy with endogenous credit money', in G. Deleplace and E.J. Nell (eds), *Money in Motion: The Post Keynesian and Circulation Approaches*, London and New York: Macmillan and St. Martin's Press, 532–45.

Minsky, H.P. (1957a), 'Monetary systems and accelerator models', *American Economic Review*, **47** (6), 859–83.

Minsky, H.P. (1957b), 'Central banking and money market changes', *Quarterly Journal of Economics*, **71** (2), 171–87.

Minsky, H.P. (1991), 'The endogeneity of money', in E.J. Nell and W. Semmler (eds), *Nicholas Kaldor and Mainstream Economics: Confrontation or Convergence?*, New York: St. Martin's Press, 207–20.

Moore, B.J. (1979), 'Monetary factors', in A. Eichner (ed.), *A Guide to Post Keynesian Economics*, White Plains: M.E. Sharpe, 120–38.

Moore, B.J. (1985), 'Contemporaneous reserve accounting: can reserves be quantity constrained?', *Journal of Post Keynesian Economics*, **7** (1), 103–13.

Moore, B.J. (1988), *Horizontalists and Verticalists: The Macroeconomics of Credit Money*, Cambridge: Cambridge University Press.

Moore, B.J. (1991), 'Marx, Keynes, Kalecki and Kaldor on the rate of interest as a monetary phenomenon', in E.J. Nell and W. Semmler (eds), *Nicholas Kaldor and Mainstream Economics: Confrontation or Convergence?*, New York: St. Martin's Press, 225–42.

Moore, B.J. (1996), 'The money supply process: a historical reinterpretation', in G. Deleplace and E.J. Nell (eds), *Money in Motion: The Post Keynesian and Circulation Approaches*, London and New York: Macmillan and St. Martin's Press, 89–101.

Nell, E.J. (1967), 'Wicksell's theory of circulation', *Journal of Political Economy*, **75** (4), 386–94.

Niggle, C.J. (1991), 'The endogenous money supply theory: an institutionalist appraisal', *Journal of Economic Issues*, **25** (1), 137–51.

O'Donnell, R. (1989), 'The unwritten books and papers of John Maynard Keynes', *Review of Political Economy*, **24** (4), 767–817.

Palley, T.I. (1994), 'Competing views of the money supply process: theory and evidence', *Metroeconomica*, **45** (1), 67–88.

Parguez, A. (1985), 'La *Théorie générale*: la révolution inachevée dans la théorie de la monnaie et du capital', in A. Barrère (ed.), *Keynes aujourd'hui: théories et politiques*, Paris: Economica, 257–76.

Parguez, A. (1996), 'Beyond scarcity: a reappraisal of the theory of the monetary circuit', in G. Deleplace and E.J. Nell (eds), *Money in Motion: The Post Keynesian and Circulation Approaches*, London and New York: Macmillan and St. Martin's Press, 155–99.

Parguez, A. (1997), 'Government deficits within the monetary production economy or the tragedy of the race to balance budgets', University of Ottawa, mimeo.

Parguez, A. (2001), 'Money without scarcity: from the horizontalist revolution to the theory of the monetary circuit', in L.-P. Rochon and M. Vernengo (eds), *Credit, Interest Rates and the Open Economy: Essays on Horizontalism*, Cheltenham and Northampton: Edward Elgar, 69–103.

Parguez, A. and M. Seccareccia (2000), 'The credit theory of money: the monetary circuit approach', in J. Smithin (ed.), *What is Money?*, London and New York: Routledge, 101–23.

Pollin, R. (1995), 'Financial intermediation and the variability of the saving constraint', University of California–Riverside, mimeo.

Pollin, R. (1996), 'Money supply endogeneity: what are the questions and why do they matter?', in G. Deleplace and E.J. Nell (eds), *Money in Motion: The Post Keynesian and Circulation Approaches*, London and New York: Macmillan and St. Martin's Press, 490–515.

Realfonzo, R. (1998), *Money and Banking: Theory and Debate (1900–1940)*, Cheltenham and Northampton: Edward Elgar.

Rochon, L.-P. (1997), 'Keynes's finance motive: a re-assessment. Credit, liquidity preference and the rate of interest', *Review of Political Economy*, **9** (3), 277–93.

Rochon, L.-P. (1999a), *Credit, Money and Production: An Alternative Post-Keynesian Approach*, Cheltenham and Northampton: Edward Elgar.

Rochon, L.-P. (1999b), 'The creation and circulation of endogenous money: a circuit dynamique approach', *Journal of Economic Issues*, **33** (1), 1–21.

Rochon, L.-P. (2000), 'The creation and circulation of endogenous money: a reply to Pressman', *Journal of Economic Issues*, **34** (4), 973–9.

Romer, C.D. and D.H. Romer (1990), 'New evidence on the monetary transmission mechanism', *Brookings Papers on Economic Activity*, no. 1, 149–98.

Rousseas, S. (1989), 'On the endogeneity of money once more', *Journal of Post Keynesian Economics*, **11** (3), 474–8.

Rousseas, S. (1992), *Post Keynesian Monetary Economics*, Armonk: M.E. Sharpe.

Screpanti, E. (1997), 'Banks, increasing risk, and the endogenous money supply', Monte dei Paschi di Siena *Economic Notes*, **26** (3), 567–87.

Smithin, J. (ed.) (2000), *What is Money?*, London and New York: Routledge.

Weintraub, S. (1978), *Capitalism's Inflation and Unemployment Crisis*, Reading: Addison Wesley.

Wells, P. (1983), 'A post Keynesian view of liquidity preference and the demand for money', *Journal of Post Keynesian Economics*, **5** (4), 523–36.

Winnett, A. (1992), 'Some semantics of endogeneity', in P. Arestis and V. Chick (eds), *Recent Developments in Post-Keynesian Economics*, Aldershot and Brookfield: Edward Elgar, 47–63.

Wray, L.R. (1990), *Money and Credit in Capitalist Economies: The Endogenous Money Approach*, Aldershot and Brookfield: Edward Elgar.

Wray, L.R. (1996), 'Money in the circular flow', in G. Deleplace and E.J. Nell (eds), *Money in Motion: The Post Keynesian and Circulation Approaches*, London and New York: Macmillan and St. Martin's Press, 440–64.

Wray, L.R. (1998), *Understanding Modern Money: The Key to Full Employment and Price Stability*, Cheltenham and Northampton: Edward Elgar.

8. Thinking of the Economy as a Circuit

Biagio Bossone[1]

INTRODUCTION

A good monetary theory after Schumpeter (and definitely after Keynes) is one that sheds light on how money interconnects with production, exchange and capital accumulation, and one that helps identify policies to improve the stability and efficiency of that interconnection. Both purposes can best be achieved if time enters the theory in a meaningful sense, that is, if full acknowledgment is given to the fact that events happen sequentially, and that human decisions take place under substantial uncertainty and ignorance of the future.

The links between money and the real economy in a world with time have been studied systematically by the theory of the monetary circuit.[2] This non-orthodox strand of macroeconomics studies the features of a monetary production economy modelled in the form of a circuit process, which begins when money is advanced by banks to firms that use it to buy inputs for production, and unfolds as production and exchange take place, incomes and savings are generated, and firms sell output and financial liabilities to income earners. The circuit closes when the firms that embarked on production use the proceeds from sales of output and financial liabilities to pay back their maturing bank debts.

Monetary circuit theory studies how production and income generation interrelate with the creation and use of bank money. Production can start when banks lend money to firms, and equilibrium holds if all the money lent and used in production re-flows back to firms, thus enabling them to pay off their outstanding maturing debt, or if the banks roll over the unpaid credits. Key to such representation of the economy is the functional separation that circuit theory operates between banks and firms.

This theory provides a powerful means to understand the integration of the real and monetary sectors of the economy and to analyse it through the interaction of different types of agents, in a context where 'before' and 'after' matters, that is, where decisions taken by agents operating upstream in the process affect decisions from agents operating downstream.[3]

The various variants of monetary circuit theory developed in the literature, however, have devoted limited attention to the role of non-bank financial intermediaries in the economy,[4] while their macroeconomic focus has kept crucial microeconomic aspects of finance (and their potential aggregate impact) out of the analysis.[5] As a consequence, circuit theory has largely ignored the function that banks and non-bank intermediaries play as core links of individual decisions and agent interactions, and has left unexplored relevant areas of banking and finance, such as the impact of banks and non-bank intermediaries on economic efficiency and stability, the role of non-bank intermediation in coordinating individual choices in the markets for funds and capital goods, and the differential welfare cost of alternative banking regulatory regimes. More generally, the theory has disregarded the role of non-bank finance in the overall circuit process and, in particular, in determining the economy's equilibrium.

This chapter illustrates the implications that derive from *thinking the economy as a circuit* when the underlying theoretical framework is adapted to incorporate the microeconomic and financial dimensions of the economy.

The next section describes how the adapted framework works, making explicit the choice structure and the interrelationships of agents operating in a multi-sector, sequential economy with risk and uncertainty. The third section discusses the implications of the adapted circuit framework, including: the possibility for the economy to achieve multiple equilibria, the existence of various sources and transmission mechanisms of financial instability across the circuit, the identification of the different roles of banks and non-bank intermediaries, and the effect of alternative regulatory regimes for banks and payment systems on the efficiency of the money supply process. The fourth section uses the adapted circuit framework to speculate on the future of banking in a rapidly changing financial environment. The last section concludes the chapter.

THE CIRCUIT OF BANKS, PRODUCTION, AND FINANCE

This section describes a circuit process where production, exchange, saving and investment, carried out from households and firms under uncertainty, are integrated via money creation and finance allocation carried out by banks and non-bank intermediaries. The process described essentially adapts the traditional circuit framework in two major respects. It models the economy as a set of self-interested, specialised individual agents using limited knowledge rationally, and includes banks and financial intermediaries as agents specialised in evaluating and taking financial risks.

How the Circuit Works: The Basic Sequence

The economy has four sectors: firms, households, banks and non-bank financial intermediaries, and two commodities: one for household consumption and the other for capital accumulation by firms. Economic activity is a one-period process with three phases in a specific sequence: an opening phase (circuit begins), an interim interval, and a closing phase (circuit ends). The stylised sequence of the circuit process is as follows (see also Figure 8.1).

1. At circuit start (I), banks negotiate with firms the conditions for one-period loans. Banks credit firms' deposit accounts with the negotiated loan amounts. Firms execute production using capital and labour inputs. Loans are used to pay wages, implying that the funds credited by banks on the firms' bank accounts are transferred from these accounts to those of wage earners. Loans can also be extended by banks to households to support consumption.[6]
2. In the interim interval (II), household incomes are spent on consumption goods and saving assets. Savings go into bank deposits and/or into long-term securities issued or traded by financial intermediaries. Firms wishing to add to their capital stock (investing enterprises) bid for funding from the intermediaries. These evaluate the creditworthiness of firms and allocate funds to the viable firms in exchange for securities. The financed enterprises purchase the capital goods desired. All money transfers and payments for goods and securities take place through book-entries on accounts held with the banks.
3. At circuit end (III), firms use their proceeds from output sales to pay off their bank debt and the money originally created is destroyed. Firms that do not succeed in selling all the output produced, try to borrow from the capital market to repay the banks or ask the banks to roll over their outstanding debt.

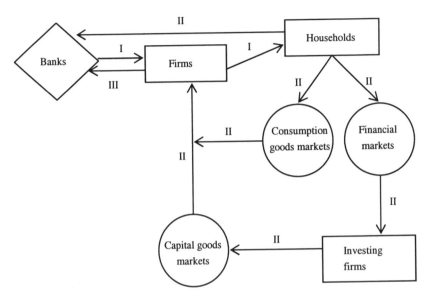

Figure 8.1. Flow of funds in the circuit model

How the Circuit Works: An Illustrative Model

A simple formal model can be used to represent in a more rigorous and compact format the circuit process just described. The model is for illustration purposes only and is not used to derive equilibrium properties, or to run comparative static or dynamic analyses. It aims at providing a framework to make explicit the agents' different roles and interactions in the circuit. The model uses standard choice-theoretic assumptions. Based on given prices and information sets, individual agents optimise their objective functions involving satisfaction from intertemporal consumption for households and profits for non-household agents. All monetary variables in it are expressed in nominal terms, and the relative prices of goods are assumed to be constant throughout the circuit cycle. In the model, the relative prices of goods are assumed constant. The interest rate determines the economy's resource allocation to current and future consumption and the demand for capital goods. The agents behave as follows.

Households
Households supply labour services to firms and receive wage income, *w*. Labour supply is linear in leisure and thus varies proportionately with

income. Households smooth intertemporal consumption based on expectations of lifetime income. Consumption, c, is positive in permanent income, y^e, and negative in the return on financial wealth, r_L:

$$c_h = c(y_h^e, r_L) \tag{8.1}$$

with $c_y' > 0$ and $c_r' < 0$. Consumption spending includes also deferred payments (with interest) from consumers to firms. Saving is current income minus consumption:

$$s_h = w_h - c_h \tag{8.2}$$

Households invest a share z of savings in securities purchased through financial intermediaries, and hold the remaining share as transaction deposits with the banks:

$$s_h = s[z_h + (1 - z_h)] \tag{8.3}$$

Share z is positive in rate of return, r_L, and negative in income variability, σ:

$$z_h = z(r_L, \sigma_h) \tag{8.4}$$

with $0 \le z \ (\le \bar{z}) \le 1$, $z_r' > 0$ and $z_\sigma' < 0$. However, z can be bounded from above ($z \le \bar{z}$) if the financial intermediaries ration their supply of investment funds and cut their demand for saving funds correspondingly.

Firms
Firms employ labour and capital to satisfy the demand for consumption and capital goods from households and firms, respectively. Firms finance production with short-term bank credit at the beginning of the circuit and repay banks at the end of the circuit. Production costs are a share of the total production value of consumption and capital goods, c and I respectively:

$$w = \sum_{h=1}^{H} w_h = v(c^s + I^s) \tag{8.5}$$

where v can be thought of either as a distributional parameter or as reflecting the value added from production ($0 < v \le 1$). The production technology of firm f has constant returns, implying that the firm's profits vary linearly with production. Firm f seeks to maximise profits. It uses bank loans to finance production and output sales. The supply of goods is based on, and adjusts to, expected demands (equations (8.6) and (8.7)), although bank credit rationing may cut supply short of expected demand (see below).

$$c^s \leq E[c^d] = E[\sum_{h=1}^{H} c^h] \qquad (8.6)$$

$$I^s \leq E[I^d] \qquad (8.7)$$

With supply adjusting to demand, the interest rate determines the allocation of resources (from the households) to current and future consumption. The demand for the capital good increases with the difference between marginal capital efficiency μ and cost of funds r defined below; μ is decreasing in aggregate capital K, consisting of inherited capital plus new investment:

$$I^d = I^d (\mu - r_L) \qquad (8.8)$$

$$\mu = \mu(K_0 + I) \qquad (8.9)$$

with $I' > 0$ and $\mu' < 0$. Corporate gross income of firm f is given by output sales minus total wages:

$$y_f = I + c - w \qquad (8.10)$$

Actual sales of c and I are the least of their respective market demands and supplies:

$$c = \min(c^s, c^d) \qquad (8.11)$$
$$I = \min(I^s, I^d) \qquad (8.12)$$

Sales of c include also deferred payments (at an implicit interest rate) from consumers. Net corporate income y_f^n equals revenue minus debt service:

$$y_f^n = I + c - \lambda C R_b^s \qquad (8.13)$$

If y_f^n is negative, the circuit closes only if firms borrow new money, or manage to have their old loans rolled over by the banks. Any positive y_f^n is saved (see equation (8.22)).

Banks

Banks are any agents that have enough reputation with the public to be able to issue liabilities that are redeemable on demand by claim holders, transferable, and usable as means of payment. Banks possess technologies and information to select and monitor the risk of borrowing firms and use various sorts of incentives and enforce mechanisms to ensure loan repayments. Since bank technologies and information are specific to the bank–borrower relationship, bank loans are not liquid.

Banks provide short-term loans to firms to finance production:

$$CR^s = \sum_{b=1}^{B} D_b^s = \sum_{b=1}^{B} CR_b (r_S - \psi_b) \qquad (8.14)$$

In equation (8.14) banks supply loans CR^s by issuing deposits D^s (with $CR' > 0$). Loans allow firms to finance input acquisition and output sales. The supply of loans is positive in the difference between the price of the loan, r_S, and the default risk of the borrower, ψ. The latter varies directly with both the amount of the loan and the lending rate:

$$\psi_b = \psi_b (CR_b^s, r_S) \qquad (8.15)$$

with $\psi_{CR} > 0$ and $\psi_r > 0$. The bank and the firm negotiate r_S and the bank sets CR^s where r_S equals the firm's marginal risk of default. The bank seeks to strike the interest rate that maximises its risk-adjusted profits. With the assumed production technology, and if r_S is consistent with positive expected profits, the firm has an incentive to borrow as much credit as the bank is willing to lend. The supply of loans determines the output produced by firms:

$$CR^s = C^s + I^s \qquad (8.16)$$

Bank deposits are created when the negotiated loans are credited on the borrowers' account. The loans give borrowers access to new purchasing power in the form of deposits that can be used for payments. Deposits are acknowledgments of debt by the banks to those who receive them as a result of payments and fund transfers. Banks commit to honouring such debt as of when funds are drawn on the loan accounts by the borrowers.

Total bank deposits equal the stock of credit outstanding CR at all times of the circuit period:

$$CR = D = \sum_{b=1}^{B} D_b \qquad (8.17)$$

with $CR \le CR^s$. Firstly, all deposits equal credit issued at circuit start (see above). Secondly, if all deposits are used to purchase goods from the producing firms, the latter appropriate the money borrowed initially and pay off their bank at the end of the circuit, so that $CR = D = 0$ in equation (8.17). Thirdly, if a positive stock of deposits is held on bank accounts at the end of the circuit, corporate incomes are reduced equivalently, causing an equal stock of loans to default and to remain outstanding at the end of the circuit, that is:

$$0 < D/CR^s = CR/CR^s \le 1$$

If bank b's loans exceed the deposits held on its accounts as a result of deposit transfers to other banks, b needs to finance the balance; it can do so by borrowing from other banks the following amount:

$$\sum_{B=1}^{n} CR_{Bb}$$

We thus have:[7]

$$CR_b^s - D_b \le \sum_{\beta=1}^{B} CR_{\beta b} \qquad (8.18)$$

with $\beta \ne b$. No cash circulates in the economy and all payments consist of deposit transfers across bank accounts (book entries). Banks extend credits to each other in the form of credit lines, overdraft, or netting arrangements; thus, payments do not entail transfers of outside money between banks, unless the receiving banks request the paying banks to settle their debts in central bank money, or unless the economy's settlement rules require interbank credit/debit balances to be settled in central bank money.[8] Deposits are *destroyed* (and liquidity is withdrawn from the system) when loans are repaid to the banks.[9]

At the end of the circuit, the banks receive debt payments from the borrowing firms. If firms are unable to pay off their debt, banks decide whether to renew (or roll over) their original loans.

$$y_b = r_S[(1 - \overline{\psi}_b)\lambda CR_b^s] \tag{8.19}$$

Equation (8.19), where $\overline{\psi}_b$ is the *ex-post* rate of default on bank debts, defines bank income as the interest earned on actually repaid loans. Bank income is invested in the capital market (equation (8.22)).

Non-bank financial intermediaries

The non-bank financial intermediaries, or non-banks, constitute the financial market of the economy. They aggregate investment funds and allocate them to users. They are specialised in assessing the risk and profitability of alternative investment options and the creditworthiness of the investing enterprises demanding funds.

The demand for capital good I generates a demand for non-bank loans LF:

$$LF^d = I^d \tag{8.20}$$

$$LF^s = S - \sum_{h=1}^{H} s(1 - z_h) \tag{8.21}$$

Equation (8.21) indicates that the supply of funds from non-banks may not exceed aggregate long-term saving. This is defined as the difference between total aggregate saving (equation (8.22)) and bank deposit holdings (equation (8.4)). All savings (from corporate and financial incomes including bank profits) are re-invested in the capital market.

$$S = \sum_{h=1}^{H} s_h + \sum_{f=1}^{F} y_f^n + \sum_{b=1}^{B} y_b + \sum_{i=1}^{I} y_i \tag{8.22}$$

A constraint on the supply of investment funding could result from non-banks deliberately borrowing less than what investors are willing to invest (owing to risk considerations), and hence intermediating less than the aggregate funds available, thereby rationing investment firms.[10] Alternatively, a shortage of investment funding could result from investors having a higher liquidity preference.

In equation (8.23), non-banks supply funds until the price they charge reaches its risk-adjusted maximum level (equation (8.24)), where the risk-adjustment factor is a convex function ϕ in r (equation (8.25)).

$$LF^s = LF^s(r, r^*) \tag{8.23}$$

$$r^* = [r - \phi]_{\max} \tag{8.24}$$

$$\phi = \varphi(r) \tag{8.25}$$

with $LF_r \geq 0$ if $r \leq r^*$ and $LF_r < 0$ if $r > r^*$, and with $\phi' > 0$, $\phi'' > 0$.

Non-banks charge a competitive intermediation fee q on the interest r_L that they pay to households on one side and pass on to the borrowing firms on the other:

$$r = r_L + q \tag{8.26}$$

Interest rate r_L is determined by the supply and demand for funds:

$$r_L = r_L(LF^d - LF^s) \tag{8.27}$$

with $r' > 0$. Non-banks earn income y_F:

$$y_F = qLF \tag{8.28}$$

which they fully save.[11] The investment actually funded in the economy is the least between the supply and demand for long-term funds:

$$LF = \min(LF^s, LF^d) \tag{8.29}$$

Assuming that equilibrium prices exist, the real and financial conditions for equilibrium are, respectively:

$$c^s + I^s = \sum_{h=1}^{H} c_h + I^d = \sum_{j=h,f,b,i}^{H,F,B,I} y_j \tag{8.30}$$

where producers sell all their output and investing firms raise enough funds to settle their contract obligations with capital goods producers, and:

$$CR^s(1 + r_S) = LF + c \tag{8.31}$$

requiring that at circuit end all deposits are destroyed, all money incomes are spent in consumption and investment, and firms pay off their debt.

In equilibrium, banks advance the credit needed by firms to produce at their maximum capacity consistent with their debt service capacity; firms formulate correct expectations as to the demand for consumption and capital goods; households supply all labour necessary for the firms to support production, and use income to optimise intertemporal consumption; and financial intermediaries allocate all savings from investors to investing firms.

In each period, the economy's equilibrium requires that firms sell their output and that the investing enterprises raise enough funds to settle their contract obligations with the capital-goods producers. If output remains unsold, firms need to finance their debt-service obligations. From the financial standpoint, at the end of the circuit all deposits must be destroyed, all money incomes must be spent in consumption and/or investment, and firms must pay off their debt. If deposits are left outstanding at the end, banks need to roll over the credit positions left open by the borrowers who have not settled their obligations. The circuit closes when producers use the proceeds from output sales to clear their debt with the banks and when debts are renewed.

At the end of the circuit, producing firms – as a group – can appropriate no more than the money originally injected in the system. This equals the initial bank loans but does not include the money needed to pay interest. Thus, firms as a group may at most be in a position to pay off the principal debt to the banks, while they need additional money to be able to settle the interest debt share (unless banks accept payments in kind). Injection of new money and conversion of short-term interest debt obligations into longer-term obligations are necessary to allow firms to pay off their initial bank debt and to allow interest debt payments and circuit closure.[12] This payment problem has nothing to do with the capacity of the firms either to produce, and sell, additional output or to extract a larger surplus from production by lowering the relative price of labour. It exclusively rests on the liquidity constraint inherent in a circuit process, whereby a given stock of money – which does not cover for interest payments – is advanced by the banks to the firms at the beginning of the circuit.[13] In the aggregate, interest payments require new money from the banking system.

IMPLICATIONS OF THE CIRCUIT FRAMEWORK

Several implications derive from thinking of the economy as a circuit. They include the possibility for the economy to achieve multiple equilibria, the identification of various sources and transmission mechanisms of financial instability across the circuit, the identification of the different roles played by the banks and the non-banks in the economy, and the effects of alternative regulatory regimes for banks and payment systems on the efficiency of the money supply process.

Macroeconomic and Structural Implications

Equilibria: neo-Keynesian, post Keynesian or new Keynesian?

The adapted circuit framework discussed in the previous section allows to identify different channels through which decisions from agents operating at various stages of the circuit can affect the economy's equilibrium. The framework points to various sources of potential shocks to the economy and proves flexible enough to support alternative theories of macroeconomic equilibrium.

Firstly, labour relations underpinning equation (8.5) and bank–firm negotiations embodied in equations (8.14)–(8.15) clearly have a crucial role in determining the aggregate level of resource use in the economy, since they basically set how much production and consumption can take place at each round of the circuit, and on what terms. The circuit framework can therefore easily lend itself to modelling economies with a large role of the banking relationship in production and investment decisions. Also, the circuit framework can incorporate neo-Keynesian mechanisms of income determination whereby resource employment levels are the result of class conflicts. Note in both cases that low-employment equilibria would result from failures taking place at the beginning of the circuit, in line with traditional monetary circuit theory (Graziani, 1988a).

Secondly, information imperfections in banking and financial markets can lead to credit rationing phenomena that are so central to the new Keynesian theory of finance. The lack of information on fund users may discourage lending and investment funding. Required risk premia on individual fund users, or transaction costs involved in dealing with them, may be so high as to make *ex ante* returns on investable funds riskier (owing to moral hazard and adverse selection). Under these circumstances, banks and non-banks may ration their fund supply (equations (8.14)–(8.15) and (8.21)–(8.22)). Bank rationing constrains production, while non-bank rationing makes funding inadequate to support the demand from fund users. By reducing their demand for long-term savings, non-banks force investors either to hold larger shares of bank deposits than desired or to reduce consumption. Both outcomes prevent the circuit from closing at the level of activity initially planned by the banks and the firms.[14]

Thirdly, failures to close the circuit round at the level of production and investment initially anticipated (that is, equation (8.21) takes the inequality sign) may also be caused by households' high liquidity preference owing to uncertainty, as in post Keynesian models: as households perceive uncertainty to increase, they reduce their portfolio long-term asset shares z_i's in equation (8.4) and ration funds to the non-banks (equation (8.22)). The resulting increase in the interest rate on long-term funds (equation (8.27)) reduces current consumption (equation (8.1)) and hence output (equation (8.10)). When households or investors demand more deposits, some net liquidity is withdrawn from circulation,[15] and firms are forced into debt default unless an equal amount of new liquidity is issued to them.[16] The circuit breaks down if banks do not offset the *leakage* from higher liquidity demand.

What do banks (and non-banks) really do?

The circuit process stylised above marks the important, different functions played by the *credit* market, where liquidity is created to finance production, and the *financial* market, where the existing liquidity is allocated from investors to fund users. This implies a distinctive role for the banks and the non-bank financial intermediaries, respectively, whereby:

1. Banks operate upstream in the circuit process. They allow the circuit to start by providing new liquidity to production and output sales. This liquidity is in the form of banks' own liabilities, or debt claims drawn on the banks themselves, which are made available to borrowers. Banks do not intermediate existing liquidity, but *add* to the system's liquidity every time they extend new credit to firms through deposit creation while simultaneously maintaining full liquidity of depositors' claims. In other words, when banks create claims that borrowers use as money for transactions, existing depositors do not part with the liquidity stored in their bank deposits; they retain at all times the power to exercise their related liquidity option by mobilising deposits on demand, and banks are at all times obliged to comply with their obligations. This implies that the economy's stock of deposits must grow when deposit-issuing banks extend new loans (and until old credits are retired). In other words, banks cannot be intermediaries (Graziani, 1988b).

2. Non-banks operate downstream in the circuit process. Unlike banks, they act truly as intermediaries: they collect existing liquidity (bank deposits) from investors with long positions and allocate it to fund users with short positions. Unlike banks, the funds intermediated or invested by non-banks do not represent claims drawn on themselves. In fact, such funds always

consist of claims on banks (that is, deposits). As such, they can only move across bank accounts. Thus, while non-banks can transfer funds across agents with different liquidity preferences, in no case can they create liquidity.[17] By funding investment, non-banks enable producing firms at circuit end to appropriate the money spent in production and to service their short-term debt obligations to banks.[18]

The peculiar functions that characterise banks as such are that they issue debt claims on themselves that are accepted by the public as money, and that they inject money into the economy by lending out claims on their own debt.

This characterisation of banks bears two implications. Firstly, as of the instant bank money is created through lending, it is *simultaneously* an asset and a liability both for the issuing bank and for the borrower who is issued the loan.[19] Secondly, banks issue claims on real resources *yet* to be produced; therefore, they carry a potential for generating production but also for engendering inflation. Which of the two effects prevails after that money has been issued is ultimately a function of how well banks select and manage their risks.[20]

An interesting implication is that money supply can be seen as a decentralised process that is inherently associated with bank risk-taking and with interbank lending decisions.

The circuit framework shows that finance is key in smoothing the circuit process and in determining the level and the efficiency of capital accumulation, while banks contribute to determining the level of economic activity at circuit start and decide whether or not to extend credit to troubled (and otherwise defaulting) firms. Therefore, banks are ultimately responsible for discriminating between illiquid but solvent firms that deserve temporary credit support and insolvent firms that need either to undergo restructuring or to exit the market. In this context, credit decisions reflect the trade-off between ensuring short-term financial stability and allowing breakdowns in the circuit to occur, with a view to forcing financial discipline into the system.

The power of banks

The circuit framework clarifies that banks command *net* real resource transfers from the firm sector: they extract *seigniorage*.[21] As noted, at the end of the circuit firms as a group can at most appropriate just enough money to pay off their principal debt. When firms repay the principal no net real resource transfer is involved from them to the banks. Interest payments, however, require firms to give in a share of output in return for no additional real resources from the banks; hence, the net resource transfer.[22]

That there is a net real resource transfer from firms to banks is explained by the nature of the interest rate on bank loans. Since banks finance loans by issuing new deposit claims, the interest charged on the loans is not a compensation for foregone consumption or intermediation services. Such interest rate (net of the resource costs to process lending and remunerate deposits) is a pure *rent* that banks extract from borrowers by virtue of their exclusive power to create money. Such exclusivity rests on the government and society confining – by law and convention – the acceptance of money only to liabilities issued by licensed agents. No rent would be involved if, hypothetically, all the agents in the economy issued their own liabilities and had them accepted as money.

On the other hand, seigniorage cannot be extracted by non-bank intermediaries, since these can only reallocate existing liquidity across agents. Unlike interest on commercial loans, but like payment for production inputs, interest payments on a company's obligations to a financial intermediary represent a production cost item against the company's revenues. As such, they represent a compensation to investors for parting with liquidity and to intermediaries for providing intermediation services. Therefore, they do not involve *net* real resource transfers from the company to the investors or the intermediary.

This is not to deny that intermediaries can have quasi-monopolistic powers enabling them to earn excess profits and thus to extract positive rents from fund users. Yet, unlike in the case of the bank-money market, where restricting entry is the interest of society, the markets for financial intermediation services can function at their best under perfect competition, earning zero excess profits or rents.

The same argument explains why changes in the degree of competition of the banking market alter bank seigniorage: more competition means that banks need to compete to attract deposits, *inter alia*, by raising their remuneration. This reduces seigniorage or, to be more precise, redistributes bank seigniorage to depositors.

The way money enters the circuit also entails a direct relationship between seigniorage and bank size. Size is here defined as the bank's share of the loan/deposit market. When bank A extends a loan to a borrower, it stands a chance that the new deposit claims are transferred to other banks. The smaller the size of A, the higher the probability of claims being transferred to other banks. When claim transfers occur, bank A incurs open interbank debit positions that it becomes liable to offset when it is so required by creditor banks or by the extant payment system rules. In fact, banks extend credit to each other at terms (prices and limits on maximum amounts) that normally vary with the size and the quality of the borrowing banks. Typically, the smaller is the size of A, the tighter (that is, more costly and more limited) is its largest open net debit position acceptable to other banks. With respect to larger banks, therefore, smaller banks must hold relatively larger reserves against their debit positions and enjoy lower money-creation capacity.[23] With interbank credit limits set to zero or with full collateral requirements on interbank credit, banks would have no money-creation capacity. On the other hand, less stringent interbank debit limits lower banks' demand for reserve assets and increase bank money creation capacity. In the extreme, with unlimited interbank credit, banks would have no incentive to hold reserve assets.

With limited interbank credit, it is convenient for a bank to expand its size. A larger size increases the re-deposit capacity of the bank, reduces the bank's obligations arising from lending, and increases its seigniorage as a result. By broadening its deposit base (through both larger deposits and more depositors), the bank increases the number of payments settled within its own books and, all else being equal, decreases the number and volume of its interbank debit positions. Also, the bank may increase its lending facing a lower probability of losing deposits to other banks, and a higher probability that deposits will flow back to its own books from other banks as a result of payment activity (see Appendix 1).[24]

The exclusive seigniorage power of banks implies that the net real resource extraction from firms through interest payments stimulate firms to make enough productive use of the money borrowed from the banks so as to generate enough surplus to service their debt. This incentive effect is discussed by Heinsohn and Steiger (1983).

Firms may save on net transfers by raising their output price or by extracting more surplus from production inputs (that is, through lowering parameter v in equation (8.5)): higher prices ration output demand from the market and make a larger share of produced output (surplus) available for bank debt servicing. Moreover, assuming a constant nominal bank interest rate, higher output prices improve the firms' terms of trade vis-à-vis the banks. As a result, relative price adjustments shift some of the firms' rent burden to third parties (namely, consumers and investing enterprises) and reduce the rents (until banks adjust the interest rate level on their loans).

However, unlike in the case of financial interest payments (which, as noted, do not involve net real resource transfers to lenders), relative price adjustments cannot entirely offset the firms' *net* real obligations to banks altogether (unless output prices rise to infinity).

Arguably, where producing firms operate in a competitive and dynamic economy and have access to investment financing, one might expect the supply-side incentive to dominate the rent-shifting effect. On the other hand, in more stagnant economies with limited competition and where firms rely on internal sources to finance investment, the incentive from interest rates to raise productivity might be weak and relative price adjustments through inflation could be an easier option, possibly leading to loan interest rates–output price spiralling effects.

Banks accumulate equity ownership
Firms settle their bank debt by transferring real resources to the banks. Real resource transfers may include direct sales of output, payments out of gross profits, and transfers of fixed asset (for instance, real estate) and of equity claims. Settlements may also involve transfers of funds borrowed from the financial market, but this solution is not sustainable over time.

While direct output sales can make up only for a small share of bank debt settlements, transfers of fixed asset claims are limited by the firms' own stocks of marketable assets. Thus, in the long run, firms can settle their debt only by using their gross profits and/or by selling equity to the banks or the public. Equity sales allow firms to transfer to the banks claims on their future income as well as control over their future income-earning capacity.

For given (desired) levels of profitability, the use of profits to settle bank debt requires that firms extract larger surpluses from the owners of inputs, or that they use inputs more intensively through productivity growth. Using profits may thus be hampered by mutually inconsistent distributional plans by firms and input owners, obstacles to productivity growth, and slow business activity.

When profits are constrained by any of these factors, the firms' demand for liquidity driven by interest debt-service requirements generates equity transfers from the firms' original owners to the banks and/or to the public. Exchange of corporate control may take place, which may take various forms depending on the institutional characteristics of the economy involved: where banks dominate the financial system (and are not prohibited from owning corporate shares) enterprise ownership claims tend over time to accumulate in the bank portfolios, with such claims likely being exchanged in exclusive (bilateral) settings under non-competitive and non-transparent conditions. On the other hand, where financial systems are more market based, corporate equity is absorbed by the non-bank public in more competitive and transparent contexts.

Exchange of corporate control can be influenced by the business cycle. By compressing corporate profits, economic slowdowns likely generate preferences for non-competitive transfers of ownership from firms to banks, since exclusive bank–firm relationships make it relatively easier and cheaper for both to convert debt into equity within the same bank portfolios. With sustained economic activity, however, larger corporate profits and the public's greater appetite for risk and need for risk diversification should encourage transfers of ownership to households, to other firms, and to non-bank financial institutions through competitive markets.

Whether corporate ownership is largely transferred to the banks or the public has a different impact on the system's liquidity. If firms transfer ownership to the banks, the interest debt is settled directly as debt is exchanged for equity and no additional money is needed in the circuit to make interest payments. On the other hand, if corporate ownership shifts to the public or to (financial and non-financial) non-bank entities, interest payments need to continue to be made from the firms to the banks, requiring new money to be injected in the system.

Policy Implications

Bank money creation entails a *forward-looking* process that goes from credit to output generation and debt settlement. To the extent that the money advanced via lending is backed by output *ex post*, the economy gains can mobilise more real resources than if loans had to be backed by output upfront (which is the case when loans are financed with fully collateralised borrowing).

On the risk side, however, a system where banks create money is riskier than if banks were to fully cover their credit. Because banks issue liquid liabilities to finance illiquid assets, they bear liquidity risks and can spread their risks to the economy.

Governments introduce rules and policies to reduce such risks. In doing so, policy makers need to resolve important risk–efficiency tradeoffs. Two issues are taken up in this section with the purpose to assess how policies aimed to reduce bank risks interact with bank incentives to create money: the first deals with the payment systems' settlement rules, and the second discusses the recurrent proposals to narrow the scope of banking.

Do payment system's settlement rules matter?
Interbank credit in a circuit process allows banks to create the money needed to finance economic activity by supporting banks' mutual debit positions arising from deposit transfers (payments).[25] Each bank must be sufficiently

creditworthy to get credit from the other banks and, in turn, must be willing to extend credit to the others (if these are sufficiently creditworthy) as deposits move across their books.

Different payment and settlement rules may alter the cost for the banking system to create money. Under *correspondent banking* arrangements, banks hold accounts with their correspondents through which they clear (incoming and outgoing) payments. Correspondents extend credit to their client banks and to other correspondents through credit lines or overdraft agreements under preset terms and limits. Up to these limits, correspondents commit to making good all incoming payments from their clients, until new funds are credited to the client accounts and overdrafts and credit lines are repaid.[26] The cost of money creation is determined by the prevailing type of interbank credit agreements. The reciprocity of such agreements and the adoption of netting contracts between correspondents can make the cost of interbank credit (and hence of money creation) much cheaper than if banks were to settle their (gross) mutual obligations in central bank money (see below in this section).

Under *multilateral net settlement* rules, banks are required periodically to use central bank money to settle their multilateral net payment obligations outstanding at the time of settlement. This requirement does not prevent banks from using the interbank credit implicit in the netting arrangement to create the money needed to finance transactions during the interval between settlement cycles. In fact, net interbank debit (credit) positions may in principle be very small, or even zero, and yet banks' mutual gross obligations could be as large as necessary to satisfy deposit transfers of any desired size. Multilateral netting rules thus provide a convenient way for banks to create money.

Under *gross settlement* rules, banks are required to settle each (gross) interbank deposit transfer in central bank money. Gross settlement virtually eliminates settlement risk as well as the possibility of systemic transmission of the failure of individual banks to settle. But this comes at a price. Recent studies have focused on the efficiency costs of gross settlement rules,[27] including payment gridlock problems and suboptimal intertemporal consumption effects (Kahn and Roberds, 1998).

The circuit approach suggests that gross settlement also reduces the banks' power to issue money and makes bank money creation more costly to the economy than the alternative rules discussed above. Under gross settlement, banks can mobilise deposit claims to execute payments only if they have or receive sufficient cover funds in their account with the central bank. They therefore need to possess enough reserves, or to borrow reserves intra-daily from the central bank, before issuing and transferring deposits to each other. In the event that central bank intra-day lending requires collateral, this has to be raised by the banks at a cost and may also carry a considerable opportunity cost. On the other hand, if the central bank does not require collateral but charges penalising interest rates, these would still impose an extra cost on the borrowing banks.[28]

As a result, the banks must pre-accumulate more resources (for any given volume of deposits that need to be mobilised) or they must curtail their overall lending, since issuing and mobilising deposits costs more to them than under alternative settlement rules.[29] These replace a regime where banks can create money by exchanging IOUs with a *cash-in-advance* regime that imposes a tighter real resource constraint on money creation.

Can banks be narrowed?

Risk reduction lies at the heart of the various 'narrow banking' proposals often recurring in the literature and the policy debate, especially in the aftermath of banking crisis episodes. These proposals aim to remove liquidity and solvency risks from the banking business by requiring deposit-issuing banks to fully back their deposit liabilities with safe short-term assets and by prohibiting such banks from taking any other type of risk. The proposals also hold that all other intermediaries be prevented from issuing demandable debt.[30]

Advocates of narrow banking note that the volume of safe assets outstanding outside of the banking system exceeds that of bank demand deposits. They consider this as evidence of a large unsatisfied demand for safe assets that banks fail to match because of existing distortive incentives (such as deposit insurance or bailout expectations) that encourage banks to hold illiquid loan portfolios (Kareken, 1985). They conclude that narrowing the scope of banks would correct these distortive incentives and make banks safer and better places to keep investor money.

Thinking in circuit terms suggests that narrowing banks would eliminate the unique role of banking and the important efficiency effects that go with it. If banks create money through lending to production, a high leverage is intrinsic to their incentive structure whereby the liquid debt claims created stand necessarily against the less liquid assets financed. The high leverage allows the economy to issue money much more conveniently than if money had to be fully covered.

To see this, consider how money would have to be injected into the economy, and production financed, under narrow banking. One option is through specialised non-banks. These may not issue demand deposits and, by construction, do not have access to bank lending, but they can borrow or purchase money from the central bank against collateral or in exchange for securities, and on-lend it to firms. Under this option, the resource requirement to finance overall non-bank lending would obviously be higher than if banks could lend by issuing demandable debt.

Alternatively, non-banks can buy securities from producing firms and finance them by issuing non-demandable debt. Such type of financing requires ultimate lenders to be willing to hold larger shares of relatively less liquid claims than demand deposits, thus requiring higher returns, lest some firm financing plans go unfulfilled or new money has to come from the central bank (at the extra cost discussed above).

Both options show that there is a natural incentive to conventional banking that narrow banking would suppress. In other words, there would always be an incentive for some agents to specialise in directly issuing the money that goes into their lending, instead of intermediating it, thus making the supply of such money cheaper and more elastic. Regulations aimed at transforming all banks into narrow banks would create market incompleteness and increase the cost of providing money to the economy.

WILL BANKS SURVIVE?

Having discussed the distinctive role of banking and finance in a market economy, one might wonder if the distinction will remain in the future, in the face of the rapid transformation of the financial environment owing to technological and institutional changes. This question arises spontaneously when observing that almost everywhere in the industrial world, over the last two decades, traditional banking (deposit and lending) activities have lost important market shares. Such a decline is the result of the impressive growth of commercial paper markets and the money market mutual funds thrift industry, the increasing ownership of banks by securities firms and commercial enterprises, and the proliferation of quasi-monies or money substitutes offering transaction services comparable to those offered by banks on deposits. Correspondingly, banks have had to diversify their activity from traditional deposit lending to non-bank intermediation and financial services provision.[31]

As many believe, the quantitative decline reflects a qualitative change in traditional banking, which has lost importance vis-à-vis other forms of financial intermediation. Banks as we have come to know them, it is argued, will either disappear or become practically indistinguishable from other financial institutions.

Is this necessarily so?

In the industrial world, non-bank financial intermediaries have taken away considerable business from commercial banks. Increases have been observed in the market share of institutions holding securities instead of loans. At the same time, banks themselves have heavily shifted their activity from traditional banking to other financial intermediation services (Allen and Santomero, 2001). Lending to production, in particular, has become less important as more and more firms can directly access the market for short-term funds. Also, following financial liberalisation, domestic banking sectors have undergone profound reorganisation, with banks consolidating into fewer and larger units.

An interesting interpretation of the disintermediation phenomenon is the core-deposit theory of Berlin and Mester (1998). Liberalisation has led banks to pay market rates on an increasing portion of their funds, core deposits have shrunk, and relationship lending has become less feasible. As a result, banks have lost some of their comparative advantage vis-à-vis non-banks.[32]

Circuit theory suggests an alternative hypothesis to explain disintermediation and consolidation. As liberalisation reduces the demand for core deposits, banks tend to run increasing interbank open debit positions associated with lending. Therefore, banks incur higher liquidity holding costs to protect themselves against the risk of defaulting on interbank obligations.[33] This puts pressure on banks to reduce lending and/or to expand their scale in an attempt to win larger deposit market shares from competitors. In any case, banks seem bound to become less in number and bigger in size.

But, can one imagine a world where non-bank intermediaries replace banks altogether?

In an environment where bank lending for production is less relevant, banks perform their key money creation function through alternative (and more wholesale type of) instruments. These include credit to non-banks (including credit card issuers and industrial corporations offering financial intermediation services) and contingent credit.

By lending to non-banks, banks indirectly supply the economy with fresh money to absorb production and services. This is typical of bank lending to intermediaries that provide credit for consumption, second-hand asset purchases, and financial services (including financial activities for speculation and hedging). This credit is essential as industrial productivity growth requires ways to expand and accelerate consumption of durables and physical capital renewal, and the demand for financial investment and risk- and portfolio-management services increases rapidly. Banks advance short-term loans to intermediaries with ready and deep access to the capital market. The intermediaries on-lend the loan proceeds (on longer-term conditions) to households and firms planning to buy durable goods, second-hand assets, or financial services. As sales are executed, the selling firms encash the sale proceeds and invest the income, which generates capital market funds. The intermediaries can refinance their position from the capital market and match their asset–liability maturity, and the system overall has more liquidity in it. A new flow of funds takes place in the circuit wherein the selling firms are net investors, the buyers of goods and services are fund users, and banks remain the suppliers of money. Banks thus are essential for the growth of the economy's real and financial sectors.

Banks can create money also through *contingent liabilities* (such as guarantees and warranties) that they issue to protect financial and non-financial institutions against adverse contingencies. These liabilities are stand-by commitments to issue money to their holders if and when these contingencies happen. Their diffusion confirms the continuing uniqueness of banks: first of all, they enable the economy to use the existing liquidity more efficiently by supporting the extension of quasi-money and short-term borrowing instruments to an extent that would not be feasible without banks' stand-by commitment guarantees. Secondly, through these types of liabilities banks act as backup sources of liquidity for all other institutions in the system (Corrigan, 1982, 2000), and are in a position to support circuit closure in the event of payment failures. This underscores the banks' continuing importance in spite of the historical decline of their traditional activities. It also emphasises their key role as market agents specialised to validate the creditworthiness of issuers of quasi-monies and short-term borrowing instruments.

In short, while the development of modern financial markets enables a growing number of fund users to raise money from non-bank sources, banks play a key role as lenders for those firms that do not have direct access to financial markets and are crucial in supporting capital market activities through their money-creation function. Through money creation, banks complete the economy's financial market structure by transforming liquidity and maturity (at a risk).

Also, while financial market development enables the economy increasingly to economise on bank money through money substitutes, until the public becomes willing to borrow such substitutes and use them for payments banks will remain special and not replaceable. By using money market mutual fund shares as an example of quasi-money, Appendix 2 explains why quasi-monies are not quite money yet.

The fact that technological and institutional development enables agents to economise on the use of bank money, and that as a result traditional banking can consolidate into a smaller sector of activity, does not reduce the importance of bank money, or of banks as money producers. The contrary appears to be true, considering that in contemporary advanced economies an increasing volume of quasi-monies and liquid financial instruments rest on a tinier base of bank money, and stand ready to be converted into bank money if need be. This enhances the importance of banks and their money.

CONCLUSION

Thinking of the economy as a circuit proves extremely helpful to explain how money interconnects with production, exchange, and capital formation in a process where time is relevant, meaning that decisions, actions, and events happen sequentially and that agents are recognised as having to cope with limited information and an unknown future.

In this chapter, we have suggested that when the circuit framework is placed on microeconomic foundations and is adapted to incorporate banks and non-bank intermediaries as agents specialised in evaluating and taking financial risks, the circuit can be used to shed light on important aspects of macroeconomic equilibrium, financial structure, and banking and payment system policies.

The adapted framework shows how the economy responds to shocks originating from sources insisting on different junctures of the circuit process. These include class conflicts, shifts in liquidity preference and demand expectations, and credit-rationing phenomena associated with financial risks and imperfect information.

The adapted framework provides a consistent understanding of the distinctive functions and roles that banks and non-banks play in the economy, along the circuit process. In particular, it has offered very powerful reasons as to why banks are special and irreplaceable entities in a market economy, and why they have unique powers that are not shared by non-bank intermediaries.

The adapted framework also offers useful valid insights into policy issues. It shows that moving toward gross settlement rules may bear significant efficiency costs by making the supply of bank money less elastic and more costly than under alternative rules. Moreover, it has shown that attempts at eliminating bank liquidity and solvency risks by suppressing conventional banking would likely result in serious efficiency costs.

Finally, the adapted framework offers valid reasons to believe that banks are not going to lose their uniqueness even if the financial system undergoes important structural changes that lead to a consolidation of the conventional banking business.

APPENDIX 1

A simple numerical example can illustrate how seigniorage increases with bank size. As the model in the second section clarifies, when a bank issues a loan, and part of the newly issued money is deposited with other banks, the issuing bank incurs new interbank liabilities that are financed through credits from the banks where the money was deposited. To the extent that part of the loan is re-deposited with the issuing bank, and that the interest rate on deposit liabilities to the public is lower than the rate of charge on interbank liabilities, the issuing bank saves on its charges in proportion to the amount re-deposited. On the other hand, the bank runs an interbank credit position vis-à-vis the other banks, which equals the share of the loans issued by them and deposited with it.

The seigniorage of each bank can thus be calculated as the difference between the bank's interest income on loans and interbank credits and the charges paid on interbank liabilities.

The interest income on loans is the product of the bank's loan and lending rate. Interbank interest income is obtained applying the bank's market share and lending rate to the loans issued by the other banks. The bank's expenses on interbank liabilities are the product of the rate of charge and the bank's loans deposited with the other banks (calculated using the market share of the other banks).

In the following numerical exercise the lending rate is 8 per cent, the rate of charge is 6 per cent, no interest is paid on deposit liabilities to the public, and all banks, except our bank of interest (bank A), issue loans totalling 100 units. The seigniorage of bank A is calculated for different combinations of bank A's loan and deposit market shares (Table 8.1).

The results show that seigniorage is more sensitive to changes in the deposit market share than to changes in the loan market share. This is because an increase in the former increases the bank's re-deposit capacity, thereby raising its income on interbank loans, and symmetrically reduces the other banks' re-deposit capacity, thus decreasing its interbank debit charges.

The example does not take into account the effect of market power on interest rates and charges associated with bank relative size, whereby lending rates tend to rise and deposit rates tend to decrease as the market becomes more concentrated (less competitive). All else equal, both effects increase seigniorage.

Table 8.1. Seigniorage and size of bank A

A's loan market share	A's deposit market share	A's loan income	A's income on interbank credits	A's charges on interbank liabilities	Seigniorage (3)+(4)−(5)
(1)	(2)	(3)	(4)	(5)	(6)
10	0.10	0.8	0.6	0.54	0.86
10	0.20	0.8	1.2	0.48	1.52
20	0.10	1.6	0.6	1.08	1.12
20	0.20	1.6	1.2	0.96	1.84
40	0.10	3.2	0.6	2.16	1.64
40	0.20	3.2	1.2	1.92	2.48
40	0.40	3.2	2.4	1.44	4.16

APPENDIX 2

Money Market Mutual Funds (MMMFs) pool savings from many individuals and invest them in high-grade, short-term securities, offering market returns on share accounts that permit check writing and wire funds transfer privileges. Although providing shareholders with deposit-like transaction services, a close inspection at MMMFs shows that they do not make banks and their money-creation function any less special. Firstly, when MMMFs issue shares, they receive bank deposits that they hold with their bank or banking department: deposits are not replaced by mutual fund shares, but shift from individual to mutual fund portfolios. Secondly, when MMMFs buy securities, they sell deposits that securities issuers use to finance their spending plans: deposits are not replaced by mutual fund shares to finance expenditure. Thirdly, when a shareholder instructs her mutual fund to make a payment on her behalf to a third party, the mutual fund debits the shareholder's share account and transfers equivalent deposits from its own banking account to the third party: deposits are not replaced by mutual fund shares as transaction devices, and payments continue to be executed as deposit transfers on the books of the banks. Of course, a mutual fund can finance its payment obligations through a line of credit from its bank or by liquidating its own securities. Both options, however, involve deposit transfers: mutual funds do not create money; they only transfer it from investors to users.

Mutual funds with many shareholders allow investors to economise on bank deposits (as banks do with central bank money). This reduces the total stock of deposits demanded by the economy and increases their velocity of circulation. However, banks stand ready to purchase securities from mutual funds (against deposits) in the event of liquidity shortfalls: banks are backup sources of liquidity for mutual funds.

Finally, nothing prevents the public from accepting mutual fund shares as payment instruments. In this case, mutual fund shares would become full-fledged money and, like banks, mutual funds would have an incentive to lend out newly issued shares.

NOTES

1. This chapter elaborates on two previous articles on the theory of the monetary circuit (Bossone, 2001a, 2001b). The author wishes to express his deep intellectual indebtedness to Augusto Graziani, whose work in this field has greatly inspired this research. The usual disclaimer applies.
2. Monetary circuit theory has its major proponents in Europe – most notably France, Belgium, Italy and Switzerland – where different groups of scholars are active under Schmitt, Parguez, Cartelier, De Vroey, Cencini, Graziani and Messori, to cite just some of the leading names. On the other side of the Atlantic, Lavoie is a circuitist from Canada. In the United States, a circuit-compatible interpretation of the saving–investment process was propounded long ago, and was later reiterated, by Davidson (1965, 1990), although this author is not regarded (and cannot be regarded) as a circuitist. Although the major contributions to circuit theory do not constitute a fully unified body of economic knowledge, and indeed considerable diversity exists across them, some basic and important common features are clearly distinguishable and provide foundations for an integrated theory of money and production. The literature on the monetary circuit has grown rich since the pioneering work of Schmitt (1959); however, many publications are in languages other than English (see Graziani and Messori, 1988). Interested English-language readers should refer to Lavoie (1985), Graziani (1990, 1996), Cencini (1995) and Rochon (1999).
3. As Graziani (1990, p. 7) emphasises: 'The theory of the monetary circuit emerges as a reaction to the standard neoclassical interpretation of economic equilibrium as the result of individual choices taken by isolated and independent agents. The model of the circuit is built instead so as to stress the existence of the relationships among macro-actors, going beyond individual choices. In this perspective, marginal theory of distribution is rejected, in favour of a theory stressing the power of banks, in that they provide the necessary means of payment, and the power of firms, in that they determine the allocation of productive resources. In this view, the level of employment . . . is determined by decisions taken jointly by banks and firms'.
4. Schmitt (1975) and Cencini (1995) investigate both the monetary and financial dimensions

of the circuit, although they do not develop specific microeconomic behavioural assumptions. They also investigate the international monetary implications of circuit theory.

5. One notable exception on both counts is Messori (1988). The role and the microeconomics of finance in a sequential monetary production economy with limited information and risk are further studied by Messori and Tamborini (1993, 1994).

6. We shall come to this point in the fourth section.

7. To keep the model simple, banks here do not remunerate deposits and have access to unlimited and costless interbank lending. Without these assumptions, any bank aiming to increase its lending can offer a competitive return on its deposits and expand its deposit base. The assumption above emphasises the role of interbank lending in supporting bank money creation.

8. The absence of the central bank from the model emphasises that bank-money creation can take place independently of the traditional money multiplier process, which requires a pre-existing form of outside money. But even when central bank money base is included, the demand for it does not necessarily imply a multiplier process of bank-money creation (although, of course, *ex post*, the money stock produced by the banks is always a multiple of the base). When the money base is included, it can be seen as a higher-powered reserve asset that banks hold in a certain proportion to their liquid liabilities as a liquidity insurance instrument. In fact, banks can always create money, provided that the supply of the base is sufficiently elastic for them to keep their desired proportion of reserves to liquid liabilities.

9. In fact, demand deposits can be converted into term deposits or other types of bank liabilities while funds are kept with banks, based on holder preferences. This implies that, although bank loans are issued in the form of demand deposits, they do not have to necessarily stay in that form until loans are repaid. This also explains both why the largest share of bank liabilities typically consist of term deposits and why total demand deposits in any economy are usually only a small fraction of total bank loans.

10. In this case, equation (8.21) would still take the equality since a decrease in the borrowing (and lending) of the non-banks would force higher holdings of bank deposits until the term on the right-hand side of the equation equals the term on the left-hand side. On the investor side, this corresponds to actual z's being upper-bounded by $\bar{z}$'s in equation (8.4) as a result of the lower supply of non-bank securities.

11. The proceeds of the non-bank financial institutions should, in fact, partly feed into payments for inputs used in intermediation activity, while only profits could be retained as savings. However, as the income of input suppliers would have the same destination of corporate income, these proceeds may be left out of the model without loss of generality and no result alteration. For the same reason, banks are assumed not to bear production costs.

12. The sequence would be: banks lend short-term funds to firms → firms pay interest to banks → banks invest interest income in the capital market → firms borrow from the capital market and clear off the bank debt → the newly created money re-flows to the issuing banks and is destroyed. Thus, as banks inject fresh money, firms are in a position to convert their short-term interest debt obligations into long-term liabilities via the financial market.

13. In fact, increasing productivity or decreasing the real value of wages can only increase firms' real profits (or material surplus) but can in no way help them raise additional cash, if the overall stock of cash is given.

14. In the above model, rationing can occur also in the interbank market, since banks can reduce their exposures or cut their credit limits to other banks. This would constrain their money-creation capacity.

15. In a model with a central bank and a public sector, banks could either deposit the funds with the central bank or invest them in government debt. In the latter event, the re-injection of funds into the economy would depend on the spending decisions of the government.

16. Firms can use previously accumulated savings (either their own accumulated profits or funds borrowed from the capital market) to discharge their obligations with the banks. In this event, however, these same savings would be withdrawn from their possible use in

investment funding by enterprises: firms producing capital goods would not appropriate the money needed to discharge their own obligations and the initial problem would reappear. While it is true that funds are always in the circuit (if the economy is closed), irrespective of who uses them, the simultaneous and competing demands for the funds from investing enterprises and producing firms would exceed supply. Some agents could raise money only at higher rates and some might be rationed.

17. In principle, however, agents could conventionally accept non-bank liabilities as money for transaction purposes. In this (hypothetical) case, the intermediary would de facto become a bank.

18. This function was well recognised already in the 1930s by Bresciani-Turroni (1936).

19. Banks do not create value and the newly issued money takes on value only when and if it is associated with new production (Schmitt, 1975; Cencini, 1995).

20. This conclusion differs from neoclassical models where banks play a passive and neutral role on prices (see for instance Fama, 1980).

21. For an analytical discussion of seigniorage in an economy with a banking sector, see Baltensperger and Jordan (1997).

22. Banks may temporarily shift the obligations to the future by refinancing the firms' debt over longer-term maturity, but at some point firms would have to relinquish real resources anyway, as term lenders would not postpone their credit exposure indefinitely.

23. Contrast this with the extreme case of a system with only one bank. Money would circulate as book-entries within the same bank's balance sheet. In this case, irrespective of how fast existing deposits change hands, and abstracting from inflationary and confidence problems, the bank could create new money at will, unimpeded by debit-offsetting requirements. Note that in this case the bank would be in a position to extend loans of any maturity, with no concern as to asset–liability maturity mismatch. Related to size is also the degree of competition among banks, which limits seigniorage both by restraining the equilibrium level of the interest rate on bank loans and by raising the equilibrium interest rate on deposits.

24. As an alternative to expanding their scale, banks could join in clearinghouse arrangements with others and accept each other's payments by extending reciprocal credits. (I am grateful to F. Mishkin for pointing this out to me.) However, whereas in the case of a clearinghouse arrangement individual banks' seigniorage would be limited by interbank credit limits and conditions, a single bank that would clear the same volume of payments in its own books would not be subject to the same limitations: by eliminating the costs of interbank lending, the clearinghouse would internalise the benefits from centralising the accounts. Moreover, the clearinghouse argument does not invalidate – and in fact supports – the conclusion that seigniorage increases with size.

25. Smith and Weber (1998) show, analytically and historically, the welfare superiority of payment systems with interbank credit.

26. Assume that banks A and B hold correspondent accounts with one another and agree on mutual credit lines. If A's borrower pays B's client out of his loan account, A runs a liability vis-à-vis B. Bank A may finance its liability by drawing its credit line with B. Bank B can do the same for its payments to A. In fact, the two banks can create money up to the limit of their mutual credit lines, with no central bank money involvement.

27. See Kahn and Roberds (1998) for a review of the literature and a contribution to the issue.

28. A bank could alternatively borrow reserves from other banks, but this option is not feasible for the banking system as a whole, which either holds enough reserves or suffers a net shortage of reserves and has to borrow them from the central bank.

29. Should the reverse hold, there would be a serious presumption that the central bank would be subsidising interbank lending under real gross settlement rules by not charging a high enough interest rate to protect itself against credit risk.

30. For a survey of the literature on narrow banking and a comprehensive evaluation of the costs and benefits of narrow banking, see Bossone (2001c).

31. For an analysis of the decline of traditional banking in the United States, see Edwards and

Mishkin (1995). Howells and Hussein (1997) and Arestis and Howells (1999) provide evidence for the United Kingdom. For a recent analysis, see Allen and Santomero (2001).

32. The concept of *core deposits* must be used cautiously. In a circuit process, increases in the interest elasticity of the demand for deposits do not imply destruction of existing deposits, but simply their increasing velocity of circulation. In principle, to the extent that banks extend sufficient credit to each other, and/or that their size allows them to minimise interbank exposures, the decline of core deposits should not upset lending.

33. Larger reserve holdings are also needed in those systems using gross settlement rules, as discussed earlier.

REFERENCES

Allen, F. and A. Santomero (2001), 'What do financial intermediaries do?', *Journal of Banking and Finance*, **25** (2), 271–94.

Arestis, P. and P. Howells (1999), 'The supply of credit money and the demand for deposits: a reply', *Cambridge Journal of Economics*, **23** (1), 115–19.

Baltensperger, E. and T.J. Jordan (1997), 'Seigniorage, banking, and the optimal quantity of money', *Journal of Banking and Finance*, **21** (6), 781–96.

Berlin, M. and L.J. Mester (1998), 'On the profitability and cost of relationship lending', *Journal of Banking and Finance*, **22** (6–8), 873–97.

Bossone, B. (2001a), 'Circuit theory of banking and finance', *Journal of Banking and Finance*, **25** (5), 857–90.

Bossone, B. (2001b), 'Do banks have a future? A study on banking and finance as we move into the third millennium', *Journal of Banking and Finance*, **25** (12), 2239–76.

Bossone, B. (2001c), 'Should banks be narrowed?', *IMF Working Paper*, WP/01/159.

Bresciani-Turroni, C. (1936), 'The theory of saving: I. The forms of the saving process', *Economica*, **3** (9), 1–23.

Cencini, A. (1995), *Monetary Theory, National and International*, London and New York: Routledge.

Corrigan, E.G. (1982), 'Are banks special?', *Federal Reserve Bank of Minneapolis Annual Report*, 5–24.

Corrigan, E.G. (2000), 'Are banks special? A revisitation', *The Region*, **14** (1), 14–17.

Davidson, P. (1965), 'Keynes's finance motive', *Oxford Economic Papers*, **17** (1), 47–65.

Davidson, P. (1990), 'Finance, funding, saving and investment', in L. Davidson (ed.), *The Collected Writings of Paul Davidson, Volume 1: Money and Employment*, London: Macmillan, 365–72.

Edwards, F.R. and F.S. Mishkin (1995), 'The decline of traditional banking: implications for financial stability and regulatory policy', *Federal Reserve Bank of New York Economic Policy Review*, **1** (2), 27–45.

Fama, E.F. (1980), 'Banking in the theory of finance', *Journal of Monetary Economics*, **6** (1), 39–57.

Graziani, A. (1988a), 'Le teorie del circuito e la *Teoria generale* di Keynes', in A. Graziani and M. Messori (eds), *Moneta e produzione*, Torino: Einaudi, 95–115.

Graziani, A. (1988b), 'Il circuito monetario', in A. Graziani and M. Messori (eds), *Moneta e produzione*, Torino: Einaudi, xi–xliii.

Graziani, A. (1990), 'The theory of the monetary circuit', *Économies et Sociétés* ('Série Monnaie et Production', 7), **24** (6), 7–36.

Graziani, A. (1996), 'Money as purchasing power and money as a stock of wealth in Keynesian economic thought', in G. Deleplace and E.J. Nell (eds), *Money in Motion: The Post Keynesian and Circulation Approaches*, London and New York: Macmillan and St. Martin's Press, 139–54.

Graziani, A. and M. Messori (1988) (eds), *Moneta e produzione*, Torino: Einaudi.

Heinsohn, G. and O. Steiger (1983), 'Private property, debts and interest or: the origin of money and the rise and fall of monetary economies', *Studi economici*, **38** (21), 3–56.

Howells, P. and K. Hussein (1997), 'The demand for money: total transactions as the scale variable', *Economics Letters*, **55** (3), 371–7.

Kahn, C.M. and W. Roberds (1998), 'Payment system settlement and bank incentives', *Review of Financial Studies*, **11** (4), 845–70.

Kareken, J.H. (1985), 'Ensuring financial stability', in J. Beebe and D. Payne (eds), *The Search for Financial Stability: The Past Fifty Years*, San Francisco: Federal Reserve Bank of San Francisco, 53–77.

Lavoie, M. (1985), 'Credit and money: the dynamic circuit, overdraft economics, and Post-Keynesian economics', in M. Jarsulic (ed.), *Money and Macro Policy*, Boston: Kluwer-Nijhoff Publishing, 63–84.

Lavoie, M. (1999), 'The credit-led supply of deposits and the demand for money: Kaldor's reflux mechanism as previously endorsed by Joan Robinson', *Cambridge Journal of Economics*, **23** (1), 103–13.

Messori, M. (1988), 'Agenti e mercati in uno schema periodale', in A. Graziani and M. Messori (eds), *Moneta e produzione*, Torino: Einaudi, 285–330.

Messori, M. and R. Tamborini (1993), 'Money, credit, and finance in a sequence economy: foundations of a macroeconomic model', *Occasional Papers*, Dipartimento di scienze economiche, Università di Roma "La Sapienza", 20.

Messori, M. and R. Tamborini (1994), 'Moneta, finanza e credito in un'economia sequenziale', in G. Vaciago (ed.), *Moneta e finanza*, Bologna: Il Mulino, 55–100.

Rochon, L.-P. (1999), 'The creation and circulation of endogenous money: a circuit dynamique approach', *Journal of Economic Issues*, **33** (1), 1–21.

Schmitt, B. (1959), 'L'équilibre de la monnaie', *Revue d'économie politique*, **69** (5), 921–50.

Schmitt, B. (1975), *Théorie unitaire de la monnaie, nationale et internationale*, Albeuve: Castella.

Smith, B.D. and W.E. Weber (1998), 'Private money creation and the Suffolk banking system', *Federal Reserve Bank of Minneapolis Working Paper*, 591.

9. Pricing, Investment and the Financing of Production within the Framework of the Monetary Circuit: Some Preliminary Evidence

Mario Seccareccia[1]

INTRODUCTION

With the publication of the major volume edited by Deleplace and Nell (1996), the recent books by Realfonzo (1998) and Rochon (1999a), as well as important summary articles by Rochon (1999b), Parguez and Seccareccia (2000) and Bossone (2001), English-speaking economists have been treated with a comprehensive exposition and analysis of the theory of the monetary circuit. Admittedly, the basic concepts and underlying framework have been well known for over a century, with their origins to be found in the works of the advocates of the Banking school and of Marx (see Seccareccia, 1999). Except for some obvious advances with the adoption of Keynes's analysis of the 'finance motive' among post Keynesian writers (see Rochon, 1997), however, most post-war developments have focused on money primarily as a *stock* variable under the control of the monetary authorities rather than as a *flow* variable arising as an outcome of the endogenous interaction of economic agents with the banking sector.

The purpose of this chapter is to address two important aspects of the literature on the monetary circuit that have not been sufficiently explored. These pertain to the flux–reflux principle at the heart of the theory of the monetary circuit. On the 'flux' side, an important question still remains to be settled. This has to do with what bank credit actually finances. As discussed in a separate contribution to the Deleplace and Nell volume (Seccareccia, 1996), this issue is far from being a trivial one, since its consequences are of critical importance to the closure of the circuit. On the 'reflux' side, instead, the role of the well-known phenomenon of business saving or 'internal finance' is critically important to the analysis, yet is often only vaguely mentioned by circuit theorists. Indeed, business saving (or firms' net cash flow) is usually presented as a purely passive outcome of how households allocate their incomes between consumption and saving in the commodity market. Our intention is to modify somewhat this general view. After a presentation of the questions at issue and their theoretical implications, an attempt is also made to test the empirical relevance of the theory using Canadian, as well as some limited American, observations.

THE BASIC MODEL OF THE MONETARY CIRCUIT AND ITS APPLICABILITY

Despite some important insights to be found in Joan Robinson's *The Accumulation of Capital* (1956), the modern post-war development of the literature on the monetary circuit can be traced to a number of writers in continental Europe, especially in France and Italy, who recognised both the institutional irrelevance of much of the neoclassical analysis of the monetary system along the lines of the Friedmanite revival of the quantity theory and sought to develop a competing theory of the monetary economy based on the fundamental heterodox principle of endogenous money (see Bellofiore and Seccareccia, 1999). While important French economists such as Bernard Schmitt and Alain Parguez have been engaged in the most sustained and substantive research in this field over the last few decades, Italian circuit writers such as Augusto Graziani have perhaps provided the most celebrated synthesis of this approach. We shall briefly sketch out the basic properties of the approach proposed by Graziani (1987, 1990, 1994b) and identify at least two serious problems with the underlying model.

In his original 1987 article (which was further refined in 1990 and 1994), Graziani begins by distinguishing between 'initial finance' and 'final finance'. All productive activities in a monetary capitalist economy require initial financing. This ought to be so not only in a growing economy that is characterised by a positive rate of net investment as, for instance, the neoclassical theorists of loanable funds would surmise. As pointed out, among others, by Parguez and Seccareccia (2000), even in a stationary environment, albeit highly uncharacteristic of capitalist economies, in which the flows of income and production are presumed to remain unchanged over time, the flow of production would require financing. Since the proceeds from the sale of their output at the end of the circuit are assumed to go toward extinguishing their debt previously advanced by the banking system, firms would require a regular infusion of initial finance at the start of each subsequent production cycle.[2] Much like the Sisyphean metaphor in Greek mythology, business enterprises are perpetually engaged during discrete intervals in a circular process of acquiring or extinguishing their debts vis-à-vis the banking system. To guarantee their financial viability, qua capitalist firms, such a process would have to be repeated continually on the basis of the specific conjuncture in which they may find themselves.

At the beginning of the production cycle, business enterprises require short-term (or initial) finance that will allow them to purchase the necessary circulating capital, largely in the form of wages and raw materials, needed to undertake production. Once this prior liquidity is provided to finance total output, regardless of whether it be in the consumption or capital goods sector, the household patterns of expenditures will determine the volume and composition of the monetary reflux to the banking system. It is in this framework, however, that one set of problems arises and that has already been discussed at greater length in the Deleplace and Nell volume (see Seccareccia, 1996). With the exception of such writers as Parguez (1980), most circuit theorists adopt a model that is akin to the old-line nineteenth-century 'real bills' doctrine of financing activities, albeit for important logical rather than institutional reasons. According to this traditional banking principle, prudent bank behaviour would dictate that credit-money ought to go only toward the financing of short-term production requirements. Long-term financing of fixed capital formation would be expected to bypass altogether the banking system and to result either from the build-up of equity via internal finance and/or through the selling of securities to households.

Unlike, perhaps, the more ambiguous position of some post Keynesian writers such as Moore (1985, 1988) and Davidson (1988), this espousal of what, on the surface, appears to be a 'real bills' view of the credit system has nothing to do, however, with any belief in the validity of this nineteenth-century doctrine to explain modern financing decisions of individual banks.[3] For instance, Graziani (1994b, p. 76) does not exclude the fact that, at the purely microeconomic level, firms may be borrowing to finance the purchases of elements of fixed *and* working capital. The adoption by many circuit writers of what seems to be a peculiar version of the 'real bills' financing rule ensues exclusively from the internal macroeconomic logic of their analysis. Indeed, when the non-financial business sector is consolidated macroeconomically into a single sector, these circuit writers argue that the only element that requires financing in advance of production is working capital and, more precisely, the wage bill (or what Marx had described as the 'variable capital' requirement of business enterprises). All other purchases of inputs (whether it be raw materials or plant and machinery, that is, Marx's elements of 'constant capital') would appear purely as internal transactions within the non-financial business sector and, therefore, would not necessitate financing via bank credit. Hence, even if an individual firm acquires credit advances for the purchases of, say, a capital equipment, the logic of monetary circulation would impose that this credit-money go ultimately toward the specific financing of machinery production, and thus of labour costs, of firms in the capital-goods sector. What, at first glance, appears as the financing of investment by one firm, in fact, turns out to be a concurrent credit transfer to another firm in the capital-goods sector that would, in turn, be used for the financing of the latter's wage bill. It is hypothesised that, in the aggregate, all initial finance, other than for wages, cancels itself out and, consequently, bank initial financing of production could be represented simply as:

$$\Delta M = \Delta(wL) \qquad (9.1)$$

where ΔM is the increase of credit-money (relative to outstanding business debt) at the beginning of the period of the circuit that is advanced to firms to cover their additional variable capital $\Delta(wL)$ needs, that is, the change in the wage bill (w = average wage and L = the level of employment), with $\Delta(p_K K)$, the purchases of newly produced fixed capital goods K (at the price p_K) being excluded from possible initial financing at the aggregate level.[4]

There are, however, a number of problems with this specific assumption. One of these questions has already been summarised partly by Lavoie (1987) and by Seccareccia (1996) and, therefore, will not be elaborated here in much detail. This has to do with the important question of how firms, producing fixed capital goods, can realise a money profit and obtain sufficient money revenues to reimburse the banks when ΔM only goes toward the financing of $\Delta(wL)$.

The argument can be briefly stated as follows: assuming a simple classical world in which the propensity to save out of workers' income is zero, the monetary accumulation of fixed capital would be realised in such a 'real bills' world only if some other sector is constantly unable to repay fully its debts or is systematically running deficits. For instance, government deficits, regardless of how they may be incurred, could be a factor in generating a sufficient cash flow internally to build up corporate equity.[5] Without some other net debt in the system, the closure of the monetary circuit within the private enterprise sector can ensue only if firms' purchases of $\Delta(p_K K)$ are financed by the creation of credit-money at the beginning of the circuit. Any other financing rule, as the one stipulated in equation (9.1), would result therefore in some firms not realising sufficient monetary revenues to acquire the newly produced fixed capital goods. Since all emissions of credit-money originate from the banking sector, as a group, firms cannot get back more than what was initially advanced to finance their working capital requirements. Barring the possibility of net debts emerging in other sectors, under this restrictive 'real bills' assumption, growth could only be realised at the end of the period of the circuit if the wage bill expands with net additions to fixed capital arising, somehow, via internal financing.[6] Given the importance of the phenomenon of internal financing in a growing economy, with few exceptions such as Nell (2002) it is surprising that this theoretical conundrum has not been more fully explored by circuit theorists.

Moreover, the financing of investment cannot be rejected on the logical ground that, even if firms were to do so, the creation of additional credit-money would be *fully* compensated by a *reduction* in the financing of working capital requirements in the capital-goods sector, as for instance Graziani (1994b, p. 76) contends. In a decentralised system in which firms and households interact and where there is a limited demand for cash and/or liquid deposits on the part of economic agents, it is obvious that this compensating effect would not fully work itself out. Therefore, even if ideally one can imagine a monetary production economy in which only changes in the wage bill would be financed, and transactions between households and firms would go instantaneously toward extinguishing the latter's debts, there would always be a non-negligible demand for cash in the system that would necessitate that ΔM finances *more* than merely changes in the wage bill for the closure of the monetary circuit. Indeed, it is only by borrowing to finance also purchases of elements of constant capital and, in particular, to finance expenditures on capital-goods equal to the gap between the aggregate value of total output of the capital-goods sector and its own sectoral wage bill, that the monetary circuit can be closed.[7] In this case, equation (9.1) would be revised so as to take into account the fact that firms finance a portion, say, α of investment, with this latter coefficient (as discussed below) empirically also varying on the basis of the net indebtedness of other sectors, namely government or households, from whose net spending private firms can then finance 'internally' the additional purchases of fixed capital goods.

Though recent writings (see Rossi, 2001) have sought to explore more carefully certain important aspects of the question, a further related problem is the pricing issue, which has not been fully articulated satisfactorily by circuit writers. Following Seccareccia (1984) and Graziani (1987), let us assume a simple two-sector model in which, during a given period, L_K of total employment (L) has been apportioned for the capital-goods sector and L_C for the consumption-goods sector. Assuming linear production processes, the physical quantity supplied of consumption goods is Q_C^S (which is equal to $a_C L_C$, where a_C

is average labour productivity in the consumption-goods sector). On the other hand, the monetary flow of demand for these consumption goods ($p_c Q_c^D$), when we consider both labour income, wL, and rentier income, iB (where i is the rate of interest, and B is the stock of securities, including liquid deposits, held by households), becomes:

$$p_c Q_c^D = wL + (1 - s_r)iB \qquad (9.2)$$

where the propensity to save out of wage income is zero and the propensity to save out of rentier income, s_r, is assumed to be positive and less than one. Defining B as some multiple γ of the wage bill, wL, and supposing market clearance of the consumption-goods market, whereby $Q_c^D = Q_c^S$, we obtain the following price equation for consumption goods:

$$p_C = [1 + (L_K/L_C)][1 + (1 - s_r)i\gamma](w/a_C) \qquad (9.3)$$

which suggests that consumer prices would depend on unit labour costs (w/a_C) in the consumption-goods sector, on the level of rentier income and rentier propensity to consume, and on the way in which total employment is distributed between the two sectors (L_K/L_C). Fluctuations in the inter-sectoral allocation of employment, for example, because of variations in L_K arising from exogenous changes in investment would impact directly on the level of consumer prices, p_C.[8] In much the same way, a change in rentier income would also exert pressure on prices, albeit less than would a comparable change in labour income, owing to the postulated lower propensity to consume out of rentier income.

There is, however, an obvious difficulty with this representation. As is shown by Seccareccia (1984), such an analysis must assume implicitly that prices are purely demand-determined and result from a market-clearing process in the context of competitive markets in which no involuntary inventories of finished goods are held. Indeed, after presenting a one-sector variant of this simple pricing model, Graziani (1990) discerns some difficulty with his formulation and seeks to allay fears about the restrictive nature of his findings. As Graziani (1990, p. 22) writes:

> It should be noticed that the preceding [market clearing] equality may seem as being in the nature of an equilibrium condition in a perfectly competitive market. It might as well be interpreted as being a condition imposed by firms enjoying an oligopolistic position and being therefore able to sell finished products at a price high enough to secure the desired profit margins.

Unfortunately, this general inference about the model's applicability is not possible within the confines of Graziani's original model, since it provides no theory about how prices are set to satisfy a specific target rate of return of the type, for instance, illustrated by Parguez (1996).

A feature common to all heterodox pricing models, whether it be the classically inspired models of the neo-Ricardians or the more fashionable Kaleckian representations, is that, for reproducible goods, prices are not affected by changes in demand, unless the underlying costs and/or mark-ups are sensitive to such variations. The only possibility for the latter to arise within Graziani's canonical model would be if firms' mark-ups are systematically related to variations in L_K/L_C. This would be so, however, only if firms would be targeting a certain cash flow or rate of internal finance along Eichnerian lines. It is only by subscribing to some variant of the Eichner-type pricing models of internal financing of investment that the formal logic of much of the established literature on the monetary circuit can be justified. As we have previously mentioned, this literature links the initial creation of credit money to the financing of a critical element of working capital – the wage bill. Investment in fixed capital, on the other hand, is assumed to be financed internally from the cash revenues arising from the monetary reflux.

Internal financing is a generally recognised phenomenon that numerous post Keynesian researchers of Kaleckian pedigree have tried conceptually to integrate within their pricing models. As shown by Seccareccia (1984), the predicted link between investment and pricing is very significant empirically.[9] For now, simple graphical illustration would suffice to highlight the extent to which inflation and investment move in tandem. Figure 9.1 displays some simple aggregate time series on the rate of inflation (choosing as measure the rate of change of the consumer price index) and business fixed capital formation as a percentage share of GDP for the period 1961–2001 in Canada. Though it is not a one-to-one relation between the two time series, the association is remarkably close.[10]

While there may be significant correlation, however, the build-up of corporate equity through pricing does not fully finance fixed capital formation within an oligopolistic environment. Credit creation also needs to fill the financing gap between desired investment and net cash flow. This is not only based on the recognised fact that bank credit has historically also gone toward financing the purchases of the newly produced fixed capital, but evidence from flow of funds data would suggest that internal financing as a share of capital expenditures is significant but not very high.[11] A notable proportion of corporate investment in North America is done via debt creation rather than through the build-up of corporate equity.

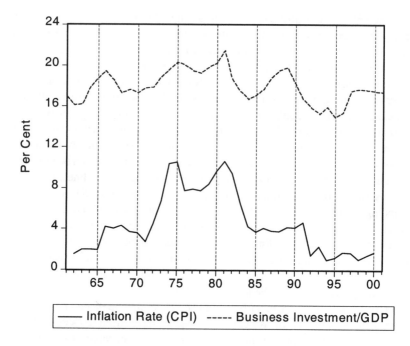

Figure 9.1. Investment and inflation in Canada, 1961–2001

To reconcile this fact with the circuit approach, one must modify somewhat equation (9.1) so as to take this phenomenon into account. As a group, firms borrow to finance their circulating capital needs as previously stipulated. In addition, they may also finance a portion α of their fixed capital requirements, $\Delta(p_K K)$. The remaining portion of the required funds $(1 - \alpha)\Delta(p_K K)$ could be obtained internally through changes in their net cash flow, $\Delta\pi$, owing, say, to some other sector's growth in its net indebtedness position vis-à-vis the banking system. In this way, taking account of this element of the monetary reflux, equation (9.1) now becomes:

$$\Delta M = \Delta(wL) + \Delta(p_K K) - \Delta\pi \qquad (9.1.A)$$

Defining $\Delta(p_K K)$ simply as I_F, business investment in fixed capital, we could then re-write equation (9.1.A) as:

$$\Delta M = \Delta(wL) + I_F - \Delta\pi \qquad (9.1.B)$$

Equation (9.1.B) describes the more general financing rule that both deals with the concerns previously expressed about the need to finance investment expenditures, I_F, while concomitantly taking into account the phenomenon of internal financing, $\Delta\pi$.[12] In this case, equation (9.1.B) should be seen as describing the credit demands on the banking sector of one particular, yet crucial, sub-system – the non-financial business sector, which is composed of firms producing either consumption or fixed capital goods. As discussed by Steindl (1982) and Seccareccia and Sharpe (1994), however, a surplus generated in one sector, $\Delta\pi$, necessarily represents a bank-financed deficit in some other sectors, whether it be the household or government sectors. Indeed, Seccareccia and Sharpe (1994) found empirically that business sector surpluses, $\Delta\pi$, originate from such important variables as money-financed primary deficits of the public sector. Unfortunately, the development of such a complete model of the monetary circuit is outside the focus of the present chapter.

One last issue on the 'efflux' side that ought to be addressed before analysing the empirical relevance of our particular theoretical model of business sector initial financing has to do with the role of the rate of interest. All other things being equal, an exogenous increase in the loan rate of interest would put upward pressure on the non-financial business sector for financing. While an increase in the loan rate facing each firm would put downward pressure on individual credit demand, for the non-financial business sector as a whole the effect would be to increase its demand for credit. Macroeconomically, a firm cannot reduce its net debt position unless some other agent (or sector) is deepening its indebtedness. This growing debt accompanying an increase in the rate of interest could arise for a number of possible reasons. Firstly, an increase in the rate of interest would mean that the overall reflux to the banking sector would be rising as long as there is no concomitant increase in the interest rate on deposits, the latter interest income flow being an amount of money that banks must also advance to depositors during the period of the circuit. Secondly, even if there were a proportional increase in both the loan and the deposit rates (thereby entailing a constant interest spread or bank mark-up), it could still create short-term problems for firms. This is because an increase in the rate of interest would favour rentiers whose propensity to save and preference for liquidity would be high. A shortfall in the cash flow accruing to business firms because of this redistribution in favour of rentier income could force firms to increase their demand for short-term credit in order to continue with their planned spending. Hence, in agreement with authors such as Wray (1991), variations in the rate of interest ought to impact positively on the demand for funds and, therefore, equation (9.1.B) can be reformulated as follows:

$$\Delta M = \Delta(wL) + I_F - \Delta\pi + \Delta(iM_0) \qquad\qquad (9.1.C)$$

where i is the rate of interest and M_0 is the volume of outstanding loans or debt being rolled over from the end of the previous period. From equation (9.1.C), it ensues that monetarist austerity policies of high interest rates ought to impact perversely on the demand for credit-money, as it would be in a macroeconomic state of Ponzi finance *à la* Minsky (of the type described, *inter alia*, by Seccareccia, 1988).

Before generalising our particular formulation so as to take into account other elements of the monetary reflux, it would be useful at this stage to provide a simple visual illustration of the relation between the dependent variable, ΔM, and the four independent variables of equation (9.1.C), namely, $\Delta(wL)$, I_F, $\Delta\pi$ and Δi. Figure 9.2 shows the relation between the average annual first-difference in total business credit, ΔM, provided by the financial system and changes in the sum of wages, salaries, and supplementary labour income, $\Delta(wL)$.[13] Except for the very brief period between 1974 and 1976 where the two series bifurcated slightly, the 'real bills' principle of a close association between business credit advances and demand for this important element of firms' circulating capital is clearly evidenced in the chart. In much the same way, Figure 9.3 displays a similar close connection between changes in credit advances (in millions of dollars) and the flow of business fixed capital formation, I_F.[14] For a measure of changes in retained earnings, $\Delta\pi$, no such measures are readily available at the aggregative national accounting level and, therefore, as a reasonable substitute, a measure of changes in corporation profits (before taxes) was used as proxy.[15] Though the link is not as strong as with the two previous variables, what the graphical evidence seems to suggest in Figure 9.4 is that our profits variable, $\Delta\pi$, does appear to be *negatively* correlated with credit creation at the aggregate level, as suggested by equation (9.1.C). Finally, and as expected, Figure 9.5 positively connects changes in bank credit with changes in the prime lending rate, the latter variable having been scaled appropriately so as to capture the common variation with ΔM. At the purely graphical level, therefore, there appears to emerge some stylised facts in support of a relation between pricing and the internal financing of investment.

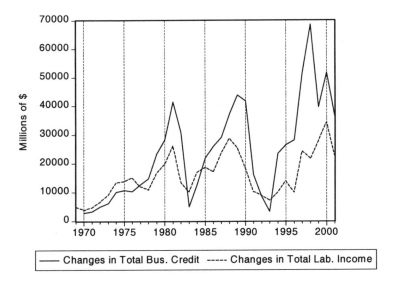

Figure 9.2. Changes in total business credit and changes in total labour income in Canada, 1969–2001

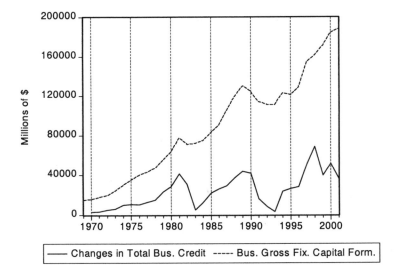

Figure 9.3. Changes in total business credit and flow of investment in Canada, 1969–2001

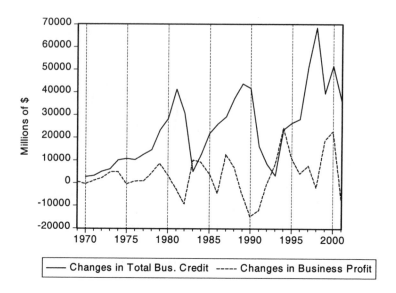

Figure 9.4. Changes in total business credit and changes in corporation profits before taxes in Canada, 1969–2001

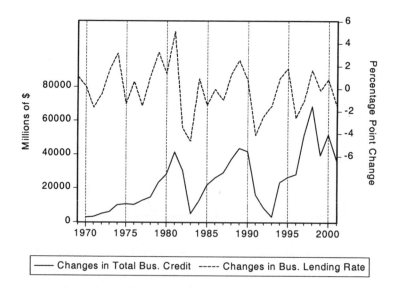

Figure 9.5. Changes in total business credit and changes in chartered banks prime business loan rate in Canada, 1969–2001

Thus far, we have pointed to the various elements of the 'efflux' of credit-money within the framework of the monetary circuit, namely, $\Delta(wL)$, I_F, $\Delta(iM_0)$, but have focused on only one, though critical, element of the monetary reflux, $\Delta\pi$, whose effect is to allow firms to reduce their level of indebtedness. Yet, there are at least two other elements of the reflux or 'final financing' within the non-financial business sector that need to be accounted for. Firstly, there is the increment of consumption expenditures, ΔC_H, arising from the additional income accruing to households. Secondly, there is the increment of household savings that are captured by firms via the selling of securities in the financial capital markets, ΔS_H^*, where S_H^* is the volume of household savings *not* held in the form of bank deposits or cash. Like $\Delta\pi$, these latter two elements of the reflux to the non-financial business sector would be used to reduce the latter's overall outstanding debt with the banking sector. From this, it follows that at the end of the period of the circuit we have:

$$\Delta M = [\Delta(wL) + \Delta(iM_0) - \Delta C_H] + [I_F - \Delta\pi - \Delta S_H^*] \qquad (9.1.D)$$

In addition, equation (9.1.D) can be further re-organised as:

$$\Delta M = [\Delta S_H - \Delta S_H^*] + [I_F - \Delta\pi] \qquad (9.1.E)$$

or simply:

$$\Delta M = \Delta M_H + [I_F - \Delta\pi] \qquad (9.1.F)$$

where ΔS_H is the net increase of total household saving during the period of the circuit, and ΔM_H is the net accumulation of bank deposits and cash balances held by households, the latter revealing the degree of household liquidity preference. Abstracting from the possibility of other sectors' indebtedness to the banking sector, equation (9.1.F) depicts how the overall net accumulation of business debt ultimately reflects decisions by firms to accumulate capital (relative to their net cash flow, $\Delta\pi$) and by households to accumulate liquid assets, ΔM_H, over time. Any changes, for instance, in household portfolio preference would thus directly impact on the net indebtedness position of firms, ΔM. As with the preceding graphical illustrations, Figure 9.6 provides some casual empirical evidence in support of this hypothesis. Using various broad measures of monetary aggregates, such as $\Delta M2$, $\Delta M2+$, and $\Delta M3$ for Canada, it is evident from the chart that these series are all closely correlated with our indicator of change in total business credit.[16] At least for the time period of the analysis, an increase in household acquisition of bank deposits generally resulted in a concomitant rise in business indebtedness.

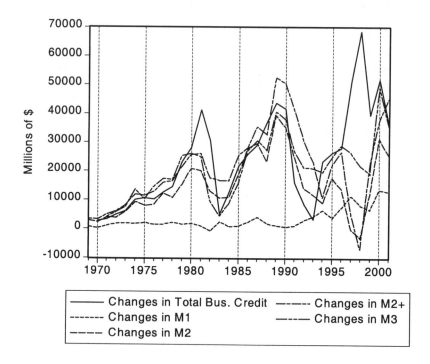

Figure 9.6. Changes in total business credit and changes in selected broad monetary aggregates in Canada, 1969–2001

These theoretical and empirical results lead to a fundamental difference in the view of the role of banks in a monetary capitalist economy. Within the mainstream textbook interpretation, the function of banks is that of intermediation. Banks are assumed merely to collect the proportion of saving that households choose to hold in the form of bank deposits, from which the former can then provide bank loans to business enterprises. Hence, as pure financial intermediaries, it follows that 'deposits make loans'. Within this traditional view of the monetary system, the unhealthy exception would arise only when banks try to deny their intermediation role and seek to over-extend credit in relation to their reserves. During situations of severe over-extension of bank credit, characterised by states of financial instability and crises, central banks are ultimately forced to intervene as lenders of last resort (as with the fire-fighter analogy in Rochon (1999b, p. 14)) so as to supply the necessary liquidity to the previously undisciplined banking system. It ensues for orthodoxy that the natural function of banks is to engage in financial intermediation with the anomaly, often leading to problems of liquidity and to financial crises, being when banks engage in net monetary creation.

Within the framework of the monetary circuit, this traditional view is completely stood on its head. Instead of financial intermediation, the normal function of banks is that of creators of credit-money that they provide *ex nihilo* to firms for the financing of production. Hence, as creators of money, 'loans make deposits'. It is only when households choose to withhold their savings from the financial capital markets and seek to hold a significant proportion of their saving in the form of bank deposits that difficulties of reimbursement appear. This forces banks into the uneasy 'intermediation' role of re-financing debt or acquiring by default business assets (in the case where $(I_F - \Delta\pi)$ is insignificant) equivalent to the net accumulated household bank deposits, ΔM_H. It is only in this anomalous theoretical case of incomplete closure of the monetary circuit that the traditional neoclassical view that 'deposits make loans' would apply. Hence, what was the exception for the traditional view of banks becomes the rule, and what was supposedly the rule in terms of financial intermediation now becomes a sign of systemic malfunction and failure of the elemental flux–reflux principle to be fully realised within the monetary circuit.

SOME FURTHER STATISTICAL EVIDENCE

To estimate the various empirical relations postulated above more rigorously, standard econometric tests were run on the previous, albeit limited, aggregate data displayed in Figures 9.2 to 9.6. The first set of empirical relations estimated pertains to equation (9.1.C). The following linear equation was empirically estimated using simple OLS procedure applied to the original annual data for the period 1969–2001:

$$\Delta M = a_0 + a_1 \Delta(wL)_t + a_2(I_F)_t + a_3 \Delta\pi_t + a_4 \Delta i_t + \varepsilon_t \qquad (9.4)$$

where ε_t is the error term. As the previous charts had already illustrated, the results of our simple tests (shown below) merely strengthen what had been inferred graphically:

$$\Delta M = -5872.58 + 0.95\Delta(wL)_t + 0.18(I_F)_t - 0.39\Delta\pi_t + 1624.57\Delta i_t \qquad (9.4.A)$$
$$\quad (-1.71) \quad (3.38) \qquad (4.49) \quad (-2.48) \qquad (2.13)$$

where:

Adjusted R^2 = 0.79
D.W. = 1.41

and with the t-ratios being displayed in parentheses below the estimated coefficients. All other variables were found to be highly significant with the appropriate sign. Moreover, since there was some evidence of serial correlation, the Cochrane–Orcutt type procedure was applied to correct for any suspected first-order autocorrelation, with the following estimated results:

$$\Delta M = -5858.69 + 0.96\Delta(wL)_t + 0.17(I_F)_t - 0.41\Delta\pi_t + 1364.26\Delta i_t \qquad (9.4.B)$$
$$ (-1.15) \qquad (2.75) \qquad\quad (3.40) \qquad (-2.48) \qquad (1.80)$$

where:

Adjusted R^2 = 0.79
D.W. = 1.91
$\rho = 0.30$
    (1.40)

An effort was also made to re-estimate these equations in log-linear form. As shown in Table 9.1, the results were not as robust even though the same empirical relations gleaned. Moreover, because of possible non-stationarity in the time series, adjustments were made to the original data so as to render the series stationary. Table 9.2 summarises the results of the re-specified estimated equations subsequent to tests of unit roots done on the time series data for each variable. The tests suggested that ln I_F was not a trend stationary process and therefore necessitated adjustment by means of first-differencing of the original time series. The results in Table 9.2 offer, once again, some support in favour of our hypothesis. In much the same way, a stronger analysis was undertaken to determine whether each data series was a trend stationary or a difference stationary process by means of the augmented Dickey–Fuller test. Subsequent to the analysis, some variables (such as $\Delta\ln M$, $\Delta\ln(wL)$ and $\Delta\ln I_F$) required second-differencing to pass the test. These latter weaker empirical results using the transformed data series are displayed in Table 9.3. In much the same way, comparable test procedures were applied to available quarterly data for the United States between 1973 and 2000. Once again, as shown in Table 9.4, although the evidence was rather weak, the signs were all in the direction suggested by our theoretical framework and, therefore, were still generally supportive of the pattern of monetary flows that was found in Canada.

Table 9.1. Estimated log-linear empirical relations for Canada

Dependent variable	Constant	$\Delta \ln (wL)$	$\ln I_F$	$\Delta \ln \pi$	$\Delta \ln i$	Adjusted R^2	D.W.	ρ
$\Delta \ln M$	−0.21	0.92	0.02	−0.07	0.06	0.70	0.83	
	(−1.82)	(5.36)	(2.20)	(−2.80)	(2.19)			
$\Delta \ln M*$	−0.04	0.80	0.01	−0.07	0.04	0.81	1.82	0.65
	(−0.18)	(4.23)	(0.33)	(−3.6)	(2.27)			(4.22)

Note
* Estimated equation adjusted for first-order autocorrelation using the Cochrane–Orcutt procedure.

Table 9.2. Estimated log-linear empirical relations using stationary data

Dependent variable	Constant	$\Delta \ln (wL)$	$\Delta \ln I_F$	$\Delta \ln \pi$	$\ln i$	Adjusted R^2	D.W.	ρ
$\Delta \ln M$	−0.09	0.20	0.33	−0.08	0.06	0.72	0.91	
	(−2.57)	(1.03)	(3.06)	(−2.59)	(3.74)			
$\Delta \ln M*$	−0.07	0.40	0.21	−0.09	0.05	0.83	1.80	0.61
	(−1.54)	(1.63)	(2.35)	(−3.34)	(2.33)			(3.89)

Note
* Estimated equation adjusted for first-order autocorrelation using the Cochrane–Orcutt procedure.

Table 9.3. Estimated log-linear empirical relations using stationary data

Dependent variable	Constant	$\Delta^2 \ln (wL)$	$\Delta^2 \ln I_F$	$\Delta \ln \pi$	$\Delta \ln i$	Adjusted R^2	D.W.
$\Delta^2 \ln M$	0.005	0.62	0.08	−0.04	0.07	0.47	2.00
	(0.81)	(1.80)	(0.80)	(−0.99)	(2.46)		

Note
Δ^2 represents second differencing of variable.

Table 9.4. Selected estimated results using US quarterly data for 1973–2000

Dependent variable	Constant	$\Delta (wL)$	I_F	$\Delta \pi$	Δi	Adjusted R^2	D.W.	ρ
ΔM	−2.45	0.16	0.01	−0.03	1.05	0.27	0.74	
	(−1.01)	(2.30)	(1.18)	(−0.77)	(1.61)			
ΔM^*	−3.82	0.04	0.01	−0.02	0.81	0.58	2.05	0.67
	(−0.74)	(0.73)	(1.83)	(−0.98)	(1.85)			(8.93)

Dependent variable	Constant	$\Delta \ln (wL)$	$\ln I_F$	$\Delta \ln \pi$	$\Delta \ln i$	Adjusted R^2	D.W.	ρ
$\Delta \ln M$	−0.001	0.75	0.001	−0.07	0.06	0.30	0.84	
	(−0.03)	(2.99)	(0.19)	(−2.70)	(2.19)			
$\Delta \ln M^*$	−0.03	0.42	0.006	−0.01	0.03	0.59	1.84	0.68
	(−0.44)	(1.86)	(0.56)	(−0.77)	(2.66)			(9.73)

Note
[*] Estimated equation adjusted for first-order autocorrelation using the Cochrane–Orcutt procedure. The data for commercial and industrial loans at all commercial banks, as well as the US prime lending rate, were obtained from the web site of the Federal Reserve Bank of St. Louis, while the national accounting data was obtained from the Bureau of Economic Analysis of the US Department of Commerce.

These overall empirical findings appear generally to be compatible with the modified structure of the circuit model presented above. The positive estimated coefficients for $\Delta(wL)$ are consistent with the generally accepted version of the monetary circuit as presented by Graziani (1990). On the other hand, the positive estimated coefficients for I_F and the negative coefficients for $\Delta\pi$ may not be. For instance, the significance of many of the coefficients of I_F would suggest a possible association between credit advances to firms, ΔM, and business fixed capital formation. These results conflict with the established model of the monetary circuit. Likewise, the negative coefficients for $\Delta\pi$ seem to detect the importance of internal financing in reducing firms' overall demand for credit. In much the same way, the positive estimated coefficients of the interest rate variable are in accordance with the generally accepted view among theorists of the monetary circuit. Indeed, while an increase in the prime rate may create obvious disincentives for individual firms to borrow, for the system as a whole the evidence suggests that it would *increase* the demand for credit. Being the sole purveyor of credit-money, the banking system cannot take in more money than what it advances initially. For a given monetary flow of payments for wages and investment purchases, an exogenous increase in the rate of interest pushes up the demand for credit. Interest payments, like wage payments, are financed by initial advances of credit-money to the non-financial business sector.

Finally, an attempt was also made to estimate the generalised version of our circuit model that adjusts for the effects of other elements of monetary reflux. To capture these residual effects, two empirical specifications of equation (9.1.F) were estimated:

$$\Delta M_t = b_0 + b_1[\Delta M_H]_t + b_2[I_F - \Delta\pi]_t + \xi_t \qquad (9.5)$$
$$\Delta M_t = b_0 + b_1[\Delta M_H]_t + b_2[I_F]_t + b_3[\Delta\pi]_t + \xi_t \qquad (9.6)$$

with ξ as the error term, and where ΔM_H is the net change of a broad monetary aggregate ($M2$, $M2+$ and $M3$). The best results were obtained with our widest definition of M_H for which data were available for the complete period of our study (namely, the $M3$ variable):

$$\Delta M_t = -1053.74 + 0.40\,[\Delta M3]_t + 0.19\,[I_F - \Delta\pi]_t \qquad (9.5.A)$$
$$(-0.23) \qquad (1.50) \qquad\quad (3.18)$$

where:

Adjusted R^2 = 0.58

$D.W. = 0.94$

Although the evidence is slightly weaker, the signs and the direction of change are all as expected from our theoretical framework. Furthermore, after adjusting for first-order autocorrelation by means of the Cochrane–Orcutt type procedure, the results improved slightly:

$$\Delta M_t = -4484.32 + 0.51 \, [\Delta M3]_t + 0.19 \, [I_F - \Delta \pi]_t \qquad (9.5.B)$$
$$\quad\;\; (-0.52) \qquad (2.02) \qquad\qquad (2.36)$$

where:

Adjusted $R^2 = 0.66$
$D.W. = 1.64$
$\rho = 0.55$
$\quad (3.17)$

Econometric results were obtained when the composite variable $[I_F - \Delta \pi]_t$ was decomposed into its two components and then estimated separately. Though somewhat less robust (especially with respect to our corporate profit variable), as displayed below, the signs were consistently in the direction suggested by our theory:

$$\Delta M_t = -1084.42 + 0.40 \, [\Delta M_H]_t + 0.19 \, [I_F]_t - 0.18 \, [\Delta \pi]_t \qquad (9.6.A)$$
$$\quad\;\; (-0.23) \qquad (1.47) \qquad\quad (3.12) \qquad (-0.79)$$

where:

Adjusted $R^2 = 0.56$
$D.W. = 0.94$

Once again, after an adjustment for first-order serial correlation, there was a net improvement in the empirical results:

$$\Delta M_t = -4062.26 + 0.52 \, [\Delta M_H]_t + 0.19 \, [I_F]_t - 0.22 \, [\Delta \pi]_t \qquad (9.6.B)$$
$$\quad\;\; (-0.44) \qquad (1.98) \qquad\quad (2.09) \qquad (-1.09)$$

where:

Adjusted $R^2 = 0.65$

$$D.W. = 1.63$$
$$\rho = 0.55$$
$$(3.10)$$

Other similar results, with $\Delta \dot{M}2$ and $\Delta M2+$, obtained using log-linear specifications, are provided in Table 9.5.

Table 9.5. Generalised version of the credit-money equation estimated in log-linear form using Canadian data

Dep. variable	Const.	Δ ln M2	Δ ln M2+	Δ ln M3	ln $(I-\Delta\pi)$	ln I	ln $\Delta\pi$	Adjusted R^2	D.W.	ρ
Δ ln M	−0.19	0.75			0.02			0.49	1.04	
	(−1.58)	(5.42)			(1.85)					
Δ ln M*	−0.18	0.59			0.02			0.60	1.79	0.56
	(−0.76)	(3.18)			(0.093)					(3.36)
Δ ln M	−0.22		0.77		0.02			0.43	0.98	
	(−1.64)		(4.79)		(1.88)					
Δ ln M*	−0.23		0.61		0.02			0.56	1.75	0.58
	(−0.85)		(2.59)		(1.00)					(3.50)
Δ ln M	−0.22			0.78	0.02			0.51	0.86	
	(−1.63)			(5.36)	(1.85)					
Δ ln M*	−1.91			0.49	0.15			0.74	1.89	0.96
	(−3.47)			(3.72)	(4.11)					(21.3)
Δ ln M	−0.17	0.74				0.02	−0.02	0.48	1.01	
	(−1.31)	(5.14)				(1.58)	(−0.67)			
Δ ln M*	−0.04	0.53				0.01	−0.04	0.60	1.76	0.57
	(−0.13)	(2.84)				(0.29)	(−1.33)			(3.30)
Δ ln M	−0.21		0.76			0.02	−0.02	0.41	0.95	
	(−1.38)		(4.50)			(1.62)	(−0.58)			
Δ ln M*	−0.07		0.54			0.01	−0.04	0.56	1.69	0.59
	(−0.21)		(2.26)			(0.35)	(−1.36)			(3.43)
Δ ln M	−0.16			0.75		0.02	−0.05	0.52	0.79	
	(−1.05)			(5.05)		(1.27)	(−1.41)			
Δ ln M*	−0.09			0.63		0.01	−0.05	0.68	1.72	0.63
	(−0.31)			(4.01)		(0.43)	(−1.92)			(3.81)

Note

* Estimated equation adjusted for first-order autocorrelation using the Cochrane–Orcutt procedure.

CONCLUSION

This chapter has explored some well-known issues within the literature on the monetary circuit. The assumption that investment is *not* directly financed through bank credit but rather exclusively through the build-up of equity during the reflux phase of the circuit has been analysed. While the existence of the phenomenon of internal financing through corporate pricing rules may be compatible with this hypothesis, our preliminary empirical evidence supports the view that business purchases of fixed capital are also partly financed by bank credit. However, in conformity with the more established literature on the monetary circuit, increases in corporate profits and, therefore, in retained earnings, appear to be ploughed back into extinguishing their bank debts previously incurred to purchase fixed capital goods and, as a consequence, reducing firms' demand for credit-money. Moreover, as emphasised by most circuit theorists, increases in bank deposits are an obstacle to the closure of the monetary circuit and, therefore, are positively correlated with the evolution of business debt. Owing to the small sample size, the evidence provided has obvious limitations. Although further research is necessary, especially in evaluating its sensitivity to model specification and studying its applicability further to data internationally, this preliminary work offers some useful insights into the possible underlying mechanism of monetary circulation.

NOTES

1. The author would like to thank Riccardo Bellofiore, Claude Gnos, Augusto Graziani, Marc Lavoie, Warren Mosler, Alain Parguez, Bernard Vallageas and L. Randall Wray for their helpful comments. The usual disclaimers apply.
2. This issue was addressed quite eloquently by Graziani (1987). With respect to Keynes's finance motive, Graziani (1987, p. 35) writes that '[w]hen the level of output is constant, the revolving fund gives the undeniable, but illusory, idea that production is self-financed and that no external support is needed. In fact, it cannot be claimed that the revolving fund be automatically renewed each time. The very existence of a revolving fund requires a discretionary decision to be taken by banks again and again'.
3. This reveals an obvious difference between certain post Keynesian and circuit writers. At the aggregate level, purchases of raw materials necessitate financing in Moore (1985, 1988) but not in Graziani and some other writers on the monetary circuit. For a defence of this latter view based on the distinction between 'nominal' and 'real' emissions, see Schmitt and Cencini (1982).
4. Graziani (1994a, p. 277) is quite categorical: 'The analysis of money creation makes clear that money is initially created in order to cover current costs of production. The circuit approach thus helps to dispel a recurring mistake in the literature, according to which finance supplied by banks is confused with the financing of fixed investment. Of course investment needs to be financed in the sense that capital goods currently produced have to be sold to some agent wanting to keep them as real wealth. Investment finance can be supplied by household savings

as well as by profits. In no case is it supplied by banks. The role of banks is to supply credit and to finance the formation of money balances, not of financing investment'.

5. According to Denis (1995, p. 850), this view on the origin of business profit was first articulated most coherently by Kenneth Boulding in 1950, who had given it a more lucid treatment than either Kalecki or Keynes in *A Treatise on Money*. Following Boulding, Denis (1995) distinguishes between 'paid profits' and 'verified profits'.

6. For the sake of argument, this excludes the obvious phenomena where firms produce capital goods for their own use and/or for the desired build-up of inventories. For further analysis see Vallageas (1996).

7. For instance, in the simplest case in which all household income goes toward the purchase of consumption goods, the net profit of the consumption-goods sector would equal the portion of household income paid out in the capital-goods sector. Hence, at best, what could return to firms in the capital-goods sector is the monetary value of the wages initially paid out by this latter sector. Abstracting from the possibility of net indebtedness emerging in other sectors (such as government), this gap could only be filled through net borrowing by firms wishing to acquire the capital goods.

8. In Graziani's (1987) article, his theoretical model is developed along similar lines set out here in which his parameter $b/(1 - b) = L_K/L_C$ in our equation (9.3). In his 1990 article, instead, his previous employment ratios, b and $(1 - b)$, are transformed into sectoral shares of total output under the more restrictive assumption of a one-commodity world. His conclusions are, however, the same as those derived above.

9. Kaleckian models of 'internal financing' *à la* Steindl have traditionally been formulated with respect to the investment function, as described, for instance, in a recent article by Dutt (1995). However, during the 1970s, post Keynesian writers such as Eichner, Harcourt and Kenyon, developed Steindl's original insights into well-articulated pricing models.

10. The original pricing equation estimated was not significantly different from our equation (9.3), using the employment ratio L_K/L_C. For further details see Seccareccia (1984, especially pp. 193–208). However, even with the data presented in Figure 9.1, the correlation is remarkably strong with the following simple OLS regression results:

$$\Delta P_t/P = -6.42 + 0.61 \, (I_F/GDP)$$
$$(-1.50) \quad (2.65)$$

with:

Adjusted $R^2 = 0.79$
D.W. $= 1.98$
$\rho = 0.81$
   (8.75)

where the terms in parentheses are the t-ratios and ρ is the auto-regressive factor to correct for first-order serial correlation.

11. For instance, according to the Federal Reserve's flow of funds accounts, debt ratios of US non-financial corporations have been very high during the post-war period, while net new equity sales as a percentage of capital expenditures average at around 4.5 per cent throughout the twentieth century.

12. Theoretically, $\alpha(I_F) + \Delta\pi_t = I_F$, and therefore $(1 - \alpha)I_F = \Delta\pi_t$, but problems of statistical classification and measurement would preclude the possibility of any simple empirical validation. The coefficient, α, ought to vary between zero and unity depending upon whether the net indebtedness of the non-business sector (which is generating a positive $\Delta\pi$) is sufficient for the financing of the planned purchases of the capital goods, I_F.

13. The measure of total business credit was obtained from the Cansim database, series B2325, while labour income data were taken from Statistics Canada, *National Income and Expenditure Accounts* (13–001).

14. The latter series is obtained from Statistics Canada, *National Income and Expenditure Accounts* (13–001).
15. As with previous aggregate series, data on corporate profits (before taxes) were also obtained from Statistics Canada (13–001).
16. As depicted in Figure 9.6, narrower monetary aggregates such as $\Delta M1$ (that is, currency plus demand deposits) would not be strongly correlated with changes in business credit since the former variable is highly sensitive to the portfolio behaviour of the public. Indeed, one ought to expect that the broader the monetary aggregate, the less sensitive it would be to the composition of the public's portfolio and, therefore, the stronger it would impact on and vary with changes in firms' indebtedness. Time series for the various monetary aggregates were obtained from the Bank of Canada series available from Statistics Canada, where $M2$ = sum of currency, demand deposits, non-personal notice deposits, and personal saving deposits held in chartered banks; $M2+$ = $M2$ plus deposits at other financial institutions, including trust and mortgage loan companies, deposits and shares at credit unions and *caisses populaires*, deposits at Province of Ontario Savings Office and Alberta Treasury branches, holdings of money market mutual funds and annuities issued to individuals; and $M3$ = currency plus total chartered bank deposits held by the general public.

REFERENCES

Bellofiore, R. and M. Seccareccia (1999), 'Monetary circuit', in P.A. O'Hara (ed.), *Encyclopedia of Political Economy*, London and New York: Routledge, vol. II, 753–6.

Bossone, B. (2001), 'Circuit theory of banking and finance', *Journal of Banking and Finance*, **25** (5), 857–90.

Davidson, P. (1988), 'Endogenous money, the production process, and inflation analysis', *Économie appliquée*, **41** (1), 151–69.

Deleplace, G. and E.J. Nell (eds) (1996), *Money in Motion: The Post Keynesian and Circulation Approaches*, London and New York: Macmillan and St. Martin's Press.

Denis, H. (1995), 'Profits payés et profits constatés', *Revue d'économie politique*, **105** (5), 847–58.

Dutt, A.K. (1995), 'Internal finance and monopoly power in capitalist economies: a reformulation of Steindl's growth model', *Metroeconomica*, **46** (1), 16–34.

Graziani, A. (1987), 'Keynes' finance motive', *Économies et Sociétés* ('Série Monnaie et Production', 4), **21** (9), 23–42.

Graziani, A. (1990), 'The theory of the monetary circuit', *Économies et Sociétés* ('Série Monnaie et Production', 7), **24** (6), 7–36.

Graziani, A. (1994a), 'Monetary circuits', in P. Arestis and M. Sawyer (eds), *The Elgar Companion to Radical Political Economy*, Aldershot and Brookfield: Edward Elgar, 274–8.

Graziani, A. (1994b), *La teoria monetaria della produzione*, Arezzo: Banca Popolare dell'Etruria e del Lazio.

Lavoie, M. (1987), 'Monnaie et production: une synthèse de la théorie du circuit', *Économies et Sociétés* ('Série Monnaie et Production', 4), **21** (9), 65–101.

Moore, B.J. (1985), 'Wages, bank lending and the endogeneity of credit money', in M. Jarsulic (ed.), *Money and Macro Policy*, Boston: Kluwer-Nijhoff Publishing, 1–28.

Moore, B.J. (1988), *Horizontalists and Verticalists: The Macroeconomics of Credit Money*, Cambridge: Cambridge University Press.

Nell, E.J. (2002), 'Monetizing the classical equations: a theory of circulation', *Cambridge Journal of Economics*, forthcoming.

Parguez, A. (1980), 'Profit, épargne, investissement: éléments pour une théorie monétaire du profit', *Économie appliquée*, **33** (2), 425–55.

Parguez, A. (1996), 'Financial markets, unemployment and inflation within a circuitist framework', *Économies et Sociétés* ('Série Monnaie et Production', 10), **30** (2–3), 163–92.

Parguez, A. and M. Seccareccia (2000), 'The credit theory of money: the monetary circuit approach', in J. Smithin (ed.), *What is Money?*, London and New York: Routledge, 101–23.

Realfonzo, R. (1998), *Money and Banking: Theory and Debate (1900–1940)*, Cheltenham and Northampton: Edward Elgar.

Robinson, J. (1956), *The Accumulation of Capital*, London: Macmillan.

Rochon, L.-P. (1997), 'Keynes's finance motive: a re-assessment. Credit, liquidity preference and the rate of interest', *Review of Political Economy*, **9** (3), 277–93.

Rochon, L.-P. (1999a), *Credit, Money and Production: An Alternative Post-Keynesian Approach*, Cheltenham and Northampton: Edward Elgar.

Rochon, L.-P. (1999b), 'The creation and circulation of endogenous money: a circuit dynamique approach', *Journal of Economic Issues*, **33** (1), 1–21.

Rossi, S. (2001), *Money and Inflation: A New Macroeconomic Analysis*, Cheltenham and Northampton: Edward Elgar.

Schmitt, B. and A. Cencini (1982), 'Wages and profits in a theory of emissions', in M. Baranzini (ed.), *Advances in Economic Theory*, Oxford: Basil Blackwell, 137–46.

Seccareccia, M. (1984), 'The fundamental macroeconomic link between investment activity, the structure of employment and price changes: a theoretical and empirical analysis', *Économies et Sociétés* ('Série Monnaie et Production', 1), **18** (4), 165–219.

Seccareccia, M. (1988), 'Systemic viability and credit crunches: an examination of recent Canadian cyclical fluctuations', *Journal of Economic Issues*, **22** (1), 49–77.

Seccareccia, M. (1996), 'Post Keynesian fundism and monetary circulation', in G. Deleplace and E.J. Nell (eds), *Money in Motion: The Post Keynesian and Circulation Approaches*, London and New York: Macmillan and St. Martin's Press, 400–16.

Seccareccia, M. (1999), 'Money, credit and finance: history', in P.A. O'Hara (ed.), *Encyclopedia of Political Economy*, London and New York: Routledge, vol. II, 763–6.

Seccareccia, M. and A. Sharpe (1994), 'Canada's competitiveness: beyond the budget deficit', *Économies et Sociétés* ('Série Monnaie et Production', 9), **28** (1–2), 275–300.

Steindl, J. (1982), 'The role of household saving in the modern economy', *Banca Nazionale del Lavoro Quarterly Review*, **35** (140), 69–88.

Vallageas, B. (1996), 'L'apport de l'analyse financière des flux à la théorie post-keynésienne des circuits et à la mesure des profits', *Économies et Sociétés* ('Série Monnaie et Production', 10), **30** (2–3), 9–54.

Wray, L.R. (1991), 'The inconsistency of monetarist theory and policy', *Économies et Sociétés* ('Série Monnaie et Production', 8), **25** (11–12), 259–76.

10. Money as Finance and Money as Universal Equivalent: Re-reading Marxian Monetary Theory

Riccardo Bellofiore and Riccardo Realfonzo

> But in what way are gold and silver distinguished from other forms of wealth? Not by magnitude, for this is determined by the amount of labour embodied in them. But rather as autonomous embodiments and expressions of the social character of wealth . . . Credit, being similarly a social form of wealth, displaces money and usurps its position. It is confidence in the social character of production that makes the money form of production appear as something merely evanescent and ideal, as a mere notion (Marx, 1981, pp. 707–8).

MONEY IN A MONETARY ECONOMY

It is well-known that in the nineteenth century the dominant conception of the nature and function of money can be traced back to Ricardo. He puts forward a commodity-money theory, where money is in the last instance reduced to coined gold; bank deposits and the notes issued by central banks are no more than surrogates of gold. Ricardo is one of the authors for whom 'the logical source of the exchange value or purchasing power of money is the exchange value or purchasing power of that commodity, considered independently of its monetary role' (Schumpeter, 1954, p. 288). Thus Ricardo defines banking activity in terms of pure brokerage, establishing that banks' collection of deposits is the previous necessary condition for lending. It is no accident that Ricardo – and all of the currency school with him – closely links credit supply to the balance of payments and therefore to the inflows and outflows of gold. In short, Ricardo implicitly brings the capitalist economy back to a barter economy, in which the function of money is merely to overcome the problems of direct barter. Money is simply the particular commodity that serves as the oil easing the circulation of goods (indirect barter).

In our re-reading of the Marxian monetary model a triangular structure of the operators (banks, capitalist firms, and wage workers) is employed (see Bellofiore and Realfonzo, 1997; Bellofiore, Forges Davanzati and Realfonzo, 2000). The banks advance money-capital; the firms use it to buy labour power from workers and alone are entitled to production decisions. In this model, Ricardo's metallist theory of money is untenable; and the same must be said of his view of bankers as mere middlemen. This point may be clarified by describing the course of the capitalist circuit from its outset.

In order for production to begin, firms must purchase labour power. Unless appeal is made to the wage fund approach, there are no commodities with which to pay the workers. Hence, as Marx notes on several occasions, the wages are advanced in monetary terms. Money available in advance becomes a condition essential to the production of commodities. The alternative hypothesis – where firms share with the workers the commodity output after production – is proper to the co-operative view of the economy, which was foreign to Marx's concerns. If in a true monetary economy money cannot be a commodity, it may be concluded that capitalist money must necessarily be seen as a pure symbol, that is, sign-money.

In a model allowing for class division between entrepreneurs and workers, money is first of all issued by banks to finance production. The alternative idea, present even in the post Keynesian camp, that money consists of liabilities issued by firms, does not escape from a barter-like approach. These liabilities are either means of final payment or promises to pay. The former case, where firms pay workers by issuing liabilities accepted by them as final payment, looks very close to a situation of seigniorage. We would be far from the world of equal rights among social agents presupposed by Marx; command over labour power would rest on judicial discriminations, resembling the overt exploitation of feudalism. If firms' liabilities are seen as promises to pay, as paper titles, when paying wages firms would remain in debt to wage earners, and we would have merely a postponement of the final payment in commodities. Therefore, the economic process is depicted either as a precapitalist form of direct command over direct workers or as a great barter exchange.

In a true monetary economy the final means of payment are the liabilities of the banking system. Banks act as the third party between firms and workers. When firms resort to bank credit to get production going, banks write on their balance loans to firms as an asset, and the equivalent volume of created deposits as a liability. When firms use their deposits to pay the wage earners, banks transfer the ownership of deposits to the workers. Firms remain in debt to the banks, and workers are the creditors written in the liability side of banks' balance sheet. Hence, bank money is the final means of payment allowing firms to discharge themselves of their debt towards workers, without any break in the principle of formal equality among agents (see Graziani, 1990, 1993).

BANKING AND THE CREATION OF MONEY

The creation of money in a true monetary economy can be depicted with the help of the Wicksellian framework, as found in his 1898 *Interest and Prices*. Let us start with the simplest case of a single bank in an isolated community. Payments are supposed to be made only by bookkeeping transfers or by means of the issue of notes. We are in a pure credit economy. Given that there are, by definition, no leakages out of circulation, the single bank can never find itself in trouble. Therefore, it does not need to keep reserves. The same holds good if multiple commercial banks act in concert with the same intentions to grant loans and issue banknotes: whenever all the banks move together, no individual bank ever has to face a negative balance at the clearing house. Things change if we consider multiple banks that do not expand loans in step: now, the bank that expands faster than the others experiences outflows higher than inflows, and it must find some way of dealing with its debts. In this case, either there is some bank of banks (a central bank) issuing a universally accepted final means of payment, or again we have to face the problem of how payments are eventually extinguished in a decentralised system. The final clearing could be seen as reached through direct, two-party, payments in commodities – though it also could be reached through reciprocal credits among banks. In an unregulated international arrangement we may have national monetary areas alongside a world barter, or mere credit, system.

Let us then go on to an open economy with a pyramidal structure and 'mixed' sign-monies. At the apex, there is a monopolistic note-issuing bank, whose customers are mostly contained within the national (political) borders. Moreover, the bank normally has the state behind its privileges. At the base, there are competing commercial banks, whose liabilities circulate among a clientele covering only a share of the deposit market. Here we have a hierarchy between two types of money. The commercial banks can find themselves having to make payments in the central bank's money, which they do not themselves produce, and which we suppose to be legal tender. They will therefore hold assets from the central bank in readiness for the redemption of their liabilities: hence they will maintain a desired reserve ratio so as to be able, if need be, to obtain credit from the central bank. The central bank, in turn, can be required to settle uncompensated foreign purchases. This will induce it to hold reserves of some commodity as a final means to extinguish its debts – unless central banks are eager to grant each other unlimited credit. In a situation of this sort, therefore, the conclusions reached for the single bank and for banks expanding at the same pace in a closed economy, no longer apply. Both the commercial bank and the single national central bank are obliged to keep reserves: the former, in legal tender; the latter, in commodity money.

We reach, however, different conclusions if we consider the case of a closed economy with multiple monies, which is equivalent to the fiction of the global economy with a world central bank. Of course, the overall amount of credit extended by the commercial banks still depends on the amount of high-powered money chosen by the central bank. Yet now there is no need for the sole central bank to set aside some reserves in commodity 'money'. Supposing the commercial banks are not acting in concert, they need to hold reserves; but, in a closed economy, the central bank does not, and can expand its liabilities at will. In other words, we return to the case of the 'single' bank. This picture can be easily adapted to the case of the global economy with a three-tier banking structure.

If we now allow for a convertibility of commercial banks' liabilities in some metallic currency within national borders, or for an external drain of commodity 'money', the reserve ratio of the commercial banks or of the national central banks in an open economy rises. The role of the commodity money may be thus empowered. But this recognition does not compromise severely the independence of the banking system as a whole from commodity money. A convertibility of the legal tender in a closed economy – or in the global economy with a world central bank – has no inner necessity, and could only be the outcome of an exogenous institutional intervention in the monetary system. And it must always be remembered that even in a free banking arrangement, or in an unregulated world system, the conversion of banks' liabilities in commodities is only one of the instruments by which an imperfect offsetting of debt–credit relationships at the clearing house can be overcome, since commercial or central banks may give each other enough credit to resolve the difficulty.

Thus, in open economies not only individual banks but also the banking sector in a given 'national' area has to keep some reserve ratio. It is so because national banking systems are here considered to be side by side as competing single actors, just like commercial banks within a country. In a similar framework, which is not unlike the framework that Marx observed in his times, the creation of money is in the last instance linked to the note-issuing banks' reserve stocks of precious metals. However, let us remember that even in an open economy, so long as the note-issuing banks are following uniform policies allowing the commercial banks to follow their lead, the extension of loans becomes autonomous from the metallic base.

It is clear that in the view we are supporting banks supplying finance create a purchasing power that did not exist before the loans were granted. For the banking sector as a whole, loans make deposits. There is no money 'multiplier' in this outlook. In the case of inconvertible legal tender, the same base money that the central bank provides to the system arises from an act of lending either to commercial banks or to the state. When there is convertible fiat money, the power of commercial banks to create deposits is indeed limited by the imposition from above of a constraint to collect commodity money: however, this convertibility must be interpreted as an exogenous intervention on the working of the banking system 'in pure theory'. Individual banks growing at different rhythms may well be constrained by the necessity of collecting some high-powered money.

METALLISM IN THE TIME OF MARX

The contrast between commodity-money theorists and sign-money theorists often parallels the debate between metallists and cartalists. The former are convinced that gold is capitalist money and that banknotes and bank deposits are mere substitutes – fiduciary money, whose value is in the last instance determined by the metal into which they are convertible. The latter reject the commodity-money approach and maintain that the means of payment in a monetary economy consists of the records in the banks' bookkeeping entries. According to this framework, payments among agents take place by means of credit transfers (see Realfonzo, 1998). The metallist position was widespread during Marx's lifetime (owing, among other things, to Ricardo's support), and was adhered to by authors working along different, and even diverging, lines. It found followers among the exponents of the currency school and it greatly appealed to the majority of the supporters of the banking school and the free banking school.

Towards the end of the nineteenth century, Karl Menger became the most noted exponent of this approach. Menger systematises a way of describing money that had been around since the mercantilists. Thus, it is useful to refer to his work in order to understand the ideas that were the most firmly rooted when Marx was writing.

In his famous essay 'On the origin of money', Menger (1892) defines money as a particular commodity selected by the market. Money is not the result of an explicit agreement among agents, nor of state intervention. How then, Menger asks, can one explain the move from the primitive system of direct barter to the general adoption of a medium of exchange? The degree of 'marketability' varies from commodity to commodity with the different spread of supply and demand, as well as with the intrinsic characteristics of the commodity that may limit its availability, spatially and/or temporally. For this reason, with the development of transactions, dealers find it more convenient to exchange their goods for more marketable commodities as soon as possible, even if they do not want to consume them. As these dealings continue to take place, a spontaneous process of selection is established and the most marketable commodities become generally accepted as intermediary in exchanges. Historically, precious metals have proved themselves to be money par excellence given their superior marketability: they are in continuous demand, geographically well-distributed, divisible, non-perishable and transportable; and can be stored at low cost. Whoever possesses precious metals is sure of being able to exchange any quantity of them, in any market, at stable prices.

MONEY-COMMODITY AS THE UNIVERSAL EQUIVALENT

The Marxian description of the capitalist process as a monetary sequence may be shown to be compatible with a theory of banks as providers of finance to production (see Bellofiore, 1989; Graziani, 1997a, 1997b). However, there are elements of money-commodity theory in Marx. This may be partly explained by the fact that in Marx's time gold currencies were routinely employed in exchange. It must also be pointed out that, in his more explicit metallist statements, Marx was often more concerned with concrete economic issues and a realistic picture of the contemporary system of payment rather than with the pure logic of a monetary capitalist economy. In the third volume of *Capital* he always started from a model with the simultaneous coexistence of a metallic base money, central bank notes, and credit money. A hierarchy among these monetary forms was imposed by the international market and by legal provisions.

The fundamental characteristic of money as put forward by Marx in the first volume of *Capital* is its being the universal equivalent. In exchange two commodities reveal themselves to be at the same time equal, as crystals of congealed abstract labour time, and unequal, as different use values. Now the value of each commodity is not placed in direct correlation to that of the other commodities, but to the value of a particular commodity. Exchange-value, as the necessary form of appearance of value, remains fixed in the metamorphosis of the commodity with the universal equivalent: 'the value of every commodity is now not only differentiated from its own use-value, but from all use-values, and is, by that very fact, expressed as that which is common to all commodities. By this form, commodities are, for the first time, really brought into relation with each other as values, or permitted to appear to each other as exchange values' (Marx, 1976, p. 158). Marx goes on to say that the commodity that has actually assumed the role of the universal equivalent is gold. 'It becomes its specific social function, and consequently its social monopoly, to play the part of universal equivalent within the world of commodities' (ibid., p. 163). The universal equivalent is the representative of abstract social wealth, 'the social expression of the world of commodities' (ibid., p. 160).

To understand Marx's connection between the notion of abstract labour and the money-commodity as the universal equivalent we must go back to the first chapter (whose position in the whole was so crucial for Marx that he took pains to restate the argument in four different steps between 1867 and 1875) where a value-form approach is clearly put forward (see Messori, 1997). According to Marx (1978, p. 140):

> *Products of labour* would not become commodities, were they not products of separate *private labours*, carried on independently of one another. The *social interconnection* of these private labours exists materially, insofar as they are *members of a naturally evolved social division of labour* and hence, through their products, satisfy wants of *different kind*, in the totality of which the similarly *naturally evolved system of social wants* consists. This *material* social interconnection of private labours carried on independently of one another is however only *mediated* and hence is realised only through the *exchange* of their products. The product of private labour hence *only* has *social form* insofar as it has *value-form* and hence the *form of exchangeability* with other products of labour.

Now, says Marx, there is a commodity – the commodity that plays the role of the universal equivalent – that has immediately social form 'insofar as its own bodily or natural form is *at the same time* the form of its exchangeability with other commodities or *counts as value-form for other commodities*' (Marx, 1978, p. 140). The definite, useful, concrete labour producing the money-commodity is immediately social labour. The inner opposition between use value and value becomes an external opposition – the equivalent-commodity counts as value-form, the shape of exchange value, and the other commodity counts as the shape of use value. Then, the labour producing the money-commodity as equivalent, being immediately not private but social, is not abstract labour but merely represents the form of actualisation of the abstract labour contained in the other commodity, which is private labour in the process of *becoming* social labour. The social nature of abstract labour is only expected by industrial capitalists, and pre-validated by monetary capitalists. In the metamorphosis of a commodity with the money-commodity what happens is the coming into being of the latent social nature dormant in the living labour of the wage-earner producing the former, in the shape of a given amount of the concrete labour producing the money-commodity – namely, labour in direct social form.

Following this argument, we must conclude that the potential abstract labour contained in the various commodities – in as much as it is eventually actualised in exchange – is merely a quota of the labour producing the money-commodity, this latter being physiological human labour: thus justifying the reference of abstract labour to physiological labour that we find in this same first chapter, in full coherence with the social and monetary value-form approach that is peculiar to Marx. Note, however, that in this chain of reasoning the physiological labour embodied in the money-commodity only counts as the expression of abstract labour, but it is not abstract labour: because – let us repeat this fundamental and often neglected point – the labour producing the money-commodity, being *immediately* social, is not, as abstract labour must be, only *mediately* social.

The first function assigned to the universal equivalent is as 'universal measure of value'. Commodities are homogeneous entities in that they are the products of abstract labour. They differ owing to the socially necessary labour time needed for their production. It is therefore possible to compare and measure them. Gold as money 'as a measure of value is the necessary form of appearance of the measure of value which is immanent in commodities, namely labour time' (Marx, 1976, p. 188).

The universal equivalent is then also 'the means of circulation', when all other commodities than the one which is the universal equivalent being different use values contradicts their economic equivalence. The exchange of commodities between owners must allow the satisfaction of needs, the redistribution of use values. Commodities must be exchanged against money and therefore money must be exchanged against the desired use values. Owners must sell in order to buy. It is the metamorphosis of the commodities, represented by the circuit C–M–C´: Commodity–Money–Commodity.

The other function of gold as money is as 'means of payment'. When credit forms of payment are employed, the buyer remains in debt to the seller.

In other words, the credit instrument – as 'a title to money in civil law' (Marx, 1976, p. 234), a bill of exchange, for example – does not give rise to a final payment, rather it postpones it: it is a representative of future money. The intervention of metal money, which eventually settles the transaction, will be necessary to extinguish the debt–credit relationship.

Further evidence of Marx's metallist leanings in the first volume is demonstrated in his examination of state-issued paper money. This is described as a symbol of gold, circulating in as far as it represents a given quantity of the money-commodity.

> Its relation to the values of commodites consists only in this: they find imaginary expression in certain quantities of gold, and the same quantities are symbolically and physically *represented* by the paper. Only in so far as paper money represents gold, which like all other commodities has value [here the correct expression would have been: whose concrete labour represents the abstract labour of all other commodities], is it a symbol of value (Marx, 1976, p. 225).

Marx's money-commodity theory has strong roots in his abstract labour theory of value. Abstract labour as activity and value as its result need to be validated in exchange. The necessary form of appearance of value is exchange value as fixed in the metamorphosis of commodities against the universal equivalent. Gold as money allows the private labours contained in commodities to find expression in the immediately social labour producing the general equivalent. Nevertheless, Marx's metallism is not of the usual kind. He shows that capital must take the money-form in its cycle; assigns a central role to banks; finds fault with the quantity theory of money (associated with metallism since Hume); and criticises the 1844 Bank Act that put artificial constraints on the banking system, without which the money supply would have been elastic. In short, when Marx moves towards money as finance, he clearly rejects the Ricardian notion that it is merely a technical aid to ease the circulation of commodities, a veil under which it is necessary to disclose a non-monetary 'core' of economic relations. This double attitude by Marx towards money – money as the general equivalent, and money as finance or capital – is unresolved in his writings.

MONEY AS FINANCE TO PRODUCTION

It is possible to go beyond Marx's explicit statements making a distinction between money as the social value-form of the commodity, abstract wealth (*Geld, argent, danaro*), and money as purchasing power (*Münze, monnaie, moneta*). The first is latent in each commodity as ideal exchange value, and may be traced back to potential abstract labour. The second, as we showed at the beginning of this chapter and as we repeat in this section, cannot be reduced to a commodity. Purchasing power is injected into the system as finance to production. For the system as a whole, money as (initial) finance can be expended only in the buying of labour power – that special commodity whose use value is the sole non-capital, non-dead labour, present in the system, namely the living labour of the wage-earner. Money as finance is the starting point of Marx's analysis of the cycle of money-capital (see Graziani, 1997b; Bellofiore, 1989; Bellofiore and Realfonzo, 1997).

Money as capital expresses the fundamental class relation in capitalism. First of all, it is purchasing power over labour power, loaned by monetary capitalists (banks) to industrial capitalists (firms). Then capital takes the shape of productive capital, where dead labour exploits living labour within the production process; money now becomes ready to be spent as income. With the production of potential value and surplus value there is the further transformation of productive capital into commodity capital. From a macro-social point of view, commodity capital consists of one part that is to be re-transformed into money capital, and of another that remains in the form of means of production. In the end, the capitalist class finds itself in possession of a greater quantity of abstract wealth – money in our first sense, *Geld*. We have here production of (more) money by means of money. Capital, dead labour exploiting living labour, has been reproduced on an enlarged scale.

Money in our second sense plays a multiple role in this sequential process. First, it is finance to production, capital's purchasing power; then, it is a means of exchange in the expenditure of income; eventually, it takes again the shape of money capital when it flows back to firms, allowing them to repay their debt to monetary capitalists (nowadays, banks).

In order for commodities to be produced, and in order for money to be employed as means of exchange in the circulation of commodities, money must be injected into the system as finance to production: it must be advanced to pay money wages. This is a preliminary and essential condition for valorisation in the capitalist production process and for the realisation of ideal exchange values on the market. When production has still to begin, no commodities, and hence no money-commodity, as yet exist. There must be purchasing power before there can be commodities. Money cannot, therefore, have any other nature than that of an agreed, third-party, promise to pay, which is not the outcome of a labour process. Money is primarily a means of purchasing labour power, and only subsequently a means of enabling commodities to circulate and hence of income expenditure. From the point of view of initial finance, as means of purchasing labour power in advance of production, money is a pure symbol which could not, as Marx would have it, be traced back to a money-commodity without falling into the trap of infinite regress. In modern times, bank loans to firms in a pure credit system, rather than gold-money, best represent the essence of money as finance.

At the macro-social level – given the rate at which labour is pumped out from labour power and leaving aside the realisation problem – the value of money as capital may be defined as the ratio between the aggregate living labour expended by workers and the wage bill: how much labour time a unit of money spent as capital represents. A more traditional definition of the value of money outside Marxism refers to the money spent at the closing of the monetary circuit, and it is equal to the inverse of the level of consumption goods prices. Let us assume that workers spend all their wages in the goods market, and disregard capitalists' consumption. If we measure output in labour embodied, the second definition gives a lower magnitude than the former, since the part of the value added that corresponds to investment goods is not made available to workers. The second definition represents how much labour time contained in wage goods a unit of money spent as income by workers gains in the market. The difference between the former and the latter definition gives us the power of pumping out surplus labour for capital as a whole.

Within the macroeconomic view, gross profits may be considered either to be earned by the firm sector in nature or – coming closer to what appears at the surface of market relations, where all exchanges must be realised in money – to be equal to investments financed by banks through a second injection of liquidity at the end of the circuit. If we follow the second route, and we look at the money spent as income by both classes, the value of money as income is now given by the ratio of the labour hidden behind the value added and the same value added expressed in prices: how much labour units a unit of money spent as income represents. This ratio is the reciprocal of the monetary expression of value – how much value in monetary units an hour of labour time brings into life. This third definition is different from the first one employed above when we allow for a new inflow of finance for investments.

Of course, it may be objected that if workers save part of their income and spend it on the stock market, financing investment demand, they may even become owners of (all or part) of the new capital goods produced. The rate of exploitation would be reduced, and may even disappear. A reading of this sort seriously misrepresents the capitalist process. The role of the financial market in a true monetary economy is simply to allow firms to get back the part of the liquidity they injected into the system at the beginning of the circuit and were not able to recover from the goods market; it has nothing to do with financing investment demand. Moreover, the workers as a class, even when formally owners of real capital goods, will never be able to influence the level and composition of output. If they decide to 'disinvest', and hence to increase their real consumption, but at the same time firms do not increase the output of consumption goods, the outcome will merely be forced savings on the part of the workers. The debt of firms towards the workers, and workers' ownership of real capital goods, are merely fictitious.

In our reformulation, money represents a given amount of labour not only because of the eventual exchange in the commodity market, as in the original formulation of Marxian value theory, but also and basically because it is the institutional symbol of the social command over labour power (over its sectoral allocation, and over the expenditure of its use value) by the capitalist class: a command that is pre-validated by banks, and that firms ought to see confirmed in the course of the capitalist labour process and on the market if they wish to reimburse their debt and increase their abstract wealth.

MONEY IN *CAPITAL*, VOLUME III

Though, as we have shown above, Marx was a supporter of the money-commodity notion, throughout all his work we find important insights suggesting a sign-money approach.

In certain articles written for *The New York Daily Tribune* and in some sections of the *Grundrisse*, Marx appears to understand the credit nature of money and the process by which banks create money. This can also be seen in *Capital* Volume III, in the fourth and fifth sections – 'The transformation of commodity capital and money capital into commercial capital and money-dealing capital (merchant's capital)' and 'The division of profit into interest and profit of enterprise'. The fifth section is where Marx more fully elaborates upon the nature of credit and the nature of the bank.

Let us briefly recall the following aspects of Marx's monetary theory as we find it in Volume III: Interest-bearing capital; the bank as intermediary; the nature of bank lending and note issue; credit as a means to save metallic currency; clearing and commodity-money as (final) means of payment; the vanishing of commodity-money. We caution readers to recall that *Capital* Volume III was published posthumously, and it was a rough draft. Despite Engels's re-ordering efforts, some relevant chapters in the fifth section are little more than first notes and collections of quotations to be elaborated upon at a later date.

INTEREST-BEARING CAPITAL

The first question examined in the fifth, and for our purposes the most interesting, section of the book, is interest-bearing capital. Here, although Marx defines money that makes up this capital as a *sui generis* commodity, his discussion of interest-bearing capital is consistent with a definition of money as pure symbol. Interest-bearing capital is defined as a given amount of money loaned to firms to function as money capital for the purchase of labour power. This money, after the loan in favour of the productive capitalist, flows back first to the 'functioning capitalists' (Marx, 1981, p. 465) and then to the initial lender. The period of reflux '*seems* to depend simply on the contract between lender and borrower', though in reality it depends on the course of the reproductive process (ibid., p. 470).

Under average conditions the money borrowed by firms and employed by them as money capital, a value sum, has, as its use value, the capacity to produce the average profit. 'But it is as *realized* capital that the borrower has to pay it back, that is, as value plus surplus value (interest); and the latter can only be a part of the profit he has realized. Only a part, not the whole. For the use-value for the borrower is that it produces him a profit' (ibid., pp. 474–5). A part of the surplus value must therefore be given up as interest. The interest rate is a levy on surplus value. It has no other origins than the exploitation of labour power. The level of the interest rate is an 'empirical' one, since it depends on the relative level of supply and demand, on the borrower's guarantees and on the duration of the loan.

In interest-bearing capital, 'the capital relationship reaches its most superficial and fetishized form'. A given money sum seems to automatically produce a greater amount of money as directly self-valorising value: 'the product of a mere *thing*', and not of a social relation. M–M´ 'is the original and general formula for capital reduced to a meaningless abbreviation' (ibid., p. 515). Marx shows that in the eyes of the entrepreneur the interest he pays seems to be the price to be paid for the money borrowed, 'the mere fruit of property in capital, of capital in itself', without reference to the production process (ibid., p. 497). The idea spontaneously emerges that gross profits consist of two heterogeneous parts, with different sources: interest, from loan capital; profit of enterprise, from the work of supervision and management (ibid., p. 507). Reality is turned upside down. 'While interest is simply one part of the profit, that is, the surplus value, extorted from the worker by the functioning capitalist, it now appears conversely as if interest is the specific fruit of capital, the original thing, while profit, now transfomed into the form of profit of enterprise, appears as a mere accessory and trimming added in the reproduction process' (ibid., p. 516). In this inverted situation, money loses its nature of institutional symbol of a social relation, to become 'a simple thing', 'money breeding money' (ibid., p. 516).

FROM THE BANK AS MERE INTERMEDIARY...

How, and by whom, is money capital supplied to firms? And what is the nature of this money capital? Marx's inquiry starts off from a study of banking activity. Initially, a view of banks as mere financial intermediaries is put forward. Banks are those agents that keep accounts, collect and settle payments, clear debt–credit relationships, and so on.

Marx claims on several occasions that banks collect money from subjects that wish to lend, in order to pass it to firms that wish to borrow. 'The borrowing and lending of money becomes their special business. They appear as middlemen between the real lender of money capital and its borrower' (Marx, 1981, p. 528). Banks concentrate money capital for loan in large masses:

> so that, instead of the individual lender of money, it is the bankers as representatives of all lenders of money who confront the industrial and commercial capitalists. They become the general managers of money capital. On the other hand, they concentrate the borrowers vis-à-vis all the lenders, in so far as they borrow for the entire world of trade. A bank represents on the one hand the centralization of money capital, of the lenders, and on the other hand the centralization of the borrowers. It makes its profit in general by borrowing at lower rates than those at which it lends (Marx, 1981, p. 528).

From this perspective, a different but related role of the banker is to combine small sums 'which are incapable of functioning as money capital by themselves' into 'great masses and thus form a monetary power'. The previous existence of money savings is here implied as the logical condition for bank lending: bank deposits originate from the flow of money savings, and there is a priority of the collecting of deposits over banks' extension of loans.

Having defined banking activity as pure intermediation – where banks are depicted, to borrow Cannan's well-known stricture, as 'cloakrooms' – it follows that Marx considers deposits as the 'loanable funds' at the disposal of the banks. The bank, therefore, according to this first approach of Marx's, would lend what are its own liabilities. Given the hierarchy of monies we detected in *Capital*, it is consistent for Marx to look on bank's collection of metal money and notes from the central bank as the fundamental circumstance upon which loans depend.

...TO THE BANK AS THE CREATOR OF MONEY

In Chapter 25, 'Credit and fictitious capital', we find some passages that Marx would very likely have used as a frame of reference for his own definitive arguments on the issue. What is interesting to pick out here is that Marx – through Tooke, Fullarton and Gilbart – emphasises that banks, while lending others' money, 'create' credit and money capital. Consider, for instance, the following passage from Gilbart. 'The deposit system might thus, by means of transfers, be carried to such an extent as wholly to supersede the use of a metallic currency' (Marx, 1981, p. 532).

It is here that the question becomes more complicated. Marx, who initially defines banking in terms of pure intermediation, comes to realise that in reality a metal base is not needed, and that it is possible in theory to maintain that banks create money *ex nihilo*. Deposits now take a twofold aspect. On the one hand, they are loans made to banks by monetary capitalists as savers, which in turn banks themselves loan out, 'and are thus not to be found in the banks' safes, figuring instead in their books as credits held by the depositors'. On the other hand, they are 'mere book entries' that, 'in so far as the reciprocal credits of the depositors are settled by cheques on their deposits', are 'mutually cancelled' in the clearing (ibid., pp. 600–1).

According to Marx, in various occasions agents make payments without there being any use of gold or even banknotes. In Chapter 29, putting together many quotes, he shows that in this way, since the individual piece of money may be deposited with various bankers, banks multiply bank deposits. Hence, '[w]ith the exception of the reserve fund, deposits are never more than credit with the banker, and never exist as real deposits' (ibid., p. 601).

Marx seems to realise that banking activity cannot be defined in terms of pure intermediation, but also entails money creation. Banks transform non-monetary assets into money claims.

Discounting bills, Marx explains, means shifting money capital from one form to another. Engels, in editing Chapter 26, interprets Marx's rough notes in a sense that, in the following pages, seems to be confirmed by Marx himself (ibid., pp. 557–9, 587–8). Three cases of bank loans are distinguished. In the first, loans are granted without any real guarantee as collateral. 'In this case [the borrower] has received not only an advance of means of payment, but unquestionably also a new capital' (ibid., p. 587). The bank transforms a pure and simple promise of reimbursement into an opening of credit. The advance of money is also an advance of capital because there is no value to offset it. In the second case, the bank loan has a security against it: here we have a cash advance that is not an advance of capital in as much as the loan is of equal or lesser value than the collateral, for the security also is capital. Bank credit now rests on a real asset. In the third case, where the discount of real bills of exchange is at issue, there is no advance at all, but simply an ordinary purchase and sale, and even the form of an advance disappears. The firm is not beholden to give anything back to the bank, which transforms a real asset into a claim to money. All of this takes place, Marx states, unless the bill of exchange is an accommodation bill, not representing any commodities sold. In this case, the granting of a loan to a firm is an advance both of money and capital.

Marx's analysis proceeds in a similar vein when he goes on to the investigation of note-issuing banks (Chapter 33). Firstly, Marx maintains that 'a banknote is nothing more than a bill on the banker, payable at any time to its possessor and given by the bank in place of a private draft' (ibid., p. 529). Of course, if there are legally prescribed reserve constraints, the issuing bank has no capacity to put into circulation an unlimited amount of banknotes. However, Marx knows that at a purely theoretical level the issue of notes by the banking system as a whole finds no limits except for demand. A consequence of the argument is that, against Ricardo, note circulation is independent of both the will of the central bank and the level of gold reserves in its vaults that ensure the convertibility of the notes. 'So it is simply the needs of business itself that exert an influence on the quantity of money in circulation' (ibid., p. 659).

Given the possibility that the system might function properly even without any reserve of 'hard' base money, Marx deemed absurd the hindrances to note issuing imposed by the Bank Act. The 1844 law, Marx goes on to say, created an artificial bottleneck to money supply creation as well as an artificial intensification of the demand for monetary accommodation, thus provoking a tendency to an increase in the interest rate (ibid., p. 689). The Bank Act is also chastised for the fallacious desire of the legislator to link gold flows to changes in the money supply: 'it seeks to compensate for a drain of gold by a contraction of the means of circulation and for an influx of gold by an expansion of the means of circulation. When put to the test, the opposite was proved' (ibid., p. 699).

Despite these revealing insights, Marx constantly returns to a less general framework. The institutional arrangements he assumes are the ones that concretely shaped the monetary system of his time. Hence, he refers to competing central banks and does not start in his inquiry from the banking system as a whole, either at the international level (a single world bank or central banks moving in step) or in a closed-economy setting. Gold money as world money and statutory legal restrictions to reserves are supposed to be into effect. Accordingly, he retains the notion that a 'hard' money-commodity is at the base of the pyramid of credit. In a system of this kind individual (central and commercial) banks must first of all collect, respectively, gold money or legal tender in order to make loans. Reserves remain the foundation necessary to build the credit system, and the collection of deposits stays firm as remains the preliminary condition for the banks to make loans, though the deposit multiplier is recognised as a flexible one. It is no coincidence that Marx picks out the metal reserve 'as the pivot of the entire credit system' (ibid., p. 706) and defines the borrower as a 'fictitious' depositor.

THE THEORY OF CREDIT

Paralleling his inquiry on banking activity, Marx also takes a dual approach as far as credit is concerned. On the one hand there is a Ricardian standpoint, where credit instruments are seen as mere surrogates of metallic money, as if it would be impossible to do without gold. On the other hand, he proposes an alternative outlook, where credit is seen as the real money of capitalism and where a money-commodity has no role to play.

Marx was well aware of the growing importance of credit for the development of the system of payments and economic growth. Banking and credit, he writes, are 'the most powerful means for driving capitalist production beyond its own barriers' (Marx, 1981, p. 742). The credit system, on the one hand, 'develops the motive of capitalist production, enrichment by the exploitation of others' labour, into the purest and most colossal system of gambling and swindling', while, on the other hand, 'it constitutes the form of transition towards a new mode of production' (ibid., p. 572).

Marx follows a traditional route when he distinguishes between the means of circulation and the means of payment. Gold money, in his view, fulfills both functions. On the contrary, non-bank credit money, which Marx identifies with bills of exchange, plays exclusively the role of means of circulation. It 'absolutely represents real money' (that is, the 'one particular commodity', 'the universal commodity', 'the commodity par excellence, in contrast to all other commodities', gold: 'the material in whose value all other commodities are measured'). With the drain of gold the identity of credit money with gold 'becomes problematic' (ibid., p. 648). During a crisis, the 'only' means of payment is gold and the 'true' existence of value can be testified solely by the money-commodity. 'In times of pressure', in order to eventually settle debts, the pure gold standard vindicates itself as the unique real, solid money.

In a gold-standard setting, the role of credit is simply to reduce circulation costs through the saving of 'real' money. As payments come to be settled by credit instruments, a growing amount of transactions may be carried out with a given quantity of metallic money: '[c]ommodities are not sold for money, but for a written promise to pay at a certain date', and 'the reserve fund of the business community is reduced to the necessary minimum' (ibid., pp. 525, 528). The credit means of payments may considerably exceed the hard money base, until the crisis breaks out.

This picture of banking and credit has been quite widespread since Marx's day, forming the core of the traditional view of money creation as constrained by some kind of 'material' base – in a fiat paper money system, it still forms the heart of the treatment of the supply of money in any contemporary macro-textbook (the theory of bank deposits multiplier). However, if our analysis were to end here, the most interesting and original reflections on credit scattered in the third volume would be lost. In fact, Marx's insistence on the pivotal role of the money-commodity is closely connected, as our quotations show, to the phenomenon of crisis and to the institutional features of his times. In the normal workings of a monetary economy free of an 'erroneous legislation based on incorrect theories of money' (ibid., p. 649) that imposes artificial constraints on reserves, Marx fully recognises the independence of capitalist money from the metal.

It has been noted above that Marx – looking at the most common credit instruments in his days – picks out the bill of exchange as the most representative form of credit-money. In his examination of 'Credit and fictitious capital' (Chapter 25), Marx labels the bills of exchange 'the actual commercial money'. Bills of exchange, and not the money-commodity, constitute 'the real basis of credit' (ibid., p. 525).

Therefore, the true money of the capitalist economy is not metal but credit. Following this lead, Marx goes as far as to suggest that hard money could even be set aside. The reference here is to the clearing house mechanism. Insofar as debt and credit relationships between agents would not offset, the intervention of a means of payment would still be necessary. However, '[t]o the extent that they ultimately cancel each other out, by the balancing of debts and claims, they function absolutely as money, even though there is no final transformation into money proper' (ibid., p. 525). With perfect clearing, there is no need for any base money – a consequence that Marx should not have seen as merely a theoretical possibility since, several chapters later, he claims that 'even now no metal money is needed at home' and 'is required only to settle international trade and its temporary imbalances' (ibid., p. 649).

The issue of the clearing mechanism is not developed further. In Chapter 22 one is left with Marx's declaration of intent. '(Note for later elaboration) ... money is replaced by the settlement of outstanding debt certificates' (ibid., p. 492).

CONCLUSION

In spite of his important insights, Marx remains tied to his analysis of the universal equivalent as 'one particular commodity' 'against all other commodities'. There is a positive side in this, since it means a fundamental break with Ricardo's non-monetary value theory and metallist theory of money, where money is a commodity like any other (this is the reason why in the case of Marx we use the term money-commodity rather than commodity-money). Marx's labour theory of value is from the start a monetary labour theory of value, since abstract labour must find its external expression in the money-commodity to actualise itself; and since the money-commodity (which is the product of an immediately social labour and hence has no value) is opposed in nature to all the other commodities. But there is also a negative side. Marx first introduces the money-commodity as a means of circulation in the general exchange of commodities. When he goes on to the analysis of capital, the notion of money as finance comes to the fore. Following the method of the 'posit of the presupposition' he should have shown how money as means of exchange is posited by money as finance (see Bellofiore and Finelli, 1998). As a consequence, he should have also explained the limited role of money-commodity in capitalism, as well as the fact that a 'hard' money base is not a necessary condition of banking activity. Loans make deposits, without any need of a previous collection of money savings by banks and money cannot be a commodity in a true monetary economy. Instead, Marx again and again derives the characteristics of banking activity and the nature of credit from the 'foundation' laid out by the money-commodity.

Thus it is no coincidence that Marx repeatedly affirms the priority of metal. The system, he explains, has a tendency to reduce gold reserves to a minimum, 'at which it can no longer perform the functions ascribed to it' (Marx, 1981, p. 706); 'with the development of the credit system, capitalist production constantly strives to overcome this metallic barrier, which is both a material and an imaginary barrier to wealth and its movement, while time and again breaking its head on it' (ibid., p. 708). Again, '[a]s paper, the monetary existence of commodities has a purely social existence. It is *faith* which brings salvation' (ibid., p. 727). And finally, 'money in the form of precious metal remains the foundation from which the credit system can *never* break free, by the very nature of the case' (ibid., p. 741).

As we have already remarked, however, most of these statements refer to the phenomenon of crisis in an international system of payments with a hierarchy of monies – a system that for Marx had the unco-ordinated central banks as the pivot of the different national credit systems, the metal reserve as the pivot of the central banks, and gold as world money. Thus, he seldom refers to a pure credit economy with only private agents (banks, firms, wage-earners), which following Wicksell we see as the right abstraction for monetary analysis in pure theory. If there is a legal tender that is imposed by law as the legal bank reserve, it could be right to set the maximum amount of the money supply as a multiple of high-powered money. It is then no surprise that in crisis agents abandon deposits in favour of cash. Again, it is in connection with the world market that Marx writes that, when international transactions do not balance, a money-commodity must be present to clear the payments. Indeed, this is how things work if, at the international level, the payments structure is not triangular: that is, so long as there is no hegemonic power, as that of the United States in the Bretton Woods era, or there is no world bank acting as the central bank for the national banks and able to create world money, in the way Keynes envisaged. In the latter case, the world market goes back to being in part a barter economy. In this situation, Marx's conclusions should be regarded as absolutely correct.

Each time Marx conceives of a closed monetary system without any kind of base money, he comes to the conclusion that money is created *ex nihilo* by banks. On the other hand, while a correct analysis of the circuit of money capital is incompatible with a money-commodity, Marx's sequential picture of the capitalist process and his abstract labour theory of value and exploitation may be shown to be compatible with a symbolic view of money.

REFERENCES

Bellofiore, R. (1989), 'A monetary labor theory of value', *Review of Radical Political Economics*, **21** (1–2), 1–25.

Bellofiore, R. and R. Finelli (1998), 'Capital, labour and time: the Marxian monetary labour theory of value as a theory of exploitation', in R. Bellofiore (ed.), *Marxian Economics: A Reappraisal*, Vol. I *Essays on Volume III of Capital: Method, Value and Money*, London: Macmillan, 48–74.

Bellofiore, R., G. Forges Davanzati and R. Realfonzo (2000), 'Marx inside the circuit: discipline device, wage bargaining and unemployment in a sequential monetary economy', *Review of Political Economy*, **12** (4), 403–17.

Bellofiore, R. and R. Realfonzo (1997), 'Finance and the labor theory of value. Toward a macroeconomic theory of distribution from a monetary perspective', *International Journal of Political Economy*, **27** (2), 97–118.

Graziani, A. (1990), 'The theory of the monetary circuit', *Économies et Sociétés* ('Série Monnaie et Production', 7), **24** (6), 7–36.

Graziani, A. (1993), 'Money as purchasing power and money as a stock of wealth', in H.J. Stadermann and O. Steiger (eds), *Der Stand und die nächste Zukunft der Geldforschung. Festschrift für Hajo Reise zum 60. Geburtstag*, Berlin: Duncker and Humbolt, 313–20.

Graziani, A. (1997a), 'Let's rehabilitate the theory of value', *International Journal of Political Economy*, **27** (2), 21–5.

Graziani, A. (1997b), 'The Marxist theory of money', *International Journal of Political Economy*, **27** (2), 26–50.

Marx, K. (1976), *Capital: A Critique of Political Economy*, Vol. I, London: Penguin.

Marx, K. (1978), 'The value form', *Capital and Class*, (4), 130–50.

Marx, K. (1981), *Capital: A Critique of Political Economy*, Vol. III, London: Penguin.

Menger, K. (1892), 'On the origin of money', *Economic Journal*, **2** (6), 239–55.

Messori, M. (1997), 'The theory of value without commodity money? Preliminary considerations on Marx's analysis of money', *International Journal of Political Economy*, **27** (2), 51–96.

Realfonzo, R. (1998), *Money and Banking: Theory and Debate (1900–1940)*, Cheltenham and Northampton: Edward Elgar.

Schumpeter, J.A. (1954), *History of Economic Analysis*, London: Allen and Unwin.

11. How Heterodox is the Heterodoxy of Monetary Circuit Theory? The Nature of Money and the Microeconomics of the Circuit

Alberto Zazzaro[1]

INTRODUCTION

The modern theory of the monetary circuit has been presented, from its very beginning, as a heterodox macroeconomic theory, that is, as an alternative to the orthodoxy of neoclassical macroeconomics.[2] To be sure, the elements distinguishing the two theories are numerous and deep, but probably the essential ingredients that many circuitists would lay at the base of their approach are the following:

1. Whilst neoclassical theory has always held that money *logically* has the *nature* of producible stuff, circuit theory shares the chartalist view according to which money is nothing but credit, a pure symbol that in modern economies consists of bank liabilities, issued chiefly at the moment of financing industrial production.
2. To develop a model of authentic monetary economics, one must abandon methodological individualism, which is a distinctive feature of the neoclassical theoretical approach, and recognise that the economy consists of social groups with different aims and constraints.[3]

In this chapter we shall seek to show that these two theses are not entirely accurate. By contrast, we shall argue that lending greater empirical content and full internal consistency to the theory of the monetary circuit – that is, to satisfactorily solve the problems of the original circuit and the closure of the circuit – requires: (1) that the chartalist theory of money be revised and a *new* institutional theory of the origin of money be developed; (2) to introduce microeconomic elements into the circuit analytical framework.

More specifically, we will maintain the following six propositions:

1. The idea that money *logically* must always assume the form of (or be convertible to) a producible commodity does not belong to the neoclassical tradition.
2. The point originally at the centre of the debate between metallists and chartalists was essentially the *value* and/or *origin* of money (and not its *nature*), hence the different stress on the essential functions to be attributed to money.
3. To provide consistent foundations to the theory of the monetary circuit, a theory of institutional change needs to be developed, which neither metallism nor classical chartalism seems able to offer.
4. Methodological individualism, if understood in a weak form, is not the exclusive domain of neoclassical theory; if understood in a strong form, it is not the domain of all neoclassical views.
5. Many authors who in the past have contributed to develop the monetary theory of production have at least partly used a weak individualist approach.
6. The adoption of this perspective is not only perfectly compatible with the monetary theory of production but is also necessary for giving greater realism and full internal consistency to the modern theory of the monetary circuit.

CHARTALISM AND METALLISM: IS THERE AN ALTERNATIVE?

It is quite common among circuitists and post Keynesians to fit their own theory of money in the framework of the chartalist tradition, contrasting it with the metallist tradition subscribed to by neoclassical scholars. The controversy between chartalists and metallists is also widely viewed as a controversy about the nature of money. From this perspective, the metallist camp would include all those for whom money is logically a producible commodity, with its utility independent of its monetary functions. The chartalists, by contrast, would refute this logical necessity, maintaining the credit nature of money. Their view does not simply mean that money identifies a general draft on the social product, a point on which pretty much all economists agree; rather it means that "'money" is the by-product of a balance-sheet operation of a third agent who, in modern parlance, can be dubbed a "bank"' (Parguez and Seccareccia, 2000, p. 101).[4]

However, from Schumpeter (1954, 1970) onwards, what is presented as two opposing positions concerning the nature of money was and is chiefly a dispute over the value and origin of money. In turn, this led and leads each author to privilege one of the functions of money over the others and to consider this as the essence of the monetary phenomenon.[5]

The Nature of Money

As Schumpeter (1954, 1970) underlined, it was Knapp (1905) who coined the expressions metallism and chartalism. It was definitely Schumpeter, however, who gave them full analytical dignity by introducing the important distinction between theoretical metallism/chartalism and practical metallism/chartalism.

> By Theoretical Metallism we denote the *theory* that it is logically essential for money to consist of, or to be 'covered' by some commodity so that the logical source of the exchange value or purchasing power of money is the exchange value or purchasing power of that commodity, considered independently of its monetary role (Schumpeter, 1954, p. 288).[6]

Knapp gave a slightly different interpretation of metallism (of which, as Mises (1924/1981) noted polemically, Knapp was unable to explicitly identify any follower), using a very peculiar definition of commodity – an object 'capable of a use in the world of art and industry', in the words of Knapp (1905/1924, p. 4) – that is hard to find in the work of neoclassical authors.

Neither Knapp nor Schumpeter, however, though referring the metallist theory to the nature of money, offered any positive definition of chartalism, which they identified as the doctrine that opposed metallism. When they devoted themselves to developing their own positive chartalist theory of money, the two authors, though pursuing radically different lines of thinking,[7] both analysed the problem of the origin of money. Schumpeter addressed the problem of the logical origin of money, explicitly neglecting any attempt to analyse its historical origin.[8] Knapp, by contrast, unless one considers the statement 'money is a creature of law' (Knapp, 1905/1924, p. 1) as a declaration on the nature of money, addressed the theme of the historical origin of money and its formal 'validity'[9] on trade.

Schumpeter did not dwell on the distinction between payments in kind and payments in money, or between a barter economy and a monetary economy.

Rather, he focused on the problem of the logical priority of the different functions of money, attributing first place to the function of unit of account. All the payments made in the process of production and consumption, where cash payments are only a special case, imply, according to Schumpeter (1970/1990, pp. 216–17; our translation from the Italian edition), an underlying credit relationship owing 'to the non-concurrence of reciprocal obligations'. As a *means of payment*, money serves to resolve credit relationships arising with exchange: 'credit relationships ... and the accounting balances in which they express themselves represent the logical *prius*, in comparison to which money differently defined performs a function of technical support' (ibid., pp. 216–17; our translation from the Italian edition). Hence the obvious consequence that 'money is neither a good nor a commodity ... in the sense that the unit of account with which commodity transactions are recorded and regulated in a pure accounting system is not itself a commodity and does not become one for this function' (ibid., p. 239; our translation from the Italian edition).

For Schumpeter the logical origin of money is in economic calculation and its essence may be easily traced, in a socialist economy as in a capitalist economy, as a unit of measurement of the *use value* of goods, besides their *exchange value*.[10] Hence, it is the function of unit of account that defines the essence of money, and not that of medium of exchange or means of payment. From this standpoint, therefore, Schumpeter must be considered an advocate of the credit nature of money, but only in the sense that behind every economic exchange, an underlying debt–credit relationship may be detected, and not in the sense, held by circuitists, that money may be logically represented only as liabilities issued by some third-party institution.[11]

Moreover, according to Schumpeter the symbolic/accounting character of money does not stem from the logical incompatibility of commodity money with a monetary economy. The essence of money as a unit of account may be equally found both in trades in kind and in those in which money appears as an *intermediary*, whether in a socialist economy or in a capitalist economy. This is what drives Schumpeter to propose replacing the traditional monetary theory of credit with a credit theory of money. What matters for understanding the essence of the monetary phenomenon is only that for 'its *logical* deduction no mercantile antecedent is necessary', in the sense that money does not *have* to be, even at the origin, a commodity that has its own utility and its own exchange value independent of its monetary function. However, Schumpeter pointed out, it remains perfectly *possible* and 'even necessary, if people have to use it in exchange', that the unit of account, once it exists and people have learnt to work with it, 'then acquires for everyone the significance of a good' (Schumpeter, 1970/1990, p. 225; our translation from the Italian edition).[12]

For their part, metallists definitely considered reference to some 'mercantile antecedent' necessary for developing a coherent theory of money. However, they did not refute the possibility that money assumed the form of an abstract sign, a stroke of a pen devoid of any utility other than that of a monetary function and without any immediate link (for example, of convertibility) with any commodity that could be produced through human labour. This is at least the position that the founding fathers of neoclassical monetary theory explicitly adopted (including certainly Marshall, Menger, Mises, Pigou, and Rist), let alone modern neoclassical economists (such as Jones, Kiyotaki, Ostroy, Shubik, Starr, and Wright).

As regards Menger, if besides his famous work 'On the origin of money' (published in the *Economic Journal* in 1892) we also consider the posthumously published edition of his *Grundsätze*,[13] it appears evident that by the expression 'money is a commodity' he only meant that money is an exchange commodity that, like others, gains value from its utility. 'The value of metallic money derives from the value of the metal and coinage, while that of fiduciary money from the rights linked to its possession' (Menger, 1923/1976, p. 368; our translation from the Italian edition).

Moreover, so as not to be misunderstood, Menger preceded his chapter on money with those on the theory of goods, of economic goods and commodities. Putting together the definitions proposed by Menger for these three categories, the statement 'money is a commodity' could then be reproduced in the following terms: *money is anything suited to meeting human needs, available in smaller quantities than required and used for exchange*, where its absolute independence of the concept of producibility is evident.[14] However, it was the need to apply utility theory to money that forced Menger to see the nature of money in its function as *a medium of exchange*, to *logically* consider money as a mercantile product and to view as misguided those, like Wagner or Schumpeter, who attributed the essence of the monetary phenomenon to its being a standard of value (unit of account).[15]

None of this, however, in principle prevents money being presented, from its very inception, as a good without its own non-monetary utility.[16] This possibility, instead, was ruled out by the analytical construct of Mises (1924), who nonetheless adhered to Menger's monetary theory. On reading Mises's work, it seems quite hard to maintain that he was a metallist, or that he held that money could not logically in any case take on the form of a pure sign or be represented by banks' balance-sheet entries.[17]

Mises's aim was simply to present a theory of money that was able to explain its value according to the 'laws of exchange'. According to Mises, precisely because money in its most advanced forms takes on the appearance of a pure sign, it cannot but have an indirect utility, as a means of procuring goods with their own direct utility. Nevertheless, this is tantamount to maintaining that the utility of money depends on its purchasing power, that is, on its value and utility. To break the circularity of this reasoning, Mises proposed the (in)famous regression theorem, by which the value of money today depends on the purchasing power that money had yesterday. Moving backwards, however, Mises could not help reaching the *logical* conclusion that 'before an economic good begins to function as money it must already possess exchange value based on some other cause than its monetary function' (Mises, 1924/1981, p. 132).

In other words, from the *logical* standpoint, according to Mises *in origin* money can only be something (most likely a real good) having its own utility for people, independent of its monetary function. Now, whatever opinion one might have on the correctness of the regression theorem,[18] what must be stressed here is that the metallism of Mises implies in no way that money must *always* consist of (or be covered by) a producible commodity.

Finally, Rist, like Menger and Mises, also had little doubts that money could take on non-commodity forms or that money was nothing other than a draft on the social product. Rist only maintained that, from a theoretical standpoint, as money *also* acts as a store of value, in other words, as money has a *direct utility* besides having an *indirect utility*, its value (but especially the stability of its value) also depends on the value of the substance of which money is made.[19]

To conclude, with respect to the *nature* of money both parties, chartalists and metallists, may be said to have recognised that money has the nature of a social institution that identifies a credit right on existing resources. For both chartalists and metallists money may be correctly understood as the *record* of a purchasing power whose support tends to change in time with customs and technology, there being no logical link between the form or support that money takes and its intrinsic essence. For both theories, this essence may be traced in the exchange of goods (Rossi, 2001), whether they are final goods, factors of production or labour, and whether they occur in a planned economy or in a market economy. For chartalists, the essence of money lies in the contract and in its underlying debt–credit relationship and in the corresponding function of unit of account according to the logical sequence: exchange $\rightarrow$ contract/debt–credit $\rightarrow$ unit of account. For metallists, it lies in transactions costs tied to the trading of goods and in its function as medium of exchange according to the logical sequence: exchange $\rightarrow$ transactions costs → medium of exchange.

The Origin of Money, the Rise of Markets and the Problem of the Original Circuit

The divergence between metallists and chartalists concerning the *origin* of money was far more pronounced than their controversy over the nature of money.[20] For Menger, like most of the economists who are considered metallists, money is an unintentional social product that arises in the exchange of goods, where each rational individual finds it worth selling his/her commodity in exchange for another, which is not directly desired but can be traded more easily (that is, for which the difference between the supply and demand price is smaller), so as to minimise transactions costs and times of the final exchange, that is, of the acquisition of goods actually desired. With the passing of time, through experience and habit, one finds that the most tradable commodity is spontaneously established as 'money' in the community, which seeks it and uses it as a general intermediary of exchange. Thus money is the spontaneous product of an evolutionary process that arises from conscious, rational interaction between individuals, but that does not have roots in the purposeful design of some individuals.

By contrast, for chartalists money is a creature of the state. It originates in an act of imposition on the part of the authorities that, on their own initiative, establish by law what object can free people from their obligations to the state or from those protected by the law. Therefore, whatever the state and the law declare to be money, a voluntary demand for money arises in everybody and money acquires its own value, even when its material substance would be devoid of value.[21] Hence, the logical consequence that any *object* or any *sign* is able in principle to act as money – gold, bank deposits or, according to a contemporary chartalist like Goodhart (1989, 1998), shares issued by investment funds – and, often (but not in Knapp's case),[22] the practical conviction that, for the economy to work well and develop, credit money is more suitable than commodity money.

However, also regarding the origin of money, the divergences between metallists and chartalists are often less fundamental than we are led to believe by arguments similar to those outlined above. Indeed, although they are mostly presented as divergences on the *logical origin* of money (Wray, 1993, 2000; Ingham, 2000), often it is only its *historical origin* that is in dispute. More precisely, given the inevitable absence of conclusive evidence about the true origin of money,[23] the real problem under discussion is which of the possible *historical* origins of money is the most *logically* convincing. The proof is that it is possible to consistently maintain the same explanation of the *logical* origin of money, yet not agree with what monetary function must be considered *historically* antecedent to the others.

For example, whichever function of money is held to be logically essential and historically primitive – unit of account, means of payment, medium of exchange – the explanation of its introduction into exchange and its evolution may be perfectly compatible with a Mengerian evolutionary approach. Thus one may at the same time believe, along with Innes (1913) and Keynes (1930/1971), that the original forms of money are to be sought in the recording of debts and credits and in the drawing-up of price lists (in other words, that the essential function of money is to perform as a unit of account), and accept the idea that the introduction and evolution of money constitute an unintentional process aiming to minimise the costs of exchange.[24] In addition, it would be possible to continue to explain the introduction of money with the difficulties of barter, and yet maintain that the good that tends to become established as money can be none other than that 'conceived of' and used as a means of payment to rid oneself of state tariffs or sanctions.[25]

Put differently, chartalism and metallism, though diverging on what is to be considered the original function of money, may very well end up sharing the same explanation of institutional changes based on an unintentional evolutionary process resulting from individual action to minimise transactions costs. By contrast, they might also agree on a subjective teleological explanation of the origin of money where institutional changes are the result of precise human design, be it that of a 'cunning governor' – as in Knapp (1905/1924) or in Wray (1998) – or that of a 'lazy genius' able to see how to overcome the difficulties of barter – as in Crowther (1940).

Be that as it may, whichever of the two methodological solutions one adopts and whatever the function of money that is considered essential, metallism and chartalism encounter the same logical difficulty of having to precede money with the existence of an adequately developed system of exchange and market mentality. Indeed, only in this case would the introduction of money be able to ensure considerable saving of resources in exchange (metallists) or to represent an effective tool of seigniorage (chartalists).[26] Accordingly, it is true to say that the well-known difficulties that Mademoiselle Zélie encountered in the *Society Islands* or Mister Cameron in Tanganyika in obtaining the goods that they urgently needed[27] may be held to be indicative only of the difficulties that any person used to live in a market economy would experience if they were suddenly catapulted into a non-mercantile society, and not of the limits of a barter system *per se*

(Einzig, 1966; Dalton, 1982; Ingham, 1996; Bell, 2001). However, it would be equally true to say that the expedient of introducing forms of monetary taxation to persuade native populations to supply their labour without having recourse to slavery (Neale, 1976) – as conceived of by the imaginary colonial governor of Wray (1998) or as is said to have been actually used by the German governors on the Pacific islands and by their French and English counterparts in the African colonies –[28] is nothing other than the solution designed by officials from mercantile societies called upon to practice their profession in cultures that know no market, without in the least constituting proof of the state origin of money.

However, to precede the existence of money with a monetary market economy is a fault that also belongs to monetary circuit theory. Is this not perhaps the decisive element underlying the well-known problem of the original circuit?[29] At what level, one might ask, will money wages initially be fixed if until that moment exchanges in money have never yet occurred?[30]

The solution to this enigma may be sought in anthropological studies on ancient economies by Malinowski, Polanyi, Dalton and others, who convincingly showed that the relationship between money and market goes the other way round.[31] 'Trade and money were always with us. Not so the market, which is a much later development' (Polanyi, 1977, p. 123).[32]

To comprehend this statement, we need first to recall the two meanings of 'economic' identified by Polanyi: the *substantivist* meaning, which 'derives from man's dependence for his living upon nature and his fellows', and the *formalist* meaning, which 'derives from the logical character of the means– end relationship' (Polanyi, 1957, p. 243). As Polanyi underlines, the two meanings have nothing in common. The formalist meaning has a logical content and 'implies a set of rules referring to choice between the alternative uses of insufficient means' (ibid., p. 243). By contrast, the substantivist meaning of economic has an exquisitely empirical content and 'implies neither choice nor insufficiency of means' (ibid., p. 243). It is to the latter meaning that, according to Polanyi (1957, p. 244), we should refer to comprehend the position that the economic (livelihood) problem assumes in the various systems and to deduce 'the concepts that are required by social sciences for an investigation of all the empirical economies of the past and present'.

However, Polanyi continues, the concrete ways of solving problems of man's livelihood necessarily consist in institutionalised processes of interaction between people and their environment. 'The human economy, then, is embedded and enmeshed in institutions, economic and noneconomic' (ibid., p. 250). 'The instituting of the economic process vests that process with unity and stability' (ibid., p. 249). If we adopt this meaning of an economic system, substantivist and institutionalised, it is easy to realise that the market approach to trade and money is unable to supply a satisfactory picture of the evolution of such institutions.

Self-regulating market exchange is not the only way of institutionalising the economic process, the only 'form of integration' of individuals amongst one another, nor is it the only way that envisages the use of money. Reciprocity – a form of socially obligatory donation – and redistribution – the assignment of individual or group production to the authority of the community and the subsequent sharing out of goods to members of the community according to customs in force – are equally important, widespread social forms of integration, in which money may still perform its functions as a means of payment, unit of account and/or medium of exchange.[33]

However, whilst in a market economy money is general-purpose, performing all the monetary functions, in social contexts in which reciprocity and redistribution are prevailing forms of integration money is special-purpose. Monetary functions appear institutionally separated from one another, confined to limited circuits and, what is more important, always independent of their mercantile significance.[34] As a means of payment, money originates from the existence of social debts, such as those based on status, kinship, marriage and religion, and not of debts arising from market transactions. As a medium of exchange it originates from external trade with outside communities, rather than from difficulties of bartering on home markets. Finally, as a unit of account, money is a device designed for regulating the redistribution of products and the reciprocity of obligations, and not for recording exchanges that occur on the market.

Thus, in primitive societies, money is not an economic phenomenon that arises from the inconvenience of barter, but an institution that is necessary to guarantee the functioning of society and its reproduction. It is only in modern market economies that the various uses of money become interdependent and oriented to market exchanges and their self-regulation.

According to Polanyi, therefore, the monetary (market) economy does not arise when money originates (in whatever form it takes), but when the evolution of society and its institutions goes so far as to transform money into an *economic good* subject to demand and supply, that is, the moment in which a market of money is established. At this stage there may already be in force monetary equivalencies for goods established by convention, custom or law. There could be administered prices for the trade of goods, the paying of taxes or fines, that is, there could be a list of non-market prices from which market prices initially originate.

This analytical expedient, that is, the pre-existence of non-market monetary prices, would perhaps be able to solve the puzzle of the original circuit, but it does not solve the basic questions. How does a monetary economy arise? As regards the institutional change that transforms money from an institution extraneous to market exchange into market money, what does it consist of and how does it occur? Why and how do we shift from a system of fixed prices to a system of self-regulated prices?[35]

These are questions that are still mainly extraneous to the economic debate on the origin of money. Only recently were they taken up by Heinsohn and Steiger (1983, 1987, 2000), who identify the birth of the institution of private property as the essential element leading to the rise of a monetary economy.[36] Yet, even ignoring the fact that Heinsohn and Steiger only show that private property is a necessary condition for a monetary economy to arise, but not a sufficient one, their solution only shifts the problem backwards: how does private property arise?

The point is, as noted by North (1977) and Godelier (1978), albeit from diametrically opposed perspectives, that Polanyi and his followers, just like Heinsohn and Steiger, failed to propose their own theory of institutional change. Certainly, it may be agreed that the market is only one of the forms of possible institutional integration of human societies. However, to explain the prevalence of one of the forms of integration and, especially, to analyse the transition from one form to another, we need a satisfactory explanation of the role and hierarchy of the forms of integration in different societies and an analysis of the reasons behind the birth of new institutions. Thus, given the lack of a 'Polanyist' theory of institutional change, also the Polanyi theory of money can only be absorbed in one of the existing approaches to social and institutional change, be it the evolutionary (linear or multilinear) or the functionalist approach.[37]

Of course, this is not the place to further address such problems and even less to propose a theory of the institutional change. However, in conclusion, what deserves to be stressed is the need for the consistent development of a monetary theory of production that recognises the fundamentally institutional nature of money and the monetary economy. This would allow circuit theory to address explicitly the problem of the original circuit and to present an explanation of the origin and evolution of money that is really different from the Mengerian evolutionary approach.

SEARCHING FOR THE MICROECONOMICS OF THE MONETARY CIRCUIT

It is commonly held among circuitists that between neoclassical theory and circuit theory there is a still greater, insurmountable difference, which goes beyond the very theory of money and banking, or rather, which would also cause divergences in this field, and which concerns the methodological approach to economics. More precisely, what circuitists consider being the very feature of all neoclassical schools is adherence to methodological individualism, which circuit theory, by contrast, cannot but reject in its entirety.

In fact, circuitists usually claim that it is this particular methodological approach that is responsible for excluding from analysis the social classes, their interaction and the role of money in the distribution of income and wealth. It is not by chance, then, circuitists conclude, that all those who have sought to develop a monetary theory of production (not only the circuitists) have recognised these difficulties, and consequently have all started by refuting methodological individualism.[38]

What circuitists seem to support, therefore, is the idea that opting for an individualist perspective in a theoretical inquiry would be tantamount to a sharp and clear choice of field, in favour of neoclassical theory and in absolute antithesis to the monetary theory of production. Unfortunately, circuit theorists hardly ever offer an explicit definition of methodological individualism.[39] What they usually seem to have in mind, however, rather than a methodological principle, is a particular description of the economic world,[40] typical of the Arrow–Debreu general equilibrium model, by which society is understood as a set of full rational, informed and undifferentiated (if not by resource availability and by taste) agents, who act independently from one another, without any kind of strategic interaction. A world in which individuals are devoid of any type of 'power' and are not open to reciprocal influences.

Yet, it is definitely erroneous to place individualism as a methodological principle at the same level with any particular description of reality, of the functioning of the economic system and of agents' objectives and forms of behaviour. To be precise, it is possible to distinguish at least two quite different ways of understanding methodological individualism: weak individualism (like Agassian institutional individualism or partly also Popperian situational analysis)[41] and strong individualism. Now, adopting a weak individualist perspective means only denying that impersonal entities, like institutions, organisations or social classes, are endowed with anthropomorphic properties, with their own wishes, aims and driving forces that are distinct and independent of those of the individuals who constitute and belong to them. This amounts to saying that phenomena that involve such impersonal entities and their evolution can only be *explained* by making reference to the actions of single individual or groups of them, which at least in part are intentional.

Adopting a weak individualist perspective does not mean either excluding classes or other forms of social organisation from economic analysis (as is shown by the analyses of class conflict in individualist terms proposed by the North-American Marxist school of Bowles, Elster, Gintis, and Roemer),[42] or denying that existing institutions are able to affect and direct individual behaviour.[43] Even less does it mean espousing the Robbins definition of economics, or adhering to the marginalist theory of distribution, or postulating that actors always behave consciously and fully rationally, or accepting a particular theory of money and banking. It does not even mean denying the legitimacy of the study of aggregate phenomena or the conceptual autonomy of macroeconomic laws. Phenomena of fallacy of composition, such as Keynes's savings paradox, or theories like effective demand and its corollary of the independence of investment from saving, are all perfectly compatible with an individualist approach, provided that 'the aggregation of individual actions is not simply reduced to a sum', but it is recognised that 'the aggregation can certainly assume the character of a summation, but does not necessarily presume it' (Boudon, 1984/1985, p. 101; our translation from the Italian edition); above all, provided that it is seriously considered that individuals are heterogeneous and interact amongst one another, that many of their characteristics are of a relational nature, that their behaviour generates externalities and that this is why the market is not a perfect mechanism for coordinating individual choices. After all, the conceptual autonomy of aggregate magnitudes and macroeconomic phenomena is ultimately based on the possibility of associating them to observable magnitudes and hence to the possibility that they are the focus of empirical surveys.

With methodological individualism intended in this weak sense, just as starting from the individual, it is hard to deny that Wicksell, Schumpeter, Robertson, and Keynes all used, to different extents and in different forms, an individualist methodology in their work.

Of course, if we move on to a strong interpretation of methodological individualism, as the doctrine by which all concepts and social phenomena must be traced back to individuals and the effects, at times not desired, of their intentional and full rational actions,[44] the use of macroeconomic concepts and the development of independent macroeconomic thinking (that is, decoupled from its microfoundations) would have to be excluded. The fact is, however, that in this strong sense not even neoclassical theory has always been able to consistently adopt an individualist methodology. At least, not the neoclassical theory of perfect competition that, to demonstrate the theorem of the invisible hand on a purely individualist basis, has been (and is) forced to refer to the figure of the auctioneer, an institution endowed with the ability to control the formation of equilibrium prices, that is, one of those impersonal entities endowed with anthropomorphic features that an individualist approach should consider as not belonging to the real.[45]

To conclude, it is perfectly compatible with the individualist approach to consider, along with monetary circuit theorists, that the society in which we live is divided between those that have access to new issues of money (firms), those that do not have access to it (employees) and those that create new money (banks), provided only that we recognise that: (1) within this subdivision individual actions (of individual capitalists, employees, bankers) are not completely pre-assigned and the evolution of the economic system depends on them; (2) in principle we may take a step backward and analyse (from the economic standpoint) the way in which social groups are formed or, symmetrically, take a step forward and ask ourselves how the processes of social mobility are determined.

Individualism, Monetary Profits and the Equilibrium Concept

In our opinion, methodological individualism (in the weak sense) is not only compatible with circuit theory; it is also absolutely necessary to complement it. In other words, we will argue that to extend the empirical significance of the theory of the monetary circuit and especially to lend greater realism and consistency to the crucial phase of circuit closure, it is even indispensable to supplement the aggregate analysis of the macro-social circuit with a microeconomic analysis of micro-social circuits.[46]

For the time being, circuit theory offers a definitely more convincing description of the working of a modern monetary economy than its 'neoclassical' counterpart does. It also provides effective explanations of some economic phenomena like money supply, inflation, public debt or income distribution. However, there are other aspects of these phenomena and, above all, there are many other economic phenomena that are hard to address without introducing rigorous microeconomic analysis into the monetary circuit model. For example, for those interested in comparing the states of different economies (or the pattern of growth of a single economy in time) in which, following the circuit theory itself, banks may create at their own discretion the liquidity that firms need, it would be excessively restrictive to limit the analysis of the bank–firm relationship to determining the overall quantity of money that is thus made available to the economy. It would be far more decisive to enquire how banks establish *to whom* to entrust the liquidity created, that is, how the process of selecting entrepreneurial capacities and credit allocation actually occurs.[47] Besides, given a certain amount of monetary base, also the overall quantity of money that the banking system may create depends, decreasingly,[48] on the number of banks belonging to the system, a characteristic that clearly depends on microeconomic and institutional reasons. Not to mention the problems of pricing bank credit, financial securities and labour supply that can hardly be analysed without taking into account the behaviour of single agents and the bargaining process that takes place between them (or between their representative institutions).[49]

However, of even greater importance is the fact that by explicitly introducing the individual component into the analysis, we may provide a consistent, realistic solution to the main difficulty of circuit theory, namely, that of the formation of aggregate monetary profits and the payment of bank interests in monetary terms. In a nutshell, the question may be posed in the following terms: if in an economic system (closed to external exchange) the only money existing is what the banks create in financing production, the amount of money that firms may hope to recover by selling their products is at the most equal to the amount by which they have been financed by banks. Therefore, once the principal has been repaid to banks, the possibility that firms as a whole can realise their profits in money terms or can pay interest owed to banks in money terms is ruled out.

In the framework of circuit theory this problem has essentially been solved in two alternative ways: (1) firms and banks spend in advance the profits expected from their operations;[50] (2) additional money is introduced into the circuit, typically through public sector spending. Although there is little space here for a detailed examination of the arguments suggested by various circuit theorists, the limits of both solutions appear fairly clear. The first solution is based on the somewhat unrealistic hypothesis that entrepreneurs and bankers systematically spend their income before earning it, while the second plunges circuit theory into difficulties similar to those that, as the same circuitists notice, traditional neoclassical macroeconomics encounters. The latter school considers the public debt as the sole source of monetary base, and is forced to hypothesise a sort 'of obligation for public authorities to regulate their budget deficit, no longer in relation to the requirements of public spending and the tax burden, but in relation to the monetary requirements of the market' (Graziani, 1994, p. 69; our translation). It is hardly worth saying that regarding public debt as the external source of liquidity necessary for the closure of the monetary circuit may be subject to exactly the same criticism.

Having discarded the above solutions, only two other possible avenues remain to justify the existence of profits and bank interests in money terms, both of which explicitly refer to microeconomic elements: (1) the economy consists of a concatenation of micro-social monetary circuits that overlap and intersect, the opening of one allowing the closure (inclusive of profits and interests) of others in an endless sequential process; (2) the economy undergoes an endless process of change that involves the entry of new firms, the start-up of new initiatives and failure of others.

The first solution, mentioned several times by circuit theorists (see Graziani, 1988), was explicitly considered by De Vroey (1988), Messori (1988), Dupont and Reus (1989), and Smithin (1997). The second solution, however, has been surprisingly overlooked, even though it would constitute nothing other than the introduction, within the analysis of the monetary circuit, of the process of creative destruction as described by Schumpeter (1934), who is unanimously considered the most loyal forerunner of circuit theories.

Of course, considering failure as a physiological element of a monetary economy is tantamount not only to reintroducing stock magnitudes into the analysis, but especially to abandoning any concept of subjective and/or objective *equilibrium*, by which, at the end of the circuit, all the agents (banks, firms, and employees) have to balance their budget (Graziani, 1988; 1994), in favour of a systemic concept of *order*.[51] But this also means, somewhat paradoxically, that it is the very introduction of *micro* elements that forces the adoption of a genuine *macro* concept of equilibrium and the introduction of institutional features as an integral part of a monetary economy of production, that is, the two essential ingredients for developing an authentic macroeconomic theory.

CONCLUSION

The theory of the monetary circuit has had the great merit of placing at the centre of macroeconomic theory the sequential nature of the economic process, the problem of financing production, and the role performed by banks in determining the macroeconomic equilibrium and in the growth process. However, in this chapter we argued that to develop a monetary theory of production fully consistent and distinct from neoclassical theory it is not sufficient to recognise the credit nature of money, the role of banks as creators of money, or the subdivision of society into distinct social groups. We also need to recognise the basically institutional nature of a monetary economy, in order to account for its origin and its ordered functioning in a continually changing environment, in which profits, failures and social mobility are an integral part of the economic process.

NOTES

1. The author would like to thank Sergio Rossi for stimulating discussions and comments on an earlier version of this work.
2. Of course, it is always very difficult to assign a precise content to expressions that should identify a school of thought. Here we adopt a broad – and in many ways unsatisfactory – solution, but which seems appropriate to the subject matter of this chapter, and which perhaps would also be acceptable to the majority of circuitist and neoclassical authors. In particular, with the term 'neoclassical theory' we shall refer both to the Walrasian model and to the Marshallian as well as the Austrian models. With the expression 'circuit theory', instead, although the most frequent implicit reference will be the Franco–Italian circuit model *à la* Parguez–Graziani, we shall at times refer also to the post Keynesian (horizontalist or structuralist) models and, to a lesser extent, to the circuit model of the Dijon–Fribourg school.
3. See, among others, Lavoie (1987, 1992), Graziani (1990, 1994), Parguez (1996, 2001), Realfonzo (1998).
4. See also Graziani (1990), Realfonzo (1998), Parguez (2001).
5. As is well known, this basically was also the interpretation of the debate between metallists and chartalists given by Mises (1924). Similarly, with reference to the contemporary debate, Heinsohn and Steiger (1989) maintain that the differences concerning monetary theory between post Keynesians (personified in Paul Davidson) and neoclassical economists (personified in Frank Hahn) concern the origin and not the nature of money (see also Chick and Dow, 2001). The opposite opinion was espoused by Iwai (1997), who not only held that the dispute between metallists and chartalists essentially concerned the nature of money, but also emphasised that this dispute must be considered logically distinct from that on the origin and value of money.
6. In the words of Schumpeter (1954, p. 288), by practical metallism nothing else was meant than 'a principle of monetary policy, namely, the principle that the monetary unit "should" be kept firmly linked to, and freely interchangeable with, a given quantity of some commodity', a principle that could well be consistently maintained by those who considered theoretical metallism unsustainable.
7. To realise how different were the routes undertaken by these two authors, it is sufficient to read the disdainful opinion that Schumpeter (1954, 1970) held of Knapp's *Theorie des Geldes*.
8. 'Is it a valid procedure to trace as far back as we can the history of an institution in order to discover its essential or its simplest meanings? Clearly no. Primitive forms of existence are as a rule not more simple but more complex than later ones ... Logical and historical origins must, therefore, be kept distinct' (Schumpeter, 1954, p. 64). Schumpeter (1970) restates the same consideration.
9. This expression comes from Mises (1924/1981, p. 507), according to whom Knapp's theory

consisted of nothing other than statements on the formal validity of nominal monetary units, to trace back to the state's authority, with nothing being said about the validity of such units in trade, that is, about their substantive validity. A similar opinion was formulated by Weber (1922) and recently restated by Ingham (1998).

10. See Schumpeter (1970/1990, pp. 28–39). By the same token, Berti and Messori (1996, p. cv; our translation) maintain that for Schumpeter the essence of the monetary phenomenon stems 'directly from the founding operation of any economic system: the calculation aimed at the allocation of scarce resources'.

11. Schumpeter's analysis substantially coincides with what Keynes writes in his *Treatise on Money* concerning the nature and origin of money (this comes as no surprise if it is true that Schumpeter abandoned the idea of publishing his book on money after reading Keynes's *Treatise*; on this point see Graziani, 1978; Swedberg, 1991; Messori, 1997), and coincides almost word-for-word with the analysis made by Hicks in his last book (Hicks, 1989). Besides, the idea that, in general, exchange presupposes a debt relationship and an accounting record is not so far removed from contemporary neoclassical theory (Ostroy and Starr, 1990). An interesting discussion on the accounting origin of money, 'external' to economic theory, is found in Mathieu (1985). In the latter respect, it should be noted that the Italian philosopher, though clearly adopting an individualist approach, has no difficulty offering a theory of money and credit that, from the conceptual standpoint, is very similar to the most radical version (the Schmittian version) of circuit theory. On the relationship between methodological individualism and monetary circuit theory we shall return in the third section of this chapter.

12. As Schumpeter also maintained, the scarcity of money – although it is extraneous to its essence of unit of account and may be introduced only artificially into the economy by means of some institutional expedient – is a necessary characteristic to determine the monetary prices of goods. Within modern circuit theory, this feature of money has been extensively analysed by Aasland (1990). It should be noted that, for many circuitists, the scarcity principle is to be rejected with reference not only to the essence of money but also to its actual supply, but then adding, to pay homage to the more common practical experience, that banks restrict their loans to creditworthy customers (Moore, 1988; Lavoie, 1996; Parguez and Seccareccia, 2000). Yet, one wonders, if banks can re-finance themselves at the central bank with no limits, though at a positive rate of interest, why they should ever refuse anyone credit, however low the probability may be of the loan being repaid? In other words, if banks are sure that they will never be rationed by central banks, why ever should they worry about expected losses? If there is no such certainty, however, either concerning the financing of losses made by bad loans or overissues with respect to a limit set by the monetary authority, is this not perhaps tantamount to setting quantitative (elastic) limits to the potential supply of credit/money on the part of banks?

13. As Menger's son (Karl) recalls in his introduction to the second edition of the *Grundsätze*, the chapter on money coincides with the article 'Geld' that Menger wrote for the third edition of the *Handbook of Fiscal Studies* (*Handwörterbuch der Staatswissenschaften*) seventeen years after the publication of his *Economic Journal* article.

14. See Menger (1923/1976, pp. 84, 146–7, 320).

15. 'One needs . . . to consider that the measure of value . . . has as a necessary premise the formation of the price and therefore the appearance of money as a medium of exchange' (Menger, 1923/1976, p. 438; our translation from the Italian edition).

16. This point was clearly expressed by Simmel (1907/1990, pp. 226–31). Besides, the lack of any non-monetary utility of money is the underlying hypothesis of modern search models *à la* Kiyotaki and Wright (1989, 1993).

17. As is well known, Mises divided the theories of money into catallactic and acatallactic, the former being those that dealt with the problem of the value of money, and the latter those that excluded it from the analysis. An interesting, balanced re-reading of Mises's theory of money and credit with a Wicksellian (or circuitist) interpretation is proposed by Bellofiore

(1998).

18. It is well known that for Patinkin (1965) the solution proposed by Mises was totally unsatisfactory. In his view, Mises could have used utility theory more traditionally and constructed a money demand curve on the basis of the various hypothetical purchasing powers that money could assume tomorrow. Evidently, the solution suggested by Patinkin could be pursued only if one imagines that money has its own direct utility. However, if, like Mises, one accepts the idea that the utility of money is only indirect, the expected prices would affect both the budgetary constraint and the utility function (hence the map of indifference curves), preventing the construction of any demand curve (in this respect, see Butler, 1988). From this point of view, therefore, it would not be the regression theorem that would have to be rejected, but the hypothesis that money only has indirect utility.

19. 'Thus gold or silver money is merely a draft on goods, a purchasing power, and, consequently, all these signs should be equivalent to one another. It is exactly this that the public has never yet admitted, and that the economists who believe themselves modern ought to recognize with the public (sic), as it is definitely the public and not the economists that fixes the value of the products on the market, as well as that of different "currencies". And the public has discovered that all the "drafts" are not equally *sure* or *universal*' (Rist, 1951/1961, p. 150). In perfect agreement with Rist, Day (1958, p. 4) wrote that the 'superiority of gold coins did not arise out of any intrinsic superiority of money stamped on valuable metal rather than on paper, it arose out of the greater willingness of some people to accept and hold gold coins than paper notes'.

20. That the divergence between metallists and chartalists concerned (and concerns) the origin of money rather than its essence may be further borne out by the fact that a scholar external to the economic debate such as Simmel had no difficulty, in his *Philosophy of Money*, in subscribing to Menger's theory and, at the same time, maintaining that credit money is the real and purest form of money. 'Whatever may be the historical origin of money – and this is far from being clearly established – one fact is certain, that money did not suddenly appear in the economy as a finished element corresponding to its pure concept. Money can have developed only out of previously existing values in such a way that the quality of money, which forms part of every exchangeable object, was realized to a great extent in one particular object; the function of money was at first still exercised, as it were, in intimate association with its previous value significance' (Simmel, 1907/1990, pp. 179–80). '[T]he development from material money to credit money is less radical than appears at first, because credit money has to be interpreted as the evolution, growing independence and isolation of those elements of credit which already exist in fact in material money' (ibid., p. 179).

21. Wray (1998) offers effective exposure of the chartalist theory in modern terms, proposing an original application to political economy issues.

22. As Knapp (1905/1924, p. 1) declares in the very first lines of his work, 'I know no reason why under normal circumstances we should depart from the gold standard'.

23. Besides the historiographic and anthropological reconstructions so brilliantly summarised by Einzig (1966), an interesting attempt to offer some statistical evidence to test the various hypotheses on the origin of money is offered by Pryor (1977), who finds slight evidence in favour of the theory that sees money as a means of payment precede money as a medium of exchange on the economic development scale.

24. See Laughlin (1903), Liefmann (1916) or, more recently, Mathieu (1985), Ostroy and Starr (1990), Kroszner (1990), Cowen and Kroszner (1992, 1994).

25. There are traces of this possibility also in Menger (1923), who proved to be well aware of the fact that in many circumstances non-commercial payments could have preceded those of a commercial nature, even if he then preferred to define the former payments as non-monetary. See also Cassell (1923), Grierson (1977), Goodhart (1998).

26. Some chartalists detect the *ratio* of the origin of money not in the acquisition of a seigniorage power on the part of the state, but in the fixing of tariffs by law to peacefully

sanction offending behaviour in the context of a community, such as to prevent violent reprisals undertaken by the injured parties (Grierson, 1977; Goodhart, 1998). In this case, the pre-existence of a market economy would no longer be a strictly necessary hypothesis, even if the transition from money to a monetary economy would still need to be explained.

27. See Jevons (1875) and Cameron (1885).
28. See Furness (1910), Stichter (1985), Forstater (1998).
29. We should not forget that, as Realfonzo (1998, p. 28) rightly underlines, 'one of the characteristics of the [circuit theory] is to show how the economic *process* of a monetary economy develops right from the beginning'.
30. Usually, the problem of the original circuit is presented in slightly different terms: how can firms or employees purchase goods if, up to that moment, goods have never been produced (De Vroey, 1988)? In this respect, the problem identified in this chapter has an even more general significance and, indeed, there would be no point hypothesising that employees might spend their wages only at the end of the production process (Messori, 1985).
31. In circuitist and post Keynesian literature the number of references to Polanyi and his followers are increasing (see Wray, 1990, 1998, 2000; Ingham, 2000; Heinsohn and Steiger, 2000).
32. For a systematic exposition of the monetary theory of Polanyi, see Mélitz (1970) and Servet (1993). On the importance of Polanyi's work for economic theory in general, see Stanfield (1986, 1989).
33. See Polanyi (1944) and Dalton (1968).
34. See, among others, Polanyi (1957), Grierson (1977), Dalton (1982), Courbis et al. (1991).
35. As pointed out by Einzig (1966, p. 347), 'it is difficult to see why the fact that certain exchange rates were kept artificially rigid should in itself have led to the monetary adoption of any of the goods concerned. On the contrary, in so far as the existence of fixed barter ratios facilitated barter it contributed towards the survival of the moneyless system of trading'.
36. Heinsohn and Steiger's theories have been fully accepted by circuitists (see Graziani, 1994; Parguez and Seccareccia, 2000; Parguez, 2001). Interestingly, more than ten years before Heinsohn and Steiger's first contribution to the property theory of interest and money, Pryor (1972) found statistical evidence for the fact that money and property institutions are positively correlated with economic development and that loans at interest occur after the appearance of property institutions and of a general medium of exchange.
37. This is implicitly recognised by Parguez (2002, p. 47), who, as regards the evolution of banks, asks 'how could modern banks evolve out of a complex debt structure'? His answer is that '[t]here are only two alternatives: the first is the solution of Menger (1923), according to whom the banks' existence would spontaneously evolve out of a pure market process without any State intervention; the second is to explain the banks' existence by the State intervention' (ibid., p. 47).
38. A clear example of this position is Realfonzo (1998).
39. As is well known, the expression 'methodological individualism' has been used in the literature with very different meanings. For a broad exposition of methodological individualism, see Donzelli (1986) and Hodgson (1988).
40. The idea that the adoption of methodological individualism involves adhering to a precise interpretative model of reality, going so far as to impose a precise line of behaviour as regards economic/social policy and to rule out the possibility of gainfully employing macro-type concepts in the analysis, is certainly not new among economists. Schumpeter (1954, pp. 888–9) already warned against the dangers of confusing methodological individualism, 'a purely analytic affair', with political individualism, 'a laissez-faire attitude in matters of economic policy'. As to the difficulties in considering methodological individualism as a criterion to distinguish between alternative approaches and explanations of social reality, see the considerations of Dorman (1991) in response to an article by Heijdra et al. (1988).
41. For a comprehensive presentation of institutional individualism and the situational analysis

programme, in addition to the work of Agassi (1975) and Popper (1976), see Toboso (2001) and Caldwell (1991) respectively.

42. On the importance of methodological individualism for Marxian analysis, see among others Elster (1982, 1985).

43. From this standpoint, to put it in Elster's words (1982/1992, p. 180; our translation), an individualist approach would be incompatible only with statements like 'capitalists are afraid of the working class' while it would be perfectly appropriate to address statements like 'the profit of capitalists is threatened by the working class'.

44. To the doctrine by which 'all social phenomena resolve themselves into decisions and actions of individuals that need not or cannot be further analyzed in terms of superindividual factors', Schumpeter (1954, pp. 888–9) attributed the term 'sociological individualism', adjudging it 'untenable so far it implies a theory of the social process'. For a rigorous analysis of the limits of the strong version of methodological individualism, see Donzelli (1986).

45. This point is clarified by Donzelli (1986, pp. 104–6, 262–3). See also Hodgson (1988) and Leijonhufvud (1997). According to Dorman (1991), also the neo-institutionalist theories of Coase, Williamson, North and Posner are all guilty of referring to concepts of a functionalist nature.

46. The expressions 'macro-social circuit' and 'micro-social circuit' were proposed by De Vroey (1988, pp. 215–16; our translation), who defines the former as 'the set of credit operations that take place in a given economy during a given period of time' and the latter as 'a specific credit operation . . . characterised by specific amount, conditions and maturity'. The importance of enhancing macroeconomic schemes of the monetary circuit with analysis of microeconomic behaviour is convincingly maintained by Messori (1988), Messori and Tamborini (1995), and Bossone (2001a, 2001b).

47. Circuit theorists are well aware of this, as is shown by the following quote from Graziani (1988, p. 19; our translation): 'The banks for their part perform the no less delicate function of choosing the firms to which to grant funding, assessing the capacity of individual entrepreneurs to overcome competition and rivals in the capture of new markets. In many respects, it is precisely in this phase that the structure of production and the configuration of the economic system are implicitly decided' (see also Rochon, 1999). Nevertheless, in the framework of this tradition, only recently have some microeconomic analyses of bank behaviour been proposed. See Dymski (1988, 1996), Messori (1988), Hill (1995), Wolfson (1996), Zazzaro (1997).

48. This, already clear in Edgeworth (1888), was more recently shown, among others, by Olivera (1971), Selgin (1993), and Graziani (1994).

49. Once again, considering that banks create money, if one is restricted to aggregate analysis, one can only reach the conclusion that firms, in principle, could satisfy any wage claim, issue securities at almost zero cost and still keep almost the whole physical production, which banks, for their part, could requisition by setting an interest rate very close to the rate of profit.

50. The hypothesis of an anticipated expenditure of profits has been variously interpreted as the possibility that initial finance obtained by firms to pay for money wages also includes expected/desired profits, that is, that having decided in advance the goods to which they will allocate profit expenditure, firms assign a part of their employees to the production of non-wage goods and extract all the wage-earners' income via a mark-up price mechanism on wage goods (Schmitt, 1984; De Vroey, 1988; Cencini, 2001; Rossi, 2001), or that the goods produced by firms are sold in several stages within a single circuit, thereby increasing the velocity of money (Sadigh, 1988; Dupont and Reus, 1989), or again that initial finance includes fixed capital besides circulating capital (Parguez, 1980; Nell, 1986; Seccareccia, 1996). As regards anticipated expenditure of interest on the part of banks, this has been interpreted either as payment of the workforce employed in the sector (Graziani, 1988) or as a fractional sale of produced goods on the part of firms first to employees and then to banks

(Dupont and Reus, 1989). Clearly, all such solutions are fairly artificial expedients when they fail to encounter logical problems.

51. The concept of *order* belongs as much to the Austrian school, which from an *individualist* perspective introduces the concept of *spontaneous order*, as to the institutionalist school (and in some respects to the Marxist school, too), which from a *functionalist* standpoint speaks of *economic order guaranteed by institutions, customs and conventions*.

REFERENCES

Aasland, D. (1990), 'The scarcity of money: a reality, a myth – or both?', *Économies et Sociétés* ('Série Monnaie et Production', 7), **24** (6), 37–50.

Agassi, J. (1975), 'Institutional individualism', *British Journal of Sociology*, **26** (2), 144–55.

Bell, S. (2001), 'The role of the state and the hierarchy of money', *Cambridge Journal of Economics*, **25** (2), 149–63.

Bellofiore, R. (1998), 'Between Wicksell and Hayek: Mises' theory of money and credit revisited', *American Journal of Economics and Sociology*, **57** (4), 531–78.

Berti, L. and M. Messori (1996), 'Introduzione', in J.A. Schumpeter, *Trattato della moneta: capitoli inediti*, Napoli: Edizioni Scientifiche Italiane, xlvii–cxxi.

Bossone, B. (2001a), 'Circuit theory of banking and finance', *Journal of Banking and Finance*, **25** (5), 857–90.

Bossone, B. (2001b), 'Do banks have a future? A study on banking and finance as we move into the third millennium', *Journal of Banking and Finance*, **25** (12), 2239–76.

Boudon, R. (1984), *La place du désordre. Critique des théories du changement social*, Paris: Presses Universitaires de France. Italian edition: *Il posto del disordine. Critica delle teorie del mutamento sociale*, Bologna: Il Mulino, 1985.

Butler, E. (1988), *Ludwig von Mises: Fountainhead of the Modern Microeconomics Revolution*, Aldershot: Gower.

Caldwell, R.H. (1991), 'Clarifying Popper', *Journal of Economic Literature*, **140** (1), 1–33.

Cameron, V.L. (1885), *Across Africa*, London: Macmillan.

Cassel, G. (1923), *The Theory of Social Economy*, London: Macmillan.

Cencini, A. (2001), *Monetary Macroeconomics: A New Approach*, London and New York: Routledge.

Chick, V. and S.C. Dow (2001), 'Formalism, logic and reality: a Keynesian analysis', *Cambridge Journal of Economics*, **25** (6), 705–21.

Courbis, B., E. Froment and J.-M. Servet (1991), 'Enrichir l'économie politique de la monnaie par l'histoire', *Revue économique*, **42** (2), 315–38.

Cowen, T. and R. Kroszner (1992), 'German-language precursors of the new monetary economics', *Journal of Institutional and Theoretical Economics*, **148** (3), 387–410.

Cowen, T. and R. Kroszner (1994), *Explorations in New Monetary Economics*, Oxford and New York: Basil Blackwell.

Crowther, G. (1940), *An Outline of Money*, London: Macmillan.

Dalton, G. (1968), 'Introduction', in G. Dalton (ed.), *Primitive, Archaic, and Modern Economies. Essays of Karl Polanyi*, Boston: Beacon Press, ix–liv.

Dalton, G. (1982), 'Barter', *Journal of Economic Issues*, **16** (1), 181–90.

Day, A.C.L. (1958), *Outline of Monetary Economics*, Oxford: Clarendon Press.

De Vroey, M. (1988), 'Il circuito della moneta: due interpretazioni', in A. Graziani and M. Messori (eds), *Moneta e produzione*, Torino: Einaudi, 215–45.

Dillard, D. (1987), 'Money as an institution of capitalism', *Journal of Economic Issues*, **21** (4), 1623–47.

Donzelli, F. (1986), *Il concetto di equilibrio nella teoria economica neoclassica*, Rome: Nuova Italia Scientifica.

Dorman, P. (1991), 'Marxism, methodological individualism and the new institutional economics: further considerations', *Journal of Instituional and Theoretical Economics*, **147** (2), 364–74.

Dupont, F. and E. Reus (1989), 'Le profit macroéconomique monétaire', *Economie appliquée*, **42** (2), 87–114.

Dymski, G. (1988), 'A Keynesian theory of bank behavior', *Journal of Post Keynesian Economics*, **10** (4), 499–526.

Dymski, G. (1996), 'Basic choices in a Keynesian model of credit', in G. Deleplace and E.J. Nell (eds), *Money in Motion: The Post Keynesian and Circulation Approaches*, London and New York: Macmillan and St. Martin's Press, 377–98.

Edgeworth, F.Y. (1888), 'The mathematical theory of banking', *Journal of the Royal Statistical Society*, **51** (1), 113–27.

Einzig, P. (1966), *Primitive Money*, Oxford: Pergamon Press, second edition.

Elster, J. (1982), 'Marxism, functionalism and game theory: the case for methodological individualism', *Theory and Society*, **11** (4), 453–82. Reprinted in J.E. Roemer (ed.) (1994), *Foundations of Analytical Marxism*, Aldershot and Brookfield: Edward Elgar, vol. II, 307–36. Italian translation in S. Petrucciani and F.S. Trincia (eds) (1992), *Marx in America*, Rome: Editori Riuniti, 179–222.

Elster, J. (1985), *Making Sense of Marx*, Cambridge: Cambridge University Press.

Forstater, M. (1998), 'Selective use of discretionary public employment and economic flexibility', paper presented at the Post Keynesian Workshop, Knoxville, Tennessee.

Furness, W.H. (1910), *The Island of Stone Money*, Philadelphia: J.P. Lippincott.

Godelier, M. (1978), 'Introduzione', in K. Polanyi (ed.), *Traffici e mercati negli antichi imperi*, Torino: Einaudi, ix–xliv. English edition: *Trade and Market in the Early Empires*, New York: The Free Press, 1957.

Goodhart, C.A.E. (1989), *Money, Information and Uncertainty*, London: Macmillan, second edition.

Goodhart, C.A.E. (1998), 'The two concepts of money: implications for the analysis of optimal currency areas', *European Journal of Political Economy*, **14** (3), 407–32.

Graziani, A. (1978), 'Il trattato sulla moneta di J.A. Schumpeter', in *Scritti in onore di Giuseppe De Meo*, Rome: Facoltà di scienze statistiche, 457–66.

Graziani, A. (1988), 'Il circuito monetario', in A. Graziani and M. Messori (eds), *Moneta e produzione*, Torino: Einaudi, xi–xliii.

Graziani, A. (1990), 'The theory of the monetary circuit', *Économies et Sociétés* ('Série Monnaie et Production', 7), **24** (6), 7–36.

Graziani, A. (1994), *La teoria monetaria della produzione* ('Studi e Ricerche', 7), Arezzo: Banca Popolare dell'Etruria e del Lazio.

Grierson, P. (1977), *The Origins of Money*, London: Athlone Press.

Heijdra, B.J., A.D. Lowenberg and R.J. Mallick (1988), 'Marxism, methodological individualism and the new institutional economics', *Journal of Instituional and Theoretical Economics*, **144** (2), 296–317.

Heinsohn, G. and O. Steiger (1983), 'Private property, debts and interest or: the origin of money and the rise and fall of monetary economies', *Studi economici*, **38** (21), 3–56.

Heinsohn, G. and O. Steiger (1987), 'Private ownership and the foundations of monetary theory', *Économies et Sociétés* ('Série Monnaie et Production', 4), **21** (9), 229–43.

Heinsohn, G. and O. Steiger (1989), 'The veil of barter: the solution to "the task of obtaining representations of an economy in which money is essential"', in J.A. Kregel (ed.), *Inflation and Income Distribution in Capitalist Crisis: Essays in Memory of Sidney Weintraub*, New York: New York University Press, 175–201.

Heinsohn, G. and O. Steiger (2000), 'The property theory of interest and money', in J. Smithin (ed.), *What is Money?*, London and New York: Routledge, 67–100.

Hicks, J.R. (1989), *A Market Theory of Money*, Oxford: Oxford University Press.

Hill St., R.L. (1995), 'A post Keynesian perspective on commercial bank behavior and regulation', *Metroeconomica*, **46** (1), 35–62.

Hodgson, G.M. (1988), *Economics and Institutions: A Manifesto for a Modern Institutional Economics*, Cambridge and Oxford: Polity Press and Basil Blackwell.

Ingham, G. (1996), 'Money is a social relation', *Review of Social Economy*, **54** (4), 507–29.

Ingham, G. (1998), 'On the underdevelopment of the "sociology of money"', *Acta Sociologica*, **41** (1), 3–18.

Ingham, G. (2000), '"Babylonian madness": on the historical and sociological origins of money', in J. Smithin (ed.), *What is Money?*, London and New York: Routledge, 16–41.

Innes, A.M. (1913), 'What is money?', *Banking Law Journal*, May, 377–408.

Iwai, K. (1997), 'Evolution of money', University of Tokyo *Working Paper*, no. 97–F–3.

Jevons, W.S. (1875), *Money and the Mechanism of Exchange*, London: Macmillan.

Keynes, J.M. (1930/1971), *A Treatise on Money*, London: Macmillan. Reprinted in *The Collected Writings of John Maynard Keynes*, Vols V and VI, London and Basingstoke: Macmillan.

Keynes, J.M. (1933/1973), 'A monetary theory of production'. Reprinted in *The Collected Writings of John Maynard Keynes*, Vol. XIII *The General Theory and After: Part I Preparation*, London and Basingstoke: Macmillan, 408–11.

Kiyotaki, N. and R. Wright (1989), 'On money as a medium of exchange', *Journal of Political Economy*, **97** (4), 927–54.

Kiyotaki, N. and R. Wright (1993), 'A search theoretic approach to monetary economics', *American Economic Review*, **83** (1), 63–77.

Knapp, G.F. (1905), *Die Staatliche Theorie des Geldes*, Münich and Leipzig. English edition: *The State Theory of Money*, Clifton: A.M. Kelley, 1924.

Kroszner, R. (1990), 'On the microfoundations of money: Walrasian and Mengerian approaches reconsidered in the light of Richard Rorty's critique of foundationalism', in D. Lavoie (ed.), *Economics and Hermeneutics*, London and New York: Routledge, 239–61.

Laughlin, J.L. (1903), *Principles of Money*, New York: Scribner's.

Lavoie, M. (1987), 'Monnaie et production: une synthèse de la théorie du circuit', *Économies et Sociétés* ('Série Monnaie et Production', 4), **21** (9), 65–101.

Lavoie, M. (1992), *Foundations of Post-Keynesian Economic Analysis*, Aldershot and Brookfield: Edward Elgar.

Lavoie, M. (1996), 'Horizontalism, structuralism, liquidity preference and the principle of increasing risk', *Scottish Journal of Political Economy*, **43** (3), 275–300.

Leijonhufvud, A. (1997), 'Mr Keynes and the moderns', University of Trento *Discussion Paper*, no. 4.

Liefmann, R. (1916), *Geld und Gold: Ökonomische Theories des Geldes*, Stuttgart: Verlags-Anstalt.

Mathieu, V. (1985), *La filosofia del denaro. Dopo il tramonto di Keynes*, Rome: Armando Editore.

Mélitz, J. (1970), 'Polanyi school of anthropology on money: an economist's view', *American Anthropologist*, **72** (5), 1020–40.

Menger, K. (1923), *Grundsätze der Volkswirtschaftslehre*, Wien. Italian edition: *Principi di economia politica*, Torino: Utet, 1976.

Messori, M. (1985), 'Le circuit de la monnaie: acquis et problémes non résolus', in R. Arena and A. Graziani (eds), *Production, circulation et monnaie*, Paris: Presses Universitaires de France, 207–46.

Messori, M. (1988), 'Agenti e mercati in uno schema periodale', in A. Graziani and M. Messori (eds), *Moneta e produzione*, Torino: Einaudi, 285–330.

Messori, M. (1997), 'The trials and misadventures of Schumpeter's treatise on money', *History of Political Economy*, **97** (4), 639–67.

Messori, M. and R. Tamborini (1995), 'Fallibility, precautionary behavior and the new Keynesian monetary theory', *Scottish Journal of Political Economy*, **42** (4), 443–64.

Mises, L. (1924), *Theorie des Geldes und der Umlaufsmittel*, second edition. English edition: *The Theory of Money and Credit*, Indianapolis: Liberty Classics, 1981.

Moore, B.J. (1988), *Horizontalists and Verticalists: The Macroeconomics of Credit Money*, Cambridge: Cambridge University Press.

Neale, W.C. (1976), *Monies in Societies*, San Francisco: Chandler and Sharp.

Nell, E.J. (1986), 'On monetary circulation and the rate of exploitation', *Thames Papers in Political Economy*, Summer, 1–36.

North, D.C. (1977), 'Markets and other allocation systems in history: the challenge of Karl Polanyi', *Journal of Economic History*, **6** (3), 703–16.

Olivera, J.H.G. (1971), 'The square-root law of precautionary reserves', *Journal of Political Economy*, **79** (5), 1095–104.

Ostroy, J.M. and R.M. Starr (1990), 'Transaction role of money', in B. Friedman and F.H. Hahn (eds), *Handbook of Monetary Economics*, Amsterdam: North-Holland, vol. I, 3–62.

Parguez, A. (1980), 'Profit, épargne, investissement: éléments pour une théorie monétaire du profit', *Economie appliquée*, **33** (2), 425–55.

Parguez, A. (1996), 'Beyond scarcity: a reappraisal of the theory of the monetary circuit', in G. Deleplace and E.J. Nell (eds), *Money in Motion: The Post Keynesian and Circulation Approaches*, London and New York: Macmillan and St. Martin's Press, 155–99.

Parguez, A. (2001), 'Money without scarcity: from the horizontalist revolution to the theory of the monetary circuit', in L.-P. Rochon and M. Vernengo (eds), *Credit, Interest Rates and the Open Economy: Essays on Horizontalism*, Cheltenham and Northampton: Edward Elgar, 69–103.

Parguez, A. (2002), 'Victoria Chick and the theory of the monetary circuit: an enlightening debate', in P. Arestis, M. Desai and S. Dow (eds), *Money, Macroeconomics and Keynes: Essays in Honour of Victoria Chick*, London and New York: Routledge, vol. I, 45–55.

Parguez, A. and M. Seccareccia (2000), 'The credit theory of money: the monetary circuit approach', in J. Smithin (ed.), *What is Money?*, London and New York: Routledge, 101–23.

Patinkin, D. (1965), *Money, Interest and Prices*, New York: Harper and Row, second edition.

Polanyi, K. (1944), *The Great Transformation*, New York: Rinehart.

Polanyi, K. (1957), 'The semantics of money-uses', *Explorations*, October. Reprinted in G. Dalton (ed.) (1968), *Primitive, Archaic, and Modern Economies: Essays of Karl Polanyi*, Boston: Beacon Press, 175–203.

Polanyi, K. (1977), *The Livelihood of Man*, New York: Academic Press.

Popper, K. (1976), 'The logic of social science', in T.W. Adorno, G. Adey and D. Frisby (eds), *The Positivist Dispute in German Sociology*, London: Heinemann.

Pryor, F.L. (1972), 'Property institutions and economic development', *Economic Development and Cultural Change*, **20** (3), 407–37.

Pryor, F.L. (1977), 'The origins of money', *Journal of Money, Credit and Banking*, **9** (3), 391–409.

Realfonzo, R. (1998), *Money and Banking: Theory and Debate (1900–1940)*, Cheltenham and Northampton: Edward Elgar.

Rist, C. (1951), 'Vieilles idées devenues neuves sur la monnaie', *Revue d'économie politique*, **61** (5), 717–35. English translation in C. Rist (1961), *The Triumph of Gold*, New York: Wisdom Library, 144–70.

Rochon, L.-P. (1999), *Credit, Money and Production: An Alternative Post-Keynesian Approach*, Cheltenham and Northampton: Edward Elgar.

Rossi, S. (2001), *Money and Inflation: A New Macroeconomic Analysis*, Cheltenham and Northampton: Edward Elgar.

Sadigh, É. (1988), 'La spesa del profitto e le disfunzioni del sistema economico', in A. Graziani and M. Messori (eds), *Moneta e produzione*, Torino: Einaudi, 45–56.

Schmitt, B. (1984), *Inflation, chômage et malformations du capital*, Paris and Albeuve: Economica and Castella.

Schumpeter, J.A. (1918), 'Das Sozialprodukt und die Rechenpfennige: Glossen und Beiträge zur Geldtheorie von Heute', *Archiv für Sozialwissenschaft und Sozialpolitik*, **44** (3), 627–715.

Schumpeter, J.A. (1934), *Theorie der wirtschaftlichen Entwicklung*, Berlin: Duncker and Humblot, fourth edition.

Schumpeter, J.A. (1954), *History of Economic Analysis*, New York: Allen and Unwin.

Schumpeter, J.A. (1970), *Das Wesen des Geldes*, Göttingen: Vandenhoeck and Ruprecht. Italian translation: *L'essenza della moneta*, Torino: Cassa di Risparmio di Torino, 1990.

Schumpeter, J.A. (1996), *Trattato della moneta: capitoli inediti*, edited by L. Berti and M. Messori, Napoli: Edizioni Scientifiche Italiane.

Seccareccia, M. (1996), 'Post Keynesian fundism and monetary circulation', in G.

Deleplace and E.J. Nell (eds), *Money in Motion: The Post Keynesian and Circulation Approaches*, London and New York, Macmillan and St. Martin's Press, 400–16.

Selgin, G. (1993), 'In defense of bank suspension', *Journal of Financial Services Research*, **7** (4), 347–64.

Servet, J.-M. (1993), 'L'institution monétaire de la société selon Karl Polanyi', *Revue économique*, **44** (6), 1127–49.

Simmel, G. (1907), *Philosophie des Geldes*, Leipzig. English edition: *The Philosophy of Money*, London and New York: Routledge, 1990.

Smithin, J. (1997), 'An alternative monetary model of inflation and growth', *Review of Political Economy*, **9** (4), 395–409.

Stanfield, J.R. (1986), *The Economic Thought of Karl Polanyi: Lives and Livelihood*, London: Macmillan.

Stanfield, J.R. (1989), 'Karl Polanyi and contemporary economic thought', *Review of Social Economy*, **47** (3), 266–79.

Stichter, S. (1985), *Migrant Laborers*, New York: Cambridge University Press.

Swedberg, R. (1991), *Joseph A. Schumpeter: His Life and Work*, Cambridge: Polity Press.

Toboso, F. (2001), 'Institutional individualism and institutional change: the search for a *middle way* mode of explanation', *Cambridge Journal of Economics*, **25** (6), 765–83.

Weber, M. (1922), *Wirtschaft und Gesellschaft*, Tübingen: Mohr.

Wolfson, M.H. (1996), 'A Post Keynesian theory of credit rationing', *Journal of Post Keynesian Economics*, **18** (3), 443–70.

Wray, L.R. (1990), *Money and Credit in Capitalist Economies: The Endogenous Money Approach*, Aldershot and Brookfield: Edward Elgar.

Wray, L.R. (1993), 'The origins of money and the development of the modern financial system', The Jerome Levy Economics Institute *Working Paper*, no. 86.

Wray, L.R. (1998), *Understanding Modern Money: The Key to Full Employment and Price Stability*, Cheltenham and Northampton: Edward Elgar.

Wray, L.R. (2000), 'Modern money', in J. Smithin (ed.), *What is Money?*, London and New York: Routledge, 42–66.

Zazzaro, A. (1995), 'La specificità delle banche. Teorie a confronto da una prospettiva schumpeteriana', *Studi economici*, **50** (55), 113–51.

Zazzaro, A. (1997), 'Regional banking systems, credit allocation and regional economic development', *Economie appliquée*, **50** (1), 51–74.

12. Post Keynesian Controversies on Endogenous Money: An Alternative Interpretation

Pierre Piégay[1]

INTRODUCTION

The most important feature of post Keynesian monetary theory is without doubt the concept of an endogenous money supply. Although this concept serves as a rallying point, there is no consensus on how endogenous money is created. Indeed, the endogenous money supply and the determination of the interest rate are matters of some contention.[2] The controversies under examination in this chapter primarily concern banks' liquidity preference and its consequences on the creation of endogenous money.

Although Moore has characterised these controversies a posteriori as 'a quintessential storm in a teacup' (Moore, 2001, p. 14), it proves very instructive to analyse them. The second section of this chapter briefly shows how Keynes's liquidity preference theory spawned both the concept of endogenous money and the controversies under examination. In the third section we propose an alternative interpretation to these controversies. It appears that, the controversies notwithstanding, the arguments relied upon by horizontalists and structuralists are ultimately not so different. It is argued that the two schools focus on two distinct levels of analysis that are not adequately distinguished within post Keynesian monetary theory. The fourth section then provides a suitable analysis to make these distinctions clear in light of the monetary circuit approach embedded in the theory of monetary emissions.

LIQUIDITY PREFERENCE AND ENDOGENOUS MONEY

In expounding his liquidity preference theory in the *General Theory*, Keynes emphasised the link between uncertainty and the integration of money in the economy. According to Keynes, because of liquidity preference, '[w]e have now introduced money into our causal nexus for the first time, and we are able to catch a first glimpse of the way in which changes in the quantity of money work their way into the economic system' (Keynes, 1936/1973, p. 173).

In Chapters 13 and 15 of the *General Theory*, money enters the economic system because economic agents demand it for portfolio motivations. The quantity of money demanded adapts to the given stock of money exogenously supplied by the monetary authorities. Supply and demand for money together determine the equilibrium rate of interest on the money market.

In his 1937 article, Keynes underlined the link between the existence of money and the radical uncertainty of the economic environment.

> [I]t is a recognised characteristic of money as a store of wealth that it is barren; whereas practically every other form of storing wealth yields some interest or profit. Why should anyone outside a lunatic asylum wish to use money as a store of wealth? Because, partly on reasonable and partly on instinctive grounds, our desire to hold money as a store of wealth is a barometer of the degree of our distrust of our own calculations and conventions concerning the future. ... The possession of actual money lulls our disquietude; and the premium which we require to make us part with money is the measure of the degree of our disquietude (Keynes, 1937a/1973, pp. 115–16).

Thus, money integrates the economic system because of radical uncertainty. Economic agents demand a stock of liquid wealth for portfolio motivations that is exogenously supplied by the monetary authorities. Therefore, liquidity preference theory is irrelevant when we come to study the creation of the endogenous monetary flow. Portfolio allocation operations under radical uncertainty refer to demand for a stock of money created previously and focus on the characteristic of money as a store of wealth.

Insofar as liquidity preference theory refers both to an exogenously given quantity of money and to asset allocation operations, post Keynesians rejected this analysis initially.[3] Indeed, in his *General Theory*, Keynes concentrates on asset allocation operations, whereas the main objective of post Keynesians was to explain the endogenous creation of money. The originality of post Keynesian and circuitist monetary analyses lies in the fact that they develop the most innovative aspects of Keynes's insights and that they distance themselves from analyses in terms of previously existing assets.

They both try to explain how endogenous money enters the economic system without necessarily having recourse to available financial reserves.

In the *General Theory*, 'technical monetary detail falls into the background' (Keynes, 1936/1973, p. xxii). Immediately after the publication of his book, however, Keynes reintroduced the role played by the banking system in the creation of money through his 'finance motive'.[4] Within the 'finance motive' analysis, banks endogenously create money to finance an overdraft spending: 'the finance required ... is mainly supplied by specialists, in particular by the banks' (Keynes, 1937c/1973, p. 219).

In its first phase, the systematisation of this concept of an endogenous money supply led post Keynesian horizontalists to neglect the microeconomic analysis of bank behaviour on the credit market. Afterwards, post Keynesians sought to develop this weak point. According to Minsky (1983, p. 47), 'any serious theory of the resource creation process needs to examine how banking and finance do in fact operate'.

In this perspective, structuralists analyse the institutional role played by the banking system in creating endogenous money within the theoretical framework of a monetary economy. This analysis has led to the rehabilitation of liquidity preference theory after its initial rejection. Liquidity preference is no longer restricted to assets allocation by households but is extended to banks.[5] Recent developments in the analysis of banks' liquidity preference[6] supplement the analysis of an endogenous money supply by making allowance for the complexity of operations carried out by banks.

The idea of an endogenous money supply is the cornerstone of post Keynesian monetary theory. This broad consensus, however, seems to be weakened by the analysis of banks' liquidity preference. Indeed, this analysis gave rise to a controversy between horizontalists and the advocates of a more realistic vision of bank behaviour. The polemical exchanges between horizontalists and structuralists raised the question of the coherence of post Keynesian monetary theory. For Pollin (1996, p. 506) the divergences are irreconcilable, while for Lavoie (1996, p. 275) 'the differences between horizontalists and other Post Keynesian monetary theorists are matters of emphasis rather than substantial differences of opinion'.[7]

POST KEYNESIANS ON ENDOGENOUS MONEY AND BANK BEHAVIOUR: AN ALTERNATIVE INTERPRETATION

The debate between horizontalists and structuralists concerns the determination of the interest rate but it also reveals divergences about the analysis of endogenous money creation.[8]

The horizontalist point of view was initially developed in opposition to the monetarist analysis that considers the quantity of money as an exogenous variable.[9] In the Moore–Kaldor analysis, money is endogenous, while the rate of interest becomes exogenous. In an overdraft system, commercial banks create money by granting credit to borrowers. Commercial banks apply a mark-up to the discount rate pegged by the central bank in its role as the lender of last resort and meet creditworthy borrowers' demand for credit in full.

> It follows that the quantity of loans and deposits is always demand determined . . . Whenever the increase in the money stock is a by-product of increased borrowing from the banking system, . . . the increase in the supply of money is a consequence of increased loan expenditure, not the cause of it, which the central bank can influence only indirectly by changing short-term interest rates. Both the high-powered base and the money stock are then in fact endogenous (Moore, 1985, p. 15).[10]

The critics of the previous position consider horizontalism as an 'extreme' analysis,[11] which distorts the role that the banking system actually plays in the creation of endogenous money. Indeed, horizontalists seemingly assign a passive role to banks that fully and passively satisfy demand for money from borrowers. On the contrary, for structuralists, the analysis of endogenous money creation requires a detailed analysis of banks' behaviour on the credit market.

> When Moore began advocating the endogenous money approach more than a decade ago, adoption of an exogenous interest rate could be justified for reasons of expediency. It is now time to go beyond this black box approach and to examine the conditions under which 'money' is 'supplied'. This involves close institutional analysis of the behaviour of banks, nonbank banks, and the customers on both sides of the balance sheets of these. Neither Moore's black box horizontalist approach nor Keynes's approach of the *General Theory* – in which monetary details fall into the background – is sufficient (Wray, 1995, p. 280).

For structuralists, commercial banks take their liquidity preference into account. 'Banks' liquidity preference influences their responsiveness to the demand for credit. Their liquidity preference is expressed in risk assessment' (Dow, 1996, p. 497). Commercial banks' lending depends both on the creditworthiness of borrowers and on the level of perceived risk that banks wish to support. 'As the debt to equity ratio of borrowers increases, the riskiness of loans increases and commercial banks have to be rewarded with higher interest rates to encourage them to forgo liquidity and enter into illiquid industrial loans' (Hewitson, 1995, p. 296).[12] The greater the amount of credit granted, the greater the risk banks run and the greater the collateral requirements they demand. This leads to an upward-sloping money supply curve and a more detailed analysis of bank behaviour.

The horizontalist model is criticised essentially because it supposedly oversimplifies banks' behaviour in the process of creating endogenous money. However, close examination of the controversy shows that Moore does not claim that banks behave passively. Indeed, Moore states that 'individual banks, of course, do not simply react passively to borrower demand for loans. . . . However, this does not affect the basic argument that, from the viewpoint of the banking industry, the total quantity of credit money supplied should be regarded as endogenously demand determined' (Moore, 1991, p. 127).[13] Thus, it appears that despite the apparent divergences, horizontalism and structuralism may not be as incompatible as they seem. In fact, the controversy reveals that both schools focus on two different levels of analysis.

The first difference between horizontalists and structuralists is the distinction between microeconomics and macroeconomics. According to Keynes (1936/1973, p. 293):

> The division of economics between the theory of value and distribution on the one hand and the theory of money on the other hand is a false division. The right dichotomy is between the theory of the individual industry or firm and of the rewards and the distribution between different uses of a given quantity of resources on the one hand, and the theory of output and employment as a whole on the other hand. . . . As soon as we pass to the problem of what determines output and employment as a whole, we require the complete theory of a monetary economy.

In its first phase, the systematisation of the concept of endogenous money corresponds to the macroeconomic level as defined by Keynes. For post Keynesians, the purpose was to understand how banks endogenously create money within a monetary economy and without any given financial provision beforehand. Initially, close examination of banks' behaviour on the credit market was neglected because the main objective was precisely to explain the macroeconomic operation of the creation of endogenous money. Money is created because it is demanded by economic agents from banks to finance overdraft spending. Whenever banks grant the credit demanded, money is endogenously created. In the words of Moore: the supply of money is credit-driven and demand-determined.[14]

On the other hand, structuralists emphasise the microeconomic analysis of bank behaviour, focusing on the way the banking system actually responds to the demand for money expressed by borrowers on the credit market. This analysis primarily concerns banks' liquidity preference and their risk management.

Consequently, the distinction between horizontalists and structuralists is essentially a matter of emphasis. On the one side, horizontalists develop a macroeconomic analysis because they seek to explain how money enters the economic system whereas, on the other side, structuralists promote a microeconomic analysis of bank behaviour. Horizontalism and structuralism are thus complementary: banks' liquidity preference analyses are explicitly based on the central concept of endogenous money.

The second distinction between horizontalists and structuralists relies on the twofold function of the banking system. Within a monetary economy, banks create endogenous money and act as financial intermediaries. Horizontalists focus on the role of banks as creators of money while structuralists focus on their role as financial intermediaries.

Following Moore's analysis, horizontalists concentrate above all on the monetary side of banks' activities, trying to explain the endogenous creation of money within a monetary production economy.[15] Money is endogenously created by banks when they grant loans to creditworthy borrowers to finance overdraft spending. Focusing on the creation of money, one cannot envisage any discrepancy between supply of and demand for money. Indeed, movements of assets and liabilities are simultaneous and involve identical amounts: 'deposits and loans expand *pari passu*' (Moore, 1995, p. 264). Whenever banks grant the credit demanded, the supply of money induced is exactly identical to the amount of credit granted. According to Moore, it is a logical necessity[16] that, at the macroeconomic level, 'the supply and demand for money are interdependent' (Moore, 1988b, p. 381).

By contrast, the aim of structuralists is to develop a detailed study of banks' behaviour on the credit market. They focus on the analysis of the banking system as a financial intermediary to understand banks' credit granting policy and their consequences for the creation of money. They seek to explain why banks do not necessarily fully satisfy the demand for credit expressed by borrowers. Banks' liquidity preference and their financial fragility affect the volume of credit granted and nothing implies that expressed demand for credit is a priori equal to banks' supply. In looking at the financial side of the banking system, one must consider motivations, institutional rules and constraints that lead banks either to grant or to refuse credit to borrowers. Banks make allowance for prudential ratios, and evaluate and manage the risk of default by borrowers that they are able to sustain. This leads to financial considerations about interest rate fixing, collateral requirements, and the control and selection of borrowers. In this perspective, post Keynesian analyses of banks' credit granting policy get closer to new Keynesian analyses of credit rationing.[17]

These two analyses focus on two different aspects of the banking system: the first looks essentially at the creation of money; the second considers endogenous money creation from the outset, concentrating thereafter on banks' liquidity preference. However, as we have seen above, the horizontalist analysis does not mean that banks' liquidity preference does not influence their credit granting policy. Wolfson (1996) provides a post Keynesian model of credit rationing compatible with a horizontalist framework. Consequently, 'there is no incompatibility between the principle of liquidity preference and a horizontalist approach to endogenous credit money' (Lavoie, 1996, p. 291). Indeed, these two analyses are complementary as the purpose of structuralists is to buttress post Keynesian monetary theory by integrating financial aspects of the role of banks. The controversy ultimately reflects the difficulty of post Keynesian monetary analysis in distinguishing between monetary and financial operations performed by the banking system.

AN ESSAY AT DISTINGUISHING MONEY AND FINANCE

The previous section has shown that post Keynesian controversies about endogenous money supply and bank behaviour arose because the distinction is not clearly drawn between the monetary and the financial sides of the banking system. In this section, we will try to clarify such a distinction in light of the monetary theory elaborated by Schmitt.[18] As Deleplace and Nell (1996, p. 33) remind us, 'explaining the peculiarity of money, specifically how it differs from finance, is a necessary piece of any theory of a monetary economy'.

It is difficult to clearly distinguish between the monetary and the financial spheres within post Keynesian monetary theory because post Keynesians still regard money as if it were an asset. As Rossi (1998, p. 25) noticed, 'post

Keynesian analysis does not distinguish money from bank deposits, since it is based on the idea that bank liabilities are money'. One of the most fundamental elements of post Keynesian analysis is the link between the existence of money and the radical uncertainty of the economic environment. Following Keynes's liquidity preference theory and Davidson's seminal work,[19] money is considered as 'the asset that is able to discharge contractual obligations' (Heise, 1992, p. 290). Consequently, in this perspective, banks are supposed to create a liquid asset because economic agents need it to finance additional deficit spending.

On the contrary, following Keynes's above distinction between micro and macroeconomics, the objective of circuitists is to link the existence of money to the production process and to develop a macroeconomic theory of money. According to Lavoie (1987, p. 73; our translation), one of the main features of the circuitist approach is 'the emphasis put on the existence of pure macroeconomic laws and of structural relations independent of the behaviour of microeconomic agents'. Following one of the most original aspects of Keynes's theory according to which the relation of cause and effect runs from investment to saving, circuitists consider that the implementation of the production process does not necessitate any recourse to financial reserves beforehand. In line with Graziani's interpretation of Keynes's finance motive,[20] the implementation of the production process gives rise to a new creation of money by the banking system, when monetary income is created: 'money is introduced into the economy through the productive activities of the firms, as these activities generate income' (Lavoie, 1984/1995, p. 388).

Post Keynesian and circuitist analyses share a common objective: to explain the integration of money in the economy. Moreover, they both agree on the fact that money does not enter the economic system as if it were dropped from a helicopter. The endogenous money concept is intimately linked to the functioning of the monetary production economy. Nevertheless, circuitist and post Keynesian analyses diverge as far as the explanation for the integration of money is concerned. As stated by Deleplace and Nell (1996, p. 19), 'for [the circulation approach] production needs determine money creation; for [post Keynesians] production requires financial assets'.

Post Keynesians link the creation of endogenous money to the functioning of the banking system within an overdraft economy and to the radical uncertainty of the economic environment. In this perspective, production is not a specific operation as far as the integration of money is concerned.[21] Fontana (2000) considers radical uncertainty as the rallying point of post Keynesian and circuitist monetary theories. However, by doing so, he puts the stress on the characteristic of money as a liquid financial asset (money as a store of wealth). Consequently, such an approach is not appropriate to draw a clear-cut borderline between the monetary and the financial spheres, precisely because money is considered as a specific financial asset. As noticed by Kaldor and Trevithick (1981, p. 12), if the distinction between money and other financial assets relies on a liquidity scale (money being the liquidity par excellence), 'it is impossible to give an unambiguous definition of the money supply along these lines ... There is no clear dividing line between "money" and "non money" and no clear principle to guide us in finding the ideal definition of money'.[22]

On the contrary, circuitists intimately link the implementation of the production process to the endogenous creation of money. Production is a specific operation regarding the creation of endogenous money because it is the economic operation in which the monetary income is initially created. Therefore, as Rochon (1999a, p. 3) argues, 'the emphasis is on a flow approach to credit endogeneity and not on portfolio decisions, uncertainty, or contracts'. Thus, circuit theory develops both a macroeconomic and a monetary analysis because it seeks to explain the creation of the monetary income within the production process and without any given financial reserves. 'The main concern of circuit theory is the initial integration of money in the economy. ... The monetary economy is first a production economy before being an exchange economy' (Ottavj, 1981, pp. 147, 151).

From now on, the starting point of our own analysis is the explanation of the initial creation of the monetary income without needing a financial provision beforehand.[23] In his *Treatise on Money*, Keynes defined income as follows: '*Income.* We propose to mean identically the same thing by the three expressions: (1) *the community's money income*; (2) *the earnings of the factors of production*; and (3) *the cost of production*' (Keynes, 1930/1971, p. 111; italics in the original). Following Keynes's definition, the creation of monetary income takes place in the production process. Insofar as no income is available yet, the analysis begins with the explanation of the creation of money and income. 'In other words, it is mistaken to explain the origin of money by resorting to an operation that implies the existence of income, and which, therefore, necessarily presupposes the very existence of money' (Cencini, 1995, p. 12). In the same way, if it is assumed that money exists before the creation of income, then the true explanation of the creation of money is missing.

Monetary income defines the earnings of the factors of production. In an overdraft economy, commercial banks participate in the creation of endogenous money. In such a system, banks play a central role by carrying out payments on behalf of the productive economy. In a monetary production economy, banks act as an intermediary between firms and factors of production when they pay the monetary income to factors of production on behalf of firms. For the sake of clarity, we have assumed that neither income nor money exists before this payment. The production process is thus defined as the economic operation in which an available income is initially created in the economy.

In their role as monetary intermediaries, banks enable firms to pay the monetary income to their factors of production. It is not necessary for firms to have a corresponding provision of loanable funds beforehand. Indeed, banks create the endogenous money when they pay monetary income to factors of production. Money that banks create in this operation has no intrinsic value. 'The emission of money is, first of all, an operation through which banks provide the economy with a numerical standard' (Cencini, 1996, p. 20). Nevertheless, the role of the banking system is essential in this analysis. By their monetary intermediation, banks authorise the implementation of the production process and the creation of the monetary income in an overdraft system. In the *General Theory*, Keynes (1936/1973, p. 82) argues that '[i]f the grant of a bank credit to an entrepreneur additional to the credits already existing allows him to make an addition to current investment which would not have occurred otherwise, incomes will necessarily be increased'.

At this stage of the analysis, the monetary income newly created in the production process is available in the hands of factors of production. The payment of income earners enables them to acquire the final goods just produced and available. However, factors of production will not immediately consume these goods. They will instead immediately 'deposit' the monetary income they earned in the production process with the banking system. Consumption does not generally take place at the very moment of the payment of monetary income. Income earners' saving merely expresses their renouncement to an immediate satisfaction of their needs. Factors of production instantaneously save their monetary income in the form of bank deposits instead of immediate consumption. They thus obtain a financial asset, which is a claim on a future consumption. As Keynes argues in the *General Theory*:

> It is supposed that a depositor and his bank can somehow contrive between them to perform an operation by which savings can disappear into the banking system so that they are lost to investment, or, contrariwise, that the banking system can make it possible for investment to occur, to which no saving corresponds. But no one can save without acquiring an asset, whether it be cash or a debt or capital goods; and no one can acquire an asset which he did not previously possess, unless either an asset of equal value is newly produced or someone else parts with an asset of that value which he previously had. In the first alternative there is a corresponding

new investment: in the second alternative someone else must be dis-saving an equal sum (Keynes, 1936/1973, pp. 81–2).

The above description of the payment of monetary income initially created in the production process implies three agents: firms, banks and factors of production. This payment defines a complete emission of money that measures the new creation of income in the economy. Within this framework, money is properly defined as the circular flow of payment. Yet, money *stricto sensu* must not be confused with a circulatory flow of money (commodity or asset), precisely because *money is intrinsically the flow of payment*. There is actually no physical movement of money, as money does not flow outside the banking system. In this operation, the monetary payment carried out by banks (in their role as monetary intermediaries) measures the creation of new income.

This payment of monetary income by banks gives rise to a financial relationship between firms, factors of production and the banking system. This financial relationship actually registered in banks' balance sheet records the result of the payment of newly created income. 'In its own nature, money ... is defined as a circular emission whose significance lies in the mark it impresses on the economy' (Schmitt and Cencini, 1982, pp. 139–40). In their role as financial intermediaries, banks record in their balance sheets the result of the payments they make as monetary intermediaries.

In an overdraft system, as soon as entrepreneurs use their credit line, banks pay income to factors of production. As soon as this monetary emission takes place, firms become debtors of the banks and, at the same time, factors of production become creditors of the banks for the same amount. Consequently, firms enter banks' balance sheets on the assets side while income earners enter on the liabilities side. Graziani (1996, p. 143) has termed this threefold relationship 'a triangular debt–credit situation'. This financial relationship is recorded as in Table 12.1. Factors of production initially renounce their claim on immediate disposal of final goods. Consequently, monetary income becomes available in the hands of firms to finance the stocks of final goods to be sold. Indeed, before consumption takes place, final goods are actually held in stocks by firms. This temporary detention of output by firms is financed through the financial intermediation of banks that lend them income just deposited by factors of production.

Table 12.1. The bank as a financial intermediary

Bank

Assets		Liabilities	
Firms	£x	Factors of production	£x
(goods temporarily held in stocks)		*(claim on a future consumption)*	

As soon as factors of production are paid, they deposit their income earned in the production process with the banking system. As a consequence, the logical causality runs from monetary payments to bookkeeping financial entries. This means that the operation of credit does not properly bring about the creation of money. Contrariwise, the monetary flow of payment results in a credit operation recorded in banks' balance sheets. Income earners become savers, as they are creditors of the banking system. Savings on the liabilities side of banks' balance sheets are financial assets representing the claim of factors of production on current output. Financial assets thus appear as a temporary abode of purchasing power: store of wealth is no longer an intrinsic characteristic of money, it is the proper feature of savings. Credits on the assets side of banks' balance sheets record the firms' commitment to sell final goods they temporarily hold in stocks. As Schmitt argues, 'income creation is not a credit operation, but when created, income is immediately the object of a credit operation. As soon as incomes are born, they are thus lent by their holders until their "withdrawal". This means that incomes are instantaneously transformed into *savings* or, identically, into *capital*' (Schmitt, 1984, p. 158; our translation, italics in the original).

The role of the banking system is thus twofold: it is first a monetary intermediary before being a financial intermediary.[24] The financial relationships actually recorded in banks' accounting (banks as financial intermediaries) are the consequence of the monetary payments they realise on behalf of the productive economy (banks as monetary intermediaries). When production takes place, income is created as well as bank money. This creation is perfectly endogenous to the functioning of the productive economy and there is no need for any pre-existing savings to start up production. On the contrary, the overdraft payment of the monetary income by the banking system gives rise to savings on the liabilities side of banks' balance sheets.

CONCLUSION

Horizontalists initially rejected the concept of liquidity preference elaborated by Keynes in his *General Theory* because it implies an exogenous money supply. Afterwards, structuralists have reintegrated liquidity preference theory after initially dismissing it by analysing the behaviour of banks on the credit market. This has led to controversies within the post Keynesian camp about the analysis of the endogenous money supply and the determination of the interest rate. We have shown that these controversies arose because the distinction between micro and macroeconomics on the one hand, and between the monetary and the financial side of the banking system on the other hand, is not clear-cut.

Post Keynesians and circuitists have a common purpose: to explain the creation of endogenous money. Nevertheless, opinions diverge when it comes to explaining the integration of money. For circuitists the creation of endogenous money is not specifically linked to radical uncertainty and to the analysis of the institutional aspect of the banking system. It is above all closely connected with the creation of income within the production process.

Therefore, we can conclude with Arena (1996, p. 431) that 'both circuit and post Keynesian approaches may be more complementary than analogous'. Indeed, post Keynesian analysis is more precise in its institutional analysis of the banking system, while circuit theory is more precise in its distinction between monetary and financial operations carried out by the banking system. The community of purpose combined with the divergence of emphasis should result in a convergence of circuitist and post Keynesian monetary theories.

NOTES

1. The author would like to thank Xavier Bradley, Marc Lavoie, Louis-Philippe Rochon, Sergio Rossi, Martin H. Wolfson and L. Randall Wray for very helpful comments on earlier drafts of this chapter. The usual disclaimer applies.
2. See for example Palley (1998) and Moore (1998).
3. See Kaldor (1985, p. 26) and Moore (1988a, p. xiv).
4. See Keynes (1937b/1973, 1937c/1973, 1938/1973, 1939/1973).
5. See Dow and Dow (1989).
6. See for example Dow (1997), Mott (1985), Niggle (1991/1995), Palley (1991).
7. In a recent paper, Moore (2001, p. 14) adopts a similar point of view: 'the debate is really quite minor in its theoretical implications'.
8. See Hewitson (1995) for a survey. See also the debates between Howells (1995, 1997) and Moore (1997) and between Arestis and Howells (1996) and Lavoie (1999).
9. See the debate between Kaldor (1970a/1995, 1970b/1995) and Friedman (1970/1995).

10. See also Lavoie (1985, p. 71).
11. See Wray (1992, p. 1160) and Cardim de Carvalho (1995, p. 30).
12. See also Wray (1992, p. 1160): '[Banks] require higher interest rates to compensate for greater perceived risk as balance sheets expand'.
13. See also Moore (1988a, p. 24, quoted by Dow, 1996, p. 499): 'commercial bank loan officers must ensure that loan requests meet the bank's income and collateral requirements. They must in general satisfy themselves as to the creditworthiness of the project and the character of the borrower'.
14. See for example Moore (2001, p. 12).
15. See in particular Lavoie (1985) and Rochon (1999b).
16. See Moore (1985, p. 24, 1988a, p. xi).
17. See Piégay (2000) for a presentation of the convergences and the divergences between new and post Keynesian analyses of bank behaviour. See also Rochon (1999b, Ch. 7).
18. See Schmitt (1984) and Cencini (1995).
19. See Davidson (1972).
20. See Graziani (1987).
21. This leads Davidson (1972, pp. 226–7) to envisage two distinct processes of money creation: the income generating-finance process and the portfolio-change process. The former refers to the macroeconomic analysis as defined by Keynes because it involves a creation of resources, whereas the latter refers to a much more microeconomic approach because the stock of available resources is given.
22. See also Kaldor (1985, pp. 116–17).
23. This is in line with Schmitt's monetary theory. For an alternative approach of the theory of the monetary circuit, see for example Parguez and Seccareccia (2000).
24. See Rossi (1998) for an extensive analysis of the twofold nature of bank intermediation.

REFERENCES

Arena, R. (1996), 'Investment decisions in circuit and Post Keynesian approaches: a comparison', in G. Deleplace and E.J. Nell (eds), *Money in Motion: The Post Keynesian and Circulation Approaches*, London and New York: Macmillan and St. Martin's Press, 417–33.

Arestis, P. and P. Howells (1996), 'Theoretical reflections on endogenous money: the problem with "convenience lending"', *Cambridge Journal of Economics*, **20** (5), 539–51.

Cardim de Carvalho, F.J. (1995), 'Post Keynesian developments of liquidity preference theory', in P. Wells (ed.), *Post Keynesian Economic Theory*, London: Kluwer Academic Publishers, 17–33.

Cencini, A. (1995), *Monetary Theory, National and International*, London and New York: Routledge.

Cencini, A. (1996), 'Inflation and deflation', in A. Cencini and M. Baranzini (eds), *Inflation and Unemployment: Contributions to a New Macroeconomic Approach*, London and New York: Routledge, 17–60.

Davidson, P. (1972), *Money and the Real World*, London: Macmillan.

Deleplace, G. and E.J. Nell (1996), 'Introduction: monetary circulation and effective demand', in G. Deleplace and E.J. Nell (eds), *Money in Motion: The Post Keynesian and Circulation Approaches*, London and New York: Macmillan and St. Martin's Press, 3–41.

Dow, A.C. and S.C. Dow (1989), 'Endogenous money creation and idle balances', in

J. Pheby (ed.), *New Directions in Post Keynesian Economics*, Aldershot and Brookfield: Edward Elgar, 147–64.

Dow, S.C. (1996), 'Horizontalism: a critique', *Cambridge Journal of Economics*, **20** (4), 497–508.

Dow, S.C. (1997), 'Endogenous money', in G.C. Harcourt and P.A. Riach (eds), *A Second Edition of The General Theory*, London and New York: Routledge, vol. II, 61–78.

Fontana, G. (2000), 'Post Keynesians and Circuitists on money and uncertainty: an attempt at generality', *Journal of Post Keynesian Economics*, **23** (1), 27–48.

Friedman, M. (1970/1995), 'New monetarism: comment', in M. Musella and C. Panico (eds), *The Money Supply in the Economic Process: A Post-Keynesian Perspective*, Aldershot and Brookfield: Edward Elgar, 205–6.

Graziani, A. (1987), 'Keynes' finance motive', *Économies et Sociétés* ('Série Monnaie et Production', 4), **21** (9), 23–42.

Graziani, A. (1996), 'Money as purchasing power and money as a stock of wealth in Keynesian economic thought', in G. Deleplace and E.J. Nell (eds), *Money in Motion: The Post Keynesian and Circulation Approaches*, London and New York: Macmillan and St. Martin's Press, 139–54.

Heise, A. (1992), 'Commercial banks in macroeconomic theory', *Journal of Post Keynesian Economics*, **14** (3), 285–96.

Hewitson, G. (1995), 'Post Keynesian monetary theory: some issues', *Journal of Economic Surveys*, **9** (3), 285–310.

Howells, P.G.A. (1995), 'The demand for endogenous money', *Journal of Post Keynesian Economics*, **18** (1), 89–106.

Howells, P.G.A. (1997), 'The demand for endogenous money: a rejoinder', *Journal of Post Keynesian Economics*, **19** (3), 429–35.

Kaldor, N. (1985), *The Scourge of Monetarism*, Paris: Economica, French edition.

Kaldor, N. (1970a/1995), 'The new monetarism', in M. Musella and C. Panico (eds), *The Money Supply in the Economic Process: A Post-Keynesian Perspective*, Aldershot and Brookfield: Edward Elgar, 188–204.

Kaldor, N. (1970b/1995), 'New monetarism: reply', in M. Musella and C. Panico (eds), *The Money Supply in the Economic Process: A Post-Keynesian Perspective*, Aldershot and Brookfield: Edward Elgar, 207–8.

Kaldor, N. and J. Trevithick (1981), 'A Keynesian perspective on money', *Lloyds Bank Review*, (139), 1–19.

Keynes, J.M. (1930/1971), *A Treatise on Money: The Pure Theory of Money*, in *The Collected Writings of John Maynard Keynes*, Vol. V, London and Basingstoke: Macmillan.

Keynes, J.M. (1936/1973), *The General Theory of Employment, Interest and Money*, in *The Collected Writings of John Maynard Keynes*, Vol. VII, London and Basingstoke: Macmillan.

Keynes, J.M. (1937a/1973), 'The general theory of employment', in *The Collected Writings of John Maynard Keynes*, Vol. XIV *The General Theory and After: Part II Defence and Development*, London and Basingstoke: Macmillan, 109–23.

Keynes, J.M. (1937b/1973), 'Alternative theories of the rate of interest', *Economic Journal*, **47** (186), 241–52. Reprinted in *The Collected Writings of John Maynard Keynes*, Vol. XIV, London and Basingstoke: Macmillan, 201–15.

Keynes, J.M. (1937c/1973), 'The "ex ante" theory of the rate of interest', *Economic*

Journal, **47** (188), 663–9. Reprinted in *The Collected Writings of John Maynard Keynes*, Vol. XIV, London and Basingstoke: Macmillan, 215–23.

Keynes, J.M. (1938/1973), 'Mr Keynes' finance', in *The Collected Writings of John Maynard Keynes*, Vol. XIV *The General Theory and After: Part II Defence and Development*, London and Basingstoke: Macmillan, 229–33.

Keynes, J.M. (1939/1973), 'The process of capital formation', in *The Collected Writings of John Maynard Keynes*, Vol. XIV *The General Theory and After: Part II Defence and Development*, London and Basingstoke: Macmillan, 278–85.

Lavoie, M. (1984), 'The endogenous flow of credit and the Post Keynesian theory of money', *Journal of Economic Issues*, **18** (3), 771–97. Reprinted in M. Musella and C. Panico (eds) (1995), *The Money Supply in the Economic Process: A Post-Keynesian Perspective*, Aldershot and Brookfield: Edward Elgar, 385–411.

Lavoie, M. (1985), 'Credit and money: the dynamic circuit, overdraft economics, and Post Keynesian economics', in M. Jarsulic (ed.), *Money and Macro Policy*, Dordrecht: Kluwer Nijhoff Publishing, 63–84.

Lavoie, M. (1987), 'Monnaie et production: une synthèse de la théorie du circuit', *Économies et Sociétés* ('Série Monnaie et Production', 4), **21** (9), 65–101.

Lavoie, M. (1996), 'Horizontalism, structuralism, liquidity preference and the principle of increasing risk', *Scottish Journal of Political Economy*, **43** (3), 275–300.

Lavoie, M. (1999), 'The credit-led supply of deposits and the demand for money: Kaldor's reflux mechanism as previously endorsed by Joan Robinson', *Cambridge Journal of Economics*, **23** (1), 103–13.

Minsky, H.P. (1983), 'Notes on effective demand: comment on Bharadwaj', in J.A. Kregel (ed.), *Distribution, Effective Demand and International Economic Relations*, London: Macmillan, 43–9.

Moore, B.J. (1985), 'Wages, bank lending, and the endogeneity of credit money', in M. Jarsulic (ed.), *Money and Macro Policy*, Dordrecht: Kluwer Nijhoff Publishing, 1–28.

Moore, B.J. (1988a), *Horizontalists and Verticalists: The Macroeconomics of Credit Money*, Cambridge: Cambridge University Press.

Moore, B.J. (1988b), 'The endogenous money supply', *Journal of Post Keynesian Economics*, **10** (3), 372–85.

Moore, B.J. (1991), 'Has the demand for money been mislaid? A reply to "Has Moore become too horizontal?"', *Journal of Post Keynesian Economics*, **14** (1), 125–33.

Moore, B.J. (1995), 'The exogeneity of short-term interest rates: a reply to Wray', *Journal of Economic Issues*, **29** (1), 258–66.

Moore, B.J. (1997), 'Reconciliation of the supply and demand for endogenous money', *Journal of Post Keynesian Economics*, **19** (3), 423–8.

Moore, B.J. (1998), 'Accommodation to accommodationism: a note', *Journal of Post Keynesian Economics*, **21** (1), 175–8.

Moore, B.J. (2001), 'Some reflections on endogenous money', in L.-P. Rochon and M. Vernengo (eds), *Credit, Interest Rates and the Open Economy: Essays on Horizontalism*, Cheltenham and Northampton: Edward Elgar, 11–33.

Mott, T. (1985), 'Towards a Post Keynesian formulation of liquidity preference', *Journal of Post Keynesian Economics*, **8** (2), 222–32.

Niggle, C.J. (1991), 'The endogenous money supply theory: an institutionalist appraisal', *Journal of Economic Issues*, **25** (1), 137–51. Reprinted in M. Musella and C. Panico (eds) (1995), *The Money Supply in the Economic Process: A Post-Keynesian Perspective*, Aldershot and Brookfield: Edward Elgar, 556–70.

Ottavj, C. (1981), 'Circuit économique et déséquilibre', *Cahiers d'économie politique*, **6**, 147–69.

Palley, T.I. (1991), 'The endogenous money supply: consensus and disagreement', *Journal of Post Keynesian Economics*, **13** (3), 397–403.

Palley, T.I. (1998), 'Accommodationism, structuralism, and superstructuralism', *Journal of Post Keynesian Economics*, **21** (1), 171–3.

Parguez, A. and M. Seccareccia (2000), 'The credit theory of money: the monetary circuit approach', in J. Smithin (ed.), *What is Money?*, London and New York: Routledge, 101–23.

Piégay, P. (2000), 'The New and Post Keynesian analyses of bank behavior: consensus and disagreement', *Journal of Post Keynesian Economics*, **22** (2), 265–83.

Pollin, R. (1996), 'Money supply endogeneity: what are the questions and why do they matter?', in G. Deleplace and E.J. Nell (eds), *Money in Motion: The Post Keynesian and Circulation Approaches*, London and New York: Macmillan and St. Martin's Press, 490–515.

Rochon, L.-P. (1999a), 'The creation and circulation of endogenous money: a circuit dynamique approach', *Journal of Economic Issues*, **33** (1), 1–21.

Rochon, L.-P. (1999b), *Credit, Money and Production: An Alternative Post Keynesian Approach*, Cheltenham and Northampton: Edward Elgar.

Rossi, S. (1998), 'Endogenous money and banking activity: some notes on the workings of modern payment systems', *Studi economici*, **53** (3), 23–56.

Schmitt, B. (1984), *Inflation, chômage et malformations du capital*, Paris and Albeuve: Economica and Castella.

Schmitt, B. and A. Cencini (1982), 'Wages and profits in a theory of emissions', in M. Baranzini (ed.), *Advances in Economic Theory*, Oxford and New York: Basil Blackwell and St. Martin's Press, 137–46.

Wolfson, M.H. (1996), 'A Post Keynesian theory of credit rationing', *Journal of Post Keynesian Economics*, **18** (3), 443–70.

Wray, L.R. (1992), 'Alternative approaches to money and interest rates', *Journal of Economic Issues*, **26** (4), 1145–78.

Wray, L.R. (1995), 'Keynesian monetary theory: liquidity preference or black box horizontalism?', *Journal of Economic Issues*, **29** (1), 273–82.

PART THREE

THE THEORY OF MONEY EMISSIONS

13. An Internal Critique of General Equilibrium Theory

Bernard Schmitt and Curzio De Gottardi[1]

INTRODUCTION

You walk along Eighth Avenue and you look at some wonderful Florida oranges arranged on a grocer's shelf. You want to buy some in order to make a healthy drink. You see that the price of 1 lb. of oranges is $1.50. You are a curious person and you ask yourself where this price comes from. You have your opinion, but you prefer to ask one of your friends. He has just finished studying economics at one of the top NYC universities. The goal of this chapter is to show that your friend's answer is illogical. This is not because your friend did not understand the lectures well, but because the theory of the determination of prices he has learnt is faulty.

In all the universities around the world, one learns that commodity prices can be explained by general equilibrium theory (GET). This theory has lasted for more than one hundred years (Walras, 1874/1988) and it is mathematically formalised (Walras, 1874/1988; Wald, 1936/1951; Arrow and Debreu, 1954; McKenzie, 1954; Arrow and Hahn, 1971; Debreu, 1959, 1982). Therefore, how can it be faulty?

GET has received a lot of critiques.[2] Economists admit its lack of realism. In fact, the mathematical formalisation has proved that a solution of the system of equations of the general equilibrium model could exist only under strong assumptions about the agent's preferences, the nature of the goods, and the economic environment.[3] But even if this critique reduces the importance of the model, it does not destroy it because the lack of realism of a theory is not an internal critique of that theory.

The conclusion is then obvious: despite the critiques, GET remains the most fundamental theory in economics. In fact, not only is GET still the foundation of most of the macro-models, but it is also believed 'to solve the problem of the determination of the prices of the commodities resulting from the interaction of the agents of a private ownership economy through markets' (Debreu, 1959, p. vii).

However, some important authors are straightforward about their doubts about the ability of GET in determining commodity prices. Hildenbrand and Kirman (1976, p. 94) affirm that:

> understanding what prices are it does not require much of the reader. However, he may feel inclined to ask where those prices come from, how they are established or who in particular determines them? These questions are not answered in this book nor are they answered satisfactorily elsewhere for that matter. Throughout those parts of the book where prices play a role the reader should view them as being determined in some arbitrary manner and then accepted as given by the agents.

Defying Weintraub's warning,[4] we will confirm the intuition of Hildenbrand and Kirman by proving that GET does not pass 'the logical test of consistency' (Mas-Colell et al., 1995, p. 584). We will show that GET is founded on a central illogical reasoning. We will prove that once logic is restored, GET shows that equilibrium relative prices cannot be determined.

In this chapter, we will consider the Walrasian model of a pure exchange economy with two agents and two commodities. We will assume that this model satisfies the assumptions that are supposed to guarantee the mathematical existence of competitive equilibrium, that is, the mathematical existence of the relative price. We will show that in this model the demonstration of the existence of the competitive equilibrium is illogical. We will prove that once the logic of the model is restored, the model shows that the relative price cannot be determined. In other words, relative prices do not exist. We will also show that this outcome can be generalised to a pure exchange model with n agents and n commodities.

In the next section, we explain what your friend told you about the determination of the price of 1 lb. of oranges. We suppose that he chose the simplest example: he assumed the existence of an exchange economy made up of only two agents (1 and 2) and two commodities (1 and 2). He also assumed that the traditional assumptions are fulfilled. These assumptions are supposed to guarantee the existence of equilibrium and its global stability. To simplify, we suppose that your friend ignored production, welfare theorems and money. In the third section, we criticise your friend's explanation. This critique is based on almost fifty years of research (see for instance Schmitt, 1966, 1972, 1984, 1996). Recently Schmitt (1998, 2000) developed a more comprehensible way to explain the logical error intrinsic in the theory of general equilibrium. In order to meet the expectations of mainstream theoreticians, we expose this critique by using mathematical language. We will show that for a model with two agents and two commodities the system of equations is over-determined twice, that is, the system of equations counts three independent equations and one unknown. The equations are not consistent. Thus, the solution of the system does not exist. In other words, the relative price cannot be determined. This implies that your friend cannot logically explain the price of 1 lb. of oranges. At the end of the third section we will also show that our critique can be generalised to a pure exchange model with *n* agents and *n* commodities. The system of equations that characterises this model is *n*-times over-determined. The solution of the system does not exist. The *n*–1 relative prices cannot be determined. We will present our conclusions in the last section.

A MODEL OF A PURE EXCHANGE ECONOMY WITH TWO AGENTS AND TWO COMMODITIES

Commodities and Prices

Commodities[5]
A list of amounts (quantities) of commodities 1 and 2 is given by the vector $x = (x^1, x^2)$, where x^1 and x^2 are two non-negative real numbers. The vector x can be viewed as a point in the 2-dimensional Euclidean space $\Re^2_+$. Commodities 1 and 2 are completely homogeneous, scarce and desirable.

Prices
Like commodities, prices are quantifiable and directly measurable. A price is specified for each quantity of each commodity. The price for commodity i is p^i. The price vector for commodities 1 and 2 is $p = (p^1, p^2)$. By the desirability and the scarceness assumptions of the commodities $p > 0$; that is, $p^i > 0$ for every i. The relative price p^1/p^2 describes the rate at which commodities 1 and 2 have to be exchanged. The relative price p^2/p^1 is equal to $1/p^1/p^2$. Thus if p^1/p^2 (p^2/p^1) is given, p^2/p^1 (p^1/p^2) is also given. Prices are assumed to be beyond the agents' influence. In other words, agents are price-takers.[6]

Agents (Consumers)

Consumption set
The agents are completely described by their preferences and by their initial

endowments. The agents choose a bundle of commodities x, that is, a consumption vector x (or consumption bundle x) in the consumption set X. X is a closed, non-empty and convex subset of the commodity space $\Re_+^2$ ($X \subset \Re_+^2$).

Preferences

The agents are 'well behaved'. Consider the consumption vectors x and y with $x, y \in X$ and the binary relation $x \succeq y$, x 'is preferred or indifferent to' y. We suppose that $\succeq$ is complete and transitive (rationality assumption), reflexive, continuous (no 'jump' assumption), strongly monotonic (non-satiation assumption or desirability assumption) and strictly convex (agents prefer 'mixed' bundles to bundles where only one commodity is concentrated).[7] We call $\succeq$ 'preference relation'.[8]

Preferences are generally represented by utility functions.[9] The restrictions on preferences translate into restrictions on the form of utility functions.[10] Utility functions assign numbers to the bundles such that if an agent prefers a bundle to another, the first receives a higher number than the second (real value function). Utility functions are not necessary to construct consumer demand, but they permit an easier construction. A utility function for $\succeq$ is a continuous function $\mu : X \to \Re$ with the property that $\mu(x) \geq \mu(y)$ if and only if $x \succeq y$. The utility function μ that represents $\succeq$ is not unique.[11] To simplify, we choose the Cobb–Douglas (C–D) utility function.[12] The utility of agent 1 is:

$$\mu_1\,(x_1^1, x_1^2) = (x_1^1)^a (x_1^2)^{1-a}$$

and the utility of agent 2 is:

$$\mu_2\,(x_2^1, x_2^2) = (x_2^1)^b (x_2^2)^{1-b}$$

a and b are given parameters:

$0 < a < 1$
$0 < b < 1$

Wealth constraint

The agents own some quantity of the commodities called initial endowments. These endowments enable agents to exchange and to realise their choices.

The endowment for an agent is then given by a positive bundle e; that is, $e \geq 0$. Agent 1 owns $e_1 = (e_1^1, e_1^2)$ and agent 2 owns $e_2 = (e_2^1, e_2^2)$ where e_1^1 and e_1^2 are the respective quantities of goods 1 and 2 owned by agent 1, while e_2^1 and e_2^2 are the quantities owned by agent 2.

Given a price vector p, agents have to choose bundles whose exchange value is less than or equal to the value of their initial endowment (economic-affordability constraint). In other words, agents have to choose a bundle $x \in X$ in a subset β of $\Re_+^2$. Thus, the competitive budget set for an agent is

$$\beta (p,e) : = \{e \in \Re_+^2 \mid p \cdot x \leq p \cdot e\}.$$

The budget set is non-empty and bounded (because $p > 0$ and $e \geq 0$) and it is convex (because X is a convex set). The product $m = p \cdot e$ defines the agents' income.

The income function $m(p,e)$ is homogeneous of degree one in p: for every p, $\lambda m(p,e) = m(\lambda p,e)$, with $\lambda > 0$. Thus, the budget set is homogeneous of degree one in p (for every p, $\lambda \beta (p,e) = \beta (\lambda p,e)$, with $\lambda > 0$).

Preference satisfaction
Agents choose and demand the best bundles that are available in their budget set. The best bundle for an agent is an affordable bundle that optimises his consumption with respect to his preferences. The result of this optimisation, that is, the demand set, is defined by $\varphi (\succeq, e, p) : = \{x \in X \mid x \succeq y$ for all y in $\beta (p,e)\}$. The demand set is non-empty and compact (because $\beta (p,e)$ is a non-empty and compact set[13]) and it is convex (because $\succeq$ and $\beta (p,e)$ are convex[14]).

From the utility viewpoint optimisation of the agents' consumption means that agents maximise their utilities subject to their budget sets. Because strict convexity of preferences is assumed, there is only one best bundle that an agent chooses and demands (that is, the demand set is a unique point). Thus, each agent has a demand function[15] $x = x(p,e)$, $x \in X$.

The demand function is a continuous function of p (because $\succeq$ is continuous, strictly convex and strongly monotone)[16] and homogeneous of degree zero in p (because the income function is homogeneous of degree one in p).[17] This means that for every p and $\lambda > 0$, $x(p,e) = x(\lambda p,e)$. The homogeneity of degree zero of the demand is important, because it implies that in determining demand only relative prices matter. In other words, only the rate at which commodities have to be exchanged matters. Given this rate, agents determine their demands. For example, it makes no difference to the agents if the prices are $p^1 = 1$ and $p^2 = 2$ or $p^1 = \lambda p^1$ and $p^2 = \lambda p^2$ (with $\lambda > 0$). For the calculation of the quantity demanded, the agents consider only the relative price $p^1/p^2 = 1/2 = 0.5$ or the relative price $p^2/p^1 = 2/1 = 2$. The two prices yield the same information (if one is given, the other is also given: $p^1/p^2 = 1/p^2/p^1$): it is necessary to give two units of x^1 to receive one unit of x^2.

The budget set is compact and the utility function is continuous. Thus, the Weiestrass theorem applies. This theorem states that there is a well-defined maximiser of the utility function in the budget set.[18] Agent 1 maximises μ_1 under $p \cdot x_1 \le p \cdot e_1 = m_1$, and agent 2 maximises μ_2 under $p \cdot x_2 \le p \cdot e_2 = m_2$. We solve the maximisation problem for agent 1:

$$\max \mu_1(x_1^1, x_1^2) = (x_1^1)^a (x_1^2)^{1-a}$$

such that:

$$p^1 \cdot x_1^1 + p^2 \cdot x_1^2 \le m_1$$

Now take the log of μ_1. It is possible to take this log, because any monotonic transformation of μ_1 represents the same preferences.[19] The log function of μ_1 is easier to maximise than the function μ_1 itself. Applying the Kuhn and Tucker theorem and doing some algebra manipulations the following demand functions can be obtained: $x_1^1(p^1, p^2, m_1) = am_1/p^1$ and $x_1^2(p^1, p^2, m_1) = (1 - a)m_1/p^2$.

The same thing can be done for agent 2. The outcomes are: $x_2^1(p^1, p^2, m_2) = bm_2/p^1$ and $x_2^2(p^1, p^2, m_2) = (1 - b)m_2/p^2$.

The total demand for each commodities is: $x^1 = x_1^1 + x_2^1 = am_1/p^1 + bm_2/p^1$ for commodity 1 and $x^2 = x_1^2 + x_2^2 = (1 - a)m_1/p^2 + (1 - b)m_2/p^2$ for commodity 2. The value of total demand is the sum of the value of the agents' demands:

$$x_1(p^1, p^2, m_1) + x_2(p^1, p^2, m_2) = \sum_{i=1}^{2} p^i x_1^i + \sum_{i=1}^{2} p^i x_2^i = p^1(am_1/p^1) + p^2((1-a)m_1/p^2) + p^1(bm_2/p^1) + p^2((1-b)m_2/p^2)$$

The total demand function is homogeneous of degree zero in prices and it is a continuous function, because it is determined by the addition of the agents' demands, which are homogeneous of degree zero in prices and continuous.[20]

Agents have calculated their demand of x^1 and x^2 given p^1 and p^2. Now what do they offer for the same given prices? The value of their supply must be equivalent to the value of their demand. Because of the strong monotonicity of preferences (non-satiation), agents demand a consumption bundle that has to meet the constraint with equality. In fact, if an agent chooses a feasible consumption bundle x' such that $p \cdot x' < m$ (x' does not meet the constraint with equality), then there must be some feasible consumption bundle x'' such that $p \cdot x'' < m$ and which is preferred to x' (non-saturation). Thus, x' does not maximise preferences and it cannot be chosen. This implies that to obtain the consumption allocation they desire, agents have to give the totality of their initial endowment ($p \cdot x = m$).[21] Therefore, the supply of agent 1 is $e_1 = e_1^1 + e_1^2$, and the supply of agent 2 is $e_2 = e_2^1 + e_2^2$. The total supply of commodity 1 is $e^1 = e_1^1 + e_2^1$, the total supply of commodity 2 is $e^2 = e_1^2 + e_2^2$ and the value of their offers is m_1 for agent 1 and m_2 for agent 2.

Market Equilibrium

Given the supply and the demand of each good it is possible to calculate the excess demand function of the two commodities. The excess demand function of commodity 1 is defined by $z^1(p^1, p^2) = x_1^1(p^1, p^2, m_1) + x_2^1(p^1, p^2, m_2) - e^1$ and the excess demand function of commodity 2 is defined by $z^2(p^1, p^2) = x_1^2(p^1, p^2, m_1) + x_2^2(p^1, p^2, m_2) - e^2$.

$z^1(p)$ and $z^2(p)$ are homogeneous of degree zero in prices and they are continuous functions, because they result from total demand, which is homogeneous of degree zero in prices and continuous.[22] The fact that $z(p)$ depends on e is ignored, because e is supposed to remain constant. Now, if e remains constant, $m(p)$ depends only on p. This means that $z(p)$ depends only on p.

The excess demand of commodity 1 is $z^1 = x^1 - e^1 = am_1/p^1 + bm_2/p^1 - e^1$ and of commodity 2 is $z^2 = x^2 - e^2 = (1 - a)m_1/p^2 + (1 - b)m_2/p^2 - e^2$.

The value of the two excess demands are $p^1 z^1(p^1, p^2) = p^1(x_1^1(p^1, p^2, m_1) + x_2^1(p^1, p^2, m_2) - e^1)$ for the commodity 1 and $p^2 z^2(p^1, p^2) = p^2(x_1^2(p^1, p^2, m_1) + x_2^2(p^1, p^2, m_2) - e^2)$ for commodity 2.

Now it is clear that the sum of the excess demands' value must be zero, because the value of the demand of each agent is equivalent to the value of his supply. Then $p \cdot z(p) = p^1 z^1(p^1, p^2) + p^2 z^2(p^1, p^2) : = 0$. This identity is called Walras's Law.

If supply and demand for commodity 1 (or for commodity 2) are not equal, the market is not in equilibrium, but Walras's Law is still true. This means that even if equilibrium prices are not determined, it is possible to affirm that the value of total supply and total demand for the commodities are equivalent.

Walras's Law is useful, because if one of the two markets is in equilibrium, the two markets are in equilibrium. If the market of commodity 1 is in equilibrium, then $z^1(p) = 0$ and $p^1 z^1(p) = 0$. Now, $p \cdot z(p) := 0$. It follows that $p^2 z^2(p) = 0$. But $p \gg 0$, then $z^2(p) = 0$.

Walrasian equilibrium is defined by $z(p_*) \leq 0$. Now commodities 1 and 2 are assumed to be desirable. Thus, Walrasian equilibrium is defined by $z(p_*) = 0$, where p_* is the vector $p_* = (p_*^1, p_*^2)$ for which the market clears.

Existence of Equilibrium

Is it possible to determine p_*? We know that the equality between the number of equations and the number of unknowns is neither necessary nor sufficient for the existence of a solution of a given system of equations (Wald, 1936/1951). In a linear system of simultaneous equations, a solution exists if the number of unknowns is equal or larger than the number of linear independent equations. In a non-linear system of simultaneous equations (in our model demand functions are not linear) even if the number of unknowns is equal to or larger than the number of independent equations it does not imply that a real solution exists (the solution may be non-real).

But even if the equality between the number of equations and the number of unknowns is a 'rule of thumb' (Nikaido, 1989, p. 139), it is obvious that if the number of independent equations is larger than the number of unknowns, the solution of the system of equations does not exist (the equations are not consistent).[23] In other words, the fact that in a system of equations the number of independent equations is smaller than or equal to the number of unknowns is not a sufficient condition for the existence of a solution of a given system of equations, but it is a necessary condition.

For the model with two agents and two commodities there are two equations ($z^1(p) = 0$ and $z^2(p) = 0$) and two unknowns (p^1 and p^2). Because of the homogeneity of degree zero in p of the excess demand function, only one unknown has to be determined: the relative price p^1/p^2 (or the relative price p^2/p^1). But there is also only one independent equation ($z^1(p)$ or $z^2(p)$). In fact, if $z^1(p) = 0$ ($z^2(p) = 0$), then $z^2(p) = 0$ ($z^1(p) = 0$) because of Walras's Law. Thus, the number of independent equations is equal to the number of unknowns: the necessary condition for the existence of a solution of the system is satisfied. However, this condition is not sufficient.

Most of the works on the general proof of the existence of a solution (existence of competitive equilibrium) in the last fifty years apply the Brouwer (or Kakutani)[24] fixed-point theorem (Arrow and Debreu, 1954; McKenzie, 1954; Debreu, 1982, 1989).[25] We will also apply this theorem. Because of the homogeneity of degree zero in p of the excess demand function, it is possible to represent p in a convenient manner. In other words, it is possible to normalise the price vector p. The relative price $(p^1/p^2$ or $p^2/p^1)$ gives the direction of the vector p in $\Re_+^2$ and prices p^1 and p^2 give its length in $\Re_+^2$. Since only relative prices matter, only the direction matters. Thus, it is possible to choose a vector p with a direction given by the relative price and with a convenient length. Two vector normalisations are generally considered. The first and the simplest is to fix $p^1 = 1$ (or $p^2 = 1$), the second is to confine the price vector to a set called unit simplex:

$$P = \{ \sum_{i=1}^{2} \tilde{p}^i = 1 \}$$

where $\tilde{p}^i$ is the normalised price:

$$\tilde{p}^i = p^i / \sum_{i=1}^{2} p^i$$

In the two cases, only one price has to be determined in order to determine the other (in the first case one of the prices is given; in the second case if one price is given, the other is also given). The first normalisation is the most convenient to explain the price of 1 lb. of oranges and the second normalisation is generally used to prove the existence of an equilibrium.

Now consider the Brouwer fixed-point theorem.[26] Let $T(.)$ be a continuous function $T : P \rightarrow P$.[27] Then there is $x^* \in P$ so that $T(x^*) = x^*$. This means that if there is a continuous function that maps the simplex into itself, then there is some point in the simplex that is left unchanged by the process.[28] This unchanged point is the fixed point.

Suppose the existence of an auctioneer who announces normalised prices (Arrow and Debreu, 1954; Arrow and Hahn, 1971; Hahn, 1982; Debreu, 1982, 1989). Agents calculate their demands as a function of these prices and report them to the auctioneer. The auctioneer calculates the excess demand for one of the two commodities. Suppose that he makes the calculation for commodity 2, that is, he calculates $z^2(p)$. If $z^2(\tilde{p}) > 0$, he increases the normalised price of commodity 2, that is, p^2. Symmetrically, if $z^2(p) < 0$, he decreases p^2. This process continues until $z^2(\tilde{p}) = 0$. The process is called *tâtonnement*. No trading occurs if $z^2(\tilde{p}) \neq 0$.

Now it is possible to use the simplex set representation in order to apply the Brouwer theorem. Suppose that the auctioneer changes the prices of commodity i by following the continuous adjustment function $T: P \rightarrow P$

such that:[29]

$$T^i(\tilde{p}) := \tilde{p}^i + \max[0, z^i(\tilde{p}))]/(1 + \sum_{i=1}^{2} \max[0, z^i(\tilde{p})])$$

Commodities 1 and 2 are assumed to be desirable. This means that $\tilde{p}^i > 0$, for every i. Thus, $T^i(\tilde{p}) > 0$, for every i. $T^i(\tilde{p})$ is a continuous function, because $z^i(\tilde{p})$ is a continuous function. The point $T^i(\tilde{p})$ is a point in the simplex P, because:

$$\sum_{i=1}^{2} T^i(\tilde{p}) = 1$$

The function $T^i(\tilde{p})$ implies that if there is a positive excess demand for commodity 1 (commodity 2), the relative price of this commodity has to increase ($\tilde{p}^i + \max[0, z^i(\tilde{p})]$) and the relative price of commodity 2 (commodity 1) has to decrease ($T^2(\tilde{p}) = 1 - T^1(\tilde{p})$), because normalised prices are kept in the simplex.

According to the Brouwer fixed-point theorem, there is a $\tilde{p}^i_* \in P$ such that $T^i(\tilde{p}^i_*) = \tilde{p}^i_*$. $\tilde{p}^i_*$ is the normalised price at which the auctioneer stops to adjust $\tilde{p}^i$. In fact, for $T^i(\tilde{p}^i_*) = \tilde{p}^i_*$, the adjustment function says that we do not need to adjust it further, because the new adjusted price would be $\tilde{p}^i_*$. But one question still remains open: is $\tilde{p}^i_*$ the price that guarantees that the market clears? In other words, are $\tilde{p}^1_*$ and $\tilde{p}^2_*$ ($\tilde{p}^2_* = 1 - \tilde{p}^1_*$) the Walrasian prices, that is, the prices for which $z(\tilde{p}) = 0$? The answer is affirmative. This can be proved by application of Walras's Law.[30] In fact, we can cross-multiply:

$$\tilde{p}^i_* = \tilde{p}^i_* + \max[0, z^i(\tilde{p}^*)]/(1 + \sum_{i=1}^{2} \max[0, z^i(\tilde{p}^*)])$$

and rearrange the terms to get:

$$\tilde{p}^i_* (\sum_{i=1}^{2} \max[0, z^i(\tilde{p}^*)]) = \max[0, z^i(\tilde{p}^*)]$$

Then, we can multiply each side by $z^i(\tilde{p}^*)$ to get:

$$z^i(\tilde{p}^*) \, \tilde{p}_*^i \, (\sum_{i=1}^{2} \max[0, z^i(\tilde{p}^*)]) = z^i(\tilde{p}^*) \max[0, z^i(\tilde{p}^*)]$$

We can sum over 2 to get:

$$\sum_{i=1}^{2} z^i(\tilde{p}^*) \, \tilde{p}_*^i \, (\sum_{i=1}^{2} \max[0, z^i(\tilde{p}^*)]) = \sum_{i=1}^{2} z^i(\tilde{p}^*) \max[0, z^i(\tilde{p}^*)]$$

Now:

$$\sum_{i=1}^{2} z^i(\tilde{p}^*) \, \tilde{p}_*^i = 0$$

according to Walras's Law. Therefore:

$$0 = \sum_{i=1}^{2} z^i(\tilde{p}^*) \max[0, z^i(\tilde{p}^*)]$$

The second term is 0 or $(z^i(\tilde{p}^*))^2$. Now, $(z^i(\tilde{p}^*))^2$ is always positive if $z^i(\tilde{p}^*) \neq 0$. Thus, the equality can only be satisfied if $z^i(\tilde{p}^*) = 0$ for all i. Q.E.D.

Application of the Brouwer fixed-point theorem provides a general proof of the mathematical existence of a competitive equilibrium. But for the simplest model with two agents and two commodities the existence can be proven without applying this theorem.[31] Consider the first normalisation. Suppose that $p^1 = 1$. Thus, there is only one unknown: p^2. According to Walras's Law there is also only one equation: $z^2(1, p^2) = 0$. Suppose that $p^{2'}$ is very small. This implies that excess demand $z^2(1, p^{2'}) > 0$, because the relative price of commodity 1 is very low. Now suppose that $p^{2''}$ is very large, then $z^2(1, p^{2''}) < 0$, because the relative price of commodity 2 is very large. We know that $z^2(1, p^2)$ is a continuous function because the agents' demand functions are continuous. It is then clear that there must be a $p_*^2 \in [p^{2'}, p^{2''}]$, with $z^2(1, p_*^2) = 0$. Hence an equilibrium price vector must exist. Q.E.D.

The Price of Oranges

Consider the first method of price normalisation and fix the price of commodity 1 equal to 1 ($p^1 = 1$). This commodity is called the 'simplified money' (or numeraire; see Balasko, 1988, p. 7). It is clear that it is also possible to fix $p^2 = 1$. The decision is a mere convention. The number 1 is also fixed by convention. Any other number can be chosen. Given $p^1 = 1$, the auctioneer announces only one price, the price of commodity 2 (p^2). This gives the relative price (p^1/p^2 or p^2/p^1). Agents make their calculation given this relative price. The auctioneer calculates excess demand and changes p^2 (and with it the relative price) if the market does not clear. The process ends when p^2 clears the market. The previous section has shown that this price exists. Now suppose that $a = 0.5$, $b = 0.75$, $e_1 = (e_1^1, e_1^2) = (1,0)$ and $e_2 = (e_2^1, e_2^2) = (0,1)$. Suppose also that the auctioneer announces that $p = (p^1, p^2) = (1,2)$. Using the previous results, it is possible to find: $z^1(p^1,p^2) = x_1^1 (p^1,p^2,m_1) + x_2^1 (p^1,p^2,m_2) - e^1 = am_1/p^1 + bm_2/p^1 - e^1 = 0.5(1)/1 + 0.75(2)/1 - 1 = 1$ and $z^2(p^1,p^2) = x_1^2 (p^1,p^2,m_1) + x_2^2 (p^1,p^2,m_2) - e^2 = (1 - a)m_1/p^2 + (1 - b)m_2/p^2 - e^2 = (1 - 0.5)1/2 + (1 - 0.75)2/2 - 1 = -0.5$. This means that the market does not clear. Now the auctioneer decreases p^2, because $z^2(p) < 0$. The auctioneer calculates the new excess demands. The process goes on until $z^2(p_*) = 0$.

It is possible to calculate p_*^2 directly. If $z^2(1, p_*^2) = 0$, the market clears. In fact, it is possible to find p_*^2 such that $z^2(1, p_*^2) = (1 - a)m_1/p^2 + (1 - b)m_2/p^2 - e^2 = (1 - 0.5)1/p^2 + (1 - 0.75)p^2/p^2 - 1 = 0$. It follows that if $p^2 = 2/3$, then $z^2(1,2/3) = 0$. Thus, the auctioneer announces $p^* = (1,2/3)$. For this price vector, the market clears and trade takes place.

Suppose that oranges define commodity 2 and that commodity 1 is the numeraire. Suppose also that the fundamental quantity unit of commodity 2 is 1 lb. Denominate prices in dollars. It is now clear that the price (monetary price) of 1 lb. of oranges is $1.50. Q.E.D.

THE CRITIQUE OF THE WALRASIAN MODEL OF A PURE EXCHANGE ECONOMY

The Critique of the Two-Agent, Two-Commodity Model

We will criticise the model that your friend used to explain the determination of prices, that is, the model presented in the previous section. We will consider the same numerical example considered in the last sub-section. In this example we assumed that:

$$\mu_1 (x_1^1, x_1^2) = (x_1^1)^a (x_1^2)^{1-a}$$

$$\mu_2 (x_2^1, x_2^2) = (x_2^1)^b (x_2^2)^{1-b}$$

and that:

$a = 0.5$
$b = 0.75$
$e_1 = (e_1^1, e_1^2) = (1,0)$
$e_2 = (e_2^1, e_2^2) = (0,1)$

Again, we assume that agents are price-takers. We also assume that an auctioneer exists and that he announces the price vector $p = (p^1, p^2) = (1,2)$. This price vector states that the unit price of commodity 2 in terms of commodity 1, that is, the unit price of commodity 2 if $p^1 = 1$ is 2 ($p^2 = 2$). Throughout the previous section we have seen that the price vector $p = (1,2)$ implies that the exchange rate between the two commodities is 2 units of commodity 1 for 1 unit of commodity 2. In other words, we can say that the 'physical' price of 1 unit of commodity 2 is 2 units of commodity 1. Tautologically, the 'physical' price of 1 unit of commodity 1 is 0.5 units of commodity 2. Thus, the unit price of commodity 1 in terms of commodity 2, that is, the unit price of commodity 1 if $p^2 = 1$ is 0.5 ($p^1 = 0.5$). Let us call $p^1 = 0.5$ and $p^2 = 2$ unit relative prices. If we express these prices in the form of a price vector we have $p = (0.5,2)$. Now, for the calculation of their demands, do the agents consider $p = (1,2)$ or $p = (0.5,2)$?

In the previous section we have seen that if the auctioneer announces p^1/p^2, he also announces $\lambda p^1 / \lambda p^2$ ($\lambda > 0$). This means that if he announces $p^1/p^2 = 1/2$ or $\lambda p^1 / \lambda p^2 = \lambda / \lambda 2$, he announces the same rate of exchange between the two commodities. Therefore, if the auctioneer announces $p^1/p^2 = 1/2$, he also announces $p^1/p^2 = 0.5/1$. Mathematically, this is clear: if we multiply the numerator and the denominator by a number $\lambda > 0$ of a ratio between two numbers, the quotient is always the same. The economic argument is given by the fact that the demand functions are homogeneous of degree zero (see above): agents demand the same amount of commodities 1 and 2 for $p^1/p^2 = 1/2$ and for $\lambda p^1 / \lambda p^2$ ($\lambda > 0$). Thus, the price vector $p = (1,2)$ includes the price vector $p = (0.5,1)$. In other words, the unit relative price p^1 (p^2) includes the unit relative price p^2 (p^1). Therefore, it seems that the analysis of the previous section is correct: agents consider $p = (1,2)$ in order to determine their demands.

Assume that the auctioneer announces the price vector $p = (1,1)$. This price vector implies that 1 unit of commodity 1 has to be exchanged for 1 unit of commodity 2. Thus, the 'physical' price of 1 unit of commodity 1 is 1 unit of commodity 2 and the 'physical' price of 1 unit of commodity 2 is 1 unit of commodity 1. Assume that for the price vector $p = (1,1)$ the economy is not in equilibrium and that the auctioneer multiplies p^2 by 2 in order to determine p^*. The new price vector $p' = (1,2)$ implies that 2 units of commodity 1 have to be exchanged for 1 unit of commodity 2. Therefore, the new 'physical' price of 1 unit of commodity 2 is 2 units of commodity 1. It is clear that if the 'physical' price of 1 unit of commodity 2 *changes*, the 'physical' price of 1 unit of commodity 1 *also changes*. The two changes have to be inversely proportional: if the 'physical' price of 1 unit of commodity 2 is multiplied by a real number $\lambda > 0$, the 'physical' price of 1 unit of commodity 1 has to be divided by the same real number $\lambda > 0$. Therefore, the new 'physical' price of 1 unit of commodity 1 is 0.5 units of commodity 2.

It is clear that the price vector considered by the agents has to take into account *both variations* of the unit 'physical' prices. If agents consider the price vector $p' = (1,2)$, they consider only one of the two variations. If the new price of 1 unit of commodity 2 is 2, the new price of 1 unit of commodity 1 has to be 0.5. It is impossible that the new price of 1 unit of commodity 1 does not change, that is, it is impossible that the new price of commodity 1 remains 1. The variations of the unit prices of both commodities have to be compatible with the variations of the unit 'physical' prices. Thus, in our example, the analysis can only be completed if agents consider the unit relative price vector $p' = (0.5,2)$. The auctioneer does not need to announce the vector price $p = (0.5,2)$. In fact, in announcing $p = (1,2)$ he also announces $p = (0.5,2)$. In other words, the announced price vector $p = (1,2)$ gives agents all the information they require to calculate the new unit relative prices. To calculate their demands, the agents effectively need to consider these last prices. It is illogical to claim that they can consider only the new price vector $p = (1,2)$, because it permits to know what the new unit relative prices are. If agents consider $p = (1,2)$, they do not completely consider the information given by this price vector. In fact, they effectively consider only half of the information: the variation of the unit relative price of p^1. But prices are relative, thus, both variations (that is, variation of the unit relative price p^1 *and* variation of the unit relative price p^2) have to be effectively considered. Once again, it is not logical to argue that if one of the two variations is considered, the other variation is also considered because it is known. Indeed both variations have to be considered. To put it differently, it is the price vector $p = (0.5,2)$ that has to be put in the maximisation problem in order to calculate demands.

At this point, we can announce a law already announced by Walras (1874/1988):[32] $p^1 p^2 = 1$, with p^1 and p^2 defined as the unit relative prices.[33] Note that Walras (1874/1988, §45) states that $p_a p_b = 1$, for any $p_a > 0$ and $p_b > 0$. He defines (ibid., §44) $p_a = v_a/v_b$ and $p_b = v_b/v_a$ (in our notation $v_a = p^1$ and $v_b = p^2$ (p^1 and p^2 are unit relative prices)). Our analysis is the same as Walras's, but instead of considering the relative prices p_a (p^1/p^2 in our notation) and p_b (p^2/p^1 in our notation) we consider the unit relative prices.[34] Thus, in our notation the law is $p^1 p^2 : = 1$, with $p^1 > 0$ and $p^2 > 0$. Walras affirms that the agents determine their demands given p_a and p_b (ibid., §49). Our goal is not to criticise the standard (or GET) interpretation of Walras. But note that in Walras's analysis (1874/1988, section 2) agent A owns commodity (A) and determines his demand for commodity (B) as a function of p_a and agent B owns commodity (B) and determines his demand for commodity (A) as a function of p_b. The modern followers of Walras interpret this (in terms of our example) as if agent A and agent B determine their demands as a function of $p = (1,2)$. This interpretation is possible because Walras does not consider the demand for commodity (A) by agent A and the demand for commodity (B) by agent B. However, Walras always relates prices to commodities and not to agents. Thus, it is natural to suppose that if agent A demanded commodity (A), he would determine this demand as a function of price p_b (as does agent B) and if agent B demanded commodity (B), he would determine this demand as a function of p_a (as does agent A). Clearly, in this interpretation agents would determine their demands for commodities (A) and (B) as a function of the unit relative prices' vector $p = (0.5,2)$.

Let us generalise the analysis for an economy with two agents and two commodities. We call $p = (1, p^2)$ with p^2 changing from an infinitesimally small positive number to the infinite unit relative price series p^2 and $p = (p^1,1)$ with p^1 changing from an infinitesimally small positive number to the infinite unit relative price series p^1. Consider the unit relative price series p^2. Changing p^2 means changing the relative price. Given that p^2 covers all the set of the positive real numbers, it seems that all relative prices are taken into account by changing p^2. Thus, it seems that if we consider the relative price series p^2 we do not have to consider the relative price series p^1. In other words, it seems that the relative price series p^1 (p^2) is included in the relative price series p^2 (p^1). But, as we have shown in the last paragraph, if the unit price of one of the two commodities changes, the unit price of the other commodity has to change. Thus, the unit relative price series p^1 (p^2) does not include the unit relative price series p^2 (p^1). Therefore, to determine their demands, agents have to consider the unit relative price series $p = (p^1, p^2)$, with p^1, p^2 such that $p^1 p^2 : = 1.$[35]

In the previous section we have seen that the homogeneity of degree zero of the demand functions allows price normalisation. Thus, it is possible to fix $p^1 = 1$ ($p^2 = 1$) and change p^2 (p^1) in order to determine p_*. But each time that the auctioneer changes p^2 (p^1), p^1 (p^2) has to change because the law $p^1 p^2 : = 1$ has to be fulfilled. If the auctioneer announces $p = (1,2)$, agents consider the price vector $p = (0.5,2)$. If this last price vector is not p_*, the auctioneer changes p. According to the normalisation, he can announce, for example, $p = (1,4)$. But once again p^1 *reacts* to the change of p^2 because $p^1 p^2 : = 1$. Thus, agents consider the price vector $p = (0.25,4)$ and not the price vector $p = (1,4)$. To simplify: instead of using the normalisation $p^1 = 1$ ($p^2 = 1$) and changing p^2 (p^1), we directly use the normalisation $p^1 p^2 : = 1$. If p^1 is known, p^2 is also known. In other words, if the auctioneer announces p^1 (p^2), he also announces p^2 (p^1).

But if agents consider the price vector $p = (0.5,2)$ instead of considering the price vector $p = (1,2)$ what does this change? It seems that nothing changes, because the mathematical model is constructed in such a way that it works with any price vector p ($p > 0$). Agents calculate their demands for the two commodities given $p = (0.5,2)$. Thus, we have the following excess demands: $z^1(p^1,p^2) = 3 > 0$ and $z^2(p^1,p^2) = -0.25 < 0$. This means that the market does not clear and that no exchange is possible. Therefore, the auctioneer changes p in order to decrease z^1 and to increase z^2. Suppose that he decides to multiply p^2 by 4. The new unit relative price of commodity 2 is then $p^{2'} = 8$. If the unit relative price of commodity 2 is 8, the unit relative price of commodity 1, that is, $p^{1'}$ is 1/8. In other words, if p^2 is multiplied by 4, p^1 has to be divided by 4 because of the law $p^1 p^2 : = 1$. Thus, the new price vector is $p' = (1/8,8)$. p' implies that the rate of exchange between commodity 1 and commodity 2 is 64 units of commodity 1 for 1 unit of commodity 2. Given p', agents calculate their demand for the two commodities. If for p' the economy is not yet in equilibrium ($z(p^{1'}, p^{2'}) \neq 0$), the process continues. It will stop only when equilibrium is found.

But there is a 'gap' in the exchange rates between commodity 1 and commodity 2, that is, in relative prices. In fact, in changing the price vector from p to p', the auctioneer does not announce the exchange rate of 16 units of commodity 1 for 1 unit of commodity 2. Clearly, he could announce this rate by multiplying p^2 only by 2. In fact, in this case the price vector would be $p' = (0.25,4)$. But in changing the price vector from p to p', the auctioneer would not announce the rate of 8 units of commodity 1 for 1 unit of commodity 2. This analysis by recurrence goes on until the auctioneer announces an infinitesimally small increase of p^2. But, even in this limit case, he would not be able to avoid the 'gap' in the exchange rates. In fact, if the auctioneer multiplies p^2 by a number in order to obtain an infinitesimal increase of p^2, one relative price of the two is still missing because p^1 has to be divided by the same number. $p^1 p^2 := 1$ is valid even for an infinitesimal change in p^1 (p^2). Clearly, the relative price would not miss if and only if an infinitesimal change of p^1 (p^2) would leave p^2 (p^1) constant. But this is not possible because the law $p^1 p^2 := 1$ would be violated.

If the auctioneer announces all possible vectors $p = (p^1, p^2)$, with $p^1 p^2 = 1$, only half of the existing relative prices will be announced. Thus, $z(p^1, p^2)$ is a function only because half of the relative prices are not taken into account. If they were, $z(p^1, p^2)$ would not be a function because some of the elements of the function's domain (some of the relative prices) would not have their corresponding image. Clearly, without functions the whole mathematical model would make no sense. Moreover, the Brower (or Kakutani) fixed-point theorem certainly would not apply. Therefore, it would not be possible to prove the existence of a solution.

However, it is possible to take into account all relative prices without invalidating the mathematical formalisation. In fact, two continuous excess demand functions can be considered: the first one is derived by fixing $p^1 = 1$ and changing p^2 from an infinitesimally small positive number to the infinite (unit relative price series p^2), the second one is determined by fixing $p^2 = 1$ and changing p^1 from an infinitesimally small positive number to the infinite (unit relative price series p^1). It is clear that if we consider the unit relative price series p^1 there are two excess demands, one for each commodity $(z^1(p^1,1), z^2(p^1,1))$. Thus, the determination of the relative price has to satisfy two conditions: $z^1(p^1,1) = 0$ and $z^2(p^1,1) = 0$. But in the previous section we have seen that one of these excess demand equations is dependent. Therefore, it is possible to take into account only one of the two equations. Obviously, the same argument applies if we consider the relative price series p^2. Only one of the two equations $z^1(1,p^2) = 0$ and $z^2(1,p^2) = 0$ is independent. Thus, there are four equations, but only two of them are independent. Suppose that $z^1(p^1,1) = 0$ and $z^2(1,p^2) = 0$ are the independent equations. If these two excess demands are taken into account, all relative prices are taken into account.[36]

The Brower fixed-point theorem applies because $z^1(p^1,1)$ and $z^2(1,p^2)$ are two continuous functions. Therefore, there exist p^1 and p^2 so that $z^1(p^1,1) = 0$ and $z^2(1,p^2) = 0$. However, this theorem applies only if we consider the two series separately. In other words, it applies only if we consider two different determinations. Throughout the previous section we have seen that GET considers exchanges as being relative. Thus, for two commodities there is only one exchange, that is, there is only one relative price to determine. But $z^1(p^1,1) = 0$ and $z^2(1,p^2) = 0$ are two independent equations. Hence, the equations are not consistent, that is, they do not fulfill the necessary condition of the existence of a solution. The relative price p^1/p^2 (or p^2/p^1) cannot be determined. This proof also indirectly shows that the fixed-point theorem does not apply if we consider the two determinations simultaneously.

However, the system is not only 1-time over-determined (2 independent equations and 1 unknown); it is 2-times over-determined (3 independent equations and 1 unknown). In fact, the equations $z^1(p^1,1) = 0$ and $z^2(1,p^2) = 0$ are not a sufficient condition to determine the relative price. Another condition must be satisfied. To simplify, consider commodity 1 and agent 1. Even if the demand for commodity 1 for $p = (p^1,1)$ is equal to the demand for commodity 1 for $p = (1,p^2)$, that is, $x^1(p^1,1) = x^1(1,p^2)$,[37] nothing guarantees that agent's 1 demand for commodity 1 for $p = (p^1,1)$, that is, $x_1^1(p^1,1)$ is equal to agent's 1 demand for commodity 1 for $p = (1,p^2)$, that is, $x_1^1(1,p^2)$.[38] Clearly, the exchange between commodities 1 and 2 is possible only if the relative prices determined for the two unit relative price series is the same. This is true only if the agent demands the same amount of commodity 1 for $p = (p^1,1)$ and for $p = (1,p^2)$. Therefore, there is a single relative price that clears the market only if three conditions are satisfied, that is, if $z^1(p^1,1) = 0$, $z^2(1,p^2) = 0$, and $x_1^1(p^1,1) = x_1^1(1,p^2)$.[39] In other words, there are three independent equations for only one unknown. The equations are not consistent. The system of equations is 2-times over-determined. The relative price p^1/p^2 (p^2/p^1) cannot be determined. Obviously, if the relative price cannot be determined, the unit price of the commodities cannot be determined. Thus, the price (monetary price) of 1 lb. of oranges cannot be determined. Q.E.D.

The Critique of the Price-Taking Behaviour

The critique
In the previous section we have seen that in GET agents are assumed to be price-takers. GET assumes that the economy has so large a market that 'accepting prices as beyond ones' influence seems reasonable' (Hildenbrand and Kirman, 1976, p. 13). In other words, agents act in a competitive market. The authors agree that the price-taking behaviour (or competitive behaviour) is puzzling. In fact, relative prices can only be determined by the actions of the agents. But this means that these actions must influence prices. Thus, agents are not price-takers. Arrow and Hahn clearly state that the theorists 'face a problem, endemic for perfect competition models, of how prices are

changed. For, if no one can affect the terms on which he may transact, it is hard to see, without the "as if" auctioneer, how these terms ever come to be different' (Arrow and Hahn, 1971, p. 266).[40] However, despite these remarks, the most prominent authors, Arrow and Hahn included, start their analyses from the price-taker assumption ('we begin our systematic study of equilibrium in economies where agents act as price takers' (Mas-Colell et al., 1995, p. 545)). Moreover, as we have seen in the previous section, the assumption of the price-taker behaviour is fundamental for the proof of the existence of equilibrium presented in the most important papers on this topic (see above).

The price-taker behaviour assumption is a 'theoretical putsch' trying to give a logical consistency to GET. This methodology can be strongly criticised. It is clear that equilibrium prices have to be determined respecting the agents' freedom. There is a widespread confusion between perfect competition and price-taking behaviour. Some recent papers[41] denounce this confusion and support the idea that 'perfect competition should be distinguished from price-taking behavior' (Serrano and Volij, 2000, p. 80). Even if agents act in a perfect competition environment, they must be able to choose not only the quantities that they want to exchange, but also the rate at which they want to exchange these commodities, that is, relative prices. Like Serrano and Volij, we think that the 'Walrasian model of perfect competition is not "closed", since it does not explain the source of the fundamental variable, the equilibrium price' (Serrano and Volij, 2000, p. 80). In other words, the model can be 'closed' only if the 'prices are not exogenously given, they emerge from bargaining' (Makowski and Ostroy, 2001, p. 480).

Even if in the first part of this section we have proven that the price-taker assumption cannot save GET, in this section we criticise this assumption. We show that if agents are free to choose, the equilibrium relative prices cannot be determined. In showing this, we will interpret relative prices in the same wrong way as in the previous section. In other words, we will ignore the critique that we have raised in the first part of this section.

Consider the price vector $p = (p^1, p^2) = (1,2)$. At the end of the previous section we have seen that for this price vector the economy is not in equilibrium because $z(1,2) \neq 0$. Now, if equilibrium is not reached, there is no exchange; and, if there is no exchange, agents do not accept $p = (1,2)$. Thus, it seems that $p = (1,2)$ is not imposed. But the price-taker behaviour implies that any time that a price vector p is announced by the auctioneer, agents maximise their utility taking p as given. If all the calculations always depend on a given price vector, the agents are *never* free to choose the price vector, that is, they are never free to choose the exchange rate at which they wish to exchange the commodities. Note that even if an announced p would be the equilibrium price vector p_*, p would result from the initial imposition of the auctioneer. Therefore, the exchange rate is always imposed to the agents.

In the previous section we have shown that if p is imposed, then prices are determined.[42] But what happens if the exchange rate is not imposed? In other words, is it still possible to determine the equilibrium price vector p_* if the exchange rate is not imposed?

The choice of the consumption bundles of the agents, that is, the demands x_1 and x_2 can still be calculated by the maximisation of the utility function subject to the budget constraint (see the previous section). But in a non-imposed exchange rate economy each agent chooses his own price vector p. Let us call the price chosen by agent 1 p_1, the price chosen by agent 2 p_2, the exchange rate (or relative price) chosen by agent 1 $r_1 = p_1^1 / p_1^2$ and the exchange rate (or relative price) chosen by agent 2 $r_2 = p_2^1 / p_2^2$. In the previous section we have seen that demands for commodities depend on relative prices. Thus, to make things easier, we write down the excess demands for the commodities as a function of the exchange rate r_1 and r_2. The excess demand function for commodity 1 is $z^1(r_1,r_2)$ and the excess demand function for commodity 2 is $z^2(r_1,r_2)$. The market clears if $z^1(r_1,r_2) = 0$ and $z^2(r_1,r_2) = 0$. But are these two equations dependent or independent?

In the previous section we have seen that if $r_1 = r_2$, that is, if the exchange rate is imposed, Walras's Law applies and the two equations are dependent. But if agents choose freely their exchange rate, that is, if the exchange rate is not imposed, it is not possible that $r_1 = r_2$ before the bargaining process. And if $r_1 \neq r_2$, Walras's Law is not valid. In the example under critique agent 1 owns, before the bargaining process, the whole quantity of commodity 1 and agent 2 owns the whole quantity of commodity 2. Recall that the agents' preferences are supposed to be convex. This means that agents prefer mixed consumption bundles than extreme ones. Thus, at the beginning of the bargaining process, agent 1 demands a large quantity of commodity 2 and offers a small quantity of commodity 1 and agent 2 demands a large quantity of commodity 1 and offers a small quantity of commodity 2.[43] It is then obvious that we cannot have $r_1 = r_2$. For the determination of commodity demands, having $r_1 = r_2$ is the same as having $p_1^1 = p_2^1$ and $p_1^2 = p_2^2$. This is because demands are homogeneous of degree zero.[44] But if $r_1 \neq r_2$, we *effectively* have $p_1^1 \neq p_2^1$ and $p_1^2 \neq p_2^2$, that is, we have $p_1^1 \neq p_2^1$ and $p_1^2 \neq p_2^2$ even for the determination of demands.[45] If $r_1 \neq r_2$, there are two values of the excess demand for commodity 1: $p_1^1 z^1(r_1,r_2)$ and $p_2^1 z^1(r_1,r_2)$ and there are two values of the excess demand for commodity 2: $p_1^2 z^2(r_1,r_2)$

and $p_2^2 z^2(r_1,r_2)$. Thus, Walras's Law is not valid.[46]

If Walras's Law is not valid, $z^1(r_1,r_2) = 0$ and $z^2(r_1,r_2) = 0$ are independent. Therefore, the system of equations does not satisfy the necessary condition for the existence of a solution. The system of equations is 1-time over-determined. The equations are not consistent. Hence the relative price cannot be determined.

However, as in the first paragraph of this section, the system is not only 1-time over-determined, but it is 2-times over-determined. $z^1(r_1,r_2) = 0$ and $z^2(r_1,r_2) = 0$ are not a sufficient condition for the realisation of the exchange. In fact, $z^1(r_1,r_2) = 0$ and $z^2(r_1,r_2) = 0$ do not imply that the value of the effective demand (supply) of agent 1 is equal to the value of the effective supply (demand) of agent 2.[47]

In the previous section we have seen that the equality of the value of supply and the value of demand for each agent is implied by the maximisation under constraint. Obviously, this equality implies the equality of the value of effective supply and the value of effective demand for each agent.[48] Following the previous section, if $z^1(p_1,p_2) = 0$ (or $z^2(p_1,p_2) = 0$), the equality of the value of supply and the value of demand for both agents implies that the value of effective demand (supply) of agent 1 is equal to the value of effective supply (demand) of agent 2.[49] But if $r_1 \neq r_2$, the first equality, even if it is still true, does not imply that if $z^1(r_1,r_2) = 0$ and $z^2(r_1,r_2) = 0$ the value of effective demand (supply) of agent 1 is equal to the value of effective supply (demand) of agent 2. Therefore, if $r_1 \neq r_2$, the equality between the effective value of supply (demand) of agent 1 and the effective value of demand (supply) of agent 2 becomes a condition that has to be fulfilled in order to have an exchange. In other words, if this condition is not fulfilled, the exchange cannot take place because the agents would, in fact, give (receive) more than what they receive (give). The condition can be expressed in the following mathematical terms: $p_1^2 x_1^2(r_1) = p_2^2(e_2 - x_2^2(r_2))$.[50]

The conclusion is straightforward. The system has three independent equations ($z^1 = 0$, $z^2 = 0$ and $p_1^2 x_1^2(r_1) = p_2^2(e_2 - x_2^2(r_2))$[51] and one unknown. The system is 2-times over-determined: for three independent equations there is only one unknown. The equations are not consistent. Hence the relative price cannot be determined. If the relative price cannot be determined, the unit price of the commodities cannot be determined. Thus, the price (monetary price) of 1 lb. of oranges cannot be determined. Q.E.D.

The permutation

It seems possible to combine the price-taker behaviour and a kind of agents' freedom. Suppose that the auctioneer exists and that he announces the price vector $p = (1,2)$. We will say that this vector is compatible with the freedom of the agents if they permute p^1 and p^2. To permute means that agent 1 interprets the announced prices as $p^1 = 1$ and $p^2 = 2$, and agent 2 interprets the price as $p^2 = 1$ and $p^1 = 2$.

In the previous section we have assumed that agent 1 owns commodity 1, agent 2 owns commodity 2 and the agents' preferences are such that they prefer mixed consumption bundles than extreme ones (convexity of the preferences). Thus, agent 1 desires some quantity of commodity 2 owned by agent 2 and agent 2 desires some quantity of commodity 1 owned by agent 1. For agent 1 the relative price of commodity 2 is high and for agent 2 it is the relative price of commodity 1 that is high. Note that the relative price 1/2 (2/1) is a low (high) price for both agents because the agents permute prices.

Even if the behaviour of the auctioneer is compatible with the freedom of the agents, the relative price cannot be determined. In fact, the system of equations is 2-times over-determined. The proof is almost the same as the one previously given.

Suppose that the auctioneer announces $p = (p^1,p^2)$. Let us call the exchange rate (or relative price) interpreted by agent 1 $r_1 = p^1/p^2$ and the exchange rate (or relative price) interpreted by agent 2 $r_2 = p^2/p^1$. As we have done above, we write down the excess demands for the commodities as a function of the exchange rates r_1 and r_2. The excess demand function for commodity 1 is $z^1(r_1,r_2)$ and the excess demand function for commodity 2 is $z^2(r_1,r_2)$. The market clears if $z^1(r_1,r_2) = 0$ and $z^2(r_1,r_2) = 0$. These two equations are independent because $r_1 \neq r_2$. Therefore, it is not true that if $z^1(r_1,r_2) = 0$ ($z^2(r_1,r_2) = 0$) then $z^2(r_1,r_2) = 0$ ($z^1(r_1,r_2) = 0$). The equations are not consistent; the system of equations is 1-time over-determined. The relative price cannot be determined.

But, once again, the system of equations is not only 1-time over-determined; it is 2-times over-determined. In fact, the conditions $z^1(r_1,r_2) = 0$ and $z^2(r_1,r_2) = 0$ are not sufficient to guarantee the determination of the relative price. As seen above, another condition must be satisfied: the value of effective demand (supply) of agent 1 has to be equal to the value of effective supply (demand) of agent 2, that is, $p_1^2 x_1^2(r_1) = p_2^2(e_2 - x_2^2(r_2))$.[52] Thus, there are three independent equations and only one unknown. The equations are not consistent; the relative price cannot be determined. The unit price of the commodities cannot be determined. Thus, the price of 1 lb. of oranges cannot be determined. Q.E.D.

Generalisation of the Critique

So far the analysis has considered a model with two agents and two commodities. In the first two parts of this section we have shown that in a model with two agents and two commodities the relative price cannot be determined because the system of equations is 2-times over-determined. This outcome can be generalised for a model with n agents and n commodities. Consider a model with three agents and three commodities. For three commodities, there are two relative prices to be determined:[53] p^1/p^2 and p^1/p^3. Three excess demand functions can be found: $z^1(r_1,r_2,r_3)$, $z^2(r_1,r_2,r_3)$ and z^3 (r_1,r_2,r_3).[54] Given that the exchange rates are not imposed, Walras's Law does not apply. Thus, there are three independent equations: $z^1(r_1,r_2,r_3) = 0$, z^2 $(r_1,r_2,r_3) = 0$ and z^3 $(r_1,r_2,r_3) = 0$. In order to determine the two relative prices, two other conditions have to be satisfied: the value of effective supply of agent 1 has to be equal to the value of demand of agent 2 for commodity 1 plus the value of demand of agent 3 for commodity 1, that is, $p^1_1(e_1 - x^1_1(r_1))$ $= p^1_2 x^1_2(r_2) + p^1_3 x^1_3(r_3)$ and the value of effective supply of agent 2 has to be equal to the value of demand of agent 1 for commodity 2 plus the value of demand of agent 3 for commodity 2, that is, $p^2_2(e_2 - x^2_2(r_2)) = p^2_1 x^2_1(r_1) +$ $p^2_3 x^2_3(r_3)$. If these two conditions are not fulfilled, the exchange cannot take place because agents would effectively give (receive) more than what they effectively receive (give).[55] Thus, there are five independent equations for two unknowns. The system of equations is 3-times over-determined. The equations are inconsistent; relative prices cannot be determined.

Consider a model with n agents and n unknowns. For n commodities $n{-}1$ relative prices have to be determined: p^1/p^2, p^1/p^3, ..., p^1/p^n. In this model there are n excess demand functions: $z^1(r_1,r_2, ...,r_n)$, z^2 $(r_1,r_2, ...,r_n)$, ..., z^n $(r_1,r_2, ...,r_n)$. Walras's Law does not apply because the exchange rates are not imposed to the agents ($r_1 \neq r_2 \neq r_3 \neq ... \neq r_n$). Thus, there are n independent equations: $z^1(r_1,r_2, ...,r_n) = 0$, z^2 $(r_1,r_2, ...,r_n) = 0$, ..., z^n $(r_1,r_2, ...,r_n) = 0$. In order to determine the $n{-}1$ relative prices we need to add to these n independent equations $n{-}1$ other independent equations: $p^1_1(e_1 - x^1_1(r_1)) =$ $p^1_2 x^1_2(r_2) + p^1_3 x^1_3(r_3) + ... + p^1_n x^1_n(r_n)$, $p^2_2(e_2 - x^2_2(r_2)) = p^2_1 x^2_1(r_1) +$ $p^2_3 x^2_3(r_3) + ... + p^2_n x^2_n(r_n)$, ..., $p^{n-1}_1(e_{n-1} - x^{n-1}_1(r_{n-1})) = p^{n-1}_1 x^{n-1}_1(r_1) +$ $p^{n-1}_2 x^{n-1}_2(r_2) + ... + p^{n-1}_{n-2} x^{n-1}_{n-2}(r_{n-2}) + p^{n-1}_n x^{n-1}_n(r_n)$.

Therefore, there are $n+(n{-}1) = 2n{-}1$ independent equations and $n{-}1$ unknowns. The system of equations is n-times over-determined ($2n{-}1 - (n{-}1)$ $= n$). The equations are inconsistent; relative prices cannot be determined. Obviously, if the relative price cannot be determined, unit prices (monetary prices) of the commodities cannot be determined. Q.E.D.

CONCLUSION

GET tries to show mathematically that relative prices can be determined, that is, that relative prices exist. But the mathematical proof fails because of a central illogicality. Weintraub (1985) is right in saying that all efforts produced in order to falsify GET are the result of a confused mind. However, he is right only if relative prices exist or if they could exist. If formal logic is opposed to the existence of relative prices, the critique of GET is not an effort of a confused mind, but it is a genuine effort to avoid illogical reasoning. No other scientific subject fears illogicalities as mathematics. No mathematician, even a mathematical economist, can accept to reason using a variable whose existence is denied by logic. We have proven that relative prices are theoretical monsters because not only they do not exist, but they also cannot exist if not as pure and simple contradiction.

We are tempted to conclude that GET is a failure. But this is not true. The object of the mathematical proof proposed by the authors of GET is the existence of relative prices. Their analysis is so rigorous that it reveals the illogicality on which the very concept of relative price is built. The object of the proof is thus inversed: it establishes rigorously that relative prices cannot exist. In a quite paradoxical sense the proof furnished by GET gives more than what could be hoped because it shows the truth at one and the same time in theory and in the real world. If relative prices could exist in theory, their existence in the real world would remain doubtful. GET would still be precious because it would explain the pure case. Obviously, the theoretical explanation of relative prices would only be an approximate explanation of the real relative prices. But any other explanation of these prices will be denied. However, since a mathematical proof establishes that relative prices are variables that contradict themselves, the importance of GET is fundamental because it definitively shows that relative prices cannot exist in theory and in the real world. We can measure the progress made thanks to GET. When economists will understand GET, they will begin the explanation of the determination of prices from another conception of prices.

How can we doubt that prices exist? They are everywhere around us, milliard a day. But it is a fact that the prices that we can observe are monetary prices. It would be absurd to criticise GET because it determines relative prices that are not monetary prices. In fact, if relative prices were not the terms of a contradiction, GET could determine equilibrium relative prices without considering money. It could then be free to introduce money and determine monetary prices (see above). However, given that relative prices are illogical, monetary prices have to be explained in another way.

Obviously, they must be directly monetary, because if they were not, they would still be relative. But are not the units of money like the units of the other commodities? This is impossible because if money were a commodity, then monetary prices would be relative.

The theory that determines prices in monetary units that are not commodities but 'pure' numbers is already advanced, but it is not the object of this chapter.

We can only conclude in saying that the two great intuitions of the adherents to GET are confirmed in the new theory: prices are numerical and they are determined in an exchange; but these exchanges are not relative, they are absolute.

NOTES

1. The authors would like to thank Patrick Gagliardini and Sergio Rossi for their helpful comments on an earlier version of this work. Curzio De Gottardi gratefully acknowledges financial support from the Swiss National Science Foundation while he was a Visiting Post-doctoral Researcher at the New York University (Stern School of Business). The usual disclaimers apply.
2. See for example Hahn (1982, 1989), Walker (1997) and Costa (1998).
3. See for example Saari and Simon (1978) and Saari (1985).
4. 'To ask about the falsifiability of the Arrow–Debreu–McKenzie model is not to be hard-headed, positivistic, or rigorous. It is to be confused' (Weintraub, 1985, p. 119).
5. A commodity may be a good or a service.
6. It is clear that this assumption makes no sense for two agents since they can influence the price. The simplified model of two agents and two goods is only an interpretation 'of a theme in an inappropriate context' (Hildenbrand and Kirman, 1976, p. 13).
7. The strict convexity of $\succsim$ implies that commodities 1 and 2 are infinitely divisible. The strict convexity assumption can be interpreted in terms of diminishing marginal rates of substitution between the two commodities.
8. $\succsim$ is a preordering or quasi-ordering relation because it is reflexive and transitive. See Debreu (1959, p. 7).
9. For every $\succsim$ (rational, reflexive and continuous) in any subset X there exists a continuous utility function. For a proof see Debreu (1959, pp. 56–9), Hildenbrand and Kirman (1976, Appendix to ch. 2), Mas-Colell et al. (1995, pp. 47–8) and Starr (1997, pp. 85–8).
10. See Mas-Colell et al. (1995, pp. 49–50).
11. See Mas-Colell et al. (1995, p. 9).
12. Varian (1992) and Mas-Colell et al. (1995) use the C–D utility functions in their examples. It is possible to use other utility functions. See for example Creedy (1987, pp. 41–9).
13. For a proof see Hildenbrand and Kirman (1976, p. 43, p. 151 and mathematical appendix I, property 16).
14. For a proof see Hildenbrand and Kirman (1976, p. 152).
15. The analysis deals with a single point for each p and e. With the convexity assumption the analysis would deal with a set of vectors for each p and e. In this case there would not be a function (point-to-point mapping or single-valued mapping), but a correspondence (point-to-set mapping or multi-valued mapping). See Debreu (1959), Hildenbrand and Kirman (1976, mathematical appendix III), Nikaido (1989) and Mas-Colell et al. (1995, mathematical

appendix).

16. For a proof see Hildenbrand and Kirman (1976, pp. 151–2 and mathematical appendix III).
17. For a proof see Mas-Colell et al. (1995, p. 52).
18. For a proof of the Weiestrass theorem see Debreu (1959, 1.7) and Starr (1997, pp. 54–5).
19. See Varian (1992, p. 95).
20. For a proof see Hildenbrand and Kirman (1976, p. 153, Appendix to ch. 6 and mathematical appendix III).
21. This permits the simplification of the maximisation problem. In fact, it is possible to maximise the utility subject to an equality constraint (max $\mu(x)$ such that $xp = m$). See Varian (1992, p. 99).
22. For a proof see Hildenbrand and Kirman (1976, p. 153 and mathematical appendix III).
23. If the number of independent equations is smaller than the number of unknowns, the solutions of the system are infinite (see Deschamps, 1988).
24. The Brower fixed-point theorem applies for single-valued mapping (or point-to-point mapping), that is, for the functions. Kakutani generalised the Brower fixed-point theorem. He showed that the theorem applies also for multi-valued mapping (or point-to-set mapping), that is, for the correspondences. See note 14.
25. For an exhaustive list of these works see Debreu (1982) and Mas-Colell et al. (1995).
26. A proof of this theorem is given in Starr (1997, pp. 57–62).
27. Note that P is a non-empty, compact and convex set. The theorem applies only if the set P has these properties. See Mas-Colell et al. (1995, p. 952) and Starr (1997, pp. 57–62).
28. If instead of having a function we would have a correspondence, the Kakutani fixed-point theorem (see note 23) would apply only if the correspondence is upper hemi-continuous (u.h.c.) and convex-valued, that is, the graph of the correspondence is closed (see Hildenbrand and Kirman, 1976, pp. 188–9; Nikaido, 1989; Mas-Colell et al., 1995, p. 953).
29. See Varian (1992, p. 321), Mas-Colell et al. (1995, pp. 586–9), Starr (1997, p. 35). The use of this adjustment function allows for a simplification of the proof of the existence of competitive equilibrium. For a general detailed proof see Debreu (1982).
30. See Varian (1992, p. 321).
31. See, for example, Mas-Colell et al. (1995, pp. 584–5).
32. To avoid confusion we do not call this law Walras's Law.
33. Instead of considering the unit relative prices, we can consider p^1 if $p^2 = 2$ and p^2 if $p^1 = 2$ (in this case, in our example, instead of considering the vector $p = (0.5,2)$, the agents would consider the vector $p = (1,4)$). Note that the law $p^1 p^2 := 1$ would not apply ($p^1 p^2 = 1$ is true only if we consider the unit relative prices). The law would be $p^1 p^2 = 4$. Our analysis would remain the same; only the numerical example would change. Thus, instead of considering the unit relative prices, we could consider the following relative prices: $p = (2,p^2)$ and $p = (p^1,2)$. Note that any other relative prices $p = (p^1, \lambda)$ and $p = (\lambda, p^2)$, with $\lambda > 0$ can be considered (with law $p^1 p^2 = \lambda^2$).
34. In our view an analysis with unit relative prices is easier to understand.
35. The only point of intersection between the two unit relative price series is given by $p = (1,1)$.
36. Note that the law $p^1 p^2 := 1$ is violated because p^1 (p^2) is fixed. But this law is valid only if we consider the two unit relative prices (or the two unit relative price series) while considering only one price vector (or only one series of relative price vectors). In other words, it is the same to consider $p = (p^1, p^2)$ with $p^1 p^2 := 1$ or to consider (simultaneously) $p = (p^1,1)$ and $p = (1,p^2)$ with $p^1 p^2 \neq 1$.
37. $x^1(p^1,1) = x^1(1,p^2)$ because $e^1(p^1,1) = e^1(1,p^2)$, $z^1(p^1,1) = 0$, and $z^1(1,p^2) = 0$ (we consider e^1 as a function only to simplify).
38. The same analysis applies for agent 2. In this case, we would have the equation $x_2^1(p^1,1) = x_2^1(p^1,1)$. Obviously, we need to take into account only one agent because if $x_1^1(p^1,1) = x_1^1(1,p^2)$ ($x_2^1(p^1,1) = x_2^1(p^1,1)$), then $x_2^1(p^1,1) = x_2^1(p^1,1)$ ($x_1^1(p^1,1) = x_1^1(1,p^2)$). In other words, $x_1^1(p^1,1) = x_1^1(1,p^2)$ and $x_2^1(p^1,1) = x_2^1(p^1,1)$ are two independent equations because $e^1(p^1,1) = e^1(1,p^2)$, $z^1(p^1,1) = 0$ and $z^1(1,p^2) = 0$.

39. Instead of considering commodity 1, we can consider commodity 2 and perform the same analysis. But we need to take into account only one of the two commodities. The analysis is like the one done for the agents (see note 37). But instead of considering the demands of the agents, we have to consider the demands for the commodities.

40. See also Walker (1997).

41. See for example Serrano and Volij (2000), Makowski and Ostroy (2001).

42. Prices are determined because we ignore the critique raised in the first part of this section.

43. Note that the choice of the exchange rate by the agents is not mathematically formalised in the model exposed in the previous section because agents are supposed to be price-takers (they do not have to choose the exchange rate). The utility functions do not permit to determine the exchange rates, which the agents will choose. To pursue our critique, we do not need to formalise this choice mathematically. We only need to prove that the exchange rates chosen by the agents are not the same. The assumption of convexity of the preferences implies that each agent wants to own at least some quantity of the commodity that he does not own. Obviously, agents will choose the most favorable exchange rate. Given that before the bargaining process agent 1 owns commodity 1 and agent 2 owns commodity 2, it is intuitively easy to see that at the first move of the bargaining process agent 1 will offer a small quantity of commodity 1 and will demand a large quantity of commodity 2. Agent 2 will do the opposite: he will offer a small quantity of commodity 2 and he will demand a large quantity of commodity 1.

44. For example, the demands for the commodities are the same in the following four cases: agent 1 considers $p = (1,2)$ and agent 2 considers $p = (2,4)$, agent 1 considers $p = (2,4)$ and agent 2 considers $p = (1,2)$, both consider $p = (1,2)$ and both consider $p = (2,4)$.

45. For example, the demands for the commodities are not the same in the following four cases: agent 1 considers $p = (1,2)$ and agent 2 considers $p = (1,3)$, agent 1 considers $p = (1,3)$ and agent 2 considers $p = (1,2)$, both consider $p = (1,2)$, both consider $p = (1,3)$.

46. It seems that Walras's Law is valid only if $p_1^1 z^1(r_1,r_2) = p_2^1 z^1(r_1,r_2)$ and $p_1^2 z^2(r_1,r_2) = p_2^2 z^2(r_1,r_2)$, that is, only if $p_1^1 = p_2^1$ and $p_1^2 = p_2^2$. But these two last conditions are not necessary. In fact, if $r_1 = r_2$, that is, if $p_1^1/p_1^2 = p_2^1/p_2^2$ Walras's Law is valid because we are interpreting the exchange rate in the same way as in the previous section: the demands of the agents are homogeneous of degree zero (they are the same if the price vector is p or λp, with $\lambda > 0$).

47. In the previous section we have seen that the agents offer the entire amount of their initial endowment and that they demand a part of it. Thus, the agents effectively offer only a part of their initial endowment and they effectively demand only a part of the commodity that they do not own. Thus, agent 1 effectively offers $e_1 - x_1^1(p^1,p^2)$ and effectively demands $x_1^2(p^1,p^2)$ and agent 2 effectively offers $e_2 - x_2^2(p^1,p^2)$ and effectively demands $x_2^1(p^1,p^2)$. The equalities of the value of effective supply and the value of effective demand are: $p^1(e_1 - x_1^1(p^1,p^2)) = p^2 x_1^2(p^1,p^2)$ for agent 1 and $p^2(e_2 - x_2^2(p^1,p^2)) = p^1 x_2^1(p^1,p^2)$ for agent 2.

48. For example, consider agent 1. $p^1 x_1^1(p^1,p^2) + p^2 x_1^2(p^1,p^2) = p^1 e_1$ clearly implies that $p^1(e_1 - x_1^1(p^1,p^2)) = p^2 x_1^2(p^1,p^2)$.

49. It is easy to see that for $p = p_* = (p_*^1, p_*^2) = (1,2/3)$, we have $p_*^2 x_1^2(p_*^1, p_*^2) = p_*^2(e_2 - x_2^2(p_*^1, p_*^2))$. But note that even for $p = p_*$, we have $p_*^1 x_1^1(p_*^1, p_*^2) + p_*^2 x_1^2(p_*^1, p_*^2) \neq p_*^2 e_2$ and $p_*^1 x_2^1(p_*^1, p_*^2) + p_*^2 x_2^2(p_*^1, p_*^2) \neq p_*^1 e_1$. In other words, at equilibrium it is the value of effective demand (supply) of agent 1 that is equal to effective supply (demand) of agent 2 and not the value of demand (supply) of agent 1 that is equal to the value of supply (demand) of agent 2.

50. It is also possible to consider $p_2^1 x_2^1(r_2) = p_1^1(e_1 - x_1^1(r_1))$, $p_1^1(e_1 - x_1^1(r_1)) = p_2^2(e_2 - x_2^2(r_2))$, or $p_2^2 x_2^2(r_2) = p_1^2 x_1^2(r_1)$. But obviously these four equations are dependent because $p_1^2 x_1^2(r_1) = p_1^1(e_1 - x_1^1(r_1))$ and $p_2^1 x_2^1(r_2) = p_2^2(e_2 - x_2^2(r_2))$.

51. Note that if these conditions are satisfied, $r_1 = r_2$.

52. The analysis is the same as above.

53. If p^1/p^2 and p^1/p^3 are known, p^2/p^3 is also known. The choice to determine p^1/p^2 and p^1/p^3 is

arbitrary. We can also determine p^1/p^2 and p^2/p^3 or p^2/p^3 and p^1/p^3.

54. For each agent there are three different exchange rates r. Consider agent 1. The three exchange rates are $r_1^{1,2} = p_1^1 / p_1^2$, $r_1^{1,3} = p_1^1 / p_1^3$, $r_1^{2,3} = p_1^2 / p_1^3$. To simplify our notation, r_1 includes $r_1^{1,2}$, $r_1^{1,3}$ and $r_1^{2,3}$. The same simplification applies to agents 2 and 3.

55. Note that if $p_1^1(e_1 - x_1^1(r_1)) = p_2^1 x_2^1(r_2) + p_3^1 x_3^1(r_3)$ and $p_2^2(e_2 - x_2^2(r_2)) = p_1^2 x_1^2(r_1) + p_3^2 x_3^2(r_3)$, then $p_3^3(e_3 - x_3^3(r_3)) = p_1^3 x_1^3(r_1) + p_2^3 x_2^3(r_2)$. In other words, these three equations are dependent.

REFERENCES

Arrow, K.J. and G. Debreu (1954), 'Existence of an equilibrium for competitive economics', *Econometrica*, **22** (3), 265–90.

Arrow, K.J. and F.H. Hahn (1971), *General Competitive Analysis*, San Francisco and Edinburgh: Holden-Day and Oliver & Boyd.

Aumann, R. (1964), 'Market with a continuum of traders', *Econometrica*, **32** (1–2), 39–50.

Balasko, Y. (1988), *Foundations of the Theory of General Equilibrium*, Orlando and London: Academic Press.

Bowels, S. and H. Gintis (2000), 'Walrasian economics in retrospect', *Quarterly Journal of Economics*, **115** (4), 1411–39.

Cencini, A. (1982), 'The logical indeterminacy of relative prices', in M. Baranzini (ed.), *Advances in Economic Theory*, Oxford and New York: Basil Blackwell and St. Martin's Press, 126–36.

Costa, M.L. (1998), *General Equilibrium Analysis and the Theory of Markets*, Cheltenham and Northampton: Edward Elgar.

Creedy, J. (1987), *General Equilibrium and Welfare*, Cheltenham and Brookfield: Edward Elgar.

De Gottardi, C. (2000), *Offre et demande: équilibre ou identité?*, doctoral dissertation, University of Fribourg.

Debreu, G. (1959), *Theory of Value: An Axiomatic Analysis of Economic Equilibrium*, New York: John Wiley.

Debreu, G. (1974), 'Excess demand functions', *Journal of Mathematical Economics*, **11** (1), 15–23.

Debreu, G. (1982), 'Existence of competitive equilibrium', in K.J. Arrow and M.D. Intriligator (eds), *Handbook of Mathematical Economics*, Amsterdam: North-Holland, vol. II, 697–743.

Debreu, G. (1989), 'Existence of general equilibrium', in J. Eatwell, M. Milgate and P. Newman (eds), *General Equilibrium: The New Palgrave*, London: Macmillan, 131–8.

Debreu, G. (1992), 'Economic theory in the mathematical mode', in K.G. Maeler (ed.), *Nobel Lectures: Economic Science, 1981–1990*, Singapore: World Scientific, 87–102.

Deschamps, P. (1988), *Cours de mathématiques pour économistes*, Paris: Dunod.

Geanakoplos, J. (1989), 'Arrow–Debreu model of general equilibrium', in J. Eatwell, M. Milgate and P. Newman (eds), *General Equilibrium: The New Palgrave*, London: Macmillan, 43–61.

Hahn, F.H. (1982), 'Stability', in K.J. Arrow and M.D. Intriligator (eds), *Handbook of*

Mathematical Economics, Amsterdam: North-Holland, vol. II, 745–93.

Hahn, F.H. (1989), 'Auctioneer', in J. Eatwell, M. Milgate and P. Newman (eds), *General Equilibrium: The New Palgrave*, London: Macmillan, 62–7.

Hildenbrand, W. and A.P. Kirman (1976), *Introduction to Equilibrium Analysis*, Amsterdam and New York: North-Holland and Elsevier.

Makowski, L. and J.M. Ostroy (2001), 'Perfect competition and the creativity of the markets', *Journal of Economic Literature*, **39** (2), 479–535.

Mas-Colell, A., M.D. Whinston and J.R. Green (1995), *Microeconomic Theory*, New York: Oxford University Press.

McKenzie, L.W. (1954), 'On equilibrium in Graham's model of world trade and other competitive systems', *Econometrica*, **22** (2), 147–61.

McKenzie, L.W. (1989), 'General equilibrium', in J. Eatwell, M. Milgate and P. Newman (eds), *General Equilibrium: The New Palgrave*, London: Macmillan, 1–35.

Negishi, T. (1989), 'Tâtonnement and recontracting', in J. Eatwell, M. Milgate and P. Newman (eds), *General Equilibrium: The New Palgrave*, London: Macmillan, 281–96.

Nikaido, H. (1989), 'Fixed point theorems', in J. Eatwell, M. Milgate and P. Newman (eds), *General Equilibrium: The New Palgrave*, London: Macmillan, 139–44.

Rubinstein, A. (1982), 'Perfect equilibrium in a bargaining model', *Econometrica*, **50** (1), 97–109.

Saari, D.G. (1985), 'Interactive price mechanisms', *Econometrica*, **53** (5), 1117–31.

Saari, D.G. and C.P. Simon (1978), 'Effective price mechanism', *Econometrica*, **46** (5), 1097–125.

Schmitt, B. (1966), *Monnaie, salaires et profits*, Paris: Presses Universitaires de France (also Albeuve: Castella, 1975).

Schmitt, B. (1972), *Macroeconomic Theory: A Fundamental Revision*, Albeuve: Castella.

Schmitt, B. (1984), *Inflation, chômage et malformations du capital*, Paris and Albeuve: Economica and Castella.

Schmitt, B. (1996), 'A new paradigm for the determination of money prices', in G. Deleplace and E.J. Nell (eds), *Money in Motion: The Post Keynesian and Circulation Approaches*, London and New York: Macmillan and St. Martin's Press, 105–38.

Schmitt, B. (1998), *Critique à la théorie de l'équilibre général (I)*, University of Fribourg, unpublished.

Schmitt, B. (2000), *Critique à la théorie de l'équilibre général (II)*, University of Fribourg, unpublished.

Serrano, R. and O. Volij (2000), 'Walrasian allocations without price-taking behavior', *Journal of Economic Theory*, **95** (1), 79–106.

Smale, S. (1989), 'Global analysis in economic theory', in J. Eatwell, M. Milgate and P. Newman (eds), *General Equilibrium: The New Palgrave*, London: Macmillan, 162–6.

Starr, R.M. (1997), *General Equilibrium Theory: An Introduction*, Cambridge: Cambridge University Press.

Varian, H.R. (1992), *Microeconomic Analysis*, London and New York: Norton, 3rd edition.

Wald, A. (1936/1951), 'Über eigene Gleichungssysteme der mathematischen

Ökonomie', *Zeitschrift für Nationalökonomie*, 637–70. Translated as 'On some systems of equations of mathematical economics', *Econometrica*, **19** (4), 368–403.

Walker, D.A. (1997), *Advances in General Equilibrium Theory*, Cheltenham and Northampton: Edward Elgar.

Walras, L. (1874/1988), *Eléments d'économie politique pure*, in A. Walras and L. Walras, *Oeuvres économiques complètes*, Paris: Economica, vol. VIII.

Weintraub, E.R. (1985), *General Equilibrium Analysis*, Cambridge: Cambridge University Press.

14. IS–LM: A Final Rejection

Alvaro Cencini

INTRODUCTION

In his defence of the IS–LM interpretation of Keynes's *General Theory* at a conference held in honour of Sir John Hicks, Patinkin (1990a, p. 120) maintained that in considering the IS–LM framework 'we must distinguish between two distinct, though related, questions: 1) Is it a valid representation of the *General Theory*? 2) Is it a valid and useful analytical construct?'

In this chapter we take up the first question only insofar as it may be of some help in answering the second. Our main concern is whether Hicks's conceptual representation is 'a valid and useful analytical construct' or a useless analytical tool incapable of helping us apprehend the real world of economics.

Referring to the interpretations put forth in the aftermath of the publication of Keynes's *General Theory* (in particular those of Joan Robinson, Champernowne, Harrod, Hicks, Lange, Lerner, Meade, Robertson and Reddaway), Patinkin (1990b, p. 213) claims that they are all 'simultaneous-equation interpretations of the *General Theory* [that] can essentially be regarded as variations of IS–LM'. This allows Patinkin (ibid., p. 213) to infer that 'Keynes's approval of these reviews also constituted his consistent approval of the IS–LM interpretation of the *General Theory*'. If he is right, then it may be argued that Keynes himself was the first to approve of the neoclassical interpretation of his theory. Hence, it is not surprising that supporters and critics of the great British economist have often engaged in lengthy, sterile debates about what he really had in mind when writing to Hicks that he had next to nothing to say against his interpretation. However, the truly important thing is not whether Keynes consciously accepted the neoclassical version of his theory. We shall probably never be able to establish beyond doubt whether he was aware that by approving those interpretations he was also endorsing a version of his theory that transformed it into a particular case of a more general theoretical framework. What really matters is if, so transformed, Keynes's theory retains its peculiarity and proves to be a valid analytical instrument for the understanding of economic reality.

The IS–LM representation has often been criticised, mainly on the ground that it is an oversimplification of Keynes's theory. Vercelli (1991, p. 200), for example, points out that 'the IS–LM model offers a profoundly distorted representation of Keynes's *General Theory*', even though it may be taken to offer 'a fairly faithful analytic representation of some aspects of the *fixprice* heuristic model'. The Italian economist's conclusion about the IS–LM model is even more ambiguous. He admits that 'it may well be useful for teaching or as a preliminary step in analysis' (ibid., p. 200), but immediately adds that 'one should always be aware of its considerable distance, not only from reality, but also from Keynes's general heuristic model itself' (ibid., p. 200). Vercelli's position is emblematic: it clearly shows the dilemma many economists are faced with concerning Hicks's IS–LM analytical construct. Lacking a valid alternative to neoclassical analysis, they still do not know how to avoid the use of Hicks's model, which, despite its 'considerable distance' both from reality and from Keynes, seems to retain 'its continued analytical usefulness as it enters its second half-century' (Patinkin, 1990a, p. 132).

The aim of this chapter is to provide the elements for a new criticism of the IS–LM apparatus. Even though post-Keynesian economists have been relentless in rejecting Hicks's interpretations, they have mostly done so on ideological grounds, without providing any decisive argument against its self-consistency. If it is true, as Patinkin (1990b, p. 228) claimed, that Keynes's *General Theory* 'was a pioneering work that introduced new concepts . . . and new ways of thinking', we should be able to prove that the IS–LM interpretation reduces it to an elaboration of old concepts along old ways of thinking. Most of all, we should prove that the IS–LM analysis suffers from a logical inconsistency that deprives it of any epistemological value. This is what we shall attempt to do in the fourth section of this chapter. Following this short introduction, the next section is devoted to a concise analysis of the reasons that have made Hicks's interpretation so successful, while in the third section we explain why the post-Keynesian criticism of IS–LM has failed to prove objectively beyond dispute.

THE REASONS FOR IS–LM SUCCESS

Hicks's IS–LM interpretation of Keynes's *General Theory* has its origin in a paper published in *Econometrica* (April 1937) and read at a meeting of the Econometric Society held in Oxford in September 1936. As emphasised by Hicks himself, it was an attempt to convey Keynes's theory to econometrists and mathematical economists, and it rested on the assumption that, in the short period, money wages can be taken as given. Even though 'it is no more than a part of what Keynes was saying, or implying, that can be represented in that manner' (Hicks, 1982, p. 100), Hicks's interpretation was highly appreciated and soon became the most generally accepted version of Keynes's theory.

For the sake of historical correctness, let us add here that, as first pointed out by Solow (1984), at the famous meeting of the Econometric Society two other papers were presented, by Harrod and Meade respectively, in which Keynes's theory was formulated in terms of the same basic equations. According to Young's circumstantial study, other economists had proposed '"IS–LM-type" approaches to Keynes's *General Theory* as early as June 1936, for example ... Champernowne and Reddaway' (Young, 1987, p. 9). Moreover, from Hicks's letter to Meade dated 6 September 1936 it is clear 'that not only did Hicks see both Harrod's and Meade's papers, he waited to see what Harrod had written before even starting his own paper' (ibid., p. 33).

In short, what Hicks attempted to do was to show that Keynes's *special theory* differs from the classical theory only insofar as the demand for money is made to depend on the rate of interest – $M = L(i)$ – while saving is not made to be determined by the rate of interest – $I = S(Y)$. His aim was therefore to reduce Keynes's analysis to a special case yielding 'the startling conclusion that an increase in the inducement to invest, or in the propensity to consume, will not tend to raise the rate of interest, but only to increase employment' (Hicks, 1982, p. 107). Having done this, Hicks was then able to show that Keynes's special theory may be transformed into a *'general theory'* on condition that the demand for money be made to depend both on the rate of interest and on income. The introduction of the 'transaction motive' into the demand for money function transforms Keynes's special theory into a much more orthodox model, which allows Hicks to represent it with the aid of a diagram of a neoclassical nature (Figure 14.1).

The LL curve – known today as LM – relates the liquidity preference to the money supply and shows the combinations of income – I in Hicks's notation – and interest rate (i) that allow for equilibrium in the money market. Since it is assumed that the demand for money increases when the rate of interest falls and varies positively with income, the LM curve is upward sloping and gets steeper 'the higher the income elasticity and the smaller the interest elasticity of the demand for money' (Vane and Thompson, 1992, p. 7).

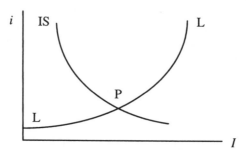

Figure 14.1. Hicks's diagram

The IS curve is the locus of combinations between interest rate and income allowing for the equality of saving and investment. It has a negative slope and implies that the equilibrium level of real income is a function of the rate of interest. Since national income depends on aggregate demand and aggregate demand is closely related to the multiplier, '[t]he slope of the IS curve depends on the responsiveness of investment to changes in the rate of interest and the value of the multiplier' (ibid., p. 4).

The point of intersection between the IS and LM curves defines the simultaneous achievement of equilibrium on the goods and money markets. Hicks's IS–LM diagram is therefore the clearest attempt to show that Keynes's contribution can be reassessed in terms of general equilibrium analysis and thus emptied of its intended revolutionary content.

Being an earnest neoclassical economist, Hicks interpreted Keynes's theory according to the principles of neoclassical economics and it is not surprising to read in his 1937 article that in his IS–LM diagrammatic representation of Keynes's *General Theory* income and the rate of interest 'are determined together; just as price and output are determined together in the modern theory of demand and supply' (Hicks, 1982, p. 109). Later on, in a paper published in the *Journal of Post Keynesian Economics*, and significantly titled 'IS–LM: an explanation', Hicks was to be extremely clear about the neoclassical origin of his diagram: 'It will readily be understood, in the light of what I have been saying, that the idea of the IS–LM diagram came to me as a result of the work I had been doing on three-way exchange, conceived in a Walrasian manner' (Hicks, 1980–81/1982, p. 320).

The neoclassical interpretation of Keynes's *General Theory* initiated by Hicks, Harrod and Meade, further developed by Lange and Modigliani, and taken over and re-elaborated by Clower, Leijonhufvud, Tobin and Samuelson was to give rise to the neo-Keynesian approach to macroeconomics. Despite notable differences between the analyses proposed by these authors, they all aim at formalising Keynes's theory in order to make it workable in mathematical terms. Thus, while it is true that Hicks's attempt to interpret Keynes's theory along the path of general equilibrium analysis was worked out with the explicit aim of reducing Keynes's contribution to a particular case of Walras's approach, it is also true that the success of IS–LM may be explained by the attractiveness it exerted on the majority of economists because of its apparent simplicity and 'mechanicity'.

Keynes's thought was too complex and in part counter-intuitive to be easily grasped. It was presented with the aid of very few and allegedly self-evident (if not tautological) equations and based on a macroeconomic approach that did not seem to be always consistent with the microeconomic perception of the real world that was supposed to be at the core of economics. Hicks's interpretation, on the contrary, had the great advantage of relying on a set of equations, of being easily represented by a simple geometrical diagram and of incorporating the microeconomic approach that was triumphally gaining acceptance among economists. It is not surprising, therefore, to find in *The New Palgrave Dictionary of Money & Finance* the following interpretation of Keynes's contribution to economic analysis: 'The main analytical innovation of Keynes's *General Theory* was to develop an alternative concept of equilibrium that allowed modified versions of supply and demand analysis to be applied to macroeconomic questions without assuming a state of ideal co-ordination' (Howitt, 1992, p. 633). As Howitt's quotation clearly shows, the core of Keynes's message is reduced to a simple application of the law of supply and demand to the general framework of aggregate output. If this were true, Keynes's revolution would be significantly played down, since it would merely amount to a particular case of neoclassical analysis.

Though some of them do not go as far as Howitt, North-American Keynesians still believe Hicks's interpretation to be respectful of Keynes's thought and a very useful instrument both at a teaching and at a research level. In a 1994 interview, Tobin, for example, does not hesitate to claim that 'the IS–LM model is the tool of first resort . . . it's a start and lots of times it's exactly right' (Tobin, in Snowdon, Vane and Wynarczyk, 1994, p. 129).

As shown by Keynes's correspondence with Reddaway, Harrod, Hicks and Meade, the author of the *General Theory* never rejected either the neoclassical interpretation of his analysis or the IS–LM representation proposed by Hicks. The responsibility for the various attempts carried out by generations of economists to reconcile Keynesian and Walrasian economics within a neoclassical synthesis may thus be ascribed to Keynes himself. It may be deemed rather unfortunate that 'Keynes made no public protest when they [IS–LM and related diagrams and algebra] began to appear' (Kahn, 1984, p. 160), yet this would not have been enough to foster the success of IS–LM had Keynes's followers succeeded in proving that Hicks's model is logically inconsistent. The wide acceptance of IS–LM is due both to its clear and simple mathematical formulation and to the failure of its critics to show that it has to be rejected on logical (and not ideological) grounds.

ARGUMENTS AGAINST THE POST KEYNESIAN CRITICISM TO IS–LM

The IS–LM interpretation was not unanimously accepted by economists. Most of the Cambridge followers of Keynes were critical of Hicks's model and some were uncompromisingly opposed to this neoclassical version of Keynes's theory. Others rejected Hicks's diagram but accepted Walras's theoretical framework. Among the economists who, in the name of Keynes, openly criticised Hicks's IS–LM without resisting the temptation of general equilibrium analysis, Leijonhufvud is an example of ambiguity that is worth recalling. In fact, while he rejects Hicks's model on the ground that it 'ignores the sequence of events within the period' (Leijonhufvud, 1984, p. 37) and goes as far as defining it as 'a singularly inadequate vehicle' (Leijonhufvud, 1967, p. 298) for interpreting Keynes's theory, he claims that what distinguishes Walras's system from Keynes's is merely the presence of the auctioneer: 'The only thing Keynes removed from the foundations of classical theory was the *deus ex machina* – the auctioneer which is assumed to furnish, without charge, all the information needed to obtain the perfect co-operation of the activities of all traders in the present and through the future' (ibid., pp. 308–9). Hence, far from proving the inconsistency of Hicks's model, Leijonhufvud endorses a neoclassical reinterpretation of Keynes, which makes him an objective ally of the famous Oxonian economist. Indeed, this conclusion is corroborated by the fact, put forth by Young, that Leijonhufvud's own contribution is actually a simple variation of Hicks's (see Young, 1987, pp. 153–7).

As for the Cambridge followers of Keynes who may be associated with the post-Keynesian school, they have always explicitly and sometimes vehemently attacked Hicks's IS–LM. Among the numerous criticisms advanced, let us quote Pasinetti's. In his analysis of the economics of effective demand, the Italian economist defines Hicks's procedure as being 'typically un-Keynesian' (Pasinetti, 1974, p. 46) and shows how Keynes's concepts are manipulated in order to justify a neoclassical interpretation of the *General Theory*. Having described the various modifications introduced by Hicks into Keynes's system, Pasinetti concludes that '[a]t the end of this, apparently innocuous, manipulation, Hicks has in fact broken up Keynes's basic chain of arguments. The relations have been turned into a system of simultaneous equations, i.e. precisely into what Keynes did not want them to be' (ibid., p. 46).

As is clear from Pasinetti's line of reasoning, post-Keynesian criticism developed essentially as a defence of Keynes's originality, emphasising the differences between his analysis and the reinterpretation suggested by Hicks and his supporters. 'The Hicks reinterpretation also helps to illustrate how the replacement of causally ordered relations with a system of simultaneous equations is not used only as a purely formal device but as a medium to introduce a basically different interpretative model of economic reality' (ibid., p. 47).

The most insightful among the post-Keynesian economists are well aware that Keynes's theory is deeply at odds with the neoclassical system of general equilibrium. The two approaches are mutually exclusive and not simply different alternatives that may equally well be applied to the economic reality. It is only fair to admit that post-Keynesian economists have been almost alone in having 'determinately insisted on Keynes's irreconcilability with traditional economics' (Pasinetti, 1983, p. 208). Yet, none of these authors has provided an internal criticism to the IS–LM analysis or has been able to show that Keynes's theory can in no circumstances be interpreted according to Hicks's model. The arguments put forth by Kahn, Joan Robinson, Minsky, Davidson, Pasinetti and many others may prove that Hicks's interpretation does not respect the profound nature of Keynes's message, and that Hicks's assumptions are just a way of transforming Keynes's theory into a variant of the quantity theory of money. Their reasoning may also show that it is possible, following Keynes, to develop a macroeconomic theory substantially opposed to the world of Walrasian or non-Walrasian general equilibrium analysis. However, all these assertions may always be discarded by claiming that they are neither less arbitrary nor more 'scientific' than those put forth by neoclassical economists. The dispute could thus go on for ever between those who believe Keynes had an entirely new vision of the economic world and those who maintain that his contribution can perfectly be integrated into the general framework of neoclassical analysis.

Now, the post-Keynesian point of view would be very much reinforced if it were possible to show that Hicks's interpretation suffers from an internal contradiction. Indeed, it is our contention that the IS–LM approach is logically flawed on several grounds, which are closely related to the shortcomings of the neoclassical theory it stems from. In the next section we shall try to prove our point, with a view to introducing the reader to a new approach that, going beyond post-Keynesian analysis, leads to the monetary macroeconomic theory of production Keynes failed to bestow on his fellow economists.

THE FUNDAMENTAL SHORTCOMINGS OF THE IS–LM APPROACH

As Kaldor stated in an interview quoted by Young, when he met with Hicks in Cambridge and was first shown the IS–LM diagram he 'was duly impressed by it . . . because it separates the monetary side and the real side very neatly' (Young, 1987, p. 55). The separation between monetary and real sides is certainly one of the main features of Hicks's interpretation of Keynes's theory. This is not surprising, of course, since Hicks was by his own admission a neoclassical economist whose general equilibrium analysis was based, like that of his fellow economists, on the 'postulate of homogeneity', that is, on the strict dichotomy between real and monetary variables. Yet, this immediately raises a serious doubt about the very possibility of inserting the IS and LM curves into the same diagram. Outwardly, this is easily done, since each curve defines an equation whose terms are a function of income and the rate of interest. On reflection, however, it appears that while the IS curve is a locus of *real* equilibrium points, the LM curve represents *money* equilibrium points. According to Hicks, income and interest rate are expressed in money terms both with regard to LM and IS. This is logically necessary in order for the two curves to represent a set of equations whose variables are not too numerous to make the system indeterminate. If income and interest rate were defined in two different ways (monetary for LM and real for IS), the equations would be outnumbered by the variables, and the two curves could not be joined together in one and the same diagram. But is it correct, from a neoclassical point of view – which is that of Hicks – to consider real variables such as I and S as functions of monetary ones?

The existence of a true problem here is confirmed by Hansen, the author who has been most associated with Hicks in the diffusion of the IS–LM analysis and whose work 'marks the beginning of the institutionalization and conventional acceptance of Hicks's SILL diagram for the purpose of both interpreting and representing Keynes's *General Theory*' (Young, 1987, p. 117). In his *Monetary Theory and Fiscal Policy*, in fact, Hansen (1949, p. 72) puts forth a system of five equations where 'the various functions [are expressed in] real terms'. Like Hicks, Hansen is well aware that in order for his system to be determinate he has to express income and the interest rate either in money *or* in real terms. Now, since both Hicks's and Hansen's approaches are essentially neoclassical – together with Modigliani's they open the way to what is known as the 'neoclassical synthesis' – they are necessarily based on the homogeneity postulate. But, if money and real variables are strictly separated how is it possible to maintain either that I and S are functions of monetary variables or that L and M are functions of real variables?

Within general equilibrium analysis the neoclassical dichotomy is too central a concept to be simply discarded. Yet, as soon as we accept it we are no longer entitled to mix up real and monetary variables. Unless money and real variables are mutually integrated – which is logically unacceptable within the neoclassical framework of analysis – it is impossible to relate real saving and real investment to money income and to the money rate of interest. Likewise, it is idle to look for a functional relationship between supply of and demand for money on one side, and real income and real interest rate on the other side. In his effort to interpret Keynes's theory according to general equilibrium principles, Hicks failed to understand how far Keynes's monetary analysis had gone in dismissing the neoclassical dichotomy. Properly carried out, a monetary analysis of production leaves no room for a theory developed in real terms only and, therefore, cannot be represented using any model that, like IS–LM, rests on the neat separation between the monetary and the real side. Hence, we are led to the conclusion that the fundamental heterogeneity of real and monetary variables repeatedly endorsed by Hicks, Hansen, Modigliani and many other neoclassical-oriented economists is a major obstacle to the scientific acceptability of the IS–LM diagram.

The neoclassical dichotomy has more far-reaching consequences than jeopardising Hicks's interpretation of Keynes's *General Theory*. As shown by Schmitt and De Gottardi (this volume), the logical impossibility of determining prices through direct exchange is the best possible proof that no economic theory may be constructed on the basis of the separation between real and monetary variables. In order to realise Keynes's purpose, the monetary theory of production must be founded on the integrated analysis of the roles played by banks and producers. Economic magnitudes such as prices, income, profits, capital, interest rates and so on are simultaneously monetary and real and cannot be determined separately either in purely monetary or real terms. For the time being, let us simply observe that this 'integrated' analysis leaves no room for the IS–LM dichotomous representation of economic reality. Our first criticism of Hicks's interpretation leads therefore to the unsatisfactory conclusion that either (1) IS and LM pertain to two separate worlds so that they cannot be related to one another within the same co-ordinated system of reference, or (2) monetary and real aspects are the two sides of one and the same reality, in which case it is meaningless to represent them by the interplay of two distinct curves. But let us now try to show that Hicks's representation may be further criticised in each of its components.

About IS

Derived from the goods market, the IS curve is usually represented as in Figure 14.2.

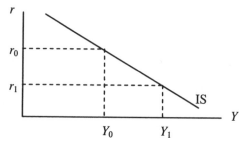

Figure 14.2. The IS curve

For any given level of the rate of interest (r) there is a level of national income (Y) at which the market for goods is at an equilibrium. Now, two interpretations of the IS curve are possible. It may be said that national income increases when the rate of interest decreases since investment is directly related to total income and inversely related to the rate of interest. It may be claimed also that there is an increase in the interest rate when national output decreases. Not very different in substance from the first interpretation, this second interpretation shows with greater clarity the absurdity of the IS curve. The reduction of national output to zero, in fact, would define the highest possible level of the rate of interest, while a zero level of interest rate would lead to the greatest possible level of national income. The absurdity of the IS curve is confirmed by the observation that in the fixed-price Keynesian model of income determination both consumption and investment are ill conceived. A quick glance at the consumption function and at the 45° line diagram highlights the fact that it is illogical to assume that consumption and investment may be positive when national income is zero. Once it is admitted that both (economic) consumption and investment can be positive only if 'fed' by a positive income, the Keynesian 45° line diagram becomes totally useless just like the IS curve derived from it.

As economists well know, the relationship between saving and investment has long been a subject of high controversy. Keynes's claim that these two magnitudes are always necessarily equal was the object of an intense dispute during which the author of the *General Theory* endeavoured in vain to convince his adversaries that his identity was much more than a simple tautology. Robertson and Ohlin were the opponents with whom Keynes discussed in the most rigorous and passionate way the interrelations between *S, I* and the rate of interest. By his analysis, Keynes mainly purported to prove that it is the level of income and not the rate of interest that ensures the equality between *S* and *I*. 'The novelty in my treatment of saving and investment consists, not in my maintaining their necessary aggregate equality, but in the proposition that it is, not the rate of interest, but the level of incomes which . . . ensures this equality' (Keynes, 1973b, p. 211). Robertson and Ohlin, on the contrary, defended the view that the equality between *I* and *S* is a condition of equilibrium, which may be satisfied only through a variation in the interest rate. Now, even though it is indisputable that most of the controversy was about the theory of interest, it is possible to interpret it differently by emphasising the opposition between identities and conditional equalities.

In his article on 'Alternative theories of the rate of interest' published in the *Economic Journal* (June 1937), Keynes reaffirms the necessary equality of *S* and *I* – '[a]ggregate saving and aggregate investment, in the senses in which I have defined them, are necessarily equal' (ibid., p. 211) – but makes it clear that the stated identity is not of a 'nominal' kind: saving and investment are not merely two different names for the same thing (ibid., p. 211). On the other hand, Keynes also claims that the necessary equality of the two terms is compatible with any realised level of income. Taken together, these two claims suggest an entirely new, 'macroeconomic' conception of production, saving and investment. Literally, they mean that for any given level of income, that is, of production, the amount globally saved can never be unequal to global investment.

With a view to fending off the difficult and revolutionary concept of the logical identity between *S* and *I* (and between total demand and total supply), Ohlin had recourse to Myrdal's distinction between *ex ante* and *ex post* magnitudes, maintaining that *S* and *I* are necessarily equal only once equilibrium is achieved, whereas they may, and usually do, differ during the search for equilibrium. Ohlin's attempt was to show that Keynes's identity is not opposed to the existence of a process of adjustment through time. Objectively, Ohlin's interpretation aims at replacing Keynes's identity with a conditional equality, that is, to transform Keynes's macroeconomic analysis into a neoclassical general equilibrium analysis based on the microeconomic adjustment between *S* and *I*. Now, the phase of adjustment that, *ex ante*, should allow for saving and investment to find their equilibrium is a mere figment of imagination if production has not yet taken place. In fact, if no income is actually available, 'virtual' or 'desired' saving and investment have no real meaning. *Ex ante*, these magnitudes do not really exist since no income is available to make them positive. It is thus useless to study their mutual interaction.

Even if we were to accept the existence of *ex ante S* and *I* in the form of planned saving and investment, this would not imply that their actual or realised values are the result of their reciprocal adjustment. Let us follow Keynes. Having admitted that '[p]lanned investment – i.e. investment *ex ante* – may have to secure its "financial provision" *before* the investment takes place; that is to say, before the corresponding saving has taken place' (ibid., p. 207), he adds that '[i]t is, so to speak, as though a particular piece of saving had to be earmarked against a particular piece of investment before either has occurred' (ibid., pp. 207–8). This is a very clear and deep argument indeed. Planned investment may be decided before production actually takes place, which is obvious. But it may also secure its financial provision before then. Keynes observes, however, that in this case an equivalent amount of future saving is earmarked against the planned investment. As he immediately explains, this means that '[t]here has, therefore, to be a technique to bridge this gap between the time when the *decision* to invest is taken and the time when the correlative investment and saving actually occur' (ibid., p. 208). Hence, planned investment can find a financial backing before saving takes place provided banks are willing to bridge the gap between the present and the future through their financial activity. If this happens, investment is financed 'in advance' with respect to the *ex ante* equality between saving and investment.

To make things clearer, Keynes argues that '"finance" has nothing to do with saving. At the "financial" stage of the proceedings no net saving has taken place on anyone's part, just as there has been no net investment.

"Finance" and "commitments to finance" are mere credit and debit book entries, which allow entrepreneurs to go ahead with assurance' (ibid., p. 209). What Keynes is telling us is, therefore, that *ex ante* investment may be financed by banks and that, even though saving has not yet been determined, this does not introduce any discrepancy between saving and investment. This argument is not easy to grasp. The only true financing of investment is saving and this can occur only *ex post*, once investment and saving have actually taken place. Nevertheless, planned or *ex ante* investment and its financing by banks is a possibility that cannot be discarded. Now, Keynes maintains that the two expenditures, 'finance' and investment, must not be taken to have the same meaning. *Ex ante* banks advance an income not yet formed, *ex post* investment is backed by an equivalent sum of income actually formed and saved. But, if this may be intended to mean that *ex post* saving and investment are necessarily equal, what about their *ex ante* relationship?

Keynes claims both that planned investment is financed by banks and that 'finance has nothing to do with saving'. Since he distinguishes investment from the decision to invest, we may infer that in his mind the *ex ante* relationship between saving and investment is replaced by the relationship between planned investment and its financial provision. We could thus be led to conclude that there are two distinct relationships, each of which implies the necessary equality of its terms. Yet, this could be interpreted as implying that investment financed by banks is entirely different from investment financed by saving, which is certainly not what Keynes would have been prepared to admit. While it is true that Keynes distinguished planned from actual investment and 'finance' from saving, it would be ingenuous to claim that he considered the two investments and the two expenditures as distinct and unrelated. Indeed, when he speaks of the financial intervention of banks, he explicitly affirms that this technique is necessary to bridge the gap between the time when the decision to invest is taken and 'the time when the *correlative* investment and saving actually occur' (ibid., p. 208; our emphasis). The existence of this correlation has far-reaching consequences, one of which is the fact that actual saving can retroactively modify the size of *ex ante* investment.

Let us take a very simple numerical example, where the unit is understood to be a monetary unit. Suppose planned investment is equal to 100 units in period p_0. This means that in p_0 firms plan to invest 100 units and that, if banks agree to do so, they provide a financial backing of the same amount. Suppose now that at the end of the given period global saving is actually equal to 80 units. Global investment is thus also set at the level of 80 units. Does this imply that the economy ends up with two distinct investments of a different nature? Certainly not, since the only investment that actually takes place is equal to 80, which therefore cannot exceed 80 units even though the amount of investment is initially set at 100 units. The exact amount of income actually saved in p_0 is crucial here. Since only 80 units are globally saved, macroeconomic investment must be equal to 80. This means that only 80 units out of the 100 advanced by banks in p_0 are in fact financing planned investment. The other 20 units are absorbed by consumption, which reduces the production of investment goods to 80 units (the remaining 20 units of production goods being indirectly purchased by wage-earners, an indirect purchase that transforms them into consumption goods 'by destination'). Finally, it is clear that saving and investment are always necessarily equal, *ex post* and *ex ante*.

To be sure, the concept of retroactivity that we have introduced in our example is not to be found in Keynes's work. Developed by Schmitt in 1984, it derives from the analysis of profit. Now, as the new, quantum theory of emissions shows, macroeconomic saving is determined by the amount of invested profit (Schmitt, 1984, pp. 165–75; Cencini, 1984, pp. 201–12). Indeed, related to investment, *ex post* saving defines that part of current income that is spent by firms in order to finance the production of investment goods. In our numerical example, this means that the production of investment goods taking place at t_0 (instant of period p_0 when productive services are paid) is only partly financed by the expenditure of profits, expenditure that reduces investment from 100 to 80 units. If the profit realised by firms at t_1 (instant of p_0 when current income is finally spent) is only equal to 80 units, the production of p_0 must be reinterpreted. What happens at t_1 reacts on what happened at t_0. Since the initial expenditure of firms (100 units) is backed by 80 units of profit only, what was planned as a production of investment goods is in part transformed into a production of (future) consumption goods. In the following period, the investment goods unsold in p_0 will in fact be replaced by an equivalent production of consumption goods. If, instead of the planned figure of 100 units, macroeconomic saving does not exceed 80 units, this means that 20 units of money income are spent by wage-earners in the purchase of future consumption goods. This forward purchase takes the form of a loan extended by wage-earners to firms. The investment goods that wage-earners purchase today indirectly (through their loans to firms) will then be replaced by an equivalent amount of consumption goods produced in a subsequent period.

It is important to reiterate here that invested profits are the measure of macroeconomic investment as well as of macroeconomic saving. In a monetary economy, net saving can exist only if part of current income is actually and irreversibly transformed into capital. This happens today when a positive income is spent on the factors market. In fact, this is precisely the expenditure that is carried out by firms when they invest their profits (realised or advanced) in the production of investment goods.

The inclusion of the expenditure of profits within the payment of wages is one key result of quantum macroeconomic analysis. It clearly shows that net saving and net investment are simultaneously determined by one and the same transaction and can therefore never differ.

Now, although it is true that no functional relationship can be established *ex ante* between saving and investment on one side and income and the rate of interest on the other, is it nevertheless correct to claim that planned investment and planned saving are dependent on the fluctuation of the market rate of interest? Of course, this is neither what Keynes suggested, nor what many of his followers would be prepared to accept. Undoubtedly, Keynes repeatedly rejected the idea that S and I may be made equal through variations in the rate of interest. Yet, a novel interpretation of Keynes's monetary theory of production is possible, in which the fundamental identity of S and I coexists with their *ex ante* variation, if only within the boundaries of the income actually formed in t_0. In the period between the instant when income is formed and the later instant when it is finally spent, the decision to save depends on the rate of interest and may adjust to the decision to invest. Whatever the impact of interest rates on the behaviour of consumers and firms, it remains true – as maintained by Keynes – that once macroeconomic saving is actually determined it can no longer differ from investment. However, the identity between S and I allows for a degree of freedom between firms' envisaged decision to invest and consumers' decision to save. An adjustment may occur between these two sets of planned decisions, but once saving has found its final macroeconomic value, investment can only match it, whether or not the process of adjustment has been successful in satisfying the desires of firms and consumers. Indeed, S and I are the two opposite facets of the same reality. Once one is determined, the other cannot differ from it. To be precise, S and I are simultaneously determined, investment being financed by that part of income that is not definitively consumed, and macroeconomic saving being formed through the investment of the same part of current income. Hence, the adjustment between firms' and consumers' decisions cannot have any bearing on the logical identities of S and I and of total supply and total demand. In no way can Keynes's fundamental identities be transformed into conditions of equilibrium.

Finally, it is important to notice that S and I are always equal, not only *ex post*, but also *ex ante*. True, in the interval between t_0 and t_1 an adjustment may occur between what firms plan to invest and what income holders are prepared to save. But, whatever the decisions taken by these agents, at each point of the interval t_0–t_1 the amount of macroeconomic saving (determined by the amount of invested profit) sets the limit to investment, so that no difference can ever be found between the two. Macroeconomic saving and macroeconomic investment are thus jointly determined. Hence, it is only at t_1 that the amount of macroeconomic saving is definitively established and that S and I find their final numerical expression. Before t_1, that is, *ex ante*, S and I may differ from their *ex post* level; yet, they define a whole series of possible 'equilibrium' values. No adjustment ever takes place between S and I, which are always equal *ex ante*, *ex post*, and '*ex* anything else' (Keynes, 1973b, p. 222).

In order to avoid a possible misunderstanding, let us observe that our analysis is only partially backed by Keynes's own statements. Thus, we would be wrong in claiming that Keynes always considered his identities as the necessary result of his conceptual analysis rather than as mere tautologies implicit in his nominal (that is, purely conventional, terminological) definitions. It cannot be denied, in fact, that Keynes himself presented his identities as deriving naturally from his nominal definitions of income, consumption, saving and investment: 'these two amounts [S and I] are necessarily equal, since each of them is equal to the excess of income over consumption' (Keynes, 1936/1973a, p. 63). By contrast, our aim is to show that, interpreted along the lines of the quantum theory of emissions, Keynes's analysis reveals its true originality and its deep-seated opposition to the neoclassical approach and to any attempt to integrate it into a neoclassical synthesis. The identities between global demand and global supply, and between saving and investment acquire their full meaning only once it has been proven that production is a creation whose result is simultaneously monetary and real, and which defines the same time dimension as the time dimension defined by the final expenditure of the money income it generates. It is quantum time that establishes the retroactive simultaneity of what happens at t_0 and at t_1, and it is quantum analysis that makes a conciliation possible between the identity between S and I and the variations of desired S and planned I.

In the light of the quantum monetary analysis it is not an exaggeration to claim that Keynes's theory of interest is inadequate. For fear of being forced to abandon his attempt to determine income independently of full employment, Keynes rejected the classical theory of the rate of interest. Unfortunately, this led him to give a tautological definition of his identities, without formulating a valid alternative to Böhm-Bawerk's theory of interest.

Now, the quantum theory of emissions shows that, once they are given their full epistemological status, Keynes's identities are perfectly consistent with Böhm-Bawerk's theory. In particular, Keynes's identities are in no way opposed to the fact that interest derives from the accumulation of capital, and the fundamental expression of the rate of interest is given by the ratio between profits and capital (Wicksell's *natural* rate). In fact, macroeconomic saving is finally determined by the total amount of invested profits (realised and advanced), which is precisely why S and I can never differ. Now, whilst the existence of a market or money rate of interest influenced by the supply of and demand for loanable funds does not explain the origin of interest, it may account for the adjustment between investment and saving decisions. It remains true, of course, that it is not because of this adjustment that S and I are always necessarily equal. The identity of S and I is established in quantum time and cannot be jeopardised by the variation, taking place in continuous time, between planned saving and investment. This clearly means that it is not because of the variation in the interest rate that S and I are necessarily equal: even if the rate of interest failed to bring the decisions to save and to invest into equality in chronological time, the emission occurring at t_1 would unfailingly establish the identity of S and I. Yet, it is significant that, within the boundaries of the emission occurring at t_0 and t_1, the interest rate influences the reciprocal adjustment of firms' and consumers' plans. Thus, the agio between the market and the natural rate of interest plays an important role in the decision to invest, and the fluctuation of the market rate has an impact on the decision regarding the supply of loanable funds.

Keynes's rejection of *ex ante/ex post* analysis as an attempt to transform the identity between S and I into a condition of equilibrium is uncompromising and shows clearly the substantial difference between his own analysis and that put forward by Ohlin, Robertson, Hicks and all those authors who read the *General Theory* with neoclassical spectacles. It also provides the proof that Keynes's analysis cannot be represented by Hicks's IS–LM diagram. If I and S are always equal, whatever the level of income actually produced, it is no longer possible to consider saving and investment as functions of income. For a given level of income and interest rate, for example, we do not necessarily find only one possible value of the identity between S and I. There is only one actual value, of course, but it cannot be determined before S and I actually take place. Even if decisions are influenced by the level of income and of the rate of interest, no function can be established between S and I since every assumption we may make as to their possible correlation can always be overruled by the actual decision of consumers and firms. We are thus led to the conclusion that *ex post* IS can only be represented by a series of unrelated points (Figure 14.3). Each point defines the level of IS in any given period when saving and investment actually occur, and is independent of any other point.

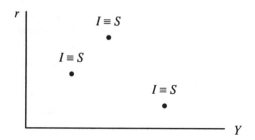

Figure 14.3. The 'ex post' diagram

Ex ante no IS curve can be drawn as a function of Y and r. Income of p_0 is determined by the production taking place at t_0 and does not vary between t_0 and t_1. In this interval of time an infinity of combinations between S and I are possible, which most of the time do not satisfy both desires: the firm's to invest and the income holders' to save. Each combination defines an *ex ante* equality between S and I and, were it possible to know the amount of planned saving at each time point, it would also be possible to draw a curve representing the various levels of $S = I$ corresponding to different levels of the interest rate (Figure 14.4).

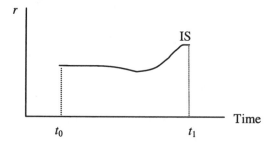

Figure 14.4. The 'ex ante' diagram

The implications for the IS–LM diagram can easily be imagined, but before considering them any further let us propose a few critical remarks about the LM curve.

About LM

To some extent, the critique of the LM curve is straightforward. To assume that the money supply is exogenously determined by the monetary authorities is, in fact, clearly inconsistent with the way money is in fact issued by banks. What Hicks was not aware of is that money is a flow created by banks for each payment, and which exists only for an instant. Hence, there is no such thing as a quantity or mass of money. But, if money is a flow and if money flows do not convey any stocks of money, can there be a money supply and a demand for money? Yes, provided the demand for money is conceived of as a request for payments to be carried out and the money supply as the capacity of banks to satisfy this request. Even in this case, however, money should not be confused with income and the monetary intermediation carried out by banks with their financial intermediation. Thus, the capacity to carry out payments should not be mistaken for the capacity to finance them. Banks create the monetary vehicle, the 'means of payment', and the economy gives money its real content. If the demand for money applies to money income and not to vehicular money, then it has to be confronted with production, the very source of money income. But, if this is done, double-entry bookkeeping immediately shows that the totality of the sum deposited with banks is always necessarily lent by them, that is, the sum total of money income created by production is subjected to an equal demand (exerted by consumers and firms). In these conditions, it is obvious that no adjustment can ever take place between supply of and demand for money, which makes the LM curve an anachronistic and mistaken representation of monetary reality.

Considering the crucial importance of the point here at issue, which threatens the whole body of monetarist and neoclassical analyses, let us look a little more closely at the nature of money and income.

First introduced by Adam Smith, the concept of vehicular or nominal money has been given a full explanation by Bernard Schmitt, who, referring to double-entry bookkeeping, has shown that, as a spontaneous acknowledgement of debt issued by banks, money is a purely numerical form, an 'asset–liability' of no intrinsic value. As such, money can be issued at near to zero cost and without there being any logical limits to its emission (except, of course, those set by production). Applied to this context, money supply simply defines the capacity that banks have to provide the economy with a numerical form. Whatever the amount needed, banks can issue it through a bookkeeping double-entry that is costless and instantaneous. Thus, with respect to nominal money, money supply does not define – as wrongly assumed by the monetarist school – a given stock or a quantity of money.

Actually, money is immaterial and the very idea of it being a quantity is seriously wrong and misleading.

The distinction between money as a number and money income – very familiar to classical economists – may sound strange to modern economists, who do not even seem to understand it properly. Is it not true, in fact, that every time a monetary transaction is carried out by banks it implies a total cost at least equal to the amount involved? If we leave aside transactions costs, it seems obvious that a payment of 100 units involves a total expenditure of 100 units and, therefore, an equivalent total cost. For what reason should there be another intermediation (purely monetary) intertwined with the transfer of 100 units of money income from the payer to the payee? Using double-entry bookkeeping, banks transfer the sums deposited with them from one client to another. Is that not enough to allow us to conclude that money income is the only reality here and that, insofar as it is the object of a deposit, it is a stock? In fact, while no one disputes the fact that money income is a stock, it can be shown that the distinction between the deposit and its object is not that between the bank's accounting books and the inflows of money income. Money income is the deposit and not the object of the deposit. Indeed, the object of the bank deposit (that is, of the money income that makes it up) is that part of current output which it 'contains'. Since money income is a stock whose value is positive and since banks cannot create it *ex nihilo*, it is not surprising to find that money income owes its positive value to its real content: the output it is made to define through the payment of its cost of production. Hence, it would be mistaken to claim that income is a stock of money issued by banks (or the monetary authorities) and whose mass or quantity defines the money supply.

Going back to the distinction between money as such and money income, we can now say that nominal or vehicular money is a 'form' whose creation is necessary if we are to give physical output a numerical expression. It is because banks are made to issue this numerical form that they perform a monetary intermediation. Without it, physical output would simply be a heap of heterogeneous objects. Thanks to banks' monetary intermediation, physical output is made homogeneous and becomes the object of a deposit. The reason why this all-important intermediation goes unnoticed is because it is always associated with a financial intermediation. Since every payment relates to an income – which is either created, destroyed or transferred in the operation – we are easily led to forget the monetary intermediation that allows the transaction to occur. Our microeconomic perception of economic reality encourages us to think that it is enough to own a positive income to finance a payment. Yet, we should always keep in mind that no money income could ever exist if banks did not give a numerical form to physical output, and that no payment could take place if banks were not able to transfer their deposits, a process that requires both a monetary *and* a financial intermediation.

As far as supply of and demand for money are concerned, we have to analyse whether or not a functional relationship between them may exist. Let us start with numerical money. If we were to maintain that the higher the income actually produced the higher the amount of numerical money required to express it, we would merely formulate a tautology. Moreover, supply of and demand for numerical money would never differ so that no interactive adjustment could ever occur between them. In fact, since vehicular or nominal money is not a stock, there is no point in talking about its supply and its demand. But what about money income?

This time we are confronted with a stock, a bank deposit of a given positive amount that cannot be modified at will and at zero cost. Yet, it must also be remembered that the available money income is not the making of banks, not even of central banks. A mere double-entry in the central bank's bookkeeping is obviously not enough to create a positive amount of riches in the form of national money income. Production is what is needed to give a real content to money creation. This means that the supply of money income is determined by production or, more precisely, by the monetisation of production. Money income is thus the result of a payment by which current output is given its numerical form. But if the supply of 'real' money is defined by the amount of income generated by production, would there be any sense in considering the money supply as a function of national income? Income is the 'real' money supply and its level is a function of production only in the very strict sense that output is precisely defined by the amount of income of which it is the real 'content'. Hence, the supply of money income is determined by the amount of bank deposits formed at the very instant when production is given its numerical form, that is, through the payment of its costs. For every given period the amount of the 'real' money supply is thus perfectly determined by the amount of deposits formed with banks. Can there be an excess demand, positive or negative, for money income? Apparently yes, particularly if we were to consider only the demand explicitly exerted by consumers. On further reflection, however, things do not work out this way. Saved income, in fact, is also subjected to a necessary demand since, according to double-entry bookkeeping, the entire amount deposited with banks (that is, entered on the liabilities side of their balance sheets) is lent out by them (that is, it is balanced by an equivalent entry on their assets side). What is not demanded by consumers is lent to firms, which need it to finance their debt to banks. On the whole, the amount of money income is demanded in its totality and no adjustment occurs between the supply of and demand for money income.

From what we have just seen it becomes immediately obvious that no LM curve can logically be drawn with respect to bank money. Hicks's mistake was to believe that money could be created by banks already endowed with a positive value. Keynes himself was not entirely aware of all the consequences of his monetary theory of production. In particular, his analysis of what he called the liquidity preference is not at the level of his most subtle intuitions and resembles more to a baffling attempt to show that the rate of interest is not determined by the supply of and demand for loanable funds than to a serious piece of monetary theory. Were banknotes and coins to be entirely done away with, the liquidity preference would no longer play any role, yet the system would remain substantially unchanged and work just as well as before. Keynes's fundamental contribution is to be found elsewhere. His basic identity between total income (Y) and total demand ($C + I$), for example, is clear evidence of the necessary equality between the supply of and demand for money income. As soon as it is realised that money as such is issued by banks as a valueless numerical form and that it is through its association with current output that it is transformed into income, Keynes's analysis acquires its full meaning. Production, which from a physical point of view is a time-consuming process of transformation, becomes a proper subject of inquiry only once it is expressed in money. Now, since the association between money and production can only take place via payments and since payments are instantaneous events, from a monetary point of view production is also an instantaneous event (see Schmitt, 1984). Income is thus formed at the very moment the macroeconomic costs of production are paid for. In fact, while the payment of the microeconomic costs of production requires the expenditure of a positive income, wages – the only macroeconomic cost of production – are paid out of a purely nominal sum of money. This is so because human labour alone is the source of economic value, that is, in neoclassical terms, of a new utility resulting from the creative power of the human mind and from the capacity of human labour to give a new form to matter and energy.

Confirmed by the way banks actually enter the payment of wages in their books, this analysis may be traced back to Keynes's concept of wage-units as well as to some of the intuitions to be found in Smith, Ricardo and Marx. Taken to its extreme consequences it shows that from a monetary viewpoint economics is a true, independent science. This is not to deny, of course, that economics is also a social science. Yet, it is only when money enters the picture that economics acquires a proper status. Production is the clearest example of this dual nature. While it may be analysed as a social process – but, as such, it pertains equally well to sociology, psychology, political studies and other related sciences – it may also be investigated in its monetary aspect, as a specific economic event. When this is done, it is soon realised that production is a very peculiar process indeed. Although closely related to the physical world, the world of economics is immaterial in the sense that, being a purely numerical form, money has merely a numerical dimension. What makes economics such a difficult science to master is precisely the fact that it is simultaneously concerned with an immaterial form and its physical content. In order to understand the specific economic aspect of production, it is necessary to go beyond its physical characteristics. Only then is it possible to accept the idea that, economically speaking, production is an instantaneous process by which current output is given its numerical form and becomes the object of the bank deposits formed through the payment of wages. As noticed by Keynes, national income is the definition of national output and, therefore, of total supply. For any given period, production is determined at the very moment wages are paid. At the same instant the money income thus formed is available as a bank deposit. Then, banks being forced by double-entry bookkeeping to lend their deposits, money income is also necessarily subjected to an equivalent demand as soon as it is formed. It thus follows that, instead of being represented by a curve, LM is reduced to a point for any level of realised income.

About IS–LM

Thanks to what we have found about the nature of IS and LM, it is now easy to see that Hicks's diagram has nothing to do with the actual working of a monetary economy. Once IS and LM are properly understood, it becomes evident that they cannot be represented by two intersecting curves. Neither IS nor LM is a function of the kind assumed by Hicks. Once the production of a given period has actually taken place, LM may be represented by a single point, while IS is still numerically undetermined. At the moment income is finally spent, LM is again nothing more than a single point, and so is IS, the amount of macroeconomic saving being fully determined and necessarily equal to investment. In no circumstances is it possible, therefore, to verify the neoclassical and Keynesian claim that the equilibrium level of income is determined, together with the equilibrium level of interest rates, at the intersection between IS and LM.

It is worth observing here that Hicks himself provides the elements for a substantial criticism to his IS–LM diagram. In his 1980 article, in fact, he refers to the distinction between stocks and flows, claiming that while the IS curve is a flow relation, the LM curve 'is, or should be, a stock relation' (Hicks, 1980–81/1982, p. 329). In the same paragraph he states that the distinction between the two categories 'is a question of time reference' (ibid., p. 329). Thus, IS is defined as a flow relation because it 'must refer to a period' (ibid., p. 329), whereas LM is defined as a stock relation since it refers 'to a point of time, not to a period' (ibid., p. 329). But, if this is indeed the case, how can one still maintain that IS and LM can be part of the same diagram? If IS relates to a finite period of time whereas LM is verified at a point in time, the two do not pertain to the same category of events and to the same temporal framework. Unfortunately, Hicks did not develop his analysis far enough to reach the logical conclusion that IS and LM are autonomously determined and, therefore, functionally unrelated magnitudes. This would have been possible only if he had foreseen that production is an instantaneous event. As shown by Schmitt, this implies that the whole period of chronological time during which physical production actually takes place is 'emitted' as a 'quantum of time' at the moment physical output is given its numerical form. Through the payment of wages output is issued as a quantum: 'It [economic output] is neither physical matter nor materialised labour: it is a quantum of time' (Schmitt, 1984, p. 94; our translation).

This implies that LM refers to quantum time whereas IS is supposed to define an adjustment taking place in chronological time. The conclusion is thus unavoidable: IS and LM belong to two different time frames and can therefore never be gathered together in the same diagram.

> From the moment analysis is able to take time into consideration, it [the analysis] becomes aware of a 'devastating' truth: magnitudes L and M are defined in quantum time; on the contrary, variables I and S pertain to continuous time. The intersection of the two representative curves, on which professors have relentlessly and mercilessly drawn the attention of generations of students, is thus a pure figment of one's imagination (ibid., p. 568; our translation).

CONCLUSION

It is possible, as maintained by Young (1987, p. 178), that Keynes was ambivalent or rather 'agnostic, preferring not to reject specifically the variant interpretations of his *General Theory* – made by the members of his General Theory group and others, such as Hicks, Champernowne, Reddaway and Kaldor – in order to get, as he put it in his 1937 *Quarterly Journal of Economics* paper, his "simple fundamental" and "basic ideas" across'.

Anyway, far from helping the understanding of his fundamental and basic ideas, the IS–LM interpretation of his theory reinforced the belief that general equilibrium could naturally represent the general analytical framework for all of economic analysis, from monetarism to Keynesianism.

As a matter of fact, Keynes was constantly put under pressure by his fellow economists, who tirelessly tried to convince him that his theory could safely be reinterpreted along more orthodox lines. He resisted this temptation only partially, perhaps because he saw it as a necessary sacrifice towards having his new ideas accepted. Unfortunately, he was wrong. The neoclassical interpretation became the most widely accepted one and the novelty of his message was almost entirely lost. In this respect, therefore, it seems justified to share Skidelsky's claim that 'Hicks emptied the *General Theory* of its real bite, he generalized and increased its acceptability, whilst laying the basis for the neoclassical synthesis. . . . I do not think it captured the essence of what Keynes was trying to say' (Skidelsky, in Snowdon, Vane and Wynarczyk, 1994, p. 84).

In this chapter we have attempted to show that Hicks's interpretation suffers from a logical inconsistency deriving from the very nature of the IS and LM relationships. This has given us the opportunity to discuss the meaning of Keynes's identity between saving and investment, and to defend it against the neoclassical attempt to transform it into a condition of equilibrium. It is a fact that even today economists are not unanimous as to the analysis of S and I. Yet, it is also difficult to deny that hardly anybody is prepared to take over Keynes's identities in order to show that, far from being nominal tautologies, they are the building blocks of modern macroeconomics. Even the most faithful followers of Keynes accept the idea that I and S are equal only at equilibrium, unaware that, in so doing, they are advocating a neoclassical interpretation of Keynes's theory. The analysis of the debate between Keynes, Robertson, Ohlin and Hicks shows how difficult it was for Keynes to get his message across. Things are not radically changed today, even though the development of banking has laid down the basis for a new understanding of Keynes's monetary theory of production. It is precisely through a rigorous analysis of bank money and production that it is possible to derive a monetary macroeconomic theory encompassing that of Keynes. By referring to this theory – built up by Bernard Schmitt in the last fifty years – we have shown that the LM relationship is of a very peculiar nature and cannot be represented by a curve made up of an infinite series of money equilibrium points. In particular, if LM is meant to define the equilibrium points between the supply of and demand for money income and not simply of nominal, valueless money, it is logically impossible to consider it as a function of income, the rate of interest and time. This is so for at least two reasons. Firstly, because – as claimed by Keynes – current national income defines current total supply and is always necessarily equal to total demand, whatever the level of income itself and of the interest rate. Secondly, because income results from production and production is not a function of time. In economics, production is a process by which current physical output is given its numerical, social form. This is the very reason why the theory of production has to be 'monetary'. And, since every payment is an instantaneous event, production itself is instantaneous.

Finally, Hicks's neoclassical representation pertains to an imaginary world where money plays no essential role and where it is assumed that real magnitudes are determined through a system of simultaneous equations reproducing as best they can the infinite multiplicity of the actual world. Keynes's attempt to reinstate economics as an autonomous and specific science distinct from mathematics and from the other social sciences was jeopardised by this predominant microeconomic approach. Most economists missed the originality of his monetary analysis and none of them truly believed in the possibility of doing away with the concept of equilibrium. Today, Schmitt's new, quantum theoretical approach provides the elements for an irrefutable vindication of Keynes's intuitions. Emphasis is placed again on the monetary aspect of production and circulation, and conventional functional relationships are replaced by conceptual identities. The final rejection of Hicks's IS–LM model depends upon the understanding of this quantum-theoretical approach to monetary economics. Let us hope economists will not miss its importance and that Hicks's diagram will soon be deemed an unfortunate accident in the history of economic analysis.

REFERENCES

Böhm-Bawerk, E. (1959), *Capital and Interest*, South Holland: Libertarian Press, 3 vols.

Cencini, A. (1984), *Time and the Macroeconomic Analysis of Income*, London and New York: Pinter Publishers and St. Martin's Press.

Cencini, A. (2001), *Monetary Macroeconomics: A New Approach*, London and New York: Routledge.

Clower, R.W. (ed.) (1969), *Monetary Theory: Selected Readings*, Harmondsworth: Penguin.

Hansen, A. (1949), *Monetary Theory and Fiscal Policy*, New York: McGraw-Hill.

Hicks, J.R. (1937/1982), 'Mr. Keynes and the "classics": a suggested interpretation', in *Money, Interest and Wages: Collected Essays on Economic Theory*, Oxford: Basil Blackwell, vol. II, 100–15.

Hicks, J.R. (1980–81/1982), 'IS–LM: an explanation', in *Money, Interest and Wages: Collected Essays on Economic Theory*, Oxford: Basil Blackwell, vol. II, 318–31.

Howitt, P.W. (1992), 'Macroeconomics: relations with microeconomics' in P. Newman, M. Milgate and J. Eatwell (eds), *The New Palgrave Dictionary of Money & Finance*, London and Basingstoke: Macmillan, vol. II, 632–5.

Kahn, R. (1984), *The Making of Keynes's General Theory*, Cambridge: Cambridge University Press.

Keynes, J.M. (1936/1973a), *The General Theory of Employment, Interest and Money*, London: Macmillan. Reprinted in *The Collected Writings of John Maynard Keynes*, Vol. VII, London and Basingstoke: Macmillan.

Keynes, J.M. (1973b), *The Collected Writings of John Maynard Keynes*, Vol. XIV *The General Theory and After: Part II Defence and Development*, London and Basingstoke: Macmillan.

Leijonhufvud, A. (1967), 'Keynes and the Keynesians: a suggested interpretation', *American Economic Review*, **57** (2), 401–10. Reprinted in R.W. Clower (ed.) (1969), *Monetary Theory: Selected Readings*, Harmondsworth: Penguin, 298–310.

Leijonhufvud, A. (1984), 'Hicks on time and money', *Oxford Economic Papers*, **36** (supplement), 26–46.

Modigliani, F. (1944), 'Liquidity preference and the theory of interest and money', *Econometrica*, **12** (1), 45–88.

Ohlin, B. (1937), 'Some notes on the Stockholm theory of savings and investment', *Economic Journal*, **47** (185), 53–69.

Pasinetti, L.L. (1974), *Growth and Income Distribution*, Cambridge: Cambridge University Press.

Pasinetti, L.L. (1983), 'Comment on Leijonhufvud' in D. Worswick and J. Trevithick (eds), *Keynes and the Modern World*, Cambridge: Cambridge University Press, 205–11.

Patinkin, D. (1990a), 'In defense of IS–LM', *Banca Nazionale del Lavoro Quarterly Review*, **43** (172), 119–34.

Patinkin, D. (1990b), 'On different interpretations of the *General Theory*', *Journal of Monetary Economics*, **26** (2), 205–43.

Robertson, D. (1933), 'Saving and hoarding', *Economic Journal*, **43** (171), 399–413.

Schmitt, B. (1984), *Inflation, chômage et malformations du capital*, Paris and Albeuve: Economica and Castella.

Schmitt, B. and C. De Gottardi (2002), 'An internal critique of general equilibrium theory', in this volume.

Snowdon, B., H.R. Vane and P. Wynarczyk (eds) (1994), *A Modern Guide to Macroeconomics*, Aldershot and Brookfield: Edward Elgar.

Solow, R.M. (1984), 'Mr. Hicks and the classics', *Oxford Economic Papers*, **36** (supplement), 13–25.

Vane, H.R. and J.L. Thompson (1992), *Current Controversies in Macroeconomics*, Aldershot and Brookfield: Edward Elgar.

Vercelli, A. (1991), *Methodological Foundations of Macroeconomics: Keynes and Lucas*, Cambridge: Cambridge University Press.

Young, W. (1987), *Interpreting Mr. Keynes: The IS–LM Enigma*, Cambridge: Polity Press.

Worswick, D. and J. Trevithick (eds) (1983), *Keynes and the Modern World*, Cambridge: Cambridge University Press.

15. Circuit Theory as an Explanation of the Complex Real World

Claude Gnos[1]

INTRODUCTION

The theory of the monetary circuit as developed over the last three decades by French and Italian writers – most notably Alain Barrère (1973), Bernard Schmitt (1966, 1975, 1984), Alain Parguez (1975) and Augusto Graziani (1990, 1996) – is gaining audience among post Keynesians. *Money in Motion* edited by Deleplace and Nell (1996) has provided evidence of this growing audience, which undoubtedly derives from the extensive reference circuitists make to Keynes's heterodoxy, a feature that they share with post Keynesians. Actually, in the words of Arestis (1996, p. 113), the circuit school is recognised as being 'a strong component of the endogenous money thesis'.[2] However, a number of obstacles stand in the way of any widening of this audience, including the question of the epistemological status of the model of the monetary circuit.

In light of Davidson's pioneering work *Money and the Real World*, post Keynesians are habitually vigilant about the realism of economic theories.[3] By contrast, the monetary circuit may appear an oversimplified and rather abstract model. For instance, Arestis and Howells (1999) observe that the emphasis circuit theory places on the role of firms in the expansion of bank loans and deposits (when firms ask banks for credit to meet their production costs until they can recoup money from sales) is not consistent with reality.

> [T]he greater part of loan demand in the UK depends upon the decisions of households rather than firms. . . . [D]emand then depends upon whatever it is that drives households' demand for credit and this is unlikely to be costs of production (Arestis and Howells, 1999, p. 117).

Victoria Chick (2000, p. 132) even suspects circuitists of departing from actual facts in order to refine the formal structure of their model. They supposedly adopt an 'extreme position, in the interest of having clear-cut macroeconomic aggregates, in which firms are borrowers from banks and households are deposit-takers' (ibid., p. 132).

The purpose of this chapter is to show that these harsh judgments rely primarily on misunderstandings that, fortunately, can be cleared up. With reference to Keynes, Kaldor and Lawson, Arestis writes that '[t]he task of a social science is the elaboration of the deep structures and relations which underpin social phenomena' (Arestis, 1996, p. 116). I shall try to show that this is precisely the goal of the circuit school: the emphasis placed on firms as bank-borrowers and on households as deposit-takers is not some arbitrary device or a priori assumption; it derives from the deep structures and relations underpinning modern economies. To make my point, I shall compare the way circuit theory depicts relationships between banks, firms and households with the diversity of observable relationships and practices. The objective is to show that the latter are 'surface phenomena' complying with the deep structure and the causal factors established by the former.

The next section focuses on the financing of firms' and households' expenditure. In the third section we address another aspect of the question under examination: the emphasis placed by circuitists on the flux and reflux of money wages faced with the actual diversity of firms' expenses and the formation of profits. The last section concludes.

THE FINANCING OF FIRMS' AND HOUSEHOLDS' EXPENDITURE

The monetary circuit, in its modern Franco–Italian version,[4] is defined with reference both to Keynes's principle of effective demand and finance motive. Endorsing Keynes's principle of effective demand, circuitists highlight the role of entrepreneurs who decide on the level of firms' activity (and hence on the amount of employment) as a function of their expected proceeds from sales and of their expected costs. It is true that, contrary to post Keynesians, circuitists have not developed an extensive analysis of the context of uncertainty in which entrepreneurs make their decisions. But this is essentially a difference of focus between the two schools, not an incompatibility (see Fontana, 2000). With reference to the finance motive, circuitists notably stress the role of bank credit in financing production costs, and so the role of the production process in the expansion of bank credit and money creation.

The model singles out the payment of factor costs (more specifically the payment of wages as stressed in the third section of this chapter) by firms, considering that this payment in itself forms the net incomes in the economy as a whole. Then, it is argued, when recipients spend their incomes, firms are paid back and money incomes are cancelled. The very concept of the monetary circuit refers to these successive outlays and receipts met by firms and the resulting formation and cancellation of money incomes.

Notice that a number of circuitists, notably Parguez and Seccareccia (2000), consider that firms' outlays and receipts involve the circulation of money units in the form of bank liabilities from firms to households and then back from households to firms. These authors argue that in response to firms' demand for credit banks issue 'debts upon themselves' (that is, bank deposits), which act as a counterpart to the services sold by households (and bought by firms) and then to the goods sold by firms (and bought by households). With reference to bookkeeping and the double-entry method, Schmitt (1984, 1996) analyses more closely the way bank money intervenes in the circuit.[5] He observes that, strictly speaking, banks do not issue deposits that they supposedly lend to firms. On the contrary, deposits are the effect of loans (as the saying goes, 'loans make deposits'). This is so because, when creating money, banks debit and credit accounts with purely numerical units of money. This distinction is not merely semantic. Being made of purely numerical units, bank money cannot be the actual object or content of households' income. Households are essentially paid in real goods and services just as they would be in a non-monetary economy. This is obviously the case since firms will have to sell goods to them in order to repay bank loans. Nonetheless, households do not obtain goods physically at the very moment they are paid in money units. This means that they save their income in the form of bank deposits until they spend it on buying goods in the market. This confirms then that, contrary to what casual observation may suggest, bank deposits do not constitute the money in the form of which households receive their income but an asset in the form of which they save it (at least temporarily). Just as Keynes (1937a/1973, 1937b/1973) pointed out in his presentation of the 'finance motive', the payment of factor cost by firms defines an investment generating an equivalent saving. Circuit theory is consistent also with Keynes's analysis in the *General Theory* (1936/1973, pp. 81–5) whereby deposits are a source of funding for banks matching the credits that banks grant to borrowers. As a matter of fact, so long as depositors save their income, they postpone their purchase and consumption of the goods and services that are the objects of the production processes initiated by firms: depositors are the actual creditors of borrowers (firms) through banks.[6]

Let us now consider the supposedly excessive emphasis that circuitists place on the role of the payment of factor costs by firms in the expansion of bank loans and so in the expansion of bank deposits.

To examine this point, we need to look closely at the economic operations that banks finance. When a bank extends credit to a firm for the purpose of financing its factor costs, this credit is backed by goods in the making and that the firm will later sell to income recipients (in accordance with the analysis of money creation outlined above). Hence the sale of the goods produced will allow the firm to recoup its outlay and thereby to pay back its bank loans. When banks meet demand for credit from households for the purpose of buying produced goods, the situation is fundamentally different. In this case the credit granted is backed by income that the borrower will earn in the future and will have to part with in order to pay back the bank loan. At the present time, the borrower spends someone else's income, even when banks create additional money instead of drawing from pre-existent deposits. This is so because the present money income that the borrower spends is not simply composed of the money units he is credited with by banks but is defined with reference to produced goods (see above and also Rossi, this volume). So long as income recipients hold bank deposits, they save their income and any additional money creation for the benefit of consumers amounts de facto to lending the saved income to the borrower.

To check this argument, let us consider the way the transactions we have just referred to are currently recorded in banks' balance sheets.

Table 15.1. Loans and deposits resulting from the payment of factor cost financed by money creation

		Banks	
Assets			Liabilities
Loans to firms	£w	Deposits of households H1	£w

Table 15.1 depicts the effect of the payment of factor cost (£w) by firms for the benefit of households H1. Firms are assumed to have been granted credit financed by money creation by banks to pay for factor costs. As stated above, this credit is backed by goods in the making that firms will later sell to income recipients. Symmetrically, these same goods form the real content of households' income that is saved in the form of bank deposits.

Let us assume that households H1 do not spend their entire income in the current period but keep holding bank deposits (£y=w–x). Goods are sold to H1 for £x, and firms are able to refund banks for this same amount;[7] firms remain indebted to banks for £y=w–x. We then have the situation shown in Table 15.2.

Table 15.2. The effect of households' purchases financed out of income

Banks

Assets		Liabilities
Loans to firms	£y=w–x	Deposits of households H1 £y=w–x

Suppose now that households H2 ask banks for credit in order to finance purchases of produced goods. Then, in proportion as households H2 spend the borrowed money (£z) in purchasing goods, firms are paid back and can refund their bank loans. Ultimately, the situation is shown in Table 15.3.

Table 15.3. The effect of households' purchases financed by money creation

Banks

Assets		Liabilities	
Loans to firms	£y–z	Deposits of households H1	£y
Loans to households H2	£z		

Table 15.3 confirms my argument. When banks create money in response to a demand for credit from households, the operation amounts to superposing financial transactions among households on the process of income creation and cancellation that ties firms and households. Here, a part of the deposits held by households H1 covers equivalent loans (£z) to households H2: the latter have borrowed (though implicitly, through banks) and spent the income saved by the former: they have bought produced goods in their place. All in all, although banks grant credit to households as well as to firms, money creation has different effects in both cases. The money created for the payment of factor costs forms the income of households, whilst the money created for the benefit of households enables financial transactions (be they implicit) among households the object of which is this same income. So, the relation tying financial transactions among households to income links the credit granted to households to the credit granted to firms

for paying factor costs. This is why circuitists may credit firms with a leading role in the expansion of bank loans and deposits despite the fact that most bank credit (and money creation) does not go towards financing production. Further, it should be noted that the proportion between bank loans granted to consumers and bank loans granted to firms may be all the greater, in practice, because firms do not systematically have recourse to bank loans in order to finance factor costs. This is another aspect of the financing of firms' outlays that we will now consider.

In fact, firms often use pre-existing cash to finance their factor costs. Does this not run counter to the model of the circuit, which emphasises the role of banks, and behind banks the role of depositors, in financing factor costs?

To examine this point, let us consider banks' balance sheets anew. This time round, starting with the situation depicted in Table 15.1, consider firms F1, which have made profits that they currently hold in the form of bank deposits (£p). Below I shall explain that profits are wages transferred from households to firms; so, firms literally take the place of households on the liabilities side of banks' balance sheets. Let us call F2 the firms that have produced the goods that profits allow firms F1 to buy (these goods are the real side of profits). Firms F2 have paid £p for the factor costs of these goods by means of bank loans: they figure on the assets side. For simplicity, we assume that the current output (worth £w as measured by its factor cost) is made up of the goods produced and sold (at a profit) by F1 and the goods still unsold by F2. So, households' deposits and loans to firms have been cancelled up to £w–p.

Table 15.4. Firms holding deposits as a consequence of the formation of profits

Banks	
Assets	Liabilities
Loans to firms F2* £p	Deposits of firms F1 (profits) £p

Note
* These loans are granted for the payment of factor costs of the goods constituting the real side of profits.

Starting from the situation depicted in Table 15.4, let us suppose that instead of spending their profits on the purchase of the produced goods still available, firms F1 spend them in financing new output (up to £p). The new situation is shown in Table 15.5.

Table 15.5. The effect of spending profits in financing new output

Banks

Assets		Liabilities
Loans to firms F2 (unchanged) £p	Deposits of households[*]	£p

Note
[*] Deposits earned in the production of the new output by F1.

The loans to firms F2 on the assets side correspond to output that these firms have not yet sold since profits were not spent on buying goods, just as stated above. The deposits of households correspond to the newly produced goods (they were paid for producing them). By using their profits to pay factor costs for these newly produced goods, firms F1 did not need to raise new loans from banks. Suppose now that the latter goods are sold to households. What happens? We are back to the position shown in Table 15.4: firms F1 recoup their deposits, that is, their profits. This means that during the period from the payment of wages out of profits to the sale of the newly produced goods, profits were not actually spent but literally immobilised by firms F1, which abandoned (at least temporarily) the idea of spending them on goods. Profits were converted from liquid into illiquid assets (although not materialised since firms do not sell bonds to themselves). Of course, factor costs were paid out of pre-existent deposits but households obtained money, the purchasing power of which derived entirely from the newly produced goods. This confirms the validity of the circuit scheme. Although banks do not necessarily finance factor costs from scratch, they nonetheless credit households with money, the purchasing power of which is not transferred from the deposits held by firms. Households receive and save newly formed income. A new circuit is thus initiated. Put simply, the way firms F1 paid for factor costs only exempted them from increasing their bank borrowings. To analyse this situation further, let us now refer specifically to Keynes's finance motive.

Keynes insisted that firms have to secure finance when they decide to start production. Such finance may be provided by banks (which notably grant overdraft facilities) or also by the market (Keynes, 1937a/1973, pp. 208–9). In the latter case, firms borrow money from the general public, which saves part of its income in the form of bank deposits. So, pre-existent bank deposits are used just as in the case of the payment of factor costs by means of profits examined above;[8] the only difference here is that firms explicitly issue claims so as to avail themselves of finance. Keynes argued that such finance, which takes the form of an 'advance provision of cash' (ibid., p. 208), does not exhaust any pre-existent savings but, as soon as it is actually spent (invested) on a new production, on the contrary, generates new net saving attached to the new net investment (ibid., p. 209). In this way, Keynes confirmed that the payment of factor costs generates incomes that are not transferred from pre-existent deposits, although the money necessary for making this payment had been borrowed from pre-existent deposits. To account for this puzzling situation, Keynes distinguished between credit in the sense of 'finance' and credit in the sense of 'saving'. Credit in the sense of finance is, from the viewpoint of entrepreneurs, a 'demand for liquid cash in exchange for a deferred claim' (ibid., p. 210). This means that deposit holders convert their cash into illiquid assets (as already stated above with reference to firms holding profits). Credit in the sense of saving corresponds to the fact that income, being paid in money, is necessarily deposited with banks (even bank notes represent deposits with the issuing central bank) and hence defines a credit granted by depositors to banks. The question, then, is to determine who ultimately benefits from this credit. When banks create money in response to demand for credit from firms, the answer is clear enough: firms are the recipients. When firms use pre-existent cash the answer is less obvious since firms do not then borrow money from banks. Nonetheless, the answer is unchanged. We have seen already that book entries in banks' balance sheets have to be interpreted with reference to the economic operations involved. So long as income recipients do not spend their money on goods, they do not exercise its purchasing power. This means that firms have in hand the goods that are in the making or stocked in their stores until these goods are sold: saving by income recipients conditions firms' investment. Therefore, firms actually benefit from credit granted by income recipients, although the operation is not completely accounted for in banks' balance sheets (firms have not become explicitly indebted to banks). The circuit scheme is not impeded; on the contrary: depositing their money incomes with banks, households de facto extend credit to firms through banks.

THE FLUX AND REFLUX OF WAGES FACED WITH THE DIVERSITY OF FIRMS' EXPENSES AND THE FORMATION OF PROFITS

The theory of the monetary circuit gives a pre-eminent role to the flux and reflux of money wages (as considered with reference to firms' outlays and receipts). A priori, this is also a questionable feature. A first issue relates to the flux. In reality, firms pay not only for wages but also for capital goods they use in the production process. Moreover, it may be argued that capital goods constitute an original factor of production for which firms pay interest, with the latter being an income supplementary to wages in the economy as a whole. A second issue relates to the reflux and the formation of profits: how would firms be able to make profits from the sale of the goods produced if they injected only wages into the economy?

Let us consider the flux first. In producing goods or services, firms incur various charges: they purchase output from other firms and also pay factor costs. Certainly, in practice, this expenditure may be financed in a number of ways. To finance plant and equipment, firms generally prefer to use cash raised by the issue of long-term bonds and equities, and to plough back part of their profits. To finance the purchase of unfinished goods and raw materials, and the payment of factor costs, they resort by preference to bank loans and also to their own cash balances (if any); they may also raise funds on the money market. Regardless of these usages and practices, circuit theory strictly divides the payment of wages and the purchase of manufactured goods into two separate categories. The former generates incomes whilst the latter spends incomes. Is circuit theory right to do so?

We have already partially answered the question under examination in the previous section when checking (in accordance with Keynes's analysis of the finance motive) that although firms may use pre-existent cash to pay for wages, they do not actually spend pre-existent incomes in doing so. New incomes are then formed in the economy. As for the firms' purchases of manufactured goods by means of newly created bank money, this is similar to the purchase of manufactured goods by households who spend newly created money borrowed from banks: they actually spend part of the current income. To check this last point, let us consider anew banks' balance sheets (Table 15.6). With reference to the situation depicted in Table 15.1, we assume that the current output (as measured by factor cost, £w) is bought partly by households (£x) and partly by a number of firms, F1, which borrow £y from banks to that end. Since, in this case, firms (including firms F1) sell their entire output (w=x+y), they recoup in full the money spent to pay for factor costs and may repay the corresponding bank loans. Then the situation is as follows. Firms F1 remain indebted to banks for £y (they borrowed £y to buy goods) whereas households are the banks' creditors for the same amount (they save £y). Current income has been spent and households are creditors of firms through banks. In other words, households' savings have been lent to those firms (F1) buying manufactured goods with newly created money borrowed from banks.

Table 15.6. The effect of firms' purchases of manufactured goods financed by money creation

	Banks		
Assets			Liabilities
Loans to firms F1[a]	£y	Deposits of households[b]	£y

Notes
[a] Loans granted for purchases of manufactured goods.
[b] Deposits formed in the current production.

It is true that households had been already creditors of firms through banks as soon as wages were paid; but, now, since the produced goods have been sold, the loans are backed not by goods but by incomes (profits) firms F1 will earn in the future. When these firms will have earned profits, they will be able to repay banks, and households' deposits will again correspond to loans made to firms backed by produced goods (which are the real side of F1's profits). The whole process may be described step by step in the following banks' balance sheets. In Table 15.7 (similar to Table 15.4 above) firms F1 that make profits in a new period of time take the place of households for £p whilst simultaneously firms F2 figure on the assets side as borrowers for the same amount of money (£p is the factor cost of the manufactured goods constituting the real side of profits and produced by firms F2 in the new period). Then (Table 15.8), firms F1 repay the £y borrowed from banks so that £y is deducted from their profits deposited with banks. Therefore, households' deposits (£y) are again covered by equivalent goods for the production of which firms F2 paid £y as factor costs. Firms F1 purchased in place of households goods that constituted the real side of wages paid in the previous period; they now make up for them with goods constituting the real side of their profits.

Table 15.7. Firms holding deposits as a consequence of the formation of profits in a new period

	Banks	
Assets		**Liabilities**
Loans to firms F2*	£p	Deposits of firms F1 (profits) £p

Note
* Loans granted for the payment of factor costs of the goods constituting the real side of profits.

Table 15.8. The effect of the reimbursement of bank loans previously contracted to finance firms' purchases of manufactured goods

	Banks	
Assets		**Liabilities**
Loans to firms F2[a]	£p	Deposits of households[b] £y
		Deposits of firms F1 (profits) £p–y

Note
[a] Loans granted for the payment of factor costs of the goods constituting the real side of profits.
[b] Deposits formed in the previous period.

What the analysis confirms here is that despite the diversity of actual practices, the circuit scheme remains adequate. When starting production, firms purchase manufactured goods and pay factor costs as well. As compared with this diversity of expenditure met simultaneously by firms, the circuit scheme is not a simplified model though. The reality is that the start of production entails the superposition of different phases of the circuit (and so different individual circuits). When buying manufactured goods, firms spend pre-existing incomes (even when they spend newly created money). This spending is part of the reflux phase of a circuit previously initiated. Simultaneously, the payment of wages initiates a new circuit.

The next issue relates to the definition of factor costs. Do factor costs simply come down to wages, as argued by circuitists, or should they also include interest that is currently paid for capital? This is a time-honoured issue in economics that circuit theory allows us to clarify. As stated above, the expenses met by firms starting production fall into two separate categories. On the one hand, firms pay for labour, which is in no way a manufactured good. Therefore, the payment of wages does not exhaust any pre-existent incomes that might be lent by their recipients to firms; on the contrary, this payment forms households' income. On the other hand, firms purchase capital goods, which are outputs of industry. So, as stated above, they conduct financial transactions; they exchange current income, which they spend on capital goods, against income they will make over to lenders in the future. This latter income will have to repay the initial loan and pay interest proportional to the time elapsed. Where will it come from? Firms' income is profit, derived from sales in the market where it is made at the expense of buyers. Therefore, although interest is usually predetermined when firms borrow money, it is of the same nature as dividends paid to shareholders out of profits. It does not constitute an original factor cost similar to wages: the payment of interest does not form an income supplementary to wages in the economy as a whole. Here again, circuit theory is consistent with Keynes's analysis regarding labour 'as the sole factor of production, operating in a given environment of technique, natural resources, capital equipment and effective demand' (Keynes, 1936/1973, pp. 213–14).

Let us now precisely consider the formation of profits. According to circuit theory, the payment of wages generates the income that households will spend on goods. At that point, wages are repaid to firms; there is no additional money with which to pay profits to firms, that is, proceeds in excess of factor costs. A number of writers opt for a solution proposed by Kalecki and put in a nutshell by Joan Robinson (1964, p. 9): 'Workers spend what they get; capitalists get what they spend'. But this solution raises a difficulty: firms cannot pay profits to themselves. To overcome the difficulty, it has been suggested that individual firms simply anticipate the formation of their profits (for a detailed presentation of this solution see Renaud, 2000). Anticipating profits, a number of firms, let us call them F1, will borrow money from banks and buy goods (capital goods in all likelihood) from other firms, F2 (F1 and F2 may as well stand for two sectors of production), repaying the factor costs of the goods they buy and paying firms F2's profits in addition. So, firms F1 sell (at a price including profit plus factor cost) the goods they have produced to households and to firms F2, with the latter spending the profits they have made. Then firms F1 are able to pay back to banks the money that they borrowed to spend their profits in advance; ultimately, their profits consist of the goods they have bought with the borrowed money. Unfortunately, the question cannot be settled in this way. One can rightly suppose that firms borrow money from banks and spend in advance the profits they expect to make. But this is not sufficient to solve the problem under discussion: being anticipated, the formation of profits is not explained but presupposed. How can we sort things out?

In the history of economic thought, two competing explanations have been suggested. On one view, profits have been considered as a part of current output, surplus to the goods consumed by workers (this is notably what the Marxian theory of surplus value claims). Then, profits are real and the question of their monetary 'realisation' is secondary. In this framework, Marx had already suggested that capitalists get the money that they spend. On the other view, profits have been considered as the result of a transfer of income from consumers to firms, occurring when prices exceed factor cost. This approach was initiated by James Steuart, an eighteenth century writer, who promoted the notion of 'profit upon alienation'.[9] This was also Keynes's approach in formulating the principle of effective demand by which 'entrepreneurs will endeavour to fix the amount of employment at the level which they expect to maximise the excess of the proceeds over the factor cost' (Keynes, 1936/1973, p. 25).[10] The theory of the monetary circuit is consistent with this latter approach. If firms sell the goods produced at a price that just pays back factor cost, they make no profit. As soon as they sell goods at a price exceeding the factor cost, they earn a profit. But, in this case, neither the existence of a surplus in output nor in the money available in the economy needs to be presupposed. Firms clearly benefit from a transfer from buyers that is both nominal and real. As mentioned in the previous section, firms literally take the place of wage-earners on the liabilities side of banks' balance sheets (see Table 15.4) and then spend the corresponding income in their place. So, profits, nominal and real, are included in the circuit of money wages. There is no need then to look for any additional quantity of money. That many circuitists appear to be preoccupied by this last question is probably to be explained by the fact that they roughly consider aggregates: how could wages amounting in the current period to £w pay for £w+p, where p stands for profits? But this is not the right way to analyse the situation, even if we consider the economy as a whole. Adopting a macroeconomic view does not exempt theorists from considering the real world: whatever the period of time we consider (be it, for example, a month or a year) firms again and again pay wages and sell goods, production processes overlapping one another, so that firms have no difficulty gaining profits out of wages provided buyers are prepared to purchase goods at prices exceeding factor costs. So, we have a confirmation that the existence of profits does not run counter to the basic scheme. Note that profits are partially re-allocated among firms. This is the case when firms F1, in the example given in the previous section, buy goods sold by firms F2 at a price exceeding their factor costs: firms F2's profits are paid by firms F1 out of their own profits earned at the expense of households. Note also that although profits are gained from sales firms can spend them in advance thanks to bank loans. We may surmise also that the additional money created will help raising prices and so allow firms (as a whole) to make greater profits. But, as shown above in the case of households asking for credit, the spending of incomes in advance amounts to superposing financial transactions on the process of income creation and spending encapsulated in the circuit; it does not condition the formation of incomes.

CONCLUSION

A priori, the circuit scheme, which singles out the payment of wages by firms (which borrow from banks to that end) and then the spending of wages by households, may appear an oversimplified and abstract model if set against the complexity of the economic transactions in the real world. We have endeavoured here to show that, in fact, the many-sided financing of firms' and households' expenditure, the diversity of firms spending and even (in this respect) the formation of profits are surface phenomena consistent with the deep structure and the causal relationships constituting the circuit.

At the beginning of this chapter, we emphasised that the theory of the monetary circuit preferentially refers to Keynes's principle of effective demand and finance motive. Another reference, which this chapter makes obvious, is to Keynes's statement in his *Treatise on Money* that:

> Human effort and human consumption are the ultimate matters from which alone economic transactions are capable of deriving any significance; and all other forms of expenditure only acquire importance from their having some relationship, sooner or later, to the effort of producers or to the expenditure of consumers (Keynes, 1930/1971, pp. 120–1).

This confirms that circuit theory, which emphasises the formation of wages paying for human effort and their spending on consumption (savings sooner or later end in consumption), is consistent with Keynes's methodology[11] and, so, is undoubtedly destined to interact with the post Keynesian research project.

NOTES

1. Helpful comments by Per Gunnar Berglund, Louis-Philippe Rochon and Sergio Rossi are

gratefully acknowledged.
2. See also Rochon (1999a, 1999b).
3. 'Theories should be *relevant* in that they should represent reality as accurately as possible and should strive to explain the real world as observed empirically. Orthodox economic theory does not adhere to this basic premise, in that it is formalistic and makes inappropriate *a priori* assumptions. Post-Keynesian theory, by contrast, begins with observation and proceeds to build upon "realistic abstractions" rather than "imaginary models"' (Arestis, 1996, p. 116).
4. The concept of the circuit in economics can be traced back to the Physiocrats, a group of eighteenth-century French economists and political philosophers.
5. See also Cencini (1995) and Rossi (1997, 1998, 2001).
6. Among post Keynesians, Moore also insists on this point. According to him, depositors are bank creditors and 'ultimately the creditors of bank borrowers'; banks are thus 'simply one type of financial intermediary' (Moore, 1988, p. 20). By contrast, consistently with their own view, Parguez and Seccareccia (2000) deny that bank credit is financed by depositors.
7. In a recent article, Pressman (2000) denies that bank credit has to be reimbursed as soon as firms get the money back. He is right insofar as practice is concerned: firms may well roll over their existing debts to finance a new production. But, as Rochon (2001) puts it, '[this] makes little difference, and does not affect the core of the monetary circuit'.
8. Keynes also evoked the fact that the entrepreneur 'may be in a position to use his own resources' (Keynes, 1937a/1973, p. 217).
9. See Schumpeter (1954).
10. See Gnos (1998).
11. Remarkably enough, in his *Treatise on Money*, Keynes continued his story in proposing 'to break away from the traditional method of setting out from the total quantity of money irrespective of the purposes on which it is employed, and to start instead . . . with the flow of the community's earnings or money income, and with its twofold division (1) into the parts which have been *earned* by the production of consumption goods and of investment goods respectively, and (2) into that parts which are *expended* on consumption goods and on savings respectively' (Keynes, 1930/1971, p. 121).

REFERENCES

Arestis, P. (1996), 'Post-Keynesian economics: towards coherence', *Cambridge Journal of Economics*, **20** (1), 111–35.
Arestis, P. and P. Howells (1999), 'The supply of credit money and the demand for deposits: a reply', *Cambridge Journal of Economics*, **23** (1), 115–19.
Barrère, A. (1973), *Déséquilibres économiques et contre-révolution keynésienne*, Paris: Economica.
Cencini, A. (1995), *Monetary Theory, National and International*, London and New York: Routledge.
Chick, V. (2000), 'Money and effective demand', in J. Smithin (ed.), *What is Money?*, London and New York: Routledge, 124–38.
Deleplace, G. and E.J. Nell (eds) (1996), *Money in Motion: The Post Keynesian and Circulation Approaches*, London and New York: Macmillan and St. Martin's Press.
Fontana, G. (2000), 'Post Keynesians and Circuitists on money and uncertainty: an attempt at generality', *Journal of Post Keynesian Economics*, **23** (1), 27–48.
Gnos, C. (1998), 'The Keynesian identity of income and output', in A. Jolink and P.

Fontaine (eds), *Historical Perspectives on Macroeconomics: Sixty Years After the General Theory*, London and New York: Routledge, 40–8.

Graziani, A. (1990), 'The theory of the monetary circuit', *Économies et Sociétés* ('Série Monnaie et Production', 7), **24** (6), 7–36.

Graziani, A. (1996), 'Money as purchasing power and money as a stock of wealth in Keynesian economic thought', in G. Deleplace and E.J. Nell (eds), *Money in Motion: The Post Keynesian and Circulation Approaches*, London and New York: Macmillan and St. Martin's Press, 139–54.

Keynes, J.M. (1930/1971), *A Treatise on Money*, London: Macmillan. Reprinted in *The Collected Writings of John Maynard Keynes*, Vols V and VI, London and Basingstoke: Macmillan.

Keynes, J.M. (1936/1973), *The General Theory of Employment, Interest and Money*, London: Macmillan. Reprinted in *The Collected Writings of John Maynard Keynes*, Vol. VII, London and Basingstoke: Macmillan.

Keynes, J.M. (1937a/1973), 'Alternative theories of the rate of interest', *Economic Journal*, **47** (186), 241–52. Reprinted in *The Collected Writings of John Maynard Keynes*, Vol. XIV, London and Basingstoke: Macmillan, 201–15.

Keynes, J.M. (1937b/1973), 'The "ex ante" theory of the rate of interest', *Economic Journal*, **47** (188), 663–9. Reprinted in *The Collected Writings of John Maynard Keynes*, Vol. XIV, London and Basingstoke: Macmillan, 215–23.

Moore, B.J. (1988), *Horizontalists and Verticalists: The Macroeconomics of Credit Money*, Cambridge: Cambridge University Press.

Parguez, A. (1975), *Monnaie et macroéconomie*, Paris: Economica.

Parguez, A. and M. Seccareccia (2000), 'The credit theory of money: the monetary circuit approach', in J. Smithin (ed.), *What is Money?*, London and New York: Routledge, 101–23.

Pressman, S. (2000), 'A note on money and the circuit approach', *Journal of Economic Issues*, **34** (4), 969–73.

Renaud, J.-F. (2000), 'The problem of the monetary realization of profits in a Post Keynesian sequential financing model: two solutions of the Kaleckian option', *Review of Political Economy*, **12** (3), 285–303.

Robinson, J. (1964), *Studies in the Theory of Business Cycles*, Oxford: Basil Blackwell.

Rochon, L.-P. (1999a), 'The creation and circulation of endogenous money: a circuit dynamique approach', *Journal of Economic Issues*, **33** (1), 1–21.

Rochon, L.-P. (1999b), *Credit, Money and Production: An Alternative Post-Keynesian Approach*, Cheltenham and Northampton: Edward Elgar.

Rochon, L.-P. (2001), 'The Keynesian multiplier from the perspective of the theory of the monetary circuit', paper presented at the Eastern Economic Association Conference, New York.

Rossi, S. (1997), 'A book-keeping analysis of a monetary economy', in S.P. Dunn, G. Fontana, C. Forde, E. Jenkins, K. Petrick, A. Roy, G. Slater and D. Spencer (eds), *The Second Annual Postgraduate Economics Conference: Papers and Proceedings*, Leeds: Leeds University Press, 141–52.

Rossi, S. (1998), 'Endogenous money and banking activity: some notes on the workings of modern payment systems', *Studi economici*, **53** (3), 23–56.

Rossi, S. (2001), *Money and Inflation: A New Macroeconomic Analysis*, Cheltenham and Northampton: Edward Elgar.

Schmitt, B. (1966), *Monnaie, salaires et profits*, Paris: Presses Universitaires de France (also Albeuve: Castella, 1975).

Schmitt, B. (1975), *Théorie unitaire de la monnaie, nationale et internationale*, Albeuve: Castella.

Schmitt, B. (1984), *Inflation, chômage et malformations du capital*, Paris and Albeuve: Economica and Castella.

Schmitt, B. (1996), 'A new paradigm for the determination of money prices', in G. Deleplace and E.J. Nell (eds), *Money in Motion: The Post Keynesian and Circulation Approaches*, London and New York: Macmillan and St. Martin's Press, 105–38.

Schumpeter, J.A. (1954), *History of Economic Analysis*, New York: Oxford University Press.

16. Money and Banking in a Monetary Theory of Production

Sergio Rossi[1]

INTRODUCTION

Ever since Cannan's (1921) famous article, the nature of bank deposits has been puzzling a number of scholars who have explored the characteristics of modern money (see, for example, Keynes, 1930/1971; Lerner, 1947; Schneider, 1952/1962; Schumpeter, 1970). More recently, this issue has regained interest within academic circles on account of the ongoing research programme aiming to forge ahead Keynes's (1933/1973) monetary theory of production. In this respect, over the past decade or so the two most active fringes of monetary economists have been post Keynesians (see, for instance, Davidson, 1990; Arestis and Howells, 1996, 1999; Chick, 2000) and circuitists (see for example Graziani, 1990, 1994; Lavoie, 1994, 1999; Parguez and Seccareccia, 2000).[2] Deleplace and Nell (1996) have provided an open confrontation between these two strands of thought, which share a number of principles of monetary economics although their emphasis on the functions of money is different. In fact, as clearly summarised by Fontana, 'Post Keynesians in general have emphasized that money is a liquid store of wealth held by agents to provide an escape route from an uncertain future. . . . Circuitists have stressed that in modern economies money serves as the means of payment' (Fontana, 2000, p. 44).

Now, as Fontana cogently argues, 'there is an urgent need to build a more general monetary theory that allows for money being store of wealth and means of payment' (ibid., p. 45). This is what this chapter intends to do. More precisely, in an attempt to build a bridge between the liquid store of wealth and the means of payment conceptions of money, this chapter suggests that Smith's (1776/1970) famous distinction between money proper and money's worth[3] may be useful in order to disentangle, at the conceptual level, the two principal functions that the thing called 'money' carries out

339

within a modern production economy. To put it differently, building on a distinction between monetary flows and stocks that gets rid of all physical conceptions of the money creation process (see Gnos, 1999),[4] this chapter concentrates on the two important functions of modern banking, namely the emission of money as such and the transfer of money balances between economic agents. It is argued that despite the advances in the theory of endogenous money, as well as the persevering attempts to carry on Keynes's monetary theory of production, the nature of modern banking still awaits to be fully explored and understood. In particular, there are two questions that call for a more elaborate theory of money and banking at the macroeconomic level.[5] First, on ontological grounds, can one and the same 'thing' be a means of payment as well as a temporary abode of purchasing power? In the negative, what does it bring to distinguish analytically the two 'things' that carry out these two functions at different points in time? Recent contributions within the post Keynesian and circuitist traditions have pointed out that '[n]o one aspect of money can stand on its own as a complete account of what money is and what money does in a modern economy' (Fontana, 2000, p. 28).[6] Yet, so far both have failed to bring to light the distinction between bank money (that is, money proper) and bank deposits (money balances),[7] perhaps because from a common-sense point of view money and deposits are synonyms and coextensive (cash is irrelevant here).[8]

The aim of this chapter is to explore the positive distinction that exists in modern banking between money and deposits, in connection with the working of a monetary production economy. The following section focuses on the bookkeeping nature of bank money, and explains the distinction between money proper and money's worth following what may be called a modern approach to Keynes's monetary theory of production. Next, the money-purveying and the credit-purveying functions of modern banking are investigated by referring to banks' double-entry system of accounts. Some final remarks conclude the chapter.

THE MEANING OF BANK DEPOSITS

Consider the process of money creation. According to pretty much all economists, money is created when a bank grants a credit to one of its clients and is destroyed when this loan is reimbursed to the bank.[9] In the meantime, money circulates between agents, who accept it as a means of payment on the basis of its purchasing power. Let us focus exclusively on the point at issue here, namely, the origin of money's worth. Parguez and Seccareccia (2000, p. 101) maintain that the value of modern money stems 'from the certainty that accepting bank debt as payment is to acquire a right on the existing as well as future output that will be created by the agents who have been granted bank credit'. So far, so good: every seller of goods and services is aware of the fact that bank deposits have a positive purchasing power and hence accepts them. Yet, a problem arises when one wants to grasp the source of 'the society-wide certainty that any temporary holder of bank debt has a right to acquire present and future real resources generated by initial spending of those debts' (Parguez, 2001, p. 72). To put it clearly, is it 'the social production of trust and confidence' that can *explain* the value of money, as claimed by post Keynesians and many others who focus on the agents' behaviour (see, for instance, Dow and Smithin, 1999, p. 80; Ingham, 2000, p. 29), or do people accept money *because* the latter has a positive exchange value independently of their beliefs? Generally speaking, the purchasing power of money is explained by referring to the universal acceptability of the latter, on the basis of the traditional social-consensus argument,[10] which has also been recast in terms of credibility of the banking system. 'Banks are deemed to be so creditworthy that no holder of their debts would ever ask for reimbursement either in kind or in the debt of another agent' (Parguez and Seccareccia, 2000, p. 103). In addition, the endorsement of bank money by the state is often said to provide further guarantee to the banks' acknowledgment of debt entered on the liabilities side of their balance sheets (Wray, 2000; Bell, 2001).

Now, confronted with the historical evolution of the material that has been used to represent money – especially in the present days of nearly full dematerialisation of the money stuff driven by information technology (see Dembinski and Perritaz, 2000) – economists may wonder whether, at the macroeconomic level, there is nothing more fundamental than the 'general acceptability' hypothesis in order to explain the purchasing power of bank money. In particular, one might be led to ask if Smith's distinction between the value of money and money proper – which he portrayed as the great wheel of (output) circulation – can be given a modern interpretation with respect to bank accounting. In fact, referring to the rigorous apparatus of double-entry bookkeeping, the macroeconomic theory of money emissions developed by Schmitt and his school provides an explanation of the value of money that is not determined by trust, confidence, or social convention. In a nutshell, this theory considers that banks issue money as a mere numerical form, deprived of purchasing power.[11] As we shall see later on, it is through its association with production that money is given a positive value, and not as a result of the social acceptance of the banks' acknowledgement of debt. In this framework, therefore, money creation may be seen as the application of banks' double-entry bookkeeping to express, and record, payments in their numerical form, that is, in the form of an 'asset–liability' entered on a bank's balance sheet (see, for example, Schmitt, 1996a; Cencini, 2001). 'It is because money is at once an asset (credit) and a liability (debt) that it is treated as a balance sheet operation' (Bell, 2001, p. 150). To put it in Schmitt's own words, 'the meaning of money creation [is that] the bank creates $+x$ and $-x$ units of money in one and the same "impulse"' (Schmitt, 1996a, p. 134). As a matter of fact, when banks provide transactions services to the public, they make payments as demanded by their clients (hence the endogenous nature of modern money), debiting and crediting them through 'bookkeeping entries [that] are used to allow economic units to exchange one form of wealth for another' (Fama, 1980, p. 43).[12]

It is at this juncture that the liquid store of wealth function of modern money, on which post Keynesian literature has focused, can be made fully consistent with the means of payment function underlined by circuitists, provided that the latter recognise that the monetary circuit they focus upon is, in fact, the circuit of income (in the form of bank deposits) and not the circuit of money as such (money proper).[13] Going beyond the negative, yet necessary, task of criticising alternative approaches to a monetary production economy, let us proceed step by step in order to point out some 'first principles' for the construction of a more general monetary theory in macroeconomic terms.[14]

The first step forward in this direction is to draw a conceptual distinction between money as such and bank deposits. To show the nature of this distinction, which is yet unperceived in monetary economics literature,[15] let us start from the tabula rasa. To be sure, this research strategy will avoid the temptation to explain a deposit formation by having recourse to a pre-existent deposit (whose origin would remain unexplained). Further, to understand the scope of the above distinction, let us consider the payment of the wage bill, since '[i]f there were no workers to remunerate, then money could not circulate and hence exist' (Rochon, 1999, p. 31).[16] We shall address here neither the reasons lying behind the actual amount of the workers' remuneration nor the distribution of income between workers (that is, wages) and capitalists (profits).[17] We abstract therefore from any value judgement about income distribution, to concentrate on a positive analysis of the income-generating process as recorded by the banks' double-entry system of accounts. Indeed the only purpose of this section is to draw a distinction between money and deposits that is not merely rhetoric.

When one considers the result of the payment of a wage bill, say, of x units of money, in bookkeeping terms, one has to start from the double entry recorded in Table 16.1.

Table 16.1. The result of a payment on the factor market

Bank

Assets			Liabilities
Firm	£x	Workers	£x

There is no need to explain the mechanics of the transaction entered in the bank's balance sheet. However, it is worth exploring the very payment that gives rise to this double entry. In the case in point, post Keynesians and circuitists agree that firms have to finance their expenditure on the factor market by obtaining a loan from banks. As Lavoie (1984, p. 774) puts it, '[t]hese flows of credit then reappear as deposits on the liability side of the balance sheet of banks when firms use these loans to remunerate their factors of production'. In fact, this is the loans to deposits causality put to the fore by both strands of thought, first spelled out by Withers back in 1909 (see Realfonzo, 1998, Ch. 6).

Now, to focus exclusively on the point at issue in this section, one has to consider that in the income-generating process depicted in Table 16.1, the money creation process carried out by the bank only provides the economy with the number of money units asked for by the firm (on the assumption that the firm's creditworthiness satisfies the benchmark set by the banker). It is production that gives a purchasing power to money, which, as such, is a mere numerical form of no value whatsoever. 'Banks, therefore, do not create value as they issue money, and their newly issued money takes on a real value only if it is associated with new production' (Bossone, 2001a, p. 870, fn. 19). The remuneration of labour, in fact, associates physical output with a number of money units in the payment of the wage bill. This creates exchange value and gives bank money its purchasing power. As Marx (1939/1973, p. 217) pointed out, '[p]roduction is not only concerned with simple determination of prices, i.e. with translation of the exchange values of commodities into a common unit, but with the creation of exchange values'. If we abstract from the monetisation of production, banks are unable to create purchasing power on their own. Dissociated from physical output, bank money would be 'a mere phantom of real wealth' (ibid., p. 234).[18] So, bank deposits are a 'liquid, multilaterally accepted asset' (Chick, 2000, p. 131), because they are the organic *result* (that is, a stock magnitude) of two intimately related *actions* (or flows): (1) creation, on the monetary side, of the numerical form of payments (money proper) by the banking system, and (2) production, on the real side, of physical output (money's worth) by the non-bank public, that is, firms and workers taken together.[19] So, the flow of money and the flow of production are complementary aspects of the same (income-generating) process. 'From the beginning, banking and productive systems thus contribute to the determination of a unique macroeconomic structure' (Cencini, 1997, p. 276).

In sum, from this point of view money as such is a flow, whose result is a stock (of liquid wealth) in the form of bank deposits. These deposits have a positive purchasing power in so far as they are the alter ego of physical output until the latter is sold on the market for produced goods and services. Consequently, contrary to the 'cloakroom theory of banking' *à la* Cannan (1921), the purchasing power of bank deposits does not originate in some 'central mystery of modern banking' (Chick, 2000, p. 131). According to the theory of money emissions, bank deposits are the alter ego of physical output, and come to light as soon as the latter is monetised via the remuneration of wage-earners by firms. At the macroeconomic level, the purchasing power of bank deposits has therefore nothing to do with the agents' trust and confidence in the banking system. In this framework, let us emphasise it, money balances are net worth because they are the form in which physical output exists before its final consumption takes place on the goods market.[20] Then, when output is sold on the market for produced goods, an equivalent (some would say identical) sum of bank deposits are destroyed, since depositors transform a liquid store of wealth into a physical value-in-use, or, to put it in the phraseology of Fama (1980), they exchange a monetary form of wealth for a real form. This exchange, taking place on the product market, destroys a sum of bank deposits equal to the amount of money wages adding up to the production cost of output sold. In fact, the firm recovers on the market for produced goods the income (in the form of deposits) that the bank did lend to it for the payment on the factor market (see Table 16.1). This destruction occurs independently of the firm's behaviour, that is, of the firm's decision to reimburse the bank loan: when physical output is released from its monetary form, the corresponding bank deposit is transformed into real goods or services and hence ceases to exist as such. Now, two cases may occur at this stage, depending on the existence of profits or not (see Rossi, 2001, Ch. 7; Gnos, this volume; Bailly, this volume). Since this issue lies beyond the scope of this chapter, let us assume that the firm does not earn a profit on output sold (for a reason that does not matter here) and that it does not make a loss either. Suppose also that this firm does not sell all produced output. In this case, the price of the output sold is equal to its production cost ($x - y$, with $y > 0$). The exchange on the product market thus gives rise to the double entry recorded in the second line of Table 16.2,[21] where the last line indicates the end-result: the firm could reimburse the bank for an amount equal to $x - y$ (hence the destruction of an equivalent sum of bank deposits) and has thus a remaining debt of y.[22]

Table 16.2. The result of a payment on the product market (zero profit)

Bank

Assets			Liabilities
Firm	£x	Workers	£x
Workers	£x–y	Firm	£x–y
Firm	£y	Workers	£y

A further point can then be noted as regards the distinction between money and deposits. Money as such exists each time a payment is carried out, so that one might argue that '[m]oney and payments are one and the same thing. No money, if correctly defined, exists either before or after a given payment' (Schmitt, 1996b, p. 88). Money balances, on the other hand, have a positive duration in time, and are saved in the form of bank deposits – a part of which may be represented by bank notes –[23] until they are transformed into use values as noted above. More precisely, bank deposits exist *between* payments, whereas money as such only exists *within* payments – which are instantaneous events on account of the fact that it takes an instant, that is, a zero duration in time, to enter a payment in the banks' system of accounts.[24] To be sure, this is tantamount to distinguishing monetary flows and stocks: money as a means of payment is a flow ('money on the wing' in Robertson's (1922/1937) language), while money as a store of wealth (that is, bank deposits) is a stock ('money at rest') – it is indeed a temporary abode of purchasing power. However, it should be emphasised that, contrary to a widely held belief, money 'on the wing' is not a stock of money in motion. In fact, the causality runs from money as a flow (means of payment) – the *primum mobile* – to bank deposits (stock of wealth).

To conclude this section, a last point can be inferred from the preceding analysis. When one considers that money proper is the *means* of payment, that is, the form in which payments are made, one notices that the *object* (or content) of any payment is not money as such, but output in the form of a bank deposit (a liquid stock of wealth). In short, a distinction has to be drawn between form and substance. Owing to today's (nearly) full dematerialisation of the money stuff, the form is issued by the banking system at a trifling cost. In fact, bank money is entirely non-dimensional, since it is a mere numerical form, that is, a double entry in the banks' bookkeeping. By contrast, the substance of monetary transactions is the result of human effort, that is, production,[25] and as such implies what Keynes dubbed the disutility of labour – measured in terms of wage-units (see Carabelli, 1992; Bradford and

Harcourt, 1997).[26] It is then possible to clarify Fama's quotation according to which 'bookkeeping entries are used to allow economic units to exchange one form of wealth for another' (Fama, 1980, p. 43). As is shown by the theory of money emissions, which has a clear affinity with Ricardo's (1823/1951) work on this point, the transformation of wealth (from a real to a monetary form, or vice versa) is an absolute exchange, whereby a single object, that is, output, changes its form as a result of the payment entered on the bookkeeping system of banks. Let us explain this point at some length, since at first sight it may seem an extraordinary statement indeed. Consider again the payment of the wage bill (see Table 16.1). Workers earn a claim on a deposit in exchange for the physical output that they have produced over the relevant period, which gives rise to a stock of new goods that are stored with the firm in order to be sold on the product market. In this situation, money proper, that is, the numerical form in which the workers' remuneration takes place, is a mere vehicle of the output produced by wage-earners: it allows the newly produced goods to be physically deposited in the firm, while their monetary alter ego is entered as a deposit in the bank's bookkeeping on behalf of wage-earners. In other words, physical output is the real content of the firm's debt to the banking system – for the payment of the wage bill – and the corresponding bank deposit of wage-earners is a positive net worth for them as well as for the economy as a whole (Figure 16.1).

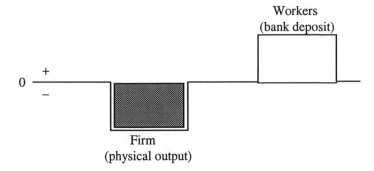

Figure 16.1. The result of an absolute exchange on the factor market

Similarly, when output is sold on the market for produced goods, an absolute exchange of the opposite algebraic sign is recorded in the bank's bookkeeping (see Table 16.2). The object of the payment is thus transformed from its monetary into its real form. By spending their bank deposit on the product market, workers (or more generally depositors) obtain the alter ego of their deposit, namely the chosen goods or services.[27] Here, too, money proper is the vehicle of the transformation by means of which a claim on a bank deposit is surrendered by those willing to obtain a physical output, that is, value-in-use. When this happens, an equivalent bank deposit is destroyed because the firm recovers it and can therefore reimburse the bank that had paid out wages (Figure 16.2).

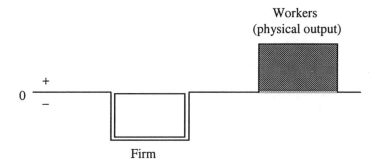

Figure 16.2. The result of an absolute exchange on the product market

In this framework, therefore, money proper and physical output are the twin aspects of the same reality: a net worth existing in the form of bank deposits until final consumption occurs on the product market. As stated by Cencini (1995, p. 16), 'money takes the place of the physical product and becomes its numerical form, so that the exchange between money and output defines their integration: money and output become the two complementary faces of a unique object'. The macroeconomic analysis of production from a 'bank money' point of view acquires thus a new light that may contribute to elaborate a more general monetary theory of production and exchange, by distinguishing money from deposits, that is, money as a means of payment from money as a stock of (liquid) wealth.

THE BANKS' INTERMEDIATION PROCESS

Let us reconsider the money creation process in connection with the payment of wages (or the wage bill), as seen from the banks' point of view. Again, what is of interest here is the interpretation of the bookkeeping entries in the balance sheet of the bank that carries out the monetisation of current production (see Table 16.1). Two points can be noted in this section. They have been clearly illustrated by Fischer's analysis of the functions of modern banking within a monetary economy. 'Banks do two things in this economy. First, they act as financial intermediaries. ... Second, they provide transactions services, making payments as demanded by the households' (Fischer, 1983, p. 4). Although the Fischer framework basically concerns exchanges of already produced goods, it may also serve as a gambit to investigate a monetary economy of production.

First, as already noted in the previous section, banks create the monetary form in which payments are made, and recorded, by them. In this respect, they act according to the principle that 'loans make deposits', as has been so clearly underlined by post Keynesians and circuitists as well (see, for example, Lavoie, 1999; Fontana, 2000; Rochon, 2001). As can be inferred from the analysis of the bank's bookkeeping in Table 16.1, starting from the tabula rasa, the payment on the factor market on behalf of the firm leads to the formation of an entirely new bank deposit. In fact, as soon as the bank enters the payment of the wage bill on its balance sheet, workers are credited with a deposit (entered on the liabilities side of the bank's account) and the firm is debited by the same amount (entered on the assets side of the bank's account). As seen from the bank's point of view, this operation, crucial as it is for the monetisation of current production, is nothing other than the use of double-entry bookkeeping to provide the non-bank public with a number of units of money proper.[28] To be clear, what originates in the bank, and in the banking system as a whole, is the creation of the monetary form in which payments are made. So, this 'money-purveying' function – as Keynes labelled it in his early drafts of *A Treatise on Money* (1930/1971) –[29] may be called in modern language a monetary intermediation: when making a payment, the bank delivers the exact number of money units asked for by the economy,[30] and enters them as an 'asset–liability' on its balance sheet. As noted by Bossone (2001a, p. 870, fn. 19), 'this money creation process is made possible by the peculiar nature of bank money which is, at the same time, an asset and a liability for both the issuing bank and the borrower'.[31] Again, we may notice here the nature of monetary transactions, which are absolute exchanges: each payment has as its object a good or service (perhaps in the form of a financial asset) that is produced within the (non-bank) economy and that the payment literally transforms. In the payment of wages, the monetary intermediation of the bank carrying out the operation transforms (that is, changes the form of) the real thing produced by wage-earners into a sum of money balances (that is, bank deposits).

Now, as already noted, the purchasing power of bank deposits does not originate in the banking system alone, independently of production. It is, in fact, the joint result of the banking and productive systems (see the previous section). More precisely, the material result of the monetisation of current production is physical output moulded by its monetary form. It is as such that it is deposited with the banking system as a whole. This is precisely the point that matters here: for every deposit entered on the liabilities side of a bank's balance sheet there is a corresponding, and simultaneous, entry on the assets side testifying a loan to the public, so much so that banks lend at once all the income saved by their clients in the form of bank deposits.[32] Consequently, in this case the relevant 'banking proverb', as identified by Schumpeter (1970) in his posthumous work, is that deposits make loans. However, to avoid any possible misunderstanding, let us point out that this causal link between deposits and loans is not a restatement of the classical loanable funds theory, according to which bank loans depend on *pre-existent* savings (that is, bank deposits). The deposits-to-loans causality results here from the fact that no deposit holder can spend this deposit *at the very instant when it is formed*, that is, when it is entered on the bank's account.[33] So, the act of saving of the newly formed deposit by its original owner implies that this amount is immediately lent by the bank where it is recorded. This loan is independent of the agents' forms of behaviour and has nothing to do with them – so much so that depositors are not necessarily aware of it – because it follows directly from the basic and essential rule of double-entry bookkeeping, a point that Moore (1988, Ch. 12) has recast in terms of 'convenience lending'. To quote Cencini (1995, p. 71) on this point, '[t]hrough the financial intermediation of banks, savings are instantaneously lent by their initial owners and spent by their borrowers'. This is precisely the 'credit-purveying' function of modern banking, as Keynes dubbed it in the *Treatise*'s early drafts.[34]

It is therefore correct to claim that banks are financial intermediaries, as claimed by the neoclassical school, even if their distinguishing characteristic with respect to other (non-bank) financial intermediaries is to act also, and foremost, as monetary intermediaries in so far as they are involved in the money creation process. As Bossone (2001a, p. 866, fn. 12) argues:

> One could think of the bank as having two separate departments – a *monetary* department and a *financial* department – with the financial department holding a deposit account with the monetary department. ... The distinction between the monetary and financial function of the bank emphasizes that the latter simply intermediates bank liabilities issued under the former.

In this respect, Pesek and Saving (1968, p. 144) recognised indeed that:

> Essentially, commercial banks engage in two basically different business functions. First, and most important, commercial banks produce and sell demand deposit money for cash or on credit. In this, the commercial banks are unique among all financial institutions. Second, commercial banks serve as financial intermediaries ... In this second function, the commercial banks compete with

many other institutions, such as savings and loan associations and mutual savings banks.

However, Pesek and Saving did not succeed in clearly focusing on the specific function of monetary intermediation carried out exclusively by banks, because they were led astray by the view that money is produced and sold. In fact, as shown in the previous section, being a means of payment of a mere numerical form, money proper is not produced and hence cannot be sold: it is entered on the system of banks' accounts as an asset *and simultaneously* a liability, that is, an 'asset–liability' of no value of its own. If money were actually produced, it would have to be included in the set of goods and services defining national output. But this would also imply that monetary transactions are 'dyadic' exchanges – of the same kind as those occurring in a barter economy –[35] which have been epitomised by Clower's view that *'money buys goods and goods buy money; but goods do not buy goods'* (Clower, 1967, p. 5).[36] If this were true, the famous Ricardo problem of finding an invariant measure of value would have no solution indeed. Clearly, including money among the set of produced output is bound to raise the problem of measuring goods by means of goods, a problem that Ricardo tried to solve without success until his death. Whilst one may claim that bank notes are the result of a production process (namely, the material result of the printing press) whose costs participate in the definition of national income, the paper is only the physical support (a representative sign) of the means of payment *proprio sensu*.[37] Essentially, the means of payment is the economic measure (or the monetary form) of produced goods and services, because, being a number of money units, it does not have to be measured. As a matter of fact, in a monetary economy of production the result of the payment on the factor market is a sum of bank deposits that are the monetary measure of current output in terms of the wage bill. This measure occurs through an absolute exchange where physical output is transformed into money income thanks to the monetary intermediation of the domestic banking system, which issues the numerical vehicle in order for the transaction to take place (see Figure 16.1). By the same token, when the reverse transformation takes place, on the market for produced output, a bank's monetary intermediation is required to obtain the physical objects that the purchasing power of money balances allows the bank's clients (that is, depositors) to buy (see Figure 16.2).

On the whole, there is therefore a two-way causality between loans and deposits, so much so that banks' double-entry bookkeeping can be referred to in order to explain that loans make deposits as well as that deposits make loans, depending on the focus of the analysis. The first reasoning refers to the fact that deposits result from the income-generating process originating in the loans that banks grant to firms, while the second refers to the fact that all the savings entered as a deposit on the liabilities side of a bank's balance sheet are immediately lent to creditworthy borrowers to finance their deficit spending. In short, banks are monetary and financial intermediaries as well.

CONCLUSION

The distinction between money and deposits pointed out in this chapter may be helpful for clarifying Keynes's original intuition that 'the money-of-account is the *description* or *title* and the money is the *thing* which answers to the description' (Keynes, 1930/1971, p. 3). Coupled with the claim that '[m]oney of account, namely that in which debts and prices and general purchasing power are *expressed*, is the primary concept of a theory of money' (ibid., p. 3), this passage might indeed suggest that money proper is a nominal form, that is, a mere counter (to use Hicks's own words, as quoted above), and that the thing which is counted is a bank deposit (that Keynes unfortunately simply called money, a slippage that may explain why the distinction between bank money and deposits has been unnoticed so far). In fact, when considered in light of what may be called a modern view of Keynes's monetary theory of production, the meaning of bank deposits is to represent physical output in its monetary form – as a result of the payment on the factor market for the current production of goods and services. As such, bank deposits are the bridge between present and future that has been so cogently emphasised by Keynes himself and by those post Keynesians who have been in the front line to investigate agents' forms of behaviour under conditions of uncertainty.[38] In this connection, one may then also consider the construction of a microeconomic theory of banks' behaviour, as attempted by Rochon (1999, Ch. 8), where the issues of uncertainty, liquidity preference, and Kalecki's principle of increasing risk can be investigated following Keynes's insights. Post Keynesians have gone a long way indeed into these important issues concerning a monetary production economy. Their analyses on these topics have provided sound thinking on the idea that 'money matters', a central tenet shared at present by all heterodox schools of thought. Were they to distinguish analytically money proper from bank deposits along the lines shaping the research presented in this chapter, a more general monetary theory that allows for money being means of payment as well as store of wealth would be provided with solid, and positive, macroeconomic foundations, doing away with all sociological or psychoanalytical explanations of money's worth, which, let us note it in passing, eventually deprive monetary economics from its own object of enquiry.[39] This might enable the economics profession to further understand the working of our monetary production economies, in order to try to make them work better by a useful, realistic, policy-oriented analysis of inflation and unemployment based on the nature of bank deposits.[40]

NOTES

1. The author would like to thank Biagio Bossone, Alvaro Cencini, Claude Gnos, Pierre Piégay, Louis-Philippe Rochon and Alberto Zazzaro for their helpful comments on an earlier version of this work. The usual disclaimer applies.
2. The post Keynesian school has ramified into a structuralist view and an accommodationist view, which has also been labelled the horizontalist approach (see Moore, 1988; Pollin, 1991; Palley, 1996; Rochon, 1999). Since the latter approach to money and credit is close to the monetary circuit approach (see Parguez and Seccareccia, 2000; Parguez, 2002), in this chapter we shall identify post Keynesians with the structuralist school.
3. In a nutshell, money proper is, in Smith's language, the great wheel of output circulation, whereas money's worth is the purchasing power of money, that is, the goods and services a given sum of money will buy. 'The great wheel of circulation is altogether different from the goods which are circulated by means of it. The revenue of the society consists altogether in those goods, and not in the wheel which circulates them' (Smith, 1776/1970, p. 385). As Smith puts it, 'the wealth or revenue . . . is equal only to one of the two values which are thus intimated somewhat ambiguously by the same word, . . . to the money's worth more properly than to the money' (ibid., p. 386). In modern banking, as we shall explain later on, the distinction between money proper and money's worth is the distinction between a numerical form and its real content.
4. Generally speaking, monetary flows are interpreted as a money stock in motion. This idea derives from physics: a flow of (say) water is indeed a moving stock. By contrast, we shall argue that, in modern banking, a flow of money is not a stock 'on the wing' (Robertson, 1922/1937, p. 29).
5. To avoid any possible misunderstanding, let us underline that our analysis is situated at an abstract, macroeconomic level. Phenomena that are of a microeconomic nature, such as agents' (complete or incomplete) information and uncertainty, lie beyond the scope of this investigation. This is not to deny that these phenomena have to be taken into account for the construction of a more general monetary theory of production and exchange.
6. See also Rochon (2000).
7. See, however, Sawyer (this volume) for a breakthrough.
8. 'To Post Keynesians, money is bank liabilities, that is, deposits' (Chick, 2000, p. 130). The same definition is given by circuitists, who claim that 'money is also a liability, i.e., bank deposits used as purchasing power' (Rochon, 2000, p. 974). Certainly, the fact that this definition conforms to the statistical definition used by central banks and international financial institutions does not provide an incentive to further investigate the nature of bank money.
9. See Dalziel (2001, pp. 28–37) for a recent exploration of this view.
10. Using neoclassical language, 'one person gives up goods (objects that appear as arguments of utility functions, directly or indirectly) for fiat money only because the person believes

that someone else will subsequently give up goods for fiat money at an acceptable rate of exchange' (Wallace, 1980, p. 49). In this framework, money has also been compared to ordinary language, in the sense that both are said to be valuable because of people's willingness to use them for (facilitating) social interactions (see Tobin, 1963). As is maintained also by Moore (2001, p. 17), '[money's] usefulness and value is based entirely on social convention. Money is like a language. It is acceptable to me only if it is acceptable to you'.

11. As Fama observes in his famous *Journal of Monetary Economics* article, the essence of the transactions services provided by the banking system is to rely on mere numerical units – integers having a concrete economic meaning, as we shall see later on – to carry out monetary transactions within the economy (Fama, 1980, pp. 39–43). This was indeed already pointed out by Hicks back in 1975: 'money is now a mere counter, which is supplied by the banking system just as it is required' (Hicks, quoted in Laidler and Parkin, 1975, p. 742).

12. Although Fama refers here to an exchange between two distinct things (that is, a relative exchange), and not to an exchange between two distinct forms of the same thing (as in an absolute exchange), the principle that he describes applies also to absolute exchanges, as we shall see at the end of this section.

13. See Cencini's (1997) critical review of Graziani (1994) on this point.

14. Contrary to Fontana (2000, p. 45), who deems it impossible 'to establish any one set of principles that are broad enough to support a unique theoretical structure [which allows for money being store of wealth and means of payment]', it will be shown here that such a theoretical synthesis may be accomplished, provided that one is willing to abandon firmly held beliefs and reconsider the whole theoretical structure afresh.

15. Sawyer (this volume) is a noteworthy exception, although his approach and conclusions differ considerably from those presented in this chapter.

16. This is a point on which circuitists are unanimous (see for example Lavoie, 1987). From the viewpoint of the theory of money emissions, the Rochon claim has to be stated the other way around: if there were no production, money could not exist and hence circulate. Note however that money proper is not a thing and hence cannot circulate. The circuit of money, in fact, is reduced to a double entry (an asset–liability) in the bank's bookkeeping system.

17. These issues are addressed by Gnos (this volume) and Bailly (this volume).

18. Bank advances (for consumption purposes) allow to obtain, and spend, today a purchasing power that a future production will create.

19. We abstract here from the state, which, however, can be added to the group of firms (namely those of the public sector) without altering the results of our analysis.

20. See Rossi (1998, pp. 33–5) for elaboration on this point.

21. Workers, or more generally depositors, are entered on the assets side of the balance sheet because they are debited for the expenditure of a sum $(x - y)$ of bank deposits.

22. Circuitists have focused on this point to note that it poses 'a problem for the closure of the monetary circuit: hoarded saving represents a leakage' (Rochon, 1999, p. 35). However, as will be shown in the next section, since in this framework income is saved in the form of bank deposits, the latter are not withdrawn from circulation. Owing to their bookkeeping nature, in fact, these deposits remain entirely available within the banking system until they are finally spent on the market for produced goods and services. What Rochon labels 'hoarded saving' is therefore immediately lent – although depositors are not aware of it – by the bank where these savings are recorded (on the liabilities side of its balance sheet) to those firms that can recover their production costs neither on the product market nor on the financial market through the sale of securities. This is indeed a point recognised by the circuit school, as noted by Rochon: 'At the end of the monetary circuit, firms owe banks the exact amount that households have decided to entrust to banks as saving deposits. Banks will use these funds to refinance firms' debt under longer term conditions' (ibid., p. 36). See Rossi (2000, pp. 608–9) for further elaboration.

23. As pointed out by Eichner (1991, p. 845), the notes issued by the central bank are recorded on the liabilities side of its balance sheet. Bank notes are therefore the physical representation of a bank deposit, namely, a deposit in the central bank.

24. As clearly argued by Cencini (1988, p. 74), 'since it is through payments that money circulates, . . . the displacement of bank deposits does not require an interval of time greater than zero, for it occurs at the very moment the account of the payee is credited by the amount transferred by the payer'.

25. As Keynes wrote in *A Treatise on Money*, '[h]uman effort and human consumption are the ultimate matters from which alone economic transactions are capable of deriving any significance; and all other forms of expenditure only acquire importance from their having some relationship, sooner or later, to the effort of producers or to the expenditure of consumers' (Keynes, 1930/1971, p. 134).

26. This issue lies beyond the scope of the present chapter. See Rossi (2001, Ch. 5).

27. Note that bank deposits are fungible assets for the general public.

28. As noted by Moore (2001, p. 17), '[i]ndividual units of money as the medium of exchange are perfectly homogeneous', a point already made by Keynes (1936/1973, p. 41). Now, Carabelli (1992, p. 23) observes that Keynes did not explain why money is homogeneous. She thus puts forward an explanation based on an analogy between the role of money in the economic process and the role of ordinary language in present-day societies. However, as pointed out by Bradford and Harcourt (1997, p. 129, fn. 16), this analogy is forced and unnecessary. Since money as such is a mere counter, issued by the banking system as an 'asset–liability', each unit of money is essentially identical to any other unit of money existing at the same time, because their origin and nature are the same.

29. See Keynes (1973, p. 91).

30. Recall the endogenous nature of modern money.

31. See also Bossone (2001b, p. 2252).

32. As Keynes wrote in connection with the saving–investment relationship, '[t]he prevalence of the idea that saving and investment, taken in their straightforward sense, can differ from one another, is to be explained, I think, by an optical illusion due to regarding an individual depositor's relation to his bank as being a one-sided transaction, instead of seeing it as the two-sided transaction which it actually is. It is supposed that a depositor and his bank can somehow contrive between them to perform an operation by which savings can disappear into the banking system so that they are lost to investment, or, contrariwise, that the banking system can make it possible for investment to occur, to which no saving corresponds' (Keynes, 1936/1973, p. 81). With respect to the bookkeeping nature of bank money, this point has been further clarified by Moore. 'Since bank liabilities are only as good as the bank assets behind them, bank depositors are ultimately the creditors of bank borrowers' (Moore, 1988, p. 20). In fact, when one considers the remuneration of wage-earners from the bank's point of view, one notes that, owing to double-entry bookkeeping, the deposits of workers are immediately balanced by an equivalent loan to firms in order to finance their costs of production. This may be seen as a modern restatement of Keynes's finance motive (see Bradley, 1993; for a different interpretation of it see Graziani, 1987; Rochon, 1997).

33. The actual period of time elapsing before this deposit is spent (on the market for produced goods) does not interest us here. This duration varies according to agents' behaviour and, as such, may be influenced by uncertainty within a non-ergodic economic system (see Davidson, 1988). In fact, a deposit may be spent on the market for produced goods *before* it is actually formed: this is indeed the role of bank advances. Yet, even in this case it remains true that the deposit holder cannot spend this deposit when it is formed. Since he has already spent the deposit in advance, he has to reimburse the bank when it becomes available and, therefore, cannot spend it twice: the reimbursement of a bank loan destroys a deposit of the same amount (Howells, 1995, p. 100; Arestis and Howells, 1999, p. 118).

34. See Keynes (1973, p. 91). Of course, banks assess the creditworthiness of potential borrowers before entering any new loan commitment, but this issue is not germane to the

present analysis.

35. As Ingham (2000, p. 23) argues, '[b]arter exchange of commodities, whatever the complexity of the system, is essentially bilateral; but, monetary relations are trilateral. . . . It has been the fundamental error of economic orthodoxy to subsume monetary exchange under the general rubric of pure dyadic exchange'. As a matter of fact, in a monetary economy '[e]very transaction involves three parties, buyer, seller, and banker' (Hicks, 1967, p. 11).

36. Recall that the Clower aphorism serves to make money useful in general-equilibrium models of monetary economies, in which production is a bilateral exchange between two distinct objects, namely, a sum of monetary assets, on one side, and a productive service, on the other side. This contrasts with the conception of absolute exchange pointed out in the preceding section.

37. Simmel (1907/1978) was aware of this point and hence made a distinction between the essence of money and the material used to carry out its functions.

38. See Keynes (1936/1973, p. 293) and more recently Minsky (1994, pp. 154–5), among many others.

39. Investigating the psychoanalytical concept of the role of money in contemporary society, Dostaler and Maris (2000, p. 251) conclude that '[m]oney cannot be analysed in isolation from one's vision, not only of the functioning of the economy but of the whole of social life, including its psychological components'.

40. See Rossi (2001, Ch. 6).

REFERENCES

Arestis, P. and P. Howells (1996), 'Theoretical reflections on endogenous money: the problem with "convenience lending"', *Cambridge Journal of Economics*, **20** (5), 539–51.

Arestis, P. and P. Howells (1999), 'The supply of credit money and the demand for deposits: a reply', *Cambridge Journal of Economics*, **23** (1), 115–19.

Bailly, J.-L. (2002), 'On the macroeconomic foundations of the wage–price relationship', in this volume.

Bell, S. (2001), 'The role of the state and the hierarchy of money', *Cambridge Journal of Economics*, **25** (2), 149–63.

Bossone, B. (2001a), 'Circuit theory of banking and finance', *Journal of Banking and Finance*, **25** (5), 857–90.

Bossone, B. (2001b), 'Do banks have a future? A study on banking and finance as we move into the third millennium', *Journal of Banking and Finance*, **25** (12), 2239–76.

Bradford, W. and G.C. Harcourt (1997), 'Units and definitions', in G.C. Harcourt and P.A. Riach (eds), *A 'Second Edition' of The General Theory*, London and New York: Routledge, vol. I, 107–31.

Bradley, X. (1993), 'La "finance" et le circuit de la monnaie', *Revue française d'économie*, **8** (1), 67–88.

Cannan, E. (1921), 'The meaning of bank deposits', *Economica*, **1** (1), 28–36.

Carabelli, A. (1992), 'Organic interdependence and Keynes's choice of units in the *General Theory*', in B. Gerrard and J. Hillard (eds), *The Philosophy and Economics of J.M. Keynes*, Aldershot and Brookfield: Edward Elgar, 3–31.

Cencini, A. (1988), *Money, Income and Time: A Quantum-Theoretical Approach*,

London and New York: Pinter Publishers.

Cencini, A. (1995), *Monetary Theory, National and International*, London and New York: Routledge.

Cencini, A. (1997), 'Review of Graziani's *La teoria monetaria della produzione*', *Structural Change and Economic Dynamics*, **8** (2), 272–7.

Cencini, A. (2001), *Monetary Macroeconomics: A New Approach*, London and New York: Routledge.

Chick, V. (2000), 'Money and effective demand', in J. Smithin (ed.), *What is Money?*, London and New York: Routledge, 124–38.

Clower, R.W. (1967), 'A reconsideration of the microfoundations of monetary theory', *Western Economic Journal*, **6** (1), 1–8.

Dalziel, P. (2001), *Money, Credit and Price Stability*, London and New York: Routledge.

Davidson, P. (1988), 'A technical definition of uncertainty and the long run non-neutrality of money', *Cambridge Journal of Economics*, **12** (3), 329–37.

Davidson, P. (1990), 'Money and general equilibrium', in L. Davidson (ed.), *The Collected Writings of Paul Davidson*, Vol. I *Money and Employment*, London and Basingstoke: Macmillan, 196–217.

Deleplace, G. and E.J. Nell (eds) (1996), *Money in Motion: The Post Keynesian and Circulation Approaches*, London and New York: Macmillan and St. Martin's Press.

Dembinski, P.H. and C. Perritaz (2000), 'Towards the break-up of money: when reality – driven by information technology – overtakes Simmel's vision', *Foresight*, **2** (5), 453–66.

Dostaler, G. and B. Maris (2000), 'Dr Freud and Mr Keynes on money and capitalism', in J. Smithin (ed.), *What is Money?*, London and New York: Routledge, 235–56.

Dow, S.C. and J. Smithin (1999), 'The structure of financial markets and the "first principles" of monetary economics', *Scottish Journal of Political Economy*, **46** (1), 72–90.

Eichner, A.S. (1991), 'Money and credit', in *The Macrodynamics of Advanced Market Economies*, New York: M.E. Sharpe, 803–63.

Fama, E.F. (1980), 'Banking in the theory of finance', *Journal of Monetary Economics*, **6** (1), 39–57.

Fischer, S. (1983), 'A framework for monetary and banking analysis', *Economic Journal*, **93** (conference supplement), 1–16.

Fontana, G. (2000), 'Post Keynesians and Circuitists on money and uncertainty: an attempt at generality', *Journal of Post Keynesian Economics*, **23** (1), 27–48.

Gnos, C. (1999), 'The endogenous view of money: the nature of money at issue', University of Burgundy, mimeo.

Gnos, C. (2002), 'Circuit theory as an explanation of the complex real world', in this volume.

Graziani, A. (1987), 'Keynes' finance motive', *Économies et Sociétés* ('Série Monnaie et Production', 4), **21** (9), 23–42.

Graziani, A. (1990), 'The theory of the monetary circuit', *Économies et Sociétés* ('Série Monnaie et Production', 7), **24** (6), 7–36.

Graziani, A. (1994), *La teoria monetaria della produzione* ('Studi e Ricerche', 7), Arezzo: Banca Popolare dell'Etruria e del Lazio.

Hicks, J.R. (1967), *Critical Essays in Monetary Theory*, Oxford: Clarendon Press.

Howells, P.G.A. (1995), 'The demand for endogenous money', *Journal of Post Keynesian Economics*, **18** (1), 89–106.

Ingham, G. (2000), '"Babylonian madness": on the historical and sociological origins of money', in J. Smithin (ed.), *What is Money?*, London and New York: Routledge, 16–41.

Keynes, J.M. (1930/1971), *A Treatise on Money*, London: Macmillan. Reprinted in *The Collected Writings of John Maynard Keynes*, Vols V and VI, London and Basingstoke: Macmillan.

Keynes, J.M. (1933/1973), 'A monetary theory of production'. Reprinted in *The Collected Writings of John Maynard Keynes*, Vol. XIII *The General Theory and After: Part I Preparation*, London and Basingstoke: Macmillan, 408–11.

Keynes, J.M. (1936/1973), *The General Theory of Employment, Interest and Money*, London: Macmillan. Reprinted in *The Collected Writings of John Maynard Keynes*, Vol. VII, London and Basingstoke: Macmillan.

Keynes, J.M. (1973), *The Collected Writings of John Maynard Keynes*, Vol. VII *The General Theory and After: Part I Preparation*, London and Basingstoke: Macmillan.

Laidler, D. and M. Parkin (1975), 'Inflation: a survey', *Economic Journal*, **85** (340), 741–809.

Lavoie, M. (1984), 'The endogenous flow of credit and the Post Keynesian theory of money', *Journal of Economic Issues*, **18** (3), 771–97.

Lavoie, M. (1987), 'Monnaie et production: une synthèse de la théorie du circuit', *Économies et Sociétés* ('Série Monnaie et Production', 4), **21** (9), 65–101.

Lavoie, M. (1994), 'Money and credit', in P. Arestis and M. Sawyer (eds), *The Elgar Companion to Radical Political Economy*, Aldershot and Brookfield: Edward Elgar, 278–82.

Lavoie, M. (1999), 'The credit-led supply of deposits and the demand for money: Kaldor's reflux mechanism as previously endorsed by Joan Robinson', *Cambridge Journal of Economics*, **23** (1), 103–13.

Lerner, A.P. (1947), 'Money as a creature of the state', *American Economic Review*, **37** (2), 312–17.

Marx, K. (1939/1973), *Grundrisse*, Harmondsworth: Penguin.

Minsky, H.P. (1994), 'Financial instability hypothesis', in P. Arestis and M. Sawyer (eds), *The Elgar Companion to Radical Political Economy*, Aldershot and Brookfield: Edward Elgar, 153–8.

Moore, B.J. (1988), *Horizontalists and Verticalists: The Macroeconomics of Credit Money*, Cambridge: Cambridge University Press.

Moore, B.J. (2001), 'Some reflections on endogenous money', in L.-P. Rochon and M. Vernengo (eds), *Credit, Interest Rates and the Open Economy: Essays on Horizontalism*, Cheltenham and Northampton: Edward Elgar, 11–30.

Parguez, A. (2001), 'Money without scarcity: from the horizontalist revolution to the theory of the monetary circuit', in L.-P. Rochon and M. Vernengo (eds), *Credit, Interest Rates and the Open Economy: Essays on Horizontalism*, Cheltenham and Northampton: Edward Elgar, 69–103.

Parguez, A. (2002), 'Victoria Chick and the theory of the monetary circuit: an enlightening debate', in P. Arestis, M. Desai and S. Dow (eds), *Money, Macroeconomics and Keynes: Essays in Honour of Victoria Chick*, London and

New York: Routledge, vol. I, 45–55.

Parguez, A. and M. Seccareccia (2000), 'The credit theory of money: the monetary circuit approach', in J. Smithin (ed.), *What is Money?*, London and New York: Routledge, 101–23.

Pesek, B.P. and T.R. Saving (1968), *The Foundations of Money and Banking*, London and Basingstoke: Macmillan.

Palley, T.I. (1996), 'Accommodationism versus structuralism: time for an accommodation', *Journal of Post Keynesian Economics*, **18** (4), 585–94.

Pollin, R. (1991), 'Two theories of money supply endogeneity: some empirical evidence', *Journal of Post Keynesian Economics*, **13** (3), 366–96.

Realfonzo, R. (1998), *Money and Banking: Theory and Debate (1900–1940)*, Cheltenham and Northampton: Edward Elgar.

Ricardo, D. (1823/1951), 'Absolute value and exchangeable value', in P. Sraffa and M. Dobb (eds), *The Works and Correspondence of David Ricardo*, Vol. IV *Pamphlets and Papers: 1815–1823*, Cambridge: Cambridge University Press, 357–412.

Robertson, D.H. (1922/1937), *Money*, Cambridge: Cambridge University Press.

Rochon, L.-P. (1997), 'Keynes's finance motive: a re-assessment. Credit, liquidity preference and the rate of interest', *Review of Political Economy*, **9** (3), 277–93.

Rochon, L.-P. (1999), *Credit, Money and Production: An Alternative Post-Keynesian Approach*, Cheltenham and Northampton: Edward Elgar.

Rochon, L.-P. (2000), 'The creation and circulation of endogenous money: a reply to Pressman', *Journal of Economic Issues*, **34** (4), 973–9.

Rochon, L.-P. (2001), 'Horizontalism: setting the record straight', in L.-P. Rochon and M. Vernengo (eds), *Credit, Interest Rates and the Open Economy: Essays on Horizontalism*, Cheltenham and Northampton: Edward Elgar, 31–65.

Rossi, S. (1998), 'Endogenous money and banking activity: some notes on the workings of modern payment systems', *Studi economici*, **53** (3), 23–56.

Rossi, S. (2000), 'Review of Rochon's *Credit, Money and Production: An Alternative Post-Keynesian Approach*', *Kyklos*, **53** (4), 607–9.

Rossi, S. (2001), *Money and Inflation: A New Macroeconomic Analysis*, Cheltenham and Northampton: Edward Elgar.

Sawyer, M. (2002), 'Money: means of payment or store of wealth?', in this volume.

Schmitt, B. (1996a), 'A new paradigm for the determination of money prices', in G. Deleplace and E.J. Nell (eds), *Money in Motion: The Post Keynesian and Circulation Approaches*, London and New York: Macmillan and St. Martin's Press, 105–38.

Schmitt, B. (1996b), 'Unemployment: is there a principal cause?', in A. Cencini and M. Baranzini (eds), *Inflation and Unemployment: Contributions to a New Macroeconomic Approach*, London and New York: Routledge, 75–105.

Schneider, E. (1952/1962), *Money, Income and Employment*, London: Allen and Unwin.

Schumpeter, J.A. (1970), *Das Wesen des Geldes*, Göttingen: Vandenhoeck and Ruprecht.

Simmel, G. (1907/1978), *The Philosophy of Money*, London: Routledge.

Smith, A. (1776/1970), *An Inquiry into the Nature and Causes of the Wealth of Nations*, Harmondsworth: Penguin.

Tobin, J. (1963), 'Commercial banks as creators of "money"', in D. Carson (ed.),

Banking and Monetary Studies, Homewood (Illinois): Richard D. Irwin, 408–19.

Wallace, N. (1980), 'The overlapping generations model of fiat money', in J.H. Kareken and N. Wallace (eds), *Models of Monetary Economies*, Minneapolis: Federal Reserve Bank of Minneapolis, 49–82.

Withers, H. (1909/1930), *The Meaning of Money*, New York: Dutton.

Wray, L.R. (2000), 'Modern money', in J. Smithin (ed.), *What is Money?*, London and New York: Routledge, 42–66.

17. On the Macroeconomic Foundations of the Wage–Price Relationship

Jean-Luc Bailly

INTRODUCTION

Keynes is often criticised for assuming that wages and prices are sticky. His detractors argue that this assumption rules out any accurate account of the mechanisms that determine wage and price levels in the different markets, and that Keynesian theory is seriously flawed in that it is unable to account for adjustments between wages and prices. In the absence of any explicit demonstration in Keynes's writings of the axiological relationship between wages and prices, the hypothesis that they are anything other than absolutely flexible is often taken to be devoid of any real theoretical basis.

Neoclassical economists or their sympathisers have argued from this that Keynesian macroeconomics is not as all-encompassing as it is made out to be. Its analytical scope is, they say, confined to situations where wage and price stickiness is the rule. Moreover, they claim that this assumption means that Keynes's theory is unable to account for the interdependence between the labour market and the goods market. In response to these attacks, some Keynesians argue that the hypothesis of fixed wages is a purely methodological device employed notably in Chapter 3 of the *General Theory* (Keynes, 1936/1973) and cast about for microeconomic underpinnings for the macroeconomic dimension.

The fact is though that the debate about any Keynesian postulate as to wage stickiness touches upon the very profound conceptual issue of measurement in economics. Keynes develops the idea that it is not prices that determine the equilibrium of aggregate supply and demand. The principle of effective demand set out in the *General Theory* refutes that prices charged in the different markets determine current income, but shows instead that equality between aggregate supply and aggregate demand defines the domain within which prices are determined.

It is not so much a question of the stickiness of wages on the one hand and of prices on the other, but rather a question of the relationship between prices and wages. This clearly derives from the very definition of the unit of measurement in a monetary economy of production. Having been formed in the production process, income cannot be something other when spent in the goods markets. That is to say, prices themselves are measured in wage-units and the sum total of prices charged cannot differ from the sum total of wages, as we shall see in the next section. An essential function of prices is to allow current output to be distributed between workers and the owners of capital. Now, because prices themselves are wage-units, it follows that profit, although not of the same nature as wages, is formed within wages. A consequence of this is that profit is strictly limited to half of output, as we will show in the third section. The last section concludes.

WAGES AND PRICES

In the *General Theory* Keynes makes a deliberate break with the assumptions of orthodox neoclassical economics. He analyses a wage economy, that is, an economy where workers are not independent of each other. Being a wage-earner, each worker is tied in with the others and his position within the general division of labour is reflected by the money income he earns.

> In dealing with the theory of employment I propose, therefore, to make use of only two fundamental units of quantity, namely, quantities of money-value and quantities of employment. . . . We shall call the unit in which the quantity of employment is measured the labour-unit; and the money wage of a labour-unit we shall call the wage-unit (Keynes, 1936/1973, p. 41).

This short excerpt raises a question about the relation of cause and effect between the labour-unit and the wage-unit. Is the wage-unit defined on the basis of the labour-unit, or is it the other way around? In short, we must inquire what exactly is the status of the wage-unit.

Effective Demand and the Wage-Unit

Admittedly, Keynes states that 'the wage-unit, can thus be regarded as the essential standard of value' (ibid., p. 302). However, he refers throughout the *General Theory* alternately to the labour-unit and to the wage-unit as the standard of measurement. The wage-unit has no clearly established status as a unit of measurement. Chapter 4, 'The choice of units', is typical of this indecision.

> For, insofar as different grades and kinds of labour and salaried assistance enjoy a more or less fixed relative remuneration, the quantity of employment can be sufficiently defined for our purpose by taking an hour's employment of special labour in proportion to its remuneration; *i.e.* an hour of special labour remunerated at double ordinary rates will count as two units (ibid., p. 41).

This passage reads as if it is wages that are used to characterise the different types of labour. In other words, the economic value of the output of labour is not determined by its physical performance but by its *remuneration*. Here, it is because it is expressed homogeneously in money-units that output has an economic value and that the labour that has gone into its manufacture can be measured in economic terms. It is not therefore because different types of labour are of different standards or take different lengths of time that wages differ.

However, Keynes's viewpoint is not as firm and final as it might appear. A few lines farther on, he writes:

> This assumption of homogeneity in the supply of labour is not upset by the obvious fact of great differences in the specialized skill of individual workers and in their suitability for different occupations. For, if the remuneration of the workers is proportional to their efficiency, the differences are dealt with by our having regarded individuals contributing to the supply of labour in proportion to their remuneration (ibid., pp. 41–2).

Of course, the different types of labour appear homogeneous because of their remuneration. However, the argument is circular. If remuneration is based on physical productivity, then the unit of measurement is the labour-unit and output is gaged in terms of this. Conversely, if the contribution that individuals make to supply is measured by their remuneration, then the wage-unit is the unit of measurement of output and, through output, of the labour-unit. There is no way of saying whether the wage-unit is the yardstick for labour or labour is the yardstick for the wage-unit.

This lack of clarification in Keynes's work has left scope for the interpretation whereby the wage-unit is comparable to a price, or more specifically, the wage-unit is the price of the labour-unit.[1] This approach is not unfounded as Keynes himself claims to support what he terms the first postulate of classical theory, namely that *'[t]he wage is equal to the marginal product of labour'* (ibid., p. 5; emphasis added).

It may be thought that, as in general equilibrium theory, prices homogenise real wealth. Different types of labour – real wealth – can be compared because of the price of the labour-unit. Hansen (1953/1967, p. 32; our translation) writes that, '[a]s for the wage-unit, it is the income paid in exchange for a labour-unit, that is, the nominal wage paid for a standard hour's work'. According to Hansen, wage-unit and wage-rate are one and the same thing.

If the wage is a price, it is determined in a market, namely, the labour market. This immediately raises a question: in what units is the price of labour expressed? This leads on to the further question: in a wage economy, what are the terms of exchange in the labour market?

In a moneyless economy made up of independent workers who are not wage-earners, since there is no money, the workers would be remunerated from their own physical output. They receive their production directly from themselves, and it is then up to them to exchange the goods they have for other goods that better meet their needs. Strictly speaking, in this type of entirely hypothetical 'real' economy, there is no labour market as such. Each worker trades his output with others, but he does not sell his labour to anyone.

In a wage economy things are different. The first obvious difference is that workers are remunerated in money and not directly in kind. From this simple observation, it is often concluded that workers do not produce directly for themselves but for their employer. This, it is said, explains why wage-earners exchange their labour (or labour force) for a money wage. Wage economies are purportedly characterised then by the existence of a labour market with suppliers of labour on the one hand and suppliers of money wages on the other. On this argument, the money wage is said to be the *nominal* price of labour, while its *real* price is supposedly determined on the goods market.

It is widely argued that, as they are not remunerated by the goods they have manufactured, wage-earners are separated from their output, meaning their real output, by money. The separation is seemingly a radical one as it leads to two separate definitions of workers' income: the nominal wage and the real wage.

Thanks to their money wages, workers are able to purchase the physical products to which they have given rise. From this point of view, in a sense, they are ultimately remunerated by the physical goods produced, meaning that the labour supplied corresponds to the units of physical goods. Money is then a simple medium facilitating exchange. However, this last assertion is contradicted by the distinction drawn between real and nominal wages.

Everyone accepts that, in the labour market, wage-earners receive a nominal wage. However, as the wage is a relative price, it is also determined relative to the quantity of goods that workers procure. This is the same as saying that the actual purchasing power of wage-earners will depend on the general price level of the products. The immediate conclusion from this is that money is not purely and simply a medium between labour and output, since the nominal/real distinction is precisely the sign that there is no transitive relationship between the monetary remuneration of labour and its so-called real remuneration. The interposition of money between the labour market and the goods market, it is argued, could produce a distortion between the real output of labour and its nominal output. It is precisely this distortion that is termed the monetary illusion[2] by which the correspondence established in production between labour and money wages no longer pertains in the relationship between labour and physical goods, observed in the product market. It follows from this that, in a wage economy, the labour market would be a three-cornered affair. Money and physical goods being two separate entities, the labour market would comprise on one side a supply of labour, and on the other side, facing it, two separate supplies: a supply of money and, independently in another area, a supply of physical goods. First labour would be exchanged against a money asset and subsequently against physical goods. Neither exchange takes precedence over the other and the correspondence between the two prices cannot be established in any fixed manner; it is random. The very measurement of output and therefore of income would be wanting since, depending on whether it was gaged at the moment it was formed in its nominal form or at the moment it was spent in its real form, it would not be of the same amount.

Keynes's statement of the principle of effective demand contradicts this picture of the wage relationship in our monetary production economies.

> Furthermore, the *effective demand* is simply the aggregate income (or proceeds) which the entrepreneurs expect to receive, inclusive of the incomes which they will hand on to the other factors of production, from the amount of current employment which they decide to give (Keynes, 1936/1973, p. 55).

Firms employ workers because they expect to recoup with a profit all of the income they pay out to their employees. Wage levels and employment levels are dependent neither on working hours nor on physical productivity but on the *expectations* of entrepreneurs expressed in money terms. That is, the principle of effective demand stands the traditional analytical perspective on its head. Contrary to the neoclassical claim, income is not defined *ex post* in real terms but is given immediately and definitively in money terms in remunerating production factors. It follows that the unit of economic measurement cannot be inferred from relative exchanges of physical goods and services; it is immediately monetary and absolute.

By virtue of the principle of effective demand as stated above, aggregate supply results from firms' expectations about expenditure that will be made in the goods markets. The amount of wages paid is inferred from the expected amount of sales and not from the quantity of labour relative to the quantity of money paid out in wages. Current output is therefore defined by the circular flow of money income formed when wages are paid. Purchasing power exerted in the goods market is strictly identical to that arising from production, whatever the level of prices. No discrepancy can be observed therefore between 'nominal' income formed when wages are paid and 'real' income spent by households. Income formation and income expenditure concern strictly the same subject-matter. For this reason, the wage-unit as an income-unit is the unit of measurement of output because it expresses the identity between what is produced and what can be purchased. The true status of the wage-unit is to be understood in the analysis of production.

The Wage-Unit as the Fundamental Unit of Measurement

The production process is only meaningful in terms of its purpose, which is to meet the needs of individuals.

> Human effort and human consumption are the ultimate matters from which alone economic transactions are capable of deriving any significance; and all other forms of expenditure only acquire importance from their having some relationship, sooner or later, to the effort of producers or to the expenditure of consumers (Keynes, 1930/1971, pp. 120–1).

Consumption is what makes all production purposeful. The two processes are inseparable because the production process encompasses all the operations necessary to make goods available to consumers. However, it is not confined to the performance of labour.

> Utility then is not the measure of exchangeable value, although it is absolutely essential to it. If a commodity were in no way useful – in other words, if it could in no way contribute to our gratification – it would be destitute of exchangeable value, however scarce it might be, or whatever quantity of labour might be necessary to procure it (Ricardo, 1823/1951, p. 11).

And certainly labour is only taken into account in economics when it is embodied in entities of some useful *form*, which is socially validated by the payment of wages. Hence, emphasising the useful character of products, Say defines the purpose of production.

> Production is never the creation of matter, but the creation of utility. It is not measured by the length, volume or weight of the product, but by the utility imparted to it (Say, 1803/1972, p. 51; our translation).

Irrefutably, it is not matter that individuals destroy in the act of consumption. What is consumed is the *form* given to matter by human labour. In economics, matter only exists inasmuch as it is encapsulated in a previously imagined form and human labour is only taken into account inasmuch as it is embodied in a form that fulfils the needs of individuals: 'both lessons [classical and neoclassical] are true when combined: labour fits matter into the utility form' (Schmitt, 1984, p. 447; our translation).

Production is characterised by: (1) performance of a physical activity that transforms matter: labour; (2) the creation of previously conceived physical utility forms; and (3) entering the products in a homogeneous numerical form. To produce is therefore to create a previously imagined space that fulfils certain types of relationships that people establish among themselves to meet their needs as consumers. The economic space is not the same as the physical space; it is *created* by people as they produce.

In a wage economy the different types of labour are reduced to a common abstract form – the money wage – which immediately makes them part of certain quantitative relationships. Each wage, each wage-unit, appears from the outset as part of a homogenous whole, the aggregate money income. Again, different types of labour are not related to each other by their concrete character but by the abstract form that their output takes on. It is this form that Marx calls 'value form' (Marx, 1867/1965).

It remains true, nonetheless, that each wage-earner produces to meet his own needs. However, because he contributes to the formation of national income proportionally to the size of his own remuneration, the output of his labour is set directly in proportion to that of others. It follows that the output of each wage-earner is only of utility to him insofar as it is to others. From the instant that wages are paid, utility is grasped in an abstract numerical form, the money form, which constitutes the finite space within which the different economic operations unfold.

Useful products are defined in two inseparable but distinct forms within the economic area, the *physical form* of the objects and a numerical form, the *money form*. Two questions follow from this: (1) what is money?; (2) by what process are the two forms of output integrated?

In the *General Theory*, Keynes asserts on several occasions that money is only useful as a medium of exchange. It is certain then that it is not added to goods to form national wealth and that it is primarily a unit of account. However, although he lays down this principle, Keynes does not follow it through to its conclusion and does not complete his criticism of the quantity theory (Friboulet, 1988, pp. 25 ff). It is Schmitt (1975) who demonstrates the bank credit character of money and as such that it is of no intrinsic value and appears first as a purely numerical form.

> The correspondence between money and products must be understood for what it is. It is not a relation between values, since money is devoid of any positive value, whatever the definition given to that term. The correspondence is between products on one side and money on the other, and in no way between the value of products nor the value of money. The monetary value of products is not the relation between the value of money and the value of products, but the simple money measurement of products: only the relation is a value or equivalence, the terms of the relation being purely physical ones (Schmitt, 1975, pp. 31–2; our translation).

It is, then, the concrete association of money with products that defines money as the economic unit of measurement. As a pure form created by banks, money only really exists in society insofar as it is attached to the objects formed in production and the objects themselves only exist as economic goods insofar as they are recorded in money units. The correspondence between money and products is effected in a specific operation: the payment of wages. As soon as it encompasses useful objects, the nominal money unit is transformed into an income unit thus becoming *real*. Hence it can be the subject of demand for its own sake as it is *value*. The wage relation means that goods and money are not defined in two disjointed areas needing to be brought together in the market.

Of course, when wages are paid, an exchange takes place. However, this is not a transfer of wealth between two agents, the worker on one side and the employer on the other. As we pointed out, money has no value until it is associated with the physical product. Likewise, labour (or the force involved) has no economic existence until it is embodied in some utility form. The utility form is itself economically undetermined, or even non-existent until embodied in some abstract numerical form. From this it is inferred that no relative exchange of labour against money, nor of labour against manufactured goods can be observed. Labour markets 'do not really exist' (Lavoie, 1992, p. 217) but it is not because, as Eichner (1986) argues, labour cannot be preserved – a number of market services, like transports, are in this position – but rather because labour (or its force) is not a good and accordingly has no price, and the wage-unit is not the price of labour.

In fact, when workers are wage-earners, they are not separated from their product; they receive their own product individually and directly *in money form*. The exchange presiding the formation of wages is unipolar; to use Schmitt's expression, it is an *absolute exchange* because it is not a transfer of wealth but a creation of wealth. In the production process, wage-earners engage in an exchange with themselves in that they convert their labour into a physical product that is itself converted into a money wage by firms and banks. Wage-earners do not sell their labour (or their force) to anyone; their income does not consist of wealth somehow produced outside of their productive activity. They receive in payment the very product to which they have given rise and not some wealth previously accumulated. Wages do not exist before production; they stem from the conversion of labour into a product with a utility and a monetary form.

> The real product arises in money, for if it arose before, it would instantaneously be nil, being merely the result of production–consumption. The interposition of money being the only way to separate consumption from production, the product only arises within money. The product arises 'inside' money and is destroyed upon 'exiting' money, at the moment the former leaves the latter (Schmitt, 1984, p. 461; our translation).

Money and utility do not exist independently of one another; their effectiveness lies in the wages that make up the national income. Of course, wage-earners will not ultimately obtain all of the wealth they have formed. Even so, the payment of wages is a crucial operation as it is at this moment that physical goods are fully grasped in the money form.

A unit of measurement is invariably defined by the relationship between a number and an object.[3] The payment of wages is precisely that material operation by which useful objects and money are brought into relation. The unit in which the integration of utilities and of money is achieved is what Keynes called the *wage-unit*.

It is true that as holders of money income, workers do not hold the useful objects and to obtain them they must spend the money they hold. At the instant that wages are paid out, goods and money form a double-sided stock: (1) physical assets on the one hand, deposited in firms; (2) monetary assets on the other, deposited in banks on the accounts of households. Each of these types of assets exists in respect of the other and holding one precludes holding the other.

It is sure too that workers will not finally gain possession of the entire product to which they have given rise. The economy has other sources of 'primary' income apart from wages: profit, which corresponds to the participation of the owners of capital in production. Because of the very existence of this non-wage income, it might be thought that the quantitative relations resulting from the payment of wages might be 'renegotiated' in the goods market. It is true that when holding money, wage-earners do not hold the useful goods deposited in firms. It may be asked whether the equivalence relation formed in the course of production cannot be questioned, or at least distorted in the goods market because of the discrepancy that there can be between prices and wages. This amounts to asking whether prices do not directly influence wages.

Prices and Wage-Units

As stated above, the principle of effective demand assumes that the income spent in the goods market is strictly equal to the income formed in the production process. 'Income = value of output = consumption + investment' (Keynes, 1936/1973, p. 63).

A first consequence of this double equality is that the purchasing power exercised on the product market is strictly identical to that formed in production and this is so whatever *the level of practised prices in the markets*. The price level, and therefore the distribution of output, is part of the framework of determinants meeting the rationale of succession of actions over time. The sequence 'formation – expenditure of income' means that the *determination* of prices does not affect that of costs. Along with Barrère (1995, p. 409; our translation) we can say that '[t]he money wage "anchors" the price level of commodities'.

One of the important contributions of circuit theory is to have established that in our monetary economies of production, aggregate demand cannot differ from aggregate supply. When they receive their wages, receiving the money form of their output, workers are at that instant solvent claimants of goods deposited with firms for the exact amount they have received in payment. It can be inferred that the wage-unit measures not only the national income as it is formed but also as it is spent on the goods market.

The very logic of the income circuit precludes any lag between production and consumption from calling into question the measurement of output in wage-units. This is the same as saying that when measured in wage-units, national income is one and the same thing and that whether viewed from the standpoint of its formation or its spending, it is both the value *and* the price of what is produced and purchased. In other words, from the principle of effective demand follows the identity of the nominal wage and the real wage, which identity holds fundamentally because the wage-unit is not the counterpart of the goods produced, like two things set down facing one another and then exchanged. The wage-unit is the unit of what is produced and identically the measuring unit of what is purchased, the result being that prices themselves are measured in wage-units. More exactly still, prices can be said to be wage-units as viewed no longer in their formation but in their spending.

To obtain goods, income holders must destroy the numerical form in which they are packaged. In other words, they must convert their money assets into physical goods. The expenditure of income on the goods market appears then as a second absolute exchange (the first being the payment of wages).

> The creation of income and its destruction are therefore two absolute exchanges of opposite sign. The first, which we could call positive absolute exchange, defines the transformation of current output into money income, whereas the second, negative absolute exchange, defines the transformation of income into physical output (Cencini, 1988, p. 91).

Each wage-holder has the power to purchase his own output in whatever utility form it may be. When worker *A* purchases output *y* of worker *B*, and vice versa, he actually buys his own output in the form of a certain quantity of *y*. The exchange of goods *x* produced by *A* for goods *y* produced by *B* is included in that *A* received the money form of goods *x* and not the actual goods *x*, and that *B* received the money form of goods *y* and not goods *y*. In spending his wage (or part of his wage) on the purchase of goods *y*, the producer of *x* exchanges goods *x* for goods *y* as he gives up, by the same token, goods *x* (or part of those goods) that he produced. Having used up his purchasing power in acquiring goods *y*, he leaves the other the power to buy goods *x*. In the form of *x* or *y*, each wage-earner takes his share of the aggregate output corresponding to his involvement in producing the aggregate income and that is expressed by his wage. The (nominal) money wage is indifferently the money envelope of goods *x* and/or *y* (real wage). The nominal wage is identical to the real wage; they have strictly the same subject-matter.

The exchange directly meets the division of labour, which is itself expressed by the remuneration of those involved in production. Thus there are not two measurements of output but a single one, the reason being that demand for a good defines supply of the same good in a different form and supply of a good defines demand for the same good in another form. Any exchange is, in fact, a conversion: each agent converts his money assets into the real form of goods inscribed in the money he holds.

Thus, what is termed the inflexibility of the wage–price relationship is not the opposite of the flexibility of relative prices of neoclassical theory but rather the sign of the immanence of the monetary measurement of output. The incomplete flexibility, the stickiness in Davidson's expression (1994), results from money imposing a timing constraint; expenditure of money income can only occur after its formation. Product prices are not therefore a factor in determining national output.

The relative prices of different products stem from the quantitative relationship uniting goods and money when wages are paid. The physical content of a wage-unit may be different from one firm to another. Two firms producing similar items may well pay their employees different wages, either overall or on the basis of their different skills. Nevertheless, 'equilibrium' (that is, the realisation of firms' expectations) supposes that each firm recovers the money-units corresponding to the units of physical goods manufactured. Exchanges are made in the goods market in keeping with a strict law: the quantity of money spent by wage-earner A from firm F for the purchase of a good y produced by a wage-earner B from firm F' is strictly equal to the quantity of money spent by B to buy the output x (or a part of it) of firm F.

The wage bill defines an area with strictly defined borders within which current prices are determined. It follows that the system of prices *practised* cannot vary infinitely. Whether firms' *forecasts* are realised or not does not alter the fact that the firms *expect* a certain level of profit and therefore a certain level of employment in view of the supply price they think they can charge (Dos Santos Ferreira and Michel, 1991).

However, prices have an essential function in that they allow the distribution of output between wage income and non-wage income. Whereas wages express the share that workers take in the formation of output, prices charged in the goods market bring out the share of the current output to be paid to capital: profit.

PRICES AND PROFIT

The quantum theory of production developed by Schmitt (1984) allows us to understand that profit is not a surplus and that, being macroeconomically net, it is 'a nested category of nominal wages'. This analysis of profit is summarised briefly with a simple numerical example.[4]

Profit and Wages

Let us consider a firm F_1 with an output of 100, that is, it pays 100 wage-units to worker L_1. In order to show that profits are formed within wages, we consider that L_1 spends his wage entirely with F_1 alone and that the only customers of F_1 are L_1 and the holders of dividends and interest paid by F_1, D_1.

It is supposed that F_1 expects[5] to make a profit of 20 wage-units, leading it to present its products in the market at a price such that the holders of wage income can only acquire for their own account 80/100 of the product to which they have given rise. F_1 must therefore sell its output at a price of $100/80 \times 100 = 125$.

Given that L_1 has only 100, it cannot spend 125 on purchasing the output of F_1. However, because of the practised price, the output of F_1 is divided into two categories: wage-goods and profit-goods.

We have already noted that profit is not additional to nominal wages and so it is logical that it should not appear immediately as a constituent part of output. It is not the remuneration of labour, but the remuneration of the contribution of owners of capital to production. 'Accommodated' in the actual output of F_1, and therefore 'carried' by nominal wages, profit results from a transfer of a part of the purchasing power formed when wages are paid.

A firm can only make a profit by selling its production in the goods market. But, at the same time, the subject-matter of profit is a fraction of output, that is, profit-goods. It is this fraction of output that we now need to understand.

In our example, when F_1 recovers 100 on the product market, it has recouped all of its production costs. However, because of the practised price, it has only delivered 80 to L_1, whereas the wage-earners' income is destroyed fully and definitively. The result of the distribution made on the goods market is such that the aggregate output is shared out among wage-goods, the 80 consumed by L_1, and profit-goods, the 20 held by F_1. The income formed within F_1 is indeed 100, but by spending 100, L_1 has only obtained 80. Hence L_1 has destroyed a purchasing power of 80 for its own account, while 20 continue to exist in the economy. The explanation behind all this is that any income is initially formed as a wage, but national income is not made up of labour earnings only. Income distribution on the goods market reveals that a fraction of production, here 20 wage-units, is 'capital income'.

The 20 in profit-goods are initially formed and monetised indistinctly within the aggregate current income, the proof being that L_1 receives 100 from F_1 and not 80. The profit-goods category can only show itself as such *post factum*, once F_1 has recouped 100 in money and having given out part only of the output to workers, here 80. Thus when L_1 gives back 100 to F_1, because of the practised price for wage-goods, a division of output occurs. At the outcome of the process, L_1 has consumed the equivalent of 80 and F_1 has obtained 20. Wages are destroyed while F_1 has caught 20 for the benefit of its assigns.

The feedback principle pointed out by Schmitt (1984) allows us to understand that the division of output effected on the goods market reflects, backwards, upon production. The division of output into wage-goods and profit-goods can be set against the division of workers between those engaged in producing wage-goods and those engaged in producing profit-goods. The latter are obviously paid in the same way as the others, but they will not purchase the goods they have manufactured; they will only buy wage-goods. It can be understood then that there is no need to imagine that the profit-goods drawn off by F_1 are monetised with the help of an advance payment of extra credit relative to wage costs,[6] nor by using previously accrued funds. In addition, the amount of profit, although expected, is not determined beforehand: it results from *the sale of wage-goods* at a price above their cost of production. It is because L_1 spends 100 on the market for produced goods that profit is 20; if he spent less, then profit would be lower.

Expecting a profit of 20, F_1 sets its level of production at 100 wage-units counting that at a unit price of 1.25 it will recoup all of its outlay and this without supplying all of its output to the holders of wage-income. To enjoy a monetary profit of 20, F_1 must sell the wage-goods it has produced at a price of 100, that is, 80×1.25. We assume that it achieves this goal and recoups 100 while L_1 spends 100 in purchasing wage-goods. The result of the operation is that F_1 has covered all of its production costs and has not delivered its whole product to the wage-earners.

The profit is certainly net. The 20 captured from L_1 relate to effective purchasing power that is not exerted. Nonetheless, the bank account of L_1 is empty, that is, like the 80, the 20 in money are destroyed, and yet their subject-matter remains and constitutes the physical form of profit to which corresponds a monetary form. To explain this we shall use strictly the same data as before, to which we shall add dividend and interest holders, D_1, who, it is assumed, receive all of the profit made. Suppose that D_1 spend their entire income in purchasing profit-goods.

Following these assumptions, F_1 may ask its bank to credit the account of D_1 for the amount of profit. As noted above, money is bank credit-money, and so banks are able to create money forms in connection with utility forms. The money created is additional to that issued for the payment of wages, so that the purchasing power of each wage-unit is divided accordingly, by 1.25 in our numerical example. In fact, the money created as profit is added to the wages issued.

It may be asked, however, whether the definition of output in wage-units is not contradicted by the formation of monetary profit. The fact is that if we look at the aggregate flow of money-units, there are more money-units in the economy than wage-units, although the measurement in wage-units is not contradicted. What has changed in the operation is that the purchasing power of each money-unit has been divided by 1.25. The wages corresponding to profit-goods have been voided of purchasing power and destroyed without the wage-earners obtaining the goods they represent. The money created as profit is in fact a *duplication* (Schmitt, 1998, p. 76) of that destroyed from wages; the money form of profit duplicates the money form of wages.

Finally, there is no discrepancy between the number of wage-units and the purchasing power available in the economy. The 'monetary' illusion stems from the fact that the same wage-units are counted twice over, once in the hands of wage-earners and once in the hands of interest and dividend holders.

If we apply this analysis to our numerical example, a problem is left outstanding. We claimed that the profit expressed in wage-units is 20. It would be quite unrealistic to think that profit-goods are proposed separately from other goods on the market and that their unit prices are different from those of wage-goods. Thus, as the profit is 20 in value and the unit price of sale is 1.25, D_1 should have 25 and not 20. It can be asked then why profit is 20 and not 25. The answer is straightforward.

Having drawn off 20, F_1 pays these 20 to D_1. The latter spends them on profit-goods, which are sold like other goods at a unit price of 1.25. Thus D_1 obtains $20/1.25 = 16$ in value. Given that F_1 does not make a profit on profits, it pays back the benefit of 4 in dividends and interest, which will again be spent, and their holders obtain $4/1.25 = 3.2$, and so on. The process is repeated until the sum in value equals 20. In fact, if it pays interest and dividends only once, F_1 directly takes out 25 for the benefit of its assigns. The dividends and interest measured in wage-units are not 25 but $25/1.25 = 20$.

Finally, F_1 sold $80 + 20 = 100$ in value at an aggregate price of 100 wage-units. It is true that as the unit price was 1.25, the total revenue resulting from the sale of all the output of F_1 is 125, that is, prices 'may be macroeconomically greater than the corresponding values' (Schmitt, 1998, p. 68; our translation). In fact, the gap between the value of output and prices arises from the fact that profit is counted as wages and as dividends and interest on one side and that the same units of money are counted several times in the circular flow of dividends and interest. Expressed as wage-units, nominal income is therefore strictly equal to real income.

Profit is not the outcome of gratuitous labour, contrary to the belief of a number of circuit theorists[7] who, either implicitly or explicitly, introduce the Marxian theory of surplus value of labour. From there on, if profit is not the result of the surplus value of labour, the issue of its monetisation[8] is pointless. Profit is not monetised separately from the remainder of current output, but when wages are paid. A consequence of this is that as profit is a 'telescopic' category of wages, it comes up against an objective limit.

Profit is Objectively Limited to Half of Current Output

The duplication mechanism referred to above is sufficient in itself to show that the amount of profit cannot be greater than that of wages and therefore that the volume of profit-goods cannot exceed half of aggregate output.

Nonetheless, it may be helpful to set out the question in a simple arithmetic form. To understand the objective limit of profit within income, the relations used above are expressed in a more general form.

Let w_i be the amount of wages paid by any firm F_i. The wage production cost for all the output of F_i, wage-goods and profit-goods included, is therefore w_i. Profit-goods are designated w_π. As these make up a fraction of the output of F_i, we have the relation:

$$w_\pi \leq w_i$$

Let p_i be the multiplier coefficient applied to wages. This coefficient expresses the proportions in which F_i wishes output to be attributed to labour or to capital to remunerate and/or maintain it. Here we retain the assumption that profit is fully redistributed in the form of dividends and interest, which we designate d_i.

Working within the perspective of the principle of effective demand, we must bear in mind that firms determine the level of employment they provide on the basis of their *expected* total sales revenues, in the perspective of achieving maximum profit. Coefficient p_i applied to wages allows us to express the *money price* of output, which is nothing other than the sum total of wage income and non-wage income: $w_i + d_i$.

All goods, whether profit-goods or wage-goods, are presented on the market at the same unit price. In other words, the same coefficient p_i applies to the entire output of F_i, the sale price of the product is therefore $w_i.p_i$.

When profit-goods are sold, F_i will recoup:

$$w_\pi p_i = d_i \tag{17.1}$$

d_i may also be expressed as the difference between the sale price of the product and the amount of wages paid:

$$d_i = w_i.p_i - w_i \tag{17.2}$$

We assume that F_i sells all of its output to its employees and assigns; its total sales revenue, S, may therefore be calculated in either of two ways. Either:

$$S = w_i + d_i \tag{17.3}$$

or:

$$S = p_i.w_i \tag{17.4}$$

As $w_i + d_i = p_i.w_i$, p_i may be expressed as:

$$p_i = \frac{w_i + d_i}{w_i} \qquad (17.5)$$

Combining (17.1) and (17.2), $w_\pi p_i = w_i.p_i - w_i$, yields a second expression for p_i, namely:

$$p_i = \frac{w_i}{w_i - w_\pi} \qquad (17.6)$$

The proportion of output to which dividend holders are entitled can then be written:

$$w_\pi = \frac{w_i(p_i - 1)}{p_i} \qquad (17.7)$$

From this expression we can already deduce that profit is positive when $p_i>1$.
   In (17.7) we can replace p_i by its expression (17.5), giving:

$$w_\pi = \frac{w_i.d_i}{w_i + d_i} \qquad (17.8)$$

which relation is at maximum equal to ½ $(w_i + d_i)$,[9] so that:

$$w_i \le \tfrac{1}{2}(w_i + d_i) \qquad (17.9)$$

As we have seen, w_π is a fraction of w_i, meaning that:

$$w_\pi \le w_i \qquad (17.10)$$

Thus, when profit is maximum, we obtain:

$$\tfrac{1}{2}(w_i + d_i) = w_i \qquad (17.11)$$

As $w_i + d_i = w_i.p_i$, we can write:

$$\tfrac{1}{2} w_i.p_i = w_i \qquad (17.12)$$

From this we can deduce that profit is maximum when:

$$p_i = 2 \tag{17.13}$$

Generally:

$$1 \le p_i \le 2 \tag{17.14}$$

When $p_i = 2$, the share of profit-goods in output can be deduced from expression (17.15):

$$w_\pi = \frac{w_i(p_i - 1)}{p_i} \tag{17.15}$$

by replacing p_i by 2, we obtain:

$$w_\pi = \tfrac{1}{2} w_i \tag{17.16}$$

Generally, we have:

$$w_\pi \le \tfrac{1}{2} w_i \tag{17.17}$$

Spelled out, this reads: *the volume of profit-goods, w_π is at most equal to half of the wages paid out by F_i.* We can draw the general conclusion that the *gross profit* made by each firm within its own output cannot be greater than half of the value of that output, *whatever the price charged* in the markets for goods and services.

If we substitute the maximum value for p_i in (17.2), namely $d_i = w_i.p_i - w_i$, we get:

$$d_i = w_i \tag{17.18}$$

and hence generally:

$$d_i \le w_i \tag{17.19}$$

This amounts to saying that, expressed in money-units, profit is at most equal to the amount of wages paid. This result is representative of the fact that money lent by banks to households holding dividends and interest is, in fact, a duplication of money-units issued for the remuneration of employees engaged in producing profit-goods.

What is true for one firm holds for the set of firms. Each firm forms its profit within its own output, and so the amount of profit formed by one has no effect on that made by others. Being internal to the output of each firm, profit is macroeconomically net. It being the case that the profit specific to one firm cannot exceed half of its output, we can then say that the *aggregate net profit* of all firms making up an economy *cannot be greater than half of the national output.*

This conclusion is not dependent on the means of regulation nor on the state of competition. Whether regulation is liberal or not, whether competition is perfect or not, the limit to profit within national output is given objectively by the very nature of today's economies based on wage earnings. Thus the stickiness of the wage–price relationship cannot be explained by institutional factors peripheral to the economic domain – state intervention or welfare protection, and so on – but rather by the very foundations of our monetary production economies. The inflexibility observed in the different markets does not stem from imperfections in their operation, but essentially from the fact that *the share of wage-goods in national output cannot be less than half of current output.*

However, it might be thought that the form of competition could call these conclusions into question. Many authors, post Keynesians in particular, defend the idea that the more or less monopolistic position of a firm directly influences the amount of profit it can make. This point of view seems to be based on a confusion about the very concept of profit, which is wrongly taken to be the same as the commercial gain that a firm can make.

Profit and Extent of Monopoly

It is true that, market conditions permitting, a firm can freely set the selling price of its products. *Prima facie*, it might be argued that because of its market power, a firm can charge monetary prices allowing it to form a commercial gain so that it can distribute dividends and interest that are greater than the amount of wages it has paid out. This will give the impression, as in Kalecki (1971), that the degree of monopoly is an explanatory factor of profit and therefore that the monopoly coefficient can be interpreted as equivalent to the gross profit margin (Lavoie, 1992). If this were so, and the question of the workings of the economy could be 'reduced' to asymmetrical powers and forms of behaviour of the different players, then we could consider along with Cartelier[10] (1996, p. 665) that the Keynesian scheme of equilibrium, characterised by asymmetrical markets, were at best a special case of Walrasian general equilibrium. We can confirm that this is not so.

Imagine that a firm F_1 producing for 100 wage-units can, because of its market power, sell all of its output by applying a coefficient $p_1 = 2.5$ to its wage costs. If it sells all of its output, it will achieve total sales revenue $S = 100 \times 2.5 = 250$.

Given that it has paid out 100 in wages and formed a redistributed profit of 100, since p_1 is at least equal to 2, it cannot achieve total sales revenue of 250 from just the wage income and non-wage income it has formed. Let us confirm this point.

F_1 pays wages for $w_1 = 100$ to L_1 who spends them all with F_1. It applies a coefficient $p_1 = 2.5$ to set the selling price of its product and so remunerates the owners of capital. According to equation (17.17), the volume of profit-goods, w_π is at most equal to $\frac{1}{2} w_i$. Here $w_\pi = \frac{1}{2} \times 100 = 50$.

On this basis, F_1 may pay total dividends and interest, d_1, equal to w_1, but because the price of profit-goods is 2.5, it credits the accounts of its assigns, D_1, for a total of 125. If we stopped at this point, the total sales revenue of F_1 would be $100 + 125 = 225$ and not 250. The wage-earners would obtain $100/2.5 = 40$ and the dividend and interest holders $125/2.5 = 50$. There would thus be 10 unsold, which is why the total sales revenue that F_1 can make from the income it has paid out alone cannot be 250. If, however, and this is our hypothesis, F_1 achieves total sales revenue of 250 and therefore sells up all its output, holders of other income formed outside F_1 have purchased some of the output.

Let us suppose that another firm F_2 employing L_2 has produced $w_2 = 50$. Of this 50, L_2 spends 25 with F_1. The total sales revenue of F_1 is therefore $S = 100 + 125 + 25 = 250$.

By spending 25 with F_1, L_2 obtains $25/2.5 = 10$ of the output of F_1. F_1 has therefore sold up all of its output. Moreover, it can redistribute an extra 15 to its assigns. It follows that the dividends and interest paid are greater than w_1, indeed, $d_1 = 125 + 15 = 140$. It is certain too that D_1 cannot spend with F_1 the 15 extra received and so spends them with F_2, which, let us assume, applies a coefficient of $p_2 = 2$. Let us look at what happens for F_2.

Having 50 and having spent 25 with F_1, L_2 spends 25 with F_2 and obtains $25/2 = 12.5$ of the output of F_2. D_1, for his part, spends 15 in purchasing wage-goods that F_2 did not purchase and obtains $15/2 = 7.5$. F_2 therefore recoups 40 including 20 that are definitively voided and 20 to which coefficient p_2 is applied to form non-wage income: $d_2 = 40$.

The total commercial sales revenue of F_2 will really be $25 + 15 + 40 = 80$ and not 100 as expected by applying $p_2 = 2$. This comes about because, owing to the prices charged by F_1, F_2 is unable to sell part of its output to households, 10, which the firm itself bought when it paid out wages. It has a monetary loss of profit, but nonetheless more than covers the cost of production of wage-goods and its total profit is 40 and not 50. It keeps 10 as a physical stock.

Finally, it turns out that when F_1 applies $p_1 > 2$, it distributes higher dividends, but this is to the detriment of holders of wage income L_1 and holders of dividends D_2. It can be seen that the dividends and interest paid by F_1 do not coincide with the net profit it really formed. The terms are not synonymous and do not designate the same things. For part, 10, the dividends and interest paid by F_1 are a monetary loss of F_2.

It seems that the more or less monopolistic degree of the firm cannot be used as a criterion for determining profit, even if it is a factor that contributes to forming expectations with less uncertainty. Enjoying a more or less monopolistic position, it can be seen that charging prices in excess of two wage-units, a firm earns a 'rent'. This 'rent' does not result from any increased value of the product supplied and, as Ricardo (1823/1951, p. 63) puts it, '[c]orn does not become dearer because a rent is paid; on the contrary, it is because corn is dear that a rent is paid'. Whether or not the 'rent' is paid back to D_1 is not very important here. The increased gap between the amount of wages and of prices is not reflected by any increased macroeconomic profit and does not affect the aggregate profitability of capital.

The stickiness of wages and prices arises essentially because profit cannot come from anywhere but wages, the amount of which fulfils the principle of effective demand. It is formed as an indivisible whole within wages *even before* being distributed among the different agents.

CONCLUSION

Analyses based on the microeconomic study of individual markets and hinging on the more or less monopolistic positions of firms cannot enable us to understand that profit is objectively limited to half of the output of each firm. They are deficient in being incapable of explaining the endogenous inflexibility of the wage–price relation that arises because current income is determined in the circular flow of wage-units formed in production. The principle of effective demand requires that no income can be engendered in the goods market. All income being formed in production, it cannot be determined in the relations of exchange observed in individual markets.

There is indeed a degree of inflexibility in the relation between wages and prices, but this is not because of exogenous factors, nor because of factors inherent to the labour market; it is part and parcel of our monetary economies based on wage-earning. The fundamental relation behind wages and prices is not down to the behaviour of players in the different markets, nor to socio-institutional constraints that are exogenous to the markets. From that, the issue of price levels relative to wages can be raised in a perspective that cannot be reduced to the workings of markets alone and to the interplay of forces exerted in the markets.

There are not two fields for determining economic magnitudes, one macroeconomic and the other microeconomic. It is pointless to look for microeconomic foundations for determining wages and product prices, as if they were determined in separate spaces whose connections needed to be discovered. The strict definition of the wage-unit as a unit of measurement allows us to understand that prices are not formed in transactions on the goods market by virtue of supposed microeconomic laws of behaviour. Prices are not variables formed in relative exchanges made by agents acting independently of each other. They are, in fact, values and their determination arises from the necessary and constantly confirmed equality between aggregate supply and aggregate demand.

NOTES

1. We do not address the definition of the labour-unit, or the hour of 'normal' work, which is, to the best of our knowledge, still unresolved.
2. See Patinkin (1965/1972, pp. 313 ff).
3. Frege (1884/1969) is of particular interest on this point.
4. We do not repeat here the entire demonstration that can be found in Schmitt (1984).
5. The firm *acts* on its forecasts about the future state of the market. Income holders are free to purchase or not the products on offer, so the firm's expectations may not concur with the income holders' choices.
6. Contrary to the argument of Parguez (1980).
7. Namely Poulon (1982), Parguez (1986) and Zerbato (1990).
8. See Ferrari (1991).
9. This can be confirmed by using remarkable identities. $(a+b)^2 = a^2 + 2ab + b^2$. From this $2ab$ $\leq (a+b)(a+b)$. It follows that $\dfrac{2ab}{a+b} \leq (a+b) \Rightarrow \dfrac{ab}{a+b} \leq \dfrac{1}{2}(a+b)$.
10. According to Cartelier (1996, p. 665; our translation, emphasis added) '[u]nder the assumption of an inflexible nominal wage, which is of no consequence for the Walras's model, it appears that any Keynesian equilibrium may be the outcome of Walrasian trial and error. . . If, during the Walrasian trial and error process, the economy *encounters* a Keynesian equilibrium, it will keep to it'.

REFERENCES

Barrère, C. (1995), 'Une problématique keynésienne pour l'économie industrielle', in *Nouvelles perspectives de la macroéconomie. Mélanges en l'honneur du Doyen Alain Barrère*, Paris: Publications de la Sorbonne, 393–412.

Cartelier, J. (1996), 'Chômage involontaire d'équilibre et asymétrie entre salariés et non-salariés', *Revue économique*, **47** (3), 655–66.

Cencini, A. (1988), *Money, Income and Time: A Quantum-Theoretical Approach*, London and New York: Pinter Publishers.

Davidson, P. (1994), *Post Keynesian Macroeconomic Theory*, Aldershot and Brookfield: Edward Elgar.

Dos Santos Ferreira, R. and P. Michel (1991), 'Keynes' aggregate supply function and the principle of effective demand', *Recherches économiques de Louvain*, **57** (2), 159–87.

Eichner, A.S. (1986), *Towards a New Economics: Essays in Post-Keynesian and Institutionalist Theory*, London: Macmillan.

Ferrari, J.M. (1991), 'La théorie du circuit est-elle pertinente pour l'analyse du profit?', *Revue française d'économie*, **6** (3), 143–81.

Frege, G. (1884/1969), *Les fondements de l'arithmétique*, Paris: Seuil.

Friboulet, J.-J. (1988), *Profit, investissement et inflation. Essai sur le Traité de la monnaie*, Berne: Peter Lang.

Gnos, C. and B. Schmitt (1990), 'Le circuit, réalité exhaustive', *Économies et Sociétés* ('Série Monnaie et Production', 6), **24** (2), 63–74.

Hansen, A.H. (1953/1967), *Introduction à la pensée keynésienne*, Paris: Dunod.

Kalecki, M. (1971), *Selected Essays in the Dynamics of the Capitalist Economy*, Cambridge: Cambridge University Press.

Keynes, J.M. (1930/1971), *A Treatise on Money*, London: Macmillan. Reprinted in *The Collected Writings of John Maynard Keynes*, Vols V and VI, London and Basingstoke: Macmillan.

Keynes, J.M. (1936/1973), *The General Theory of Employment, Interest and Money*, London: Macmillan. Reprinted in *The Collected Writings of John Maynard Keynes*, Vol. VII, London and Basingstoke: Macmillan.

Lavoie, M. (1992), *Foundations of Post-Keynesian Economic Analysis*, Aldershot and Brookfield: Edward Elgar.

Marx, K. (1867/1965), *Le capital* ('Bibliothèque de la Pléiade'), Paris: Gallimard.

Parguez, A. (1980), 'Profit, épargne, investissement: éléments pour une théorie monétaire du profit', *Economie appliquée*, **33** (2), 425–55.

Parguez, A. (1986), 'Au cœur du circuit ou quelques réponses aux énigmes du circuit', *Économies et Sociétés* ('Série Monnaie et Production', 3), **20** (8–9), 23–39.

Patinkin, D. (1965/1972), *La monnaie, l'intérêt et les prix*, Paris: Presses Universitaires de France.

Poulon, F. (1982), *Macroéconomie approfondie: équilibre, déséquilibre, circuit*, Paris: Cujas.

Ricardo, D. (1823/1951), *On the Principle of Political Economy and Taxation*, London: Macmillan. Reprinted in P. Sraffa and M. Dobb (eds), *The Works and Correspondence of David Ricardo*, Vol. I, Cambridge: Cambridge University Press.

Say, J.-B. (1803/1972), *Traité d'économie politique*, Paris: Calmann-Lévy.

Schmitt, B. (1975), *Théorie unitaire de la monnaie, nationale et internationale*, Albeuve: Castella.

Schmitt, B. (1984), *Inflation, chômage et malformations du capital*, Paris and Albeuve: Economica and Castella.

Schmitt, B. (1998), *Le chômage et son éradication*, University of Fribourg, unpublished.

Zerbato, M. (1990), 'Intérêt, profit et bouclage monétaire du circuit', *Économies et Sociétés* ('Série Monnaie et Production', 6), **24** (2), 97–106.

18. Involuntary Unemployment and Investment

Xavier Bradley

INTRODUCTION

Investment or the process of capital accumulation has always played the key role in any thorough explanation of unemployment. This is particularly the case for Keynes, who tried to prove that a lack of investment is responsible for the existence of an *involuntary* unemployment.[1] To reach this objective, Keynes based his analysis on the concept of income rather than on those of prices and volumes, explicitly rejecting the traditional dichotomy between the theory of value and the theory of money.[2] For this reason, any analysis of investment founded on the circuit of incomes has to take into account the Keynesian system when it deals with the dysfunctions of the economy. On the other hand, Keynes's analysis cannot be directly adopted in its original form because, in spite of announcing a profound reconstruction of economic analysis, he fell back on traditional conceptions at crucial stages; in particular, Keynes's definition of investment is surprisingly vague and therefore 'very unsatisfactory for the purposes of a causal analysis, which ought to be exact' (Keynes, 1936/1973, p. 39).

Our objective here will be to identify why at crucial points Keynes did not stand to his own objectives. This will enable us to propose solutions consistent with a macroeconomic analysis of money incomes.

INVESTMENT AND THE CIRCULATION OF INCOME IN KEYNES'S ANALYSIS

In his writings on unemployment, Keynes always insisted that the unemployed would not find any job unless the level of investment could be increased. In the *General Theory*, Keynes (1936/1973, pp. 135–7) explained that the marginal efficiency of capital decreases with the accumulation of capital. The declining marginal efficiency of capital (or m.e.c.) is compared to the interest rates that, for reasons specific to the characteristics of money,[3] will stay at the same level or will not decrease as fast as the m.e.c. does. This implies that investment is brought to a standstill before all workers willing to work at current conditions have found a job. To overturn this tendency, Keynes advocated a programme of investment, encouraged or even engineered by the government,[4] together with a redistribution policy so as to increase the marginal propensity to consume.[5]

The peculiarity of such a policy is that, once the initial investment programme is under way, the working of the multiplier process will automatically lead the system to full employment. This means that, although entrepreneurs would not invest spontaneously for fear of unprofitability, nevertheless they would not incur any loss should their fears be overcome. The unavoidable conclusion therefore is that there is no real structural malfunction in the economy; it is only psychological tendencies that have to be overcome. The m.e.c. does not emerge as an objective error-free computation but rather as the reflection of what the entrepreneurs are imagining at the present time. If there is a genuine structural problem in the economy, the unprofitability of investment projects will constitute a symptom of a malfunction and if entrepreneurs are to go on with these projects, they will eventually incur a real loss. Keynes's use of the concept of involuntary unemployment tends eventually to shift the responsibility of unemployment from the workers to the entrepreneurs or to the *rentiers*. A true involuntary unemployment should not have its origin in the behaviour of *any* economic agent. The concept of involuntary unemployment[6] must indeed mean that some workers willing to work cannot find a job but, to have any significance, it should also mean that entrepreneurs and investors cannot develop their activities as much as they would like to do.

Keynes (ibid., p. 62) defined investment simply as a transaction between entrepreneurs; however, this in turn raises the question of the definition of an entrepreneur. Surprisingly, instead of addressing the problem, Keynes (ibid., pp. 61–2) declared that he had nothing to add to traditional discussions on this matter: the frontier between investment and consumption goods depends on the use of the goods by their buyer. In view of the importance of the concept of investment in Keynes's system, this low-key approach is quite amazing. The origin of this lack of precision lies in fact in a conception of income that tried to combine traditional and innovative material.

Keynes (ibid., Ch. 10) developed his analysis of the role of investment when dealing with the multiplier process. The study of this mechanism is extremely useful both to highlight the inconsistency of Keynes's conception of investment and to help devise a solution. The multiplier process is based on the idea that an increase in the volume of a specific variable will cause an increase in the volume of another variable by a multiplying coefficient greater than one.[7] This multiplication is entirely based on investment driving saving in spite of their being always equal; as Keynes emphasised,[8] the level of income will vary to keep saving at the same level as investment. The fundamental condition for the working of the multiplier is that spending a certain amount of income will not destroy it but will rather transfer it from one agent to another. In Keynes's framework, spending keeps the momentum in the formation of income whereas saving will stop it. This principle, however, is supposed to coexist with a different kind of income formation: the creation of new incomes through investment. We end up therefore with a circuit of incomes that has the following features: *creation* of incomes through investment, *transmission* and *conservation* of incomes through consumption spending, *hoarding* of incomes through saving.

This circuit suffers from an evident dissymmetry: two different channels are available for the *formation* of incomes but there is no corresponding *destruction* of incomes. The logical problems raised by this construction can be illustrated by the question of the length of the period: as saving only keeps incomes without destroying them, any lengthening of the period of observation would increase the chances of the savings being spent; such a circuit is therefore highly explosive because there is no real device that will limit or compensate the formation of incomes.

A LOGICAL CONCEPTION OF THE CIRCUIT OF INCOMES

Contrary to what he advocated, Keynes has not been able to distance himself from the traditional dichotomy between monetary and real variables. In the traditional approach, this dichotomy originated from interpreting any transaction as a variant of the fundamental operation of exchange. Along this line, money spending is viewed as an exchange between a certain amount of money and a certain amount of goods; this explains why barter played such a significant role in the presentation of the basic traditional analysis. Focusing on *income*, Keynes shifted the emphasis from exchange to production.[9] Considered in the perspective of production, consumption appears quite clearly as its symmetrical operation; this means that goods enter the economic system through production and leave it through consumption. Now, a consistent working of the income circuit, that is, dichotomy-free, would imply that the formation/creation of incomes comes about through production and that the use/destruction of incomes is performed through consumption. But, in the multiplier process, Keynes chose to interpret consumption as a conservation of incomes, thereby reintroducing a dichotomy between money incomes and 'real' goods. This is another instance of dissymmetry in Keynes's scheme: production brings on goods and creates incomes but consumption is supposed to preserve incomes while withdrawing goods from the economic system.

Considering, as Keynes did, that income spending does not destroy incomes but, on the contrary, preserves them, leads to the conclusion that income spending is a transfer from one agent to another. In this perspective, the formation and the use of incomes are, from a global point of view, identical in nature; these operations are therefore *relative* as they only differ in the view of the agents involved; in addition, it also appears that economic agents are functionally interchangeable.

By contrast, if we adopt the conception of two symmetrical spending operations, one that creates and the other that destroys incomes,[10] then each of these payments will have a *net* effect for the whole economy and not just for individual agents. Aggregating economic agents will not neutralise the effect of each of these operations that are therefore *absolute* and not relative to the position of individual agents. Of course, in the economic system, there are pure transfers of existing incomes; but, indeed, it is important to distinguish these relative transactions, incomes passing from one agent to another without increasing or decreasing the global level of incomes, from those that have a net effect on the economy. If we want to keep the word *exchange* to designate all these operations, we can contrast *absolute exchanges*,[11] net creations or destructions of incomes, with *relative exchanges*, mere transfers of incomes.

From this distinction, a precise meaning can also be assigned to the functions of economic agents. The functions are no longer *relative* to the point of view of the individual agent; they depend on the role played in each (absolute) operation of creation or destruction of incomes.

If the positions were relative we would have a transfer in each direction; this is not the case because the income creation corresponds to the availability of a new batch of goods entering the economic system. This is the key feature to understanding the whole process. The creation of incomes does involve the formation of a claim for the factors and the formation of a debt for the firm but the object of the claim and the debt is that batch of goods that did not pre-exist in the property of the firm. The destruction of incomes implies the annulment of the claim and the debt but this means that the factors obtain in kind what they indirectly owned through the system of claims and debt. At the end of the process, the situations are not symmetrical because the factors will have obtained new goods whereas the firm will get back to its initial situation (provided of course that there are no losses and profits). In a sense, the process is neutral for the firm but has a net positive effect for the factors.

It is quite clear that the firm and the households are not interchangeable in these operations: new incomes cannot be *created* on the firm and existing incomes cannot be destroyed definitely to allow the firm to *consume* goods, that is, to allow goods to leave the economic system.

SPENDING AND THE INSTANTANEITY OF THE CIRCUIT OF INCOMES

It is of interest to note that Keynes did try to examine in detail the payment linked to producing. Initially Keynes elaborated the concept of *finance*[12] only to study the consequences on the rate of interest of the relationship between banks and firms when the latter want to produce investment goods while lacking financial reserves; however, he did stress that the concept of 'finance' should be extended to any kind of production.[13] Moreover, as Keynes considered the rate of interest to be a monetary phenomenon,[14] 'finance' was specifically designed to approach the relationship between money and production.

Writing closely after the publication of the *General Theory*, Keynes wanted to keep the framework elaborated in his latest book. *Finance* being just a component of the *finance motive*, the problem was approached through the motives for the demand for money; this was unfortunate because applying the traditional concepts of supply and demand to analyse the creation of money led Keynes to consider money as a kind of asset. The choice of the word *finance* is quite revealing: Keynes based the whole process on the creation of a *financial* relationship between the firm and its bank; after this initial creation, the financial stocks were supposed to be motioned from one agent to the other.

This concept of finance deals specifically with the situation following the *decision* to pay but preceding the effective payment;[15] the key feature is therefore the initial relation preceding the advent of the stocks. Keynes described it as a bi-directional financial relationship between the firm and its bank. Unfortunately, this hardly constitutes an adequate description of a *creation* because it would imply that the bank owes something to the firm that itself owes the *same* thing to the bank; here, until the firm actually spends, nothing has effectively been created. But is it not possible to rescue the creation by contrasting the time dimension of each side of the balance sheet? Apparently, the asset of the bank seems to have a definite term whereas the firm seems to hold a claim on demand. Unfortunately, this argument is not valid: the bank has not to provide anything on demand; the firm has only the possibility at any moment to pass on to another agent its claim on the bank. On this account, the debt of the firm may have a maximum term but it will be cleared, either before or in due term, as soon as the firm obtains an equivalent claim on the bank.

Keynes (1973, p. 223) justified his approach by referring to the example of a bank authorising an overdraft. However, if an agreement is indeed signed between the bank and its customer to set the rules for future payments, the signing of the contract does not start an effective process of payment. The fact that the overdraft facility may never be used in the future proves that, at the stage of the agreement, nothing has yet been created.

We can therefore safely conclude that it is the actual payment that takes prime place, but this operation will necessarily involve a third element: the firm can only pay an agent distinct from the bank. Three different economic agents will therefore participate in the payment: the payer, the monetary intermediary (the bank) and the payee.

To characterise finance, Keynes stressed that the bank will restore its 'liquidity position' when the payment is made through a 'revolving fund'.[16] The idea of a revolving fund implies an operation going full circle; this is coherent with the restoration of the initial liquidity position. Still, this approach would clearly appear meaningless should we accept that the payment consists in a transfer of wealth from the firm to the workers. It would also be an unsuitable instrument to describe the relations between the firm and its bank. Robertson was at ease to pinpoint the inconsistency (Keynes, 1973, pp. 228–9): if the overdraft facility is utilised by the bank's customer, the bank effectively owes something to the depositor but holds a claim on its customer, hardly a position where the bank restores its liquidity. In the traditional transfer perspective, Keynes's analysis appears totally mistaken. However, it could be that Keynes's embarrassment in identifying the proper operation of creation is an indication that monetary relations are definitely not a segment of financial relations. Keynes would have erred only in applying traditional instruments, the old conception of flows as stocks in motion, to describe a reality that does not fit into this framework. If incomes are first created then destroyed, a flow can no longer be interpreted as a moving stock:

the creation will not require any pre-existing stock whereas the destruction will not preserve the stock. Consequently, the 'revolving fund' would not concern the situation before nor after the payment but would belong to the payment itself. It would be within the payment that a complete revolution is accomplished. In this interpretation, the complete movement cannot stretch through time; it must be confined to the payment itself, to the instant of the payment. This is consistent with the fact that incomes are *created* in the payment of wage-earners and not merely transferred from the firm. Conversely, the use of incomes for consumption by households will destroy these incomes instead of transferring them to the firm.[17] This perspective is at odds with that of the Keynesian multiplier where the consumer effectively obtains something while passing his income on to another agent who, in his turn, can use this income all over again. In this respect, the expression *revolving fund*[18] used by Keynes is misleading because it conveys the idea of a pre-existing *fund* circulated, transferred, through the economic system. But, if a payment were just a transfer, another operation would have to be identified to explain the formation of the asset. Because it stresses on the *revolving operation*, the term *circuit* gives an adequate description of the phenomenon: being a complete process, the circuit of incomes allows explaining the formation of assets without having to assume any pre-existing assets.

THE NATURE OF PRODUCTION

The idea that flows are just stocks in motion takes its roots in the prominence given to *objects* and *services* that are considered the basic elements of the economic system. This explains that relative exchanges are usually considered the essential operations in the system: physical objects result from a combination of physical ingredients and the whole process seems to require an interpretation in terms of an exchange between the inputs and the output.

A deeper inquiry shows however that this approach is inadequate to describe economic phenomena. Of course any economic process is necessarily linked to a physical process but nevertheless these operations belong to distinct domains not to be confused. This is apparent in the fact that interpretations trying to build economic relations on the physical process of transformation will only consider the ingredients that are the *property* of someone; free elements are never taken into account from an economical point of view although they may be crucial to physical transformations. Labour is obviously only one of many contributing factors to the physical shape and characteristics of the goods; however, when focusing on economic relations, labour[19] emerges as the sole source of the capacity for the members of the community to *appropriate* the goods. By making goods available, economic agents obtain the rights to acquire these goods. Consequently, in studying a production process from the economic point of view, it is only new and existing *possessions* that should be considered.

In an auto-consumption economy where individuals consume the result of their own activity, there is no need to measure the capacity to acquire things: goods are instantaneously acquired as soon as available. However, in a community where activities are numerous and collectively organised, it is a necessity to measure individual contributions to the creation of purchasing power or capacity to appropriate. This measurement process also enables relative exchanges to take place: instead of acquiring the goods immediately in kind, the factors of production obtain money incomes that will give them access to anything available in the community. In this perspective, the payment to the factors of production emerges as the endowment with the power to acquire goods newly available in the community; therefore it cannot be interpreted as a transfer because the capacity to acquire did not pre-exist in the property of the firm. It is now easier to understand why a valid payment has to involve three kinds of economic agents. The factors of production produce the new purchasing power whose object is located in the firm organising the physical process; but this newly created purchasing power has to be measured, certified for the whole community, by a neutral agent, a bank representing the whole banking system. Thanks to the monetary payment, the purchasing power created within a particular firm by individual workers is incorporated in the global income of the economic community whereas the goods made available in that firm are incorporated in the stock of the community.

To interpret, as Keynes did with his *finance* concept, the creation of money through a relationship limited initially to the firm and the bank misses the key nature of the process. This dichotomic approach analyses the situation within the instant of the payment with categories belonging to the situation in-between payments; consequently, production, the creation of purchasing power, and money, the quantitative and social measure of this purchasing power, are artificially separated. In fact, the creation of money is intimately connected to production; they are two constituents of the broader phenomenon of the creation of *incomes*. On the side of the factors of production, the money income indicates the number of units of purchasing power endowed to these factors. On the firm's side, a parallel measuring operation forms the counterpart of the money income; by this process the goods newly made available become the object of the purchasing power: in the firm is formed a monetary receptacle that associates monetary units, that is, economic units of measure, to the goods. The function of the first branch of the payment carried out by the bank is therefore to measure the purchasing power, created in the property of the factors, and its content, the goods located in the firm.

We have only dealt with the first part of the income creation but the complete process of the payment leads to a situation characterised by a creditor position on the bank account of the factors, a debtor position on the bank account of the firm and a stock of goods on sale in the firm. We need therefore to explain how this situation of financial claims and debts can be reconciled with the concept of a complete revolution or circuit.

Although the factors of production receive a purchasing power, they postpone the final appropriation of the goods. On the opposite side, instead of handing over the goods immediately, the firm will set up a stock. This implies that the purchasing power is not *suspended* until a future use but, on the contrary, immediately exerted by the firm to detain temporarily the goods. In a sense, the claim and the debt are compensated to liberate the goods for the firm; this completes the circuit, the revolving process, of creation and destruction of incomes. But this completion establishes a financial relationship that calls for a reconstitution of the circuit in the future. The firm obtains the purchasing power only by committing itself to provide the goods on demand; symmetrically, the factors renounce the immediate use of the purchasing power in exchange for a claim to a future use.

Apparently, the working of the circuit seems limited to overdrafts. How then can we account for the common practice of banks requiring that firms back the payment of wages with a financial reserve? In fact, focusing on the overdraft situation is only a means of discerning the fundamental operations. Payments result in financial relations that then can be imputed on existing relations. The financial *consequence* of the 'creation' payment is always that the firm will be indebted to the bank that, in its turn, is indebted to the payees. Now, if, prior to the payment, the firm is endowed with a financial reserve, it holds a claim on other agents. Following the payment, the firm will compensate its new debt by its old claim whilst the bank will have a claim on the debtors of the firm rather than on the firm itself. The existence of a financial provision will therefore only influence the identity of the agent indebted to the bank without affecting the nature of the payment that creates new incomes; this is confirmed by the fact that when the stock of goods is completely cleared, the firm will regain its financial provision.

This approach allows explaining the payments of wages with or without pre-existing financial reserves; it is therefore comprehensive whereas an interpretation exclusively based on transfers of assets cannot explain the *creation* of these assets.

CONSUMPTION AND THE FORMATION OF PROFITS IN THE CIRCUIT OF INCOMES

After being paid, the wage-earners have yet to collect the goods they need; for this, they must now pay the firm in order to acquire the goods in stock. A creation followed by an immediate final use of the capacity to acquire only occurs with an auto-consumption, which precisely excludes money incomes and the intervention of banks. When the banking system is indeed involved, the complete process requires the working of two circuits: the first one leads to a *temporary* destruction while the second one operates the *final* destruction of the incomes created earlier. In-between these payments, the economic agents concerned are indebted or hold financial claims whilst a stock of goods is waiting to be cleared. In this framework, contrary to what Keynes (1936/1973, p. 293) argued, it is finance, not money, that bridges the present and the future, that is, the 'initial' and the 'final' circuits.

Now, let us examine the operation of this final circuit. As in the case of the 'initial' or 'creation' payment, a complete revolving process will involve two complementary branches. From the product angle, the goods have to be transferred to the consumers. This is done through the first stage or branch of the circuit; the complementary second stage will mark the final appropriation of the goods. From the monetary angle, the first phase of the payment creates the receptacle for the goods, that is, recreates the association between the goods and the monetary units of measure, whereas the second phase of the payment empties the receptacle, that is, operates the effective use of the purchasing power. The positions are exactly symmetrical to what they were in the 'creation' payment.

The working of the circuits that create and destroy incomes raises the question of the formation of profits. If the wage-earners receive the purchasing power through a payment by the firm, how could profits be formed in the economy? Indeed there would be no place for profits should production be identified with the physical transformation process. However, the productive role of labour does not concern the material shape of the goods but only establishes a power of appropriation on these goods; it is therefore quite possible that, once produced, the purchasing power could be redistributed amongst economic agents. Moreover, the existence of two distinct circuits, initial and final, leaves room for the formation of secondary incomes.

In the financial situation following the formation of its profits, the firm has gained a creditor position. At first sight, this financial situation invites an interpretation in terms of an external transfer of property, that is, a firm harnessing incomes distributed by one or several other firms; here profits appear to be in the nature of a surplus. This is precisely what Keynes did in his *Treatise on Money*:[20] incomes formed in one sector of activity are supposed to spill over to be spent in addition to the incomes of another sector. Unfortunately, this approach is unable to solve two problems: (1) sectors are supposedly identified before the formation of profits but there is no physical criterion to discriminate between types of goods; (2) if profits are just a surplus gained from other firms, no net profits can be formed by the firms taken as whole.

The difficulty in interpreting the formation of profits is that internal and external operations are intertwined. To say that an internal process of distribution is at work means that the beneficiaries of the firm are able to capture a share of the purchasing power created by the workers of this firm. This means that the formation of profits is in fact a redirecting of incomes: initially all incomes are created in the property of the workers but, owing to distribution operations, some incomes will be re-routed to other households. The beneficiaries have therefore the capacity to acquire a portion of the corresponding stock of goods; yet, they are not interested in obtaining 'own' goods but rather, by selling the captured goods, they want access to goods available elsewhere or to obtain financial assets. For this reason, profits are commonly reckoned only once the whole stock is cleared. Unfortunately, this gives the impression that the secondary operation, the exchange of the captured goods for other incomes, is the prime constituent in the formation of profits whereas the truly fundamental internal re-routing goes totally unseen.

The re-routing of incomes means that the conditions of use of the incomes react on the initial formation of these incomes: in a retroactive way, the incomes will be formed in the property of the firm's beneficiaries. The firm cannot directly benefit from this re-routing process because, if it were, this firm would become both the payer and the payee in the same operation. Although resulting from a distribution process, profits are nevertheless money incomes; this means that the internal process of distribution must involve a complete circuit for the profits. However, this circuit operates in opposite directions as compared to the circuit of primary incomes. This is quite clear for the formation of profits: these originate in the spending of 'primary' incomes. But, by symmetry, profits must therefore be spent, employed, in the operation that creates 'primary' incomes. This means that the corresponding goods are actually appropriated by the spending of the captured incomes. Consequently, profits are not initially formed in kind, as a stock of goods, but are actual incomes, albeit destroyed for a definitive use immediately after their formation; the retroaction or reinterpretation process plays therefore a key role in the circuit of profits because it conditions the formation of profits as an internal partition process. The exchange with incomes distributed by other firms is only subsequent to the appropriation of *profit-goods*.

As for any payment, the formation of each unit of profits must involve a complete circuit, a revolving process; it cannot therefore be interpreted simply as an empty payment unrelated to the product. This circuit will necessarily concern one unit of product with two complementary branches but, at the same time, the process must result in the appropriation of a unit of good by the firm's beneficiaries. The only possibility is that, instead of one isolated empty payment, the process requires two payments for the same content, that is, the same unit of good. When a consumer pays for the goods, the first branch of the circuit forms a receptacle for the goods whereas the second branch liberates the goods for the final appropriation. Even in the case of the formation of profits, the first stage of the payment will create the receptacle to receive a unit of product; this guarantees that the payment is not empty. The distinctiveness of the operation concerns the second stage; here to liberate the unit of good, the consumer is required to carry out another payment of one unit, allowing the beneficiaries to appropriate the corresponding unit of good. Instead of being directly liberated from its receptacle, the same unit of good will fill in another receptacle; two units of debt share the same product. The conclusion is therefore that the capture into profit of one unit of wages cannot take place unless one uncaptured unit of wages is still available to back the profit formation. The startling consequence of this feature is that profits cannot exceed half the amount of incomes[21] initially created by the firm. Consequently, the behaviour of the consumers can only determine the actual amount of profits within the limits from zero to half the global income.

THE INVESTMENT OF PROFITS

The use of the circuit concept to analyse investment raises an important logical difficulty. Would it not be incoherent to have a firm benefiting from the spending of captured incomes to accumulate a stock of capital? Is that not a circular analysis involving the confusion on the same agent, and for the same incomes, of the payer and the payee? Before drawing conclusions let us examine in details the new elements introduced by investment.

As an operation that builds up a stock of capital goods, investment differs from consumption, which, on the contrary, results in the destruction of a stock. The acquisition of consumer goods removes these from the economic system whereas the purchase of capital goods maintains them in the system; in a sense, investment is a modification in the ownership of an existing stock. The difference observed in the stocks when consumed or invested must in some way be reflected in the circuits of incomes. Originally, profits are formed by a partition of the incomes created in a firm whereas spending these profits results in a partition of the stock of goods.[22] The partitioned goods are then sold to consumers in exchange for incomes issued elsewhere. The firm may use these incomes to distribute dividends and interests but, in the case of investment, the incomes issued elsewhere will be spent on equipment.[23] A hasty interpretation would conclude that the investment process is completed once the stock of equipment is in place but this would neglect the economic relations involved in the operation.

What are the features of the spending operation? Firstly, an investment requires an inter-firms transaction: the purchase of goods available in another firm. Of course a firm may produce by itself the equipment it needs but this situation would in fact involve a logical division of the firm in two different departments coexisting in the same company. If we consider the balance sheet of the firm, we can plainly see that the equipment is recorded at its market value;[24] the transaction is therefore to be interpreted as an inter-firms relation, whatever the financial links between the two concerns. Secondly, the most apparent consequence on the internal situation of the firm is the accumulation of a stock to be maintained. The spending of the incomes cannot therefore be interpreted as a simple use, destruction, of incomes, which would clear the stock out of the system, as consumption would do.

The first point just considered focuses on the logical necessity of an external detour by the purchase of goods to another firm or department; this operation allows a firm to overcome the impossibility, due to the distinction between the payer and the payee, to accumulate its own stock of goods. But what is exactly the effect of this operation on the circuits of incomes of the accumulating firm? It is at this stage of the analysis that the second point will prove useful. We saw that, in the formation of profits, the initial capture of 'internal' incomes triggers a retroactive mechanism re-routing incomes and leading to the appropriation of the profit-goods on behalf of the firm's beneficiaries. If a firm is able to spend profits to accumulate equipment goods, it must also benefit from a kind of re-routing process of the profits that were initially destined to its beneficiaries. On the one hand, a second re-routing of the same initial incomes is excluded because these incomes have already been spent in favour of the beneficiaries and because a re-routing process would require a supplementary transaction of some kind between the firm and its beneficiaries. On the other hand, an inter-firms relation is a complex transaction; it involves not only an operation on goods already available, it also implies a reinterpretation of the initial production of these goods. When a firm buys raw materials, it is substituted to its supplier to sell the products. We can say therefore that the inter-firms relation reacts on the initial creation of incomes when the raw materials were produced in the first place.

Now, from this perspective, the purchase of equipment appears as a key operation in the investment process. Of course this transaction gives access to suitable physical types of goods; but much more important is the fact that spending incomes on equipment will react on the conditions of production. As part of an investment process, this reaction, instead of affecting the initial production of the equipment goods, will in fact influence the formation of a new series of profits obtained on a new batch of products. In other words, the purchase of equipment, as the final stage of a process involving past profits, will trigger a new process establishing a link with current profits. This will enable the firm to spend these current profits on the formation or financing of the stock of capital goods. Thanks to the purchase of equipment, the firm is then able to capture, on its own behalf, the new profits (related to the second batch of products) and will exchange these profits for those of the first batch that were destined to the beneficiaries: the whole procedure amounts to a re-routing, in favour of the firm, of the profits initially destined to the beneficiaries.

The involvement of two different production batches connected through an external process guarantees that the interpretation of the investment circuit is not flawed with a vicious circle: the firm is finally able to spend for itself although this was not possible directly. In a sense, the process results in changing a stock of consumer goods into a stock of capital goods. To succeed in this operation, the firm needs the intervention of other agents, of an external production and two internal productions. But considered globally, the proceedings boil down to profits gained on a first batch of production and used on the production of a second batch, which will then constitute a stock of fixed capital.

INVESTMENT AND INVOLUNTARY UNEMPLOYMENT

Let us now see what can be gained by the preceding analysis in contrast with that of Keynes. If investment involves spending incomes, then it seems that it must be carried out at a stage posterior to the production associated with the creation of these incomes; this was not acceptable to Keynes because it would leave open the possibility of an alternative use of incomes that could still justify a decision to produce. Keynes thought that investment would come into being as soon as equipment is produced;[25] it is therefore identified with the decision to produce a certain type of good. This led to the idea of a causal asymmetry between investment and saving:[26] investment was supposedly positioned on the side of the creation of incomes whereas saving was located on the side of the use of incomes. Unfortunately, this approach is not satisfactory for several reasons.

- The whole framework rests eventually on the physical characteristics of the goods but in many cases the same goods can either be consumed or invested.
- If some equipment is left unsold, the producing firm will incur a loss; in this situation, consumption is indeed forced on the owners of the loss-making firm without involving any investment. The physical characteristics of the goods reflect expectations as to the conditions of sale but it is the effective sale that eventually determines the true economic nature of the operation.
- Keynes's interpretation indiscriminately lumps together in the same category the constitution of a stock of goods for sale and that of a stock of capital goods.[27] But a firm producing a new stock of equipment is on the supply side of the economy whereas a firm willing to accumulate a stock of capital is on the demand side. For the supplier, whoever buys the goods on sale is indifferent; as recognised by Keynes,[28] it is the economic function of the purchaser that will determine the nature of the operation, investment or consumption; investment is therefore a component of demand.

There is an interesting intuition in Keynes's analysis: investment does entertain a relation with the production process. However, this is not, as Keynes would have it, the consequence of a choice on the type of goods to be produced but rather because spending profits to accumulate goods will react on a new production set. It is therefore the conditions of income spending, here spending in an inter-firms transaction, that determine the economic nature of the goods although of course certain physical characteristics will suit better a future use in production. The supplying firms will always adjust to the characteristics of demand; it is therefore the investors that are the driving force to form capital goods when they choose to accumulate instead of distributing dividends.

The use of the adjective *involuntary* to characterise unemployment requires the identification of a mechanism of compulsion. By considering that the economic nature of the goods is determined by their physical characteristics, that is, on the supply side, Keynes appeared to exonerate income holders of the responsibility of unemployment. However, in Keynes's system, the behaviour of economic agents did intervene at the earlier stage of the determination of the rate of interest and the m.e.c.[29] Involuntary unemployment will be a relevant concept only on condition that involuntariness is proven comprehensive; this implies that unemployment will arise whatever the behaviour of *all* economic agents. Keynes was not far from that notion with his peculiar characteristics of money stifling demand; in Chapter 17 of the *General Theory*, Keynes argued that the demand for money is a *Danaïd Jar* preventing the purchasing power turning into a demand for products.[30] Unfortunately, the Keynesian 'special properties of money' depend on viewing money as an asset and are totally incompatible with the characteristics of credit money;[31] this attempt at a structural explanation is not satisfactory so that Keynes's explanation rests entirely on the behavioural content of this analysis. If a compulsion mechanism does indeed exist, the physical characteristics of the goods should, in contrast to Keynes's approach, be a result of this mechanism and not its cause.

If the proposed analysis is correct, investment cannot constitute a compulsion mechanism; the reason is that the beneficiaries explicitly give up the use of the profits *for the time being* to allow the formation of a stock of capital goods, very much like wage-earners deposit their incomes to allow the formation of stocks to be cleared later. Here, provided the supplying firms correctly anticipate these decisions, it is only the distribution of employment amongst branches rather than the global level of employment that is in question.[32] Still, the conditions of the formation of the stock of capital goods are such that profits are spent through an operation that establishes a link between two circuits of profits and two batches of production. A sort of 'knot' or 'intersection' of circuits is created and, although the beneficiaries are involved in each individual circuit of profits, they are bypassed by this 'intersection'. This has no immediate negative consequences but all future operations concerning these capital goods will recreate the 'knot' and therefore at first by-pass the owners; supplementary operations will then be required to reinstate the households into the proceedings. These supplementary operations constitute the core of the dysfunctional process that may lead to involuntary unemployment.

To say that part of the economic activity is predetermined, with the consequence that the labour resources cannot be employed elsewhere if these activities are abandoned, implies that the conditions of incomes creation predetermine the use of a portion of these incomes. The only conceivable operation of this kind would be an organic relationship between the productions, and therefore the incomes, of two different periods. Now, there is an obvious candidate for this role: it is the amortisation of the stock of capital.

THE RELATIONSHIP BETWEEN PROFITS AND THE AMORTISATION OF CAPITAL

Any stock of goods is temporary; however, a stock of capital can truly be characterised as *fixed* when the stock, in normal conditions, is maintained by continually replacing obsolete capital. In a sense, stocks of consumer goods are also renewed but there is no organic link between two successive batches. Only the amortisation of capital goods will predetermine the value to be produced although it is usually combined with a net investment when only improved equipment is available. It is therefore the value of capital that is fixed and not the equipment as such. How is it then that, through amortisation, firms, which are intermediary agents, could by-pass households?

When a stock is cleared, the incomes that were accumulated are released to allow the amortisation of the stock or final appropriation of the goods. But more important, this recreation of incomes reproduces the initial conditions of formation of the stock. In the case of consumer goods, members of the households' category have a claim that allows a direct appropriation. The case of the amortisation of fixed capital is a more complex variant: when a firm does accumulate a stock of capital goods, this cannot constitute a final operation precisely because the goods are maintained in the economic system. Here, the incomes linked to the stock will be recreated through a new production process involving this capital. The equipment participates in the process that should give the owners of a firm a right on a portion of the goods made so available; as the consumers buy the entire stock, they also obtain that part which really belongs to the owners of the firm. The allowance for depreciation included in the price of goods is precisely intended to compensate the owners for this loss. But then, is not the whole process simply an exchange between the owners of the firm and the consumers?

Obviously, an exchange does take place in the amortisation process. Still, we can alter slightly the previous question: is amortisation *limited* to an exchange between the owners of the firm and the consumers? Here the emphasis is shifted from the existence of the exchange, which is certain, to the channel of this exchange. There may be room for compulsion if the exchange cannot be *direct*, a pure compensation, but requires a detour for its completion.

At the first stage of the process, the price of the goods provides for the formation of profits for depreciation to be spent in replacement of the obsolete equipment. If the amortisation process or *gross* investment were perfectly sound, the operations would end up here because of the direct exchange between the incomes that come out of the decaying capital and the portion of current profits assigned to amortisation. Through the finished goods, the consumers would then indirectly obtain, hence profits being *gross*, the used capital in exchange of an equivalent portion of the current activity; the owners or beneficiaries of the firm would lose some capital during the production process but this would be compensated or replaced by the newly acquired equipment.

In present conditions, spending profits in an inter-firms transaction will indeed start a retroactive process intersecting with the circuit of the profits assigned to amortisation. At that stage, however, the incomes recreated are not yet available to the beneficiaries because, in the present state of banking procedures, no operation has been designed to deal with the specificity of capital accumulation, which is treated like an ordinary financial relation. Consequently, the beneficiaries are excluded from the initial spending of profits that forms the stock of capital. When the stock is cleared through depreciation, the profits accumulated in the stock cannot therefore be released in favour of the beneficiaries, who are prevented from exchanging directly with the consumers. The relationship established by the incomes emerging from the stock of capital will therefore recreate an intersection of profit circuits severing the link with the beneficiaries. But then how, in spite of this, will the consumers eventually obtain the final goods? In a sense, a process is needed to transform *net* profits back into *gross* profits; in other words, a detour is necessary to re-establish a link between the depreciation of capital and the beneficiaries, allowing the exchange with the consumers. What is the nature of this diversion?

While studying investment, we saw that spending profits of a past period to purchase equipment will necessarily spark off a connection with the retroactive process of current profits. Amortisation is confined to the current period but the incomes recreated from the stock of fixed capital were formed in a previous period. Consequently, the new net profits are exchanged for the recreated profits that are then re-connected with the beneficiaries. Now, at last, it becomes possible for the beneficiaries to abandon the recreated profits to the consumers. But why should this process be considered a malfunction of amortisation? In fact, the detour or intermediate process needed to complete the amortisation is parasitic on the process of profit formation; there is an overaccumulation or overinvestment because *in addition to* the portion of current profits assigned to amortisation, an equivalent amount of current profits, initially free of use, has to be invested to complete the process; in other words, there will be a reduction in the amount of profits available for distribution to the beneficiaries of the firm. This whole process leads therefore to a decrease in the rate of profit; or, to put it differently, a portion of current profits will be predetermined, escaping the free decision of the owners of the firm.

An innocuous amortisation process would only link current gross profits and formerly accumulated profits. But the present dysfunctional amortisation is a two-part process: current net profits are linked to formerly accumulated profits and these are then linked to current 'free' profits that thereby become gross profits. During this process, a duplication in the purchasing of equipment will take place: instead of a strict compensation of the loss of value in the stock of capital, there is an additional or overaccumulation of capital for exactly the same amount. The depreciation of capital is compensated twice; gross investment induces a net investment of the same amount, an overinvestment.

FROM OVERINVESTMENT TO UNDERINVESTMENT

The idea that there may be a situation of overinvestment in the economy is not unfamiliar; it is, in fact, the basic tenet of all analyses of business cycles. But, usually, overinvestment is viewed as the consequence of expectational errors. These errors are then attributed either to the entrepreneurs themselves or to the interventions of governmental or monetary authorities sending wrong signals to the entrepreneurs; Keynes's conception of overinvestment clearly belongs to the former category of explanation: for him, overinvestment is caused by the poor quality of (long-term) expectations.[33] Expectations may indeed be inaccurate and lead firms to invest too much; however, if a real structural problem does exist in the economic system, it should persist even when expectations are error-free.

Amortisation induces a supplementary investment but in what way is it an excessive investment? As the stock of fixed capital increases in the economy, so will the need to compensate for depreciation but this requires supplementary investment that feeds on profits that should be free to use. There is therefore a competition between spending profits for supplementary investment and distributing dividends. Initially, this phenomenon will stay unnoticed because the amount of profits going to supplementary investment and lost to dividends can be offset by an increase in the overall amount of profits. However, we have emphasised earlier that the formation of profits is a process requiring the intervention of uncaptured units of wages; more specifically, each unit of profit needs a relay by a unit of uncaptured wages in a mechanism that bears some resemblance with that of a unit of amortisation requiring the relay of a unit of supplementary investment. The consequence of this need for preserved uncaptured wages alongside captured wages, that is, profits, is that profits cannot extend to the entire national income (independently of the social feasibility of such a situation where workers would be deprived of any remuneration); thus the total amount of profits in the economy cannot theoretically exceed half the global income. Given this limit, the increasing needs of overinvestment will no longer be compensated for by the extension of the mass of profits. Consequently, the percentage of profits *available for dividends* will sooner or later start to decrease and at this stage the negative influence of overinvestment in the economy will become apparent.

At this point, we join up the Keynesian perspective of a disconnection between the rate of profit and the rate of interest. Entrepreneurs cannot make any difference between normal and supplementary investments; the overinvestment channel will therefore no longer be applicable once the *accurately* expected profitability of these projects falls below the rate of interest. Of course, the management in individual firms will only blame the desires of the public without identifying the macroeconomic dysfunctional nature of this phenomenon.

At this stage of the analysis, we have two problems to consider. What is the reason for the disconnection between rates of profits and rates of interest? Is it possible to amortise through a channel other than that of overinvestment?

We saw the structural reason for the dwindling profitability of investment projects but what about the level of interest rates? The rates of profits in the industry certainly influence the rate of interest so that a decrease in the latter will probably cause a partial decrease of the former. Nevertheless, interest rates are also determined by payments of interest between economic agents, especially households, without involving any circuit of profit; the key point is that these payments are not affected by the overaccumulation process. Consequently, the rates of interest will not decrease or not as much as the rates of profit. When this happens, the owners of firms should rationally decide to shelve their investment projects, including overinvestment, and instead put their money on financial markets or in the banking system. But then, what will become of the amortisation process? This is precisely where financial operations come to play against production and lead to involuntary unemployment.

Overinvestment is a duplication process whose function is to transform *net* profits into *gross* profits. But, what could be the use for net profits if they are not invested? These profits cannot be distributed to the beneficiaries because this would make amortisation impossible; as attested by accounting procedures, the amount of profits available for distribution is determined after constituting the provisions for depreciation. If profits are not spent to buy equipment and if they are not distributed, the only option left is to lend them through the financial system. If not invested by another firm, these funds will be borrowed and added on to the amount spent by consumers; this will reconstitute the profits but this time the link with the beneficiaries will be re-established. In a sense, net profits are transformed into gross profits through the financial system but without any production corresponding to this transformation. As long as amortisation takes place through the overinvestment process, there is no ill effect on unemployment precisely because goods must be produced to accumulate new stocks of fixed capital. But, if this demand for equipment fails, no other activity will recycle the left over resources precisely because there would be no profits available to justify, in the eyes of entrepreneurs, an alternative production. The economic system is faced with the following dilemma: either to invest profits to use the labour resources thus provoking a further decrease in profitability or to lend the profits to maintain profitability thus increasing joblessness.

The financial channel of amortisation cannot be used forever because the indebtedness of households cannot increase indefinitely. More and more borrowers will be unable to pay high interests; this will force the banking system to write off increasing amounts of claims. In parallel, some firms may reduce amortisation. In this situation, unemployment soars to huge numbers. Finally, once the stock of (financial and material) capital has lost enough value, the pressure on profits will ease and the rates of profit will again exceed interest rates. The problem will nevertheless sooner or later reappear with overinvestment exerting its pernicious effects.

CONCLUSION

Income formation and income expenditure involve a relationship between the households and their products through the agency of firms and banks. In a sense, households produce for themselves but, in a monetary economy with specialisation and division of labour, there is a need for a monetary intermediary and a production intermediary. If households are willing to participate in a production process so as to gain access to the goods available in the economy, a demand is inherent in any offer to work at market conditions. In this perspective, *involuntary unemployment* can only result from the breaking of the causal link between the demand for goods and the supply of labour.

Keynes saw that an economy can suffer from involuntary unemployment and that this is not the sign of any unwillingness to work at current market conditions. But, although he did put a great emphasis on the concept of *monetary economy of production*, he failed to see that payments are oriented to form circuits of incomes.[34] Of course, if actual circuits were limited to the basic production–consumption circuit, involuntary unemployment could never happen. But in developed economies, the presence of a stock of capital implies that income circuits include a redistribution process, a profit circuit. Consequently, the causal link between the supply of labour and the demand for goods depends on the profitability of the production–consumption circuit. Lacking a precise circuit conception, Keynes was not able to provide a full analysis of the formation and spending of profits and particularly to understand that, instead of being a supplement of incomes, profits originate from a partition of primary incomes. Without the adequate tools to account for a global insufficient profitability, Keynes could only stray into psychological arguments like the excessive thriftiness of income-earners or the timorous attitude of investors.

A falling global profitability as well as involuntary unemployment are signs of a deep structural problem. The origin of this malfunction is to be found in intersecting circuits that ought to stay independent. The investment of profits transforms the working of the circuits by creating a link between profits of two different production periods. This link is reproduced through amortisation that will then provoke an overaccumulation of capital; this process causes a reduction in the rate of profit that will in its turn lead to the decline of productive investment in favour of purely financial operations, this tendency being accompanied by soaring unemployment. When the financial burden reaches unbearable levels, amortisation will itself be affected and once the stock of capital has been reduced to a level allowing again sufficient profitability, unemployment will decrease; but then the whole process of amortisation will start another trend of overinvestment leading to the same fate. This problem cannot be overcome by forcing investment (either by forcing private firms to invest or by nationalising private firms); in this respect, the failure of the Keynesian economic policies was unavoidable. However, the policy of slashing public services and easing the industrial legislation can do no better[35] to deal with the fundamental problem of capital overaccumulation. The only effective solution would be to take into account the working of circuits of incomes as well as the nature of capital accumulation and to reform the payment system to make it possible to amortise without over- or underinvestment.

NOTES

1. The concept of involuntary unemployment is introduced by Keynes in Chapter 2 of the *General Theory* (*GT* hereafter) (Keynes, 1936/1973, p. 15).
2. See Keynes (1936/1973, p. 293).
3. See Chapter 17 of the *GT*.
4. See Keynes (1936/1973, pp. 164, 220–1, 320, 378).
5. See Keynes (1936/1973, p. 325).
6. Initially, Keynes insisted on what involuntary unemployment is not by contrasting it with other forms of unemployment; from this perspective, Keynes stressed that neither the unemployed nor the other wage-earners are responsible for the existence of involuntary unemployment. On the other hand, the positive definitions of involuntary unemployment give a quite ambiguous picture by putting to the fore the increase in employment that would correspond to a reduction in real wages (Keynes, 1936/1973, p. 15). On this point see Corry (1997).
7. A multiplier equal to one would still make sense but this would shift the emphasis from the multiplier to the multiplicand. For a critical analysis of the multiplier concept see Schmitt (1971) and Bradley (1994).
8. See Keynes (1936/1973, pp. 82–4, 110–11, 117–18), but also Keynes (1973, pp. 211–12).
9. Of course, production was not ignored by the traditional approach but rather was viewed as a particular kind of exchange.
10. The idea of the creation–destruction symmetry is not unfamiliar to the post Keynesian tradition; see for example Kaldor and Trevithick (1981, p. 7). But to break the mould of the traditional dichotomy one has to go a step further by applying it not just to money but also to incomes.
11. Schmitt (1984, pp. 336–76).
12. This concept is studied in four articles published in June 1937 (Keynes, 1973, pp. 208–10), December 1937 (ibid., pp. 216–23), June 1938 (ibid., pp. 229–33) and September 1939 (ibid., pp. 278–85).
13. In the December 1937 article (Keynes, 1973, p. 220) and again in September 1939 (ibid., p. 283).
14. See Keynes (1936/1973, pp. 164–74) and Keynes (1973, p. 206).
15. Keynes (1973, pp. 207–9, fn. 1, 216, 219, 233, 284).

16. 'As soon as it is "used" in the sense of being expended, the lack of liquidity is automatically made good and the readiness to become temporarily unliquid is available to be used over again' (Keynes, 1973, p. 219).
17. For the moment, we do not consider profits.
18. See Keynes (1973, pp. 209, 219, 230, 232, 283–4).
19. Keynes (1936/1973, p. 214) did mention labour as the sole factor of production but he did not elaborate on his conception. As he only referred to the classical theory of labour (ibid., p. 213), he gave the impression that no new perspective could be given to what then appeared to be an old-fashioned approach.
20. See Keynes (1930/1971, p. 125).
21. On this question see Schmitt (1984) and Bailly (this volume).
22. Thus, if we say that profits are spent by the beneficiaries or invested by the firm, it really means the spending of the incomes obtained in exchange for the profit-goods.
23. It is true that a firm may borrow the funds needed for investment. However, given the fact that the firm will have to repay this loan with its profits, it appears that borrowing to invest only allows a firm to advance its future profits.
24. From the accounting point of view, this operation may involve a large degree of imprecision in costs imputation.
25. 'But no one can save without acquiring an asset, whether it be cash or a debt or capital-goods; and no one can acquire an asset that he did not previously possess, unless either an asset of equal value is newly produced or someone else parts with an asset of that value which he did not previously have. In the first alternative there is a corresponding new investment: in the second alternative someone else must be dis-saving an equal sum' (Keynes, 1936/1973, pp. 81–2). In the *GT* (ibid., p. 113), describing the multiplier mechanism, Keynes clearly identified investment with the production of investment goods. See also Keynes (ibid., pp. 116–17, 126–7).
26. 'Saving is in fact a mere residual. . . . [T]he act of investment in itself cannot help causing the residual or margin, which we call saving, to increase by a corresponding amount' (Keynes, 1936/1973, p. 64).
27. 'Investment, thus defined, includes, therefore, the increment of capital equipment, whether it consists of fixed capital, working capital or liquid capital' (Keynes, 1936/1973, p. 75).
28. 'The criterion must obviously correspond to where we draw the line between the consumer and the entrepreneur' (Keynes, 1936/1973, p. 62).
29. See Keynes (1936/1973, p. 245).
30. '[M]oney is a bottomless sink for purchasing power, when the demand for it increases, since there is no value for it at which demand is diverted – as in the case of other rent-factors – so as to slop over into demand for other things' (Keynes, 1936/1973, p. 231).
31. On this point see Moore (1988).
32. See Keynes (1936/1973, p. 379).
33. More precisely, their volatile nature and their dependence on the herd mentality. See Keynes (1936/1973, Ch. 12).
34. Although a circuit of incomes appeared explicitly in the *Treatise on Money* (Keynes, 1930/1971, p. 121), Keynes could not build a coherent and thorough analysis on this basis because he conceived of his circuit as a circulation of assets between economic agents; flows are just stocks in motion.
35. These 'liberal' policies can accelerate the reduction in the stock of capital and therefore the recovery but they cannot avoid the malfunctioning of the economy.

REFERENCES

Bailly, J.-L. (2002), 'On the macroeconomic foundations of the wage–price relationship', in this volume.

Bradley, X. (1994), 'Le multiplicateur d'investissement et l'épargne des revenus', *Recherches économiques de Louvain*, **60** (1), 87–105.

Corry, B. (1997), 'Keynes's use of the term "involuntary unemployment": a historical perspective', in *Capital Controversy, Post-Keynesian Economics and the History of Economic Thought: Essays in Honour of Geoff Harcourt*, London and New York: Routledge, vol. I, 212–15.

Kaldor, N. and J. Trevithick (1981), 'A Keynesian perspective on money', *Lloyds Bank Review*, 139, 1–19. Reprinted in M. Sawyer (ed.) (1988), *Post-Keynesian Economics*, Aldershot and Brookfield: Edward Elgar, 101–19.

Keynes, J.M. (1930/1971), *A Treatise on Money*, London: Macmillan. Reprinted in *The Collected Writings of John Maynard Keynes*, Vols V and VI, London and Basingstoke: Macmillan.

Keynes, J.M. (1936/1973), *The General Theory of Employment, Interest and Money*, London: Macmillan. Reprinted in *The Collected Writings of John Maynard Keynes*, Vol. VII, London: Macmillan.

Keynes, J.M. (1973), *The General Theory and After – Part II: Defence and Development*, in *The Collected Writings of John Maynard Keynes*, Vol. XIV, London and Basingstoke: Macmillan.

Moore, B.J. (1988), *Horizontalists and Verticalists: The Macroeconomics of Credit Money*, Cambridge: Cambridge University Press.

Schmitt, B. (1971), *L'analyse macro-économique des revenus*, Paris: Dalloz.

Schmitt, B. (1972), *Macroeconomic Theory: A Fundamental Revision*, Albeuve: Castella.

Schmitt, B. (1984), *Inflation, chômage et malformations du capital*, Paris and Albeuve: Economica and Castella.

PART FOUR

FURTHER CONTRIBUTIONS TO
MONETARY ANALYSIS

19. Keynes and the Classics: Notes on the Monetary Theory of Production

Heinrich Bortis[1]

INTRODUCTION

This chapter deals with the *principles* of *long-period* classical–Keynesian political economy, which encompasses a monetary theory of production. Dealing with principles raises deep-going methodological problems and may lead to misunderstandings. Most importantly in this chapter it will be suggested that theorising on classical–Keynesian lines at the most fundamental level should be done on the basis of the labour value *principle*. Seemingly, this is to think little of the efforts that have been, rightly, made by Sraffa and the Sraffians to overcome the obvious fact that the labour *theory* of value only holds in very specific circumstances, that is, if the ratio of fixed to circulating capital is the same in all sectors of production. In this chapter it will be suggested, however, that labour values and prices of production are not exclusive, but intimately linked and hence complementary. Both are valid at different levels of abstraction. In fact, the labour values are essential or constitutive to prices, and the prices of production bring them into concrete existence though in modified form. This very simple point touches upon most controversial issues and justifies some introductory remarks on method.

Very broadly and tentatively, one may distinguish between two different, but complementary concepts of social science, which comprises economics and political economy. The first, conventional, notion of science considers the theoretical economist as a model builder, possibly in view of establishing testable propositions. He endeavours to *explain* economic phenomena starting from given premises and engages in the search for empirical regularities within economic phenomena. Even at the macroeconomic level, theoretical explanation is frequently complemented by empirical means, with the Phillips curve, the work done on the Keynesian consumption function, and the close association between price levels and quantities of money perhaps being most prominent. At the sectoral and microeconomic level, explanatory models and empirical investigations abound. However, scientific work always rests upon fundamental principles, which, as a rule, are taken for granted. Neoclassical analysis is based upon the marginal principle; Keynesians rely upon the principle of effective demand. This leads to a second notion of science. Here the theorist attempts to distil principles or fundamentals in view of *understanding* how socio-economic systems essentially function. For example, the question is about the fundamental forces governing prices, distributional outcomes or employment levels. In this sense, Ricardo wrote on the principles of political economy, Marshall on the principles of economics. Based upon the principle of effective demand, Keynes aimed at establishing a general theory of employment, interest and money. In a sense principles – the marginal principle, the surplus principle, the principle of effective demand – form the basis upon which theoretical work dealing with phenomena takes place. As such, principles have a metatheoretical character. Principles are not about visible characteristics of phenomena to be brought to the open by theories but represent the fundamental forces (probably) constituting phenomena like prices, distributional outcomes or employment levels. In fact, one should not hesitate to say that the principles underlying the great theoretical systems are metaphysical since they tell us what is (probably) essential for our object of enquiry, that is, the economy and its relation to society as a whole. In Bortis (1997) the two concepts of science have been associated respectively with pure and applied theory, relying thus upon Keynes, who made this distinction in a more specific context in his *Treatise on Money* (Keynes, 1930/1971): Volume one is on the *pure* theory of money, Volume two on the *applied* theory of money.

In this chapter we shall adopt the second notion of science, and this introductory section is about a few characteristics of pure theory. We shall use the expressions *metatheoretical* or *metaphysical* to designate the preoccupation with *principles* underlying some specific approach to economic phenomena, for instance neoclassical or classical–Keynesian. As already suggested, principles represent the essential elements underlying a certain phenomenon, or the constitutive elements of an object. As such, principles also denote the fundamental and ultimate causal forces governing phenomena like prices, employment levels, and distributional outcomes, for example. To distil such principles the whole of society and man must be considered, and all the information available must be examined, scientific and non-scientific, theoretical and empirical and historical, whereby the objectively given material is dealt with by reason based upon a metaphysical vision that, in turn, is associated with intuition. This implies, as, in our view, Keynes suggested, that science and metaphysics interact: principles guide scientific work, and the results of science eventually modify the scientist's fundamental outlook and may induce him to adopt another approach in his scientific work, based upon a different set of principles. The notion of principles is closely associated with Aristotle's' essentialist theory of knowledge: the human mind does not remain at the surface of phenomena but tries to understand the essential or constitutive forces behind, perhaps better, inside, the phenomena. Here, the distinction between essentials and accidentals is crucial as is the comprehensive point of view implying that all the relevant information – with the history of economic thought perhaps being most important – has to be taken into account if a complex problem is investigated (for example, the formation of prices or the determination of involuntary unemployment). Only what is considered to be essential or constitutive to a phenomenon is included in the model, which is a picture, in fact a *reconstruction* or *recreation* of what *probably constitutes* a phenomenon (for example, prices, quantities and employment levels in political economy). This recreation is performed by reason interacting with intuition and is analogous to the recreation of constitutive aspects of nature by the late Cézanne by the means of colour or to the representation of essential information for the user of the underground through a map. Consequently, metatheories or sets of principles have *not* to be realistic in the scientific sense, since they are not reflections or copies (*Abbilder*) of certain spheres of the real world that can eventually be associated with testable propositions. In their being reconstructions of essential aspects of real world phenomena, principles illuminate these phenomena from inside and initiate the formation of empirically testable theories. In this sense, Walras's general equilibrium model contributes to understanding how Adam Smith's invisible hand might work in principle. With the Walrasian model in the background neoclassical economists have built simplified textbook theories of value, distribution and employment upon the marginal principle, which is behind all demand and supply curves. In many instances, the Cobb–Douglas production function or Samuelson's surrogate production function are used to elucidate the implications of the marginal principle – the Walrasian model is too complex for an easily understandable exposition of the neoclassical principles and their implications. Ricardo attempted to establish the principles of value and distribution in line with the social and circular process of production, that is, the labour value principle and the surplus principle. Keynes endeavoured to derive principles embodying the essential features of the phenomena of employment, interest and money occurring in monetary production economies. A striking instance is the *logical* theory of the multiplier, which states how output and employment are governed in principle in monetary economies (Keynes, 1936/1973, p. 122). Sraffa developed the concept of the standard commodity to set out the fundamental principles of value and distribution in the classical approach in an immediately evident way. The classical–Keynesian model to be set forth in this chapter is also a set of principles and represents, as such, a piece of pure theory independent of space and time picturing how the relevant causal forces work in principle in a monetary production economy.

Owing to the existence of differing sets of principles associated with specific approaches to economic problems, the question as to the choice of the approach arises. The vision of man and of society – a metaphysical concept – seems to be most important in determining what is considered essential and what is accidental (Bortis, 1997, Ch. 2). Therefore, the neoclassical economist will arrive at principles differing from those of the classical–Keynesian political economist. Regarding distribution, the former will put the marginal principle to the fore, the latter the surplus principle. The difference between the exchange-based neoclassical approach and the production and labour based classical system are brilliantly set forth at the level of principles in Pasinetti (1986a). The fact that different sets of principles coexist implies that sets of principles cannot be proved or disproved by conventional scientific methods: one cannot conclusively prove whether liberalism is superior to middle-way humanism (Bortis, 1997, Ch. 2) or to socialism, or not. In a sense, conventional science is based upon *deductive* reasoning starting from *given* premises that, eventually, lead to the setting up of testable propositions. When dealing with principles this type of reasoning has to be replaced by reasoning aiming at essentials and based on *inference*. The premises now comprise information located in various spheres of the real world, taken in the broadest sense. The point of view must be global, and a vision is required to broadly classify the information considered. The knowledge so obtained is bound to be probable to a greater or less degree, depending mainly upon the robustness of the vision and of the quality of the information considered. The logic of probability set out by Keynes (1921/1988) provides the formal basis to reconcile metaphysics and science: scientific results complemented by the vision are used to distil (metaphysical) principles that, in turn, provide a broad framework for scientific work. The immense impetus given by the principle of effective demand underlying Keynes's *General Theory* to macroeconomic reasoning and to empirical macroeconomic work is a striking instance. This suggests that Keynes's conception of metaphysics is not speculative or dogmatic but modern, in the sense that full account is taken of the results of sciences. One can only establish the (probably) essential features of specific real world phenomena (for example, prices, distributional outcomes, employment levels), if, as far as is humanly possible, account is taken of all the relevant information, theoretical and empirical-cum-historical, most importantly, the history of economic thought. This incidentally implies that all serious scientific work is important. From the metaphysical standpoint, theories are essentially complementary. For example, even for the classical–Keynesian political economist, Walras's general equilibrium theory is of immense importance, because this theory greatly helps to understand the implications of Adam Smith's invisible hand and the conclusions that should eventually be drawn for further theoretical work and for policy making.

In this chapter we attempt to set forth the essential features of a monetary production economy along classical–Keynesian lines, that is, the social process of production, the surplus principle of distribution and the importance of the uniform rate of profits to organise an economy, the labour principle of value, the determination of employment through effective demand, and last, but not least, the crucial importance of money to run the socio-economic system of production and exchange. Regarding method and content the starting point is provided by Pasinetti's outstanding work on the 'Theory of value – a source of alternative paradigms in economic analysis' (Pasinetti, 1986a). Here the fundamental differences between exchange-based neoclassical pure theory and production or labour-based classical theory is set forth at the level of *principles*, illuminating thus the basic options in economic theory open at present. In this chapter we suggest that the classical principles ought to be elaborated and to be brought together with Keynes's, adapted to the classical long-period method. The classical–Keynesian set of principles set out in this chapter are intended to constitute a preparatory and tentative contribution to an alternative to the neoclassical Walrasian system. Moreover, the classical–Keynesian principles set out here ought to strengthen the theoretical foundations of the system of middle-way political economy, tentatively sketched and put into a wider context in Bortis (1997). Finally, it is hoped that the principles suggested in this chapter may contribute to enhancing the coherence of heterodox economic thinking – comprising for example Keynesian, post-Keynesian and humanist Marxist strands – by providing a fundamental theoretical framework.

The Problem

In his celebrated article entitled 'Mr. Keynes and the "classics"', Hicks (1937) associated Keynes's theory of employment, interest and money (Keynes, 1936/1973) with neoclassical economics – classical theory in Keynes's terms – which, fundamentally, is based on exchange. This combination of theoretical approaches, summarised by the IS–LM diagram, subsequently gave rise to Samuelson's neoclassical synthesis, combining exchange-based Marshallian marginalist equilibrium theory and Keynes's theory of effective demand. In retrospect these developments seem unfortunate since they distorted Keynes's original intention to work out a monetary theory of production (Keynes, 1933/1973) associating his theory of effective demand and involuntary unemployment with *money and finance in relation with the social process of production*. It must be mentioned, however, that Keynes greatly favoured the development of the neoclassical synthesis because he kept the Marshallian framework to the largest possible extent, presumably for reasons of persuasion. Moreover, Keynes naturally thought in Marshallian terms because Alfred Marshall had been his teacher.

Classical political economy in the sense proper, that is, Ricardo's system of economic theory, precisely puts the social process of production to the fore. There is a division of labour and final commodities are produced with labour using commodities taken from nature. Therefore, traditional classical theory would seem to be a natural complement of Keynes's monetary theory of employment, because a monetary theory of production, implying fixed prices (the classical natural prices for example) and quantity adjustments, might potentially obtain. In fact, Keynes, in spite of his critical stance towards Say's Law, had considerable sympathy for classical political economy, even in the *General Theory*. Indeed, direct and indirect labour produces the social product, which is measured by labour commanded (Keynes, 1936/1973, pp. 37–45); capital or past labour constitutes the environment within which labour works (ibid., p. 213).

Thus, considering the content of theories, it seems not entirely fanciful to attempt to combine the classical (Ricardian) theory of value and distribution, which is rooted in production, and Keynes's theory of employment, interest and money conceived of as a part of a monetary theory of production. But such an undertaking raises a serious methodological problem (Bortis, 1997, pp. 103–17). Most importantly, Ricardian political economy is, fundamentally, of a long-period nature. Ricardo mostly abstracts from temporary and rapidly changing elements of reality, for example market prices, and uniquely considers stable, that is, constant or slowly changing, elements of socio-economic reality, namely, technology and institutions, which partly *govern* behaviour with near-certainty. This implies considering long-period equilibrium situations: market prices coincide with the prices of production and profit rates are the same in all sectors. Contrariwise, Keynes's general theory of employment is of a short-period nature. Productive capacities are given. Their utilisation depends on short-period effective demand. In the present, money is held and investment decisions are taken on the basis of short- and of long-period expectations respectively, which are continually revised when moving into an uncertain future. Put in a nutshell, Ricardo's long-period theory is – like Quesnay's, Leontief's and Sraffa's theories – about the functioning of the socio-economic system, that is, the technological and institutional system; Keynes's theory deals with the behaviour of producers and consumers in the short run and the coordination of this behaviour by the socio-economic system through effective demand.

These opposing views may be brought together on the basis of an appropriate analytical framework. The problem is to adapt the behavioural elements of Keynes's short-period theory to a long-period institutional basis and to combine it with long-period classical system theory. This should result in a classical–Keynesian system of economic theory of which classical and Keynesian theory would constitute different aspects (for a preparatory and tentative attempt to set up such a system see Bortis, 1997). Three points, related to system and behaviour, to money and saving, and to investment respectively, are relevant for adapting Keynes's short-period theory to the long run in order to make it compatible with classical long-period theory.

The institutional system – the material basis and the institutional superstructure – and the behaviour of individuals within this system are complementary, and there is mutual interaction. This is the main tenet of Bortis (1997). In principle, the institutional system only determines global magnitudes or magnitudes that depend upon the system as a whole. Behaviour, however, refers to specific instances. For example, in a classical–Keynesian view, the system governs output and employment as a whole, behaviour determines who is employed or unemployed or which enterprises survive in the long term and which enterprises are squeezed out of the system. Since institutions and technology are associated with duration, they constitute in a natural way the persistent or slowly evolving factors governing long-period prices and quantities in classical–Keynesian political economy (Bortis, 1997, Chs 3–4). The long-period considerations of this chapter therefore constitute a synthesis of classical and Keynesian institutionalism at the level of principles. The central problem to be dealt with hereafter is about the functioning of the institutional–technological system regarding the determination of long-period prices and quantities (see also Bortis, 1997, pp. 142–204). The analyses of business cycles and of the functioning of markets, which are at the level of behaviour (ibid., pp. 204–35), are just alluded to.

The relationship between money and uncertainty, and the associated theory of interest, enabled Keynes to establish the principle of effective demand. Saving depends primarily on actual income, which is something *certain,* not on the rate of interest associated with future consumption, which is in turn dependent on future incomes and prices, all of which are *highly uncertain.* This leads straightaway to 'the logical theory of the multiplier, which holds goods continuously, without time-lag, at all moments of time' (Keynes, 1936/1973, p. 122). Hence the causal forces associated with the multiplier principle are independent of the length of the time-interval considered and, consequently, this principle – as any principle by the way – may also be applied to the long run, which means determination of prices and quantities by technology and institutions, that is, by persistent and slowly changing factors (Bortis, 1997, Ch. 4). Incidentally, the multiplier principle is associated with a specific aspect of Keynes's monetary theory of production: autonomous expenditures set economic activity into motion and final goods are exchanged against money, which represents effective demand. The latter governs the scale of economic activity and, hence, the extent of involuntary unemployment.

In a monetary production economy, money is of fundamental importance, not primarily as a store of value, but because money is necessary to run the system of social production and circulation as well as for the expansion of this system through net investment. Indeed, all the production, investment and consumption plans are set up in terms of money. Goods are always exchanged against money, which means that there is circulation of goods and money.

To establish a Keynesian theory of employment, implying the existence of involuntary unemployment, one must show that the neoclassical price mechanism is unable to bring about a tendency towards full employment. In the neoclassical view uncertainty plays, in principle, no role since, ideally, the behaviour of producers and consumers is *governed* by the law of supply and demand. In an underemployment situation, real wages would decline, profits and investment increase; simultaneously labour would be substituted for capital. A strong tendency towards full employment would arise. It is here that the significance of the capital theory debate emerges (Harcourt, 1972). No 'well-behaved' demand curves for 'factors of production' necessarily exist if the process of production is of a social nature, that is, if production of commodities goes on by means of commodities *à la* Sraffa–Leontief. In this case it is, in principle, impossible always to associate larger quantities of capital with lower interest rates, and vice versa. Moreover, no persistent tendency towards full employment exists. Hence the exchange-based law of supply and demand cannot provide a solution to the great problems of economic theory if production is a social process. This clears the way for the classical–Keynesian multiplier approach to output and employment determination, which is based upon fixed prices and quantity adjustments.

Further, Keynes treats investment at a behavioural and psychological level: the fate of each investment project is uncertain, and investment decisions are based on long-period expectations, which are governed, in varying degrees, either by optimism or by pessimism. The aggregate of investment decisions governs the level of investment, which, together with other autonomous variables, determines short-period employment *via* the multiplier. Obviously, in the short run, only the income effect of investment is relevant since, by definition, the capital stock is given.

The post Keynesian (Kaleckian) medium-term theory of investment is also based upon an interaction between entrepreneurial behaviour and the functioning of the system: higher volumes of investment are associated with larger profits and profit rates that, in turn, induce entrepreneurs to invest more, and vice versa. There is thus an interaction, a double-sided relationship, between investment and profits. If left unfettered, this mechanism may be completely unstable: the upswing will come to an end at the full-employment ceiling and the downswing will touch the bottom at the lowest possible level of employment, which obtains at zero gross investment; incidentally, this mechanism was pictured by Hicks (1950), who put to use Harrod's (1939) multiplier–accelerator model.

The treatment of investment in the long run is associated with the fact that capitalist systems are not completely unstable. Cyclical movements seem to take place around a remarkably stable long-period trend, as suggested by the near-constant average unemployment rates over longer periods of time in many countries. Such long-period trends may, of course, change their position as time goes by. In any case, as Garegnani (1983, p. 78) has emphasised, the position of the trend is crucially important since it matters whether cyclical fluctuations take place around a trend implying a relatively high or a relatively low level of permanent or long-period unemployment.

The clue for inserting investment in an appropriate way into a synthesis of the proportions-based classical theory of value and distribution with Keynes's theory of employment dealing with the scale of economic activity lies in the notion of long-period equilibrium (Bortis, 1997, pp. 75–103). The conventional view starts from a disequilibrium situation in the present, which, in a stationary state, would work out and produce an eventual tendency towards a future equilibrium situation. This equilibrium concept is untenable once historical time is introduced as Joan Robinson emphasised time and again (Robinson, 1956): an economy cannot get into an equilibrium if there is uncertainty about the future and if, as a consequence, expectations are liable to disappointment. The equilibrium position must, therefore, be sought in the present. The first step is to abstract from temporary and rapidly changing short- and medium-term elements of reality, that is, behavioural elements related to markets and to business cycles (Bortis, 1997, p. 106, scheme 3). This is to dig deeper to bring into the open the permanent or slowly evolving elements of the real world made up of the technological and economic structure, that is, the material basis of a society, and the social, political, legal and cultural superstructure erected thereupon. Technology and institutions represent the stable features of social reality the classical economists, Ricardo in the main, had in mind when they conceived of labour values (and prices of production) as the natural and fundamental prices from which actual or market prices temporarily deviate (Ricardo, 1821/1951, p. 88). The classical notion of equilibrium prices and quantities, as implied in the price and quantity systems (19.18) and (19.25), complemented by the supermultiplier relation (19.40), is, therefore, a *system equilibrium*, not a market equilibrium. The latter conceives of the market as an autonomous subsystem surrounded by a social, political and legal framework. The former, however, implies that prices and quantities are directly or indirectly governed by the entire socio-economic system, that is, by technology and institutions, which form a structured entity. This is the main tenet of Bortis (1997).

To conceive of the long run as being situated in the present has already been envisaged by Marshall. In fact, Robertson (1956, p. 16), relying on Guillebaud, mentions that 'Marshall used the term "the long period" in two quite distinct senses, one which stands realistically for any period in which there is time for *substantial* alterations to be made in the size of plant, and one in which it stands conceptually for the Never-never land of unrealized tendency'. In Bortis (1997, pp. 81–9), it is suggested that, appearances notwithstanding, Marshall's second definition of 'the long period' is relevant for long-period analysis, not the first one. Indeed, with the usual first meaning of this notion, the long-period equilibrium is located in the future and would come about if the persistent economic forces could work out undisturbed, that is, if there was a stationary state or a steadily growing one. This first of the Marshallian definitions is largely irrelevant because 'in the long run we are all dead'; moreover, there are no 'stationary conditions and steady states'; and, finally, there are the results of the capital theoretic discussion: lower factor prices cannot, in principle, be associated with larger factor quantities. The second meaning of 'the long period', however, allows us to locate the long-period equilibrium in the *present* and to associate it with an institutionally governed system equilibrium (Bortis, 1997, Chs 3–4). This takes us back to the classics and Marx, whose approach to economic problems has proved so immensely fruitful.

The institutional system equilibrium is thus located in the present. This has important implications for the treatment of uncertainty in relation with saving and future consumption on the one hand and with investment and future earnings on the other. Indeed, it has been suggested above that saving depends on actual income, which is a known magnitude, and that the deviation of the medium and short-term investment volume from its institutionally determined long-period counterpart is governed by the difference between realised profits and normal (satisfactory) profits, which are also known (Bortis, 1997, pp. 207–14). Now, Keynes (1936/1973, p. 148) argues thus regarding uncertainty:

> It would be foolish, in forming our expectations, to attach great weight to matters which are very uncertain. It is reasonable, therefore, to be guided to a considerable degree by the facts about which we feel somewhat confident... For this reason the facts of the existing situation enter, in a sense disproportionately, into the formation of our long-term expectations; our usual practice being to take the existing situation and to project it into the future, modified only to the extent that we have more or less definite reasons for expecting a change.

Now, institutions and technology are precisely facts of the existing situation on which we have little reasons for expecting a change or on which the direction of change is broadly known, as is the case with technology, where moreover changes occur, as a rule, at the margin. Regarding investment, the difference between the normal (satisfactory) rate of profits and the realised rate of profits, constitutes a *given* fact that is very important for investment decisions, and the importance of this fact increases if the difference is larger and more durable (Bortis, 1997, pp. 207–14). In a sense, then, *Keynesian long-period analysis* could be called *Keynesian Institutionalism*, which differs from the traditional system-based institutionalism, of the German Historical School in the main, by its explicit theoretical foundations.

The output and employment trend may be conceived of as a (hidden) fully adjusted situation characterised by normal prices and quantities and normal degrees of capacity utilisation (ibid., pp. 75–89, 142–204). Normal or long-period prices and quantities, *including investment volumes*, depend on the entire institutional system, that is, on the material basis and the institutional superstructure. As such, normal prices and quantities constitute a system equilibrium. Since normal output does not, as a rule, correspond to full-employment output, permanent involuntary unemployment obtains. Normal prices are, in turn, governed by the conditions of production and distributional arrangements. The latter imply that normal prices are, in principle, associated with an equal (target) profit rate, r^*, which entrepreneurs consider satisfactory and that, therefore, enters their price calculation. In the sense of Sraffa the magnitude of the normal profit rate is governed by the basic rate of interest set by the central bank.

Cycles around the trend are shaped by an interaction of the income and of the capacity effect of investment (ibid., pp. 204–20). The income effect, based upon Kalecki's double-sided relationship between investment and profits, brings about the upswings and downswings; the capacity effect explains the turning points. In fact, in the course of the upswing, driven by the income effect of investment, capacities gradually rise above the long-period trend level of effective demand, with the realised profit rate (r) exceeding the normal rate (r^*). As the capacity effect works out, r starts to diminish and falls below r^*, because output exceeds long-period effective demand, initiating thus the downswing, and vice versa.

In this view, the uniform profit rate, associated to the notion of normal prices, emerges as an ingenious device to deal with long-period uncertainty: if the realised profit rate exceeds the uniform normal rate, entrepreneurs invest more, and vice versa (ibid., pp. 207–14). This very simple device allows disposing of the concept of the 'marginal efficiency of capital', which is associated with uncertainty and expectations. Indeed, investment decisions are now decisively based on comparisons between the *objectively given* realised and normal profit rates, which enables us to evacuate largely the subjective and psychological elements of Keynes's analysis that Sraffa disliked so intensely, and provides a very strong link between Sraffa and Keynes. In fact, Keynes (1936/1973, p. 148) himself argues 'that the facts of the existing situation enter, in a sense disproportionately, into the formation of our long-term expectations; our usual practice being to take the existing situation and to project it into the future, modified only to the extent that we have more or less definite reasons for expecting a change'. Moreover, Keynes made an important step towards Sraffa's uniform rate of profit in Chapter 17 of the *General Theory*, where, in long-period equilibrium, all own rates of interest are equal with the own rate of money ruling the roost. Significantly, the notion of the *own rate of interest* is Sraffa's, who developed it when criticising Hayek's *Prices and Production* in 1932 (Roncaglia, 2000, pp. 26–9). Hence, it is Chapter 17 of the *General Theory,* based upon the concept of the own rate of interest, which has to be stripped of marginalist remnants and the uniform, long-period, own rate of interest would have to be associated with the surplus principle and to be explained by institutional factors with central bank policy playing a crucial role, as Sraffa has indeed suggested.

Taking up the notions of realised and normal profits implies going back to Keynes's *Treatise on Money* (Keynes, 1930/1971). Here we also find the normal prices that are at the centre of Sraffa's work and that can be built into Pasinetti's vertically integrated system. The normal prices are, in principle, independent of output levels and are, as such, the natural complement to the Keynesian fix-price theory of output and employment, where movements towards underemployment equilibria are based upon quantity adjustments. Hence theorising in the spirit of Sraffa and Keynes also implies bringing Keynes's *Treatise on Money* closer to his *General Theory*.

This point has important consequences for the nature of long-period investment. Indeed, in the long run, *r* must equal *r**, hence the income effect of investment based upon Kalecki's double-sided investment–profit relationship is not relevant here. Only the capacity effect is significant. As we shall see later on, autonomous variables – government expenditures and exports – set economic activity in the consumption and investment goods sectors into motion to govern a long-period equilibrium. This implies that, if the long run is considered, *investment*, like consumption, must be *induced*, depending upon the capital stock required to produce long-period output (Bortis, 1997, pp. 81–9, 144). In the long run, employment and output are governed by long-period, institutionally determined, effective demand, which grows at the rate of growth of the autonomous variables, that is, government expenditures and exports. Net investment leads to an expansion of the capital stock and hence to growth; replacement investment is required to maintain the existing capital stock. Hence, in the long run, investment is linked to the social production *system*. This definitely clears the way for bringing together the classical theory of social and circular production, and the associated theory of value and distribution, and Keynes's monetary theory of output and employment determination on the basis of Pasinetti's vertically integrated model, which implies the horizontal and circular interindustry model.

The Labour Value Principle and the Uniform Rate of Profits

At a fundamental level the labour values and the uniform rate of profits are both essential features of a monetary production economy. This gives rise to three kinds of problems we want to deal with briefly in this section: the labour value principle and the uniform rate of profits, the meaning of labour values, and the social significance of the uniform rate of profits.

First, to put to use simultaneously the labour value principle *and* the uniform rate of profits requires abstracting from specific conditions of production that are considered accidental features of a monetary production economy if fundamentals or principles are considered. This abstraction is carried out later on and is maintained throughout this chapter in order to put to the fore in a simple and widely accessible form the fundamental forces at work in a monetary production economy. We may recall that this way of proceeding is legitimate since our investigation is at the level of essentials or principles and the corresponding pure theory is not a reflection but a reconstruction of what is regarded essential to prices and other economic phenomena.

Secondly, we use the labour value principle in a broad humanist sense, not in the spirit of class struggle as was certainly largely justified in the nineteenth century. In a monetary production economy labour values are obviously essential to prices. This does not mean, however, adopting a labour *theory* of value, which evidently does not hold at the level of appearances. In fact, labour values are modified through the conditions of production leading to prices of production that, in turn, deviate from market prices. Hence observed prices are not proportional to labour values, which, however, constitute the essence of prices. It is in this sense that we put to use the labour value *principle*, which holds at the fundamental level of analysis, where only essentials are considered and accidentals – market conditions and conditions of production – are abstracted from. Further, the labour value principle and the associated surplus principle allow us to deal in a comprehensive way with the problem of distributive justice associated with the structure of wages, profits and rents, and with the size of the surplus comprising profits, ability rents and land rents. The labour value principle may also be associated in a straightforward way to the study of social relations, for example between people working in the profit and non-profit sectors respectively. Also, at the level of principles, part of the social surplus over ordinary wages is due to additional labour time of the persons working in the profit sector. This is the *quantitative* part of the surplus. More importantly, however, is the *qualitative* part of the social surplus made up of the surplus wages, exceeding ordinary wages. Surplus wages are due to special abilities, of some artisans, managers, surgeons, or lawyers for instance. In part, profits may also be interpreted as a reward for good management (on the social importance of profits see also Bortis, 1997, pp. 158–75).

In this chapter the somewhat antiquated notions of productive (surplus producing) labour and unproductive labour (paid out of the surplus) are replaced by the more modern terms 'profit sector' and 'non-profit sector' associated with the agents working in these sectors.

To conclude it has to be emphasised that in a humanist view the social surplus has nothing to do with exploitation. The surplus is socially necessary because its use ought to maintain, and improve, the orderly function of society as a whole and, thereby, to create the preconditions for surplus creation. In a sense there is an interaction between the creation of value and surplus value in the profit sector and the use of the surplus. Both may mutually enhance each other if the surplus is used in a socially appropriate way. Socially inappropriate uses of the surplus (for example through corruption) may, however, lead to a deterioration of the socio-economic situation in the sense that labour productivity stagnates or even decreases while involuntary unemployment increases.

Third, in a monetary production economy a socially appropriate profit rate

– compatible with full employment (see below) – has, as a result, nothing to do with exploitation. At a fundamental level the uniform (normal, target, satisfactory) profit rate is a highly important social institution that greatly contributes to the good and proper functioning of a monetary production economy. This classical notion is also fundamentally important for the project of combining Keynesian and Sraffian (classical) elements of analysis. The importance of the normal rate of profits for investment under uncertainty has been alluded to in the introductory section. Moreover, the uniform profit rate (r^*) is a powerful social tool to organise competition in the classical sense: capital circulates between sectors to bring about a tendency towards the equal profit rate; simultaneously, these capital flows steered by r^* tend to create a tendency toward a fully adjusted situation, that is, stock equilibrium, characterised by normal prices and quantities. As such, r^* and the normal prices contribute to governing structures or *proportions* between vertically integrated final goods sectors and, subsequently, in horizontal interindustry models. Most importantly, the normal rate of profits r^* and distribution in general are a crucial determinant of the *scale* of economic activity as suggested in Bortis (1997, pp. 142–204). Finally, interests and profits, seen as parts of the social surplus, may be associated without difficulties with a theory of *endogenous* money.

The normal rate of profits and profits in general are also important for micro-cum-macro reasons (see also Bortis, 1997, pp. 158–75). Profits provide a source of own funds for investment. At a given normal rate of profits, firms introducing better techniques of production and/or new products strengthen their competitive position. Moreover, in a Schumpeterian vein, these firms will get profits above the normal level, which constitute a kind of ability rent. In this sense, profits are also a reward for good management. Finally, the rate of profit usually contains a risk premium.

Hence the normal rate of profits renders decentralised decision taking regarding prices and quantities possible and is, as such, fundamental for the orderly functioning of a monetary production economy. The associated normal prices do not stand in contradiction to the labour values but render these operable, though in an imperfect way. Indeed, labour values are basic principles that cannot be rendered operable in the real world directly, that is, in their pure form. In the real world we need workable, though imperfect, approximations to labour values and associated profit rates. These are given by normal prices and the normal rate of profits. This implies that there is no contradiction between Ricardian–Marxian labour values and Sraffian prices of production. In the latter, differing conditions of production, which are abstracted from in the former, are taken into account in order to render labour values operable. The practical advantages of the prices of production are immense, because decentralised decision taking regarding prices and quantities is now possible. Normal prices, in fact, emerge from the normal cost calculation carried out within individual firms. These represent historical realisations of the theoretical normal prices of the Sraffa type, which are principles. Firms may also decide on the quality of products and on the techniques of production to be used. However, labour values would have to be calculated by the central planning bureau and to be imposed upon firms. In principle the vector of direct labour has to be multiplied by the Leontief inverse (relations (19.4) and (19.5) below). Such calculations are necessarily more or less imprecise. As a consequence, a heavily distorted price system comes into being, which is still more distorted through subsidies. Some firms realise 'profits', others make losses, which, perhaps, partly explain the interfirm debt–credit relations that occurred in the socialist economies. Moreover, the introduction of new products and new production technologies as a rule disturbs the plan; hence the technological stagnation above all in the consumer goods industries in socialist economies and the fact that product quality frequently was not in line with consumers' wants, which, in turn, led to stocks piling up. All this suggests that Sraffa's prices of production are not only very important theoretically because they provide a neat solution to the transformation problem if production is seen as a social and circular process. Sraffa prices are also of immense practical relevance (on this see also Harcourt (1981)).

Finally, it should be noted that the labour value principle and the uniform profit rate are probably the most appropriate starting points for social ethical considerations. We may indeed start, as Pasinetti does, from a natural state of affairs where two important social ethical postulates are, in principle, fulfilled: first, distributive justice is brought about through an ethically appropriate wage structure and a socially appropriate uniform rate of profits; second, there is full employment in the sense that there is no system-caused involuntary unemployment (there may be, however, structural unemployment due to disproportions between sectors of production). Socio-economic reality may now be seen as an alienated deviation from the social ethical norm (Bortis, 1997, pp. 39–53). The latter serves as a reference and a starting point to study specific problems. For example, if there is heavy involuntary unemployment, there may be a pressure on the wages of less qualified workers. Consequently, profits may get associated with exploitation. Such deviations from the ethically desirable *natural* state may become institutionalised and hence *normal*. Inversely, the natural state of affairs may be appropriately considered the ethically desirable form of the (alienated) normal state. In theoretical work this means that the same variables and parameters may refer to an alienated or to a natural state of affairs. Looked at in this way all the scientific work in the social sciences, be it theoretical, empirical or historical now involves an ethical dimension. As Keynes reminded us, social sciences are *essentially* moral sciences.

Some Crucial Issues

In this chapter we attempt to elaborate the principles underlying long-period classical–Keynesian political economy, that is, the pure theory of a monetary production economy, and, as a by-product, to strengthen the analytical basis of the classical–Keynesian system that, in a tentative and preparatory way, is presented and put into a wider context in Bortis (1997). Among other features, this chapter intends to clarify somewhat the analytical links existing between horizontal Sraffa–Leontief interindustry land models and vertically integrated Ricardo–Pasinetti labour models. These links are taken for granted in Bortis (1997), which is based on the intuitive insight that Keynes and Sraffa somehow belong to a wider theoretical system.

This view has of course been upheld in an analytically rigorous form by Pasinetti since the 1950s. However, Pasinetti (1986b, pp. 3–4) looks at the Keynes–Sraffa issue from another angle and his aim is different in that he focuses on structural change:

> Sraffa's *Production of Commodities* is centered on theories connected with the price system (mainly theories of value and distribution). It does not deal with the economics of physical quantities, which are taken as given. This is the major aspect of differentiation from the theories which, from Keynes to the post-Keynesians have (quite independently from Sraffa) shared the same critical attitude to prevailing theory and have pursued the same aim of reconstructing economic theory along the lines of the old classical economists. Keynes and the post-Keynesians, in striking contrast with Sraffa, have concentrated on movements of macro-economic magnitudes through time, while neglecting the relations at the interindustry stage and normally taking the price structure as given.

Pasinetti (ibid., p. 4) then goes on to say that he is:

> going to adopt an approach to economic reality which is the same as Sraffa's, but [is] considering an economy which is moving through time. [The aim is to go] *beyond* Sraffa's assumption of given physical quantities and thus reach out for a link, and a harmonization along classical lines, with the economic theory that has stemmed from Keynesian and post-Keynesian analysis.

Pasinetti's analysis is based on the fact that an 'economic system may be considered from different points of view. [One is Sraffa's approach emphasising] the circularity of the production process. [The second aspect] is the point of view of effective demand [from which] one can investigate the final product and immediately relate it to its direct and indirect [labour] requirements' (ibid., pp. 10–11). And Pasinetti (ibid., p. 14) concludes:

> The vertically integrated concepts thus emerge as becoming essential precisely at the point of going over to dynamic analysis. ... There is therefore complementarity (not incompatibility!) between vertically integrated sectoral analysis and inter-industry analysis. [The] appropriate combination of the two approaches, or more specifically the finding of an appropriate way of, alternatively, going back and forth, from one approach to the other, that one can pave the way to a truly modern version of classical economic analysis – an economic analysis that may encompass, at the same time, the circular process of production and the evolution of economic systems through time.

The crucial point is that Pasinetti (ibid., pp. 14–16) sees that this conclusion, obtained:

> through a chain of arguments starting from Sraffa, can also be reached by starting from the other end, i.e. from a Keynesian analysis. [It] is not difficult to realize that what has allowed Keynesian and post-Keynesian analysis to deal with technical (in striking contrast with inter-industry) analysis is precisely the fact that, by being conceived in macro-economic terms, it had necessarily to be conceived in vertically integrated terms. Unfortunately Keynesian analysis, though capable in principle of overcoming the limitations of given technical coefficients, when extended to the long run, has not been carried beyond the stage of macro-economic analysis.
>
> But there is no need for Keynesian dynamic analysis to be carried out only in macro-economic terms. The singling out of the concept of vertically integrated sectors allows the possibility of its complete disintegration into as many sectors as there are final goods. And this allows the possibility of breaking it down to a complete scheme of structural dynamics.
>
> Here therefore is the clear way to analytical development. It has become a common place by now that Keynesian analysis must be developed beyond its macroeconomic original conception, ... namely in its being broken down into as many vertically integrated sectors as there are final commodities. The analytical device of the sub-systems can then complete the so much sought-after relations and links with the field of investigation concerning the circular process of production.

It is well known how immensely fruitful Pasinetti's (1981) *Structural Change and Economic Growth* has been since its appearance more than twenty years ago. For example, we gain, in a classical environment and in a structurally changing economy, profound insights into the nature of technical change (pp. 61 ff. and 206 ff.), the basic functions of the price system (pp. 133 ff.), the significance of the rate of interest (Ch. 8), the meaning and the implications of the choice of techniques (pp. 188 ff.), and one could go on.

This very brief sketch of Pasinetti's work enables us to situate broadly this chapter, and Bortis (1997), with respect to Pasinetti's writings. In general terms, we have insisted on the fact that Pasinetti's combination of interindustry analysis and vertical integration provides the analytical basis for bringing together classical and Keynesian elements of economic analysis. This idea has been presented in Bortis (1997), where, however, the classical side has been taken for granted and, consequently, has not been elaborated (Bortis, 1997, Ch. 3), whilst the Keynesian long-period employment side has been put to the fore (ibid., Ch. 4). In this chapter, therefore, we attempt to clarify and to strengthen the *classical* analytical basis of Bortis (1997), in view of providing an outline of a more complete classical–Keynesian system of political economy. This system should provide the starting point for an alternative to the Walrasian–neoclassical framework. Needless to say, given the immense complexity of the problem, the present contribution is bound to remain tentative and preparatory, as is the whole of Bortis (1997).

Our aim, then, is to elaborate a classical–Keynesian system of political economy in which all the great problems of political economy are dealt with, most importantly distribution, value, employment and money. This means that our purpose differs from Pasinetti's (1981) endeavour to deal with *Structural Change and Economic Growth*. The difference of aims entails a difference of method. *Specifically, we want to maintain, in opposition to Pasinetti, a Keynesian aggregate macroeconomics in order to be able to deal with the scale of economic activity, that is, with the level of employment.* Moreover, Keynesian macroeconomics has, in turn, to be combined with *classical macroeconomics, dealing with proportions and structures*, which enable us to picture the *social process of production*, which is basic in classical political economy, and to tackle the issues of *value and distribution within this process*. Here, the labour value *principle* is of fundamental importance, as is the uniform rate of profits as a most powerful tool to organise a monetary production economy. The analytically difficult task consists, therefore, in combining the labour value principle and the uniform profit rate, which are both *essential* features of a monetary production economy. At the level of principles or metatheory this can only be done within a vertically integrated framework if the analysis is to be kept manageable. Relaxing this assumption and introducing prices of production is a matter of economic science operating through theories. In a classical–

Keynesian framework the theoretical results will not modify qualitatively the conclusions reached at the level of principles. By contrast, the neoclassical principles derived from Samuelson's (1962) surrogate production function break down once we leave the realm of labour values.

To deal with these problems, proportions and structures are, in the spirit of Ricardo and Marx, dealt with in the simplest possible way. It is, in fact, assumed that the *proportion* of circulating to fixed capital is the *same* in all sectors, although the *absolute* quantities of labour embodied in fixed and circulating capital respectively *differ* between final good sectors. This assumption, which will be justified later on, and the fact that the *same quantity of labour* may be embodied in *qualitatively very different goods*, ensure the *heterogeneity* of the various consumption and capital goods. Simultaneously, the fundamental importance of labour appears in a pure form. Only labour values are *essential* to price, not the *accidental* conditions of production and exchange, which merely modify the labour values and lead to prices of production and to market prices. This is not to say that the latter are unimportant. Prices of production – and the associated uniform profit rate – and market prices render labour values *operable* in the real world, although in a modified form. Particularly, the uniform rate of profits is a powerful tool to organise monetary production economies, because decentralised decision making regarding prices and quantities is rendered possible and competition may be organised in an orderly way. The labour value principle, however, is part of a system of pure theory enabling us to deal with essential aspects of a monetary production economy.

Hence to postulate uniform ratios of fixed to circulating capital and, consequently, the labour principle of value is *not* to criticise the *scientific* work done, by Sraffa, Pasinetti, Steedman and others, on the basis of non-uniform ratios of fixed to circulating capital, quite the contrary. In fact, these authors deal with economic phenomena and their models must be realistic in the sense that they reflect these phenomena. However, this chapter is on principles, that is, on the fundamental forces governing economic phenomena. Principles illuminate phenomena from inside and, as such, need *not* reflect these in a realistic way.

Specifically, in this chapter we consider the *principles* governing the economic aspects of the socio-economic-cum-political *system* made up of institutions and technology. Institutions and technology form a system because the various social and individualistic institutions are complementary and broadly ordered through the famous classical–Marxian 'material basis – social superstructure' scheme. To deal with socio-economic system outcomes at the level of principles implies abstracting from the vagaries of the market and even from historical realisations of the conditions of production, which means that the prices of production are proportional to labour values. Hence our analysis is of a long-period nature: only permanent or slowly evolving factors (technology and institutions) are considered, abstracting thus from more or less rapidly changing short- and medium-term *behavioural* elements associated with the market place or with business cycles respectively.

In this chapter, as in Bortis (1997), we oppose exchange between individuals and production as a social and circular process. It is natural, therefore, that we *start* from the exchange/production dichotomy that is set forth in Pasinetti's (1986a) 'Theory of value: a source of alternative paradigms in economic analysis', specifically his labour or production model (ibid., pp. 421–7). This model is completed by the neat integration of interindustry and vertically integrated models in Pasinetti (1981, pp. 109–12).

It should be mentioned that our analytical treatment of employment differs from Pasinetti's. Indeed, we consider that condition (16) in Pasinetti (1986a, p. 422) must always be fulfilled, at any level of employment, because it guarantees non-trivial solutions. Involuntary unemployment must enter, consequently, in the form of an employment scalar, smaller than unity, which the quantity vector in the system (14) in Pasinetti (1986a, p. 422) has to be multiplied with (see also Bortis, 1997, pp. 150–2). Such a treatment of employment completes, in our view, Pasinetti's preoccupation with *structural change* in a very useful way, because the employment level heavily determines the social climate within which structural change goes on. For example, with massive involuntary unemployment prevailing structural changes will be resisted precisely because of the fear of even more unemployment.

Starting, then, from Pasinetti (1981, pp. 109–12, 1986a), this chapter on Keynes and the classics is written in the *spirit* of Sraffa and Keynes, who, respectively, represent the surplus principle and the principle of effective demand, and the theoretical implications of these principles. No precise literal correspondence with these authors is sought; this, incidentally, would be impossible as noted above.

Based on the classical–Keynesian model of a monetary production economy sketched in this chapter, one may subsequently attempt to work out a comprehensive alternative to the Walrasian exchange-based model (for a tentative and preparatory contribution to classical–Keynesian political economy in a wider context see Bortis, 1997). Starting from the suggestions made in this introduction, in the next two sections we consider the classical view of production as a circular, social, and vertically integrated process (second section), and its implications for the pure theory of distribution and value (third section). While this theory implies dealing with *proportions* (relative prices) and *shares* (in a given income), Keynes's theory of employment deals with the scale aspect of economic activity where absolute (money) prices and quantities are put to the fore. This leads to defining *classical* and *Keynesian* macroeconomics (fourth section). It has already been mentioned that the former is about proportions within production and circulation (for example proportions between industries and sectors, relative prices and income shares), while the latter is about the scale of economic activity associated with certain levels of employment and involuntary unemployment. In the fifth section the problems of value and distribution are addressed within a framework of classical macroeconomics, which pictures the social process of production and the associated circulation of intermediate and final goods at a given scale of economic activity. The sixth section is about Keynesian macroeconomics, which deals with the forces governing the scale of economic activity, that is, output and employment levels, with proportions given. In the seventh section some extensions of the basic model are briefly considered; for example, the relation between values, prices of production and market prices is very briefly touched upon. The concluding section alludes to the fundamental importance of the modern founders of classical–Keynesian political economy, Keynes and Sraffa, who, together with Kalecki, are the great figures of Shackle's *Years of High Theory*.

Hence classical and Keynesian macroeconomics are to be combined to yield a *monetary theory of production* as envisaged in Keynes (1933/1973), in contrast to the neoclassical real exchange model. The monetary theory of production implies that *money is essential* in a modern economy, because the social process of production and the processes of circulation simply could not go on without money, as Davidson and others have emphasised time and again. The basic reasons are that in a monetary production economy consumption, production and investment plans are always in terms of money; production and investment take time and monetary outlays and receipts do not coincide; in the sphere of exchange, commodities are always exchanged against money.

Moreover, since our analysis is at the level of pure theory, we do not consider concrete institutional set-ups but only examine how the institutional and technological system works in principle. This implies that the long-period equilibrium is in the *present* and that the corresponding prices and quantities are all governed by technology and institutions, which represent the permanent or slowly evolving factors of classical political economy (Bortis, 1997, pp. 84–9, 103–17). Dealing with principles means representing probable (Keynes, 1921/1988) causal relations in their pure form or setting up pure theories, *independent* of historical realisations. Therefore, there are *no leads and lags* to be found here. These would only appear in applied models picturing historical realisations of principles; here, such realisations are merely used to illustrate the principles or pure theories in some instances.

THE STARTING POINT: THE SOCIAL PROCESS OF PRODUCTION

The way in which classical and Keynesian elements of political economy must be combined emerges from the very nature of the social process of production. Indeed, Marx suggested conceiving of this process as an interaction between man (labour) and nature (land). In this interaction labour is evidently the active element while land is passive. In the seventeenth century already William Petty suggested that 'labour is the father of value, and land the mother'. The land and labour features of production give rise to distinguishing *three* kinds of basic goods, absolutely necessary for production: land basics, labour basics, and labour–land basics. *Land basics* are primary products taken from nature, for example iron ore or crude oil, which are made ready for productive use in the form of steel or petrol respectively. Subsequently, land basics or primary goods are used to produce intermediate products: wheat, flour, leather, bricks for instance. Primary products and intermediate products represent part of the means of production that are converted into final products, specifically: bread, shoes, houses, various machines and equipment; generally: private consumption goods, private and public capital goods, and goods made up for state or public consumption. *Labour basics* are *final* products and correspond to the socially necessary consumption goods required to maintain the persons who are active in the 'profit sector' and who, through the social surplus, enable to build up and to maintain a 'non-profit sector', including the state, that is, the political institutions. Finally, *labour–land basics* are machine tools, that is, machines to make machines, representing past labour, and enable the labour force operating in the 'profit sector' to enter into contact and interact with nature through the social process of production, that is, to extract primary goods, nature or land basics, with the aim of transforming them, passing through intermediate products, into final products, including labour basics. The primary land basics move between industries in horizontal interindustry models to produce, in a first stage, primary goods entering the production of all goods, as is pictured by *Sraffa's model* in which *inputs and outputs coincide*. Since the output of land basics enters the production of all intermediate and final goods, necessary technical relations exist between land basics and the final output. The prices of nature basics are thus determining the prices of final products. Hence the fundamental relations between value and distribution may be studied within the social process of production of *primary products or land basics* as Sraffa (1960), with intuitive insight and analytical ability, did indeed on the basis of a model implying non-uniform compositions of capital. In fact, land basics contain, potentially, all final outputs, including labour basics, that is, necessary consumption goods.

The output of land basics is, in a second stage, taken up to produce all intermediate goods. In a third stage, primary and intermediate goods are transformed into final goods consisting of labour basics, labour–land basics and non-basics. The latter make up the social surplus: gross investment, consumption exceeding the socially necessary consumption of the workers and employees of the 'profit sector', comprising the necessary consumption of the 'non-profit sector' and the non-necessary consumption of the entire population, social and state consumption (for example for cultural purposes in the broadest sense).

This view of production – primary products are, passing through intermediate products, transformed into final goods – explains the triangular structure of the Leontief matrix in which Sraffa's land basics are located in the upper left corner. Land basics are produced with land basics and hence the corresponding transaction table and the coefficient matrix form a square matrix. The output of primary goods is distributed to the industries producing intermediate and final goods. Intermediate goods require as inputs land basics and other intermediate goods. The corresponding coefficients form another square matrix beginning at the lower right-hand corner of the Sraffa land basics matrix. Final goods are produced with land basics and intermediate goods. Therefore, primary products enter the production of all goods; intermediate products enter the production of other intermediate goods and of final goods. The latter are only outputs. Hence for intermediate goods some positions to the left of the main Leontief diagonal are positive. By definition, for final goods only the net output vector contains positive elements. The broadly triangular structure of the Leontief matrix thus emerges, with zero positions dominating to the left of the main diagonal.

The vector of net outputs has zero positions for primary and intermediate products. The lower part of this vector is occupied by the final outputs. These are made up of private and public investment (capital) and consumption goods. For each product, primary, intermediate and final goods, there is a specific capital good. Moreover, among the capital goods there is a particular type, that is, machine tools or machines to make machines, a point emphasised by Lowe (1976). Machine tools are, in association with labour, capable of reproducing themselves and of producing the corresponding investment goods for each industry, that is, for all primary, intermediate and final goods industries. *Obviously, the machine-tool sector is of basic importance for the social process of production.* As suggested, this sector enables man (labour) to enter into contact and to interact with nature (incidentally, in traditional societies, this role was held by the blacksmith, who always occupied a privileged position in pre-modern societies because it is he who produced the tools and the weapons). Because of their fundamental importance in the social process of production machine tools may, therefore, conveniently be called labour–land basics. The presence of the machine-tool sector also implies Sraffian 'production of commodities by means of commodities', not only among the processes linking primary and intermediate goods to final goods, but also on the *final* product side. The basic two-sector model put to use in the capital theory debate – a capital good (machine tool) sector producing a capital good for itself and for the consumption goods sector – is a striking example (Garegnani, 1970; Harcourt, 1972).

The second type of final goods consists of consumption goods. These are of three broad types: necessary consumption goods, non-necessary consumption goods and goods for social and state consumption.

Historically, the *nature* aspect of production associated with the notion of land basics was put to the fore in the fundamental 'zigzag' *tableau économique* of Quesnay (*le grand tableau ou tableau fondamental* reproduced and explained in Oncken, 1902, pp. 386–402) and subsequently taken up in the interindustry models of Leontief and Sraffa. The *labour* aspect of production is set out in Ricardo's vertically integrated labour model, elaborated by Pasinetti (1981, 1986a). Labour basics also appear in the vertically integrated two-sector (consumption and investment goods) models of Smith (1776/1976, Book III), Marx (1867–94/1973–4, vol. II, Chs 20–1), Robinson (1956) and Kalecki (1971).

In this framework, we may remark that only labour and land are, in their capacity as basic and original 'factors' of production, capable of producing a surplus. By the help of his *tableau économique*, Quesnay attempted to show that only land produces a surplus. Ricardo, however, argued that both land and labour concur in producing the surplus. Nevertheless, his fundamental prices are labour values because rent is eliminated by an ingenious device. Indeed, Ricardo argues that prices are formed where the conditions of production are most difficult. Here rent is zero and labour time, uniquely, determines value. As a consequence land rents are of a differential nature, arising in more favourable conditions of production. It is this Ricardian device of determining value that is adopted in this chapter. This is done by introducing the notion of the mark-up over ordinary or normal wages. This mark-up allows to include various elements in the social surplus: normal profits, profits higher than normal (for example, owing to outstanding management), land rents, and, very importantly, labour rents that accrue on account of exceptional abilities in the main. The issue of value and distribution within the framework of the social process of production is taken up in the next section.

SOCIAL PRODUCTION, VALUE AND DISTRIBUTION

The social process of production is of immense complexity, and so are the problems of value and distribution, which are closely associated with this process. The complexity of the social process of production appears from its two aspects. In horizontal models of the Sraffa–Leontief type primary and intermediate products move between industries to enable, in association with direct labour and fixed capital (past labour), the production of final goods. In vertical production models labour is put to the fore. At the different stages of production labour uses up primary and intermediate goods to produce final goods.

In order to represent the essentials of social production and the associated processes of value and distribution, that is, to bring to the open the fundamental causal forces at work, all accidental elements have to be left aside. Most importantly, we consider a vertically integrated economy and the conditions of production are assumed to be such that the labour value principle emerges. A very simple fundamental (metaphysical) model picturing essentials will emerge and the conclusions obtained from this model will not be qualitatively modified if the simplifying assumptions are given up to carry out studies at the scientific level. However, the metaphysical model will provide a foundation and a framework for scientific activities. According to Aristotle, metaphysics is the ordering science.

Let us now consider how the processes of price formation and distribution take place *in principle* within the framework of the social process of production. In this process Sraffa–Leontief interindustry prices are transformed into Ricardo–Pasinetti vertically integrated prices proportional to direct and indirect labour.

The starting point is a Leontief price system:

$$\mathbf{p}\mathbf{A} + w_n \mathbf{n}_d k = \mathbf{p} \tag{19.1}$$

where **A** is the broadly triangular Leontief coefficient matrix sketched in the previous section. The coefficients:

$$a_{ij} = x_{ij}/X_j \qquad (19.2)$$

indicate the amount of good i required to produce a unit of good j. **p** is the (row) price vector. Firstly, we have the prices of primary goods or land basics, subsequently the prices of intermediate products, which are followed by the prices of final products, that is, private and public consumption and investment (capital) goods.

The expression:

$$w_n \, \mathbf{n}_d \, k \qquad (19.3)$$

denotes value added and its distribution between wages and gross profits. (We use the symbol k instead of the profit rate and the value of the different capital goods in order to be able to include at a later stage land and labour rent elements – in the case of labour, ability rents – in excess of ordinary wages w_n.) $\mathbf{n}_d$ is the (row) vector of direct labour per unit of output for all products, primary, intermediate and final, in this order. Complex labour is reduced to simple labour through the existing wage structure, where the determination of the socially appropriate wage structure constitutes a most complex problem of social ethics. w_n is a scalar denoting the wage rate per unit of simple labour time in terms of money, and k is the mark-up on labour costs such as to ensure a satisfactory (target or normal) rate of profits on fixed capital and to allow for the depreciation of equipments. The mark-up, k, is the same in all industries and sectors. This implies *abstracting from specific conditions of production*, which means that the *proportion* between the value of fixed capital and the wage bill (circulating capital) are postulated the same in all sectors, although *absolute magnitudes diverge*. The implications of this procedure of abstraction will be brought out below.

Starting from the Leontief interindustry price system the Ricardo–Pasinetti price system based on vertical integration can now be derived. Relation (19.1) may be rewritten as:

$$\mathbf{p}(\mathbf{I}-\mathbf{A}) = w_n \, \mathbf{n}_d \, k$$

where **I** is a unit matrix (the main diagonal is made up of the element '1', all other positions of this square matrix are '0').

Multiplying on both sides by the Leontief inverse, $(\mathbf{I}-\mathbf{A})^{-1}$, and transposing this matrix as well as the vectors **p** and **n**$_d$, which now become *column* vectors, yields:

$$\mathbf{p} = w_n \left[(\mathbf{I}-\mathbf{A})^{-1} \right]' \mathbf{n}_d \, k \qquad (19.4)$$

The relation:

$$\mathbf{n} = \left[(\mathbf{I}-\mathbf{A})^{-1} \right]' \mathbf{n}_d \qquad (19.5)$$

indicates that the column vector of vertically integrated labour **n** is derived from multiplying the column vector of direct labour **n**$_d$ by the *transposed* Leontief inverse. This procedure may be called the Pasinetti transformation (Pasinetti, 1981, pp. 109–12). Each line of the transposed Leontief inverse contains the quantities of *all* goods required *directly and indirectly* to produce a unit of the good considered. As a result, each **n**$_i$ designates the total amount of labour required to produce one unit of a primary, intermediate or final good.

Combining relations (19.4) and (19.5) yields the Ricardo–Pasinetti prices for final outputs based upon vertical integration:

$$\mathbf{p} = w_n \, \mathbf{n} \, k \qquad (19.6)$$

Before going on, the implications and the meaning of abstracting from specific conditions of production have to be explained, first technically and then as to the wider meaning. From relations (19.11) and (19.16), it emerges that the direct and indirect labour used to produce a consumption (or a primary or intermediate) good, n_i, and the capital good used to produce it, n_{iK}, must be the same, in fact equal to unity as implied in relation (19.16). Technically, this means that *for each good* (consumption, intermediate or primary good) *the corresponding capital good row of the transposed Leontief inverse in the equation system (19.4) must be multiplied by a specific coefficient so as to make the corresponding ratio* n_{iK}/n_i *equal to unity* (ratios smaller or greater than unity would also be possible), bearing in mind that the absolute values of n_{iK} and n_i may differ widely. This very simple device allows doing analytical work at the level of basic principles while at the same time maintaining the presence of heterogeneous goods that is required to allow for the social character of the process of production. The heterogeneity of goods is also ensured by the fact that a certain quantity of abstract labour may produce widely differing goods. Hence, on the one hand, the abstraction from specific conditions of production to bring out essentials leaves all the crucial characteristics making up the social and circular process of production intact. On the other hand, it is intuitively evident that reintroducing differing conditions of production – that is, differing n_{iK}/n_i – for scientific purposes would not basically alter the conclusions. Precisely, with classical–Keynesian theory the fundamental principles remain intact when the level of abstraction is lowered to tackle real world problems at the level of phenomena. We shall see that this is not the case with neoclassical theory (on this see also Bortis, 1997, pp. 289–90). Finally, in the above abstraction procedure some coefficients will be greater than unity and others will be smaller than unity. Hence a value of 1 for n_{iK}/n_i appears as a broad average of real world production conditions.

It has already been suggested that to abstract from specific conditions of production means passing from scientific models to metaphysical models (metamodels) embodying principles. Abstracting from all accidentals, which in this instance also comprise the historically variable conditions of production, enables the theorist to state the principles in the simplest possible way and to draw conclusions that are immediately evident and are, as such, generally accessible to a wider audience, for example historians and policy makers. This evidently favours the integration of political economy into a wider framework of social theory and policy.

As suggested, the crucial point is that the conclusions drawn from the set of principles (the metaphysical model) will remain valid if the model is made more realistic (if, for example, differing conditions of production are considered or if the mark-up is not only on wages but also on intermediate and primary products, as would be the case if production is not vertically integrated). This emerges from the price system (19.1). Indeed, if the proportions between circulating and fixed capital were not uniform, the scalar k in relations (19.1) and (19.3) would have to be replaced by a square matrix containing the various sectoral mark-ups on the main diagonal with zero positions elsewhere. Or, when the economy is not vertically integrated, the mark-up would be on wages *and* intermediates and primaries; the price system (19.1) would become:

$$[\mathbf{pA} + w_n \, \mathbf{n}_d]k = \mathbf{p}$$

The model would become immensely complicated while the conclusions would only be quantitatively, and not qualitatively, modified.

The *macroeconomic* counterpart of the sectoral price system obtains if we multiply in relation (19.6) the column vectors $\mathbf{p}$ and $\mathbf{n}$ by the quantity (row) vector $\mathbf{q}$:

$$Y = w_n N k \qquad (19.6.A)$$

where Y is the nominal gross national product and N the number of workers and employees in the 'profit sector' if we interpret w_n as the average wage rate.

In the second place, p_c, the money price of a bundle of necessary consumption goods, is selected as a *numéraire*. This implies that the real social product is $Q = Y/p_c$, a certain number of bundles of necessary consumption goods. We now obtain the Kalecki–Weintraub price equation put to use by Bortis (1997):

$$p_c = w_n n k = w_n (1/A) k \qquad (19.7)$$

Overall labour productivity, A, is the inverse of the macroeconomic labour coefficient, n, with $A = Q/N$ and $n = N/Q$, where N is the labour force active in the 'profit sector'. The social product may be measured most appropriately in terms of (productive) labour embodied if the capital composition is uniform. Indeed, if in relation (19.7) both sides are multiplied by Q and divided through $w_n k$, the social product is measured by N, which may be interpreted as labour time. As already suggested, this procedure implies that the 'reduction problem' is solved; as a consequence w_n represents the value created by a unit of simple labour.

If the ratios of fixed to circulating capital were different, k would have to be interpreted as the weighted average of the sectoral mark-ups. In this case, the social product would simply have to be measured in terms of the above mentioned bundle of labour basics (necessary consumption goods) having a money price p_c. Indeed the simplifying assumption of uniform compositions of capital can be given up whenever the analytical aim pursued requires this, for example if one deals with structures and structural change as does Pasinetti (1981).

The prices (19.6) and (19.7) refer only to produced goods and, as such, reflect the social effort that has been made to produce them. This effort is represented by vertically integrated labour coefficients, n_i for each good i, in the system (19.6) and its macroeconomic equivalent n in (19.7). The effort made to produce good i starts with the production of primary goods, with value added being n_{iP}, and, passing through intermediate products (value added is n_{il}), terminates with the final products, with direct labour in the last stage of production being n_{id}. Hence:

$$n_i = n_{iP} + n_{il} + n_{id} \qquad (19.8)$$

and:

$$n = n_P + n_l + n_d \qquad (19.9)$$

for all final goods if the n's in (19.9) are conceived of as vectors and for the economy as a whole, in relation with the social product, if the n's in (19.9) are seen as scalars.

Combining (19.9) with (19.7) yields:

$$p_c = w_n (n_P + n_l + n_d)\, k \qquad (19.10)$$

This relation implies that, with vertical integration of the social process of production, value added in primary and intermediate goods sectors is also *variable* capital in Marx's sense, which greatly simplifies the presentation of price formation. In fact, with vertical integration, labour values enter the final product in a logically distinct sequence, starting with the value added in the fundamental layer of primary goods or land basics, going through the intermediate layer and ending up with the final product layer.

The price equations (19.6), (19.7) and (19.10) further imply that distribution is a social and political process synthesised by the mark-up, k. Indeed, equation (19.7) implies a wages share $1/k$ and a property share $1-(1/k)$ (made up of profits and of land and labour rents). The social forces determining k are the relative strength of employers and workers, eventually represented by associations, the amount of involuntary unemployment; the political element comes in through state intervention. The above price equations imply that prices and the price level depend upon technology, synthesised by n and A, and distribution, represented by w_n and k. Specifically, distribution is logically prior to production and price formation. These latter processes can only start if a structure of money wages and a rate of profits are given.

The process of distribution occurs at each layer where the social effort of value creation is performed, as can be seen from relation (19.10).[2]

These remarks on the nature of prices allow us to assess the influence of land and labour basics on prices. If the conditions of extracting land basics get more difficult, the corresponding labour coefficient for primaries, n_P, will increase, and, as a consequence, the prices of all intermediate and final products will rise. This will reduce real wages and may trigger distributional conflicts, as indeed happened whenever oil prices rose sharply. The latter implies that labour basics are price determining through income distribution. The wage–price spiral is a case in point.

Two issues remain to be addressed in this section: the significance of the mark-up, k, and the fundamental importance of the machine-tool sector. To bring out the meaning of the mark-up, k, we start by considering the price equations for consumption goods, taking account of the fact that each private or public consumption good is produced by vertically integrated labour assisted by a specific capital good (the same holds for all other goods: private and public investment goods, primary and intermediate goods). The price equation for a consumption good can be written as follows:

$$p_{ic} = w_n \, n_{ic} + r \, (w_n \, n_{iK} \, k)$$

or:

$$p_{ic} = w_n \, n_{ic} \, [1 + (r \, w_n \, n_{iK} \, k)/(w_n \, n_{ic})]$$

and:

$$p_{ic} = w_n \, n_{ic} \, [1 + (r \, n_{iK} \, k)/n_{ic}] \qquad (19.11)$$

Since we abstract from the differing conditions of production to bring out the basic principles, the proportions of fixed to circulating capital, n_{iK}/n_{ic}, are the same in all sectors, although absolute magnitudes may differ as is required with heterogeneous goods. As suggested above, this implies that the mark-up on circulating capital, k, is the same in all industries and sectors. Hence the expression in square brackets of relation (19.11) equals k, which allows us to bring out the economic meaning of the mark-up more precisely *for the case when property incomes consist of profits only*:

$$k = 1 + (r \, n_{iK} \, k)/n_i$$

Hence:

$$k = n_i/(n_i - r \, n_{iK}) \qquad (19.12)$$
$$1/k = (n_i - r \, n_{iK})/n_i = 1 - r \, (n_{iK}/n_i) \qquad (19.13)$$

and for the economy as a whole:

$$1/k = (n - r \, n_K)/n = 1 - r \, (n_K/n) \qquad (19.14)$$

Relations (19.13) and (19.14) tell us that all values are created by labour active in the 'profit sector' and that profits are proportional to past labour embodied in fixed capital goods. Moreover, since according to relation (19.7) the real wage is in terms of necessary consumption goods (labour basics), distribution must be regulated in the labour-basics sector, with the price and distribution equations having the same structure as relations (19.11) and (19.13). At this stage, it has to be repeated that normal profits have nothing to do with exploitation but are socially necessary (see also Bortis, 1997, pp. 158–75).

The price equations for the capital goods entering the production of consumption goods, primary and intermediate goods, have exactly the same structure as the price equations for the consumption goods represented by relation (19.11):

$$p_{iK} = w_n \, n_{iK} \, [1 + (r \, n_{iK*} \, k)/n_{iK}] \qquad (19.15)$$

There is one important difference, however. In producing the capital goods required to produce consumption goods, labour is assisted by a specific capital good, that is, machine tools or machines to make machines (Lowe, 1976). In expression (19.15) this specific capital good is marked with a star (K^*). Hence machine tools assist labour in producing all the capital goods required (in the production of each consumption good labour is assisted by a specific capital good). *However, machine tools also assist labour to produce machine tools.* Hence we have a final fundamental equation:

$$p_{iK*} = w_n \, n_{iK*} \, [1 + (r \, n_{iK**} \, k)/n_{iK*}] \qquad (19.16)$$

This relation fixes the proportion between the value of fixed and circulating capital that must hold in all price equations, that is, n_{iK**}/n_{iK*}. We should recall here that we abstract from the conditions of production in order to put to the fore two essential features of a monetary production economy, that is, the uniform profit rate and the fact that all value is created by labour. However, the uniform ratio between fixed and circulating capital is not chosen arbitrarily. This ratio is determined in the basic *technology determining* sector of a monetary production economy, that is, the machine tool sector. In a way, this is in analogy to the Ricardian proposition that the rate of profits is governed in the agricultural sector, which produces the necessary consumption goods.

According to relation (19.16) the ratio of fixed to circulating capital may be unity with absolute values being the same, which would simplify all the price equations set forth above. However, this proportion need not be unity, and absolute values of fixed and circulating capital may vary since machine tools may produce machine tools of differing shapes. But even if the absolute values in all the n_{iK}/n_i proportions were the same, the heterogeneity of produced goods would be possible since machine tools are capable of producing capital goods, including machine tools, of different *qualitative* shapes, which, in turn, can produce qualitatively different consumption goods, always in association with labour of course. In fact, the same *quantity* of labour may be associated with very different qualitative realisations in the form of heterogeneous goods. This is in analogy to Pasinetti (1981), where the vertically integrated labour coefficients are associated with differing and changing structures.

The treatment of value and distribution within the social, circular and vertically integrated process of production suggested here and in the previous section enables us to deal with three problems associated, in our opinion, with Sraffa's model of circular production, value and distribution. Firstly, the notion of land basics or primary products enables us to deal with the problem that, with Sraffa, inputs equal output. Indeed, in the upper left-hand corner of the Leontief matrix, iron ore is transformed into steel, crude oil into petrol, and so on; the outputs of land basics are subsequently transferred to all intermediate and final goods sectors. Secondly, treating fixed capital goods as final products, all produced by machine tools and labour, rather than treating fixed capital goods as joint products, renders the whole analysis of value and distribution within social and circular production much easier; specifically, profits may now be calculated on fixed capital by way of a mark-up on circulating capital, which includes direct wage costs and the costs of intermediate and primary goods, which also become wage costs if there is vertical integration. Thirdly, the social and circular process of production implies, in fact, production of commodities by means of commodities *and labour*. This means that the feature of circularity appears in three instances in the social process of production. In the first place, there is production of primary commodities by primary commodities and labour in the upper-left Sraffa corner of the Leontief system. Secondly, in the realm of final products, there is production of commodities by means of commodities in the capital goods sector, where all specific capital goods are produced by machine tools, which also produce and reproduce themselves. Thirdly, and perhaps most importantly, necessary consumption goods, which are final goods, have to move the all, even to the most remote corners, of the social and circular production system, because of the fact that there is production of commodities by means of commodities and labour, a fact pictured by relation (19.5) above, which indicates the Pasinetti operation of calculating vertically integrated labour by multiplying the transposed Leontief inverse by the vector of direct labour.

PROPORTIONS AND SCALE: CLASSICAL AND KEYNESIAN MACROECONOMICS

Classical and Keynesian macroeconomics represent two aspects of the social process of production and of the associated processes of circulation of money, means of production and final goods respectively. It has already been suggested that classical macroeconomics deals with *proportions* in relation with the social and circular process of production and with the associated theories of values and distribution at a *given scale* of economic activity. Keynesian macroeconomics, however, treats of the *scale* of output and employment, that is, economic activity, with *proportions given*. This is valid only at the level of principles. In the real world, set in historical time, proportions will vary if activity changes.

The classical and Keynesian elements of economic analysis may now be brought together within the wider framework of a monetary theory of production. The essential feature of a monetary production economy is neatly represented at the outset of the second volume of Marx's *Kapital* (p. 31):

$$M - C \dots P \dots C' - M' \tag{19.17}$$

In the first stage, producers dispose of money and finance, M (G in original) and buy means of production, that is, commodities and labour force, C (W in original). These are transformed into final products, C' (W'), in the vertically integrated labour view of the social process of production, P, which implies the horizontal land aspect of production. The final goods, C', are transformed into money, M' (G'). At this second stage of circulation, M' – effective demand in money terms – governs C', the amount of final goods that may be exchanged against money.

The classical proportions aspect emerges, in the first place, in the sphere of distribution. Before production can start, distribution must be regulated: the normal (satisfactory, target) profit rate used in the price calculation of firms, and a wages structure, ideally based upon an evaluation of work places, must be given. Hence a Ricardian touch comes in through the primacy of income distribution, which indeed emerges as the primary and fundamental problem of classical–Keynesian political economy. In a wider view the determination of the wage, profit, and rent structures and the corresponding shares in national income is a central problem of distributive justice, which, in turn, forms the kernel of social or political ethics.

As production goes on, normal absolute prices and money incomes are formed. This gives rise to a new set of proportions, that is, relative prices and shares in a given income. The spending of incomes determines another set of proportions: absolute and relative quantities, the latter giving rise to specific proportions that must hold between final product sectors, for example between the consumption and the investment goods sectors (hence if wages are entirely consumed and profits saved and equal investment, the wage bill in the investment goods sector must equal profits in the consumption goods sector). Fundamentally, that is, at the level of principles, proportions must be such that the processes of production and circulation pictured by scheme (19.17) may go on smoothly; specifically, entrepreneurs must be able to cover the costs of production and to realise the normal rate of profits. This represents a Sraffian element in classical macroeconomics.

The classical proportions aspect is in direct relation with the *circuit* of monetary flows and of final goods flows, which take place between producers and private and public consumers. The breadth of the circuit is given. This implies that the scale of economic activity, measured in terms of employment, is also given; economic activity may go on at an employment level of 70, 80 or 90 per cent, for example, implying corresponding levels of involuntary unemployment.

It is evident from scheme (19.17) that money is absolutely necessary to run the system of social production and circulation. There is not exchange of goods against goods, but always goods against money. For example, when the steel sector delivers steel to the machine-tools sector, the steel sector does not get machine tools in return, but money. This gives rise to flows of commodities and money in the opposite direction, that is, to circuits of goods and money. It has already been suggested that the surplus principle – interest as part of the social surplus – that is implied in scheme (19.17), seems naturally associated with a theory of *endogenous* money.

Long-period Keynesian macroeconomics is, precisely, about the *scale of economic activity*, that is, *the breadth of the circuit*, with proportions in principle given.[3] Keynesian models, whether comprising one or several sectors, are necessarily based upon vertical integration, which puts the labour aspect of production to the fore. The result of the social process of production is the social product, which, as a consequence, contains final goods only. The processes of distribution and formation of values or prices that go on within the vertically integrated process of production are now completed and the process of circulation of final goods and of money may start. The latter gives rise to real and monetary flows between enterprises, households, the social sphere (where most diverse associations are located, mostly non-profit organisations) and the state.

It is at the second stage of the process of circulation, $C' - M'$ in scheme (19.17), that the scale aspect of classical–Keynesian political economy emerges: *the level of economic activity, that is, the scale of output (C', to wit, the social product, Q) and of the associated level of employment (N), is governed by effective demand (M').* The employment level so determined is associated with a definite level of involuntary, system governed unemployment.

This very simple monetary theory of production implies that the social processes of production and circulation could not go on without money, which is an indispensable measure and representative of value and an equally indispensable means of transaction. All public and private consumption and investment plans realised in historical time are in terms of money, which represents the link between the past and the future. However, in a monetary production economy (Keynes, 1933/1973) with extensive division of labour and, consequently, with social production, there are no exchanges of goods against goods, as is the case in a real exchange economy, but always goods against money. For example, the steel industry delivers steel to most parts of the machine industry without buying the machines produced there. Or, workers occupied in the machine industries do not exchange labour time for machines; in fact, these workers 'exchange' their salaries against goods that they have not directly produced, for example necessary consumption goods. In a way, one could conceive of an exchange of input values (labour time) C, represented by M, against output values C', and its counterpart in money terms M', within the two processes of circulation set forth in scheme (19.17), whereby money *represents* value. Since $M' > M$ in this scheme, a surplus value amounting to $M'-M$ must have been produced within the social process of production, P, as Marx has argued at the outset of the first volume of his *Kapital*. Hence workers are remunerated in money form for their contribution to the productive effort in the social process of production. Money wages represent, in turn, a claim on a part of the common result of production that can be chosen freely. As a consequence, the social process of production within which final goods embodying value (labour time) are created could not function without money, which represents these values and enables thus their circulation; as such money – which includes, of course, the financial sector – is also a social institution.

Hence the vertically integrated production model, which implies the horizontal interindustry model (as developed in the two previous sections) and the associated processes of circulation synthesise classical and Keynesian pieces of analysis and represent, as such, a monetary theory of production. For analytical purposes, it is appropriate to abstract from differences in the conditions of production such that these are similar but not equal in the various sectors and industries. In fact, while the ratio between the value of fixed capital and of circulating capital – consisting of wages only in a vertically integrated model as emerges from relations (19.4) to (19.7) – is assumed to be the same in all sectors and industries, the absolute magnitudes of these capitals are postulated to be different. This allows for the existence of heterogeneous goods. Given these specific proportions between fixed and circulating capital, all economic activities now stand in a direct relation to labour: the fundamental prices are labour values; profits and rents arise because the labour force in the 'profit sector' produces a quantitative and qualitative surplus value (qualitative surplus value arises in the form of surplus wages due to specific abilities, for instance). This in turn implies that the social product is measured by labour time. Hence the postulate of equal ratios between fixed and circulating capitals, not absolute magnitudes thereof, allows us, in a Ricardian–Marxian vein, to discuss fundamentals, that is, the essential features related to production, value, distribution, employment and money in a very simple way. Different conditions of production, cyclical movements of prices and quantities, and the vagaries of the market are merely associated with historically variable forms of appearance (*Erscheinungsformen*) of invariable basic principles. For instance, the Sraffian prices of production, themselves principles, though non-fundamental, show how the fundamental Ricardian labour values can be historically realised through prices based upon normal cost calculation.

THE PROPORTIONS ASPECT OF CLASSICAL– KEYNESIAN POLITICAL ECONOMY

Complementarity is a fundamental feature of the social process of production. The social product is the result of a common effort of all industries and sectors. These come into being on account of the division of labour that, in principle, is rendered possible by the different dispositions and abilities of the social individuals associated with their social nature. Between the various sectors and industries given but not invariable proportions must prevail if the process of production is to go on in an orderly way. This requires cooperation between producers. Coordination is also required at the level of the firm; some coordination may be required at the level of industries through producers' organisations, or even at the macroeconomic level regarding distributional issues in the main, for example wage structures or the level of the normal profit rate or the hierarchy of profit rates.

The essentially social character of production implies that, at a fundamental level, all the great problems of political economy, namely, value, distribution, employment, accumulation and growth are also social, in a way macroeconomic, problems. In this section it is suggested that value and distribution are associated with the proportions aspect of production; in the next section employment is shown to be related with the scale aspect. The analytical starting point is provided by Pasinetti's (1981, 1986a) vertically integrated labour system, which, as suggested in the fourth section, implies the Leontief–Sraffa nature-based horizontal model.

Before going on, a definitional problem concerning the terms *normal* and *natural* has to be clarified. In fact, Sraffa's system exhibits *normal* variables and Pasinetti's model contains *natural* variables (see also Bortis, 1997, pp. 47–53, 86–7). Pasinetti's *natural* system characterises an economy with ethically desirable properties: there is full employment and the income distribution implied might reflect the principle of distributive justice. In fact, the variables and parameters appearing below are formally, but not materially, equivalent to Pasinetti's and reflect ethically imperfect real world situations. For example, permanent involuntary unemployment and a very unequal – ethically inappropriate – distribution of incomes may prevail. Since we attempt to come to grips with the fundamental causal forces at work, we speak in a Sraffian vein of *normal* variables and parameters in this framework, which implies that the 'natural' is the 'normal' in its ethically desirable form. Given this, it is suggested below that Pasinetti's vertically integrated approach can be associated with a theoretical system comprising normal variables, specifically, a uniform profit rate and normal prices.

Based upon a vertically integrated framework and taking account of the previous sections, the main purpose of this section is to picture the determination of prices and quantities within the social, and circular, processes of production and circulation. In fact, as we shall see below, the proportions model only determines *relative* prices and quantities (see on this Pasinetti, 1981, p. 23, fn. 30). Absolute prices and quantities are, at first, arbitrary and are fixed once the money wage level and the level of employment are determined. This implication of the circulation model is a first justification to speak of the proportions aspect of political economy. In the first place, this implication means that the level of money wages – governing absolute prices – and the level of effective demand – governing quantities – are determined outside the technical–economic sphere, that is, in the social and political realm. Relative prices are important for the determination of the wage structure, which is independent of the absolute wage level. However, when the determination of the social surplus and of the scale of activity is considered, *absolute* prices and quantities move to the fore, as is natural in a monetary production economy where all economic calculations are in money terms and where commodities are always exchanged against money.

The social and circular process of production stands at the heart of a monetary production economy and is complemented by the processes of circulation of goods (means of production and final goods) and money (see scheme (19.17)). The economy is looked at from the point of view of vertical integration. This means that final products are linked to labour, which now stands for direct and indirect labour, the latter being used to produce primary and intermediate goods. It has already been suggested that the vertical (Ricardo–Pasinetti) view of the social process of production implies the horizontal or interindustry aspect of production as pictured by Sraffa's and Leontief's models; at each vertical stage of production the horizontal aspect of production is implied.

It has also been mentioned that the social process of production can only start if distribution is already determined. Indeed, *the regulation of distribution is a precondition for production, and for price and income formation.* The structure of money wages and the normal (target, satisfactory) profit or hierarchy of profit rates both enable monetary costs and hence prices to come into being. With monetary costs given, firms are able to carry out price calculations. In fact, the wage structure and the normal profit rate are both required to represent the efforts undertaken within the social process of production in the form of prices of production, to regulate distribution at each stage of the vertically integrated process that transforms primary products into final goods and, simultaneously, to organise the social process of production, that is, to bring about the appropriate structures or proportions, and to render possible competition in the classical sense, that is, to create a tendency of realised profit rates towards a uniform profit rate. For these reasons the average money wage rate, w_n, and the mark-up, k, which is, in turn, governed by the normal rate of profits, must be predetermined and, consequently, appear at the end of the price vector in system (19.18) below. Indeed, once distribution is determined, the prices of intermediate products at each stage of vertical production leading from primary to final products are known, and so are the final product prices p_i ($i = 1, \ldots, m$) appearing in this system. In the fundamental model exhibiting principles, these prices are proportional to labour values and reflect the social effort that has been made to produce the final goods.

Incomes are thus formed simultaneously with prices. This leads to *monetary* flows associated with the formation and the spending of incomes. These aspects of the process of production are exhibited by the price system (19.18), which, like all the other equations and equation systems set forth in this section, is taken in a slightly elaborated form from Pasinetti (1986a) and also follows from the third section above.

$$
\begin{bmatrix}
1 & 0 & \cdots & 0 & -n_1 \\
0 & 1 & \cdots & 0 & -n_2 \\
\vdots & \vdots & \ddots & \vdots & \vdots \\
0 & 0 & \cdots & 1 & -n_m \\
-c_1 & -c_2 & \cdots & -c_m & 1
\end{bmatrix}
\times
\begin{bmatrix}
p_1 \\
p_2 \\
\vdots \\
p_m \\
w_n k
\end{bmatrix}
= 0
\qquad (19.18)
$$

The number of final goods produced in an economy is m. These goods are for private and state consumption and investment. Some of them may be exported, and imports may be equal to, fall short of or exceed exports. As suggested in the fourth section, the final goods consist of labour basics (necessary consumption goods), labour–land basics (machine tools) and non-basics.[4] The p_1, ..., p_m represent the corresponding prices of production. The average nominal income produced by a worker (a labour unit) in the 'profit sector' is $w_n k$, which equals nominal average labour productivity pA. w_n is the money wage rate and k the mark-up over prime costs at normal capacity utilisation. In a vertically integrated economy wage costs equal prime costs since labour comprises direct and indirect labour. p is the money price of a bundle of necessary consumption goods and stands, as such, for the general price level. $A = Q/N$ is labour productivity in real terms. The size of the social product, Q, is expressed by the number of bundles of necessary consumptions goods and N is the labour force in the 'profit sector'. In this sector a qualitative and quantitative surplus over wages occurs, which, in nominal terms, equals $w_n(k-1)$ and accrues to capital, in the form of profits, and to land owners and to specially skilled or organised labour, in the form of rents. Since working time is assumed to be given, N stands either for the number of workers and employees or for working time measured in hours, in months, or in years. As already suggested, those working in the 'non-profit sector' in the widest sense (for example civil servants, teachers in state schools, entertainers and artists), while not economically productive, are of course socially and politically productive; if appropriately organised, the 'non-profit sector' ought to contribute to the good and proper running of society and of the state. This point has been particularly emphasised by the political economists of the German Historical school in the late nineteenth and in the early twentieth century.

The n_i (= N_i/Q_{if}) are the vertically integrated labour coefficients comprising direct and indirect labour time, N_i, for example man years, in relation to the full-employment output (Q_{if}) of good i. The indirect part of N_i is embodied in primary and intermediate products. The c_i (= Q_{if}/N_f) represent demand coefficients, which indicate how the average nominal income, $w_n k$, or total income in real terms, N_f, that is, in terms of labour time, is spent. Part of income is consumed, and part is paid in taxes and saved. Since saving equals investment in long-period equilibrium (Bortis, 1997, pp. 81–9), the demand coefficients c_i relate to the demand for private and public consumption and investment goods.

Multiplying the first m rows in system (19.18) yields a corresponding number of sectoral price equations. These equations picture the formation of prices within enterprises and the payment of incomes to households. The price equations contained in system (19.18) are all based on vertical integration and, therefore, correspond to the equation system (19.6):

$$p_i = w_n \, n_i \, k = w_n \, (1/A_i) \, k \qquad (19.19)$$

with $i = 1, 2, \ldots, m$ and where A_i is sectoral labour productivity Q_i/N_i.

These prices represent the *essential* features of the classical theory of value and distribution. In their being proportional to the quantity of labour embodied directly and indirectly in the production of one unit of output, they reflect the *social effort* that has been made to produce a commodity. Hence prices, fundamentally, are not indicators of scarcity as is the case with exchange-based neoclassical theory. In the classical view, goods can always be produced if the labour required is devoted to the production of these goods – this is a tenet of Pasinetti's work. To this a Keynesian argument adds: with the scale of economic activity being governed by effective demand (see below), the possibility of permanent involuntary unemployment arises. In such a situation it would be possible to produce more of all commodities if effective demand increased. It is plain that it is entirely inappropriate to speak of the prices as scarcity indicators while part of the fundamental factor of production, that is, labour, remains idle.

In relations (19.19), the level of money wages, w_n, determines the value of the various commodities in money terms. Money prices and money wages are proportional and this has implications for the theory of inflation: distributional conflicts may give rise to wage–price spirals. With prices given, workers and employees in the profit sector may attempt to increase the wages share through imposing higher money wages. This would reduce the mark-up, k. If entrepreneurs want to maintain their income share, determined by the prevailing normal rate of profits for example, they will put up prices, starting thus the wage–price spiral.

The labour value principle gives rise to a distributional issue associated with the notion of distributive justice. This emerges from the set of relative prices that can be derived from the absolute prices (19.19):

$$p_i/p_j = n_i/n_j \qquad\qquad (19.19.\text{A})$$

Here, the distribution aspect is associated with the evaluation of labour and, consequently, with the wage structure, which, in turn, represents a particular dimension of distributive justice. With the technical conditions of production and the socially necessary direct and indirect labour time given, a rise in n_i/n_j signifies that labour producing good i is valued relatively higher than labour in sector j. As a consequence, the money wage rate i will rise relative to the rate j. It should be evident that the determination of the wage structure is an immensely complex issue of distributive justice, with various factors playing a role, the evaluation of work places within enterprises and trade-union activity perhaps being the most important. Presumably, the most important factor leading to a distortion of the wage structure is involuntary unemployment, as is indicated by the emergence of the working poor and of precarious work places in times of prolonged crisis.

In the system of absolute prices (19.19) the determination of the surplus over wages (k) is associated with another dimension of distributive justice, that is, the determination of various shares in a given income. Since, in a Ricardian vein, price formation relates to the most difficult conditions of production, the surplus over normal or ordinary wages w_n is made up of various elements: normal profits and differential rents, that is, rents on land, but also rents on special skills, for instance of sportsmen, physicians and lawyers, and privileges associated with the corporative organisation of certain professions. Hence the mark-up, k, governs the share of ordinary wages and of various surplus shares in income.

In the second and third sections we have also suggested that, in a Ricardian–Sraffian vein, distribution must be regulated in the sectors producing basic goods: land basics (raw materials, energy resources and agricultural primary products), labour basics (necessary consumption goods) and labour–land basics (machine tools, that is, machines to make machines). Basic goods are required in the production of all goods. Their prices exert, therefore, a determining influence on the prices of non-basics, which, as a result, are determined by the conditions of production in the basic sectors. This also holds for distribution. For example, the profit rate determined in the basic goods sectors will govern profit rates in the non-basic sectors.

The distributional aspects just considered imply that *long-period* distribution – the shares of wages, profits and rents in the *given* income and their structures – is entirely governed by institutions, for example trade-unions, entrepreneurial and professional associations, the government including the civil service, and habits and customs that have developed historically. Hence the surplus principle of distribution is associated with a complex social process involving *part–whole relationships* between parts of society (individuals and social groups) and society as a whole. Distribution must be of a social nature since production, as pictured by the Sraffa–Leontief model set forth above, is essentially a social process. Since part–whole relationships are crucial, the determination of shares in a given income and of wage structures embody relations between parts of society and society as a whole. Consequently, the *wage rate* for some kind of work is a *share* in a *given* national income, determined by effective demand, and *not* the price of labour that, eventually, brings about an equilibrium between supply and demand in the labour market in general or on some specific labour market.

The prices of production are also of a social nature since they are determined by distributional arrangements reflected in the money wage rate, w_n, by the mark-up, k, and by the (social) conditions of production pictured by the triangular Leontief matrix sketched in the third section and synthesised through vertical integration by the labour coefficient, n_i, or labour productivity, A_i. This appears clearly from price equations (19.4) to (19.7). Hence, in the classical approach to economic problems, value and distribution are macroeconomic, not microeconomic, phenomena. The reason is that with the production of each good the *whole* production system enters the scene. This is perhaps the main tenet of classical macroeconomics.

The strategic position of distribution in economic theory and reality emerges from system (19.18). Only once a wage structure and the surplus over wages (k) are fixed, can the problems of value (equations (19.19) and (19.37)) and employment (equation (19.40)) be tackled. This expresses the Ricardian–Sraffian idea that the regulation of distribution is logically prior to the determination of value, and Keynes's view that distribution is, *via* consumption, a crucial determinant of employment and capital accumulation. Ricardo (1821/1951, p. 5) was certainly right when he claimed that to 'determine the laws which regulate . . . distribution, is the principal problem of political economy'. In another context a similar point was made by Keynes

(1936/1973, pp. 372–3): 'The outstanding faults of the economic society in which we live are its failure to provide for full employment and its arbitrary and inequitable distribution of wealth and incomes. . . . [U]p to the point where full employment prevails, the growth of capital depends not at all on a low propensity to consume but is, on the contrary, held back by it'.

As suggested above, the classical theory of value and distribution implies the *creation of incomes* in the social process of production and their subsequent *distribution*. This emerges from the system of equations (19.19), which are derived from system (19.18). The last equation of this system, namely:

$$c_1 p_1 + c_2 p_2 + \ldots + c_m p_m = w_n k \tag{19.20}$$

indicates in what proportions incomes are spent on the various goods. The c_i coefficients (defined by expression (19.26) below) represent the fractions of real income – measured in terms of labour time, man-years N_f for example – spent for a certain quantity of each good i (if N_f is interpreted as a number of workers and employees (labour units), the c_i would represent per capita demand for a specific good). The $c_i p_i$ coefficients are expenditures in money terms on the various goods and services per person employed in the profit sector, indicating the way in which average money income, $w_n k$, is spent. This becomes immediately evident if in relation (19.20) the definition of c_i (relation (19.26) below) is taken into account:

$$\sum_{i=1}^{m} c_i p_i = \sum_{i=1}^{m} \frac{Q_{if}}{N_f} p_i = w_n k \tag{19.21}$$

As such, equations (19.20) and (19.21) picture yet another part of the flows of money, goods and services in a monetary production economy. The average income, $w_n k$, is consumed, paid in taxes and saved, and subsequently spent on private and public consumption goods and on investment goods, whereby both consumption and investment may be financed in part by the financial sector with saving passively adjusting. In this process, the enterprise sector delivers goods and provides services, and receives the sales receipts. In these processes proportions between sectors are established.

The economic meaning of relation (19.21) emerges more clearly if the equations for p_i (relation (19.19) above) are taken into account:

$$\sum_{i=1}^{m}\frac{N_i}{N_f}\,w_n k \;=\; w_n k \qquad\qquad (19.22)$$

$$\sum_{i=1}^{m}\frac{N_i}{N_f}\,w_n k\; N_f \;=\; w_n k\, N_f = Y \qquad\qquad (19.23)$$

$$\sum_{i=1}^{m}\frac{N_i}{N_f} = 1 \qquad\qquad (19.24)$$

These definitions, together with definition (19.20), tell us that the spending of average income (relation (19.22)) or total income (relation (19.23)) governs the distribution of the labour force across the various sectors of production (relation (19.24)). The last two terms of relation (19.23) indicate the relationship between nominal income, Y, and real income, N_f. The latter obtains if the former is divided through the average money income, $w_n k$, which *represents* the total value per person employed in the profit sector in terms of money. Relation (19.20) indicates that the distribution of the labour force depends upon the demand coefficients, c_i, and the labour coefficients, n_i, that are contained in the prices, p_i. Both types of coefficients may, of course, change in concrete historical situations. The demand coefficients, c_i, vary in the long run because of changes in consumer preferences and in public spending *with the demand for investment goods passively adjusting*. The labour coefficients, n_i, decline because of technical progress: less direct and indirect labour is required to produce a unit of some good i. As a result, with a given effective demand and hence given output, technical progress is bound to lead to a reduction of employment. Involuntary unemployment can only be avoided if money wages rise in line with labour productivity. This confirms the conclusions following from the so-called *Freisetzungstheorie*, which suggests that technical progress may lead to technological unemployment. Already Ricardo (1821/1951, Ch. 31) had argued that the introduction of new and better machinery may be harmful to the working class. Capitalists, in fact, choose those techniques that yield the highest net income (profits); at the same time gross income (wages plus profits) may decline, which implies that the wage fund declines and fewer labourers may be put to work.

The *quantity* flows of a monetary production economy are captured by the equation system (19.25), which depicts proportions. From this system it emerges that the scale of activity, governed by the employment level N, is arbitrary. In accordance with Pasinetti (1981) we assume that full employment prevails. This assumption will be given up in the next section, where Keynes's principle of effective demand comes in to determine the long-period scale of economic activity.

$$
\begin{bmatrix}
1 & 0 & \cdots & 0 & -c_1 \\
0 & 1 & \cdots & 0 & -c_2 \\
\vdots & \vdots & \ddots & \vdots & \vdots \\
0 & 0 & \cdots & 1 & -c_m \\
-n_1 & -n_2 & \cdots & -n_m & 1
\end{bmatrix}
\times
\begin{bmatrix}
Q_{1f} \\
Q_{2f} \\
\vdots \\
Q_{mf} \\
N_f
\end{bmatrix}
= 0
\qquad (19.25)
$$

Here N_f represents the – full employment – *labour force in the profit sector*. The (full employment) quantity of profit-sector labour (N_f) represents the pivot of the quantity system. N seen as labour time has, in fact, two aspects. On the one hand, N_f, as *labour commanded*, *measures* the value of output or the level of incomes, which, as suggested above, implies that the nominal social product must be divided by $w_n k$ or pA (that is, nominal average income, which equals labour productivity in money terms) to obtain a measure of the real social product in terms of labour. This is appropriate from the social point of view since profit-sector labour creates all value, *including* surplus value. Moreover, this procedure is in line with the Ricardian–Sraffian tenet that distribution must be regulated *before* the problem of value can be addressed (the nominal average, w_n, and, thus, the wages structure and the normal or target profit rate and, consequently, the mark-up, k, must be known before production can start). While labour time (value) is the real measure of output, *money represents value* and is, as such, a social institution that enables the social processes of production and circulation to function at all. To be able to fulfil its social function, money must be legally anchored; specifically, the obligation to accept money as the ultimate means of payment or of clearing debts must be legally fixed. Hence money is not 'the most easily exchangeable commodity' of the neoclassical real-exchange model, but a socio-economic and legal institution established by the state.

The spending coefficients c_i indicate how full-employment (real) income N_f is spent and thus determines the full-employment quantities Q_{if} of private and public consumption and investment goods, that is, the structure of production, which is also a matter of proportions:

$$
Q_{if} = c_i N_f \qquad (19.26)
$$

with $i = 1, 2, \ldots, m$.

Equation (19.26) implies that in a monetary production economy *goods valued at labour time (Q_{if}) are, ultimately, exchanged against labour time (real income measured in labour time)*, not against other goods, as is the case in the neoclassical exchange model. In a way, profit-sector labour, assisted by past labour (capital), represents the economic basis of a society that produces the social surplus. As a result, effective demand originates from four sources: households, firms, society, and the state. The quantity system (19.25) seen together with the price system (19.18) renders visible the social role of *money*, which, as suggested above, *represents* the values created by productive labour and is, as such, a social institution that renders possible the social processes of production and circulation of goods and services within society at large.

On the other hand, N_f represents *labour embodied* in the quantities of the various goods produced and, consequently, in the social product. The vertically integrated coefficients of direct and indirect labour (n_i) and the quantities demanded (determined by relation (19.21)) govern the distribution of labour between the different sectors of production.

$$n_1 \, Q_{1f} + n_2 \, Q_{2f} + \ldots + n_m \, Q_{im} = \sum_{i=1}^{m} N_i = N_f \qquad (19.27)$$

where the

$$n_i = N_i / Q_{if} \qquad (19.28)$$

represent the labour coefficients, that is, the amount of direct and indirect labour required to produce a unit of output. As such, labour embodied represents the *social effort* required to produce the final goods and hence the social product.

In this view, N_f not only stands for productive labour, but also for the economic sphere of society. Indeed N_f represents the material basis of a society with social production as its core. The social surplus enables society to accumulate capital, to realise technical progress through saving labour and to erect a social, political, legal and cultural superstructure. This is reflected by the fact that the goods appearing in system (19.25) and in definitions (19.26) and (19.27) include private and public consumption and investment goods.

Mathematically, the dependence of one equation on the others implies that the determinant of the equation systems (19.18) and (19.25) is zero (this condition has been established by Pasinetti (1981, for example on p. 32)):

$$c_1 n_1 + c_2 n_2 + ... + c_m n_m - 1 = 0 \qquad (19.29)$$

If account is taken of the definition of the c_i and n_i coefficients (definitions (19.26) and (19.28)), this condition indicates, once again, the distribution of labour across the vertically integrated sectors of production:

$$N_1/N_f + N_2/N_f + ... + N_m/N_f = 1 \qquad (19.30)$$

The sectoral distribution of profit-sector labour emerges as the basic element of socio-economic structure and of the proportions aspect of classical–Keynesian political economy. According to condition (19.29) this distribution depends upon demand (c_i) and upon direct and indirect labour requirements (n_i). This conclusion also follows from definitions (19.20) to (19.24).

Working at the level of principles greatly simplifies the discussion of extremely complex macroeconomic issues, as Ricardo, Marx *and* Keynes clearly perceived. For example, in his *General Theory* Keynes (1936/1973, p. 41) states: 'In dealing with the theory of employment [and with the associated problems of measuring aggregate output and the aggregate price level] I propose . . . to make use of only two fundamental units of quantity, namely quantities of money-value and quantities of employment'. Later on, he expresses his sympathy 'with the pre-classical doctrine that everything is produced by labour, aided by what used to be called art and is now called technique, by natural resources . . ., and by the results of past labour, embodied in assets' (ibid., p. 213). Hence, to abstract from specific conditions of production enables us to discuss the great problems of political economy on the basis of principles, that is, at the level of labour values. If the level of abstraction is lowered, labour values are modified (see Bortis, 1997, pp. 125–9). For example, if differing conditions of production are considered, Ricardian labour values become Sraffian prices of production, which, in turn, differ from market prices. In fact, starting from labour values the prices of production can be exactly calculated (Pasinetti, 1977, pp. 122–50). *At the level of principles, that is, at the level of pure theory*, there is, in our view, absolutely no contradiction between Ricardo and Sraffa; in the same way there is no contradiction at all between volumes I and II of Marx's *Kapital* and volume III of this work. We are faced here with analyses of the same issues at different levels of abstraction. In this view, Sraffa shows how labour values – the essence of prices – are brought into concrete existence with unequal conditions of production and equal profit rates. However, it is of crucial importance that, in a Marxian vein, upper-layer phenomena, prices of production, market prices, wages, profits and rents (Bortis, 1997, pp. 103–17), 'can only be understood properly if the fundamentals (value and surplus value) have been grasped' (ibid., p. 127). Hence principles (fundamentals or essentials) illuminate the extremely complex appearances (*Erscheinungsformen*) of monetary production economies from inside, so to speak.

To conclude it may be mentioned that the way of abstracting has different consequences for different theoretical approaches. In fact, to abstract from specific conditions of production and to work on the basis of the labour principle of value is *simplifying* for classical–Keynesian theory, but *crucial* for neoclassical theory (Bortis, 1996, pp. 141–5, 1997, pp. 289–90). Introducing non-uniform compositions of capital associated with an equal rate of profits only modifies the labour principle of value (*values* now become Sraffian *prices of production*) and leaves the conclusions drawn from it intact. The marginalist theory of value, distribution and employment built upon a surrogate production function implying the same conditions of production everywhere (Samuelson, 1962) does no longer hold, however, once unequal conditions of production are combined with an equal rate of profits: lower factor prices are no longer necessarily associated with larger factor quantities, and vice versa, and the marginal product of capital no longer equals the rate of profits. This is the result of the capital theory debate (Harcourt, 1972).

THE SCALE ASPECT OF CLASSICAL–KEYNESIAN POLITICAL ECONOMY

The conditions (19.29) or (19.30) guarantee economically meaningful solutions for the equation systems (19.18) and (19.25), that is, positive prices and quantities. They also imply that *the proportions, that is, relative prices and quantities, are, in principle, independent of the scale of economic activity* (Pasinetti, 1981, p. 23, fn. 30, pp. 32–3). However, the independence of proportions from scale not only holds for the vertically integrated labour model of Pasinetti (1981, 1986a) but also for Sraffa's horizontal, interindustry nature model. Indeed, Sraffa (1960, p. v) emphasises that 'no changes in output . . . are considered', a point on which Roncaglia (2000, pp. 48–51) insists. The independence of the proportions and of the scale aspect in social production and circulation provides the clue for bringing together classical and Keynesian elements of economic theory on a long-period basis

(Bortis, 1997, pp. 150–2). Indeed, if the quantity vector in system (19.25) is multiplied by a scalar smaller than unity, say $1-u$ (u being the ratio of involuntary unemployment to the productive full-employment labour force), all the quantities are reduced correspondingly and a permanent involuntary unemployment of $100u$ per cent would come into being, while all the formal properties of the quantity system would be preserved. This means that the coefficient matrix of the quantity system (19.25) would remain formally unchanged and that the vector of *normal* quantities would now be given by:

$$[Q_1, Q_2, ..., Q_m, N] \tag{19.31}$$

with:

$$N < N_f \tag{19.32}$$

Let us recall here that N stands for *profit-sector* employment. Given this, condition (19.32) indicates the possibility of normal or long-period equilibrium employment being below full employment, that is, the possibility of long-period or permanent involuntary unemployment, which is determined by the socio-economic system, that is, all the institutions pertaining to the economic basis of a society, and to the political, legal, social and cultural superstructure erected on this basis. Hence, the *normal* quantities and prices entering the present analysis are embedded in the real world and differ from Pasinetti's *natural* quantities and prices, which relate to an ethically desirable situation. Given this, all the magnitudes considered in this section are, in a classical vein, governed by technology and institutions and are, as such, constant or slowly evolving if the real world set in historical time is taken into the picture (see Bortis, 1997, pp. 199–204). But let us recall, once again, that our suggestions are located at the level of principles, independent of space and time.

The employment scalar $(1-u)$ or, conversely, the long-period unemployment rate (u) are defined as follows:

$$1 - u = N/N_f \tag{19.33}$$
$$u = (N_f - N)/N_f \tag{19.34}$$

where N is the institutionally governed long-period equilibrium employment to which corresponds a long-period equilibrium output, Q, smaller than the full-employment output, Q_f. Since N is linked to Q through labour productivity at any moment of time ($Q = AN$), these definitions could also be written in terms of Q. At this stage, we may mention that two conditions must be fulfilled at the profit-sector employment level N_f: first, entrepreneurs realise the normal (target, satisfactory) profit rate, and, second, given a certain ratio of profit sector to non-profit sector employment, there is no involuntary unemployment in a society. Hence $N_f - N$ only refers to involuntary unemployment in the profit sector that falls short of overall or social involuntary unemployment. Now, if for some reason N increases, involuntary unemployment will diminish in the profit *and* in the non-profit sector since the rising social surplus will allow additional employment in the latter. This is, of course, valid only at the level of principles. In the real world employment may first rise in the non-profit sector, for example if the state launches a public work programme. In principle, the spending of the incomes thus created will, through multiplier effects, lead to an overproportional increase in employment in the profit sector (see the supermultiplier relation (19.40) and Bortis, 1997, Ch. 4).

The determinants of N and Q emerge from a macroeconomic equilibrium condition in which the various *demand components govern* normal output Q, that is, supply, and hence normal employment N. This implies that output and employment are governed by effective demand (for a tentative explanation of this proposition see Bortis, 1997, Chs 3–5).

$$AN = Q = wN + c_s (P + R) + I + G + X - tM \qquad (19.35)$$

Q is real output – the social product – measured in terms of a bundle of necessary consumption goods; Q is made up of private and public consumption and investment goods, that is, of the same goods that are listed in the output vector of the quantity system (19.25). N is labour employed in the profit sector; A is labour productivity (Q/N); w is the real wage rate w_n/p_c (w_n stands for the money wage rate and p_c for the normal price of a bundle of necessary consumption goods). The wage bill wN is entirely consumed; c_s is the fraction of the social surplus $P+R$ consumed (P represents profits, including interest, and R represents rents accruing to landowners and to labour on account of special skills or social arrangements, for instance corporative organisations); I is gross investment; G represents government expenditures; X stands for exports; M for imports; and t indicates the terms of trade.

Imports M are of two broad types both of which are related to economic activity, that is, to output Q or to income Y (with $Q = Y$ in principle):

$$M = bQ = M_1 + M_2$$

with:

$$M_1 = b_1 Q$$
$$M_2 = b_2 Q$$

hence:

$$M = bQ = M_1 + M_2 = b_1 Q + b_2 Q = (b_1 + b_2)Q \qquad (19.36)$$

M_1 are necessary imports required in the process of production. These goods are land basics, labour basics and labour–land basics (machine tools *and* the various capital goods produced with machine tools and labour). Necessary imports are, then, part of the necessary goods entering directly or indirectly as inputs in the production of all goods; necessary consumption goods, raw materials and machines to make machines are the cases in point. M_2 are non-necessary imports related to consumption out of the social surplus.

The macroeconomic (Kalecki–Weintraub) price equation implied in relation (19.35) is analogous to the sectoral price equations (19.6) and (19.19) and equals (19.7) as derived from combining the interindustry and vertically integrated approach to social production:

$$p_c = (w_n/A)k \qquad (19.37)$$

This very simple price equation has two important properties. Firstly, it is based on vertical integration, which implies that all the costs of production ultimately become labour costs. Secondly, this simple mark-up equation is directly linked with the surplus principle of income distribution, the wage and property shares being:

$$W/Y = 1/k$$
$$(P+R)/Y = 1-(1/k) \qquad (19.38)$$

Given technology, as synthesised by overall labour productivity (A), the regulation of distribution – the determination of the money wage rate w_n and of the mark-up k – must logically precede price formation. Hence, given A, the price p_c is determined once w_n and k are fixed. The determination of the wage and property shares in income is a *social* problem because *part–whole relationships* are involved. The parts are the wages (W) and profits and rents ($P+R$), the whole is the *given* income Y, which, as is evident from the supermultiplier relation (19.40), is governed by effective demand. The determination of the structures of wages, profits and rents are also part–whole issues.[5]

Normal or trend gross investment is directly associated with the maintenance and expansion of the normal capital stock, K, required for the production of the normal output, Q:

$$I = (g + d)vQ \qquad (19.39)$$

where g is the trend growth rate of the economic system, a weighted average of the trend rates of growth of the autonomous variables, that is, normal government expenditures, G, and normal exports, X (see relation (19.40) and Bortis, 1997, p. 155); d represents the fraction of the normal capital stock that is annually replaced and v stands for the normal capital coefficient K/Q. *Normal investment* is thus related to the *functioning of the entire social system*, encompassing technology and institutions. Hence, technology and institutions *determine* the normal or long-period investment volume through the principle of effective demand (the social product, Q, appearing in relation (19.39) is determined by the supermultiplier relation (19.40)). Therefore, investment – which is autonomous in the short run – represents *derived* demand in the long run. This is a central tenet of relation (19.40).

Taking account of relations (19.35) to (19.39) yields a relation for long-period (normal, trend) output Q, and, since $Q = AN$, for the long-period (normal, trend) level of employment, N (Bortis, 1997, pp. 142–204):

$$Q = \frac{G + X}{z_s[1 - (1/k)] + t(b_1 + b_2) - (g + d)v} \qquad (19.40)$$

where:

$$z_s = 1 - c_s = s_s + t_s \qquad (19.41)$$

The leakage coefficient z_s indicates the fraction of the surplus over ordinary wages that is *not* consumed, the fraction consumed being c_s. Consequently, the leakage coefficient is the sum of the fractions of the surplus paid for taxes (t_s) and saved (s_s). Since the long-period consumption coefficient c_s and the long-period tax coefficient t_s are both determined by institutions – consumption habits and tax laws – the long-period saving propensity s_s is a *pure residual* varying with the normal level of output and employment (Bortis, 1997, pp. 166–8). This is perfectly analogous to Keynes's short-period theory of saving.

Equation (19.40) may, following Hicks (1950, p. 62), conveniently be called a supermultiplier relation, 'which can be applied to any given level of [autonomous demand components] to discover the equilibrium level of output [Q] which corresponds to it'. Hence the autonomous demand components, G and X, set economic activity in motion, similarly to the expenditure of rents by the landlords in Quesnay's extended *tableau économique* (on this see Oncken, 1902, p. 394). This gives rise to two different employment mechanisms, namely, the internal mechanism set in motion by government expenditures, G, and the external mechanism initiated by exports, X (see Bortis, 1997, pp. 190–8).

Once output and employment are determined through the supermultiplier relation (19.40), the output and employment scalar $1-u$ (definition (19.33)) is also fixed. In principle, the normal quantities corresponding to a specific output and employment level obtain if the full-employment quantity vector in the quantity system (19.25) is multiplied by the employment scalar. The determination of *normal output and employment is equivalent to fixing the output and employment trend* around which cyclical fluctuations take place (ibid., pp. 149–51). It has already been suggested that the position of the output and employment trend is of considerable socio-economic and political importance, because this determines the extent of long-period (system governed) permanent involuntary unemployment. The latter is, in turn, an important element governing the social and political climate in a country.

Methodologically, the supermultiplier relation (19.40) represents the pure long-period Keynesian employment theory, picturing how output and employment are determined *in principle* by the various demand variables and parameters on the right-hand side of this equation (Bortis, 1997, pp. 142–204). According to our methodological introduction, this relation is a metatheory (a metaphysical theory) of employment taking account of scientific and other information to determine what is – probably – essential about employment determination in a monetary production economy. Determination *in principle* of some socio-economic phenomena attempts to capture the essential features of the causal mechanism at work, which are timeless and invariable. Moreover, in a pure or 'ideal-type' model the *ceteris paribus* clause is automatically implied. This amounts to saying that the predetermined variables on the right-hand side of the supermultiplier relation (19.40) are considered independent of each other. As a rule, this will not be the case if some real world situation is considered.

In principle, normal output is positively linked to the autonomous variables G and X, and to the gross investment–output ratio $I/Q = (g + d)\, v$.

The effect of exports (X) on output and employment will be particularly strong if exports mainly consist of high-quality manufactured products with a large value added, that is, a high content of direct and indirect labour (Kaldor, 1985, pp. 57–79). However, normal output will be lower if, given exports X, the technological and cultural dependence on the outside world is strong, as would be reflected in large import coefficients b_1 and b_2, and if the terms of trade (t) are unfavourable, which would show up in a high value of t. Very importantly, normal output (Q) is negatively linked with the property share in income, $1-(1/k)$, and with the leakage coefficient, z_s, associated with this share. As a rule, z_s will be larger if the distribution of property income is more unequal. Given government expenditures and gross investment, *a higher leakage* out of income $(z_s[1-(1/k)])$ reduces effective demand because *consumption is diminished*. Fundamentally, unemployment occurs because the saving–income ratio, $s_s[1-(1/k)]$, exceeds the investment–output ratio, $(g+d)v$, at full employment. Full employment could only be maintained if private and/or public consumption were increased. A redistribution of incomes, that is, raising the share of normal wages $(1/k)$, would lead to higher private consumption through enhancing spending power. In principle, a higher level of public expenditures (G) would require a tax increase: the tax rate, t_s, would have to be raised to preserve the equilibrium of the budget, which would reduce the saving coefficient s_s. If these measures are not undertaken, output, employment and tax receipts will decline, and, given government expenditures, budget deficits will occur. These will reduce the saving ratio until it equals the investment ratio at some long-period equilibrium level of output and employment involving persistent involuntary unemployment. Hence the negative association between distribution and employment emerges because the property share and the saving and the leakage ratio associated with it are too high; s_s, and thus z_s, will be higher the more unequally property income is distributed. Thus, the notion of unequal income distribution has a double dimension: the property share is high and property income is itself unequally distributed. This leads to a high leakage out of income, given by $z_s[1-(1/k)]$, to which corresponds a reduced level of output and employment.

This crucially important relationship between unequal distribution and involuntary unemployment represents, according to Schumpeter (1946, p. 517), the essence of the Keynesian revolution: '[the Keynesian doctrine] can easily be made to say both that "who tries to save destroys real capital" and that, via saving, "the unequal distribution of income is the ultimate cause of unemployment." *This* is what the Keynesian Revolution amounts to'. Indeed, Keynes (1936/1973, pp. 372–3; see also Garegnani, 1978, 1979) held that:

[the] outstanding faults of the economic society in which we live are its failure to provide for full employment and its arbitrary and inequitable distribution of wealth and incomes. [Up] to the point where full employment prevails, the growth of capital depends not at all on a low propensity to consume but is, on the contrary, held back by it [and] measures for the redistribution of incomes in a way likely to raise the propensity to consume may prove positively favourable to the growth of capital.

The inverse long-period link between employment and distribution is *the* crucial feature of the supermultiplier relation.

VALUES, PRICES OF PRODUCTION AND MARKET PRICES

The previous sections deal with principles, that is, with the fundamental forces governing prices and quantities in a classical–Keynesian view. As such, these sections exhibit aspects of the pure long-period classical–Keynesian model of production, value, distribution and employment. However, concretely existing prices and quantities are governed by a great many factors, circumstances or causal forces, fundamental and accidental. Among the accidental factors, some features of the conditions of production, of cyclical movements of output and employment and of the functioning of the market – the sphere of circulation – are particularly important. It is important to note that, in the long run, the functioning of the system *determines* the behaviour of individuals and collectives. In the medium run and in the short run, behaviour of economic agents takes place within the (institutional) system, giving thus rise to specific forms of behaviour during the business cycle and on the market. The issue of institutions and behaviour is a central tenet of Bortis (1997).

If sectoral differences in the conditions of production, expressed by differing ratios of fixed to circulating capital (n_{Ki}/n_i), are considered and if a uniform profit rate prevails in the various sectors and industries, prices are no longer proportional to the socially correct labour values. In fact, values are now transformed into Sraffian prices of production. This is required because it is impossible to calculate prices proportional to values with sufficient precision and to implement them, as has been shown by the experience of the centrally planned economies. Values are constitutive principles that are embodied in concretely existing prices or essential causal forces determining prices and appear simultaneously with other factors governing observable prices, like the conditions of production, profit rates and money wages, and market elements. Given this, the prices of production and the uniform rate of profits associated with these prices may be considered approximations to labour values and render these values socially operable. Indeed, the uniform rate of profits and the associated prices of production or the normal prices are the conceptual foundations for the long-period normal price calculation of enterprises (*Normalkostenkalkulation*): the normal price states what the calculated price is *in principle*. The normal prices calculated on the basis of permanent costs and of a normal (satisfactory, target) rate of profits approximate, in turn, the true, but largely unknown, prices of production associated with a given technique. In this view the prices of production fulfil, as suggested in the second section, at least four important social functions that are, moreover, related to the mechanism of the (medium-term) business cycle (Bortis, 1997, pp. 204–20) and to the functioning of the markets – the sphere of circulation – in a classical–Keynesian sense (ibid., pp. 220–35). Firstly, the prices of production enable decentralised decision making regarding socially appropriate prices such that the processes of production and circulation function smoothly. Each firm may calculate its price of production that covers the costs incurred in the social process of production and yields a target rate of profits on the capital invested, which, given the money wage structure, regulates the distribution of the value of the product or of the incomes created. Hence normal prices approximately capture the social effort that is made to produce the various products, and the normal profit rate (r^*) together with the money wage structure regulate the distribution of the incomes created within the social process of production. In this way normal prices ensure the normal functioning of the social process of production and of the associated spheres of circulation of means of production and final goods: firms recover their costs and realise a normal profit. Secondly, the institutionally fixed normal rate of profits, r^*, regulates the socially appropriate allocation of resources: sectors in which the realised profit rate, r_i, exceeds the normal rate (r^*) will attract resources, ultimately direct and indirect labour; contrariwise, resources will flow out of sectors where realised profit rates fall short of the normal rate r^*. The allocation function performed through the interplay of the realised and the normal rate of profits pictures the classical view of the functioning of markets: the function of the market is to implement the normal prices governed by distribution and technology. Thirdly, the comparison between the normal (target) profit rate r^* and the realised rate r enables entrepreneurs to behave rationally in the face of uncertainty about the future. Indeed, entrepreneurs will invest more if r exceeds r^* persistently, and vice versa. The investment behaviour of entrepreneurs and its coordination by the socio-economic system give rise to cyclical movements of overall output and employment levels around a long-period institutional 'trend', whereby the cycles are governed by the interaction of the capacity effect and the income effect of investment (ibid., pp. 204–20). Fourthly, competition with a given target profit rate r^* forces entrepreneurs and managers to attempt to produce goods of a given quality at the lowest possible prices. This implies saving the ultimately scarce natural resources, labour and land, through the introduction of improved techniques of production, that is, through realising land- and labour-saving technical progress.

Hence, the classical notions of the normal (uniform) profit rate and of the associated prices of production appear as ingenious devices of social organisation enabling decentralised decision making and justify the institution of private property of means of production. The latter is associated with responsibility for the proper functioning of production within each firm and hence for the entire process of production as well as with caring for the good state of the means of production (ibid., pp. 158–80). As suggested in the previous sections, this view implies that there is no contradiction at all between Ricardian–Marxian value analysis and Sraffian prices of production since the same problem, to wit, price formation, is analysed at different levels of abstraction.[6]

It has already been suggested that the existence of a normal rate of profits, r^*, and its interplay with the realised rate r greatly contributes to the orderly functioning of a monetary production economy. In the real world deviations from the normal state of affairs will, as a rule, occur. For example, in times of depression, market prices below normal prices may come into existence. Entrepreneurs may now attempt to maintain or to expand their market shares while, simultaneously, trying to maximise profits by reducing costs (mainly labour costs) as much as possible. This, as a rule, is possible in times of heavy unemployment. In this framework it is important to note that the supermultiplier relation holds in any situation; for example, prices may be long- or medium-run prices of production or short-period market prices. Hence the impact on employment of the abnormal distributional outcomes just mentioned may be captured by this relation.

Finally, in the classical–Keynesian view, the function of the market is to bring market prices into line with the prices of production calculated by the firms, which embody the normal or target rate of profits. If demand is in excess of production, market prices and realised profits are above their respective normal levels. If this situation persists, entrepreneurs will invest more, attempting thus to bring realised and normal profit rates into line. The contrary holds when normal production is in excess of demand. This is the classical view of competition, which, however, as has been alluded to above, may stop functioning if normal prices and normal profit rates – both institutions – no longer contribute to stabilising the long-period trend. In this case, the trend would itself become unstable and fluctuations around it would dominate (see Bortis, 1997, pp. 199–204).

CONCLUDING REMARKS: KEYNES AND SRAFFA

In this chapter the great problems of classical–Keynesian political economy – the economic theory of a monetary production economy – have been broadly sketched at a fundamental level, that is, at the level of principles or of pure theory, independent of space and time. At the heart of the monetary theory of production is the social and circular process of production embodying the labour and land aspects; distribution is a social and political process based upon the surplus principle and is, as such, governed by institutions; the essence of prices are labour values, which reflect the social effort made to produce commodities; output and employment are governed by effective demand through the supermultiplier; and last but not least, the processes of production and circulation, and of capital accumulation, could not go on without money. Methodologically speaking the whole analysis has been carried out at a long-period level. Only constant or slowly changing elements of reality associated with stock equilibria or fully adjusted situations have been considered. The normal prices and quantities associated with a fully adjusted situation represent a system equilibrium. The system is an institutional system, made up of a material basis on which, out of part of the surplus, an institutional superstructure may be erected. Hence, in a way, this chapter suggests how classical and Keynesian institutionalism may be brought together at the level of principles.

The theoretical foundation to bring together Keynes and the classics was laid down in the 1930s, Shackle's *Years of High Theory*, when Keynes and Sraffa set up their respective theoretical systems. In his *General Theory* Keynes asked how behavioural outcomes were coordinated by the system in a monetary production economy. He had to stay at the short-period behavioural level because his main problem was to bring to the open the importance of money, which can only be a store of value in a world of uncertainty and disappointed expectations. However, Keynes also held that a modern monetary production economy simply could not function without money and finance: all the dispositions of producers and consumers are made in terms of money in the course of time such that, as he explicitly claims, money becomes the link between the past and the future. Having explained the importance of money and the nature of interest, Keynes was able to formulate his all-important principle of effective demand, which took the form of the multiplier, and, ideally, implies fixed prices and quantity adjustments.

Sraffa, however, worked at the level of the production system from the mid 1920s onwards to initiate a revival of classical political economy. His problem was not to formulate a new principle, but to take up already known principles, that is, to reformulate Ricardo's theory of value and distribution in light of Quesnay's view of the social process of production set forth in the *tableau économique*. Hence Keynes and Sraffa worked on different problems and at different levels of analysis, and it was impossible for them to meet in order to establish a synthesis. Moreover, there was an evident lack of mutual interest in their respective economic work. Keynes was unable to understand the significance of Sraffa's long-period equilibrium and Sraffa disliked Keynes's psychological approach to investment in the form of uncertainty and expectations. Hence, regarding economic theory, Sraffa and Keynes necessarily led parallel lives (Pasinetti, 1998). Only now does the time seem ripe to bring them together in a middle-way classical–Keynesian synthesis, which can provide the starting point for an alternative to the Walrasian general equilibrium model. At the theoretical level the capital theory debate had to take place, and the approach to production based on vertical integration had to be developed. At the social and political level the breakdown of centrally planned socialism and the present and past difficulties experienced by capitalism are also necessary preconditions for putting to the fore a humanist intermediate way between liberalism and socialism. To work out such a middle-way framework was Keynes's fundamental preoccupation, as emerges, for example, from Fitzgibbons (1988), O'Donnell (1989) and Mini (1991). In this undertaking Keynes was greatly supported by Sraffa. In fact, 'all the time that the explosions of the Keynesian Revolution were going on overhead, Piero Sraffa was sapping and mining away to prepare a revolution of his own' (Joan Robinson quoted in Porta, 1995, p. 683). Given the immense social and economic problems presently prevailing – characterised by huge inequalities in income distribution, massive involuntary unemployment and growing poverty – the classical–Keynesian synthesis that can be elaborated through working in the *spirit* of Sraffa and Keynes on a Pasinettian labour principle platform of vertical integration constitutes a message of hope.

In the third and fourth sections we have suggested that, building upon Pasinetti (1986a, 1986b), the theoretical starting point for a classical–Keynesian synthesis lies in the integration of Sraffa's-cum-Leontief interindustry approach with Ricardo's and Pasinetti's vertically integrated framework.

To establish a complete classical–Keynesian system of political economy (for a preparatory and tentative attempt to do so, see Bortis, 1997, Chs 3–4) is, however, only a first step to be undertaken. In a second step, classical–Keynesian political economy must be linked to other social sciences – sociology, law and politics – to provide a system of social sciences. Moreover, the notion of the middle way must be specified. This amounts to elaborating a social philosophy that is an alternative to liberalism and socialism. In Bortis (1997, Ch. 2) the notion *comprehensive humanism*, covering the individual and social dimension of man, has been suggested and the classical–Keynesian system of political economy put in a wider context (ibid., Ch. 7). Finally, while the social philosophy of humanism underlies the humanist system of social and political sciences, social and political ethics must provide the roof, for, to extend Keynes's famous dictum, the social and political sciences are essentially moral sciences.

NOTES

1. The author is greatly indebted to Mauro Baranzini, Claude Gnos, Geoffrey Harcourt, Frederic Lee, Luigi Pasinetti, Eric Rahim, Angelo Reati, Sergio Rossi and Sebastian Schnyder for helpful and encouraging remarks. Of course, all responsibility remains with the author.
2. In Pasinetti (1981, pp. 133–8) the *distribution* and the *social effort* aspects of the price system are set forth for the natural system.
3. It has already been suggested that, in the real world set in historical time, proportions will not be independent of activity levels, as is precisely the case with economies of scale.
4. Again, if the proportions between circulating and fixed capital were not uniform, the price vector in system (19.18) would be a matrix with each column containing one price and the corresponding mark-up at the appropriate positions, and zero positions elsewhere. At the level of principles, where essentials are set out, there is no need to consider non-uniform ratios of fixed to circulating capital. However, non-uniform compositions of capital have to be considered explicitly at the level of scientific theories that are erected upon a set of principles.
5. It should be emphasised that the wage and property shares (19.38) do not correspond to the definitions of shares one usually finds in statistical yearbooks. In the surplus approach W in the wage share only contains ordinary, eventually necessary, wages of labour active in the *profit sector* of an economy. And rents, R, in the property share also contain 'surplus wages', due to special abilities or privileges, for instance. Moreover, government expenditures, G, in the supermultiplier relation (19.40) also contain the wages of all civil servants.
6. On 'layers' of reality see Bortis (1997, pp. 103–17).

REFERENCES

Bortis, H. (1996), 'Structural economic dynamics and technical progress in a pure labour economy', *Structural Change and Economic Dynamics*, **7** (2), 135–46.

Bortis, H. (1997), *Institutions, Behaviour and Economic Theory: A Contribution to Classical–Keynesian Political Economy*, Cambridge: Cambridge University Press.

Fitzgibbons, A. (1988), *Keynes's Vision: A New Political Economy*, Oxford: Clarendon Press.

Garegnani, P. (1970), 'Heterogeneous capital, the production function and the theory of distribution', *Review of Economic Studies*, **37** (3), 407–36.

Garegnani, P. (1978), 'Notes on consumption, investment and effective demand: I', *Cambridge Journal of Economics*, **2** (4), 335–53.

Garegnani, P. (1979), 'Notes on consumption, investment and effective demand: II', *Cambridge Journal of Economics*, **3** (1), 63–82.

Garegnani, P. (1983), 'Two routes to effective demand', in J.A. Kregel (ed.), *Distribution, Effective Demand and International Economic Relations*, London: Macmillan, 69–80.

Harcourt, G.C. (1972), *Some Cambridge Controversies in the Theory of Capital*, Cambridge: Cambridge University Press.

Harcourt, G.C. (1981), 'Marshall, Sraffa and Keynes: incompatible bedfellows?', *Eastern Economic Journal*, **7** (1), 39–50. Reprinted in C. Sardoni (ed.) (1992), *On Political Economists and Modern Political Economy: Selected Essays of G.C. Harcourt*, London and New York: Routledge, 250–64.

Harrod, R.F. (1939), 'An essay in dynamic theory', *Economic Journal*, **49** (193), 14–33.

Hicks, J.R. (1937), 'Mr. Keynes and the "classics": a suggested interpretation', *Econometrica*, **5** (2), 147–59. Reprinted in J.R. Hicks (1982), *Money, Interest and Wages: Collected Essays on Economic Theory*, Oxford: Basil Blackwell, vol. II, 100–15.

Hicks, J.R. (1950), *A Contribution to the Theory of the Trade Cycle*, Oxford: Oxford University Press.

Kaldor, N. (1985), *Economics Without Equilibrium*, Armonk: M.E. Sharpe.

Kalecki, M. (1971), *Selected Essays on the Dynamics of the Capitalist Economy*, Cambridge: Cambridge University Press.

Keynes, J.M. (1921/1988), *A Treatise on Probability*, London: Macmillan. Reprinted in *The Collected Writings of John Maynard Keynes*, Vol VIII, London and Basingstoke: Macmillan.

Keynes, J.M. (1930/1971), *A Treatise on Money*, London: Macmillan. Reprinted in *The Collected Writings of John Maynard Keynes*, Vols V and VI, London and Basingstoke: Macmillan.

Keynes, J.M. (1933/1973), 'A monetary theory of production'. Reprinted in *The Collected Writings of John Maynard Keynes*, Vol. XIII *The General Theory and After: Part I Preparation*, London and Basingstoke: Macmillan, 408–11.

Keynes, J.M. (1936/1973), *The General Theory of Employment, Interest and Money*, London: Macmillan. Reprinted in *The Collected Writings of John Maynard Keynes*, Vol. VII, London and Basingstoke: Macmillan.

Lowe, A. (1976), *The Path of Economic Growth*, Cambridge: Cambridge University Press.

Marx, K. (1867–94/1973–4), *Das Kapital*, Berlin: Dietz-Verlag, 3 vols.

Mini, P. (1991), *Keynes, Bloomsbury and The General Theory*, London and New York: Macmillan and St. Martin's Press.

O'Donnell, R.A. (1989), *Keynes: Philosophy, Economics and Politics – The Philosophical Foundations of Keynes's Thought and their Influence on his Economics and Politics*, London and New York: Macmillan and St. Martin's Press.

Oncken, A. (1902), *Geschichte der Nationalökonomie*, Vol. I, Leipzig: Hirschfeld (only one volume published).

Pasinetti, L.L. (1977), *Lectures on the Theory of Production*, London: Macmillan.

Pasinetti, L.L. (1981), *Structural Change and Economic Growth: A Theoretical Essay on the Dynamics of the Wealth of Nations*, Cambridge: Cambridge University Press.

Pasinetti, L.L. (1986a), 'Theory of value: a source of alternative paradigms in economic analysis', in M. Baranzini and R. Scazzieri (eds), *Foundations of Economics: Structures of Inquiry and Economic Theory*, Oxford and New York: Basil Blackwell and St. Martin's Press, 409–31.

Pasinetti, L.L. (1986b), 'Sraffa's circular process and the concept of vertical integration', *Political Economy – Studies in the Surplus Approach*, **2** (1), 3–16.

Pasinetti, L.L. (1993), *Structural Economic Dynamics: A Theory of the Consequences of Human Learning*, Cambridge: Cambridge University Press.

Pasinetti, L.L. (1998), 'Piero Sraffa: an Italian economist at Cambridge', in L.L. Pasinetti (ed.), *Italian Economic Papers*, Vol. III, Oxford and Bologna: Oxford University Press and Il Mulino, 365–83.

Porta, P.L. (1995), 'Joan Robinson and Piero Sraffa', *Rivista internazionale di scienze economiche e commerciali*, **42** (9), 681–9.

Ricardo, D. (1821/1951), *On the Principles of Political Economy and Taxation*, in P. Sraffa and M. Dobb (eds), *The Works and Correspondence of David Ricardo*, Vol. I, Cambridge: Cambridge University Press.

Robertson, D.H. (1956), *Economic Commentaries*, London: Staples.

Robinson, J. (1956), *The Accumulation of Capital*, London: Macmillan.

Roncaglia, A. (2000), *Piero Sraffa: His Life, Thought and Cultural Heritage*, London and New York: Routledge.

Samuelson, P.A. (1962), 'Parable and realism in capital theory: the surrogate production function', *Review of Economic Studies*, **29** (3), 193–206. Reprinted in G.C. Harcourt and N.F. Laing (eds) (1971), *Capital and Growth*, Harmondsworth: Penguin, 213–32.

Schumpeter, J.A. (1946), 'John Maynard Keynes, 1883–1946', *American Economic Review*, **36** (4), 495–518.

Smith, A. (1776/1976), *An Inquiry into the Nature and Causes of the Wealth of Nations*, Oxford: Clarendon Press.

Sraffa, P. (1960), *Production of Commodities by Means of Commodities*, Cambridge: Cambridge University Press.

20. The Pervasive Saving Constraint in Minsky's Theory of Crisis and the Dual Profits Hypothesis: Minsky as a Post Keynesian Hayekian

Alain Parguez[1]

INTRODUCTION

For some time, a debate has raged over the interpretation of Minsky's general theory of crisis. It arose because of two interrelated sets of propositions, which, at first glance, are embedded in contradiction. The first deals with the theory of interest rates. On the one hand, Minsky emphasises that the fundamental instability of the capitalist economy results from the perfect endogeneity of money. On the other hand, the boom determines an automatic rise in the level of the rate of interest because it is always spontaneously set up in the market for loanable funds by adjusting the demand for loans to an inelastic supply of loans. Minsky explains the inelasticity of the supply curve both by some exogeneity of reserves reflecting the policy of the central bank, and by the individual portfolio choices the outcome of which is the *ex ante* savings invested in banks. A loanable funds theory of interest rates is obviously inconsistent with a pure theory of endogenous money, which cannot fit an *ex ante* savings-led supply curve.

The second set of propositions addresses the hard core of the explanation of crisis. On one side, what triggers the crisis is the accelerating growth of investment beyond the 'stability threshold'. From the point of view of individual corporations' expectations, Minsky draws a fundamental borderline between sound or hedge investment plans and speculative plans. Sound finance rules when corporations expect to receive sufficient profits to meet all commitments resulting from these plans. Each new plan will generate a flow sufficiently high in all periods of the financial interval to pay both interest and the required share of the initial loan. Speculative finance prevails when for some time, at the beginning of the financial interval, investors expect to be short of profits to match their commitments. They bet that yields in the last stages of the financial interval will be high enough to allow them to meet the new financial commitments they have to incur to compensate for the lack of profits in the first stage. Minsky draws a new borderline between pure speculative plans and Ponzi plans. Such a borderline is the 'absolute instability threshold'. In the first instance, corporations expect to raise new debt sufficient to pay the required shares of the loans; beyond this, they expect to have to raise new debt to reimburse the loan as well as pay interest.

Starting from a position of sound finance, corporations are spontaneously driven beyond the stability threshold. Sooner or later corporate plans are so optimistic that they trespass the fundamental instability threshold and Ponzi finance rules. The greater the share of speculative (including Ponzi) finance in past investment plans, the more there must be a lack of profits to validate financial commitments. Beyond the stability threshold there is an accelerated growth and the effective demand for loans to meet the shortage of profits. As the economy is automatically doomed to trespass the Ponzi threshold, the rate of growth of the demand for loanable funds is driven by the law of compound interests. In the market for loanable funds, the demand for loans is colliding more and more with an increasingly inelastic supply of loans. Equilibrium is attained through an automatic rise in the rate of interest, which is the last resort engine of the crisis.

Given that Minsky explicitly addresses the endogenous theory of crisis, he relies on a macroeconomic theory of profits carved out of Kalecki's equation. In the simple economy without government, within which Minsky frames his theory of crisis, the growth of effective profits is therefore equal to the growth of investment abstracting from wage-earners' savings.[2] Beyond the stability threshold and even beyond the Ponzi threshold, the new investment plans generate an equal amount of profits validating plans that have been already undertaken. Since interest rates have not yet risen, there cannot be a shortage of profits. Kalecki's equation ignores the nature of *ex ante* expectations. Firms are not able yet to raise new debts, which prevents the induced rise in the demand for loans. There is therefore a blatant inconstancy between an explanation of crises in terms of a lack of profits rooted in the *ex ante* nature of expectations and Kalecki's theory of profits.

As regards the theory of money, we may summarise these points in the following two propositions.

Proposition 1 Money is endogenous in an economy driven by bank credit.
Proposition 2 The rate of interest is determined in the loanable funds market. Increases in the interest rate are the outcome of the growth of the demand for loans colliding with an inelastic supply.

It is clear that the first proposition contradicts the second proposition.
  With respect to the theory of crisis we then have:

Proposition 1' *Ex ante* unsound plans generate an *ex post* lack of profits.
Proposition 2' Kalecki's equation.

Proposition 1' contradicts proposition 2'. Moreover, the two contradictions are intertwined since proposition 1' requires that proposition 2 collides with proposition 1.
  There have been in the literature many attempts to explain the contradictions (see Lavoie and Seccareccia, 2001), which result from Minsky's inability to group the macroeconomic outcomes of his distinction concerning the nature of *ex ante* plans. Minsky failed to discover that the *ex ante* nature of plans was irrelevant at the macroeconomic level where Kalecki's equation rules. Some inconsistency between the microeconomic level (where such a distinction makes sense) and the macroeconomic level (where Kalecki's Law operates) plagues Minsky's theory of crisis.
  Lavoie and Seccareccia (2001) are mostly addressing the contradiction between Proposition 1' and Proposition 2', while others, like Rochon (1999), are interested in the first contradiction. There would have been in the course of time two Minskys. The first Minsky lived before the discovery of the financial instability hypothesis. He was not yet 'Minskian'. He lacked a sensible theory of endogenous money and, like Gurley and Shaw, he dallied with some slightly amended neoclassical theory of money. The first Minsky would have been reborn a Minskian when he started to unfold the general theory of endogenous crises. Now he scorned his early writings and could spell out a cogent theory of endogenous money.[3]
  Lavoie and Seccareccia's (2001) solution suggests that Minsky did not understand his own theory and was so blinded by microeconomics that he never could explore a macroeconomic analysis of the capitalist economy. Minsky would have just paid lip service to Kalecki's theory of profits, which would have been integrated in an already fully developed theory of crisis. We cannot agree with this interpretation because Kalecki's principle had not yet been introduced *ex post* to bail the microeconomic theory of *ex ante* plans out of the charge of lacking post Keynesian macroeconomic credentials. As soon

as Minsky began to spell out his theory of crisis, he emphasised its two components, the *ex ante* theory of investment plans and Kalecki's equation. Minsky never stopped to fully develop the causal link between investment spending and profits. He was quite adamant in his explanations of the consolidation of past commitments by new investment spending. He always scorned the neoclassical microeconomics for being at odds with the future of the capitalist economy. The mystery is not yet cleared.

Rochon's (1999) 'two Minsky' hypothesis collides with Minsky's own certainty and pride of the perfect consistency of his core beliefs over time. From Minsky's perspective, the second Minsky was the twin of the first just a bit older and therefore wiser relative to the imperfections of the capitalist system. The proof lies in the paramount fact that Minsky included his early writings in his collected essays on the financial instability hypothesis (see Minsky, 1982), where they appear respectively as Chapter 7 and 11. In other chapters, and therefore in later works, Minsky refers appropriately to these early writings.[4]

There are many authors who emphasise the contradiction between their early writings and their later works. Keynes is one of them, but others can be found in modern post Keynesian literature.[5] There exist authors who never addressed the consistency of their theory in the course of time. Minsky was a very rare character because he never doubted that his theory of crisis was the logical development of the theory of money and financial markets embedded in his postulated neoclassical early works. Minsky was obviously right. It will be proven that the crucial propositions of his early theory are the foundations of his general theory of crisis. Proposition 1 above sustains Minsky's theory of interest rates and explains why the boom leads to an automatic increase in interest rates inducing the crisis. There has been only one Minsky over time. Since the first is not endorsing a theory of endogenous money because he is still too much neoclassical relative to the dominant role of the loanable funds market, the second is still closer to the loanable funds school than to modern post Keynesians.

This chapter aims at answering two intertwined questions.

The first question addresses the mystery of the role of profits in Minsky's theory of crisis. The enigma can be solved by the clue given by Minsky himself when he emphasised the perfect consistency of his fundamental beliefs. From this clue, we can derive the existence of a dual theory of profits in Minsky's theory of crisis. The first theory is the Kaleckian theory of profits; the second is a neo-Wicksellian theory determining real normal profits. The crisis occurs when the neoclassical theory of value is no more superseded by credit inflation financing the rise in Kaleckian profits. As soon as firms and banks serendipity is no more entertained by credit or profit inflation, they discover at once the lack of normal profits. Firms strive to meet their real commitments by increasing the demand for loans while banks are keen to lower their supply of loans at the existing level of interest rates. To build a general theory of financial crisis out of the dual profits hypothesis, we just need to link the fall in real profits to the excess of investment relative to *ex ante* savings, which accounts for speculative *ex ante* plans.

The dual profits hypothesis bails the Minskian theory of crisis out of any contradiction. It supports Minsky's contention that his theory evolved out of an unchanged core. It is true that Minsky never endeavoured to unfold his dual theory of profits either because it was obvious from his perspective, or because he did not want to dally with the pure theoretical foundations of his work. In any case, Minsky's theory of crisis now appears as some ultimate version of the neo-Wicksellian theory of crisis, which had been developed in the 1920s and 1930s by Hayek, Myrdal and many others.

As shown by Seccareccia (1992), this theory was anything but Keynesian. Minsky himself acknowledges the legacy of the neo-Wicksellian theory of crisis by anchoring his own theory into the well-known synthesis of the Swedish school displayed by Ohlin (1937a, 1937b), who proved that the initial discrepancy between *ex ante* savings and *ex ante* investment could explain the instability of the capitalist economy. Minsky refers many times to Ohlin's paper to demonstrate, like Hayek before him, that the role of banks was to thwart the automatic market adjustment of *ex ante* investment to *ex ante* savings. Even in his last major work, Minsky (1986) maintains the distinction between *ex ante* and *ex post* macroeconomic quantities, which had been explicitly rejected by Keynes in his rebuff of Ohlin.[6] From this neo-Wicksellian perspective the peculiar theory of money in Minskian economics is no more than an enigma. Neither Wicksell nor neo-Wicksellians, like Myrdal and Hayek, believed in the necessity of postulating a discretionary power of the central bank over the supply of money. All of them would have rejected the monetarist version of his classical economics. What mattered was the existence of the loanable funds market allowing the interest rate mechanism to adjust the supply of loans to the demand for loans. Banks could obviously increase the quantity of money they wished to supply through the channel of changes in the desired structure of *ex ante* wealth. Any shift from *ex ante* desired stock of illiquid assets to *ex ante* desired stock of liquid assets is reflected by a rise in the so-called velocity of money. Such an endogeneity of money fits the logical straitjacket of neoclassical scarcity theory because it is the proof of the existence of a strong *ex ante* saving constraint. To believe that it encapsulates a sensible theory of endogenous money is to confuse the general neoclassical theory of value with its crudest and most naïve version, the monetarist model. Rebuffing Friedman is not the test since Hayek himself had explicitly scorned monetarism and its early model, the Cambridge quantity theory.

The dual profits hypothesis is therefore helping us to answer a second fundamental question addressing the minimum prerequisites for a general theory of capitalism, thereby breaking once and for all the Procuste's bed of the neoclassical scarcity theory. Since the duality hypothesis is enshrined into the saving constraint, *ex ante* savings must play no part at all, which was Keynes's most solemn wish. Bank credit can no more account for a discrepancy between effective investment and *ex ante* savings, which unravels the distinction between sound and unsound investment plans. There is no more a market for loanable funds determining interest rates by conflating a demand for excess loans and an inelastic supply of loans. Getting rid of the loanable funds doctrine unfolds the true role of banks, which is not to be pure intermediaries, in the like of Gurley and Shaw (1960) to whom Minsky refers approvingly.[7] Banks' capacity to create money financing firms' plans cannot be constrained by *ex ante* portfolio choices even in the presence of financial innovations. Ultimately, Minsky's underlying theory of *ex ante* savings led him to a very old-fashioned theory of banks in which *ex ante* deposits constrain loans.

In retrospect, Minsky's failed attempt to escape from orthodoxy is an echo of Keynes's own failure in the *General Theory*, as shown by Moore (2001). Keynes could not throw away the whole orthodox theory of saving, which is plaguing his multiplier theory. He was therefore unable to build a theory of profits germane to the capitalist monetary economy (Rochon, 1999; Parguez, 2001). His theory of asset markets in the *General Theory* (Keynes, 1936/1973, Ch. 17) is still deeply embedded into neoclassical economics (Parguez and Seccareccia, 2000). Minsky could not go beyond the Keynes of the *General Theory*,[8] because he wished to root his theory of crisis in the most orthodox parts of the *General Theory*, displaying in Minsky's own terms the Wall Street view of capitalism. A proof is given by explicit reference to Ohlin's 1937 papers in *Can 'It' Happen Again?* (Minsky, 1982, Ch. 11), addressing the Keynesian theory of investment. Unaware of Keynes's adamant rejection of Ohlin's interpretation of the *General Theory*, Minsky believes that the *ex ante/ex post* distinction is a very useful tool to understand Keynes's theory of capital.

Setting the record straight on Minsky's theory of crisis helps discover the reason behind the failure of the post Keynesian school to supersede neoclassical economics. A unified post Keynesian school does not exist, and never did. Relative to the prerequisites for escaping from the general neoclassical theory of scarcity, there is no obvious convergence between Minsky and Davidson. Since his early writings, Davidson got rid of the neoclassical saving constraint while Minsky used it as the cornerstone of his theory of crisis. It will be shown in this chapter that in Minsky's theory of crisis uncertainty fits the neo-Wicksellian explanation of crisis. Minskian uncertainty is not the non-ergodic Davidsonian uncertainty. Never had Hayek postulated a Walrasian perfect information when he unravelled the destabilising intervention of profit-seeking banks.

THE PURE THEORY OF FINANCIAL CRISIS UNDERLYING THE FINANCIAL INSTABILITY HYPOTHESIS OF MINSKY: THE DUAL PROFITS HYPOTHESIS

Most of the participants to the Minsky debate were not aware of the reason why Minsky unceasingly connected his theory with Fisher's (1933) celebrated explanation of major crises as the outcome of excess debt. Fisher is the true founding father of modern general equilibrium theory, as shown by Mirowski (1989),[9] and therefore cannot be deemed a precursor to post Keynesian economics. His theory of crisis is rooted into the failure of the interest rate mechanism to coordinate *ex ante* investment and saving. As discussed above, Minsky cannot be deemed himself post Keynesian or even Keynesian. Fisher, Hayek and Minsky share the same concern about market failures. Minsky's theory cannot be understood as long as it is not interpreted as the ultimate achievement of the neo-Wicksellian theory of crises.

Let us start from the fundamental equations from which stems the duality of profits leading to an explanation of the role of banks in market failures.

The Fundamental Equations

All the following equations are pure neo-Wicksellian vintage:

$$I_t^* = I_N + I_S \tag{20.1}$$

$$I_N = P_K^0 \alpha_0 S_t^* \tag{20.2}$$

$$K_t(1+g)^t = K_{0t}^* = \frac{(1+r)K_t(1+g)^t}{(1+g)} \tag{20.3}$$

$$I_t^* - S_t^* P_K^0 = \Delta F \qquad\qquad (20.4)$$

$$I_N - S_t^* P_K^0 = \beta\Delta F \qquad\qquad (20.5)$$

with:

$$\alpha_0 \geq 1$$
$$\beta \leq 1$$

and where I_t^*, S_t^* and P_K^0 are respectively *ex ante* aggregate investment and saving and the price level of capital goods that is consistent with long-run equilibrium. An invariant price level fits the neo-Wicksellian equality of the supply and demand price of capital goods. It reflects the purchasing power of a given amount of monetary capital, the capital fund, in terms of real capital goods. Equation (20.1) explains that aggregate *ex ante* investment splits between normal or sound investment and speculative investment. It displays the Minskian neo-Wicksellian postulate, which can be found in Hayek and Fisher, that the *ex post* or effective nature of investment is determined by its *ex ante* nature.

According to equation (20.2), sound investment is a predetermined multiple of the monetary value of *ex ante* savings. In Hayek's theory, α is equal to 1 because there is no growth. We will show that the *ex ante* savings multiplier accounts for the growth of the real *ex ante* savings. Equation (20.3) displays a paramount characteristic of the neo-Wicksellian theory, the targeted desired stock of real capital K^*. Let us assume that T is the society's expectations time span. The present value of the targeted stock of capital in T, K_{tT}^*, must reflect the present value of normal or real profits generated in the course of time. Let r_0 and g_0 be respectively the maximum and constant rate of profit, and the rate of growth of an economy that is always in its natural or optimal efficiency growth path. Aggregate real profits are growing at a rate equal to the natural growth rate. They are discounted at the natural rate of interest i_0 expressing the Hayeko-Fisherian time preference. From equation (20.3) stems the equality of the natural rate of interest and the rate of profit. Equation (20.4) explains that the discrepancy between *ex ante* savings and investment is met by an increase in the stock of loanable funds, which is split between sound investment and specific time investment.

Normal Profits and Monetary Profits

The duality of profits is a last and shrewd attempt to solve the old pre-Keynesian problem of realisation. The *ex ante* effective saving fund S_t^* is the available real surplus, which is the share of the predetermined real output society must save from consumption to attain the desired path of capital accumulation. In a monetary economy S_t^* is thus the real value of available savings for a given and constant relative price of capital goods P_K^0, reflecting the real surplus.

Let us assume that all monetary savings accrue to the owner of capital, as returned earnings, equity and recycled bank loans. Normal profits are therefore meeting four fundamental constraints:

$$\Pi^* = P_K^0 S_t^* \tag{20.6}$$

$$\frac{\Pi^*}{P_K^0} = rK_t \tag{20.7}$$

$$r = f'(K) = \Phi(g_K) \tag{20.8}$$

such that:

$$g < g_0, \qquad \frac{\partial r}{\partial g} > 0$$

$$g > g_0, \qquad \frac{\partial r}{\partial g} < 0$$

and:

$$r = r^0 \tag{20.9}$$

where K_t, r_0, F'_K and g_0 are respectively the initial capital stock, the rate of profit, the marginal productivity of capital and the natural rate of growth. Equations (20.6) to (20.9) explain that, following the neo-Wicksellian tradition, Hayek and Minsky used to conflate the classical doctrine of surplus and the neoclassical scarcity theory of value. For a given stock of capital, the available real surplus is determined by the rate of profit, which is equal to the marginal productivity of capital.

Equation (20.8) displays the dynamic production function. The marginal productivity of capital is determined by the rate of growth of capital. There is one rate of growth that allows society to benefit from the highest rate of profit. It is the natural rate of growth allowing society to enjoy all the feasible technical innovations.

Equation (20.9) is the long-run neo-Wicksellian equilibrium condition adjusting the rate of interest to the maximum rate of profit, which defines the natural rate of interest in equation (20.3) above. It is the prerequisite for the long-run equilibrium in the market for capital goods that allows the invariance of P_K^0.

In a monetary economy, real surplus is realised through the channel of current investment expenditures, according to Kalecki's principle. Following Ohlin (1937a, 1937b), Minsky postulates that *ex ante* monetary savings today are *ex post* past savings. Since *ex post* savings or profits are generated by investment expenditures, *ex ante* profits are equal to past investment. Assuming a one-period lag, as in Ohlin, Minsky got the dynamic equation that was missing in Hayek's model determining monetary profits. This equation is the Minskian interpretation of the Kaleckian equation:

$$\Pi_t = I_t^*$$ (20.10)

Henceforth, Minsky had the fundamental stability condition:

$$\Pi_t = \Pi_t^*$$
$$I_{t-1} = rK_t P_K^0$$ (20.11)

Monetary profits, Π_t, must be equal to normal profits to allow realisation of the real surplus for an economy on its natural growth path. As soon as current investment is above its equilibrium level, there is profit inflation leading to a fall in the rate of profit and a rise in the price level, P_K^t, displaying the fall in the purchasing power of monetary savings. Price inflation is the outcome of excess investment relative to the realisation condition. It appears long before true full employment, like in Hayek's model, because the economy is pushed away from its maximum efficiency frontier as shown by equation (20.8). Minsky, like Ohlin, assumes that the increase in the stock of capital is generated by investment spending in real terms that had been undertaken in the former period. According to the starting fundamental equations, real investment today accounts for *ex ante* investment, I_t^*. As long as the stability condition is fulfilled, the economy grows at its natural rate, g_0, thereby sustaining a constraint and maximum rate of profit, r_0, and allowing for a stable price level, P_K^0. In any period on the natural growth path, we have the following conditions:

$$\Delta K_t = g_0 K_{t-1} = I_{t-1}^* = I_N \tag{20.12}$$

$$I_{t-1}^* = \alpha S_{t-1}^* = \alpha_0 r_0 K_{t-1} \tag{20.13}$$

and so we have:

$$\alpha_0 r_0 = g_0 \tag{20.14}$$

$$\alpha = \frac{g_0}{r_0} = \frac{g_0}{i_0} \tag{20.15.A}$$

Equation (20.14) determines the sound finance or sound debt multiplier in terms of the two parameters defining the natural growth path or the maximum efficiency frontier, the growth rate and the rate of profit. The higher is the rate of profit generated by the rate of growth, the lower is the amount of loans firms need to undertake their normal *ex ante* investment.[10] It is proven that firms ask for loans to undertake required *ex ante* investment maintaining the economy on its natural growth path. *Ex ante* increases in debt are always validated by the growth of the real surplus it has accurately anticipated. By supplying loans banks allow for the rise in monetary profits realising the growing surplus at a constant price level.

The Minskian model leads to the stability theorem generalising the neo-Wicksellian theory of the saving constraint:

> In an economy growing on its natural path, debt is just the anticipation of the future *ex ante* savings. Investment is always financed by existing *ex ante* savings and perfectly anticipated *ex ante* savings. Since loans are backed by *ex ante* savings, pure credit in the definition of Hayek as credit granted *ex nihilo* does not exist.[11] Banks are pure intermediaries between future savers and present borrowers.

Going back to the fundamental equations, we can now spell out the two states of a capitalist economy.

The long-run equilibrium is defined as follows:

$$I_t^* = \alpha_0 S_t^*$$

$$\alpha_0 = \frac{g_0}{r_0}$$

$$\Pi_t^* = \Pi_t$$

$$r_t = r_0$$

$$P_K = P_K^0$$

$$I_S = 0$$

The inflationary boom is defined as follows:

$$I_t^* = \alpha S_t^*$$

$$\alpha > \alpha_0$$

$$\Pi_t^* < \Pi_t$$

$$r_t < r_0$$

$$P_K^t > P_K^0$$

$$I_t^* - \alpha_0 S_t^* = I_S$$

The stability condition is both necessary and sufficient because as long as α is equal to α_0, *ex ante* profits or savings are always high enough to allow investors to pay interest on outstanding debt and refund the required share of the debt. Minsky never brought about the proof of the theorem while he is raising some thorny problems that are embedded into the neo-Wicksellian theory of capital. We need first to assume that all the components of the real stock of capital have the same velocity of depreciation, v_0, which means that in each period a share, v_0, of the inherited capital stock has to be replaced. Replacement investment, being part of the *ex ante* aggregate investment, is financed partly by *ex ante* savings and partly by bank loans.

Let us also assume that bank loans are reimbursed at a velocity equal to the depreciation velocity of real capital. Since banks are financing a constant share, β_0, of aggregate *ex ante* investment, β_0 is the rate of outstanding debt to the capital stock, with the following condition:

$$\beta_0 = \frac{\alpha_0 - 1}{\alpha_0} = \frac{g_0 - r_0}{g_0} \tag{20.15.B}$$

Firms are paying to banks a rate of interest, i_b, which is the natural rate of interest. In any period the ratio of interest payments to *ex ante* profits being equal to the debt ratio, β_0, firms are never obliged to get into new debt to pay interest to banks. The excess of *ex ante* profits over interest payments is available to finance debt repayment and the required share of replacement investment. The sustainable level of v_0 is therefore determined by the equilibrium condition:

$$i_b = i_0 = r_0$$
$$r_0(1-\beta_0)K = v_0\beta_0 K + v_0(1-\beta_0)K \qquad (20.16.A)$$
$$r_0(1-\beta_0) = v_0\beta_0 + v_0(1-\beta_0)$$

or:

$$v_0 = r_0(1-\beta_0) = \frac{r_0^2}{g_0} \qquad (20.16.B)$$

As long as the economy is on its natural growth path, the velocity of depreciation of the capital stock allows firms to always meet their required debt payments. It is now proven that the stability condition is necessary and sufficient to prevent *ex ante* speculative and Ponzi investment.

The realisation principle holds as long as banks are complying with two equilibrium constraints. On one side, they have to recycle interest payments into equity capital raised by firms. On the other side, they must compensate for debt repayment by new loans financing the required share of replacement investment. Hence compensating loans prevents the fall of the debt ratio induced by debt repayment. Firms can therefore always recoup an amount of money that is equal to *ex ante* normal profits realising the surplus. Ultimately, financial commitments are neutral relative to *ex ante* savings.

THE FINANCIAL STRUCTURE AND THE NEOCLASSICAL THEORY OF ENDOGENOUS MONEY

Minsky's theory of finance is explicitly rooted in Gurley and Shaw's (1960) own theory of financial structure. Gurley and Shaw, whose neoclassical pedigree was more than authentic, could be conflated with the neo-Wicksellian school because they had obviously scorned the monetarist model.[12] In a capitalist economy *ex ante* savings are channelled to *ex ante* investment through intermediation of a complex financial structure of which banks are just a part. In any period aggregate *ex ante* financial wealth, F, is the monetary value of all stocks of financial assets including the *ex ante* stock of money. All of these assets are claims of their holders against firms or financial intermediaries. Financial intermediaries' books are balanced by claims on firms. For Minsky and Gurley and Shaw, being pure financial intermediaries, banks are always interposing themselves between *ex ante* savers and borrowers. Since banks can create money through their loans, the very nature of money creation is a specific interposition between *ex ante* savers and borrowers. In any period the stock of financial assets must be equal to the money value of the stock of capital it has financed. Assets are held by non-intermediary agents, households and corporations.

When corporations hold assets, equity or claims on intermediaries, they are just holding direct or indirect claims on themselves. The increase in the stock of financial assets account for *ex ante* savings, which are the share, s, of effective money income accruing *ex ante* to the non-intermediary sector. Let Y be the *ex ante* aggregate income. It is equal to the monetary value of output, which is itself determined by the available stock of capital and the capital–output ratio resulting from the technology embodied in the stock of capital. Income is shared between gross *ex ante* profits and wages. Profits are themselves distributed between interest payments, stockholders' income and retained profits. Minsky, like Hayek, maintains the classical assumption that all savings arise out of profits. Since profits are realising the surplus, as long as the economy is on its natural growth path, we can write the following equations, where h_0 is the share of profits, F is the available stock of assets and ΔF^* is the equilibrium increase in the aggregate demand for assets.

$$F = P_K^0 K_t \qquad\qquad (20.17.\text{A})$$

$$S^* = s_0 Y = P^0 \frac{s_0}{T} K \qquad\qquad (20.17.\text{B})$$

$$S^* = \Pi^* = P^0 r_0 K \qquad\qquad (20.18)$$

$$\Delta F^* = I_N - S^* = I^* - S^* \qquad\qquad (20.19)$$

$$\Delta F^* + S_t^* = P_K^0 \Delta K \qquad\qquad (20.20)$$

$$s_0 = r_0 T_0 = i_0 T_0 = h_0 \qquad\qquad (20.21)$$

Equations (20.17.A) to (20.21) display the equilibrium financial structure of the economy. For a given P^0, the stock of assets must always grow at the same rate as the stock of capital. Since the capital increment reflects *ex ante* investment, growth requires an increase in the stock of assets adjusting *ex ante* savings to *ex ante* investment. On the natural growth path, the rate of saving is therefore predetermined for a given capital–output ratio by the natural rate of interest. Equation (20.21) fits the preference for time root of the natural rate of interest in the neo-Wicksellian theory (equation (20.3)). The preference for time ruling over the choice between consumption and accumulation determines the saving rate and therefore the share of profit (equation (20.22)), which provides the *ex ante* savings realising the surplus (equation (20.18)) and generates the increase in the stock of assets sustaining the required capital stock increment (equation (20.19)). What is special in bank intermediation is that through their loans banks create money.

To emphasise the paramount non-monetarist nature of Minsky's theory of finance, let us assume that there is no central bank, the very Wicksellian hypothesis. Banks must always balance their books adjusting their assets (loans) to their liabilities that include the money stock, M, and their non-money liabilities, L_B, generated by financial innovations. Let D be the outstanding stock of firms' debts or loans. Whatever can be the state of the economy, we have always:

$$D = M + L_B \qquad (20.22)$$

where M and L_B are components of the aggregate financial wealth, the other parts of which being the stock of equity, E, and the stock of non-bank intermediaries' liabilities, L_{NB}, whatsoever they could be. Let m^*, l_B^*, l^* and l_{NB}^* be respectively the desired shares of M, L_B, L, and L_{NB}. These shares depend upon the relative real rates of return on assets including the implicit rate of return on money. According to equations (20.16.A) or (20.16.B), rational wealthholders do not suffer from monetary illusion. Portfolio adjustments are imposing for all assets the equality of supply and demand. The effective stock of deposits, M, results from the adjustment of the banks' supply, M^S, to the demand for money, M^D. Hence we can write:

$$M = M^S = M^D = m^* F = m^* P^0 K_t \qquad (20.23)$$

The equilibrium stock of loans is therefore:

$$D = M(1 + k_m) \qquad (20.24)$$

with the following condition holding:

$$k_m = \frac{l_B^*}{m^*}$$

From these equations, we derive the role of banks in the adjustment of *ex ante* investment to *ex ante* savings. Savings are increasing the *ex ante* stock of deposits, which trigger a fall in the ratio of debts to the money stock. Banks have to increase their stock of loans to adjust the debt–money ratio to its equilibrium level. The ratio of the increase in loans to the money stock must fit the ratio l^*/m^*. The higher is l^* relative to m^*, the greater is the stock of loans that can be reimbursed by a given stock of money. The increase in the stock of money resulting from new loans generates an equal increase in *ex ante* savings restoring the equilibrium allocation of wealth. It is therefore ultimately entirely determined by portfolio choices of wealthholders. Banks can strive to increase their money supply by engineering financial innovations increasing the relative rate of return on their non-money liabilities. Financial innovations may induce either a shift from M to L_B or (and) from L_{NB} to L_B and even E to L_B.

By employing the role of financial innovations, Minsky has encapsulated the core of what must be deemed the neoclassical theory of endogenous money:

> Money is endogenous because its equilibrium supply by banks is entirely determined by market forces generated by wealthholders' optimal allocation of their wealth. It is hereby true that *ex ante* deposits determine loans or rather that *ex ante* savings make loans.[13]

This theorem does not require the absence of a central bank. Let us now assume the existence of a central bank targeting a ratio, B, of reserves, R, to deposits. Equilibrium conditions in the market for assets and money requires that banks can always supply enough money to meet the desired stock, which determines the equilibrium level of reserves:

$$\frac{R}{B} = M = m^* F$$

$$R = BM = Bm^* F$$

(20.25)

Let us now assume that the central bank cheats market forces by supplying an amount of reserves that is lower than the equilibrium level. There is an excess demand for money and therefore, for a given structure of wealth, an excess of *ex ante* savings relative to the supply of assets. This excess demand for assets is met by banks through financial innovations increasing l^* and lowering m^*. Herein, we grasp the generalised theorem of the neoclassical endogeneity of money:

> The central bank cannot contradict market forces. Either it creates enough reserves to match portfolio adjustments or the lack of reserves is automatically compensated by financial innovations generating the equilibrium stock of money. Financial innovations overcome central bank policy because this policy is contradicting financial market forces.

This theorem explains why Hayek and Minsky have rejected the monetarist model. Too many post Keynesians have been deceived by Minsky's adamant rebuff of the textbook monetarist multiplier story. It was not the proof of his rebuff of neoclassical economics because the monetarist doctrine thrives on the ignorance of the true neoclassical theory of value and money. We may henceforth for a while abstract from the central bank. Banks' supply of money is adjusted to *ex ante* sound investment when the money multiplier is fitting the equilibrium condition:

$$(1+k_m)M = \beta_0 I_t^* = \alpha_0 - 1 \qquad (20.26.\text{A})$$

with:

$$M = m^* S_t^*$$

$$\alpha_0 = \frac{g}{r}$$

$$(1+k_m) = \frac{\alpha_0 - 1}{m^*}$$

Given these conditions, we can write:

$$l_B^* - m^* = \frac{g-r}{r} \qquad (20.26.\text{B})$$

$$f = f_0$$

Therefore, when:

$$f > f_0$$
$$\Delta F > I_N$$

we obtain:

$$\Delta F - I_N = I_S \tag{20.27}$$

As soon as banks, wishing to increase their loans, induce a rise in l_B^*, which is so high that f is now greater than f_0, the increase in the money supply is financing speculative investment. Banks achieve their targeted supply of money by accelerating the pace of financial innovations providing wealthholders with new assets, the rate of return on which is increasingly greater than the rates of return on other assets. Financial innovations lead wealthholders to shift their wealth from money, non-bank intermediaries' asset and equity to newly supplied banks' non-money assets. Equations (20.26) and (20.27) explain that to increase f above f_0, banks must induce a rise in l_B^* resulting from the fall in l_{NB}^* and l^*, which proves their ability to attract *ex ante* savings at the expense of other intermediaries and the stock market.

Banks supply new assets as long as they are profitable. Their profit margin on a new innovation is the discrepancy between their expected rate of return on new loans and the marginal cost of this innovation. The expected rate of return is the sum of the rate of interest on loans, i_B, and of the expected increase in the market value of equity acquired out of interest income. Banks' expected capital gains depend upon the expected rise in the rate of profit. Let r_D and $(\bar{r} - r)$ be respectively the rate of return on loans and the discrepancy between the expected rate of profit and its existing level, always assuming zero inflation:

$$r_D = i_B + (\bar{r} - r) \tag{20.28}$$

On the other side, newly created assets provide a yield equal to the sum of the rate of interest paid by banks, i_L, and their marginal utility, U'_L.[14] Banks may engineer innovations until the rate of return on new loans is equal to the yield of innovations supplying *ex ante* savings financing the new loans. In any period the money supply is thus sustaining the equilibrium condition:

$$i_B + (\bar{r} - r) = i_L + U'_L \tag{20.29.A}$$

or:

$$i_B - i = U'_L - (\bar{r} - r) \qquad (20.29.B)$$

Herein is the seed of excess investment. Banks wish to increase the money supply until the discrepancy between the bank rate and the rate of interest paid to savers (interest spread) is equal to the discrepancy between the marginal utility of new assets and banks' expected capital gains. For a given level of the bank rate and a given expected capital gain, a rise in U'_L generates a fall in i_L and therefore an increase in banks' profit margin, which sustains an increase in the money supply. The twin equations (20.24) and (20.25) stem from the dynamic Minskian supply function of money, U_B being banks' profit margin:

$$\Delta M^S = \Delta F = \Delta D \qquad (20.30.A)$$
$$\Delta M^S = m^* [U'_L - (\bar{r} - r)] S_t^* = \beta_0 I^* \qquad (20.30.B)$$

This suggests that:

$$\Delta M^S = m^* [U_B] S_t^* \qquad (20.30.C)$$

where:

$$\frac{dm^*}{dU_B} > 0$$
$$\beta > \beta_0$$

A rise in the bank rate induces with some delay a fall in the expected rate of profit generated by a forecasted fall in market assets' values. According to equation (20.25), there must be a lower profit margin, which shifts to the left the money supply function in Figure 20.1 (with $i_B^2 > i_B^1$). The inverse relationship between the bank rate and the money supply has been emphasised by Minsky in all his contributions to the theory of financial instability. It can be deemed the long-run supply function of money.

The money supply function displays the fundamental characteristic of the genuine neoclassical theory of money. Money has a positive value because it is scarce since its supply is constrained by the existing stock of wealth generated by *ex ante* savings and banks' profit margin adjusting wealthholders' preferences to banks' expectations. Like Wicksell, Fisher,

Hayek and the whole neo-Wicksellian school, Minsky has always implicitly rejected any explanation of money in terms of the theory of the monetary circuit. The money supply function showing that banks may sway wealthholders preferences, which has also been emphasised by Gurley and Shaw (1960), is perfectly germane to neoclassical economics (Rochon, 1999).

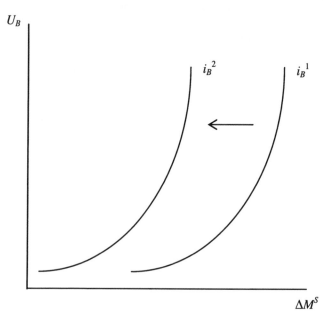

Figure 20.1. The money supply function

THE MECHANISM OF CRISIS

There are two prerequisites for a theory of endogenous cycles. There must be a robust equilibrium condition around which the economy is gravitating. The system also needs ignorance of all participants relative to the equilibrium condition. Neither firms nor banks can learn out of their past failures because so strong is their greed that they are doomed to unceasingly ignore what requires equilibrium. Both prerequisites are met by all neo-Wicksellian models and by Minsky's own theory of crisis.

Hayek had always thought that the equilibrium state was just an 'attraction' that was never attained or maintained because of greed-motivated ignorance. The ignorance postulate of the neo-Wicksellian school should convince post Keynesians that they must be cautious when they dally with 'uncertainty' and scorn neoclassical economists for their perfect information hypothesis.[15] Minsky's model enshrines a very robust equilibrium condition determining the equilibrium level of *ex ante* investment (equations (20.12) to (20.14)) and the potential thwarting power of banks (equation (20.26)). Minsky is also relying on the greed-motivated ignorance postulate, which explains why neither banks nor firms learn from their past failures. In this search for a rise in their profit margin banks are always keen to supply enough money to finance speculative investment. The central bank is doomed to fail to prevent their excess creation of money. Herein is the ultimate reason why Minsky rejects the textbook monetarist model that obviously cannot fit the theory of endogenous crisis.

Let us start from some state, t_1, just after the end of the spiralling deflation triggered by the previous crisis. The economy is very far below the stability threshold. The debt deflation has led to a collapse of the debt–capital ratio, which means that the stock of debts has fallen more than the capital stock. We have the following conditions:

$$\alpha_1 < \alpha_0 \text{ or } \beta_1 < \beta_0 \tag{20.31.A}$$

$$K_0 < K_0^* \tag{20.31.B}$$

$$g < g_0 \tag{20.31.C}$$

$$r < r_0 \tag{20.31.D}$$

$$\frac{r^2}{g} > v_0 \tag{20.31.E}$$

$$I_0^* = I_N \tag{20.31.F}$$

$$I_0^* < S_0^* \tag{20.31.G}$$

$$i_B < i_0 \tag{20.31.H}$$

Because of the deflation, the rate of growth has also collapsed until it became negative and now is just a little above zero (equation (20.31.C)). The rate of profit has been squeezed well below its normal level (equation (20.31.D)) by the scarcity of capital (equation (20.31.B)), which has moved the economy below its maximum efficiency frontier. During the deflation, *ex ante* investment was negative, an increasing share of the capital stock has not been replaced or destroyed. *Ex ante* investment is so low that it cannot absorb *ex ante* savings (equation (20.31.G)), there is no more speculation investment (equation (20.31.F)). Excess *ex ante* savings are invested into forced hoardings because there is not enough supply of other assets. To save their business, banks have been obliged to accept a rate of interest that is lower than the natural rate of interest (equation (20.31.H)), which reveals the outstanding excess supply in the loanable funds market. The compound impact of a collapse of the debt ratio allows interest rates and a repay–wait ratio lower than their equilibrium level (equation (20.31.E)) determined by equation (20.18). This explains the quasi-demise of firms' financial commitments.

Such a state is not stable because of the intertwined impact of greed and technology. Let us assume that *ex ante* investment, for a given rate of interest, is determined by the expected increase in the rate of profit. Let us also assume that firms adjust their expected increase in the rate of profit to the discrepancy between the existing level and the level they had expected to determine past investment. Dynamic investment relationships are therefore the following:

$$I_1^* = I_{(t)}(i_B, \bar{r}_1 - r_1) \qquad (20.32.A)$$

$$(\bar{r}_1 - r_1) = \gamma_{(t)}(r_1 - \bar{r}_0) \qquad (20.32.B)$$

where $I_{(t)}$ and $\gamma_{(t)}$ are changing over time. The more firms have enjoyed today a higher rate of profit than the expected level in the previous period, the more they expect an increase in the rate of profit, which sustains the growth of *ex ante* investment. Expectations are embedded into a given bank rate and the absence of inflation. A rise in the bank rate above the natural level generates an *ex ante* investment squeeze, with some delay, because of losses in asset values.

Any increase in investment determines so strong a rise in the rate of profit (equation (20.8)) that the rate of profit is always greater than its expected level. Expectations relationships $I_{(t)}$ and $\gamma_{(t)}$ are more and more buoyant. There are plenty of hoarded *ex ante* savings to finance the rise in investment. Wealthholders want to get rid of their excess stock of money ($m > m^*$) by acquiring equity. The growth of *ex ante* investment determines an equal increase in *ex ante* savings in the future, which is the Kalecki–Ohlin relationship (equations (20.10) and (20.11)).

Since the real surplus is growing faster than the realising investment, there are downward pressures on the price level. Firms' expectations are becoming so optimistic that *ex ante* investment is higher again than *ex ante* savings.

Banks are keen to provide funds to increase their profit margin by supplying new assets to wealthholders ($l_B < l_B^*$).

Sooner or later, *ex ante* investment is exceeding its equilibrium level. Firms indulge in bets on the future, which are so optimistic that they account for slowing a rise in the rate of profit in the far future that it could compensate for inadequate rates of profit in the near future. The sheer forces of greed lead firms to *ex ante* speculative investment moving the economy beyond the ignored stability threshold.

Banks and firms have the same vision of the future. Banks are ready to comply with firms' demand for funds by increasing the pace of financial innovations inducing the required portfolio adjustment. The market for loanable funds is still in equilibrium because the increase in the money supply is equal to the demand for funds (equation (20.26)), even when the debt rate becomes higher than its equilibrium level.

Beyond the stability threshold, the forces of technology impose a fall in the rate of profit because growth is less and less efficient (equation (20.5)). Monetary profits are still rising since they are generated by the increase in *ex ante* investment but they are realising a vanishing real surplus. The increasing discrepancy between realising expenditures and the real surplus is met by accelerated inflation.

Minsky and Hayek share the same theory of inflation, which has been forgotten by both mainstream analysis and many post Keynesians (Seccareccia, 1996). Inflation happens long before full employment because it is the outcome of excess investment. The equilibrium level of investment being logically independent of full employment, inflation does not depend upon pressures in the labour market. For Hayek, inflation appears as soon as *ex ante* investment is greater than *ex ante* savings, because there is no growth. In Minsky's model, inflation is the outcome of *ex ante* investment greater than its normal level meeting the stability condition, α_0 (equation (20.14)).

Inflation overcomes the impact of the Kalecki mechanism because both firms and banks and wealthholders as well can no more ignore the failure of their expectations. Firms are now striving to compensate for the lack of profits by raising new debt just to meet their financial commitments. For a while banks are willing to accommodate the inflation-induced demand for new loans because they contrive to prevent firms' failure, which would lead to a fall in their own assets. They strive to finance the required increase in the money supply by engineering new innovations raising l_B^*. Former *ex ante* speculative investment is henceforth imposing a cumulative rise in the debt rates inducing a new increase in the demand for loans to match the impact of accelerated inflation. Sooner or later, banks can no more increase their supply of loans because the supply function of money is absolutely inelastic. Any new increase in the money supply would induce a negative profit margin, because the marginal utility of new assets in now zero or negative while the expected rate of profit is shrinking relative to its existing level.

The rigidity of the money supply determines a growing excess demand in the market for loanable funds, which propels upwards the rate of interest on loans. Bank rate hikes are soon imposing an unexpected rise in the rate of interest, which is used to reckon the present value of assets. The preference for time is so low that the rate of interest is far behind its natural level.

Nothing can now prevent the collapse of *ex ante* investment as shown by the investment function (equation (20.28)). The Kalecki effect explains an equal collapse of monetary profits, which increases the profit lack to meet financial commitments. Wealthowners strive to shift their wealth away from banks, l_B^* could become negative, forcing a liquidity crunch on banks that strive to protect their solvency by requiring before-term repayment. The credit crunch is propelling the rate of interest again upwards, the deflation turns into a cumulative process. It comes to a halt when all excess debts and capital have been wiped out. Since there had been a large outflow of savings from banks this desintermediation explains why ultimately debt has fallen more than capital relative to the equilibrium state. Firms' outstanding debt has been written off leading to banks' failure to meet their own commitments (there could have been bankruptcies within the banking sector), while a share of the capital stock has been sustained by equity despite the fall in stocks. Wealthholders have been in a quandary since the start of the crisis in their search for assets. They had to choose between the two remaining assets, money and equity. In the worse case – the absolute financial crisis – bankruptcies of banks determine a flight from money, at least from bank money. The economy is again ready to start a new boom. It has learned nothing because it cannot learn from past failures.

BEYOND MINSKY: THE MINIMUM AGENDA FOR AN ECONOMY WITHOUT SAVING CONSTRAINT

The dual profits hypothesis has been useful to prove the logical consistency of Minsky's theory of crisis, because it reconciles the Kalecki effect with the *ex ante* saving constraint. From this perspective of the neoclassical synthesis, such a theory is a remarkable achievement bringing about the ultimate generalisation of the neo-Wicksellian theory of capital and money. Minsky's theory cannot therefore be deemed 'post Keynesian' as long as post

Keynesians are those who endeavour to encapsulate the crucial propositions of the *General Theory* and after into a more general and consistent theory.

There are three fundamental propositions explaining Keynes's rejection of what he dubbed classical economics:

Proposition 1 *Ex ante* savings do not exist.
Proposition 2 Effective savings is nothing but the mirror image of investment.
Proposition 3 There is no market for loanable funds determining the rate of interest.

Proposition 1 denies the saving constraint, while according to proposition 2 effective savings are independent of wealthholders' choice because they are generated by investment expenditures. Effective saving obviously includes firms' profits (Rochon, 1999; Moore, 2001). The sheer impossibility of a loanable funds market is the logical consequences of proposition 1 and proposition 2. Conflating Minsky's theory of crisis with post Keynesian economics leads to the restoration of the classical economics Keynes had explicitly rejected. Anyone who would follow this avenue could confuse the general theory of neoclassical economics with the late textbook version postulating perfect information, neutral money and a central bank-determined supply of money. The dual profits hypothesis is the last resort proof that it is not enough to rebuff the naïve Friedmanian multiplier story to jump out of the straitjacket of neoclassical economics. Dallying with a vague uncertainty is also insufficient to break up with the neoclassical theory of capital, as long as the nature of uncertainty is not speculated. It must be a Davidsonian non-ergodic uncertainty instead of being rooted in the blithe ignorance out of greed of strong equilibrium conditions.

Minsky's failure to escape from neoclassical economics emphasises the necessity of setting up the major characteristics of an economy bereft of the *ex ante* saving constraint, and therefore embodying the three crucial Keynesian propositions. Following the methodology of Rochon (1999), we can derive six fundamental propositions from the undaunted denial of the *ex ante* saving constraint:

1. Money being the existence condition of the non-despotic production process is ruled by the flux–reflux principle of the monetary circuit (Parguez and Seccareccia, 2000). It cannot be defined as an asset being held for its specific yield. The demand for money plays no part at all or a very minor and insignificant part. Money is created to be ultimately

destroyed in the reflux stage of the monetary circuit. Any reference to a demand for money function is inconsistent with the nature of money (Rochon, 1999; Moore, 2001; Parguez, 2001).

2. The amount of money that is created by banks does not depend upon wealthholders portfolio choices. The neoclassical endogeneity of money is a generalisation of the *ex ante* saving constraint.

3. Interest rate hikes are not the predetermined outcome of an excess demand for funds. Going back to Minsky's explanation of the use of the bank rate, we can draw Figure 20.2, which is the twin of Figure 20.1. Let us start from state 1, when firms and banks share the same discrepancy between the realised rate of profit and its expected level. The increase in the available supply of funds is determined by the money supply function (equation (20.26)). It has become rigid since banks can no more engineer profitable innovations to induce shifts in the stock of wealth. The demand curve of firms has a negative slope because any rise in the rate of interest generates higher expected losses and therefore lower investment. The equilibrium level of the rate of interest is i_{B1}. Let us assume a higher discrepancy between the expected rate of profit and its effective level. There is a fall in the available increase in the supply of funds because banks can no longer overcome the impact of firms' failure by supplying profitable new assets to wealthholders. The demand function has moved to the right because firms strive to meet their increased lack of profits by new loans. The equilibrium level of the rate of interest is now i_{B2}, which displays the magnitude of the rationing imposed on banks. Rochon (1999) is therefore right to suggest that this market mechanism is quite similar to the new Keynesian theory of interest rates. It is the last resort proof of the ruling role of the market for loanable funds in any theory that ignores the absolute exogeneity of interest rates in the monetary economy. The full exogeneity of interest rates means that neither their existence nor their level depends upon the market mechanisms level in Figure 20.2 (Parguez, 2001).

4. An economy without a loanable funds market is bereft of the thwarting power of banks relative to the equilibrium condition. The distinction between *ex ante* sound and speculative investment is irrelevant. The full or non-portfolio choices-led endogeneity of money means that bank loans are never recycling already existing funds. *Ex ante* wealth never makes loans and *ex ante* existing and future savings are never the sound source of finance for investment. Like Hayek, Minsky had been ensnared by the weird role of banks and credit within the neoclassical theory of portfolio choices. Disintermediation would be a sensible solution that should repeal

the thwarting role of banks by shifting wealth out of their embrace. In a pure equity economy, there would be no banks but there would be no more credit as well. Who could buy new equity when nobody may ask for new money? The usual no-banks economy should operate in the mode of some Walrasian quasi-barter system.

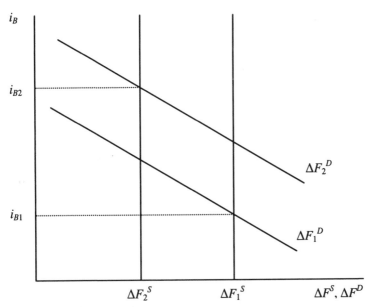

Figure 20.2. The determination of the rate of interest by the neoclassical endogeneity of money

5. Inflation can no more be explained as the mere outcome of speculative investment or excess *ex ante* investment relative to the future growth of savings. It is therefore impossible to endorse Minsky's emphasis on the thwarting impact of 'big government' or large deficits. On one side, large deficits are a cornucopia for firms indulging in speculative and Ponzi investment, because they provide them with enough monetary profits to compensate for inflation. Speculative firms could increase their profits in real terms and henceforth they would be bailed out of the constraint of asking for new loans to meet their financial commitments. There would be no interest rate hikes and crisis should not occur, which ought to sustain an increase in speculative investment accelerating the pace of inflation. On the other side, in his last contribution to the theory of crisis Minsky (1986)

puts in the front stage the direct impact of government on inflation. The profligacy of welfare programmes is shrinking the efficiency of the economy and therefore the available surplus. Since growing monetary profits are realising squeezed real surpluses, the direct outcome of big government is more inflation. Ultimately wealthholders would fly from government debt and financial instability ought to increase, because there could be a rise in the demand for assets issued by banks or a more fight from the domestic currency. Denouncing the tricky danger of stabilisation through big government, Minsky stirs a mild Hayekian echo from the road to serfdom. The proof is that his last resort recommendation is that governments should target a long-run fiscal surplus to win the confidence of wealthholders.[16]

6. At last, a true monetary economy does not fit the existence of a Ricardian pre-determined real surplus (Parguez, 2001). The realisation principle collides with the flux–reflux law encompassing the three major Keynesian propositions. The so-called surplus evolves out of internal outlays financed by the creation of money for both firms and government. There is therefore no retained earnings fund financing sound investment. Pre-existing retained earnings are the value of the classical surplus (Parguez, 1999).

CONCLUSION

In its own terms, Minsky's theory of crisis has been a very interesting contribution to the economic theory of the post-second world war period. Minsky achieved what had escaped former neo-Wicksellian writers. He could integrate their *ex ante* saving constraint into a general theory of accumulation and finance. Ultimately, the avenue had no Keynesian exit because of Minsky's undaunted faith in his distinction between the *ex ante* nature of investment. He thought of having discovered the philosopher's store of crises but he became the prisoner of the neoclassical economics he had hoped to reject. The last-resort lesson of Minsky's failed hopes is that, albeit the financial structure is a crucial part of a theory of crisis, it must not deal with a distinction between the nature of investment expenditures. The very notion of speculative investment is the neoclassical chamber of secrets because it is encompassing the *ex ante* saving constraint. It is indeed the Trojan horse of neoclassical economics.

NOTES

1. The author would like to thank without implicating them Marc Lavoie, Louis-Philippe Rochon and Mario Seccareccia who inspired this work.
2. In Minsky's model, profits are distributed between firms and their creditors who recycle their income into the acquisition of assets (their propensity to save is equal to one). Aggregate profits are thus equal to the increase in the stock of assets held by firms and their creditors including banks.
3. In his paper on 'Central banking and money market changes', Minsky (1957a) explains that through their supply of new assets, banks can partly overcome central bank control of the money supply. In his paper on the accelerator models, Minsky (1957b) explicitly endorsed the exogeneity of the money supply, which is determined by the central bank, but an increase in the velocity of circulation (resulting from financial innovations) can compensate for the rigidity of the money supply.
4. He just emphasises that uncertainty was absent from his 1957 writings.
5. For instance, Victoria Chick in her collected essays is adamant to address her evolution starting from her very orthodox early writings (see Arestis and Dow, 1992).
6. Keynes thought that the Swedish school approach was both irrelevant and contradicting the major propositions of his own theory. Keynes had in mind the very paper to which Minsky is referring.
7. In their general theory of finance published in 1960, Gurley and Shaw ignore the crucial role of money in financing the production process. Money is just one component of the pyramid of assets held by wealthholders. They extol intermediation between savers and borrowers. Banks are just participating to the intermediation function. Banks are never creating money within their framework. Referring to Gurley and Shaw is therefore believing in the old-fashioned causality: deposits make loans.
8. As far as we know, he never quoted the *Treatise on Money*.
9. Fisher's dissertation on the theory of value (1896), republished in Fisher (1926), addresses the logical requirements of a sensible formalisation of neoclassical economics.
10. There can be an increase in the desired stock of money assets, which leads to banks' recycling of effective *ex ante* deposits and loans.
11. The very notion of a pure *ex ante* creation of money is insulting the general theory of value that embedded the crucial axioms: (a) nothing can be created out of nothing; (b) value can never be created.
12. The famous monetarist model was just restating a very old story as shown by Realfonzo (1998), who proves that the money multiplier was accepted by most European economists. He obviously should have mentioned that the neo-Wicksellian school had rejected the multiplier.
13. This was shown convincingly by Rochon (1999).
14. The marginal utility of a new asset reflects its intrinsic characteristics in terms of liquidity, insurance against losses, and so on. The marginal utility of an asset is inversely related to its supplied stock.
15. The very meaning of 'uncertainty' must be explained to distinguish the Keynesian uncertainty from the neoclassical uncertainty. Sometimes, uncertainty is a self-defining buzz word. Minsky himself never explained what he had in mind when he involved the weight of uncertainty on firms' expectations.
16. All agents should target surpluses when they plan to become indebted. According to Minsky, targeted surpluses prevent the depreciation of their debt titles. This rule ensures the supremacy of wealthholders (the so-called capital market). The whole economic policy agenda is enslaved to the whimsical speculators, embodying the rentier power Keynes dreamed of 'euthanising'.

REFERENCES

Arestis, P. and S.C. Dow (eds) (1992), *On Money, Method and Keynes: Selected Essays of Victoria Chick*, London and New York: Macmillan and St. Martin's Press.

Fisher, I. (1926), *Mathematical Investigation into the Theory of Value and Prices*, New Haven: Yale University Press.

Fisher, I. (1933), 'The debt-deflation theory of great depressions', *Econometrica*, **1** (4), 337–57.

Gurley, J.G. and E.S. Shaw (1960), *Money in a Theory of Finance*, Washington: The Brookings Institution.

Keynes, J.M. (1936/1973), *The General Theory of Employment, Interest and Money*, London: Macmillan. Reprinted in *The Collected Writings of John Maynard Keynes*, Vol. VII, London and Basingstoke: Macmillan.

Lavoie, M. and M. Seccareccia (2001), 'Minsky's financial fragility hypothesis: a missing macroeconomic link?', in R. Bellofiore and P. Ferri (eds), *Financial Fragility and Investment in the Capitalist Economy: The Economic Legacy of Hyman Minsky*, Cheltenham and Northampton: Edward Elgar, vol. II, 76–96.

Minsky, H.P. (1957a), 'Central banking and money market changes', *Quarterly Journal of Economics*, **71** (2), 171–87.

Minsky, H.P. (1957b), 'Monetary systems and accelerator models', *American Economic Review*, **47** (6), 859–83.

Minsky, H.P. (1982), *Can 'It' Happen Again? Essays on Instability and Finance*, Armonk: M.E. Sharpe.

Minsky, H.P. (1986), *Stabilizing an Unstable Economy*, New Haven: Yale University Press.

Mirowski, P. (1989), *More Heat than Light: Economics as Social Physics: Physics as Nature's Economics*, Cambridge: Cambridge University Press.

Moore, B.J. (2001), 'Some reflections on endogenous money', in L.-P. Rochon and M. Vernengo (eds), *Credit, Interest Rates and the Open Economy: Essays on Horizontalism*, Cheltenham and Northampton: Edward Elgar, 11–30.

Ohlin, B. (1937a), 'Some notes on the Stockholm theory of savings and investment. I', *Economic Journal*, **47** (185), 53–69.

Ohlin, B. (1937b), 'Some notes on the Stockholm theory of savings and investment. II', *Economic Journal*, **47** (186), 221–40.

Parguez, A. (1999), 'A monetary theory of public finance', Paper presented to the Sixth Post Keynesian Workshop in Knoxville, 22–23 June, unpublished.

Parguez, A. (2001), 'Money without scarcity: from the horizontalist revolution to the theory of the monetary circuit', in L.-P. Rochon and M. Vernengo (eds), *Credit, Interest Rates and the Open Economy: Essays on Horizontalism*, Cheltenham and Northampton: Edward Elgar, 69–103.

Parguez, A. and M. Seccareccia (2000), 'The credit theory of money: the monetary circuit approach', in J. Smithin (ed.), *What is Money?*, London and New York: Routledge, 101–23.

Realfonzo, R. (1998), *Money and Banking: Theory and Debate (1900–1940)*, Cheltenham and Northampton: Edward Elgar.

Rochon, L.-P. (1999), *Credit, Money and Production: An Alternative Post-Keynesian Approach*, Cheltenham and Northampton: Edward Elgar.

Seccareccia, M. (1992), 'Wicksellianism, Myrdal and the monetary explanation of cyclical crises', in G. Dostaler, D. Ethier and L. Lepage (eds), *Gunnar Myrdal and His Works*, Montreal: Harvest House, 144–62.

Seccareccia, M. (1996), 'Post Keynesian fundism and monetary circulation', in G. Deleplace and E.J. Nell (eds), *Money in Motion: The Post Keynesian and Circulation Approaches*, London and New York, Macmillan and St. Martin's Press, 400–16.

21. A Primer on Endogenous Credit-Money

Marc Lavoie[1]

INTRODUCTION

When students enter a post-Keynesian class in monetary economics, their minds have been so much distorted by the neoclassical fallacy of an exogenous supplied stock of money that they find difficult to understand even the simplest story about demand-led endogenous money. The purpose of this chapter is to help teachers in presenting the main features of a modern financial system.

To do so, the T-accounts of banks and central banks, where assets must by necessity balance with liabilities, will be presented in a systematic way, starting from the simplest pure credit economy, with a single bank and without central banks and outside currency. Complications will be gradually introduced, such as competing private banks, a central bank and its reserve requirements, and then, at a later stage, the State with its financial requirements and its issues of government bonds. Recent developments in banking, such as capital adequacy ratios, zero-reserve requirements, repos, securitisation, and electronic money will also be discussed within the framework of the T-accounts.

A PURE CREDIT ECONOMY, WITH A SINGLE BANK

Let us begin with a pure credit economy, in which there is a single bank engaged in credit and debit operations, and where firms are forbidden to issue bonds or commercial paper. This single bank may be a private bank, set up by some private entrepreneurs, or it may be an institution set up by the State. Whatever the case may be, we assume that the State has no budget, and hence that it spends nothing and taxes nothing. The fact that this enterprise acts as a bank may either have been acquired through the spontaneous act of the markets or through some law imposed by the authority of the State. In any case, there is no currency money, no reserve requirements, no financial markets, and no central bank. The economy is also a closed one: there are no foreign transactions, no foreign reserves, and no exchange rates. Finally, neither gold nor silver are considered as reserve assets.

Within such a financial system, all financial transactions would have to transit through this single bank. There could be no leaks, and no inflows, besides the new credits granted by the bank. Every one would have an account at the single bank. That account could be either a debit, in which case the bank would make a loan L to the individual household or firm, or it could be a credit, in which case the individual household or firm would be holding a bank deposit, which is usually called money. Because there are no leaks, whatever amount of credit has to be equal to the amount of debit, that is, $L = D$ (Table 21.1).

Table 21.1. Unique bank

	Bank	
Assets		Liabilities
Loans L		Deposits D

Let us now assume that some agents, most likely firms, but perhaps also household consumers, wish to increase the amounts they borrow. Where are these loans going to come from? In the mainstream story, starting from fully loaned banks, new credits can only be granted when banks are the recipients of new deposits, a situation which occurs when the central bank purchases government bonds (from banks or from the general public) on the open market, thus giving rise to the creation of excess reserves. But in the present model, there are neither government bonds nor a central bank. How can the banks create new loans?

The post-Keynesian answer to this query is rather simple. Loans are created *ex nihilo*, at the stroke of a pen, or by punching a key on the computer, *as long as the borrower is credit-worthy*. The only limit to this process is given by the amounts of loans which can be granted to credit-worthy borrowers. This depends on the willingness of borrowers to borrow, and on the willingness of banks to grant credit-worthy status to their customers (Rochon, 1999, Ch. 8). The latter may be influenced by the degree of liquidity of the banks, to be defined in a later section.

The simplest arrangement for banks and their customers is to set up credit lines, or overdrafts, which Keynes (1930/1971, p. 41) defined as 'an arrangement with the bank that an account may be in debit at any time up to an amount not exceeding an agreed figure, interest being paid not on the agreed maximum debit, but on the actual average debit'. When the credit line is being pulled upon, the additional loan which is awarded to the borrower has an immediate counterpart in the liabilities of the bank, by the creation of an equivalent additional deposit. This additional deposit then changes hands, as the borrower uses the new credit-money to pay for some services.

In our modern world, just as in Keynes's time, it is not necessary to have money deposits to be able to spend. 'A customer of a bank may draw a cheque against his deposits, thus diminishing his *credit* with the bank; but he may, equally well, draw a cheque against his overdraft, thus increasing his *debit* with the bank' (Keynes, 1930/1971, p. 41). Similarly, recipients of cheques may use the funds to increase their credit balances at the bank, that is, their deposits, or they may use the funds to reduce their debit balances, that is, the used portion of their credit line.

This is what currently occurs with the use of debit cards. For instance, when customers use their debit cards to purchase goods, they may have no bank deposits, and hence the used portion of their credit line will be increased as the transaction occurs. Similarly, some sellers may also be in a debit position vis-à-vis the bank, and hence the payments received will be automatically applied to reduce the amounts due, as shown in Table 21.2. Under these circumstances, no change whatsoever will occur in the amount of deposits held by each transactor. This is a clear example of the reflux principle.

Table 21.2. Payments through debit balances

	Bank	
Assets		Liabilities
Debit position of purchaser	+100	
Debit position of seller	−100	

Agents who desire to spend can thus do it in two possible ways. Either they spend by depleting their money balances (the bank deposits), or they keep still their money balances while increasing their debit at the bank. As Keynes pointed out, the potential for purchasing goods and services, or what he calls the cash facilities, is made up of two components, the money deposits being held and the *unused* overdraft, that is, the portion of the credit line which has not yet been drawn upon. 'Properly speaking, unused overdraft facilities – since they represent a liability of the bank – ought ... to appear on both sides of the account' (Keynes, 1930/1971, p. 42). If we were to keep track of these unused overdraft facilities, then the bank accounting would look as shown in Table 21.3.

Table 21.3. Taking explicit account of credit lines

	Bank
Assets	Liabilities
Loans (used overdraft facilities)	Deposits
Unused overdraft facilities (potential loans)	Unused overdraft facilities (potential deposits)

Although unused overdraft facilities are still considered as off-balance sheet loan commitments, some countries, namely the United States, do have some statistical data on these (Moore, 1988, p. 25). Unused credit lines represent approximately one-half of the narrowly defined money stock, and twice the amount of used overdraft facilities. It is thus clear that those who have credit line arrangements do have access to an endogenous source of credit-money. Indeed, the Bank for International Settlements (BIS) considers that formal standby facilities and credit lines of banks ought to be taken into consideration when assessing capital adequacy ratios (BIS, 1988, p. 24).

Some authors, mainly associated with the Dijon school, sometimes make the controversial statement that the monetary circuit starts with the savings of the workers. This paradoxical statement by Keynesians is however easy to understand, within the framework of the T-accounts. Assume that new loans are demanded by producers to pay their workers. The deposits created in the process of drawing on the credit line are transferred to the accounts of the workers. As long as the workers do not spend their new incomes, they are saving it (Rossi, 1998). By contrast, when households purchase goods, the deposits are transferred back to the firms, who can then use the deposits to reimburse the advances that were granted to them. The deposits of the households do constitute savings that are lent to firms, but the economic process starts when the bank grants an advance, or a loan, to its credit-worthy customers.

A PURE CREDIT ECONOMY, WITH PRIVATELY-ISSUED BANKNOTES

Let us now assume that the customers of the unique bank would like to benefit from the convenience offered by banknotes when doing their transactions. In other words, rather than having all transactions going through a scriptural system of accounts, some transactions, presumably the more petty ones, could be done without the bank being an intermediate. In our modern financial systems, we are accustomed to banknotes being backed by the central bank or by the Treasury of the central government. Here, neither of these institutions exists. Where are the banknotes going to come from? They are going to be issued by the private bank.

In the past, privately issued banknotes were quite common. The State would grant some banks the right to issue banknotes. In our pure credit economy, banknotes would be issued by our unique bank, on demand. In other words, whenever a customer desires to have a deposit transformed into banknotes, such banknotes are created by the bank. Banknotes are purely endogenous. The new T-account of the bank would look like Table 21.4.

Table 21.4. Unique bank with banknotes

Bank	
Assets	Liabilities
Loans L	Deposits $D' = D - B$ Banknotes B

Banknotes issued by the unique bank are a liability of the bank. The bank transforms one kind of liability, the deposits, into another kind of liability, the banknote. There is no limit to the amount of banknotes that can be so created. If customers of the bank were to bring back the banknotes, they could only be exchanged for deposits at the very same bank. There cannot be an excessive creation of banknotes, in line with the reflux principle. It could happen, however, that credit is being granted to finance inflationary expenditures or wage increases. This explains why the best-known exponent of the reflux principle – Thomas Tooke, who was in favour of free enterprise in all aspects of economic life – argued in his later work that while banknotes need not be regulated, credit and loans ought to be (Arnon, 1993).

It should be noted that banks should be highly favourable to the issue of private banknotes. Whereas banknotes carry no interest rates, bank deposits do or can easily do so. As a consequence, for a given markup between the loan and the deposit interest rates, the higher the proportion of money in the form of banknotes, the larger the profits of banks. As a result, one should expect banks to favour any technological change that would transform bank deposits into privately issued banknotes. We shall see that such a transformation is starting to occur with electronic money.

THE PROFITS OF BANKS

One issue which has been momentarily ignored up to now is that of bank profits. Obviously, in a perfect world where financial transactions could be conducted at no cost, and where there would be no default risk on the part of borrowers, the condition of zero-profit for the bank would be equivalent to the interest rate charged on loans to be equal to the rate of interest paid on deposits. In the real world, borrowers are sometimes unable to face their debt commitments and must default on their loans. Banks must thus set a spread between the lending and the deposit rates, to compensate for this risk. In addition, banks, like all firms, must pay salaries to their employees, they must service the cost of their fixed equipment, and they must turn out a profit for their owners. Indeed, banks, like all firms, have a certain target rate of return, and the differential between the lending and the deposit rate (on top of service charges) will be such that banks achieve this target rate of return on the capital of their owners in normal times, net of the losses due to loan defaults.

If all the profits are redistributed to the households who own the banks, then the simple equality of Table 21.1 could still be relevant. This can be seen with the help of Table 21.5. Assume that the rate of interest on loans is i_c, while the rate of interest on deposits, which is lower, is i_d. By the end of a year, unless interest payments have been made by the borrowers or loans have been reimbursed, outstanding loans will now amount to $L(1 + i_c)$. On the liability side, outstanding deposits will have increased to the amount $D(1 + i_d)$. This implies, assuming that in the initial state deposits and loans were of equal amounts, that the profits of the banks, their own funds, are now of an amount $L(i_c - i_d)$. If all the profits are redistributed as dividends, then we are back to the second line of Table 21.5, where deposits and loans are once more equal, as they were in Table 21.1.

Table 21.5. Banks with own funds distributed as dividends

Bank

Assets	Liabilities
Loans $L(1 + i_c)$	Deposits $D(1 + i_d)$ Own funds $L(i_c - i_d)$
Loans $L(1 + i_c)$	Deposits $D(1 + i_c)$

It should also be clear, even though loans and deposits appear to grow at a rate equal to the rate of interest on loans, i_c, that there is no need for loans and money deposits to grow at that rate. For instance, if the households who are the owners of the banks decide not to save their dividends in the form of deposits, but rather decide to spend them all on consumption goods, the loans due by the non-financial firms will be reduced by an equivalent amount, and hence there will be no growth whatsoever in the amount of outstanding loans.

In general, however, one would expect the administrators of the bank to retain part of the profits, so as to constitute some reserve fund. This reserve fund is the own capital of the bank. It includes the funds initially put up by the owners of the bank when starting business (how that initial fund came about is rather mysterious however), plus the retained earnings of the bank. The own capital of the bank constitutes a liability to itself. It represents the funds which the firm owes to its owners. In general, the own funds play a role similar to deposits that would be in the hands of the owners. The own funds, just like the deposits or the credits, are an accounting entry, but in contrast to deposits, they cannot be drawn down by the owners. They would be reduced whenever a borrower defaults on a loan. In that case, a similar amount would be deducted from the loan assets and the own funds liabilities when the bad loans need to be written off (that is, when the accountants of the bank consider that the borrowers are unable to service the interest payments on their loan and are unable to ever pay back the loan). When there is too large a proportion of bad loans, own funds, that is, the net worth of the bank, can become negative, in which case the bank becomes insolvent.

In the simple world described in the first row of Table 21.5, the additional own funds of the bank have, as a counterpart, additional borrowing by the non-financial firms, as interest accrues on the books of the banks, both on the asset and the liability sides. However, even if profits are entirely retained within the bank, rather than distributed to household owners, it is still possible for loans not to rise at the rate i_c. This is because banks may decide to purchase real capital goods produced by non-financial firms (they may also decide to purchase financial assets (shares) issued by non-financial firms, if we now assume that such financial instruments exist). In that case, as the non-financial firms sell some of their produced output (or some financial assets to the bank), they will be credited in counterpart with money deposits.

This is shown in the transition from the first to the second row of Table 21.6. However, under the assumption that firms do not hold deposits, using them rather to reduce the value of their outstanding loans, it can be seen in the third row of Table 21.6 that loans outstanding will be reduced by the amount R – the value of the real assets purchased by the banks. Clearly then, the investment expenditures of the banks allow for a reduction in the debt owed to the banks by the non-financial firms.

Table 21.6. Banks with own funds and real assets

Bank

Assets	Liabilities
Loans L	Deposits D' Own funds F
Loans L Real assets R	Deposits $(D' + R)$ Own funds F
Loans $(L - R)$ Real assets R	Deposits D' Own funds F

THE LIQUIDITY OF A BANK AND CAPITAL ADEQUACY RATIOS

Another interesting feature of the pure credit economy, with no government bonds on the books of private banks, which to a large extent represents most financial systems in the world, is that the liquidity of a bank is rather difficult to assess from the standard point of view. In the standard view, the liquidity of a bank is measured by the ratio of its safe to total assets. This standard view of liquidity has already been criticised by those who point out that, through liability management, it is always possible for large banks to obtain the funds that they need to settle their accounts (Moore, 1988, p. 33).

In the pure credit economy, this criticism is highlighted. Here, there are no safe assets since banks hold no government bonds and since there is neither reserves nor central bank cash. The lending behaviour or the liquidity of a bank thus cannot be based in general on the proportion of cash or government bonds that the bank holds among its asset portfolio. Such a ratio would always be equal to zero. The only option left, then, is to measure the liquidity of a bank by the proportion of its own funds. It is the own funds of a bank, rather than its reserves or safe assets, which may play a key role in a theory of endogenous money (de Boyer, 1998). The relevant ratio to measure risk would be the L/F ratio, that is, the ratio of loans to own funds. Alternatively, if the real assets of the banks are taken into account, it would be the assets to own funds ratio, A/F.

Lately, this ratio, or rather its inverse, the own funds to assets ratio, has become the subject of intensive scrutiny, under the guidance of the BIS. The BIS has designed a *capital adequacy ratio*, that private banks ought to respect, under the guidance of central banks or their supervising agencies. The minimum ratio suggested by the BIS is 8 per cent: it is the ratio of the own funds of the banks (their capital) to a weighted measure of their assets, the weights being based on a conventional assessment of the risks associated with each kind of assets, and even off-balance items (BIS, 1988).

Some economists have argued that the maximum A/F ratios that arise from the imposition of minimal capital adequacy ratios may replace the role of reserve multipliers in a world without reserve requirements. This new multiplier would be equal to the allowed assets to own funds ratio. For instance, it has been argued that the incapability of the Japanese economy to come out of economic stagnation in the 1990s has been due to the low net worth of the Japanese banks, following the huge losses that these banks had to absorb as a consequence of substantial defaults on loans (mainly related to land and construction speculation). Because of their low net worth, it was said that Japanese banks were prevented to grant new loans, because of binding capital adequacy ratios.

Several remarks can be made in this regard. It should be noted first that the capital adequacy ratios have been set in such a manner that they would only be binding for the most risky banks. Solvent and profitable banks accumulate retained earnings that are added to their net worth, and they should have no trouble in inducing economic agents to forego deposits in exchange of newly issued bank shares, thus allowing these banks to improve their own funds to assets ratio.

What happens, however, if all banks incurred large losses, pushing the assets to own funds ratio beyond its maximum value, so that no private agent would be willing to buy bank equity? If such a situation were to occur, and there is no confirmation that it did occur in the case of Japan, it would be the responsibility of the central bank to purchase new equities issued by the banks. As a result of this transaction, the banks would increase both their own funds and their reserves at the central bank. This would allow them, as we shall see in later sections, either to reduce their borrowing from the central bank or to acquire safe assets such as government bonds. They could then resume their business of granting loans to all credit-worthy customers.

Some post-Keynesian authors argue that when banks grant new loans they are automatically decreasing their liquidity and hence are intrinsically reducing their liquidity preference, since the ratio of loans to own funds is immediately rising (Wray, 1995; Brossard, 1998). That it is true, in some sense, can be seen immediately from the first line of Table 21.6. At the very moment that a new loan is being granted, the bank commits itself to a more illiquid position. The amount of loans rises while that of own funds remains the same. Thus, at the very moment in time when a new loan has been granted, the bank is in a more risky position.

This situation is, however, only a temporary one. For the larger stock of loans and deposits will allow the bank to make additional net interest revenues (unless the new loans are being defaulted in unusual proportions), as shown in Table 21.5. These additional revenues, when they are due and integrated to the retained earnings, will thus bring the L/F ratio back to its initial level. At the end of the year, the balance sheet of the bank has increased in size, but the liquidity preference of the bank may remain the same. In other words, there is no upward pressure on interest rates charged on loans when additional loans are being granted.

A PURE CREDIT ECONOMY, WITH TWO SETS OF BANKS

We have seen that a single bank in a pure credit economy cannot encounter any liquidity problems. The unique bank could become insolvent, however, if the amount of defaulting loans were to exceed the amount of own funds of the bank, thus reducing the value of assets below that of liabilities.

What happens when there are two banks? Let us still assume that there is no central bank and no government expenditures. Let us assume that there are two banks, one specialised in making loans to corporations, and the other one specialised in collecting deposits from households. In a sense, this corresponds to the institutional framework of many financial systems. In the United States, for instance, banks located in New York have specialised in making large loans to big businesses, while the so-called country banks specialise in collecting deposits. Similarly in France, for a long time specialisation was institutionalised, with business banks (*banques d'affaires*) and deposit banks (*banques de dépôt*) (see Marchal and Poulon, 1987).

With this division of the banking business, it is impossible for each bank to reach an approximate equality between loans and deposits. The deposit bank (Bank D) consistently has excess deposits, while the business bank (Bank B) continuously has an excess of loans over deposits. In other words, at the end of each day, Bank B realises that the cheques drawn by its customers in favour of the customers of Bank D are in an amount that exceeds the cheques drawn the other way. Bank B is systematically indebted vis-à-vis Bank D. The positive balances of Bank D are exactly matched by the negative balances experienced by Bank B. As soon as the cheques are cleared, Bank B is indebted vis-à-vis Bank D, and Bank D holds an asset against Bank B, as shown in Table 21.7. In a system with only two banks, it cannot be otherwise. Still, if Bank D consents to grant loans to Bank B, the accounts will balance, and such a situation can perpetuate itself.

Table 21.7. Two banks, pure credit economy

Bank B		Bank D	
Assets	Liabilities	Assets	Liabilities
Loans to non-financial agents	Deposits	Loans to non-financial agents	Deposits
	Funds owed to Bank D		Own funds
		Advances made to Bank B	
	Own funds		

Things are just slightly more complicated in a multi-bank system. A single bank may at the same time owe funds to a bank and be owed funds by another bank. The clearing house is designed to net out these balances, and bring together all the main participants to the clearing system. Each participant then knows the amounts that it can lend to those in deficit or the amounts that it must borrow from those in surpluses. The clearing house may then act as a broker between the deficit and the surplus banks, that is, between the business banks (B) and the deposit banks (D). In the aggregate, their T-accounts will look like those of Table 21.7.

The two banks B and D, or the two sets of banks, need only make sure that they agree on a rate of interest that will be profitable to both of them. In other words, the interbank interest rate, that is, the rate of interest charged by Bank D to Bank B on the amounts due must be somewhere in between the rate of interest on deposits, which Bank D is paying to its depositors, and the rate of interest on loans, which Bank B is charging to its borrowers. If the interbank rate is set in an appropriate fashion, the rate of return of both banks will be the same, and hence the ratio of own funds to assets of both banks will be the same. Similarly, the loans to own funds ratio will also be the same in both banks, where loans now include the loans made to other banks.

CERTIFICATES OF DEPOSIT AND SECURITISATION

Although the above direct lending arrangements between banks are perfectly legitimate, some observers of the banking scene may find it rather worrying that some banks are heavily in debt towards other banks or other financial institutions. To overcome and disguise this feature, a series of arrangements have been designed, two of which we shall briefly outline.

An option for *business* banks, that is, the banks that specialise in lending to firms, is to issue certificates of deposit (CDs). Bank B, the business bank, is attracting an insufficient amount of deposits. Bank B may thus issue certificates of deposit, which would be purchased by Bank D, which has positive balances. The issued certificates of deposit would thus appear on the liabilities side of the balance sheet of Bank B, replacing the amounts due to Bank D, while the purchased certificates of deposit would appear on the assets side of the balance sheet of Bank D, taking the place of the loans made to Bank B. This is shown in Table 21.8, which is barely different from Table 21.7. But now Bank B does not 'borrow' from bank D any more, or so it appears from a legal point of view.

Table 21.8. Two banks, certificates of deposit

Bank B		Bank D	
Assets	Liabilities	Assets	Liabilities
Loans to non-financial agents	Deposits	Loans to non-financial agents	Deposits
	Sold CDs		Own funds
		Purchased CDs	
	Own funds		

The above presentation makes clear that credit relations are based on creditworthiness. As long as Bank D believes that Bank B is able to provide interest payments on its commitments, there is no reason for Bank D to refuse extending loans to Bank B, or purchasing certificates of deposit from Bank B. The same occurs at the level of the customers of a bank. Banks grant loans and renew lines of credit as long as they have faith in the ability of the borrower to make interest payments. Similarly, depositors have no hesitation to leave their deposits at a bank as long as they believe that their orders to transfer these deposits will be honoured. The credit-worthiness of a bank thus ultimately depends on the credit-worthiness of its borrowers and the confidence of its depositors. Credit-worthiness and credibility are the key elements of the system.

It should be emphasised that there are no safe assets in this pure credit economy. When deposit banks lend to business banks, collaterals in the form of risk-free government assets cannot be provided since they do not exist by definition. The credit-worthiness of the loans granted by the banks are the only collaterals available. Conventions based on trust and confidence rule the banking system.

This brings forth another fashionable arrangement, *securitisation*. Securitisation may be defined as the transformation of an asset, which would not previously be marketable, into a marketable one. In other words, the securitisation of an asset implies that this asset can now be sold on some market. A typical example of securitisation is the sale of a set of loans, previously granted by a bank, to some other financial institution. These other financial institutions are usually non-bank financial intermediaries, such as pension funds, trust companies, insurance companies, which collect vast amounts of savings from households. We can call these companies financial intermediaries, under the understanding that financial intermediaries do not create credit, in contrast to banks, being content to recycle existing assets.

Once again, this kind of arrangement arises as a result of specialisation. The non-bank financial intermediaries specialise in collecting time deposits and other long-term savings from households and even corporations. The banks specialise in finding credit-worthy borrowers. This specialization creates an imbalance in the balance sheets of banks and financial intermediaries, similar to the one shown in the top part of Table 21.9. This imbalance could be solved by banks issuing certificates of deposit, which would be bought by financial intermediaries, but securitisation seems to be the new fad in finance.

Table 21.9. Financial intermediaries with securitisation

Bank B			Financial intermediary FI		
Assets	Liabilities		Assets	Liabilities	
Loans to non-financial agents 100	Deposits 30 Funds owed to FI 70		Advances made to Bank B 70	Deposits 70	
Loans to non-financial agents 100	Deposits 30		Securitised loans 70	Deposits 70	

In the case of securitisation, banks typically sell a bunch of their loans to a financial intermediary which has collected a large amount of time deposits. The loans thus disappear from the balance sheet of the bank, and appear on that of the financial intermediary. In the example of Table 21.9, 70 per cent of the loans end up being securitised. The net result for the bank is a reduction in the size of its balance sheet: the loan made to a non-financial institution is gone, but so is its liability towards financial intermediaries. It is true that the bank is forsaking the future interest revenues to be obtained from the borrower, but the bank has collected up-front fees when initially granting the loan. In addition, the bank is now in a better position with regards to its capital adequacy ratios, as previously discussed. It has collected fees when making the loan, and it can repeat the operation without having to worry about the BIS-imposed capital adequacy ratios, thus circumventing them.

Securitisation, just like lending between banks, requires confidence. The wholesale of loans can only occur as long as the purchasers of these loans are confident that the loans will be repaid and the interest payments will be made.

THE CENTRAL BANK IN AN OVERDRAFT ECONOMY

An interesting classification, underlined by several post-Keynesian authors, is the distinction between *overdraft* economies and *auto-economies*, a distinction first made by John Hicks (1974, p. 51). In the auto-economy, agents sell their liquid assets to finance new ventures, or they issue new bonds or new shares. For this reason, these economies are often called *financial-markets* economies, but we shall call them *asset-based* economies, to underline the fact that firms in such economies are said to own the financial resources required to make their investment expenditures, whereas banks sell their liquid assets (mainly Treasury bills) to make new loans.

In the overdraft economy, by contrast, firms or households pull on their lines of credit with private banks when they require new financing means. The same distinction applies to the financial sector. When they need more high-powered money, banks borrow it from the central bank instead of purchasing it by selling government securities. As a result, when the focus of the analysis is on the balance sheet of the central bank, the distinction between an overdraft economy and an asset-based economy relies on whether the central bank has claims over the domestic financial sector. 'The overdraft economy is thus defined by a double level of indebtedness: that of the firms to the banks and that of the banks to the central bank' (Renversez, 1996, p. 475). This distinction will be quite useful in the discussions that follow, although the ultimate functioning of a modern financial system is the same regardless of it being an overdraft or an asset-based system.

Let us start then with the simplest of the two systems, the overdraft system. The overdraft system is in fact an extension of the pure credit economy, to which a central bank has been added. In the overdraft system, the operations of the central government, beyond those of the central bank, may still be assumed away, and this is mainly why the overdraft system is easier to describe than the asset-based system.

Let us then assume the existence of a central bank, and that of a network of private banks, consolidated into a single conglomerate for simplification. In this more realistic financial system, we assume that private banks cannot issue banknotes any more. Only the central bank can issue banknotes. Suppose that we start from the situation described by Table 21.1. The private bank conglomerate has loans on the asset side, and deposits on the liability side (own funds are set aside for simplification). Its depositors now wish to split their money holdings into bank deposits and banknotes. How are the banks going to provide their customers with the banknotes issued by the central bank?

The mainstream answer, provided within the framework of an asset-based financial system, is that the banks will sell government assets to the central bank, thus obtaining the banknotes that they need. These banknotes, which are said to be part of the money supply, are also part of what is called high-powered money, that is, money issued by the central bank, or central bank money. But here, in this pure overdraft economy, there is no government sector (beyond the central bank) and there are no government bonds. We assume further, in line with present institutions, that central banks will not buy any privately issued asset. Still, banks are required to obtain the banknotes, for their customers will lose all faith in the banking system if it cannot provide the banknotes that they lust for. How can the banks obtain the banknotes?

If banks cannot sell any asset to the central bank, the only way they can obtain the banknotes is by borrowing them from the central bank. This is the so-called discount window operation, whereby banks borrow from the central bank. This is what is shown in Table 21.10. The amount borrowed is exactly equal to the required amount of banknotes, that is, the amount of central bank money. The central bank has a monopoly over the provision of banknotes. As long as there is a demand for central bank banknotes by their customers, private banks are forced to go into debt vis-à-vis the central bank. Private banks cannot but be indebted vis-à-vis the central bank.

Table 21.10. Overdraft economy, with banknotes

Private banks		Central bank	
Assets	Liabilities	Assets	Liabilities
Loans L	Deposits $D' = D - B$	Loans B made to private banks	Banknotes B
	Funds B borrowed from the central bank		

LIABILITY MANAGEMENT AND THE OVERDRAFT ECONOMY

The overdraft economy is the ultimate example of liability management. Broadly speaking, liability management refers to the ability of banks to increase their lending activity by borrowing funds that appear on the liability side of their balance sheet, without being forced to sell some of their marketable assets – mainly Treasury bills. Several authors have argued that liability management is the latest stage in the historical development of banking systems (Chick, 1986). Before the advent of liability management, banks would passively wait for deposits, and only expand their lending activity if new depositors came forth. The attracted deposits were taken as a pool of funds, available for lending.

There is, however, another view of liability management – the radical view. According to this new view, liability management is *not* an innovation that would have transformed the process of banking intermediation. Rather, liability management is a permanent feature. Banks are perpetually engaged in passive liability management, as they must first consent to loans, and later search for funds to finance the deposits which are leaking out. All overdraft systems are compelled to practice liability management as a logical necessity. Any adjustment is done on the liability side, simply because no adjustment from the asset side is possible. Banks as a whole, when they are in need of banknotes for their customers, or in need of compulsory reserves as we shall soon see, cannot get them by selling liquid assets to the central bank since they hold no Treasury bills. They obtain all of their high-powered money by borrowing it from the central bank.

Most European banking systems, for instance those of France and Germany, have structurally been indebted to the central bank. The Japanese banking system is also of the overdraft type, as are most of the banking systems in the less-developed countries (Lavoie, 2001). The argument, to be found in the traditional view, that liability management would be a new phase in the development of financial systems, thus does not seem to be a correct assessment of the actual evolution of financial systems throughout the world.

An interesting feature of the overdraft economy is that it clearly shows that money and high-powered money are endogenous variables, which cannot be under the control of the central bank. In the present overdraft economy, with a demand for central bank banknotes, the banknotes must be provided and the central bank has no choice but to provide the private banks with the loans that they need. The central bank is left however with a powerful tool: that of setting the rate of interest at which the private banks will be forced to borrow the required amounts of banknotes.

The situation is identical when compulsory reserves are taken into consideration. Suppose that we are in an economy where customers only wish to use scriptural money and no banknotes. Is it still possible for the central bank to force indebtedness on the part of private banks? The obvious solution is for the central bank to impose compulsory reserve requirements. It does not matter whether the reserves are imposed upon deposits, as they are in most countries and in the United States in particular, or upon loans and other assets, as they were in France and in other European countries. Reserve requirements have consequences similar to those of central bank banknotes on the accounting structure of banks. Again, because banks in an overdraft system have no assets to sell to the central bank, banks have no choice but to borrow the required reserves, at the rate of interest charged by the central bank. As shown in Table 21.11, the adjustment to the compulsory reserve requirements is done through the liability side.

Table 21.11. Overdraft economy, with compulsory reserves

Private banks		Central bank	
Assets	Liabilities	Assets	Liabilities
Loans L	Deposits D	Loans R made to private banks	Deposits of private banks (reserves R)
Reserves R	Funds R borrowed from the central bank		

THE OVERDRAFT ECONOMY, WITH TWO BANKS OR SETS OF BANKS

Finally, let us consider the case of two banks, or two sets of banks, within an overdraft economy. Let us sweep away, again for simplification, all the complications associated with compulsory reserves and banknotes issued by the central bank, as well as the own funds of banks. In a previous section, we also considered the case of two sets of banks, but in the absence of a central bank. All discrepancies in the net claims of each bank had to be made good by a bank borrowing funds from another, usually with the help of some clearing agent, the clearing house.

The advantage with an overdraft system based on the central bank is that the private banks need not enter into contracts with each other. In other words, the risk of lending to another bank is now taken over by a public institution, the central bank. Suppose again that there are two kinds of banks, the business bank and the deposit bank. The business bank will consistently run negative balances in the clearing house, while the deposit bank will consistently accumulate surpluses in the clearing house. The clearing house is now the central bank, and what the central bank can do, in contrast to the private clearing house, is itself be the counterpart to the required lending and borrowing operations of the banks when accounts have to be settled at the end of the day.

This is shown in Table 21.12. The discrepancy, for Bank B, between loans and deposits, is exactly equal to the discrepancy, for Bank D, between deposits and loans. And this discrepancy is exactly balanced on the books of the central bank. Provided there is only a small difference between the penalty rate charged on negative settlement balances (the advances provided by the central bank to banks showing a deficiency of funds) and the rate of interest offered by the central bank on the positive settlement balances (the rate of interest on the surplus funds that banks with excess funds deposit at the central bank), there is no incentive for banks to look for the private arrangements described in Table 21.7, such as overnight lending (Henckel et al., 1999).

Table 21.12. Overdraft system, with two banks

Bank B		Bank D	
Assets	Liabilities	Assets	Liabilities
Loans to non-financial agents	Deposits of non-financial agents	Loans to non-financial agents	Deposits of non-financial agents
	Advances from the central bank (negative settle-ment balance)	Deposits at the central bank (positive settle-ment balance)	

Central bank	
Assets	Liabilities
Advances to Bank B	Deposits of Bank D

In other words, provided the central bank is content with making a small profit when running the clearing house, there is no need for private banks to settle their accounts between themselves before relying on the facilities of the central bank for final settlement.

An interesting feature of this overdraft system, with a central bank, is that the amount of high-powered money, here excluding banknotes and including only the amount of deposits which are held at the central bank, has no relationship whatsoever with the total amount of money, or money deposits, in the system. This amount of high-powered money mainly depends on how extensive are the specialisations of the private banks into loan-making and deposit-attracting activities. When banks specialise heavily, the amount of high-powered money will be large relative to economic activity. When all banks move together in step in their lending and deposit businesses, the required amount of high-powered money is quite low, and may even approach zero.

THE CENTRAL BANK IN AN ASSET-BASED ECONOMY: THE POST-CHARTALIST VIEW

Let us now abandon the overdraft economy for a while and deal with the asset-based financial system. In an asset-based economy, there are large stocks of accumulated public debt. In the past, central governments have run public deficits, and as a result there is an outstanding stock of government bonds, which is held by the central bank and by private agents, non-financial and financial ones, banks in particular.

New debt is issued when past issues have come to maturity and the central government is unable to reimburse the debt holders: this is the case of the rollover. New debt is also issued when the government runs a deficit. There are two views with regards to the financing of government deficits. According to the first view, the Treasury, the fiscal arm of government, sells bonds to private banks. According to the second view, the Treasury draws cheques from its account at the central bank, and sells bonds to the central bank in order to replenish its bank account at the central bank. The latter view is endorsed in particular by the neo-chartalists from within the post-Keynesian school (Wray, 1998; Mosler and Forstater, 1999; Bell, 2000). The former view – let us call it the post-chartalist view – sees government expenditures in a light that is akin to that of expenditures by private firms: firms need to borrow from banks to make their expenditures. The bonds issued by the government and purchased by banks play a role similar to that of the advances made by banks to firms (Lavoie, 1992, Ch. 4).

Let us suppose that the government is running a deficit, say equal to 100 units, and hence issues Treasury bills (short-run government bonds) in that amount. The bills are then bought by a private bank, in line with the post-chartalist view. The counterpart to this purchase are the deposits now credited to the government. This possibility is quite realistic, as is recognised even by neo-chartalists. Wray (1998, p. 118) for instance points out that '[w]hen new government debt is auctioned, the Treasury often designates a portion of the auction as being eligible for purchase through credit by special depositories. In this case, the special depository obtains the bond as an asset by issuing a deposit in the name of the Treasury'.

In the second stage, however, the deposits will revert to households, as soon as the planned government expenditures are made good. This is illustrated in Table 21.13, where only the relevant transactions are shown.

Table 21.13. Treasury bills sold to private banks

Private banks, first stage		Private banks, second stage	
Assets	Liabilities	Assets	Liabilities
Treasury bills +100	Treasury deposits +100	Treasury bills +100	Household deposits +100

Table 21.14. Treasury bills sold to private banks, with banknotes

Central bank		Private banks	
Assets	Liabilities	Assets	Liabilities
Treasury bills +10	Deposits of banks +10	Treasury bills +90	Household deposits +100
		Reserves +10	
Treasury bills +10	Banknotes +10	Treasury bills +90	Household deposits +90
	Deposits of banks 0	Reserves 0	

Let us now assume that households wish to keep 90 per cent of their money holdings in the form of bank deposits, and 10 per cent in the form of banknotes. Let us assume, as in the previous section, that all banknotes are issued by the central bank. Again the question arises as to how the private bank will be able to obtain the banknotes that are demanded by its customers. In this asset-based financial system, private banks do not need to borrow from the central bank to obtain the banknotes; private banks simply need to sell to the central bank some of the Treasury bills which are part of their assets.

In the present case, since households desire 10 units of additional banknotes, banks will be selling 10 units worth of Treasury bills to the central bank, thus acquiring a deposit of 10 units at the central bank (that is, their reserves have now increased by 10 units). The private banks are thus left with 90 units of Treasury bills, while their reserves have increased by 10 units, as shown in the first row of Table 21.14. In the second stage, and this is shown in the second row of Table 21.14, banks will use their reserves to provide their customers with the 10 units of banknotes that they desire, and hence their reserves will fall back to zero while the deposits held by households fall from 100 to 90 units.

THE CENTRAL BANK IN AN ASSET-BASED ECONOMY: THE NEO-CHARTALIST VIEW

Will the situation be any different if Treasury bills issued to pay for government expenditures or deficits are sold directly to the central bank, as the neo-chartalists would generally put it? The answer is no, ultimately it will not. Table 21.15 illustrates this second case, the case put forth by the neo-chartalists. The first row of Table 21.15 shows the impact of the initial sale of Treasury bills on the accounts of the central bank. This sale has no impact whatsoever on the money supply and the private economy as long as the newly acquired government deposits are not spent in the economy.

Table 21.15. Treasury bills sold to the central bank, with banknotes

Central bank		Private banks	
Assets	Liabilities	Assets	Liabilities
Treasury bills +100	Government deposits +100		
Treasury bills +100	Deposits of banks +100	Reserves +100	Household deposits +100
Treasury bills +10	Banknotes +10	Treasury bills +90	Household deposits +90

Once the expenditures of government have actually occurred, as shown in the second row of Table 21.15, the deposits of government at the central bank are now held by households or firms as deposits at private banks. But since the cheques were drawn from the central bank, the banks, the customers of which received the cheques, now detain deposits of their own at the central bank. In other words, the reserves of banks have increased by 100 units.

Banks now dispose of excess reserves of 100 units. In the mainstream story, these 100 units of excess reserves would allow the private banks to provide new loans and start the money multiplier process. The post-Keynesian story at this stage is entirely different however. In the post-Keynesian view, banks provide loans first, and search for reserves later. Banks do not wait for excess reserves to be provided to them like manna from heaven. They grant loans whenever a credit-worthy customer shows up. It follows that when banks wind up with excess reserves, they have already granted all the loans that they could have made. The fact that they now have excess reserves, or positive settlement balances, does not make their potential customers more credit-worthy.

What, then, are banks going to do with their excess reserves? The simple answer is that banks will attempt to purchase safe liquid assets with these reserves. The safest and most liquid assets are the Treasury bills. Banks will thus purchase Treasury bills. Since there is no increase in credit to private agents and hence in bank deposits, beyond the initial increase, excess reserves in the financial system will only be eliminated if the Treasury bills purchased by the banks are sold by the central bank. What we have here is an example of open market operation, but here at the initiative of the private banks.

If there are no reserve requirements and if there is no demand for additional central bank banknotes by the bank customers, banks will use the entire reserve amount of 100 units to purchase Treasury bills. In the present case, let us assume, as we did in the previous case, illustrated with the help of Table 21.14, that households now wish to hold 10 extra units of banknotes. Banks will thus purchase 90 units of Treasury bills, using 10 units of their excess reserves to acquire the banknotes that are demanded by the households. The deposits of households, once they have acquired the banknotes, will thus be reduced to 90 units. The last row of Table 21.15 is now exactly identical to the last row of Table 21.14. Whether the Treasury bills used to finance government expenditures are initially sold to the central bank or to private banks makes no difference whatsoever to the final requirements of the banking system.

Which view best describes the financial relationship between government and the banking system, the neo-chartalist view of Table 21.15 or the post-chartalist view of Table 21.14? It really does not matter. Each view may correspond better to the existing institutional arrangements. In Europe, with the new European Central Bank, central governments just cannot sell any of their newly issued securities to their national central bank or to the European Central Bank. They must sell their bonds or bills to the private banks. Similar rules apply in the United States. 'The Federal Reserve is prohibited by law from adding to its net position by direct purchases of securities from the Treasury – that is, the Federal Reserve has no authority for direct lending to the Treasury. As a consequence, at most the Desk's acquisition at Treasury auctions can equal maturing holdings' (Akhtar, 1997, p. 37). Thus, at least in Europe or in the United States, the post-chartalist view may seem to apply best on this issue.

THE GROWING REPO MARKETS

In standard textbooks, central banks are said to control the amount of high-powered money and money supply through open market operations. Such open market operations have been described in the above section. Open market operations occur on secondary markets, that is, they deal with second-hand securities, which have already been issued and sold. Open market operations are usually understood as outright purchases or sales of government bonds by the central bank. A large proportion of open market operations are however conducted on different terms.

The so-called repurchase agreements (repos, RP) and reverse repos add flexibility and security to the conduct of monetary policy. With repurchase agreements central banks can add or subtract liquidities to the financial system, but on a temporary basis, say one week. So, if at the end of the week central bankers desire to call back the previously injected liquidities, they need do nothing; the adjustment will be automatic. 'Under the RP agreement, the Desk buys securities from dealers who agree to repurchase them at a specified price on a specified date. The added reserves are extinguished automatically when the RPs mature' (Akhtar, 1997, p. 37). Reverse repos do the opposite: they allow the central bank to reduce the liquidities that would be temporarily in excess amount, and to reverse this operation automatically at the end of the purchase and resale agreement.

The repos and reverse repos, however, should be understood for what they are: both the central bank and the banks are perfectly willing to engage in these special kinds of open market operations. In the case of the reverse repo for instance, the central bank wants to drain excess reserves, in order to maintain the overnight rate (the federal funds rate in the United States) at the level of its choice, that is near the discount rate set explicitly by the central bank. The banks on the other hand want to get rid of excess funds that would draw either no interest rate (as in the United States) or a rate of interest below market rates (as in Canada) if it were to be deposited at the central bank.

Repo and reverse repo operations are now the main tool of monetary policy, having so replaced outright open market operations. The Bank of Canada for instance does not conduct traditional outright open market operations in the Treasury bill market since 1995 (Lundrigan and Toll, 1997–8, p. 36). It only enters into repo or reverse repo agreements, mainly in the overnight repo market (one-day transactions). In addition, the repo markets have taken extraordinary importance in many countries over the last few years. The growth of the repo market has been exponential in the United States, in Canada and in other countries. The explosion of the repo market and its use of Treasury bills as an alternative liquid reserve asset have been due essentially to three phenomena.

First, there have been improvements in electronic payment systems and broker systems, which induce agents in search of temporary liquidity or with provisional excess funds to engage in a repo. Second, there is the fact that, with the advent of electronic large-value payments transfer systems, electronic banking transactions (electronic cheques so to speak) are cleared immediately, but on a bilateral gross basis, rather than at the end of the day, on a multilateral net basis. This is called a *real-time gross settlement system*. Its advantage is that settlement is final as soon as the transaction occurs, whereas in the case of net settlements, payment becomes a certainty only at the end of the day, when the net accounts are settled. The disadvantage is that gross settlement requires large stocks of reserve-acting assets. The shift from net to gross settlement payment systems explains why banks have acquired large amounts of government bonds in the 1990s, and why there has been such an increase in the size of the repo market (Henckel et al., 1999, p. 14).

Third, it should be noted that from the point of view of the bank granting the liquidity, the repo is like a collaterised loan. Indeed, this is how the BIS (1988, p. 24) views repos. The loan is backed by a Treasury bill. But this Treasury bill is being held and owned by the bank (for the duration of the repo), not by the borrower. In the balance sheet of the bank, this loan will not appear as a loan, but rather as a Treasury bill. Since capital adequacy ratios attach no risk to this kind of asset, loans based on repos can totally circumvent the capital adequacy requirements.

TRANSFERS OF GOVERNMENT DEPOSITS

There are however other means, beyond repos and open market or discount window operations, at the disposal of the central bank to add liquidities to or to subtract liquidities from financial markets. Many central banks, in particular the Bank of Canada, now use transfers of government deposits between the books of the central bank and those of private banks. To increase liquidities in the banking system, government deposits are transferred from the central bank to private banks; to subtract liquidities, government deposits are transferred the other way.

These government deposit transfers are often used to compensate the flows originating from government expenditures and collected taxes. We have already seen, with the help of Table 21.14, that government expenditures financed by cheques drawn on the central bank automatically lead to the creation of excess reserves. Reciprocally, taxes collected from private agents and deposited as government deposits in the accounts of the central bank withdraw reserves from the banking system. An obvious way for neutralising these effects is to transfer government deposits the other way. For instance, if, near the deadline for income tax collection, cheques made by households to the order of the Treasury have been settled at the clearing house, the liquidities of the banks may be replenished by the central bank simply by moving government deposits back to the accounts of the private banks.

This is shown with the help of Table 21.16. Suppose households have paid their taxes with cheques worth 100 units. Private banks then lose the equivalent of 100 units of reserves, as shown in the first row of Table 21.16. But the loss can be made good by the autonomous transfer of government deposits from the books of the central bank to those of the private banks, as shown in the second row of Table 21.16. Reserves will then come back to their zero level.

Table 21.16. Transfers of government deposits

Central bank		Private banks	
Assets	Liabilities	Assets	Liabilities
	Government deposits +100	Reserves −100	Household deposits −100
	Deposits of banks −100		
	Government deposits 0	Reserves 0	Household deposits −100
	Deposits of banks 0		Government deposits +100

There is another way to neutralise the effects of government expenditures and collected taxes. Instead of setting up compensating account transfers, one could attempt to avoid account transfers altogether. This is done by setting up government accounts in private banks, thus paying government expenditures with cheques drawn on the government deposit accounts in those private banks; symmetrically, these government accounts at private banks could serve as collection points for tax receipts. Collected taxes would thus accumulate in the government accounts at the private banks, with no effect on high-powered money (Wray, 1998, p. 115). The only change is that the deposits of the private agents diminish by the amount of the collected taxes, while government deposits in private banks increase by the same amount. In the United States such a regime is in place, with the so-called Treasury and loan note option accounts at depository institutions (Akhtar, 1997, p. 20). This feature gives some additional credence to the post-chartalist view.

Still, the neo-chartalists offer an important insight: when government spends from its central bank account, there is an automatic expansion in the supply of high-powered money, unless the central bank takes the counter-acting decision to drain the excess reserves so created. In other words, government deficits financed from the central bank account tend to lower interest rates, unless other measures are taken. This runs in opposition to the standard neoclassical story, based on the IS–LM model, according to which public deficits crowd out private investment, because they lead to higher interest rates. The IS–LM model is based on the hypothesis of a given exogenously supplied money stock which is incompatible with a coherent treatment of stock–flow analysis. The correct story is that when banks acquire the excess reserves, they will try to get rid of them by purchasing Treasury bills, as illustrated in Table 21.15. The central bank will be quite content to accommodate these purchases by providing reverse repos, getting involved in open market operations, or shifting government deposits away from the banks, unless it desires to reduce interest rates.

OPEN ECONOMY CONSIDERATIONS

We have not yet taken into account the outside world. In the mainstream story, with fixed exchange rates, a balance of payments surplus leads to an automatic increase in high-powered money and in the money supply, unless the monetary authorities decide to engage into so-called sterilisation operations. The story ends by claiming that the increase in the money supply drives up domestic prices, thus eventually slowing down net exports and eliminating the surplus in the balance of payments, just as in the old gold-specie mechanism. In the Mundell–Fleming mainstream story, money is endogenous with fixed exchange rates, but this endogeneity is supply-led, in the sense that more money is being provided from abroad, regardless of the domestic demand for money.

Monetary economics based on the post-Keynesian view rejects these mechanisms and provides another interpretation, the so-called compensation approach (Lavoie, 2001). The compensation approach applies both to overdraft economies and to asset-based economies. Let us start with the case of an overdraft economy, perhaps the simplest one. Suppose that the economy is running a positive balance of payments, and hence that domestic agents have been accumulating foreign currency which they have exchanged at the central bank. The initial situation, with which all economists would agree, is described by the first row of Table 21.17. The private banks, in the name of their clients, are selling foreign currencies to the central bank, which is accumulating foreign assets; as a result the private banks are accumulating deposits, or reserves, on the accounts of the central bank.

Table 21.17. Positive balance of payments, overdraft economy

Central bank		Private banks	
Assets	Liabilities	Assets	Liabilities
Foreign reserves +100	Deposits of banks +100	Reserves +100	Deposits of exporters +100
Foreign reserves +100	Deposits of banks 0	Reserves 0	Deposits of exporters +100
Loans to domestic banks −100			Loans from the central bank −100

In an overdraft economy, however, private banks are indebted vis-à-vis the central bank. The accumulated reserves will thus be used by the banks to reduce their debt vis-à-vis the central bank. At the end of the process, as described by the second row of Table 21.17, there are no additional bank reserves; banks however have managed to reduce the amounts they owe to the central bank.

One may argue that mainstream theory is still correct, for the amount of bank deposits has risen by the amount of additional bank deposits now in the hands of the exporters, as shown in Table 21.17. But even this increase is illusory. Now that the exporters have been paid, they are in a position to reimburse the loans that were consented to them to produce and ship their exported goods. As a consequence, the exporters may also use their deposits to pay down their debts, and, with this second round of compensation effects, there would be no increase at all in the money supply.

Let us now consider the case of the asset-based economy. Let us assume again a positive balance of payments, with the consequences illustrated in the first row of Table 21.18. The situation is nearly identical to that described in the second row of Table 21.14. Once again, banks have excess reserves which they do not wish to use to increase loans since they have already, by assumption, granted all the loans that they could make to credit-worthy borrowers. Hence, private banks once more will attempt to get rid of these unwanted reserves by purchasing Treasury bills from the central bank. Simultaneously, the central bank will be quite willing to sell bonds, for it wishes to drain the excess reserves.

Table 21.18. Positive balance of payments, asset-based economy

Central bank		Private banks	
Assets	Liabilities	Assets	Liabilities
Foreign reserves +100	Deposits of banks +100	Reserves +100	Deposits of exporters +100
Foreign reserves +100 Treasury bills −100	Deposits of banks 0	Reserves 0 Treasury bills +100	Deposits of exporters +100

In the mainstream story, this action is called sterilisation. But it should be noted that the neutralisation that occurs is at the initiative of the private banks, which have no desire to keep excess reserves or to make additional loans. The central bank, unless it wishes to modify the overnight rate, will be quite happy to accommodate the purchases of the private banks. As in the case of government expenditures, the central bank can also wipe out the excess liquidities arising from the positive balance of payments by removing government deposits from its accounts at the private banks.

ELECTRONIC MONEY

Over the last years, several articles in the popular press and also in academia have underlined the dangers arising from the generalised use of electronic money, in particular an increased difficulty for the central bank to pursue an adequate monetary policy. Different people, however, have different definitions of electronic money. The debates regarding the definition of money or electronic money, and the debates regarding the ability of the central bank to still have some control over monetary policy are remindful of the debates that occurred in the nineteenth century when the usage of the cheque became widespread: were bank deposits to be counted as money or ought they be excluded? These past debates look rather silly today, and today's debates might appear in a similar light in the near future.

As a first approximation, one may consider that there are five kinds of electronic money: (a) large value transfers, done by electronic means; (b) prepaid cards, such as electronic cash, electronic purses, smart cards; (c) credit cards, such as Visa cards; (d) debit cards, that directly take funds from deposit accounts when purchases are made; (e) internet money.

Credit cards and debit cards have now been in operation for a number of years, and people understand their purpose. Debit cards act like a cheque that would be cleared instantaneously. In general, to be able to use the debit card, the bank deposit needs to have a positive balance, unless its user has a pre-arranged credit line with the bank. On the other hand, credit cards increase the velocity of money, for households can buy goods whenever they wish to, and they can pay down the amount due on their credit card the day they get paid.

Finally there is the question of prepaid cards, such as electronic purses, and internet money, which is used to pay goods purchased on the internet. It is clear that prepaid cards play the role of coins and banknotes issued by central banks. As their name indicates, prepaid cards have been paid in advance. They are plastic cash. The act of buying a prepaid cash card is similar to the act of going to one's bank and getting the automatic teller machine to withdraw a certain number of units from one's bank deposit in exchange of banknotes. It is thus clear that the attempt to generalise the use of prepaid cards is similar to an attempt by the banks to issue their own banknotes in lieu of central bank banknotes.

Exactly the same conclusion can be drawn with respect to the use of internet money. Internet money tends to reduce the amount of bank deposits and the amount of banknotes. It is as if banks were issuing their own banknotes. In other words, prepaid cards and internet money are the modern equivalent of the private banknotes that used to be issued by private banks a century or so ago. This can be demonstrated with the following T-accounts.

When agents want to have internet money, they must first obtain a deposit account in the books of some issuer of electronic money, usually a scheme operator who is itself a branch of some bank (Piffaretti, 1998). The agents thus draw on their deposit accounts at their bank, and obtain instead a deposit in the books of the issuer. The issuer in turn has a claim over the bank, which itself has a debt vis-à-vis its own branch operating the electronic scheme. This can all be seen in the first row of Table 21.19.

Table 21.19. Internet money

Bank		Bank branch issuer (scheme operator)	
Assets	Liabilities	Assets	Liabilities
	Deposits of Agent A −100 Debt towards issuer +100	Credit on Bank +100	Deposits of Agent A +100
	idem	Credit on Bank +100	Internet money of Agent A +100
	idem	Credit on Bank +100	Internet money of Agent B +100
	idem	Credit on Bank +100	Deposits of Agent B +100
	Deposits of Agent A −100 Deposits of Agent B +100		

In the second stage, the deposits of Agent A are transformed into internet money, and then, when the purchase of the good on the internet is completed, the internet money is transferred from Agent A to Agent B. The deposits of Agent A on the books of the issuer of internet money are then finally transferred back on the books of the bank.

While the deposits of the agents are on the books of the issuer of electronic money, the deposits carry no interest. In other words, there is a 'float', of which the electronic bank can take advantage. In addition, in countries where reserves on deposits still exist, there is an additional advantage for this bank involved in electronic banking. The amount that has been transferred out of the bank deposits does not carry reserve requirements any more.

It is clear from the above that internet money plays the role of privately issued banknotes. These banknotes are a debt of the bank towards the bearer of the banknote. In the case of internet money, the bank has a debt towards the issuer of internet money, and hence, indirectly, a debt towards the bearer of internet money. As with banknotes, the law of reflux applies: there cannot be an excess supply of banknotes.

CENTRAL BANKING IN A WORLD WITHOUT HIGH-POWERED MONEY

Some authors, of various persuasions, have recently argued that the electronic money revolution might erode the ability of central banks to pursue monetary policy (Palley, 2000; Spotton Visano, 2000). Here I argue that internet money does not jeopardise the ability of central banks to control the money supply – central banks never had that power in the first place. In addition, internet money does not jeopardise the ability of central banks to set short-term rates of interest – the ability of central banks to set overnight rates does not depend on their monopoly power over the supply of banknotes; rather their control over short-term interest rates depends on their ability to participate to the payment system. Fears that the generalisation of electronic money might make the central bank impotent are thus unwarranted.

The generalisation of electronic payments, in my view, has not reduced the ability of central banks to conduct monetary policy. On the contrary, it may have facilitated the work of monetary authorities. For instance, electronic large-value transfer systems (LVTS) are now widespread, and in fact, because these operations have to go through computers, it is even easier for central bankers to keep a check on them and to take them into account when deciding on the amounts of reserves that have to be added to or subtracted from the banking system. In other words, central banks are better equipped than ever to hit their targeted overnight rate of interest.

The introduction of electronic money and electronic payments has made the existing financial system even more in tune with post-Keynesian theory. We are in the so-called zero-reserve financial system, which some people call an *anchorless* or a *Keynesian* banking system (Rymes, 1998) and which others call a world *without money* (Black, 1970). What is really meant is not that deposit money is non-existent, but rather that the amount of high-powered money is zero.

In such a 'world without money', why is it still possible for the central bank to set interest rates? By setting an upper and a lower limit on interest rates, a central bank is able to have perfect control over short-term rates of interest, even if there are no reserve requirements and if banknotes have been entirely eliminated. Thus the power of the central bank to set interest rates does not depend on its monopoly over the issue of high-powered money. Rather, central banks retain the power to set interest rates either because, by law, they force private banks to settle their accounts on the books of the central bank, or because they offer this possibility to private banks, at a cost which no other institution could match.

The payment system could even be run by a private institution, provided the central bank is given full membership to the clearing house. However, the fact that central banks are the only entity to retain the power to corner the market, by forcing *all* banks to borrow from the central bank, gives central banks the greatest credibility in terms of interest rate announcements. This central banks can do, as emphasised by the neo-chartalist authors, by moving the proceeds of government taxation from private bank deposit accounts to government accounts at the central bank.

Instances of this power are offered in Tables 21.18 and 21.19. In both instances, suppose there are no reserve requirements and no demand for (central bank) banknotes. These components are thus totally absent from the liability side of the central bank's balance sheet. Let us then distinguish two cases: the case where governments run mostly budget surpluses, which can most easily be associated with overdraft financial systems (Table 21.20); and the case where governments are running budget deficits, which can most easily be associated with asset-based financial systems (Table 21.21).

In the overdraft case, start with a government asking for advances from the banking system to pay for its expenditures (200 units), at the going rate of interest. The balance sheet of private banks will look as shown in Table 21.20. These deposits will then be transferred to households, but they will soon revert in an even greater amount to the government, as households pay their taxes. On the assumption that the government is running a 50-unit surplus, the government will then be in a position to reimburse the advances that it took and will be left with a portion of its deposits (50 units). The central bank can force banks to be in a negative settlement balance position by moving some of the remaining government deposits from the private banks to its own account (here 30 units). To settle their accounts with the central bank at the clearing house, banks have no choice: they are forced to draw advances from the central bank – as they would have to do in a pure overdraft economy with central bank money or compulsory reserve requirements.

Table 21.20. A world without money: government surpluses and overdraft economies

Central bank		Private banks	
Assets	Liabilities	Assets	Liabilities
		Loans to governm. +200	Government deposits +200
		Loans to governm. +200	Household deposits +200
		Loans to governm. +200	Government deposits +250
			Household deposits −50
Advances to private banks +30	Government deposits +30	Loans to governm. 0	Government deposits +20
			Household deposits −50
			Funds borrowed from the central bank +30

A similar situation arises when the government is running a deficit. Assume that in this asset-based economy, government expenditures (200 units) are financed by issuing Treasury bills, with rates of return high enough to induce private banks to purchase them. In exchange, the Treasury will be credited with deposits on the books of these banks. This is shown in Table 21.21. Once again the deposits are first transferred to households when the government actually incurs its expenditures, but part of these funds – only part of them since we assume a government budget deficit of 50 units – will be flowing back to government deposit accounts when taxpayers pay their taxes. In the example given, the government lets 100 units of Treasury bills to mature without renewal. Once more, the central bank can force banks to be in a negative settlement balance position by moving some of the government deposits, from the tax accounts at the private banks to the government account at the central bank (here 30 units once more). To settle their accounts with the central bank at the clearing house, banks once again have no choice. This time, they must sell some of their Treasury bills to the central bank (30 units).

Table 21.21. A world without money: government deficits and asset-based economies

Central bank		Private banks	
Assets	Liabilities	Assets	Liabilities
		Treasury bills +200	Government deposits +200
		Treasury bills +200	Household deposits +200
		Treasury bills +200	Government deposits +150 Household deposits +50
		Treasury bills +100	Government deposits +50 Household deposits +50
Treasury bills +30	Government deposits +30	Treasury bills +70	Government deposits +20 Household deposits +50

It is true that the banks could refuse to renew their holdings of Treasury bills when these mature, in which case the rolled-over bonds would have to be sold to the households. Such an extreme situation will not occur, however, as long as banks are required to hold government bonds in their portfolio. This may happen either because of direct mandatory regulations, such as minimum secondary reserve requirements, or because of indirect regulations, banks being induced to hold safe assets such as government bonds since they have no adverse effect on their capital adequacy ratios. Finally, with real-time gross settlement systems, banks need ever-larger stocks of government bonds, to be able to settle their transactions with the other members of the clearing system without encountering any risk.

It must thus be concluded that, whether the government is in a deficit or surplus situation, and regardless of whether the economy is of the overdraft or asset-based type, it is always possible for the central bank to control interest rates and to force banks to be in an overall negative settlement balance position, even if there are no reserve requirements and no demand for central bank money.

In Canada, for instance, where rules oblige banks to clear payments through the central bank, banks that have negative settlement balances can settle their accounts by borrowing from the central bank at the discount rate (say 6 per cent), that is, by arranging for a collaterised overdraft. The banks that have positive settlement balances can deposit these balances at the Bank of Canada, at a rate which is 50 basis points below the discount rate (say 5.50 per cent). As a result, banks usually try to find some arrangement between themselves, those with positive balances making loans to those with negative balances. As a matter of fact, almost all of these loans are fully collaterised, since they are made in the repo market described earlier (debts are settled with repos). The rate at which these one-day loans or pseudo-loans are arranged, the overnight rate, is almost always to be found right in the middle of the band between the discount rate and the deposit rate at the Bank of Canada (here 5.75 per cent). The Bank of Canada, as do most of the other central banks, thus has a nearly perfect control over the shortest of the interest rates, although private banks generally hold no settlement balances (Clinton, 1997).

CONCLUSION

The purpose of this chapter was to elaborate a simple, yet consistent, story relating credit creation and money endogeneity. Causality is probably the most crucial aspect of economics: this is how, in many instances, theories can be distinguished from one another. The T-accounts that have been presented thus must be comprehended with the causal story that has been appended. This causal story underlines the importance of credit-worthiness and confidence, as well as the autonomy of credit creation from the previous existence of bank deposits. The coherence of the described financial system also relies on the law of reflux, the existence of credit lines, and the acquisition of own funds.

Several issues have not been dealt with. The multiplicity of financial instruments has been assumed away. Thus only the determination of interest rates of the shortest term has been discussed, while the relationship between these very short rates and the rates of assets of longer maturity has been left aside. In any case, the relationship between these rates and the various financial aggregates should be treated within a fully integrated accounting framework, where all flows and all stocks are accounted for. This is rarely done in macroeconomics, although there are some exceptions, such as Godley (1999), whose method readers would be well-advised to study.

NOTES

1. The essence of this chapter was presented in a class given to fourth-year students of the Université Pierre Mendès-France, in Grenoble, where the author was Visiting Professor in the Spring of 2000, following the initiative of Ramon Tortajada. It was also presented in the same year to the students of the graduate course, *Explorations in Monetary Economics*, at the University of Ottawa. The author wishes to thank Claude Gnos, John Kutyn and Warren Mosler for their numerous and useful comments.

REFERENCES

Akhtar, M.A. (1997), *Understanding Open Market Operations*, New York: Federal Reserve Bank of New York, Public Information Department.

Arnon, A. (1993), 'The policy implications of classical monetary theory: Between the two hands', in G. Mongiovi and C. Rühl (eds), *Macroeconomic Theory: Diversity and Convergence*, Aldershot and Brookfield: Edward Elgar, 110–22.

Bell, S. (2000), 'Do taxes and bonds finance government spending?', *Journal of Economic Issues*, **34** (3), 603–20.

BIS Basle Committee on Banking Supervision (1988), *International Convergence of Capital Measurement and Capital Standard*, Basle: Bank for International Settlements.

Black, F. (1970), 'Banking and interest rates in a world without money', *Journal of Banking Research*, **1** (3), 8–20.

Brossard, O. (1998), 'Comportements vis-à-vis de la liquidité et instabilité conjoncturelle: une réflexion sur la préférence pour la liquidité', *Cahiers d'économie politique*, (30–31), 123–46.

Chick, V. (1986), 'The evolution of the banking system and the theory of saving, investment and interest', *Économies et Sociétés* ('Série Monnaie et Production', 3), **20** (8–9), 111–26.

Clinton, K. (1997), 'Implementation of monetary policy in a regime with zero reserve requirements', Bank of Canada *Working Paper*, 97-8.

de Boyer, J. (1998), 'Endogenous money and shareholders' funds in the classical theory of banking', *European Journal of the History of Economic Thought*, **5** (1), 60–84.

Godley, W. (1999), 'Money and credit in a Keynesian model of income determination', *Cambridge Journal of Economics*, **23** (4), 393–411.

Henckel, T., A. Ize and A. Kovanen (1999), 'Central banking without central bank money', International Monetary Fund *Working Paper*, 99/92.

Hicks, J.R. (1974), *The Crisis in Keynesian Economics*, Oxford: Basil Blackwell.

Keynes, J.M. (1930/1971), *A Treatise on Money*, London: Macmillan. Reprinted in *The Collected Writings of John Maynard Keynes*, Vol. V, London and Basingstoke: Macmillan.

Lavoie, M. (1992), *Foundations of Post-Keynesian Economic Analysis*, Aldershot and Brookfield: Edward Elgar.

Lavoie, M. (2001), 'The reflux mechanism and the open economy', in L.-P. Rochon and M. Vernengo (eds), *Credit, Interest Rates and the Open Economy: Essays on Horizontalism*, Cheltenham and Northampton: Edward Elgar, 215–42.

Lundrigan, E. and S. Toll (1997–8), 'The overnight market in Canada', *Bank of Canada Review*, 27–42.

Marchal, J. and F. Poulon (1987), *Monnaie et crédit dans l'économie française*, Paris: Cujas.

Moore, B.J. (1988), *Horizontalists and Verticalists: The Macroeconomics of Credit Money*, Cambridge: Cambridge University Press.

Mosler, W. and M. Forstater (1999), 'A general framework for the analysis of currencies and commodities', in P. Davidson and J. Kregel (eds), *Full Employment and Price Stability in a Global Economy*, Cheltenham and Northampton: Edward Elgar, 166–77.

Palley, T. (2000), 'The e-money revolution: Challenges and implications for monetary policy', AFL–CIO (Washington, DC), Public Policy Department, *Economic Policy Paper*, E045.

Piffaretti, N. (1998), 'A theoretical approach to electronic money', Faculty of Economic and Social Sciences, University of Fribourg, *Working Papers*, 302.

Renversez, F. (1996), 'Monetary circulation and overdraft economy', in G. Deleplace and E.J. Nell (eds), *Money in Motion: The Post Keynesian and Circulation Approaches*, London: Macmillan, 465–88.

Rochon, L.-P. (1999), *Credit, Money and Production: An Alternative Post-Keynesian Approach*, Cheltenham and Northampton: Edward Elgar.

Rossi, S. (1998), 'Endogenous money and banking activity: some notes on the workings of modern payment systems', *Studi economici*, **53** (3), 23–56.

Rymes, T.K. (1998), 'Keynes and anchorless banking', *Journal of History of Economic Thought*, **20** (1), 71–82.

Spotton Visano, B. (2000), 'Electronic finance and exchange rate regimes: Industry changes and the question of a single North American currency', *The Political Economy of Monetary Integration: Lessons from Europe and Canada*, Conference paper, University of Ottawa, October, mimeo.

Wray, L.R. (1995), 'Keynesian monetary theory: liquidity preference or black box horizontalism?', *Journal of Economic Issues*, **29** (1), 273–80.

Wray, L.R. (1998), *Understanding Modern Money: The Key to Full Employment and Price Stability*, Cheltenham and Northampton: Edward Elgar.

22. The Gold Standard and Centre–Periphery Interactions

Matias Vernengo[1]

INTRODUCTION

The gold standard prevailed as the dominant international monetary system roughly from the 1870s to 1914.[2] This period corresponds to the dominance of the commodity export model of development in the peripheral countries. In other words, the international division of labour implied that centre countries exported manufacturing goods and imported commodities from the periphery. Therefore, an export-led strategy of development in the periphery characterised this period.

In this period few commodities dominated the exports of the periphery to the core industrial countries. For example, in Latin America the main exports by country were meat from Argentina, coffee from Brazil, copper from Chile, tobacco from Colombia, sugar from Cuba, guano from Peru, and cacao from Venezuela. The extreme dependency of the balance of payments on one single commodity implied that these peripheral countries were extremely vulnerable to changes in the terms of trade. Export revenues were essential to service the foreign debts incurred during the period, in general with British banks, and for importing essential goods to accelerate the development process.

A fall in the terms of trade implied the impossibility to serve the debt, and forced a default that led to the abandonment of the gold standard. Hence, the periphery was for most of the time off the gold standard system, and effectively in an exchange gold system.[3] This chapter will analyse the main effects of this hybrid system on the balance of payments adjustment mechanism of central and peripheral countries. It will be argued that the conventional wisdom that assumed a smooth and symmetrical adjustment of the balance of payments in the centre and periphery is incorrect. The next section discusses alternative views to the price–specie flow mechanism. The third section deals with the empirical problems of the conventional view of the functioning of the gold standard. The last section puts together an alternative in which the asymmetries between centre and periphery are directly connected to both endogenous money and effective demand.

BEYOND THE SPECIE-FLOW MECHANISM

Most economic historians tend to look at the gold standard as an idyllic time in which the stability of the international monetary system led to prosperity. Conventional wisdom tells us that the gold standard was a self-adjusting system. David Hume (1752/1969) first presented the notion of a stable and self-adjusting balance of payments in his well-known 'Of the balance of trade'. According to Eichengreen (1996, p. 25), 'the most influential formalization of the gold-standard is the price–specie flow model of David Hume. Perhaps the most remarkable feature of this model is its durability: developed in the eighteenth century, it remains the dominant approach to thinking about the gold standard'.

In the simple model developed by Hume (1752/1969), a country with a trade deficit would pay for the excess of imports over exports in gold specie, generating an outflow of gold. This outflow of gold would reduce the stock of gold in the country, thus reducing the domestic price level, according to the principles of the quantity theory of money (QTM). Finally, deflation at home would restore the international competitiveness of domestic goods, leading to the elimination of the trade deficit. In other words, the balance of payments was self-adjusting.

It is usually assumed that classical political economists in general accepted Hume's specie flow mechanism. However, a more detailed look at the views of the classical authors show that their views did not always coincide with that of Hume. David Ricardo and Thomas Tooke were among the authors that were critical of Hume's specie flow mechanism.

For Ricardo, the exchange rate is determined by the supply and demand conditions for bills of exchange. Bills of exchange denominated in pounds were used as means of payment in international trade, even by countries other than Britain. Domestic exports must generate a supply of foreign bills of exchange in the domestic market, whereas domestic imports engender a demand for foreign bills of exchange in the domestic market.

If the demand and supply of bills of exchange are directly connected to the trade activities of the British Empire, then the determinants of the trade flows are the ultimate determinants of the exchange rate. According to Marcuzzo and Rosselli (1986/1991, p. 91), however, from the time of the Napoleonic wars, London displaced Amsterdam and maintained a dominant position not only in international trade, but also in the international capital market. This means that the supply and demand of bills of exchange were also affected by capital flows.

In the case in which the demand and supply of bills of exchange are solely determined by trade flows, one can imagine a simple connection between trade flows, purchasing power and the price–specie flow mechanism. Trade is determined according to the principle of comparative advantage, as in Ricardo's famous example of wine and cloth trade between England and Portugal.[4] However, if a country does have an absolute disadvantage in the production of all commodities, as in the case of England in Ricardo's example, then this country will incur in a temporary trade deficit. This trade deficit will in turn lead to an outflow of gold, which will reduce prices – following the QTM – rendering profitable the exports of the commodities in which the country is relatively more productive.

The price–specie flow mechanism not only will allow the principle of comparative advantage to work, balancing trade flows, but also will maintain the stock of gold in each country at a certain level determining the domestic price level, and hence the exchange rate. Clearly, by balancing trade flows, and rendering the exports of the less productive country profitable, the price–specie flow mechanism determines the demand and supply of bills of exchange. If a country is sold all around, there is no supply of foreign bills in the market, constraining, as a result, the demand for foreign bills. By avoiding this situation the specie flow mechanism determines the exchange rate, which is proportional to the stock of gold in each country, and hence proportional to the price level.

Ricardo's theory, however, is independent of both the QTM and the price–specie flow mechanism, for he clearly was critical of Hume's theory of balance of payments adjustment.[5] According to Ricardo, exports of gold would not occur if the quantity of gold was at its natural level – that is, when the quantity of gold corresponded to the natural price of gold,[6] as determined by the conditions of production of gold.

To understand Ricardo's theory of balance of payments adjustment we will analyse the effects of a subsidy on the balance of payments, since this was the example used by Henry Thornton that Ricardo and Malthus also utilised in their debate.[7] The decision to send a subsidy to a foreign nation created an increase in the demand for bills of exchange denominated in foreign currency in the domestic economy. The result is a fall in the exchange rate. The price–specie flow mechanism assumes that with the fall in the exchange rate it becomes profitable to export gold. The shipment of gold reduces the stock of gold in the domestic country, and raises it in the foreign country, producing the deflationary and inflationary processes that eventually restore equilibrium.

Unlike the defenders of the specie flow mechanism Ricardo argued that once the exchange rate fell, British exporters would rush to increase the supply of bills of exchange denominated in foreign currency, paying with the proceeds of exports – which would increase as a result of the fall of the exchange rate. This rise in the supply of bills of exchange would move the exchange rate towards parity. In contrast with the specie flow mechanism, the subsidy was paid in Ricardo's theory by exporting commodities rather than exporting gold. As a result, the exchange rate does not reflect the equalisation of the purchasing power of gold in different countries.

In addition, Ricardo assumed that the rise in exports would lead to a fall of domestic transactions, and hence to a redundancy of currency. The redundancy of money would make prices rise, reducing the competitiveness of British exports. This fall in exports would imply that the exchange rate would not rise to par, and might be permanently below the initial level, that is, before the subsidy.

As it should be clear, there are two main differences between Ricardo's view of balance of payments adjustment and the specie flow mechanism. The first was already noted above, namely, the fact that gold was not exported when other commodities could be exported.[8] The second difference is that whereas for Hume the devaluation would be followed by domestic deflation, in the Ricardian theory devaluation would lead to domestic inflation.

An even more radical departure from the specie flow mechanism can be found in the works of Thomas Tooke and the Banking school. According to Tooke (1844, p. 121), 'the doctrine by which it is maintained that every export or import of bullion in a metallic circulation must entail a corresponding diminution of, or addition to, the quantity of money in circulation, and thus cause a fall or rise of general prices, is essentially incorrect and unsound'.

The reflux principle, defended by the Banking school, implied that the Bank of England, and banks in general, could not increase or decrease the amount of money in circulation, nor operate through that medium on the prices of commodities. As a result, the only way 'they can influence the exchanges, so as to arrest a drain, or to resist an excessive influx . . . [is] by a forcible action on securities, [that] is . . . a great advance in the rate of interest on the one hand, or a great reduction of it on the other' (Tooke, 1844, p. 121). Monetary policy, through the control of the rate of interest, is then the crucial instrument to direct capital flows, and to deal with balance of payments disequilibria.

Both for Ricardo and the Banking school, foreign exchanges were determined by the supply and demand of bills of exchange. However, whereas for Ricardo foreign trade was the dominant, but not unique, cause of the supply and demand of bills of exchange, for Tooke capital flows seem to have a dominant role. The control of capital flows is the only way to control foreign exchanges, that is, 'it is only through the rate of interest and the state of credit, that the Bank of England can exercise a direct influence on the foreign exchanges' (Tooke, 1844, p. 121).

It must be noted that in Tooke's analysis the rate of interest is the exogenous variable, determined by the monetary authority (Pivetti, 1991).[9] A trade deficit can be closed if the interest rate is raised sufficiently to attract capital flows. Tooke seems to believe that the possibility that there might be a situation in which no level of the rate of interest would attract capital inflows is relatively unimportant. This, in turn, appears to reflect the experience of the Bank of England that could actually command capital flows by changing the bank rate. However, if one is open to the possibility that interest rates fail to command the flows of capital, then something else must close the balance of payments.

Most classical authors remained prisoners of Say's Law, and as a result the level of activity was excluded from any role in adjusting macroeconomic disequilibria. It was only with the formal development of the principle of effective demand by Keynes that the possibility of having the level of income as the adjusting variable entered the scene. In Keynes's work the level of income works as the adjusting variable between savings and investment. In an open economy environment the level of income operates as the adjusting variable for a trade deficit (Harrod, 1933/1957). If a country runs a persistent trade deficit, and capital inflows are lacking, then a reduction in the level of income would lead to a contraction of imports, and the adjustment of the balance of payments.

Structuralist authors pointed out later that even exchange rate movements affect the balance of payments not through its impact on price competitiveness, but through its effect on income distribution and the level of activity. Krugman and Taylor (1978), building on the work by Hirschman and Diaz-Alejandro, show that depreciation leads to a contractionary adjustment if the economy has a trade deficit or if it redistributes income to higher income groups. In the first case, if the volume of imports is high and the value increases after devaluation, contraction of output may be the only way to reduce the trade deficit. In the second case, if the redistributive effect of depreciation increases the income to low spending groups (higher income groups), then a contraction of output also follows.

The picture that emerges from these alternative views to the still dominant price–specie flow mechanism is that certain countries could adjust their balance of payments deficit by attracting capital inflows by manipulating the rate of interest. For the countries for which the previous option is not open, only an output contraction would adjust their balance of payments deficit.

Before trying to analyse what are the conditions that determine whether a country would fall into the first or second category, we will discuss the operation of the gold standard system in practice.

THE MYTH OF THE GOLD STANDARD

One important limitation of Hume's model to characterise the working of the classic gold standard system at the end of the nineteenth century is the assumption that only gold coins circulate, and that there are no other capital flows. In reality, the central banks of the countries involved in the gold standard did not allow gold to move freely from one country to another. Sayers (1976, p. 28) argues that 'for almost a century before 1914 the Bank [of England] regarded itself as primarily responsible for the protection of the gold reserve ... [and] the Bank had settled to the view that it was by the manipulation of an effective Bank Rate that the Bank could protect its reserve consistently with the least harm to the business of the country'.

Bloomfield (1963, p. 2) argues emphatically against the nostalgic references to the

> good old days of the international gold standard ... [since] disequilibrating movements of short term capital, destabilizing exchange speculation, capital flight, threats to the continued maintenance of convertibility, concern as to the adequacy of international reserves and the volume of floating international indebtedness – all these at times were in evidence in the pre-1914 system and in some cases necessitated measures going well beyond routine application of discount-rate policy.

Bloomfield (ibid., pp. 7–19) documents the rise of the official holdings of foreign exchange currencies during the 1880–1914 period. This increase is attributed to the fact that monetary authorities resorted to the sales and purchases of foreign exchange against domestic currency in order to maintain the exchange rate within the limits of the gold points.[10]

Private capital flows were also crucially relevant for the working of the gold standard. So that, in contrast with Hume's model, the gold standard system was characterised by the limited amount of gold coins in circulation. The consensus has been that under the pre-1914 system these capital movements had primarily an equilibrating role in the balance of payments.

The argument goes as follows. Suppose that the exchange rate falls bellow the point that would encourage gold exports. Economic agents would speculate that the exchange rate could not fall, and that it would rise in the near future. As a result, an inflow of capital would follow, leading to the appreciation of the currency. Conversely, if the exchange rate is above its gold import point, there will be expectations that the exchange rate will fall, leading to capital outflows and the actual depreciation. This means that capital flows benignly substitute for flows of gold specie (Eichengreen, 1996).

Bloomfield (1963, p. 91) argues, on the contrary, that capital flows did not always have an equilibrating effect. In fact, for him:

> Threats to convertibility, at times induced or accentuated by disequilibrating capital flows, on more than one occasion necessitated 'extraordinary' defensive measures going well beyond discount-rate increases, which were in any case a rather weak reed for most gold standard countries to lean in normal times. For example, in a number of instances monetary authorities were forced to arrange emergency borrowings of gold and foreign credits in order to cope with dangerous drains on their reserves, and in at least two cases . . . resort was had temporarily to limited forms of exchange rate control.

Capital flows were thus controlled through changes in the rate of interest, and at times by direct capital controls. As noted by Sayers (1976, p. 29), Bloomfield's argument means that the determination of the rate of interest was directly connected to the maintenance of the fixed parity, saying 'nothing of correcting the balance of payments or the balance of trade'. The existence of destabilising capital flows leads De Cecco (1984, p. 20) to argue that the automatic stability of the gold standard system is a myth.

The fact remains that the gold standard was relatively stable from 1870 to 1914, even if the stability was somewhat exaggerated by modern economic historians. However, according to the traditional view the stability was the result of stabilising capital flows, whereas an alternative view, based on Bloomfield's empirical analysis, would suggest that the system was stable despite the existence of destabilising capital flows.

Eichengreen (1992, 1996) represents the most accomplished version of the conventional view on the gold standard. According to him (1992, p. 30), 'the key to the success of the classical gold standard lays . . . in . . . credibility and cooperation'. Credibility followed from the unquestionable commitment of the central banks of the gold standard system to maintain the parity of their respective currencies against gold. Because there were no doubts about this commitment, capital flows moved in the right direction reinforcing the stability of the system, and reducing the need of central bank intervention. In addition, Eichengreen argues – less convincingly – that the Bank of England was not the sole director of an orchestra, as Keynes suggested, but one member, albeit the most important, of a system of central banks that cooperated to maintain the stability of the system.

In this view, the commitment of the central bank to maintain the parity could not have any real effects. The absence of political constraints was an additional blessing. In fact, according to Eichengreen (1992, p. 6) 'labor parties, where they existed, rarely exercised significant influence. Those who might have objected that restrictive monetary policy created unemployment were in no position to influence it. Domestic political pressures did not undermine the credibility of the commitment to gold'. Following modern terminology, Eichengreen argues that central banks were independent and could follow their own policy choices.

It must be emphasised that even if political pressures might have existed, they could have only a short-run effect. In the long run, flexibility in the labour market would lead the economy to the natural rate of unemployment. Also, the manipulation of the capital flows through the manipulation of the rate of interest can only be admitted as a short-run device. In the long run, the natural rate of interest would prevail. Hence the commitment to convertibility, and the credibility attached to it, only meant that equilibrium was reached effortlessly. The rules of the gold standard game, to use the expression coined by Keynes (1925/1972), worked automatically.[11]

As a result, the gold standard implied that the fixed parities between currencies corresponded to the fixed parity of each currency with respect to gold. For a given supply of gold in each country corresponded a domestic price level, and this determined the purchasing power of the domestic currency against foreign currencies. Domestically each country would tend to move towards, in modern language, the natural rate of unemployment. In the absence of short-term disequilibria, the adjustment of the balance of payments would be painless, that is, it would not lead to changes in output and employment. Only the price level would be affected.

The picture that emerges from the conventional interpretation of the operation of the gold standard implies that although capital flows were unstable, and interest rate hikes and capital controls had to be occasionally used, the credible commitment to convertibility made the system relatively stable. Yet, this picture neglects the operation of the gold standard in the peripheral countries. Ford (1962) shows that in the case of Argentina the main adjusting mechanism were changes in the level of income. In fact, for him (1962, p. 189):

> Automatic income adjustment forces (provoked by factors causing balance of payments disequilibria in many cases) provided the main adjustment mechanism, whilst the gold standard 'medicine' of higher interest rates in the face of gold losses played a subsidiary role in promoting long-term adjustment. It is true, however, that for some countries (notably, Britain) the quick effects of increases in rediscount rates which were reflected in market rates of discount were of the utmost importance in easing the strain of gold losses.

In other words, for most countries, which would include all peripheral countries, the main adjustment variable was the level of activity, with the rate of interest having only a secondary role. This adjusting mechanism implies that the gold standard system enhanced the fluctuations of the external sector in the periphery. In addition, this suggests that the adjustment mechanism in the centre and periphery countries was asymmetrical.[12]

In sum, even if one believes that credibility and cooperation rendered the gold standard smooth and self-adjusting in the central countries, this proposition fails to explain the wide fluctuations and instability in the periphery of the system. In these countries, the gold standard tended to work pro-cyclically. Boom years in the centre meant capital inflows, and export-led growth. A weakening on either the exports or the capital inflows, both of which depended on the core countries performance, would imply reserve losses, domestic contraction and eventually foreign debt default and abandoning of the gold system. The details of the asymmetries between centre and periphery are analysed below.

CENTRE–PERIPHERY ASYMMETRIES

The theory of hegemonic stability, developed by Kindleberger (1973), suggests that the stability of the gold standard system resulted from the effective management by the leading hegemonic member, that is, Britain. According to Kindleberger (1973, pp. 289–90), the Bank of England stabilised the system by acting as the lender of last resort, ensuring the coordination of macroeconomic policies, and providing counter-cyclical long-term lending.

This suggests that it was the relevance of England's position in world trade and finance that allowed for the stability of the system. De Cecco (1984, p. 20) refers to the idea that 'the system was really based on sterling rather than gold'. In his own words:

> Her [England] banks in the Colonies and the City allowed long term international investment to take place; this could continue only if money sent out of England as investment came back to England in payment for English goods exported. England, moreover, as the leading country in international finance, satisfied the demand for gold induced by rising incomes in the new countries, and attracted gold from other European gold standard countries by aggregate changes in the Bank of England's discount rate.

In this view, neither credibility nor cooperation was at the centre of the working of the international gold standard. Hegemonic power was instead.

The central role of the City of London as the financial centre of the world allowed the Bank of England to manage the international monetary system. The London City could lend long and borrow short, functioning as the banker of the world.[13] Whenever the exchange rate fell to the gold export point, an increase in the bank rate would avoid the outflow of gold. The command over gold flows was asymmetric, since changes in the interest rates of other countries had less effect than the Bank of England's discount rate.

The emphasis on the relative control that the Bank of England had on the balance of payments through the manipulation of the exogenous rate of interest, however, is not extended to all countries, since it depends on its hegemonic role.[14] Capital flows could be destabilising, but the capacity of the Bank of England to tame them was crucial for the maintenance of the system. In fact, the ability to control capital flows, which is ultimately dependent on the international role of the pound sterling and the role of the City as the main financial centre of the world, allowed Britain to stay on a gold standard for more than a century, a far longer period than any other country (see Table 22.1). The average permanence of central countries on the gold standard was 58 years and a quarter. If we exclude Britain, the average permanence is still quite high, at 39 years.

Periphery countries were not as successful, and on average were on a gold standard for approximately 14 years and a half. If one eliminates the British and American Colonies, which were on an exchange gold system, the average permanence on the system falls even more. Not only the average permanence of periphery countries was much shorter; also, some countries experienced great instability. For example, Argentina and Brazil were expelled from the system in peaceful periods, while the only time Britain suspended gold convertibility before World War I was during the Napoleonic wars.

Table 22.1 also reports the per capita GDP in 1913 (in 1990 dollars), the end of the gold standard period, when almost all countries were still on the system. It is clear that the gold standard did not lead necessarily to a worse overall economic performance in the periphery. The Southern cone (Argentina and Chile) shows that some peripheral countries fared quite well during the period, reaching levels of per capita income that were close or superior to France and Germany.[15] Interestingly enough, both Southern cone countries, despite the high levels of per capita income show an enormous difficulty in maintaining the gold standard system. Argentina dropped the system three times, and Chile has the shortest permanence of all, with only three years. This clearly indicates that the main difference between central and periphery countries during the gold standard period was related to the way they adjusted to balance of payments disequilibria.

Table 22.1. Selected countries on the gold standard

Country	Type	Period	Per capita GDP (1913)[*]
Centre			
Britain	coin	1774–97, 1821–1914	4,921
France	coin	1878–1914	3,485
Germany	coin	1871–1914	3,684
United States	coin	1879–1917	5,301
Periphery			
Argentina	coin	1867–76, 1883–5, 1900–14	3,979
Brazil	coin	1888–9, 1906–14	811
Chile	coin	1895–8	2,653
Egypt	coin	1885–1914	732
India	exchange	1898–1914	673
Mexico	coin	1905–13	1,732
Philippines	exchange	1903–14	1,066
Peru	coin	1901–14	1,037

[*] 1990 dollar values.

Source: EH.Net Encyclopedia, and Maddison (2001).

In periods of recession, as in the last quarter of the nineteenth century, peripheral countries would be unable to attract enough capital, or export enough to central countries, in order to pay the interest and principal of their foreign debts, and to maintain the high levels of imports needed for the process of development. As a result, they would be forced out of the gold standard system, and would let their currencies depreciate. Additionally, for the most part a domestic recession would allow them to reduce the volume of imports. In periods of international growth, as in the first decade of the twentieth century, periphery countries would find enough outlets to their exports, and would attract enough capital to serve their debts and to import.

Central countries, on the other hand, would be able to attract funds, and/or export enough, in order to keep their external accounts in order even in periods of recession. This asymmetry explains why the average permanence of central countries was higher than for periphery countries, and also why most peripheral countries were off the gold standard in the late nineteenth century and on it in the early period of the twentieth century.

More importantly, the adjustment of the balance of payments was independent of the central and peripheral countries' fiscal stances, and of the credibility of their commitment to the gold standard system. The essential difference between centre and periphery was the ability to finance balance of payments disequilibria by issuing debt in its own currency. Britain, and to a lesser degree the other central countries, could borrow in international markets in their own currencies. Higher interest rates then actually worked in bringing the needed capital inflows. The lack of internationally accepted currencies made this sort of solution impossible for peripheral countries.[16] As a result, the only alternative left for the periphery was an income adjustment.

The asymmetry between centre and periphery also plays a role on the demise of the gold standard system. The collapse of the gold standard system can be placed before Britain declared war to the central powers (De Cecco, 1984, p. 128).[17] The reason lies in the erosion of the British position in the international monetary system. The period of the gold standard coincides with the so-called second industrial revolution, in which the United States and Germany caught up with Britain.

The capacity of the British economy to control capital flows was constrained by the increasing challenge from rival financial centres.[18] The period that goes from the abolition of the Corn Laws to the great depression of 1873 was an era of unchallenged dominance of the British economy. The erosion of the British competitive position over the next 25 years was related to unilateral free trade policies in face of the protectionist policies of competing countries.[19]

Britain was able to maintain her dominant position in face of the international challenge, as noted by Hobsbawm (1968/1990, p. 151), 'by exploiting the remaining possibilities of her traditional situation', that is, by shifting the bulk of her trading relationships to the formal and informal Empire.[20] Britain had trade deficits with Europe and the United States, and surpluses with the Empire. Britain was a long-term investor, first in Europe and the United States, then in the Empire, and the rest of the world transformed British investment in demand for British exports. However, the increasing competition by Europe and the United States started to erode the British position as creditor of the world.

The final blow was caused by the war, but the war ultimately brought down a system that was already doomed. According to Hobsbawm (1968/1990, p. 152):

Britain ceased to be the world's greater creditor nation, mainly because she was obliged to liquidate a large part of her investment in the USA ... and in turn became heavily indebted to the USA, which ended the war as the greater creditor nation in its turn.

This means that the gold standard system, based on the capacity of the Bank of England to control capital flows and ensure the fixed parities, collapsed. A new system would have to be built around the new hegemonic power, namely, the United States. From the perspective of this chapter what is crucial is that it was the existence of the peripheral countries, with their income adjustment, that allowed the gold standard system to be successful for such a long period, adding a degree of flexibility that would not be possible for central country standards.

In other words, the income adjustment would not have been feasible in central countries, mainly for political reasons. Hence, central countries relied exclusively on their ability to attract capital inflows by managing the real rate of interest. This view is compatible with the views of the classical political economy authors, in particular those of Tooke and the Banking school, according to which it was the control of the rate of interest that allowed the Bank of England to manage the system. On the other hand, the income adjustment prevailing in peripheral countries is more in line with the views developed by Keynesian and structuralist authors.

CONCLUSION

The main point of this chapter was to show that the conventional view that assumes that the balance of payments adjustment during the gold standard period was smooth and symmetric in the centre and periphery – relying on a credible commitment to the rules of the game and on international cooperation – misses an essential element of the actual operation of the system. In fact, central countries scarcely relied on well-behaved capital flows, and had to manage speculative flows by administrating the rate of interest. On the other hand, the peripheral countries' ability to manage capital flows was heavily restricted, since capital flows would not respond to changes in their interest rates as effectively. As a result, income adjustment dominated in the periphery, resulting in a higher degree of instability.

In turn, the asymmetric adjustment of centre and periphery shows the importance of alternative views on the operation of the balance of payments adjustment. Exogenous interest rates (endogenous money) in the centre – as noted by classical political economists – and income variation (effective demand) in the periphery – as emphasised by Keynesian and structuralist authors – account for the balance of payments adjustment during the gold standard period.

NOTES

1. This chapter is a heavily modified version of Chapter 5 of the author's Ph.D. dissertation. The author would like to thank, without implication, Wynne Godley, Will Milberg, Edward Nell and Lance Taylor for their comments on that occasion.
2. A country is said to be under the gold standard, according to De Cecco (1984, p. 1), 'when gold is used as the ultimate *numeraire* of that country's monetary system, and/or when other means of payments in use there, Government IOUs or bank's notes, are readily redeemable in gold at their bearers's request'. According to Eichengreen (1996, p. 9), the most accurate date to say that the gold standard was the basis of the international monetary system is the last quarter of the nineteenth century.
3. The exchange gold standard differs from the coin gold standard in that domestic currency is convertible into pounds or dollars, which in turn are convertible into gold. This, for example, was the case of India (pound–gold system) and the Philippines (dollar–gold system).
4. Brewer (1985) shows that introducing capital mobility would radically change Ricardo's conclusion, bringing about the possibility that absolute advantage rather than comparative advantage determines trade patterns.
5. According to Marcuzzo and Rosselli (1986/1991, p. 147), 'those who still relied on the price–specie flow mechanism for international adjustment evoked his ironic comments'. In support of their view they quote the following passage from Ricardo: 'is it conceivable that money should be sent abroad for the purpose merely of rendering it dear in this country and cheap in another, and by such means ensure its return to us?' (ibid., p. 147).
6. The natural price is the price that allows the producer to obtain the uniform rate of profit.
7. The example is related to the fact that Britain did effectively send subsidies to their allies during the Napoleonic wars.
8. This question bears on the crucial issue of whether gold flows were really part of the operation of the gold standard. This issue will be discussed in the next section.
9. Tooke's views would be classified in modern terms as an endogenous money position. For a modern discussion of endogenous money see Rochon and Vernengo (2001).
10. Gold points are defined as the levels of the exchange rate plus transportation costs at which it became profitable to engage in arbitrage because of a deviation between the market and mint prices of gold. According to Bloomfield (1963, p. 39), 'the gold points were not rigidly fixed even in the short run. Apart from the slight changes that might occur in the costs of shipping gold, some of the leading central banks from time to time fractionally altered their selling or buying prices of gold or took other steps that had the effect of slightly displacing the gold points or of causing exchange rate to move somewhat outside the range of those points'.
11. The expression 'rules of the game' describes the accepted rules governing the pre-1914 gold standard. The rules of the game can be summarised as follows: (a) the central bank fixes the price of gold and is committed to convert freely between domestic money and gold; (b) there are no current or capital account controls, so that exports and imports of gold by private citizens are allowed; (c) the central bank acts as a lender of last resort domestically (Bagehot's rule).
12. Fritsch and Franco (2000) raise the same point with respect to the Brazilian gold standard experience.
13. See Stallings (1987).

14. This means that the Bank of England was able to determine the long-term real rate of interest, regulating the normal rate of profits.
15. Of course, one can argue that the Southern cone is the exception that confirms the rule since most periphery countries had per capita GDP levels that were quite lower than those of the central countries.
16. The argument corresponds to what Eichengreen and Hausmann (1999) denominate the original sin hypothesis, which emphasises an incompleteness in financial markets that prevents the domestic currency from being used to borrow abroad or to borrow long term even domestically. The original sin hypothesis implies that incomplete markets are the culprits of financial crises. Taylor (1998), while also rejecting the conventional view, develops a framework that is more akin to the approach used in this chapter. Financial liberalisation is considered as the main cause of the recent wave of financial crises.
17. Eichengreen (1992) argues, on the other hand, that the collapse of the gold standard system is related to the end of the credible commitment on the part of central banks, both as a result of the war and the extension of the franchise in the inter-war period, which led, in turn, to an erosion of the political acceptance of the negative short-run effects of fixed exchange rates.
18. According to De Cecco (1984, pp. 127–70), the shift of the centre of gravity within the British financial system was also crucial for the collapse of the gold standard. In particular, the role of the joint stock banks that benefited from the City's central role in the international monetary system, without carrying any of the burdens that came with that position, is at the heart of the 1914 crisis.
19. Hobsbawm (1968/1990, pp. 138–9) argues that the period of British unchallenged dominance is related to the fact that for underdeveloped countries England was the only possible market for their production, whereas for developed countries the demand for capital goods, pushed by the second industrial revolution, made trade with Britain essential. Free trade between Britain and the rest of the world was beneficial for all the participants. However, 'after 1873 the situation of the advanced world was one of rivalry between developed countries' (ibid., p. 139).
20. Both Hobsbawm (1968/1990) and De Cecco (1984) emphasise the role of the British Empire, in particular India, and what Hobsbawm (1968/1990, p. 148) calls the informal Empire, which includes Latin American countries such as Argentina, Chile and Uruguay, in the maintenance of the stability of the gold standard.

REFERENCES

Bloomfield, A. (1963), 'Short-term capital movements under the pre-1914 gold standard', *Princeton Studies in International Finance*, 11.

Brewer, A. (1985), 'Trade with fixed real wages and mobile capital', *Journal of International Economics*, **18** (1–2), 177–86.

De Cecco, M. (1984), *The International Gold Standard: Money and Empire*, London and New York: Macmillan and St. Martin's Press.

Eichengreen, B. (1992), *Globalizing Capital*, Princeton: Princeton University Press.

Eichengreen, B. (1996), *Golden Fetters*, New York: Oxford University Press.

Eichengreen, B. and R. Hausmann (1999), 'Exchange rates and financial fragility', *NBER Working Paper*, 7418.

Ford, A.G. (1962), *The Gold Standard, 1880–1914: Britain and Argentina*, Clarendon: Oxford University Press.

Fritsch, W. and G. Franco (2000), 'Aspects of the Brazilian experience with the gold standard', in P. Acena and J. Reis (eds), *Monetary Standards in the Periphery*,

Cheltenham and Northampton: Edward Elgar, 4–31.

Harrod, R.F. (1933/1957), *International Economics*, Chicago: University of Chicago Press.

Hobsbawm, E. (1968/1990), *Industry and Empire*, Harmondsworth: Penguin.

Hume, D. (1752), 'Of the balance of trade', in R.N. Cooper (ed.) (1969), *International Finance: Selected Readings*, Harmondsworth and Baltimore: Penguin, 60–77.

Keynes, J.M. (1925/1972), 'The economic consequences of Mr. Churchill', in *The Collected Writings of John Maynard Keynes*, Vol. IX *Essays in Persuasion*, London and Basingstoke: Macmillan, 207–49.

Kindleberger, C. (1973), *The World in Depression*, Los Angeles and Berkeley: University of California Press.

Krugman, P. and L. Taylor (1978), 'Contractionary effects of devaluation', *Journal of International Economics*, **8** (3), 445–56.

Maddison, A. (2001), *The World Economy: A Millennial Perspective*, Paris: Organisation for Economic Co-operation and Development.

Marcuzzo, M.C. and A. Rosselli (1986/1991), *Ricardo and the Gold Standard*, London and New York: Macmillan and St. Martin's Press.

Pivetti, M. (1991), *An Essay on Money and Distribution*, London: Macmillan.

Rochon, L.-P. and M. Vernengo (2001), 'Introduction', in L.-P. Rochon and M. Vernengo (eds), *Credit, Interest Rates and the Open Economy: Essays on Horizontalism*, Cheltenham and Northampton: Edward Elgar, 1–8.

Sayers, R. (1976), *The Bank of England 1891–1944*, Cambridge: Cambridge University Press.

Stallings, B. (1987), *Banker to the Third World*, Berkeley: University of California Press.

Taylor, L. (1998), 'Lax public sector, destabilizing private sector: origins of capital market crises', *CEPA Working Paper*, 6.

Tooke, T. (1844), *An Inquiry into the Currency Principle: The Connection of the Currency with Prices, and the Expediency of a Separation of Issue from Banking*, London: Longman, Brown, Green and Longmans.

Name Index

Aasland, D. 236
Agassi, J. 239
Akhtar, M.A. 528, 529, 532
Allen, F. 163, 171
Amadeo, E. 137
Arena, R. 258
Arestis, P. xxiv, 33, 45, 55, 57, 58, 120, 122, 133, 137, 171, 258, 322, 323, 339, 354, 503
Aristotle 413, 436
Arnon, A. 510
Arrow, K.J. 265, 272, 273, 282–3

Baghestani, H. 62
Bailly, J.-L. xlvii, 344, 353, 407
Balasko, Y. 276
Baltensperger, E. 170
Bank for International Settlements (BIS) 509, 514, 530
Bank of England 45, 61
Baranzini, M. xxxvii
Barrère, A. 322, 369
Basu, S. xli, 110
Bell, S. xxvi, 60, 93, 101, 227, 341, 342, 525
Bellofiore, R. xxvi, xxxiii, xliii, 117, 174, 199, 203, 207, 216, 236–7
Berlin, M. 163
Bernanke, B.S. 42, 52, 55, 110, 130
Berti, L. 236
Besanko, D. 110
Bester, H. 110
Bhattacharya, S. 110
Bibow, J. xxxi
Bird, R.G. 110
Black, F. 537
Black, S. 85–6
Blinder, A.S. 42, 44, 55, 82, 104–6, 130

Bloomfield, A. 549–50
Böhm-Bawerk, E. 310
Bortis, H. xlviii–xlix, 412, 414–27 *passim*, 429, 431, 432, 439, 440, 443, 449, 452, 459, 460, 461, 462, 464, 465, 467, 468, 469, 470, 472
Bossone, B. xlii, 168, 170, 173, 239, 343, 348, 349
Boudon, R. 231
Boulding, K. 195
Bradford, W. 345–6, 354
Bradley, X. xxix, xlvii–xlviii, 354, 406
Bresciani-Turroni, C. 170
Brewer, A. 557
Brossard, O. 515
Butler, E. 237

Caldwell, R.H. 239
Calomiris, C.W. 110
Cameron, V.L. 238
Cannan, E. 339, 344
Carabelli, A. 345, 354
Cardim de Carvalho, F.J. xxv, 259
Cartelier, J. 378
Case, K. 73
Cassell, G. 237
Cencini, A. xxvi, xxxvi, xxxvii, xlv–xlvi, xlix, 168–9, 194, 239, 254, 255, 256, 259, 308, 336, 342, 344, 347, 349, 353, 354, 370
Chase, S.B. 110
Chick, V. xxviii, xxxi, 58, 118, 127, 132, 235, 322–3, 339, 343, 344, 352, 503, 521
Clarida, R. 55
Clinton, K. 541
Clower, R.W. 3, 350

Subject Index